Dictionary of Medieval Knighthood and Chivalry

Dictionary of Medieval Knighthood and Chivalry

Concepts and Terms

BRADFORD B. BROUGHTON

Illustrations by Megan Broughton Blumbergs

Greenwood Press
New York • Westport, Connecticut • London

Library of Congress Cataloging in Publication Data

Broughton, Bradford B., 1926–
  Dictionary of medieval knighthood and chivalry.
  Concepts and terms.

  Bibliography: p.
  Includes index.
  1. Knights and knighthood—Dictionaries.
2. Chivalry—Dictionaries. 3. Civilization, Medieval—
Dictionaries. I. Title.
CR4505.B76 1986   929.6′003′21   84–29036
ISBN 0–313–24552–5 (lib. bdg.)

Library of Congress Catalog Card Number: 84–29036
ISBN: 0–313–24552–5

First published in 1986

Greenwood Press, Inc.
88 Post Road West
Westport, Connecticut 06881

Printed in the United States of America

The paper in this book complies with the Permanent Paper
Standard issued by the National Information Standards
Organization (Z39.48–1984)

10 9 8 7 6 5 4 3 2 1

To my wife, June, goodwife for thirty-four years, for enduring my constant flow of information about knights while this dragon brought this book to fruition, including her staying in Potsdam without me for a year while I finished its research in Ireland, and almost without me for the eighteen months it took to write the finished manuscript.

Contents

Acknowledgments

This work has been fifteen years in the making. It began as an idea to help students understand the background of some of the literary works they were reading in medieval literature courses here at Clarkson University. Much of the material was compiled during my sabbatical leave in 1970–1971 at Trinity College, Dublin, Ireland, and written up in its first version as a narrative between an aged knight and his young son: the retired knight explaining what knowledge his young son would need in order to survive and prosper in the world he was soon to enter. Thus students could learn easily what a squire had to know, for example, before he went through the knighting ceremony. And they could readily see how satiric was Chaucer's description of the squire in the *Prologue* to the *Canterbury Tales*.

That narrative idea gave way in time to the present concept of a dictionary which would serve much the same purpose. Such a modification required a second year in the Trinity College library in Dublin during my sabbatical in 1982–1983. As modified by the information collected on that second trip, this work was intended to include numerous short biographical sketches of important figures in the medieval European world, descriptions of most of the famous battles occurring between those of Stamford Bridge in 1066 and Agincourt in 1415, and the stories of fictional knights which entertained knights and their ladies in drafty castles on dank winter evenings. It was determined, however, to confine the work essentially to the original concept, but still in dictionary format. A second dictionary volume, now underway, will deal with events and personages, both real and fictional.

For a work this long in the making, special thanks go to numerous people, including Timothy Rutenber, long-time friend, one-time student, and significant contributor to the first version of this work, for his contributions, support, encouragement, advice, and counsel. Also, particular thanks go to a group of friends at the Lecky Library of Trinity College: to Len Mathews for kindly providing me with space in which to work; to the other dedicated staff members, particularly Tony Bohan, Sean Breen, Tina Howe, Gemma O'Riordan, Ron O'Shaughnessy, and Niamh Power, who speedily got me all sorts of information whenever I requested their help; to Professor V. J. Scattergood, chairman of

English I at Trinity; and the two ever-helpful secretaries there: Mary Dalton and Geraldine Mangan, who gave me continuing encouragement and friendship.

Clarkson people also contributed a great deal to the success of this project: to my dean, Owen Brady, and my chairman, Mary Lay, my sincere thanks for the encouragement and financial support all along the sinuous path to publication; to Dennis Horn for showing me the incredible speed and magic of a word-processor on which to compose this work and constantly introducing me to new time-saving uses for it.

And finally to some very special people: my beloved and incredibly clever daughter, Megan Broughton Blumbergs, for her marvellous drawings to illustrate this work; to my always-supportive and encouraging son, Thaddeus; and finally and profoundly, to Joseph Kruger II.

Introduction

This volume, on concepts and terms relevant to the world of the medieval knight, is the first of a two-part *Dictionary of Medieval Knighthood and Chivalry*; the second volume, now in preparation, will concentrate on persons, places, and events in history and literature. The intent of this first volume is to help the uninitiated reader more easily understand the development and growth of the intricate concepts of chivalry and knighthood in a world centuries removed from our own, concepts which hold incredible fascination for the modern reader and student perhaps because they are so far removed and different. Set up alphabetically to provide a brief explanation of the ideas, concepts, terms, and some of the major figures in the period between roughly 1050 and 1400, the period called "medieval," this work is intended primarily as a reference work. Practically all of the words or phrases included contain a reference to a major work on that subject. These references, which appear at the end of an entry as, for instance, "(Bibliog. 21)," are keyed to the alphabetical bibliography at the end of the book. When the text mentions a term or person on which additional information can be found in a separate entry, an asterisk indicates a cross-reference to that entry. In addition, the appendix listing of entries by topic will aid those looking for information on a particular aspect of the subject. The listing of Feast and Saint's Days will provide a ready reference for those interested in the dates of these events.

In addition to serving as a reference work, the book should prove fascinating for someone who is merely curious about, for example, what money was circulated back then, how it was circulated, how much it was worth (see coinage), and other such questions. It explains what a medieval knight was expected to do, militarily, politically, and socially (see knighthood). It provides the type of information a knight was expected to know: weights and measures,* conduct on the battlefield, arms* and weapons, siege warfare,* names and dates of feast days (see Appendix A) by which to date documents or events. It should also answer questions about a squire's* training to become a knight, or about a castle* or the crusades,* or an ordeal,* or the types of tournaments.*

Further, it details social customs and mores of the period and provides descriptions of a coronation* ritual, the precedence* of royalty, and a definition

of and distinctions among the various ranks of the peerage (see peer), particularly
in England and France. Although chivalry* and knighthood also existed in Germany, Italy, and other European countries, this work focuses primarily on the
original development of these concepts in France and England, although included
are some terms from those other countries which a knight-errant* might expect
to encounter on his continental peregrinations. There is only limited coverage
of literary works and actual and fictional personalities, these areas being the
province of the second volume. Biographical entries included here are those
essential to the development or understanding of certain concepts (see, for instance, Henry II, Dame Nicolla de la Haye). Although focusing primarily on
chivalry and knighthood, this work also enters the world of the vassal* and
villein,* because the two classes were not immune from each other but were
mutually interdependent in a world where the knight was master and the villein
his servant.

It began when William,* duke of Normandy, brought the concept of knighthood with his invasion forces to the shores of England in 1066. Before that
time, the Anglo-Saxon thanes* were the important figures of the country; but
they were not knights. William's mounted forces brought with them the idea of
knights fighting on horseback instead of riding to an engagement and dismounting
before beginning battle. The word chivalry comes from the French *chevalier*,
meaning a mounted warrior. Seeing such figures ride around the countryside,
the native English people called them cnihts,* the Anglo-Saxon word for servant,
because they appeared to serve their overlords in military and political matters.
Their role in England grew when, to control the newly conquered land, William
erected a new type of fortress called a castle and needed men to garrison it:
knight-warriors serving a castellan-overlord. As continuous warfare was the way
of life for these knights, the love of battle, the hatred of restraint, and a sense
of arrogant superiority became deeply ingrained in their natures, especially the
French nobles on both sides of the English channel.

These men held a monopoly on the military profession. They trained for war,
bred for battle, and lived in warfare. To be an effective fighter, a man was
required to have a horse,* armor,* and weapons, all of which were expensive
and far beyond the means of the serf* or peasant (see villein). And to wield
those materials effectively, a man had to have the leisure to practice their use
continuously. This man, the *miles** or knight, was master of 11th-century France
and England; and so long as he and his class, the nobility,* held a monopoly
on the military, rebellion was impossible. The lower classes had only the short
bow* as a weapon, and this was ineffective against the armor of the knight.
Thus, until the non-noble class had money, leisure, and cheap effective weapons,
the aristocracy* was secure in its lofty place in society.

All this had emerged from the void in central political power left by the
disintegration of the Roman Empire. Such a gap was filled by a series of contractual relationships between men based on land tenure.* Weaker men took
refuge under the protection of stronger men who by virtue of their wealth and

position could offer protection. This resulted in a pyramidal structure of society in which every man was subordinated to another, every man was the vassal of another, setting up a huge structure of military and ecclesiastical land-holding aristocracy.* Each warrior in essence became an independent lord with his own vassals, subsequently owing service to the king. The lord bestowed on those beneath him a fief* or benefice, that is, a grant of land in return for service, support, and other "feudal obligations."* Such an arrangement soon became hereditary.

Even though, on a visit to Normandy in the mid-11th century, King Edward the Confessor had promised the Anglo-Saxon throne to Duke William, Saxon Earl Godwine's son, Harold, was elected to it by the Anglo-Saxon Witan upon Edward's death in 1066. William, however, was determined to have what he felt was rightfully his—the English throne—and won it at the battle of Hastings on October 14, 1066. Over the next four years he set out to establish a powerful feudal monarchy, keeping forty percent of the countryside for his own royal demesne* and imposing feudal demands on English barons,* bishops,* and abbots.* As a result, a French-speaking feudal aristocracy was established to control the Norman feudalism on English soil. Little changed among the people on the Anglo-Saxon shires* and hundreds* during this period, even under such tyrannical rulers as William's favorite second son, and successor, William II (see William).

This red-haired William Rufus, as he was known, reigned with violence, cruelty, and injustice. His death at the hands of Walter Tirel* in 1100 brought his brother Henry I, William the Conqueror's third son, to the throne. Ending his quarrel with his oldest brother, Robert Curthose, duke of Normandy (see Robert II), and by so doing bringing that French dominion under the control of the English crown, Henry I did much to unite the England of the Anglo-Saxons with the England of the Normans, by such means as instituting itinerant justices and circuit courts.* He even married Matilda, a princess of the Anglo-Saxon house of Wessex. The "White Ship disaster,"* however, deprived him of his only legitimate son, the Lord Prince William, in 1120; and thus on his death in 1135, the crown passed to Stephen of Blois, grandson of the Conqueror. That event sparked a period of anarchy as Henry's daughter, Matilda, sought to claim the throne for herself. To that end, she brought her second husband, Geoffrey of Anjou, with her to England to fight for the crown* for their son, Henry Plantagenet,* of Anjou. By 1150 young Henry had gained all of Normandy and forced the childless King Stephen to recognize him as heir. Before he ascended the throne in 1154, Henry had married the divorced wife of King Louis VII of France, Eleanor,* heiress to the duchy of Aquitaine, and thereby he acquired control over that huge section of France. By adding this to his holdings in Normandy and Maine, Henry controlled an enormous portion of France.

Once in power in 1154, Henry II restored and developed the machinery of government that his grandfather and namesake had created. He originated the English jury system (see jury duty), enlarged the jurisdiction of the royal courts,

and developed the common law. He altered the military system, replacing the
"feudal levy"* with a paid, professional body of soldiers who stood ready to
fight at any time, and he revived the concept of liability for military service of
all freeholders in England—the concept of the Anglo-Saxon fyrd.* Additionally,
he tried to control the church by exercising control over ecclesiastical courts and
insisting that "Criminous Clerks"* be tried by lay courts. After he appointed
his close friend Thomas à Becket* to the archbishopric of Canterbury, Becket
changed from being a king's man to one who vehemently defended ecclesiastical
liberties, enraging and arousing Henry's enmity and leading to Becket's murder
in the Canterbury cathedral in 1170. In the years following, Henry fought a
continuing series of battles with his rebellious sons—young Henry, Richard,*
Geoffrey, and John—who wanted autonomy in their French dominions while
their father still lived. After the death of young Henry in 1173, the three surviving
sons joined with the French monarch, Philip II, Augustus (see Philip), son of
Louis VII by his third wife, to force their father to grant their wishes. That union
finally destroyed an aging Henry, and he died in 1189, naming Richard as his
heir.

King Philip had ascended the French throne in 1180 at the age of fifteen, a
descendant of the Capetian line of French kings begun by Hugh Capet in 987.
The first four Capetian kings—Hugh (987–996), Robert (996–1031), Henry I
(1031–1060), and Philip I (1060–1108)—did little more than just keep the monarchy alive and establish hereditary succession to the throne.* Their resources
consisted entirely of the "Île de France."* The duchy of Normandy, founded
by Duke Rollo in 911, was, however, outside their province. Under strong dukes,
Normandy became the most powerful vassal of the French kings. Its Duke
William enlarged its holdings by invading England as William the Conqueror.
Louis VI, the Fat (1108–1137), increased the French royal domain by consolidating the royal authority in the Île de France by overthrowing small vassals,
supporting towns and the church against baronial opposition, and with the able
assistance of his chief minister, Abbe Suger, abbot of St. Denis,* awakening
some national spirit in the north of France. His son, Louis VII, though able and
energetic, was not the statesman his father was. His participation with his wife,
Eleanor of Aquitaine, on the disastrous second crusade to the Holy Land lost
considerable prestige for the royal house. Further loss occurred when Eleanor
sought and was granted permission to divorce him in order to marry Henry of
England, taking Aquitaine with her as her marriage portion. As a result, Louis
was overshadowed by his vassal Henry by the fact that Henry held fiefs for more
than one-third of all France.

Philip, too, was a different king than his father, Louis VII. He fought steadily
to rid France of all English control by undermining the position of the English
kings in France and repeatedly intriguing against Henry II, Richard (1189–1199),
and John (1199–1216). Finally in 1204, through a series of blunders and mis-
government by John, Philip obtained control of all the fiefs in France held by
the English king except Gascony and Poitou. By his scheming and maneuvering,

Philip earned the enmity of many continental nobles. In addition to the continual plotting of John to recover the lost land, Philip had to contend with the count of Flanders and Otto IV, emperor of the Holy Roman Empire.* The climax came at the battle of Bouvines* in 1214. That battle marked the end of the war between John and Philip which had begun in Normandy in 1202 and the end of the dispute between Frederick II of Hohenstaufen and Otto IV of Brunswick over the crown of the Holy Roman Empire. Philip and his ally Frederick decisively defeated John, Otto, and the count of Flanders. That victory allowed Philip to complete his takeover of Normandy, Anjou, and Touraine and to create for John such domestic difficulties in England that on his return he was confronted with a rebellion of the barons and was compelled to issue the *Magna Carta Libertatum** in 1215. Additionally, Philip actively supported Simon de Montfort's actions as leader of the northern French forces against Languedoc in the Albigensian crusade* in the southern portion of his country. This resulted in extending Capetian authority upon southern France. In his forty-three years on the throne, Philip II considerably increased the royal domain, forced the barons and nobles to obey the crown, and created officials similar to the itinerant justices appointed by Henry II in England to govern the royal domains.

His successor, Louis VIII, died after only three years, leaving a child king, Louis IX, to rule under the regency of the queen, Blanche of Castile.* This child matured to become one of France's greatest monarchs, known better as St. Louis. He possessed a rare combination of kingly talents and deep piety, and established a widespread European reputation for justice. He took up the cross as a crusader in 1144 and carried it all the rest of his life; he was canonized shortly after his death. He continued and refined his grandfather's system of royal officials to control the seneschals* and bailiffs,* and in a move that dealt a severe blow to the political independence of the feudal barons, insisted that appeal to the *curia regis** must be allowed from all feudal courts when certain issues were involved. At the time of his death, the French feudal lords had been reduced in power to obedience to the monarch, the country was becoming unified in spirit of patriotism and nationality, and Roman law was superceding feudal law throughout.

Thirteenth-century England saw the troubled reign of Richard's successor, John, end in 1215 with the *Magna Carta*, the feudal document that lay down the principle of limited, contractual monarchy. John's death in 1216 left his nine-year-old son, Henry III, as king to rule for fifty-six years. Henry proved to be a poor king for he was subservient to the papacy and allowed papal exploitation of England; he supported extravagantly such foreign enterprises as seeking the Sicilian crown for his son, aiding his brother Richard Earl of Cornwall* in his efforts to gain the crown of the Holy Roman Empire, and patronizing several large groups of foreign favorites of his French wife. From the turmoil in his reign emerged the beginning of the English Parliament. The leader of the baronial opposition to the king was Simon de Montfort,* son of the leader of the Albigensian crusade* in France. In 1258 he demanded of the king the "Provisions of Oxford" which included a reaffirmation of the *Magna Carta*, the dismissal of foreign favorites, the resistance of papal taxation, and the appointment of a permanent Great Council to control the crown. In the civil war that followed, the king was defeated and captured, and Simon became virtual dictator of England. In 1265, to support his regime, he summoned a Great Council, now coming to be called a parliament,* which included two knights from each shire and two burgesses for the more important towns, as well as bishops, abbots, and barons. Simon was overthrown and killed in the battle of Evesham in that same year by forces of the king led by the king's eldest son, Edward, who became the real ruler of the country until his father's death in 1272. Coming to the throne in 1272, Edward reigned until 1307; he well understood the significance of Simon de Montfort's tactics and policy and followed much of it by summoning in 1295 the Model Parliament.*

Under Edward I, England conquered Wales in 1284, sought unsuccessfully to rule Ireland, and forced an alliance between Scotland and France when Edward claimed an ancient right of suzerainty over the Scots, but his efforts were defeated by Scottish resistance led by William Wallace* and Robert Bruce. His son, Edward II, was a weak and incompetent king who had continual troubles with the barons and Parliament. His forces were defeated by the Scots at Bannockburn* in 1314, and he was deposed and secretly murdered by Parliament in 1327. His son, Edward III, followed him and reigned for fifty years.

Philip III, the Bold, succeeded his father, Louis IX, on the throne of France in 1270 and was in turn succeeded by his more famous son, Philip IV,* the Fair, who reigned from 1285 to 1314. Two of his well-known actions were to support the claims of a Frenchman, Clement V, to the papal throne, his subsequent packing of the College of Cardinals with French clergy, and moving the papacy to Avignon; and his attack on the Knights Templar.* This latter group, fat with wealth and no longer involved in the crusades, held great privileges in France. In 1307 Philip ordered them seized and prosecuted. Under torture some of their leaders confessed the charges were true, and Pope Clement V condemned the order from Avignon. All their moveable wealth was confiscated by Philip, and their lands were given to the Hospitallers.* Philip's sons followed successively to the throne, but none left a male heir; so in 1328, the throne went to Philip VI of the House of Valois, which battled the English over the French throne for a hundred years.

This strife, called the Hundred Years War, stemmed from the French King Philip IV's eagerness to break the feudal grip of England on Aquitaine in the southeast corner of France because the English presence there blocked unification of France under the French crown. He and Edward I were at war between 1294 and 1303 with no appreciable change in the situation. As an additional strain on this relationship, Edward III claimed the French throne. He was grandson of Philip IV, the Fair, through a female line of succession and had challenged the succession of Philip VI of Valois in 1328. Invoking "Salic law,"* the French excluded him from the throne, and he reluctantly did homage* to the new Valois

king for his French fiefs in 1329. Eight years later he repudiated that homage
and declared himself king of France. Between 1337 and 1360 several battles
occurred, but none was important until 1346 when the English demolished the
French in the Battle of Crécy.* That victory was due to the superior effectiveness
of the English longbow* over the French feudal cavalry charge: the longbowmen
were superior to mounted feudal knights. From there the English marched north
and captured Calais, which they held for over 200 years. A truce in the war
followed the incursion of the Black Death,* the plague that swept across Europe
in 1348 and 1349, killing perhaps one-third of the population. In 1355 the Prince
of Wales,* Edward, the Black Prince,* began another campaign in Aquitaine,
and he won another tremendous victory over the French at the Battle of Poitiers*
in 1356, in which the longbow again proved to be superior and the French lost
their king, John, and two of his sons as prisoners to the English. This resulted
in a truce in 1357, for France in defeat was falling into collapse. The resultant
treaty of Bretigny in 1360 ceded Calais and nearly all of Aquitaine to Edward
III in full sovereignty and no longer as fiefs of the French king, in return for
which Edward abandoned all claims to the French crown. Charles V, the Wise,
new French king after the death of the captured John, in 1338 repudiated that
Treaty of Bretigny by reasserting claims of sovereignty over Aquitaine. This
time, the French were well prepared to fight, for they had an extremely able
leader in Bertrand de Guesclin who cleverly allowed the English to exhaust
themselves by running all over the countryside and then launched a French
offensive. By 1374 the English held only a few ports in France, and Charles
was contemplating an invasion of England. His plans were stopped by a truce
mediated by the papacy in 1375.

The Black Prince died in 1376, a year before his father Edward III, so on the
death of the aged monarch, the crown passed to his young grandson, Richard
II. In turmoil over the defeats in France, financial disorder of the government,
and baronial attempts to enforce old manorial services on the peasantry, England
experienced the Peasant's Revolt* in 1381. Even though they were unsuccessful,
the peasants obtained considerable advantage from their revolt, and the ancient
holds exerted by serfdom over them were broken forever.

That, then, was the political panorama in which knighthood and chivalry
developed in France and England and reached their zenith around the end of the
14th century.

Dictionary of Concepts and Terms

A

"à bonne usance" (Fr. "for my own good use"), cry uttered by soldiers in pursuit of the enemy and scattering in quest of "spoils of war"*; this cry meant that each man took for his own everything that he found: the harder he worked, the more he took for profit. See *"à prix d'une esquillette;" "à butin."* (Bibliog. 181)

"à butin" (Fr. "for spoils and plunder"), cry uttered by soldiers in pursuit of the enemy and scattering in quest of "spoils of war,"* this cry meant that the spoil was to be shared according to the rank of the gatherers, as normally done. See *"à bonne usance;" "à prix d'une esquillette."*(Bibliog. 181)

"à logis, ployez les banniers" (Fr. "to your homes, furl your banners"), words used by heralds* to signify the end of the whole fête of a tournament.* (Bibliog. 78)

"à mêlée" See *mêlée.*

"à outrance" (Fr. "with utmost hostility"). See *jousts à outrance.*

"à plaisance" (Fr. "for pleasure"). See *jousts à plaisance.*

"à prix d'une esquilette." (Fr. "equal shares"). See spoils of war.

Aarvak, Arvak, in Norse mythology a fiery horse* called the "early waker" (Aarvak) that was driven by the maiden Sol to draw the sun's chariot across the sky. (Bibliog. 308)

abai, abay, act or occasion of keeping a hunted animal at bay by barking dogs. See hunting. (Bibliog. 226)

abaised, abased, charge* borne lower than its usual position, in heraldry.*
(Bibliog. 43)

abaite, setting dogs in pursuit of game. See hunting. (Bibliog. 226)

abatements, rebatements, marks of disgrace attached to heraldic arms* by
reason of a dishonorable act of the bearer. Basically, these were pieces of
differing shape cut off or out of the design on a shield.* Colored either sanguine*
or tenne,* which early writers of heraldry* called "staynaude colours," these
abatements existed only in systems of heraldry. As the use of arms was not
compulsory, and a bearer would rather relinquish his arms than publish his
disgrace by bearing them abased, no actual instance of their use has survived.

Abatements were imposed for such actions as revoking one's challenge, deserting one's sovereign's banner,* discourteously treating a maiden or a widow
against her will, boasting of one's prowess, killing one's prisoner, cowardice,
drunkenness, or lying to one's sovereign. Traitors had their own marks of disgrace: debasing or reversing one's arms, hence the term "turncoat." (Bibliog.
43)

abbot, superior or head of an abbey or monastery for men; an abbess rules a
convent.

abece, Latin alphabet of twenty-two letters, lacking *k* and *w,* and with distinct
characters for *j* and *v,* arranged in specific sequence. (Bibliog. 226)

abjuration of the realm, oath of a confessed felon (see felony) in England
promising to leave the realm and never to return. Sanctuary* seekers could
request from the coroner* the right to abjure the realm within forty days of their
sanctuary confinement. At the abjuration ceremony, the felon confessed and then
swore on the Gospels to leave the realm of England and to return only by the
express permission of the king* or the king's heirs; to hasten by direct road to
his port (see borough) of departure, not leaving the king's highway under pain
of arrest as a felon nor staying in any one place for more than one night; to seek
diligently for passage across the sea on arriving at his port, delaying only one
tide if possible, but if he could not secure passage, he was to walk into the sea
up to his knees as a token of his desire to cross it. If after forty days he still
was unsuccessful, he was to take sanctuary again at the port. Under his oath,
the felon swore to depart from the kingdom of England only and not from the
British Isles; thus an abjurer could cross to Ireland, Scotland, or Wales through
a border town and did not need to go to France or the continent through a seaport.
Such abjurations could be made only from a consecrated church or chapel, for
if a felon took sanctuary in a non-consecrated church, he could be forcibly
removed and executed; and both the coroner and the township could be subjected
to amercement* (that is, punishment by fines*) if they permitted such sanctuary.

Whenever requested by a sanctuary seeker, a coroner had to appear at any consecrated church, but not immediately upon the felon taking sanctuary. When summoned, the coroner ordered the local bailiff* (usually of the hundred*) to assemble good and lawful men of the neighborhood for the abjuration ceremony, which was interesting enough to draw a crowd without such bidding. At this ceremony the coroner gave the felon a choice: either surrender or abjure the realm. Likewise, the felon could delay in summoning the coroner, for he knew that he had forty days of guaranteed safety. He also had a fair chance of escaping; forcible rescue of sanctuaried felons was common and posed physical danger to the bailiff or chief constable* burdened with guarding the church. As a result, guarding was often inadequate despite the fact that if a felon escaped, the township or hundred (whatever jurisdiction was in charge) would be amerced. In 1311, for example, a Norfolk coroner was prevented from taking an oath of abjuration from a felon by men who beat the guards and rescued the criminal. However, some townships took so seriously the responsibility of guarding felons in sanctuary that the felon was not allowed to leave the church to relieve his bodily functions.

Few such felons surrendered, for had they intended to surrender they never would have taken sanctuary in the first place; and if they did surrender, they would be committed to jail.* Those who refused to surrender were given a choice either of abjuring the realm at once or of remaining in the church for a further period not to exceed the forty days since their first arrival. Some left immediately; others told the coroner that they would wait to abjure the realm until the fortieth day, for escape was still a strong possibility.

If at the end of forty days the felon refused to surrender, however, his privileges of sanctuary ended. Although he still could not be removed by force, his guards had to prevent food and water from being brought to him or they would suffer serious consequences. Only a few desperate men still refused abjuration after the fortieth day because the chance of escaping would be greatly reduced by their declining physical strength. For example, in 1344, after a confessed homicide in Norfolk refused to surrender or abjure at the end of his forty days, the coroner withdrew and ordered the doors to be guarded closely; five days later the felon died in the church.

To distinguish himself from an ordinary wayfarer, the abjurer had to carry in his hand a wooden cross* as a sign of the church's protection. Originally he wore just sack* cloth, but from late in the 13th century he wore a shirt, coat, and breeches. All the rest of his clothing had been forfeited, and his head and feet were bare. Having handed him the cross, the coroner led him to the highway, gave him a final warning not to stray from it, and saw him off in the right direction; sometimes he was handed from constable to constable along the road. Sooner or later, the abjurer generally left the highway and took up residence unmolested elsewhere. This was easy to do as the felon had no distinctive garb and no guards; he needed only to toss away the cross. Any abjurer, however, who left the king's road too near the place of sanctuary was open to immediate arrest and even could be beheaded with impunity. Although penalties were imposed on any who molested an abjurer on the road, some still were pursued and decapitated frequently near the land of the family which had been robbed or had lost a member or had been injured or molested by the abjurer and were unwilling to see him escape unpunished. He also could be decapitated legally if he returned to the kingdom without specific permission. No excuse was valid for an abjurer to return; if he were caught and were proved to be a returned abjurer, he could be hanged on the spot. (Bibliog. 171)

abressemine, disease of hawks. (Bibliog. 226)

abstersen, to clean a wound of pus and other impurities. (Bibliog. 226)

accolade, ceremony to mark the conferring of knighthood, consisting of an embrace, kiss, or slight blow on each shoulder with the flat blade of a sword. (Bibliog. 246)

accollé, two shields* placed side by side, touching each other but not overlapping, in French heraldry.* (Bibliog. 43)

achatour, buyer of provisions for the household of a king* or a lord. (Bibliog. 226)

achievement, hatchment, complete armorial bearings (see charge); it distinguished the whole from its parts: arms,* crest,* motto,* and so forth. See blazoning a shield. (Bibliog. 43)

ackermanni, carucarii, (L.) servants on an English baronial estate who led the unwieldy plows; they were helped by a set of drivers and young boys who tended the oxen or horses.* (Bibliog. 357)

acoupen of, to accuse someone of a crime or an offense. (Bibliog. 226)

acquiller, enquiller, to rouse the animals of the chase* (the prey) with hounds. See hunting. (Bibliog. 96)

acre, measure of land in the British Isles which, in its earliest use, referred to the amount of land one yoke of oxen could plow in one day. Later the acre was standardized at 160 square perches* of sixteen and one-half feet* each, or 43,560 square feet; the statutory acre was forty perches in length and four in width. (Bibliog. 394)

acton. See aketon.

adalid, officer in the Spanish armies whose duty was to observe the flight of birds, especially eagles, and to report to his leader on the favorable moment for battle as determined by that flight. (*El Cid*, Cantar 10–13, describes such an officer.) (Bibliog. 274)

Adam and Eve's Arms, a shield* gules* (Adam's) and a shield argent* (Eve's) which Adam later bore as an escutcheon,* his wife being his sole heiress. After the Fall, Adam bore a garland of fig leaves, which later Abel quartered* with "Argent, an apple vert,* in right of his mother." (Bibliog. 253)

adder, slaying. See asp.

addorsed, placed back to back as in the use of the wings of birds when shown in such a position in heraldry*; the term also referred to axes* (or bills*) or keys when the blades were turned outward. (Bibliog. 43)

adolencena emberbis. See youth, terms for.

adulescentulus. See youth, terms for.

adulterine castles, castles* built throughout England during the reign of King Stephen, 1135–1154. Unlicensed and spurious, these hastily constructed fortifications probably were built of earthwork and timber. Many were destroyed shortly after Henry II ascended the throne in 1154. One chronicler of the period, Robert of Torigni, abbot of Mont St. Michel, reported that most of them were destroyed after the peace treaty in 1153 that settled the succession of the throne on the future Henry II. (Bibliog. 341)

Adventurous Shield, shield* in the White Abbey destined for Galahad, the perfect knight in Arthurian legend. (Bibliog. 2)

advowson, official "patronage" of an ecclesiastical office or religious house which gave it the right to hold a benefice* or fief* and to defend its rights or to be its "advocate." (Bibliog. 100)

aesc-born, literally "ash-bearer," an Anglo-Saxon metonymic (a word used in a transferred sense: that is, the name of something closely related being substituted for the name of an object) for soldier*—"ash-bearer"—referring to the lances* made of ash wood. (Bibliog. 226)

affeer, act of establishing the amount of fine* or amercement* for one "in mercy,"* based on the individual's worth and the gravity of his offense. (Bibliog. 226)

affer, afer, aver, farm stock: cattle, domestic animals, beasts of burden common in Anglo-French and Anglo-Latin. Usually it meant a draught ox or horse,* specifically a horse used for particularly heavy work (such as a cart* horse). (Bibliog. 103)

affeted, 1. stag's antlers regularly tined and well grown; 2. hound or hawk which had been trained, tamed, reclaimed, and gentled. (Bibliog. 96)

affronty, position of a beast whose whole body showed full body and face in heraldry*; hence, facing the front. A beast whose head alone faced the viewer was described as guardant.* (Bibliog. 253)

afon, avon, to receive a gift or reward; to inherit or take possession of land, office, estate. (Bibliog. 226)

afornrider, one who rode ahead of an army as a scout or one of the vanguard. (Bibliog. 226)

agate, semi-precious stone which was the color of a lion's* skin and which protected those who carried it from snakebite and scorpion sting; when wrapped in moist tow and placed on a wound, it drew out infection and pain; if ground into a powder and given to someone in a drink, it protected him from injury and bestowed on him the eloquence, strength, virtue, and the love of God and man. (Bibliog. 258)

age of majority, legal age, for which a man had to have reached his twenty-first birthday and a girl her fourteenth birthday. (Bibliog. 264)

age of marriage. See marriage, age of.

Aggstein, impressive castle* along the Danube river in Austria. Perched on a cliff about 1,000 feet above the river, this castle was built early in the 12th century and was controlled by the dukes of Austria until its destruction in 1296. (Bibliog. 45)

agister, official of the royal forest* who supervised the pasturage of common cattle, sheep, and pigs of the villagers in the forest and who collected the fees called "agistment"* for such pasturage. (Bibliog. 262)

agistment, fees paid for pasturage of domestic animals in a royal forest.* (Bibliog. 163)

agnel. See coinage.

agueys, dents along the edge of an indented document. See Exchequer. (Bibliog. 226)

aids, auxilia, demands on tenants and serfs* in addition to a lord's right to take money from them for relief* or the *servitium debitum.** These moneys were demanded on such special occasions as when he had to pay heavy relief upon entering his inheritance, but more particularly on three distinct occasions: (a) to ransom* himself from enemy imprisonment; (b) to contribute to the expenses of knighting his eldest son; (c) to help defray the costs of marrying off his eldest daughter—once. However, the sums demanded had to be reasonable—that is, within the tenant's means and ability to pay and not so severe that the tenant could no longer maintain himself in his current social position. Often, though, kings and the major barons* of the kingdom ignored such limitations and demanded aids for such actions as reducing the king's or baron's debts or stocking his farms. Uniquely, some close vassals* were required to hold the English king's head in his boat as he crossed the choppy water of the Wash* on the eastern coast of England.

Additional burdens, particularly in France, included the chevauchee* or cavalcade, ''castle guard''* (the duty to keep open his own castle* for a visit from his lord or his monarch), and the obligation to carry the newly consecrated bishop of Paris into Notre Dame cathedral on their shoulders (required of the chief vassals of that particular bishop). See *dona*; tallage. (Bibliog. 262)

aiel, grandfather, ancestor. (Bibliog. 226)

aiguilette, aglet, aiglet, anglet, metal tag on the end of a ''point of a shield,''* or lace, sometimes the point itself, used to fasten together the pieces of plate armor.* See arming points. (Bibliog. 331)

ailettes, ailets (Fr. ''little wings''), small square shields fastened at right angles upon the shoulders, sometimes appearing at the back of the arm or at the side of the upper arm. Made of metal or leather and attached by a leather band around the neck, these long were thought to serve as protection for the neck and to minimize the effect of a sweeping cut from a sword* or other edged weapon, but their use later was determined to have been heraldic (see heraldry) and their function purely decorative. Instead of being made of metal or leather as originally deduced from their appearances on memorial brasses* decorating tombs, they were made of flimsy material and served no protective function at all. Piers Gaveston in 1313, for example, wore a pair which were garnished and spotted with pearls. (Bibliog. 27, 71)

Aix la Chapelle, town between the Rhine and the Meuse rivers; the location of Charlemagne's favorite palace. After being crowned emperor* of the Holy Roman Empire* on Christmas Day, A.D. 800, Charlemagne made Aix the real capital of the Carolingian Empire, and his son, Louis the Pious, was crowned there in 814. Later, after the Emperor Frederick (Barbarossa) I declared Charlemagne to be a saint in 1164, pilgrims flocked to its church. (Bibliog. 139)

Akershus, massive royal palace and fortress in Oslo, Norway, begun by King Haakon V Magnusson around 1300 and not completed until the end of that century. (Bibliog. 45)

aketon, acton, auqueton, gambeson, hacketon, haqueton, wambais, wambesium, wambs, plain quilted coat worn under armor* by knights but by foot-soldiers as their main body armor. It was a knee-length garment put on over the head like a shirt, quilted vertically, and had straight sleeves which ended just above or below the elbow; many had high, stiff collars fastened on either side to protect the neck. (Bibliog. 27)

alabaster, soft stone which when mixed with vinegar healed ailments of the chest and head. (Bibliog. 258)

aland, alon, alan, alant, alaunt, generic term for a large ''hunting dog''* with short ears used primarily for hunting wild boar, but no particular breed was so designated. Supposedly brought to western Europe when the Alani tribe of nomads invaded Gaul in the 4th century, this strong, ferocious animal was used as a war dog because once it seized its prey, nothing but a direct command of its master could force it to release its hold. (Bibliog. 96)

alaunt. See aland.

Alberich, dwarf who figured prominently in Germanic legend. He appeared in the *Nibelungenlied** where he sought to avenge Nibelung and Schilbung, was vanquished by Siegfried, and was forced to surrender the Tarnkappe. Later he provided Siegfried with the strength necessary to woo and win Brunhild in Iceland for Gunther. (Bibliog. 124)

Albigensian crusade, military expedition organized by Pope Innocent III (1198–1216) to crush the Cathars in southern France, for he felt they were a pernicious heresy. The Cathars believed in two gods, a god of good and a god of evil. The god of evil had originally been an angel, Jehovah, to whom God had given the job of building the earth. When he was through with that job, Jehovah decided to have his creation worship him instead of the true God, so he organized his own church, the Jews, on earth. But when God sent his son, Christ, to redeem men and bring them back to the true worship, Jehovah killed him, making the Cross a symbol of defeat and not of victory. From this initial denial the Cathars went on to deny all the sacraments of the church, and most of the tenets.

In 1209 the pope launched this crusading invasion of the fertile and warm lands of Languedoc in southern France. Led by Simon de Montfort, these northern forces encountered stiff resistance. De Montfort told his men to kill all, and so the capture of the Provencal cities was accomplished with much savagery and bloodshed. For example, when the crusaders attacked Beziers, a city of 60,000, its count refused to defend it, and thereby subjected the entire population to the swords of the crusaders who slaughtered men, women, and children. Seven thousand people sought sanctuary in the church of Sainte-Madeleine, and were butchered there; six thousand others were burnt alive in the church of Saint-Nazaire, for the crusaders had been promised a remission of several centuries of Purgatory for each ten thousand slain. Near the end of this reign of terror, de Montfort himself was killed at the siege of Toulouse when his skull was shattered by a stone hurled from the ramparts* by a woman. Shortly thereafter, the troublesome Provence was annexed to France by the expedient of having Marguerite, the eldest daughter of the Count of Toulouse, marry King Louis IX, and the youngest daughter marry Charles of Anjou, the king's brother. (Bibliog. 42, 186)

Albion, Britain.

alborium, bow* made of hazel in the 11th century. (Bibliog. 331)

Albuquerque, castle* forty kilometers north of Badajoz, Spain, built in 1354 by Alfonso Sanches, son of King Dinis of Portugal. Often besieged during the border conflicts of Castile and Portugal, it held out against Pedro the Cruel, king of Castile, 1346–1369. Its walls had square towers with pointed merlons* and extended to enclose the town on the north side. (Bibliog. 45)

Alcala de Guadaira, huge Moorish-style castle* near Seville. Its keep* and the towers were altered by Christians after it was captured by King Ferdinand the Saint in 1246 and later were emblazoned with the arms* of Castile-Leon and the knightly orders. (Bibliog. 45)

Alcantara, order of knights in Spain, instituted about 1156 by two brothers, Don Suarez and Don Gomez de Barrientes, for protection against the Moors. In 1177 they were confirmed by Pope Alexander III as a religious order of the Knights of San Julian del Pereyro knighthood* under Benedictine rule, but in 1213 when the defense of Alcantara was entrusted to them, they took for their order the name of that city. For a long time they were subject to the grand master of their kindred order of the Knights of Calatrava,* but ultimately they elected their own grand master and during the successive rule of thirty-seven grand masters, they grew in wealth and influence to rival the power of the king.* (Bibliog. 45)

alcato, a collar or gorget* of the 13th century. (Bibliog. 331)

Alcazaba of Malaga, 11th-century Moorish fortification containing a square tower and *enciente** united by a double zigzag "curtain wall"* to form a capital fortress on the Mediterranean seacoast of Granada. (Bibliog. 45)

Alcazar of Segovia, great castle* in the center of Segovia dating from the reconquest of the city in the 11th century. (Bibliog. 45)

alcube, tent* set up to shelter the king* while hunting.* (Bibliog. 161)

alectory, stone found in the gizzard of cocks and the stomach of capons who were seven years old. As large as a bean and resembling a crystal drop of water, this served as an excellent talisman,* providing protection so that nothing could hurt anyone who carried it in his mouth. When dropped into wine* it healed gravel, and when placed in the crest* of a helm* it assured victory for its wearer; it made a man amorous, a woman agreeable, and a messenger* garrulous. (Bibliog. 258)

aleior, top portion of the wall of a city on which the guards patrolled. (Bibliog. 161)

alemandina, gem which melted ice and boiled water. (Bibliog. 258)

Alençon, French castle* owned by King Henry I* of England which Count Fulk of Anjou overcame by forcing the garrison to surrender from thirst after he located and destroyed the underground conduit from the river Sarathe which provided the castle's water. (Bibliog. 129)

Alhambra, castle* in Granada, begun in the 13th century. Its *enciente** with towers incorporating part of the Alcazaba of Malaga* or palace of Granada had one of the strongest types of castle gates, the Justice Gate of 1348, which had a vaulted passage turning through three right angles. See barbican. (Bibliog. 45)

Alia-Aenor, Eleanor* of Aquitaine's accurate name.

alienated, ownership of property that had been transferred legally to another person, that is, had changed its "lien." (Bibliog. 102)

alienation, transfer of property or rights. (Bibliog. 226)

alkibrit, sulphur, used in "greek fire."* (Bibliog. 226)

allege, to make a formal declaration in court* either by way of bringing a charge, defending a charge, supporting a charge, or justifying a claim. (Bibliog. 226)

allegiance. See knighthood.

allerion, eagle* displayed in heraldry* without beak or legs; in French blazon* it was said to represent a vanquished empire.* The arms* of the duchy* of Lorraine: "Or,* on a bend* gules,* three allerions argent.*'' (Bibliog. 43)

alleron, tip of a wing of a hawk. (Bibliog. 226)

allodium, allod, allodial land, opposite of fe-odium, or fief,* these were lands which were the absolute property of their owner and were not subject to any service or acknowledgment to a superior. Common throughout northern Europe, these were unknown in England because William* the Conqueror made feudal land universal in the British Isles. See *Domesday Book*. (Bibliog. 100)

allonge, thrust with a small sword.* (Bibliog. 331)

allowance, adjustment for wind made by an archer when he shot wide on the side of the mark nearest to the wind, in order that the wind would bring the arrow* into line with the mark. (Bibliog. 100)

allume, beast when its eyes were tinctured (see colors; heraldry) gules* in French blazon.* (Bibliog. 251)

allure, walkway along the ramparts* of a castle.* (Bibliog. 341)

allusive arms, arms* which referred to or played upon the name of their bearer (for example, a family named Archer might have chosen an arrow*; a family named Bacon, a pig; a family named Corbet, crows [corbies]). (Bibliog. 251)

Almayne, Almain, Almagne, Germany.

almerie, place for storing or safekeeping, as in a pantry or buttery.* (Bibliog. 226)

almoner, member of the staff of a priest in a castle* who was in charge of offerings to the poor; he gathered leftovers from the table to make sure that they were distributed among the needy and not pilfered by the grooms and servingmen. In the 13th century the "king's almoner" was the crown official in charge of alms (see mercy) and gifts and their distribution to the sick, the poor, the captive, and those in want. (Bibliog. 128)

alms. See mercy.

alnage. See ulnage.

Alnwick, castle* built by Ivo de Vesci in Northumberland near Newcastle around 1100. It began as a motte* and bailey* castle, was fortified with stone in the 12th century, and was rebuilt by the Percy* family in the 14th century. (Bibliog. 45)

aloue, (Fr.) fief* in which the landowner owed his overlord no rents but only service in the time of major emergency. See *servitium debitum.* (Bibliog. 161)

alouten, made obedience, showed deference, bowed as in submission. (Bibliog. 226)

alphyn, monster* of varying form in heraldry,* sometimes with tufts and claws like an heraldic tiger and sometimes with forelegs like an ox. (Bibliog. 43)

Amazonia, women's land near Albania, partly in Asia and partly in Europe; it was called Amazonia after the widows of the Goths who were slain when leaving Scythia. These women donned their husbands' armor* and weapons and avenged their husbands' deaths by killing all the young males, old men, and children and taking away all the women. (Bibliog. 21)

amber, measure for liquids and grains, especially salt and ale, that varied in size; four bushels* was the most common size for dry measure, but the size of the liquid container was unknown. (Bibliog. 394)

ambesas, two ones in the game of dice or hazard, the lowest possible score. (Bibliog. 226)

ambler, saddle horse,* as distinct from war horse or destrier.* (Bibliog. 226)

ambrosino, silver coin depicting St. Ambrosius, issued in Florence between 1250 and 1310. See coinage.

ambulant, indicating that a being or creature described in heraldry* was walking. See beasts, positions of. (Bibliog. 43)

ambulary tower, movable siege tower. (Bibliog. 226)

amercement, penalty levelled against a village or hundred* for its refusal to perform an action, such as supplying a required number of men-at-arms or allowing a felon claiming sanctuary* to escape. Such a financial demand fell both on the villeins* and freemen of the locality; it differed from a fine* in that a fine originally was a set and fixed amount for a specified offence, whereas the amount of the amercement was discretional—at the discretion of the court.*

Although the sums may have appeared trifling, they were not. Normally in the king's court, the amount never dropped below half a mark,* that is, below six shillings eightpence. See coinage; money. (Bibliog. 264)

amistunte, hard stone (flint) which set fire to tow (hemp fibers) when it was struck with a bit of iron. (Bibliog. 258)

amorette, love-knot interlaced like a rosette. (Bibliog. 226)

amphisbene, serpent-like animal which lived best in the cold, had a head at each end of its body, and eyes that glowed like candles. (Bibliog. 193)

Ampoule, Sainte. See anointing.

Ampulla or Golden Eagle, vessel shaped like an eagle* containing consecrating oil used in the English coronation* ceremonies. Its head screwed off at the middle of its neck to put in the oil, and its neck was hollow to the beak to pour into a golden spoon. Including the pedestal, it was nine inches* high, had a wingspread of seven inches, weighted ten ounces,* and held six ounces of oil; it was used only for the coronation of King Henry IV on October 13, 1399. See anointing. (Bibliog. 178)

anceps, snare which caught game by the foot and lifted it into the air. (Bibliog. 96)

ancient demesne, lands in England which at the time of the conquest, William* I took for the English crown; lands in this original demesne, however, did not cease to be so regarded even if the king* had granted them away to others, for if land was recorded in the *Domesday Book** as lands held by the king, then it was and always would be part of the ancient demesne, regardless of who the current owner might be; any lands which subsequently fell to the crown by way of escheat* did not form a part of this demesne. (Bibliog. 264)

ancipiter, bird of prey. (Bibliog. 226)

anesthetic, compound which allowed cutting on a person's body without any feeling of pain. John Ardene's recipe (1370) included henbane, mandragora,* hemlock, black and white poppies, opium, and so forth. Placing the seed of any of these in wine* made the drinker sleep at once so deeply that he could not feel what was being done to him. (Bibliog. 364)

ange d'or, gold coinage* issued by Philip* IV of France in 1341, depicting St. Michael and the dragon* on one side and an elaborate cross* with four crowns* on the other; it was imitated with variations in many of the Low Countries. (Bibliog. 150)

angle, dead. See dead angle.

Anglo-Gallic money, extensive series of gold, silver, and billon* coins struck by the kings* of England in their roles as sovereigns of France from the time of Henry II (1154–1189) through the reign of King Richard II (1377–1399); by the regent, the duke of Bedford; and by Edward, the Black Prince,* son of King Edward III, who for Gascony struck billon deniers (see denarius) called "lions"; their inscription read "EDWARD FILI / H. REGIS ANGLIAE." See also coinage. (Bibliog. 150)

angon, spear* or javelin,* frequently barbed. (Bibliog. 9)

anlace, anelace, small, double-edged dagger with a blade broad at the base; it was a common arm of both the military and laity between the 13th and 15th centuries. (Bibliog. 9)

annulet, ring used frequently as a charge* in heraldry* to indicate the mark of cadency* for a fifth son. Two annulets interlaced were called a gimmel* ring. (Bibliog. 43)

anointing, a sacred action which signified sovereignty, obedience to the throne, submission to the scepter,* and allegiance to the crown and made necessary the recognition of the supremacy of the sacred oil. Kings* were the Lord's anointed because they were anointed with His oil out of the sanctuary. In the English coronation* ceremony, the archbishop dipped his right thumb into the ointment and applied it to the king—first on the summit of the head, then on the breast, the back, the right and left shoulder, and in the joints of the right and left arm and accompanied each unction with the words, "I anoint thee king with the holy oil, in the name of the Father, the Son, and the Holy Ghost."

By this consecration and anointing, the king was changed outwardly by the hand of the priest; inwardly he also was changed: cleansed, purified through the grace of the Holy Ghost. And so he became a different man with a new status and a new relation with God: he was the Lord's anointed. In granting him this consecration, God accepted him as His office-bearer in the world; the king had a place not only over his own people but now in the divine order of things. Anointing, thus, signified more than just a simple insignia; it gave the king a place set apart by God so men could not dispute it, it made him dependent upon the religious services rendered him by the clergy, and it also created for him a special place among the people: he stood alone as king.

To this ceremony gradually were added other actions, such as a coronation. Early Teutonic rulers had worn golden helmets,* but later practice called for them to put on a symbolic golden diadem after being anointed. As the clergy had the responsibility of anointing, step by step they gradually obtained for themselves the right to deliver the other insignia of dominion: sword,* ring, scepter, rod to the new king. Appropriate prayers and wordings created for this investiture were recorded so that precedents could be recalled easily for future use. Such prayers, called *ordines*, can be traced to Archbishop Hincmar (d. 883), who recorded some for others to carry on; by the next century the Frankish kings had a well-established coronation ceremony. For example, in 936, Otto I had himself solemnly anointed and crowned at Aachen; this was followed in 961 by an *ordo* drawn up at Mainz to create the norm used in Germany for several centuries which combined the Frankish *ordo* with Otto's and amplified both. The resultant model so surpassed all others for fullness, clarity, and wealth of idea that it obviously was imitated; the church of Rome, which had nothing of its own to use, adopted it as the "Roman" form from the 11th century onward.

When Clovis, the pagan warrior-king of France, was faced by disaster in his war against the invading Almanni about the year 500, so legend related, he remembered what his wife, Queen Clotilde, had said as she begged him to become a Christian as she was. He vowed, then and there, that if the threatening defeat were turned to victory, he would become a Christian. Immediately the tide of battle turned, the Almanni were routed, and their king was slain. On his victorious return to his capital, Clovis ordered elaborate preparations made for the royal baptism. On the appointed day, the crowds gathering to witness this great event were so huge that the priest with the crism for the anointing could not get through to the waiting Clovis at the font; St. Remigius, bishop of Reims, in charge of the ceremony, knelt in prayer for help. In response a dove, white as snow, appeared out of the sky, carrying in its beak an ampoule with the crism needed to consummate the sacrament. Thus Clovis, the first Christian king of the Franks, was anointed with miraculous crism divinely presented. With the remnants of this divine crism preserved in what was believed to be the original heaven-sent ampoule (known as the Sainte Ampoule) every subsequent French monarch was anointed. The Sainte Ampoule was a small phial of somewhat ordinary glass; its whitish and opaque color was attributed to the calcination of time. The body of the phial appeared less transparent than its neck because it was filled with a reddish balm of a color resembling dried roses; its shape resembled a fig, it stood about two and a quarter inches* high, and it was one inch in diameter.

Long envious that the kings of France were anointed with an oil brought down from heaven, the kings of England "discovered" a similar miraculous oil for their coronation anointing: in 1399, King Henry IV was anointed with an oil which, it was claimed, had been received by St. Thomas à Becket* from the Blessed Virgin Mary herself during his exile in France 230 years before. She presumably had appeared to Becket while he was in exile and praying at the church of St. Colombe in Sens, France. Presenting him with a golden eagle* which contained a stone flask filled with oil, she told him that if this oil were to be used to anoint future [but unspecified] kings of England, they would recover peacefully the lands lost by their predecessors: the king thus anointed would recover Normandy and Aquitaine without the use of force, would become the "greatest among kings," would build many churches in the Holy Land, and would drive the pagans from and build many churches in Babylon. Because he was in exile, Becket hid the eagle in the church of St. Gregory, where it remained forgotten and undiscovered for a long time. A vision of a certain unnamed holy man during the reign of King Edward III, while Henry de Grosmont, first duke* of Lancaster, was fighting in the Battle of Poitiers,* revealed its presence seemingly to be used for the coronation of the Black Prince.* When he received the oil, the Black Prince placed it in a chest locked safely in the Tower of London to await his coronation. However, as his death preceded his father's, he was not to become king; and so when his son Richard was to be crowned, the holy oil could not be found.

In 1399, however, Richard found the chest in the tower, which when smashed open revealed the eagle containing the ampulla of holy oil and the "writing" of the martyr Becket. When he read about the powers of this holy oil, Richard asked the archbishop of Canterbury, Thomas Arundel, to anoint him with it, but the churchman refused, saying that his anointment could not be repeated. Although the king did not insist on being anointed a second time, he carried the eagle to turn away dangers, especially on his trip to Ireland in 1399. On his return to England later that year, the eagle was taken away from him by Archbishop Arundel, who made it quite clear that it was not he for whom the oil was intended; the oil was to be kept until the coronation of Henry IV. Not only was Henry the first king anointed with this holy oil, he was the *only* English king so anointed, for it never again was used in any English coronation ritual. (See Ampulla.)

Thus traditions connected with ordaining a monarch blended inauguration ceremonies from the Teutons with anointing ceremonies of the Christians. As a result, the concept emerged that the consecration of a king included the rites of anointing, investiture with insignia, coronation, enthronement, the coronation banquet, and so on. All these were accompanied by words and gestures, by symbolic ceremonies and liturgical formulae, and by ecclesiastical anthems and music which transformed the entire performance into a worship service. It was more than mere chance, for God was looking down upon it, and future generations as well, asking whether the crown had been passed from head to head as it should be. (Bibliog. 243, 301, 308)

anoselen, to train a hawk to fly at birds. See hawking. (Bibliog. 226)

antipasis, bloodletting* on the part of the body opposite from the afflicted area: from the left elbow if the right elbow was inflamed. (Bibliog. 226)

Antipodes, land on the other side of the earth.

antrustio (L; plural: *antrustiones*), freemen among the Franks of the 6th and 7th centuries who put themselves under the personal protection and service of the king* to serve as his armed companions. These were picked fighting men who enjoyed one of the highest social ranks of the population; only the king and queen had *antrustiones*. Each *antrustio* enjoyed a triple wergild*; if one were killed, the murderer had to pay three times as large a sum to the victim's family as for the death of any other man. (Bibliog. 123)

apanage. See appanage.

apaume, appaume, position of the hand or gauntlet,* showing the open palm* in heraldry.* (Bibliog. 43)

ape wine, one of the different stages of drunkenness: when a man began to drink he was like a lamb; as he continued, he became successively like the lion, then the ape, and then the sow. Also known as wyn ape. (Bibliog. 226)

apel. See horn calls in hunting.

apothecary, merchant who sold aromatic spices which were utilized in every kitchen except the poorest. Among the substances sold were antimony, acacia, asphodel, garlic, anise, almonds, amber, balsam, acanthus, hellebore, henbane, and gum arabic. People who were troubled by nervous stomachs would carry such spices which they would eat like candy. For example, Thomas à Becket* (1118–1170) ate both ginger and clove by the handful and always diluted his wine.* (Bibliog. 161)

apothecary pound. See barleycorn.

appanage, provision made for the maintenance of the younger children of kings,* princes,* and so forth. Originally it meant assigning the income from a province, from a jurisdiction of an area, or from a lucrative office. (Bibliog. 246)

appatis, agreement between local inhabitants and soldiers* living off the countryside as one of the ''spoils of war.''* As long as they made their payments at the proper time and did not aid their own side in any way, the inhabitants of an ''appatized'' country could not be plundered or put to ransom,* nor could their lands be burned or put to waste.* This was an expensive form of protection. (Bibliog. 181)

appeal, process of law in which the plaintiff, or appealor, laid an accusation against the defendant. In no way was this concerned with reversing a judicial decision; quite the contrary, for this was the initial stage of a judicial process: the accusation of guilt. (Bibliog. 226)

Appolin, Apolin, one of the four pagan gods worshipped by the people of Sarras, that is, the Saracens*; the other three gods were Tervagant, Jupiter, and Mahommed. The Saxons, being pagan, also worshipped him. (Bibliog. 372)

apposer, officer of the Exchequer* who examined or audited accounts. (Bibliog. 226)

approver, an accused person, legally termed *probator regis,* who turned king's or state's evidence to inform on his accomplices. If a felon (see felony) defended himself successfully against the appeals* (accusations) of others who had committed felonies in his presence and he thereby secured their conviction, he escaped hanging and was given the choice of life imprisonment or "abjuration of the realm."* However, before he could be accepted as an approver and accuse others, and only then, he had to ask for a coroner* to be assigned to him for "the king's profit." In granting him that permission, the justices made him swear on the Gospels that he would accuse all those who were guilty of the same offense as he, "omitting none for favour and adding none through malice," and warned him that he would hang if he broke his oath. Then they assigned a coroner* to hear, record, and report what he had to say. After all this, the approved was returned to jail* to await the outcome of the hearings. (Bibliog. 171)

apres, apre, apree, monster* in heraldry* having the body of a bull and the tail of a bear. (Bibliog. 43)

aptalon, creature of the wild having the form of an antelope and resembling a roe-buck with two horns as sharp as sickles. It was a savage and wild beast and most difficult to approach. It drank the waters of the Euphrates River which flowed from Paradise. To capture it, one had to arrange a trap that entangled its horns in the bushes. When so trapped, it cried out for help; then the hunter ran up and bound it securely. (Bibliog. 258)

aquarius. See ewerer.

aquilino, small silver coin of the gros* class struck at Padua between 1200 and 1300, and again at Treviso by the Count of Goritz (1319–1323); it bore the inscription "Padua Regia Civitas." (Bibliog. 150)

aragonais, French mercenaries.* (Bibliog. 159)

aramanda, silver-colored, semi-precious gem found in the Red Sea, this stone overcame one's anger when it was placed in the mouth. (Bibliog. 258)

arbalest (Fr. *arbalète;* Ger. *armbrust),* weapon commonly known as the crossbow.* All varieties consisted basically of a heavy bow* mounted on a stock having a groove in the top for an arrow,* with a mechanical unit to release the string. Frequently they were made of wood or whalebone and were wrapped with sinew. The earliest crossbows were comparatively light bows that could be drawn by hand, the stock being braced against the body. As they became stronger, the bow was held on the ground by the feet while both arms were used to pull back the bowstring. Later a metal stirrup was added in which to place the foot when drawing the bow. Even later a pulley and cords were used. In that arrangement, one end of the cord was fastened to the belt and the other hooked to the stock. The arbalestier* then stooped, bending his knees, and fastened the hook on the pulley to the bowstring. He bent the bow by rising and straightening his legs. This was followed by a windlass which drew back the bowstring. See moulinet and pulleys crossbow. (Bibliog. 71)

arbalest draught, arbalest shot, range of a crossbow.* (Bibliog. 226)

arbalestier, crossbowman whose early equipment consisted of a heaume* narrow at the back; a short-sleeved hauberk* of mail; a sleeveless surcoat* bearing his arms* on his breast. Later he was protected further by a haqueton* and a basinet* provided with a collarette of iron (a bent piece of steel hinged or pivoted on either side of the basinet and falling down to protect the chin and neck) and a pavise* carried on his back. After discharging his bolt, he would turn around, and under the protection of the pavise, would wind up his crossbow* in safety to fire again. See arbalest. (Bibliog. 9)

arbalestina, a cross-shaped opening in a wall from which to shoot with a crossbow.* See arbalest. (Bibliog. 45)

arbalète à cranequin (Fr.), windlass-type crossbow,* consisting of a toothed wheel enclosed in a circular and flat case. This wheel engaged a toothed rod with a hooked end so that when the wheel was turned by means of a handle, the rod advanced to grip the bowstring, and when reversed, it drew back the string to reach the notch. See moulinet and pulleys crossbow. (Bibliog. 9)

arbalète à cric (Fr.), powerful latch crossbow,* used frequently for the defense of castles* and beleaguered places. It drew on the same principles as the windlass (see moulinet and pulleys crossbow), but because of the great strength of the steel bow,* it required double sets of pulleys and cordage to cock it for firing, one near the bottom of the stock and the other near the bowstring. It got its name from the trigger shaped like a latch and manipulated by a cog wheel and its notched bar called a "*cric,*" which had hooks at the top to grasp the string and a handle turned by the archer to wind up the "moulinet" (winch) to draw the string and bend the bow. (Bibliog. 9)

arbalète à jalet. See prodd.

arch, device* of either a single curve supported by two pillars or a double one supported by three pillars, in heraldry.* (Bibliog. 43)

archduke, title borne by the dukes* of Austria, Lorraine, and Brabant; all three archduchies had devolved to the imperial family of Austria, so the sons of that family were styled archdukes and the daughters archduchesses. See also duchies. (Bibliog. 246)

arciones, high back and front peaks of a war saddle.* (Bibliog. 331)

arcon, saddle* bow, the rising front of a war saddle. (Bibliog. 9)

arcubalista, large Roman siege engine, more commonly known as a balista.* (Bibliog. 27)

Arends groot, Brabantine and Dutch coinage* of the 14th and later centuries. (Bibliog. 150)

argasill, antelope in heraldry* with a tiger's face, tusks, serrated horns, and an antelope's body, with tufts of hair down the spine and ending in a lion's* tail. (Bibliog. 43)

argent, silver and also the moon in heraldry*; the term came from the French word for silver, *argent.* (Bibliog. 43)

argentarius, the "silverer" at the Exchequer* who presided at the testing of the silver, while the fusor* did the actual testing. (Bibliog. 144)

argento, silver coinage struck by Pope Clement V at Carpentras near Avignon early in the 14th century. (Bibliog. 150)

argh, timid, cowardly, afraid; ignoble, worthless, contemptible. (Bibliog. 226)

argus, dewclaws of a hart.* (Bibliog. 226)

Arion, Hercules's horse* given to Adrastus. Its right feet were those of a man, it spoke with a human voice, and it ran with incredible swiftness. Formerly the horse of Neptune, it was brought out of the ground by having Neptune strike the earth with his trident. (Bibliog. 308)

aristocracy, hereditary, privileged, ruling class in England, composed of warriors and chieftains, manorial lords, royal officials, and knights of the shire.* These were a narrow band of earls* and barons* whose way of life differed greatly and deliberately from that of the common freeman and who, by the 13th century, had become endowed with definite privileges. Such privileges were almost exclusively political and honorific and were attached to their honour*; they were transmissable only to the eldest son through primogeniture.* This group maintained its dominant position through the centuries by restricting its activities primarily to the practical aspects of control over men. See nobility; peer. (Bibliog. 28)

arm, the human arm in heraldry* either embowed,* bent (cut off at the shoulder and flexed at the elbow), or cubit* (cut off at the elbow); the blazon* stated whether the arm was dexter* (right) or sinister* (left). (Bibliog. 43)

arm and crown, armed all over, from head to toe. See cap-a-pie. (Bibliog. 226)

arm long, length of the lower arm, a cubit.* (Bibliog. 226)

arma patria (L.), elderly squires* who either had been unable or unwilling to gain knighthood but were permitted to carry certain arms* of war on their own besides the sword*; their *arma patria* consisted of a lance* and shield.* (Bibliog. 225)

armbrust (Ger.), crossbow.* See also arbalest. (Bibliog. 27)

armed, 1. in heraldry,* the offensive and defensive portions of a creature's anatomy when of a different tincture (see colors) from that of the body; it was used to describe possession of teeth, claws, horns, or talons; 2. when used for humans or parts of the human body, it meant encased in armor* but with no reference to carrying weapons; a man carrying weapons but without his armor was "unarmed"; 3. heads of arrows,* but barbed (see barb) was the more usual term for that usage. (Bibliog. 43)

armed all to rights, completely equipped; fully armed. (Bibliog. 226)

armed at all points, totally armed and armored and ready for combat; said of knights prepared for tournaments* or battle.

armiger, 1. after an apprenticeship as an armiger, a young man ("tiro") in pre-Conquest Normandy had knighthood* bestowed upon him by a ceremony usually described as the bestowal of arms.* Robert of Grentemesnie, for example, was an armiger of Duke William* of Normandy (William the Conqueror) for five years and then was knighted by him; 2. an armiger in heraldry* was one who bore arms*; in the time of King Edward I (1272–1307), it meant one who served as a squire* to a knight. (Bibliog. 49, 87)

armigerous, personal blazon* on the shield* of a squire* who had been granted *"arma patria,"** that is, had been granted lance* and shield. (Bibliog. 225)

arming cap, small quilted coif worn under the hauberk* to support the helm.* This was a close-fitting cap equipped with two ear laps having laces to tie it under the chin; some had padded circular projections above the ears. (Bibliog. 27)

arming doublet, aketon,* jacket worn under armor.* (Bibliog. 226)

arming nail, rivet used in making or repairing armor.* (Bibliog. 226)

arming points, laces or cords for fastening the parts of armor* together. See aiguilette. (Bibliog. 331)

armor, 1. weapons and armor collectively: armament, arms; 2. an offensive weapon; 3. military equipment in general, siege engines; 4. soldier or soldiers; a body of troops; 5. use of weapons, warfare: by armor meant by armed force; 6. protection for the human body in combat in a never-ending search for means to provide warriors with protection that could withstand better than previous efforts the weapons used against it. Each development in protection was countered with new weapons to offset the new defensive measures. Seven "periods" of armor appeared between the Saxons control of England in the 8th and 9th centuries, and the development of plate armor around the year 1400:

Saxon—up to 1066

Norman—1066–1080

chain mail*—1180–1250

chain mail, reinforced—1250–1325

cyclas*—1325–1335

studded and splinted—1335–1360

camail* and jupon*—1360–1410

Saxon armor developed almost simultaneously in various Scandinavian countries, using the same military equipment: byrnie,* helmet,* and shield* as the main bodily defenses; spear,* javelin,* sword* scramasax,* and the axe* as weapons. Norman armor used the hauberk,* helmet, and shield; its weapons included the lance,* javelin, axe, sword, mace,* and bow.* This transition period was caused by new weapons or by improvements of old ones whereby existing armor was overcome. This period's most important offensive weapon was the

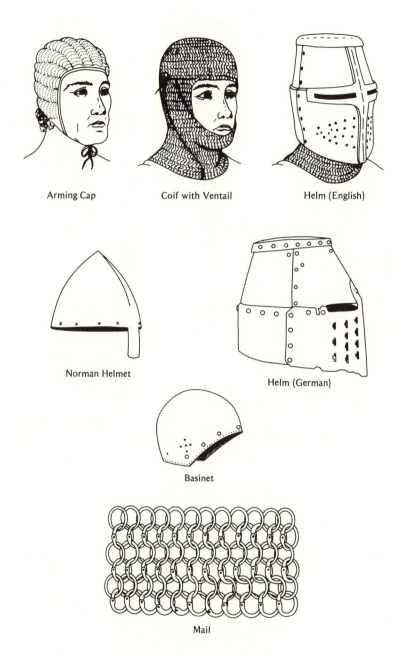

Arming Cap   Coif with Ventail   Helm (English)

Norman Helmet

Helm (German)

Basinet

Mail

Figure 1. Armor

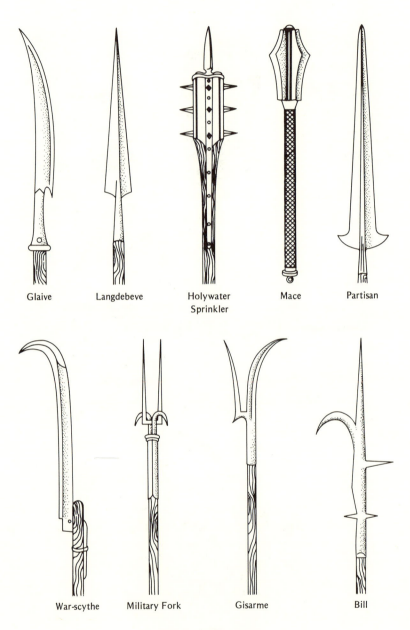

Glaive   Langdebeve   Holywater   Mace   Partisan
Sprinkler

War-scythe   Military Fork   Gisarme   Bill

Figure 2. Weapons

26

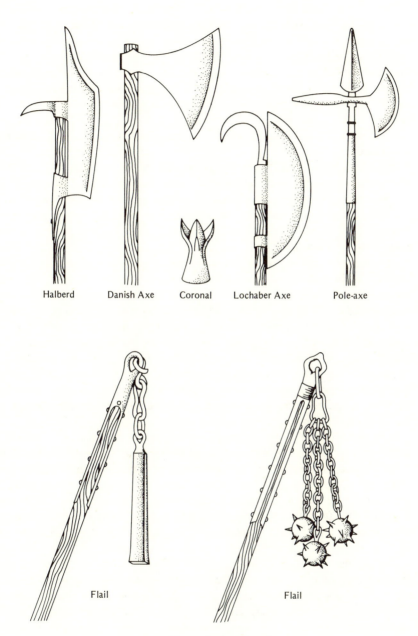

Halberd   Danish Axe   Coronal   Lochaber Axe   Pole-axe

Flail   Flail

Figure 2. *(continued)*

27

longbow,* first used decisively by the English at the Battle of the Standard* (1138). However, despite the fact that the Saxons earlier had used the shortbow, they deemed it less effective than the lance and axe. William* of Normandy's capitalizing on the Saxon's failure to use such a weapon, and his own use of large numbers of it, was largely responsible for his victory over Harold at the battle of Hastings in 1066. Practically all the Norman infantrymen were archers, and William used them as screens for his three large divisions of cavalry at that battle.

Chain mail replaced various defensive measures used previously; a heaume* was added to protect the head. Heraldry* began to appear at this time, which made identification easier, especially by the addition of a sleeveless surcoat* on which one's arms* could be represented, worn over the mail. This early mail was made only by the massive labor of coiling hand-drawn wire on a stick, cutting it, flattening the ends, piercing holes in each end, and riveting it to close each link meshed with other links. Such additional weight borne by the warrior made a horse* a necessity.

Armorers soon added reinforcements in the form of banded mail (see mail, banded). In the incipient stages of plate armor, armorers introduced reinforcing knee–cops* of plate because they recognized that the knees were particularly vulnerable. *Coif-de-mailles** were made continuous with the hauberk, probably worn over a pot-de-fer*; mail chausses* covered feet and legs; gauntlets* were made continuous with mail sleeves, mitten-like; the shield generally assumed a heater* shape. In addition, a conical helm* rested upon and was supported by the shoulders instead of being borne solely by the head; and crests* began to appear. The ordinary footsoldier wore a pot-de-fer covered with a quilted material which continued as a neck guard and pectoral, a surcoat under the hauberk, and his lower limbs frequently covered with leather.

In the cyclas period, warriors had come to realize that the use of pourponterie,* cuir-bouilli,* and a small amount of mail was proving ineffective. Thus they looked to a new form of defensive equipment: the cyclas. Basically this offered a large number of thickly padded, loose upper garments over a mixture of plate and mail. These flowing garments hampered the effect of a sword blow and mitigated the effect of a sweeping cut. And with all these layers, a lance or arrow would have to pierce in succession the cyclas, gambeson,* breastplate,* hauberk, haqueton,* and woolen shirt to wound a warrior.

This development was followed by studded and splinted armor during the transitional phase of strenuous warfare in England when the battles of Crècy* and Poitiers* figured so prominently. Armor changed as one form after another failed and was replaced. Plate armor composed of splints or separate pieces riveted together appeared after knights realized that large sheets of metal could not be adapted to the normal fighting movements of the human body. In reaction, narrow splints were used to allow great flexibility, for the backplates* and breastplates*, demi-cussarts,* demi-jambarts* with genouillieres* of plate were made of overlapping splints. Some helmets had occularia* and ventails,* some did not. Many of these defenses were adopted in reaction to the new weapon just coming into widespread use: the crossbow.* And the steel bow had increased the range of the archer from the longbow's* 250 yards* to over 300 yards.

During the sixty years of the camail and jupon period, splints, horn, bone, leather, *cuir-bouilli*,* and so on, that had not held up in battle all gave way to steel plate. At the start of the period, the basinet* was tall and pointed and came well down over the neck and sides, providing good protection for the ears and back of the head. The opening at the face was square or oval, and visors were hinged to move only up and down, not side to side as had their predecessors.

War armor was distinct from tournament* armor, for mobility was less important than safety in the joust,* and the massive weight of the tournament helms and reinforced armor suggested that the joust was too dangerous to be performed in the more mobile war armor. For example, a war helmet generally weighed about six or seven pounds,* whereas a tournament helmet could weigh as much as twenty-two pounds; breast and back plates approached seventeen pounds, as did the arm and shoulder defenses, and the leg and thigh coverings were almost that heavy in the tournaments. (Bibliog. 9, 27, 331)

armory, 1. armor* and weapons collectively, war equipment; 2. royal storehouse of weapons and armor, arsenal; 3. workshop in which arms were made or repaired; 4. the correct word used to describe the study of armorial insignia; the word ''heraldry,''* however, superceded it in popular usage, but strictly speaking, that word referred specifically to all the duties of a herald* and not just to insignia. (Bibliog. 43, 226)

arms, term freely used to refer to the complete achievement* of arms but accurately applied only to the shield* and the designs carried on it. (Bibliog. 43)

arms, bern of, an armed soldier* either mounted or on foot; a man-at-arms. See arms, lede of. (Bibliog. 226)

arms, come to, reach the age to be able to bear arms.* (Bibliog. 226)

arms, lede of, armed soldier, either mounted or on foot; a man-at-arms. See arms, bern of. (Bibliog. 226)

arms, mastery of, feat of arms; military action; deed performed in battle or tournament.* (Bibliog. 226)

arms of assumption, when the victor in a combat assumed the arms* of the loser, the arms so taken were ''arms of assumption,'' subject to the approval of the sovereign. (Bibliog. 43)

arms of England, Kings William* I, William II, and Henry I* used "gules,* two lions" (leopards*), passant* guardant* in pale or.*" Later, when Henry II* married Eleanor,* heiress to the duchy* of Aquitaine, he added a third lion, so his arms became "gules, three lions passant guardant in pale or", called the "Lions of England."* After 1340, King Edward III* bore "quarterly one and four azure* semy* of 'fleur de lis'* or" (for France) and two and three arms of England. Such arms were followed by King Richard II; but toward the end of his reign, he impaled* the imaginary arms of King Edward the Confessor, his patron saint: "azure, a cross patance* between five martlets* or." (Bibliog. 116)

arms of France, from the time of Louis VII (1137–1180), the French escutcheon* was "seme* de lis" in allusion to the king's name, Loys; but from the time of King Charles V (1364–1380), the royal insignia carried "three 'fleur de lis'* or.*" (Bibliog. 116)

arms of God, fanciful escutcheon* of the 14th century which portrayed God's figure with "a helmet* crowned or,* with roset mantling* and wreath,* a crucifix or, pierced by three nails, at the top a scroll inscribed I N R I, on the dexter* a birch, on the sinister* a scourge." (Bibliog. 99)

arms of office, arms* borne by reason of holding a certain office, such as "king of arms"*; they could be impaled* with the personal arms of the office-holder. (Bibliog. 43)

arpentier (Fr. *arpent,* land measure equivalent to one and one-half English acres*), surveyor of land. (Bibliog. 226)

Arques-la-Bataille, castle* built by William of Arques on the French coast of the English Channel in 1038. Besieged by William* the Conqueror in 1052, it was rebuilt later by Henry I* of England and was the last castle to surrender to Geoffrey*, count of Anjou (1129–1151), when he conquered Normandy. (Bibliog. 45)

array, troops drawn up and prepared for battle. (Bibliog. 163)

array, commission of, method most commonly used to obtain troops for a great war. By this method, crown commissioners surveyed the able-bodied men between the ages of sixteen and sixty in each hundred* and township within the shire,* and, under the authorization of the Statute of Winchester (1285), chose the best of them to serve at the king's wages, but the cost of their initial equipment was to be borne by the localities. These commissioners normally were men of knightly class, sometimes experienced officers of the "king's household"* who knew what they were looking for. Their efforts were helped at the beginning of each campaign by various proclamations that offered inducements to serve in the wars, such as pardons for criminal offenses, prospects for good wages, or shares in the profits of war. Although compulsion may have had to be applied to obtain men to serve in Scotland, there was no lack of eager volunteers for the campaigns in France because of the richly attractive prospects for gain across the channel. In fact, in 1359 King Edward III had so many more volunteers for his impending French campaigns than he could use that he had to reject a large number. See *arrière-ban;* spoils of war. (Bibliog. 222)

arrearage, unpaid debt; balance due on debt, wages, pension, taxes. (Bibliog. 226)

arrent, exchange of rent for a special duty, used to refer to sergeanty.* (Bibliog. 264)

arrière-ban (Fr.), also known as *levée en masse*, this was the rule that every able-bodied man in the country owed military service to his lord and was to provide himself with the weapons according to the worth of his land and chattels. Known in Europe since the days of the Carolingians, this practice never really was used until 13th-century princes* adopted it. Normally, the knight who fought because of his "feudal obligation"* formed the core of the "feudal army"* and with his tactics generally dominated battlefield into the 13th century. Mercenaries* usually served as footsoldiers. During the 13th century, though, as the pike* and longbow* came into use, princes expanded their traditional right of mobilizing all freemen to fight; and in the hands of freemen, both those weapons proved fearsome against knights and repeatedly drove feudal aristocracy* from the field. Thus with the weapons and battlefield tactics* of footsoldiers prevailing over knights, and with the costs of putting a knight into the field becoming prohibitive, the princes of Europe recruited their armies on the principle that military service had to be performed because of allegiance to the prince. This won them more battles and was far less expensive, despite the fact that the men came to be paid daily and were kept in the field far longer than in the past.

The commission of array,* the English version of *arrière-ban*, was used regularly by Edward I, II, and III to procure troops for their Welsh, Scottish, and occasionally for their continental wars. This new development affected fief-rentes* by slackening the demand for knights provided by fief-rente. Additionally, not being based on feudal tenure,* such service weakened the position of the lord who was required by fief-rentes to supply archers, pikemen, and other types of footsoldiers; the *arrière-ban* obtained these soldiers without the expenses of the fief-rente.

Among other uses, King Henry I of France assembled this *arrière-ban* against the Normans of 1059, and Louis the Fat summoned it against the German invasion in 1124. (Bibliog. 208)

arrière-garde (Fr.), the reserve forces of an army in the 14th century. Then, the army was arranged in three battles (*batailles**) or divisions: the *avant-garde,** *bataille,* and *arrière-garde;* sometimes these three formed in line, the two *gardes* serving on the wings but maintaining their names. (Bibliog. 264)

arrow, missile shot from a bow*; composed of four parts: the head or pile; the body, stele,* or shaft; the nock* or notch for the bowstring; the feathers, glued or tied to the shaft to steady the flight. Its length varied from eighteen to sixty inches.* Generally, it followed an English rule that the bow should be the height of the user and the arrows for that bow one-half the bow height. (Bibliog. 331)

arrow, bearing, an arrow* which possessed a steady and unwavering flight. (Bibliog. 100)

arrow loops, narrow vertical slots, called "*meurtrières*"* (murderesses), which pierced the "curtain walls"* at a level below the battlements.* Flaring out on the inside, these gave the defending archers room to move laterally and thus cover a broad field of fire, while presenting in return only a narrow exterior slit as a target. (Bibliog. 129)

arteler, maker of arms, weapons. (Bibliog. 226)

articles of the eyre. See feudal obligations; wardship.

artillator, maker of bows,* arrows,* darts,* and other military stores. (Bibliog. 331)

ashlar, stone with a flat surface, usually rectangular shaped; used in building castles,* especially the outer surfaces of walls which then had rubble packed in between them to form a solid core. (Bibliog. 280)

ashlar coin, ashlar* stone used for the corners of buildings or for buttresses. (Bibliog. 226)

asine, measure of capacity used principally for wine* in the 14th century; it had no standard dimensions and probably meant the load of burden of one ass; presumably equivalent to one sack* load. (Bibliog. 394)

asius, stone of Alexandria; white and light as pumice stone, its surface disintegrated and crumbled whenever it was touched; it had a salty taste, and when mixed with wine,* it was a sovereign remedy for a host of ailments such as gout, fistula, and so on. See frigius. (Bibliog. 258)

asp, venomous slaying adder which felt love and affection for its mate as though through wedlock; if one was killed, the other pursued the killer with a vengeance that passed comprehension: it always found him whether in great company of people or alone, and overcoming all difficulties and distances, it slew him. See aspide. (Bibliog. 21)

aspect, synonymous with "attitude" when referring to the position of an animal in blazon,* in heraldry.* (Bibliog. 251)

aspersed, strewn or scattered as stars, in heraldry.* See seme. (Bibliog. 251)

aspide, aspic, serpent, slaying adder, whose bite and fatal wound were so well known by the history of Cleopatra. It was crowned by a precious stone called a carbuncle and knew how to escape from enchanters who by means of magic words wished to despoil it of its gem: it would keep one ear to the ground and thus seal it, and would plug the other ear with its tail and thus not hear the magic words. There are many species of aspides: those whose bite made people die of thirst; who made people die of lethargie (the death trance); who made people bleed to death; and who made people swell up and decay of rot. See asp. (Bibliog. 193)

aspro, silver coinage* of the Knights of St. John of Jerusalem at Rhodes (see Hospitallers) in the 14th century; it also was known as the danaro. (Bibliog. 324)

assail, to attack or assault an enemy, city, person; to besiege a city; to invade and plunder property. (Bibliog. 226)

assart, clearings; land made available for pasture or lair for animals when groves of trees or thickets in the forest* were cut down, torn up by the roots, and the land was cultivated. If five or more trees close together were felled, it was called waste.* (Bibliog. 281)

Assassins, radical Muslim sect in the Ismali sect of the Shi'ites, organized late in the 11th century to fight the opponents of the Ismali by any means, including murder and poisoning. Because they used to fortify themselves for their bloody work by using hashish, they were known by their Arabic name, Hashishin— "users of hashish"—which the French-speaking crusaders pronounced as "assassin," a term which became synonymous with murder. They set up a stronghold on the border of Antioch under the leadership of Sinan Ibn Salman Ibn Muhammad, called Rashid ad-Din, and preserved their independence even in the time of Saladin.* Under Sinan, called Old Man of the Mountain by his followers, the Assassins began to act against the crusaders (see crusades). Two of them murdered Conrad of Montferrat in 1192, supposedly at the instigation of Richard

Coeur de Lion,* but this charge was disproved. At Acre on June 17, 1271, an
emissary of the Old Man of the Mountain, against whom Richard, earl of Cornwall,* tried to warn King Henry III of England, tried to stab the heir apparent
to the English throne, Prince Edward; and when royal attendants raced to the
scene of the scuffle between Edward and his would-be killer, they found that
the prince already had killed his attacker but had been wounded in the process.
His wife, Eleanor of Provence, sucked the poison from the wound to save her
husband's life. (Bibliog. 44, 139)

assault, unconditional surrender in the law of war, though not a fortress or town
taken by hot blood and force of arms. (Bibliog. 181)

assault tower. See belfry; cat.

assay, to test one's qualities in combat, the qualities of materials, the effectiveness of a horse,* or the performance of a weapon. (Bibliog. 226)

assessor, advisor of a ruler, lord, or magistrate in matters of law. (Bibliog. 226)

assise, note on a hunting horn* blown at the death of a stag which had been
hunted and brought down by staghounds. See horn calls in hunting. (Bibliog.
96)

assize, 1. session of a court* charged with the deliberation and disposition of
civil actions, especially actions concerning land tenure* and imprisonment; 2.
the deliberations of such a court, including the gathering of evidence and the
hearing of plaintiff, defendant, and witnesses before a jury and the rendering of
the decisions. Instituted by the *Magna Carta Libertatum** in 1215, these courts
were held periodically in each county* in England by the High Court of Justice,
attended by a jury. See jury duty. (Bibliog. 261)

Assize of Arms, one of the military reforms instituted by King Henry II of
England (1181) in order to recreate the ancient fyrd* as an efficient supplement
to the "feudal levies."* Its provisions required that:

1. every holder of a knight's fee (see knighthood) have a hauberk,* a helmet,* a shield,*
   and a lance* for his own use, and as many hauberks, helmets, shields, and lances as
   he had knight's fees in his demesne*;
2. every free layman who held chattels* or rent valued at sixteen marks* or more have
   a hauberk, helmet, shield, and lance; every free layman who held chattels or rent
   worth ten marks have an aubergel,* a headpiece of iron, and a lance;
3. and all burgesses and the whole body of freemen have quilted doublets and a headpiece
   of iron and a lance;

4. and every one of them swear that before the Feast of St. Hilary (January 13) he would obtain these arms, would swear allegiance to King Henry, and would bear these arms in his service according to his orders.

This assize* synthesized the great fyrd and the select fyrd (see fyrd) into a single recruitment system and thereby incorporated all those from the feudal service of knight's fees to the general obligation of freemen. Later King Henry issued a similar assize for his continental domains, as did the French kings, Philip Augustus and Philip of Flanders (see Philip). It was the beginning of a long process that undermined the system of private feudal tenures* and united knight service into the same system that governed the recruitment of footsoldiers and men-at-arms. (Bibliog. 102)

Assize of Bread and Ale, statutory regulation (1267) of reign of Henry III* that fixed the price of bread* and ale with that of grain. (Bibliog. 163)

Assize of Clarendon, legislative enactment (1166) of King Henry II* of England that increased the powers of police jurisdiction of itinerant justices and applied their sworn inquest exclusively to the settlement of criminal cases. Furthermore, it replaced the ancient processes of compurgation* and trial by "ordeal"* in the formal procedures in criminal cases with references to both the previous record and the reputation of the accused. Some of its more important provisions required that a jury of twelve men from each hundred* and four from each vill* inquire into whether any hundred or vill had any murderer, thief, or robber living in it, or anyone there sheltering such felons; any suspects so found were to clear themselves by the "ordeal of cold water."* If a suspect's lord, steward,* or vassals* stood pledge for him within three days, he was to be released on bail until his trial. Anyone arrested on suspicion was to have a speedy trial. If no jails were available in the area, prisoners were to be housed in any nearby castle* of the king or in a jail built of wood from the king's forest* if no castle was nearby. Anyone of evil reputation who was caught with stolen goods in his possession was to be punished immediately without trial; anyone else so caught was to undergo the ordeal of cold water; any accused felons of evil reputation who were acquitted of the charges were to undergo "abjuration of the realm"* within eight days and were to be outlawed (see outlaw) if they ever returned. See trial procedure. (Bibliog. 102)

assize of *mort d'ancestor*, disposition of freehold held by the heir's immediate ancestor. If a man died in seisin,* that is, in possession of a tenement [a holding], his heir was entitled to obtain possession of it against every other claimant, even if such a claimant actually had a better right to the land than the dead man had; such a right had to be exerted in person and not by the seizure of a vacant tenement. (Bibliog. 261)

Assize of Novel Disseisin, ordinance issued by English King Henry II in 1166 on the new and startling principle that if one person was disseised [dispossessed] of his free tenement (holding) unjustly and without a judgment, he was to have a remedy by royal writ; a jury was to be summoned and in the presence of the king's justices was to answer the simple question about seisin* and disseisin: who had the right to the holding. If it found for the plaintiff, he was to be restored to his possession. This concept occurred again in clause 35 of the *Magna Carta Libertatum.** See also Grand Assize. (Bibliog. 261)

Assize of the Forest, King Henry II in 1184 promulgated this assize* to protect his forests.* Its provisions forbade anyone from transgressing against his hunting* rights or his forests in any respect; and if anyone was convicted of offending these rights, full justice* would be exacted from the offender. Twelve knights were appointed to guard his property in every county* where he had venison, vert,* and forest, and four knights were appointed to pasture cattle in his woods and receive and protect the king's rights of pannage.* Dogs that intruded and harried wild animals in their forest lairs were to be mutilated (see mutilation of dogs). (Bibliog. 102)

Assize Utrum, assize* issued by Henry II of England in 1164 creating a legal process calling on twelve lawful men to determine whether [*utrum*] a particular tenement (holding) belonged to free alms [by reason of frankalmoigne*] or to a lay fee, that is, regular tenancy. See also Grand Assize. (Bibliog. 261)

assoin, pardon; free from guilt. See essoin.

astrolabe, instrument for determining the movements and positions of celestial bodies and calculating longitude and latitude; this was the most important astronomical instrument of the entire period. (Bibliog. 226)

at gaze, deer-blazoned statant* guardant,* in heraldry.* See beasts, positions of; deer. (Bibliog. 251)

at speed, running deer* in a blazon,* in heraldry.* See beasts, positions of. (Bibliog. 251)

athel-man, nobleman, knight.

atheling, member of a noble family: a prince,* a lord, baron,* a prince of the royal blood, even carrying over to refer to the heir apparent to the throne. This term was derived from an early English word, *aethel,* which came from an Old

Norse word meaning race or ancestry, especially noble ancestry or nobility,*
and carried with it the meaning of honor, dignity, might, and power. (Bibliog.
246)

athresten, to pursue game closely. See hunting. (Bibliog. 246)

attach, to arrest someone or to secure by means of sureties a person's future
attendance at court.* (Bibliog. 171)

Attachment, Court of. See Court of Attachment.

attack first, philosophical advice with three separate meanings: (a) [Scriptural]
it is better to give than to receive; (b) it is more virtuous to do well than to do
nothing; (c) the harder and more difficult a thing is to do, the more virtue there
is in doing it. (Bibliog. 31)

attaint, overturn a verdict. An assize* could be attainted, that is, the verdict of
the assize (the twelve men) could be overturned by being brought before another
set of twenty-four men. There the verdict could be reversed and the original jury
of twelve punished if the twenty-four disagreed with it; then the twelve could
be imprisoned for a year, lose their chattels, and "lose the law of the land,"
that is, they would cease to be "oath-worthy." See jury duty. (Bibliog. 261)

attaint jury, jury of twenty-four men summoned to inquire whether a previous
jury had returned a false verdict. See attaint. (Bibliog. 261)

attire, knight's whole equipment: armor,* weapons, mount. (Bibliog. 226)

attired, antlers of a stag or other member of the deer* family mentioned when
of a different tincture (see colors) than the head, in heraldry.* (Bibliog. 43)

attires, deer's* antlers, in heraldry.* (Bibliog. 43)

attributed arms, arms* invented by heralds* for someone who never could
have borne them: pre-heraldic monarchs, saints, and biblical figures. See Adam's
and Eve's Arms; arms of God. (Bibliog. 43)

aubergel, garment similar to but less costly than a hauberk.* See Assize of
Arms. (Bibliog. 102)

augmentation, mark added to an existing "coat of arms"* to commemorate
some notable achievement or special honor. Usually as a chief,* canton,* or
inescutcheon,* and often referred to as of an extra crest,* this was borne on the
dexter* of the family crest. King Richard II augmented his arms with the leg-

endary arms of St. Edward the Confessor (see arms of England) and in 1394 granted the same to Thomas Mowbray, duke* of Norfolk, to be impaled* in the same manner. (Bibliog. 43)

augustale, gold coin of Sicily issued by Frederick II in 1231 from his mints in Messina and Brindisi. It was modeled on the ancient Roman *aureii* and contained the profile portrait of Frederick in the Roman manner on the obverse and an eagle* on the reverse. See coinage. (Bibliog. 150)

aula, hall* or a manor* house but not a castle.* See steward. (Bibliog. 341)

aula regis. See *curia regis.*

aulnager, official stationed in a port (see borough) or town who measured the cloth brought in by merchants and textile manufacturers to determine whether its length and breadth (its "aulnage") conformed to statutory specifications. (Bibliog. 326)

auqueton. See aketon.

austringer, one who kept short-winged birds for hawking.* (Bibliog. 26)

auxilia. See aids.

auxilium exercitus (L.), scutage* levied in Normandy.

avant-bras, armor* for the forearm. See brassard.

avant-garde (Fr.), division of the 14th-century army. See *arrière-garde.*

aventail, mail tippet which replaced the 14th-century English coif* and was fastened inside the helmet*; it was called *camail* in France. (Bibliog. 27)

aventiure, acceptance of risk in equal combat in the hope of augmented honor and renown; it was characteristic of chivalric life (see chivalry) in the courtly romance* in High Middle German literature, as personified in Wolfram von Eschenbach's *Parzival.* (Bibliog. 124)

aver. See affer.

aversant, clenched, as a heraldic (see heraldry) fist; it was the opposite of apaume.* (Bibliog. 43)

avoirdupois, system of weights which originally applied to goods sold by weight rather than by capacity, by the piece, or by any other way; the term came from the French *aver* or *avoir* (the property of goods), and *de* (of), and *pois* or *peis*(weight). See also barleycorn. (Bibliog. 394)

avon. See afon.

axe, used commonly as a weapon on the continent but rarely as a weapon in England. Basically an agricultural tool, it was used to fell trees, oxen, and opponents; it had an ash handle and iron head. In Normandy, however, the axe was a long-handled weapon with a single curved blade; it was used by William* I on his invasion of England and by Richard I* on his crusade.* In contrast, the Danish axe was a staff weapon with a blade on one side of the head and a diamond-shaped spike on the other. (Bibliog. 9)

azure, heraldic tincture (see colors) of blue. Deriving its name from the Arabic word, *lazura*, which was introduced into the Western languages by returning crusaders (see crusades), the term meant the bright blue of the eastern sky. (Bibliog. 43)

B

Babieca, Bavieca, El Cid's famous steed. (Bibliog. 308)

bacele, ten lances* of cavalry, each of fifty to sixty horsemen, forming a division of cavalry; five baceles united to form a regiment of fifty lances (or 300 men) under the command of a "banneret knight."* (Bibliog. 331)

bachelor, young knight, a novice in arms, who was not allowed to lead a body of his retainers onto the field, that is, was not allowed to "*lever bannière*" (raise his banner*); he was a young knight, too young or having too few vassals* to display his own banner, but carried instead pennons* ending in a point* or points and followed the banner of another. See knight bachelor. (Bibliog. 17)

bacinet. See basinet.

backplate, metal protection for the back from the waist to the neck; when used with a breastplate* to cover the entire torso from waist to neck, it was called a cuirass.* (Bibliog. 9)

badge, mark of distinction, a cognizance similar to a crest,* though not placed on a wreath* or worn on a helmet.* This was a supplemental bearing quite independent of the charges* of the original arms,* and although borne often on banners,* ensigns,* and caparisons,* most frequently it was worn on the sleeves of servants and followers. Examples of badges included the broom plant, (*planta genesta**) used by the kings* of England who were descendants of Count Geoffrey of Anjou and his son Henry II (1154–1189), the Plantagenets*; King Stephen (1135–1154) used ostrich feathers; Richard I* (1189–1199) used variously a star within a crescent* (on his great seal), and a star and a crescent separate on later occasions. Both John (1199–1216) and Henry III (1216–1272) used the star within the crescent; but Edward I (1272–1307) Henry III's son, used a rose,* and his son, Edward II (1307–1327), used hexagonal castles.* At the celebrated judicial combat (see duel) at Coventry before King Richard II (1377–1399) in 1398, Henry of Lancaster (later Henry IV) appeared in blue and green embroidered with swans and antelopes, his badges; Mowbray wore crimson velvet embroidered with silver lions* and mulberry trees, his badges. (Bibliog. 43)

bagwyn, heraldic monster* resembling the argasil* but with the tail of a horse* and long curved horns. (Bibliog. 43)

Baiart, Bayard, horse* of Renaut de Montauban; its name meant bay color. (Bibliog. 191)

bailey, palisaded enclosure as part of early castles.* Often the synonymous word "ward" and the term "base-court" were used to refer to various enclosed portions of a medieval castle—to mean a guarded enclosure. (Bibliog. 341)

bailiff, official of a medieval estate. The bailiff, or beadle* as he frequently was called, was an outsider appointed by the lord to look after the interests of his employer: he collected rents, enforced duties, managed the home farm,* and took care of the domainial cattle, buildings, and agricultural implements. Often he was hired to perform such duties in consideration of a fixed rent; in that case, the bailiff was known as a firmarius.

Some manors* had both bailiff and reeve,* but most had only one man to do both jobs. Occasionally, when the bailiff had charge of two manors or more, he was given the rank and pay of a serviens (sergeant*), but little differentiated his duties from those of a simple bailiff. Regardless of his title, the bailiff stood above the other dwellers on the manor because he was a freeman and had prestige arising from his being spokesman for his lord. Furthermore, he swore before the "manor court"* and took his oath of fealty* in which he swore to protect his lord's rights. For these services he was paid well, often being the top-paid servant. Living in the manorial house at the expense of the lord so he could keep a sharp eye on the other servants, he superintended the affairs of the entire manor.

Once a year, shortly after Michaelmas (see Appendix A), the lord's auditors would appear at the manor and examine critically its financial affairs and conditions. To these men the bailiff had to explain in verifiable detail and to substantiate with tallies* and other records the full details of just how he had spent the lord's money during the past year and what he had received for every penny.* Afterwards, he would obtain from the auditors a handwritten quittance stating that on his leaving office or at the end of the year, there were on the manor so many horses,* plows, bags of feed, and so on. Two copies of this document were written on one piece of parchment which was divided in two by a wavy line: one part was given to the bailiff and the other was sewn into the roll for the year so that if any dispute arose, both copies could be checked readily. (Bibliog. 24)

balancing, hurling shot from a catapult.*

baldric, distinctive hip belt used between 1360 and 1400. From it the sword* was suspended on the left and the misericorde* on the right by a small chain.

Fastened in front by a buckle, this baldric had its free end pushed up under the sash and passed downward through the loop formed, producing an effective fastening. See Order of the Garter. (Bibliog. 9)

baleyn, whalebone used unsuccessfully by armorers* late in the 13th century as an experimental substitute for metal. (Bibliog. 27)

balinger, small, fast, naval vessel.

balista, springald, siege weapon which shot shafts and javelins* to pick off adversaries who showed themselves along ramparts* or in apertures in crenellation.* Its earliest form had a heavy frame with three vertical openings: the two on the sides contained a tightly twisted skein of cord or sinew in the midst of which was placed a lever projecting backward; the ends of these levers were joined by a cord drawn back by a windlass. A guide for supporting the missile was fastened in the lower section of the middle opening. The catch for the cord connecting the levers, and the trigger mechanism, were at the rear of the trough. The dart* or missile was placed in the trough before the cord was drawn and could be fired whenever desired, regardless of whether it had been drawn back to its fullest; this allowed the users to control the range of the missile. Sometimes balls of baked clay were used because they would shatter on impact, causing damage, and could not be used by the enemy in return. In the 12th century, a crossbow* often was referred to as the "balista." See also moulinet and pulleys crossbow. (Bibliog. 331)

balistarii, (L.) ancient term for "slingers": men who operated the balista.* These men operated their machines so far from the front line of combat that they needed no armor,* not even a helmet,* for protection. (Bibliog. 9)

balk, strip of land left unplowed as a boundary line between two furrows, or plowed portions of a field.* (Bibliog. 24)

ballard, German coin. See pollard.

ballock-knife, dagger or knife with its guard formed by two rounded lobes, often made with the wooden grip and reinforced at the top with a metal washer. First appearing in England, Scotland, and Flanders, these were widely used by the laity or the common man around 1300. (Bibliog. 27)

Balmung, one of the swords* made by Weiland the Smith for Siegfried. (Bibliog. 308)

bandcroll, small flag used to indicate the limits of a military encampment. (Bibliog. 331)

banded mail. See mail, banded.

banderolle, banderole, small streamer attached to the head of a lance*; also called a pencil. See also pennoncelle.

bane, slayer of a human. See deodand.

banner, small square or oblong flag carried at the end of a lance,* in contrast to the standard,* although the terms often were used interchangably to mean the flag of a knight, baron,* or king.* It was the symbol of resistance because troops fought as long as their leader's banner flew. A rule of the Knights Templar* which set the practice followed by most combatants stated that a knight cut off from his own banner was to continue fighting under the first Christian banner he encountered, and only when no banner could be seen was he free to seek refuge. Therefore, as it served as the sign of a successful attack or of continuing resistance, and the troops recognized that its being down marked the beginning of defeat and signalled flight, then naturally it was necessary to protect the banner with utmost vigilance and effort. The marshal* and commander of any unit would detail ten knights to guard the banner, and every deputy commander had a spare banner which was unfurled immediately when the first one had been brought down. Furthermore, it served as more than a useful and practical rallying point around which troops regrouped, more than a unique symbol; it was the sign of authority for the execution of orders and for ensuring that the fight continued to ultimate victory. (See banners displayed.)

Banners were also used to signal the need for help. At the battle of Bouvines* in 1214, after King Philip* of France had been pulled from his horse* and was in serious danger of being killed, one of his men, Waldo of Montigny, saved him by summoning a compact band of knights to rescue the king by the tactic of raising and lowering the royal banner to signal that the king needed immediate help.

Only a king, duke,* count,* or baron used both banner and pennon*; "banneret knights"* used a banner alone, and nobles who were not barons or banneret knights bore only a pennon. Such a distinction carried over into warfare.

Another Templar rule stipulated that a knight was forbidden to attack with the lance that had the banner attached to it; even the lance with the reserve banner was included in such a prohibition. Violation of this rule meant expulsion from the Templars, and if harm to the banner resulted from such an attack, the offender could be put into irons and thrown into jail.* (Bibliog. 241, 351)

bannerer, one who bears the banner* of his king* or lord.

banneret knight, knight whose pennon* was rendered square by having the points* of the bachelor's* pennon cut off in high recognition of extraordinary gallantry on the battlefield. Such a process of converting a pennon into a banner* was performed by the English king* himself on the field of battle, standing beneath his own "royal standard,"* and the knight so honored ranked above all other knights except those of the Order of the Garter.* By accepting this honor, the banneret was expected to provide and support fifty or more men-at-arms for his sovereign, but because of this expense, poorer knights often declined the honor. Although this banner bore the blazon* of the banneret himself and served as an ensign* for his followers and retainers, this dignity died with the person who gained it. Heralds* were charged with recording when such awards were bestowed and of the blazons of all the knights in the kingdom. The Roll of Caerlaverock,* for example, contained the blazon of nearly one hundred bannerets (including the king, eleven earls,* and the bishop of Durham) who were present with King Edward I on his campaign against Scotland in 1300. (Bibliog. 251)

banners displayed, an acknowledged declaration of war. To ride with one's banners* displayed was a public display of declaring open warfare against one's king. Originally a sign of a breach of the feudal contract between a lord and his vassal,* it later became a token of treason to a sovereign prince.* In 1233, for example, the "earl marshal"* declared his rebellion by unfurling his banner at Woodstock; in 1322, Roger Damory was accused of such an action and was tried by the "Court of Chivalry"* (though the court was not called that then) under the constable* and marshal.* (Bibliog. 87)

Banos de la Encina, castle* built by the caliph* Hakam II in 967–968 to guard the Guadalquiver River in Granada, but it was captured by the Christians before 1212. Its single enciente* had fifteen square towers and a double horseshoe gateway of ashlar.* (Bibliog. 45)

banwort. See bonewort.

bar, an ordinary* which like the fess* crossed the center of the heraldic field* horizontally; it normally occupied one-fifth of the field unless widened to about one-third to accommodate a supercharge (see charge). (Bibliog. 43)

bar hole, horizontal hole or recess for a timber bar used as a door bolt. (Bibliog. 280)

bar sinister, misnomer for baton* or bendlet* sinister* which was an heraldic mark of bastardy. The original term, *barre sinistre*, was merely the French translation of bend sinister, the French word *barre* meaning a bend,* not the English bar.* (Bibliog. 43, 361)

barat, baret, strife, conflict, turmoil, disturbing the peace. (Bibliog. 226)

barb, backward-turned point on a spear* or arrow* to prevent its being withdrawn from a wound. (Bibliog. 331)

Barbarossa, "Redbeard," Emperor Frederick I.

barbel, part of a helmet* protecting the chin. (Bibliog. 226)

barber-surgeons, practitioners of the art of surgery; they performed minor operations such as bloodletting,* tooth-drawing, cauterization, and so on for centuries. Until the 12th century, the practice of surgery and medicine was almost exclusively confined to the clergy. In those early times, barbers assisted monks in surgical operations, thereby acquiring a proficiency which enabled them to practice as surgeons themselves. In 1163, however, the Council of Tours under Pope Alexander III considered that any practice which involved shedding blood was incompatible with the holy office of the clergy and forbade them to involve themselves in any way in surgery. Therefore, they had to give over surgery to the barbers; the clergy kept for themselves, however, the practice of healing in medicine. Thereafter, barbers, practicing the art, called themselves barber-surgeons. In 1307 barbers were forbidden to put blood in their windows to advertise on pain of a two-shilling (see money) fine.* They also had been supervising public baths which were the frequent resort of improper characters; so in the next year, when Richard le Barbour was made "master of the barbers," he was instructed to make sure that barbers kept no brothels. Subsequently, they were appointed as keepers or porters to keep strict watch that no lepers should enter the city of London in 1375, because their surgical and medical knowledge enabled them to identify those afflicted with leprosy. (Bibliog. 392)

barbican, any outwork of a castle* by which its principal approach or the gateway of a town could be protected by the field of fire from the walls. The barbican proper was a walled extension of a gatehouse* outward which restricted the approach to only a narrow passage. For example, Walmgate Bar at York had a gatehouse strengthened by adding on its outer side two parallel high walls at right angles to the sides of the gateway. These formed a walled alleyway through which any attackers would have to pass in order to get at the gateway proper, but in crossing this barbican area, the attacking forces would be exposed to the missiles of the defenders from the ramparts* of the gatehouse and the adjacent areas on the walls. (Bibliog. 341)

barbuda, coin with the denomination of three dinheiros struck under Fernando I of Portugal, 1367–1383; it had a profile of the king,* crowned and visored on the obverse, and a cross* surcharged with a besanted* shield* and cantoned* with four castles* on the reverse. (Bibliog. 150) *barbute,* Italian helmet* imitating classical models. Although similar to the ordinary basinet,* its sides extended forward to protect the face, leaving in front only a narrow opening the width of the eyes, while fully protecting the neck. (Bibliog. 241)

bard, early British entertainer who was both musician and poet, held in highest esteem by the people. In their works, these poets celebrated the noble actions of illustrious persons in heroic poems which they sang to the sounds of the lyre accompaniment. See entertainment. (Bibliog. 334)

barded, caparisoned, fully bridled, saddled, and armored horse.* See caparisoned. (Bibliog. 241)

bardiche, Russian and Scandinavian weapon with a long, narrow, crescent-shaped blade attached to the top of a pole by a ringed haft (the handle of a weapon); the lower end of the blade was fastened to the pole further down. (Bibliog. 71)

barding, armor* for horses.* The earliest were of mail,* but then because of weight, they were changed to *cuir-bouilli,** though the chanfron* and crinet (see horse armor) were of metal. A full suit of barding consisted of headpiece or chanfron; the upper side of the neck covered by the crinet, a series of articulated plates or of narrow plates alternating with mail; sometimes a cuello, articulated plates for the lower side of the neck; peytral* (poitrel) of plate, some with bosses* on the side, covered the animal's chest and shoulders as far back as the saddle*; flanchards* protected the sides below the saddle; and a crupper (see horse armor) of several plates riveted together sometimes had a tubular plate as a tail guard attached at the root of the tail to allow it some motion. (Bibliog. 331)

barge, seagoing vessel of moderate size; war vessel attending a great ship. (Bibliog. 226)

barleycorn, standard base of the linear measures and the apothecary, avoirdupois,* and troy pounds. Linearly, three medium-sized barleycorns placed end to end were an inch* as defined by statute, and twelve of those inches were a foot.* The apothecary and troy pounds had 5,760 barleycorns, the avoirdupois pound had 7,000. (Bibliog. 394)

barnacle, 1. instrument used to pinch a horse's* nose and thus to curb it when breaking it to harness or saddle; usually referred to as "a pair of barnacles," it sometimes was called a brey or a horse brey. 2. torture instrument, used by the Saracens during the time of Louis IX's* crusade, made of two pliable pieces of wood notched at the edges with interlocking teeth and fastened together at both ends with stout strips of ox-hide. The victim of the torture would be laid on his side and would have his legs put between the teeth, lengthwise. Then another man would sit on top of the barnacle. As a result, every bone would be crushed, and at the end of three days when the legs would be inflamed, the torturers would again put the victim in the barnacle and crush the bones all over again. Just the threat of this torture would convince any prisoner to do whatever the Saracens wished. (Bibliog. 43, 355)

baron, vassal* whose homage* was given directly to the king or territorial prince*; a tenant-in-chief*; a captal (see ranking of nobles). Being derived from the Middle High German word *bar,* meaning man, this term came to mean a vassal because in doing homage, in swearing fealty* to a lord, one acknowledged oneself to be his "man." In time this word came to be applied to the principal vassals of great chiefs, showing thereby a relative superiority of status over other sworn retainers in the same group.

English Kings Henry I* (1100–1135) and Stephen (1135–1154) addressed innumerable writs to barons as a class: they were considered to be the king's greater tenants-in-chief by military service, as distinct on one hand from knights, sergeants,* and ministers of lesser rank, and on the other from the undifferentiated multitude of his *fideles* [his faithful and trusted servants.] If men ranked as barons at King Henry I's court,* it was because they enjoyed the king's confidence; they were barons because it pleased the king* to treat them as such. Whatever else barons might have been, they were first and foremost their lord's counsellors: attending his court, approving what he had done, or giving advice about events which had taken place on a fee (see knighthood). As a class, the barons of writs (charters*) doubtless were men of considerable possessions. Although many of them must have been of high birth, the quality which enabled a baron to play his distinctive role in the life of the honour* to which he belonged was not from wealth and rank alone but from his sense of responsibility, from the power of giving a reasoned opinion for his lord's guidance; essentially, it was the power of using experience and elementary legal knowledge in the interest of his lord. In this lay the chief difference between the functions of a baron and those of a mere knight in feudal society.

A knight's opinion was not often asked by his lord unless some military question was at issue. There rarely was a need for a lord to ask his knights for any other counsel, for the advice he needed in time of peace was not the advice of a military entourage nor of the knights whom he had provided with land sufficient for their maintenance alone, but rather advice from those tenants with a substantial interest in their honours and responsibilities toward men enfeoffed* under them. For example, knights thought it strange when Duke William* of Normandy came in sight of London to ask their opinion about whether he should be crowned at once or wait until his wife could be with him.

This term was applied to all tenants-in-chief of the crown whether holding by knight service or by sergeanty. These latter were the king's barons and as such possessed both civil and criminal jurisdiction, each in his *curia baronis* (baronial court, or "court baron"*) and were entitled to seats in the great council.

In time the term came to refer to the fifth and lowest rank in the English peerage (see peer). From the 13th century on, the title was reserved for those who received writs to attend Parliament,* a practice which dated from the reign of King John (1199–1216). (Bibliog. 330)

baroness, wife of a baron,* or a woman who held a barony* in her own right; baronesses in their own right usually used the title "baroness," while a baron's wife generally was called "lady." (Bibliog. 43)

baronet, order created by King James I of England on May 22, 1611: Baronets of England. It ranked below that of peer* and above that of knight; its dignity was bestowed by "letters patent"* and was hereditary, but it was limited to the male heir of the grant. Originally it was bestowed on duly qualified knights and esquires,* each of whom stipulated to maintain thirty footsoldiers in Ireland at eight pence (see penny) per day for the term of two years. Thus the cost was 240 pence (or one pound) a day for two years, or a total cost of 720 pounds (see money). Initially this was an expedient to raise money for the defense and maintenance of the new plantation in the Irish province of Ulster, but actually the money was placed into the king's exhausted treasury. (Bibliog. 253)

barony, a knight held *a* barony and he held *by* barony. Tenure* by barony appeared to be one of the modes of tenure and was the same as tenure by knight's service but for one point—the amount of relief.* Service due from the tenant was equal to an aggregate of knight's fees (see knighthood); no military service was due from a tenant himself by barony as such, but if his barony consisted of twenty knights' fees, then he owed twenty knights, but he himself did not have to serve. This same arrangement concerned the various other obligations of tenure as well: aids,* wardship,* marriage,* escheat*—all but relief. (Bibliog. 250, 261)

barrel, measure for both wet and dry products, the capacity of this nearly cylindrical wooden vessel varied according to the commodity it was to carry:

a barrel of ale contained 32 gallons*;

a barrel of beer contained 36 gallons;

a barrel of wine* contained 31–1/2 gallons, which equalled 1/8 tun* or 252 gallons;

a barrel of herring or eels contained 30 gallons fully packed;

a barrel of salmon equalled 1/2 a salmon pipe* or 1/12 salmon last* and equalled 42 gallons;

a barrel of butter weighed 256 pounds;

a barrel of soap weighed 280 pounds.

See weights and measures. (Bibliog. 394)

barrulet, diminutive of a bar* in blazon*; as one-fourth of a bar, it was one-twentieth of the field.* (Bibliog. 43)

barry, field* divided horizontally into an even number of bars*; occasionally the actual number of bars was specified in the blazon.* (Bibliog. 43)

Bartholomew, Peter. See Peter Bartholomew.

base-court. See bailey.

baselard, dagger having a hilt shaped like the capital letter *I* and long enough to be called a short sword.* Originating in southern Germany or northern Italy late in the 13th century, it soon spread all over the continent. It was used by armored knights, but as its blade grew longer it became a weapon carried predominantly by footsoldiers and civilians; its use in England was almost exclusively restricted to civilians, who wore it in front suspended from a belt; a London ordinance of 1386 forbade stranger or foreigner from carrying sword, dagger, hache* (battle axe*), or baselard. (Bibliog. 27)

baseling, inferior (debased) English coin withdrawn by King Henry II in 1158. See coinage. (Bibliog. 226)

basilisk, king of serpents; it had six feet, white spots, and the head of a cock. This creature travelled only half-erect; its eyes emitted rays carrying forth the subtlest portion of its poison which when received by the brain of man or beast infected the brain and then the heart and killed instantly. It was so venomous that its presence corrupted the air, for its odor killed birds in flight, and men died merely by glancing at it. It was hatched by a toad or a serpent from a cock's egg. After a hen laid ninety-nine ordinary-sized eggs, she then laid a tiny one which was called the cent (hundredth) or cock egg, a peculiar egg not even as large as a pigeon's egg, which contained no yoke but only albumen; if hatched it produced the basilisk. Its only enemy was the weasel, which could kill it. In heraldry,* it was depicted with a dragon's* head on the end of its tail. (Bibliog. 177)

basinet, bacinet, head covering in a variety of shapes. Originally a small hemispherical skull cap worn under a coif,* it was enlarged between 1335 and 1360 to include a grilled occularium,* breathing holes, and a projection which covered the chin and throat. This was changed during the next fifty years into a tall pointed covering which came well down the neck and sides to protect the ears and back of the head; its opening for the face was square or oval; the lacing of the *camail** to the basinet at first was fully exposed but soon was covered by an ornamental band around the neck. Visors* first added to basinets were readily removable: hinged from the center and pivoted at the sides; in time, however, they became fixed to the skull part or main part of the headpiece and hinged upward or sideways, but finally were hinged only to move up and down late in the 14th century. See helmet. (Bibliog. 9)

basse prime, denotation of the time just after the break of day ("basse" = just after) when travellers began their journeys. See canonical hours. (Bibliog. 161)

bastile, outer area of defense for a gateway. See barbican; chatelet. (Bibliog. 341)

bastion, any solid masonry projection. (Bibliog. 280)

baston, mace,* thickened at the outer end, used in a tournament* event called the "baston course,"* as well as in combat. (Bibliog. 9)

baston course, 15th-century tourney (see tournament) event in which two opponents battered each other with bastons,* or short maces.* Each combatant wore a large helmet* which did not come in contact with the head at any part and which had a grill to protect the face instead of a visor.* (Bibliog. 9)

bataille, **battle** (Fr.), formation of fighting men arranged in a series of conrois* drawn up next to each other to create a formation of two to three men deep and fifty to sixty or more knights and squires* across the front. The royal French army which advanced to crush the rebels from coastal Flanders at Cassel in 1328 was made up of ten *batailles* with 177 banners.* In a different battle, Henry of Constantinople divided his army into fifteen battles, each of twenty knights and armored cavalrymen, except for the fifteenth, which was made up of fifty men and commanded by the emperor* himself. See also *arrière-garde.* (Bibliog. 351)

bate, hawk's struggle or violent jump from the fist or from the perch or block.* See hawking. (Bibliog. 26)

baton, bendlet* couped* at either end; it usually was found borne sinister* (from sinister chief* to dexter* base*) as a mark of bastardy and incorrectly termed "bar sinister."* See heraldry. (Bibliog. 251)

battering ram, tenebra, weapon of attack consisting of huge beams joined and suspended in a sling or massive trestle, sometimes put on wheels or rollers, and rapidly run forth to batter a wall or gate; its head often was covered with a metal cap to prevent the end from splintering. Those besieged tried to counter the impact and deaden its effect by lowering woolsacks or bags of hair from the ramparts, but the attackers often turned these against the defenders by igniting them to help destroy the gate or wall they were battering. See ram. (Bibliog. 71)

battle. See *bataille*.

battle axe, weapon of the Franks in the Merovingian period; at that time it often was thrown as well as wielded by hand by the early knights against an opponent. A 6th-century battle axe had a broad, sometimes a double, blade and a short shaft. (Bibliog. 71)

battle cry, cries during battle, used as summons for aid or encouragements, and were uttered by the combatants themselves or by their heralds.* For other uses, see signs of war. (Bibliog. 350)

Battle of Bouvines. Decisive battle on July 27, 1214, in the twelve-year war between England and France ensuring the ultimate victory of King Philip* Augustus II of France over King John of England. (Bibliog. 241)

Battle of Courtrai. Near a town in Flanders in July 1302, French chivalry,* highly skilled and greatly respected, took the field against an army which awaited them on foot behind ditches and waterfilled channels, armed with a version of the halbard* called a godendag.* The French cavalry sent their footsoldiers ahead to clash with the Flemish footsoldiers but soon became impatient and, fearful that they would be robbed of the glory of victory by the lowly footsoldiers, ordered their footsoldiers to withdraw. The French cavalry then plunged through them wildly to find themselves suddenly in ditches and channels. As wave after wave fell on their downed companions in front, the Flemish used their godendags with merciless results, cutting the entire French chivalry to pieces in the greatest humiliation that chivalry ever had suffered. When the victorious Flemings stripped the slain and fished the drowned out of the Groeninghebeke River, they identified sixty-three counts,* barons,* and bannerets*; 700 pairs of knightly spurs* of gold were stripped off the heels of the fallen and hung up as a thank-you offering for victory in the church at Courtrai. Footsoldiers had proved that they could defeat mounted cavalry, that chivalry was not unbeatable.

Ingenious stories were created to explain this disaster. One blamed the defeat on cowardice of the Genoese infantry who fled from their first encounter with the Flemish as the vanguard in this battle. A second absurd story related how the Flemish cried out to the French to give them more space for a fair fight, and when the gullible knights retired many yards to oblige them, the Flemish charged suddenly while the French had their backs turned. Another declared that there had been no battle at all but that the French knights had charged into a deep morass; were engulfed to their midsections, and then the Flemish had swooped down and murdered them as they sat helpless on their sunken steeds. A fourth related that there was in front of the Flemish lines not the *trou-de-loup** but a vast ditch dug out and covered with hurdles and grass into which the French plunged unwittingly and were annihilated. (Bibliog. 241)

Battle of Crécy. Battle between the English under King Edward III and his son, Edward, the Black Prince, and the French under King Philip VI on August 26, 1346. The English had invaded France and after plundering the orchards of Normandy and sacking Caen marched toward Paris and Rouen, reaching Poissy almost in the suburbs of Paris. Philip marched to intercept the English, but Edward feigned a move toward the southwest while his carpenters rebuilt the fallen bridges to get his army across the Seine. He crossed the Somme river at low tide, ahead of the pursuing French who were cut off by the rising waters. This allowed his forces time to rest and recover from their arduous march, and to prepare for the battle which was sure to come. Their position was advantageous, for they were on a ridge over a small river; at their back was the forest of Crécy-en-Ponthieu. Edward divided his forces into three groups, the right under the Black Prince, the left under the earl of Northampton, and the reserves commanded by the king a short way behind the center of the line. Learning that their enemy was at Crécy, the French knights insisted on attacking as soon as possible. Led into the setting sun by Genoese bowmen with their crossbow strings made practically useless by a sudden rainstorm, the French cavalry ignored the fleeing bowmen who had run out of arrows, and rode over them roughly. King Philip lost control of his forces as the pride of French chivalry rode to its destruction in wave after wave of horseman trying in vain to penetrate the solid English lines of bowmen and shields, as clouds of English arrows rained death on French and Genoese bowman, knight and horse alike. Fifteen separate French assaults were attempted; all were repulsed. When the last French attack had been repulsed, Edward allowed his men to break ranks and strip the slain. Heralds accompanied them to identify the noble dead, and found that one thousand five hundred and forty-two lords and knights had fallen, and over ten thousand other warriors fell. On the other hand, the English lost two knights, one squire, and forty men-at-arms, and a few dozen Welsh who had sought to plunder corpses while the battle raged. The English had won by combining steadfastness of their dismounted men-at-arms with the splendid archery of their bowmen. The English arrow was dreaded for years to come. (Bibliog. 222, 241)

Battle of Falkirk, fought between King Edward I of England and William Wallace* of Scotland on July 22, 1298. Because they had fewer knights, the Scots used dense formations of footsoldiers armed with long-handled weapons. They had been trained with pikes* as long as ten feet* and then grouped in circular formations several ranks deep, called shiltrons.* When Edward attacked Wallace at Falkirk, these shiltrons were arranged in three ranks: the front row crouching, the second kneeling, and the third standing; thus, they presented three levels of pikes to the enemy. With such hedgehog formations, these shiltrons broke the charges of the enemy knights until the English finally brought up archers whose volleys eventually broke the Scots' formation and enabled the English knights to ride over them to victory. (Bibliog. 241)

Battle of Hastings. Decisive battle on October 14, 1066, between the English forces of Harold Godwineson, king of England, and the Normans under William I, duke of Normandy. Harold's forces were exhausted from the forced march southward after defeating an invading army of Norsemen at the battle of Stamford Bridge on September 26, and they were further depleted by the delay of Edwin and Morcar, two earls who, with their men, should have been beside him. William and his men had landed at Pevensey on the south coast of England on September 28, and had moved inland slowly. The English forces established a shield wall along the crest of a ridge at Senlac near Hastings by imbedding their large shields in the ground side by side. William's men made two charges against the impenetrable wall, but were repulsed each time. Feigning a retreat, the Normans scattered, and lured Harold's forces into breaking the integrity of their shield wall as they raced onto the battlefield in search of loot from fallen Normans. Once the wall was broken, William signalled his men to regroup and attack once again. This time the Normans were successful, and routed the tired English. Harold was killed in the battle. From here, William's forces marched virtually unopposed to take over the kingdom. (Bibliog. 131, 241, 262, 339)

Battle of Poitiers. Led by their king,* John II, in 1356, the French tried to imitate the tactics used by the English so successfully against them at Crécy ten years earlier. John ordered a force of some 300 mounted knights to smash a gap through the English line of dismounted knights and bowmen who were well positioned behind hedges on a low ridge; his remaining knights had dismounted and were ready to follow up on foot. What the French king had not realized was that his dismounted knights needed missile support to be effective. He should have sent them forward on foot to make the first breach in the lines of the outnumbered English forces and then have followed up with a cavalry charge. This oversight was not lost on the English commander, Edward the Black Prince, who ordered his knights to remount and then launched a charge that shattered the disorganized French and lost them their king, who was captured. (Bibliog. 5, 20, 346)

Battle of the Standard, also known as the Battle of Northallerton, fought between King David of Scotland and King Stephen of England on August 22, 1138; remembered primarily for the English bowmen's devastating use of the longbow.* (Bibliog. 241)

battle orders, attack orders, orders to attack given by banner* and trumpet: the first blast on the trumpet signalled each man to arm himself, the second blast to form into units around banners, and the third blast to assemble the whole army around the banner. Other uses included the signal to break camp, to herald the assault, and to give the soldiers the order to take arms. Banners also were used to give orders: to take a banner forward was the sign to begin the attack; it also was used to halt the attack and to direct the setting up of camp. (Bibliog. 351)

battle sark, Saxon body covering. See byrnie.

battled, embattled, military order for the shield* divisions and the charge forces to form their lines; these lines resembled castle* battlements* or crenellation.* (Bibliog. 251)

battlefield actions and conditions. When Jean Froissart wrote his *Chronicles* in 1367, he chose as one of his sources the work of a compatriot, Jean Le Bel, a knight and soldier* who had taken part in King Edward's campaign against the Scots in 1327. This probably was the last English campaign conducted mainly on traditional feudal lines. Le Bel described how the Scots were well able to travel in harness,* for when they entered England, they moved their whole army twenty-four miles within a day and night, because they all were on horseback: the knights and squires* were well horsed, and the common people and others were on little hackneys* and geldings. As the mountains over which they had to pass in Northumberland were harshly difficult to cross, they used no carts* or chariots. Thus they carried no provisions of bread* and wine* but lived only on meat half-cooked and had only river water to drink; they carried no pots or pans but cooked beasts in their own skins, for they counted on finding many beasts in the country they passed through. Furthermore, for utensils they carried only a sack* of oatmeal and a broad plate of metal between their saddle* and saddle cloth, and so, when they ate their half-cooked meat, they would put the plate on the fire and drop on it a paste of oatmeal and water to make a little cake in the manner of a crakenel (biscuit). Thus they could make longer journeys than other forces were able to do. In this manner the Scots entered the country, wasted* and burned all about as they went, and took a great number of beasts. They numbered 4,000 men-at-arms, knights, and squires* mounted on good horses,* and another 10,000 armed each in his own way and mounted on little hackneys which they never tied but let go to pasture in the fields and bushes.

When the King of England learned of this invasion by the Scots, he cried alarm and commanded every man to rally to his king and follow the marshals'* banners.* When they reached the Tyne River to lodge by the riverbank, they found that only a few had either axe* or bill-hook* or any instrument to cut wood to make lodgings and that many there were completely lost; some of the footmen were so far behind that they did not know which road to take. Those who knew the countryside well said that they had ridden for twenty-four English miles* so fast with no rest that their horses had no food either that day or the day before, and no oats for forage had been brought along. Most men had carried behind their saddles only a loaf of bread, but these had become soggy with the sweat of the horses. They had only the water from the river to drink, for they carried no bottles with them and no fires nor anything with which to kindle them. Such were battlefield conditions recorded by an eye-witness. (Bibliog. 76)

battlement, parapet* with crenellations* to protect the defenders; the upper portion of a castle* or fortification walls with ramparts.* (Bibliog. 280)

bauderik, sash or girdle worn over the shoulder or around the waist for carrying a sword,* hunting* horn,* or pouch. See baldric. (Bibliog. 226)

bausons, streamers of red sendal flown from the mast of a ship which everywhere (c. 1300) among seamen was a signal to indicate "death without quarter," that is, no prisoners were to be taken; any fight was to the death. At the battle of Crécy* (1346), the French displayed a fiery banner* alongside the king's standard* to indicate that no man was to be taken alive, on pain of death. (Bibliog. 381)

baviere, decorated throat protection. See gorget.

Bayard, Baiart, steed of incredible swiftness given by Charlemagne to Renaud de Montauban and the other sons of Aymon. If only one of the sons mounted it, the horse* stayed regular size, but if all four mounted it, its body became elongated to the requisite length to support all four. (Bibliog. 162)

beacon. See bekin.

beadle, lord's official representative on the manor.* For his lord, he collected all the rent moneys and paid them at the direction of the sergeant*; he summoned and supervised work-tenants; he summoned tenants to court,* told tenants the work days and boon-days (see boon-work) that they owed during the harvest season; rounded up cattle straying onto the lord's meadows and put them into the village pound until the will of the lord was known concerning them. See bailiff. (Bibliog. 24)

beadle-mead, portion of meadow granted by a lord to a hayward* as payment for his efforts. (Bibliog. 24)

bearing, heraldic term synonymous with charge.* (Bibliog. 43)

beasts of stinking flight. See hunting.

beasts of sweet flight. See hunting.

beasts, positions of. Special terms described the various positions of beasts in arms.* Three factors were involved: the position or attitude of the body, the position of the head, and the position of the tail if unusual. Eight basic body positions were used:

1. passant—walking, forepaw off the ground;
2. statant—standing stationary, all four paws on the ground;
3. rampant—standing, only one hind paw on the ground;
4. salient—leaping, forepaws aligned with each other;
5. sejant—sitting, all four paws on the ground;
6. sejant erect—sitting, only the rear paws on the ground;
7. couchant—reclining or crouching, all four legs and belly on the ground;
8. dormant—sleeping, with head lower than forepaws.

(Bibliog. 251)

beating up the river. See ruses.

beau frere (Fr.), good fellow, term used in direct address. (Bibliog. 226)

"Beau Séant" (Fr.) battle cry of the Templars* which they also bore on their banner.* Through folk etymology this cry derived from French *baucent* from Latin *balteanus*, *balteus* for "belt" thus designated because of its black and white colors. (Bibliog. 40).

Beaufort, crusader castle* in the Holy Land with a massive square keep,* a rock-cut ditch, and a "curtain wall"* which was so impregnable by reason of its location atop a sheer rock face that it held out against Saladin* for a year. Finally overcome only by starvation in 1190, it was sold by the Muslims in 1260 to the Knights Templar* but was recovered by bombardment and siege in 1268. (Bibliog. 45)

Beaumaris, last of King Edward I's Welsh castles* to be built by the great castle builder, Master James of St. George*; but after the Welsh submitted in 1296, work on it slowed, and stopped in 1330. See also castle building. (Bibliog. 45)

bec-de-corbin. See *bec de faucon.*

bec de faucon, 1. 11th-century French weapon with a slightly curved fluke resembling a bird's beak, projecting from the head of a fighting axe* or hammer*; the term often referred both to the fluke and to the whole weapon; 2. tower built across two galleys tied alongside each other for the purpose of assaulting a town defended by rivers or by the sea. (Bibliog. 27, 331)

Dormant Couchant Sejant

Statant Passant Sejant Erect

Salient Rampant

Figure 3. Principal Positions of Beasts (As shown by lions)

Becket, Thomas à, Archbishop of Canterbury (1162–1170). Son of Normans in London, Thomas rose in his career to become archdeacon of Canterbury, and a close friend of the king. In 1154 when he was 36, Henry II appointed him to be chancellor of England, and he became one of the most powerful men in the kingdom. Seeking to control the church, the king in 1162 appointed Thomas to be Archbishop of Canterbury, but the appointment did not work out as the king had wished. Thomas changed; he determined to be his own man and not to follow slavishly whatever the king wished of him. He also changed his lavish and luxurious life style, and became austere and simple. He soon found himself at odds with the king over the issue of taxation of the clergy. When the Constitution of Clarendon* in 1164 gave the king jurisdiction over "criminous clerks*," Becket openly broke with him, fled to France, and appealed to the pope for help. Pope Alexander III, at that time involved in a dispute with the Emperor Frederick Barbarossa,* chose not to disrupt his own relations with the English monarch by responding to Becket's plea. Becket remained in France for five years, openly opposing Henry's policies. He returned in 1169 to excommunicate the English bishops who had defied him by joining with the Archbishop of York in crowning the heir to the English throne, Henry's son, young Henry III, because that act was the established right of the Archbishop of Canterbury. In a rage, King Henry II ordered four knights to assassinate Becket on Christmas Day 1170. He was canonized three years later. (Bibliog. 139)

bed, piece of furniture composed of a rectangular frame (espondes) of wood fastened by loops (crepons) of red silk or leather thongs to the head and foot pieces (pecuels); it was easily assembled at night and disassembled in the morning. Its feet often curved outward like an animal's paw or bird's claw; each post usually was decorated with a knob. A number of thin padded mattresses were laid on top of a first mattress stuffed with feathers; the entire bed could be curtained off during labor or illness. Frequently, one or two of these were left standing during the day to serve as benches for the lord or his lady. (Bibliog. 161)

bedale, drinking party to which many guests were invited. (Bibliog. 226)

bedarasule, drug used in treating leprosy. (Bibliog. 226)

bedemad, manorial service consisting of mowing for the lord of the manor.* (Bibliog. 226)

beffroi. See belfry.

behourd (Fr.), tournament.* Derived from the Latin word *burdicum* or *buhurdicum*, it became the Old French *behourd, behours* from *bourdis,* meaning originally a lance,* but by mid-13th century it had come to mean tilting* between individuals; within a half-century it had come to mean *hastiludium*,* or tourneying between teams. Even after an edict against tournaments was issued by the English crown in 1234, nine more prohibitions had to be issued against them in that same year; even squires* were *behourding*. (Bibliog. 88)

bei, beigh, arm bracelet, armlet, bracelet, ring mail.* (Bibliog. 226)

bekin, biken, beacon, fire, usually on a hilltop, signalling the approach of an enemy. (Bibliog. 226)

belfry, berefreid, berefroi, huge movable siege tower with several stories connected by ladders, this apparatus offered shelter to a large number of men. The uppermost floor of the tower approximated the level of the ramparts* of the besieged castle,* so a drawbridge* would be thrown across the narrowing gap when it drew close, and the tower's occupants would race across the drawbridge onto the ramparts. This tower often was transported to the walls on rollers or logs, but frequently even the smallest ditch or incline made its approach extremely difficult. For the siege of Toulouse, Simon de Montfort ordered a tower like this containing 500 men. Scots beseigers at Carlisle in 1315 also erected such a tower which was considerably higher than the city walls. To combat it, however, carpenters within the city erected an even higher wooden tower on one of the city's towers. These two towers never met, however, because the Scots tower on wheels got mired in the swampy ground outside the city walls. (Bibliog. 341)

bell man, town crier who walked through town ringing a bell and making announcements; an officer who announced funerals and summoned guild members. (Bibliog. 226)

bella donna. See medicine.

belligeration, warfare. (Bibliog. 226)

belloculus, white stone called belloculus because it rendered one invulnerable in war (*bellum*). It had a gold spot circled with black. (Bibliog. 258)

below the salt. On trestle table for meals, a huge oval flat dish (see nef) containing salt was placed as the divider for nobility and commoner: the common people sat "below the salt." (Bibliog. 223)

beme, trumpet used in warfare and hunting.* (Bibliog. 226)

bemere, trumpeter. (Bibliog. 226)

bemish, groschen* minted at Prague and worth about one and one-half English pennies.* (Bibliog. 226)

bend, ordinary* consisting of a broad band one-fifth of the field* from the dexter* chief* to the sinister* base. When charges* were placed on a shield* in the direction of a bend, they were said to be ''in bend.'' If so charged, it consisted of one-third of the field. Its margins frequently were modified by being engrailed,* invected,* embattled,* and so on. See heraldry. (Bibliog. 43)

bend sinistre. See bar sinister.

bender, bowmaker, archer. (Bibliog. 226)

bendlet, diminutive of a bend,* normally one-half the width of the ordinary.* (Bibliog. 43)

bendy, shield* divided bendwise into an even number of divisions, that is, a field* of bends.* See heraldry. (Bibliog. 43)

benefice, fief* granted at first for life only at the pleasure of the donor, but then becoming hereditary.

benes. See boons.

berefreid, berefroi. See belfry.

berelica, gemstone which cured palpitations and stopped falling hair when drunk powdered in wine.* (Bibliog. 258)

bern, knight, soldier,* often equated with baron.* (Bibliog. 226)

bern-at-armes, men-at-arms. (Bibliog. 226)

bernage. See brenage.

berner, man in charge of the ''hounds for the hunt,''* a huntsman,* a kennelman. The term came from the French *bernier* or *brenier,* meaning one who paid his feudal dues to his lord in bran from which bread* was made to feed the lord's dogs. (Bibliog. 96)

beryl, stone, greenish like oil, which drew the rays of the sun to itself and set fire to dry material. Rings mounted with it maintained agreements between husbands and their wives and cured all sorts of maladies, especially eye problems. (Bibliog. 258)

besagews, two disc-shaped armor* plates secured by laces to the front of the shoulder and outside the elbow, respectively, to supplement the vambrace.* (Bibliog. 27)

besant, besaunt. See bezant.

bescia, land measure for turf-cutting on the fens or marshy districts in Lincolnshire around 1400. It represented the amount of land that one man could dig with a spade between May 1 and August 1. (Bibliog. 394)

Beste Glatissant. See Questing Beast.

bevor, plate armor* for the neck and chin consisting of a short cylindrical collar that extended to just below the nose and carried a short cape that just covered the points of the shoulders, introduced in the last decade of the 13th century. (Bibliog. 27)

bevy-grease. See grease.

bewits, strips of leather by which bells were fastened to a hawk's legs. See hawking. (Bibliog. 26)

bezant, besant, besaunt, 1. coins of the Byzantine Empire and their imitations; 2. simple circle as a charge* representing a roundel* when it was gold* color, imitating and signifying the gold coin of Byzantium, the bezant. (Bibliog. 43, 187)

bezoar, stone found in the stomachs of such various animals as cattle, chamois, llama, goats, horses,* porcupine, and monkeys; it was an effective cure for most ailments but worked especially well to prevent and cure seasickness. (Bibliog. 286)

biken. See bekin.

bikeren, to make an assault on, to attack. (Bibliog. 226)

bilibre, two-pound measure weighing twenty-four ounces.* (Bibliog. 226)

bill, widely used weapon of footsoldiers in the early 13th century. Derived from the agricultural tool of the same name, this weapon had an unusually long head with a long single cutting edge that was convex or flattened S-shaped, divided at the top into a vertical spike and a forward-curved hook, and at the center of the back had a horizontal fluke. (Bibliog. 27)

biller, maker of halbards.* (Bibliog. 226)

billet, oblong heraldic charge* proportioned like a building brick, usually placed on the field* with the longest dimension vertical. (Bibliog. 253)

billhook, cutting instrument with a hook-shaped point, fitted with a handle. (Bibliog. 9)

billon, metal of gold or silver (usually silver) alloyed with a considerable amount of less valuable material for use in coinage.* (Bibliog. 324)

bind, 1. hawking* term for the action of a hawk in seizing a bird in the air and clinging to it; used only in describing the seizure of a large bird at some considerable height in the air; 2. measure of quantity for eels, consisting of ten sticks.* See weights and measures. (Bibliog. 96, 394)

bipennis, Danish axe.* See also pick, military. (Bibliog. 9)

birle, cup-bearer, butler. (Bibliog. 226)

bisacuta, military pick with points on each side used for piercing through chain mail.* (Bibliog. 9)

bishop, clergyman of the highest order; the head of a diocese or See.

bittar, one who supplied water in buckets. (Bibliog. 226)

bitte, butte, bag or skin for liquids. (Bibliog. 226)

bitunen, to surround a castle* or city with fortifications; to fortify. (Bibliog. 226)

Blachernes, large palace built in the 11th century by Byzantine Emperor Manuel Comnenus on the shore in Constantinople. (Bibliog. 310b)

black, heraldic tincture (see colors) that stood for the earth; and because it was farther from light than all the other colors, and hence was nearest to darkness, it also signified grief. For the death of a prince* or a loss in battle, those defeated clothed themselves in this color; for the same reason, religious people who had no interest in vainglory clothed themselves in black. (Bibliog. 31)

Black Death, plague, believed to have been bubonic, which swept western and central Europe several times during the 14th century, killing about one-third of the population of about 20 million people. One of its repercussions created a crisis in agriculture because the lack of manpower gave rise to restrictions against peasants leaving their farms which in turn led to a consequent return to serfdom (see serf); in England this in turn led to numerous peasant uprisings like the Peasant's Revolt* of 1381. (Bibliog. 393)

Black Rood, Scottish name in the early 14th century for the piece of the True Cross which they revered highly but which King Edward I took from them to London after their defeat. It was returned to them by King Edward III in 1328 when his five-year-old daughter, Joan of the Tower, married David, son of Robert the Bruce, King of Scotland. (Bibliog. 104)

Blanchart, popular horse's* name meaning white* in such *chansons de geste** as *Aubri le Bourgoin, Bastart de Bouillon, Fierabras, Gaidon, Hugues Capet, Ogier le Danois, Otinel,* and *Renaut de Montauban.* (Bibliog. 162)

Blanche Nef. See White Ship disaster.

Blanche of Castile (1199–1252), Queen of France as the wife of King Louis VIII; her mother, Eleanor of England, was the daughter of Eleanor of Aquitaine and Henry II of England. (Bibliog. 139)

blanching of farm rent, assaying the money paid into the Exchequer* to see how many pence* short was each pound. (Bibliog. 144)

blanc, 14th-century French silver coin. (Bibliog. 226)

blazon, correct term for describing heraldic (see heraldry) arms* in their correct armorial bearing (see charge) so that they could be rendered correctly from oral description. For example, the blazon of Trinity College Dublin read: "Azure* a Bible closed clasps to the dexter* between in chief* on the dexter a Lion* passant* on the sinister* a Harp* all Or* and in base* a Castle* with two Towers* domed each surmounted by a Banner* flotant* from the sides Argent* the dexter flag charged with a Cross* the sinister with a Saltire* Gules.*" In official blazons, tinctures (see colors) and the names of charges began with capital letters, and the descriptions were unpunctuated. (Bibliog. 43)

blazoning a shield, providing the seven descriptions of arms* in proper sequential order:

1. First, the shield* surface, its tincture (color) and its field*; it should state whether the field was parted, varied, or strewn with small charges,* or plain, if just the tincture was given.
2. Next, the principal charge resting on the shield in the most prominent position.
3. Then the secondary charges, if any, resting in the field.

4. Next, all objects overlaid on all the previous charges.
5. Then all important objects on the shield which were not central (for example, canton*).
6. Then objects placed in the last-mentioned charges, and
7. Finally came any marks of cadency.*

To complete this achievement,* the shield had several accessories: the crest* or ornamentation on a helmet* displayed above the shield; the supporters or figures that upheld the shield from each side; the scroll or the extended horizontal roll below the shield that supported the supporters and served as a location for the motto.* (Bibliog. 251)

blench, to trick or deceive a deer, that is, to turn back a deer in its flight and make it retrace its steps. See hunting terms. (Bibliog. 96)

blencher, one who turned a fleeing deer back toward a hunter, to make it retrace its steps. See hunting terms. (Bibliog. 96)

block, conical piece of wood to which hawks were tethered outside during the day. It was roughly nine inches* high and six inches in diameter, had an iron staple driven into the center of its top to hold the jesses,* and a stout iron spike in its base projected about nine or ten inches downward to hold the block firmly in the ground. See hawking. (Bibliog. 26, 145)

blood-feud, revenge sought when one member of a family was slain by a member of another family. The injured family could avenge its wrong not merely on the person of the slayer but also upon his belongings, his chattel. Blood-feud demanded life or lives for life, for not all lives were of equal value. In Anglo-Saxon times, six ceorls* had to die in balance for the life of one thane.* In King Alfred's reign (849–899) it was unlawful to begin a blood-feud until an attempt had been made to exact the dead man's wergild.* Later, King Edmund (939–946) suppressed blood-feuds by allowing a slayer twelve months to pay the wer (see wergild) before he was attacked and by not allowing the feud to be extended to the slayer's kindred unless they had made his misdeed their own by harboring him. Any breach of this decree was cause for outlawry.* Such practice continued for centuries before dying out. (Bibliog. 261)

bloodletting, ancient medical practice known by such various names as phlebotomy and venisection. This procedure was controlled minutely by the phases of the moon, the state of the tides, the seasons* of the year, the motions of the planets and stars, and by the day, hour, age, sex, and temperament of the patient and stage of his disease. Spring was the best time to draw blood, but it was to be avoided totally at both the solstices and equinoxes; April, May, August, and September were the worst months for bloodletting. Furthermore, a healthy man should be bled at sunrise, a choleric man at noon, a melancholic man at sunset, and a phlegmatic man at midnight. No one under age fourteen or over sixty was to be bled. Thirty-two veins in different parts of the body and thirteen in the head alone offered locations from which to draw blood; arm veins were the most popular. One physician recommended opening a vein in the ankle to cure a rupture of the blood vessels in the lungs because he believed that the blood thereby would be diverted from the place of the rupture to the healthy parts of the circulation and thereby allow the rupture to heal quietly.

Bloodletting was considered to be the beginning of health, or so said physicians, because it strengthened the mind and memory, purged the bladder, dried the brain, warmed the spinal cord, cleared the hearing, restrained tears, relieved loss of appetite, purified the stomach, improved digestion, invited sleep, drove away disease, and prolonged life. However, as it was such a powerful contributor to health, it had to be done cautiously. The amount of blood to be drawn depended on the time of the year, the age of the patient, and state of his bodily heat. If the blood ran black at first, it was to be drawn until its consistency was like water, but not until the patient felt lassitude or weakness in his stomach. See medicine; barber-surgeons. (Bibliog. 286, 335)

boar-spear. See spear.

board lands, a demesne*: the land set aside on a manor* for the lord's own use and to provide for the wants of his household. (Bibliog. 357)

boc. See book-right.

bodel silver, payment to the lord of the manor* for housing. (Bibliog. 226)

Bodiam, quadrangular English castle* built near Hastings under a license granted by King Richard II in 1385 for the defense of the adjacent countryside against French raids. (Bibliog. 45)

bohort, bohourt, tilting* or jousting* with a lance.* See tournament.

bold, bould, edifice such as a castle* or manor*; a brave or noble warrior, a knight. (Bibliog. 226)

bolognino, silver coinage* first minted when Bologna was an autonomous republic in the 11th century and later widely copied in Italy. (Bibliog. 150)

bolt, crossbow* arrow,* sometimes called a quarrel.* (Bibliog. 9)

Bolton, castle* in North Yorkshire similar to Bodiam,* with rectangular instead of round towers built by Richard, Lord Scrope, under license granted him in 1379. (Bibliog. 45)

bombard, siege ordnance used to throw heavy stones. (Bibliog. 226)

bonacon, bonasus, heraldic (see heraldry) bull-like monster* with horns which curled inward, a short nose, and a horse's* tail. As its horns were useless for defense, it defended itself by shooting burning excrement at its enemies. (Bibliog. 43)

bonaghtie, tax or tribute levied by Irish chiefs for the maintenance of soldiers.* (Bibliog. 226)

Bonaguil, French castle* with strong rounded towers, a wall thirteen feet* thick, and a pentagonal keep* built in Aquitaine on a rocky promontory between two valleys in the 13th century. (Bibliog. 45)

bond, "feudal obligation,"* as of a lord to his tenant or the tenant to his lord; a document embodying such an obligation. (Bibliog. 226)

bondman, customary tenant, unfree villager, villein,* farmer, or husbandman. (Bibliog. 226)

bonewort, banwort, any variety of medicinal herbs such as violet and daisy used in healing broken bones and wounds. (Bibliog. 226)

book-land, special form of property used by the Anglo-Saxon kings* before the Conquest. Only with the consent and witness of his wise men could the king grant this because land so granted conferred a larger dominion than was known to the popular and customary law. Although it made no difference in the actual occupation of the soil, it was a grant of lordship and revenues and in some cases even jurisdiction and its profits. (Bibliog. 261)

Book of the Ordre of Chyvalry, William Caxton's English translation of Ramon Lull's* *Le Libre del Orde de Cauayleria*, explaining the important elements of a knight's life: the office of a knight, examination of a Squire,* ordination of a knight, significance of a knight's arms,* customs of a knight, and the honor due to a knight. See knighthood. (Bibliog. 64)

Book of Winchester. See *Domesday Book.*

book-right, tenure* by which a thane* held his land under Anglo-Saxon kings.* This was an ancient name for land taken from the common land and granted by "boc" or written charter* to a private owner which he might bequeath or sell at his discretion. (Bibliog. 261)

boon-work, *precariae* (L.), day's work given gratuitiously to a lord by his men on special occasions. Even though from August to Michaelmas (see Appendix A) his men worked one or two days more than at other times in the year, this was not enough, and they were expected to give several extra days of their time as a boon or gift to him. All the villein's* family (except his wife) were expected to contribute these boon-days. See week-work. (Bibliog. 12)

booty. See ransom.

bord fellow, table companion, close friend. (Bibliog. 226)

bord land, land held by a cottager* under feudalism.* (Bibliog. 226)

bordars, peasants (see villeins), descendants of free but dependent ceorls* of Anglo-Saxon times. (Bibliog. 261)

border, feudal tenant of the lowest class, a cottager. See feudalism. (Bibliog. 226)

bordure, small margin around the circumference of the shield* upon which charges* could be placed; generally, it occupied one-fifth of the shield and usually was added to denote the younger branch of a family. See cadency; blazoning a shield. (Bibliog. 253)

boreyne, heraldic monster* like a bonacon* but with a tongue like a spearhead, a dorsal fin, the forelegs of a lion,* and the hind legs ending in eagle's* claws. (Bibliog. 43)

borgh, surety, one who became legally responsible for the behavior of another, who guaranteed that another would perform an oath or fulfill an agreement. (Bibliog. 226)

borough, fortified burh* which afforded protection for its immediate neighborhood in time of war and a safe site in time of peace. These began to appear in numbers during the 10th century both in the English- and the Danish-controlled areas of Britain and gradually became administrative centers for their immediate localities as they became units of fiscal, police, and judicial organization. Many were royal boroughs under a royal reeve* who accounted for rents, tolls, and the profits of justice.*

Originally the term implied fortification, just as the term "port" implied a market, and not necessarily on the coast (see abjuration of the realm), but both terms came to be used synonymously with town. By the 10th century these had become part of the national defense system, and with local defense in mind, they continued for centuries to bear a military obligation that was separate from the hundreds* and the wapentakes.* After the Conquest, boroughs continued to develop, especially in the 12th century as economic growth promoted town life and the number of chartered boroughs increased greatly. One of the primary duties of borough citizenry was to serve on "watch and ward"* (see also bailey). By ordinance of 1242, each borough had to provide twelve men to watch throughout the night; cities had to provide six men at each gate. Further, borough authorities had to provision armies, sometimes to man ships, to proclaim peace, and to make arrests. In boroughs, mayors and bailiffs* performed the tasks elsewhere performed by sheriffs,* escheators,* and hundred bailiffs. (Bibliog. 163)

borsilver, payment collected from tithingmen (see tithing) or frankpledge.* (Bibliog. 226)

bos, stall for livestock. (Bibliog. 226)

bosing silver, manorial rent collected from a tenant for having a horse* and cart* and perhaps for the privilege of keeping his horse in his own stable. See manor. (Bibliog. 226)

boss, center of the small shield* or buckler* carried by footsoldiers; this hollow section projecting forward had a spike that was used as an added offensive weapon in close hand-to-hand combat. (Bibliog. 27)

bosson, "battering ram"* on wheels which struck its target of castle* wall or gate with massive force when besiegers rolled it up against its target repeatedly. (Bibliog. 33)

bot, compensation of any kind but more general than the word "wer" (see wergild). By the 12th century homicide was a deed which could be atoned by money payments; furthermore, outlawry* and blood-feuds* also had given way to "bot"—a financial settlement whereby a guilty person could buy back the peace he had broken. To do so, he had to settle with the injured party and with the king*: he had to make "bot" to the injured person and to pay "wite"* to the king. A complicated tariff was arranged to accomplish this: every wound or blow given to every person had its price. Even homicide had its price wherein the "bot" was the wergild of the slain. However, some of the gravest offenses, especially committed against the king or his peace, were said to be "botleas" (bootless)—that is, the offender could never redeem himself and therefore was completely at the king's mercy.* (Bibliog. 261)

botdragers, silver coinage* of double gros* class circulating in the 14th century in Brabant and Flanders; it derived its name from the helmeted lion* on the obverse, colloquially called "potcarrier." (Bibliog. 150)

bouche, small notch cut in the upper-right-hand corner of a knight's shield* to serve as a support his couched lance*; it came from the French word for mouth, *bouche.* (Bibliog. 27)

bouget, hard leather water bags joined by a carrying yoke.

boughs, breaking, practice of huntsman* when he was harboring* a deer: he broke boughs (bowes) or branches to mark where he had detected signs of the stag. Then during the chase, he placed twigs pointing in the direction the stag had taken so that the hounds could be brought back to the original scent if they lost it. When they harbored a deer, he placed a broken bough in front of the slot* (deer's hoofprint) with its end pointing in the direction the stag was headed; each time the harborer changed direction, he would show it with a broken twig; sometimes these branches were merely bent and left on the branch (*brisée hautes*) or broken off and placed on the ground (*brisée basses*).

When making his ring-walks around the covert, the harborer was to put a mark to every slot he came across: a stag's slot was marked by scraping a line behind the heel; a hind's slot by a line in front of the toe. A fresh footing was to be marked additionally by placing a twig or branch in the slot: for a stag, two twigs; for a hind, one twig; for a stale slot, no twig. Thus a hunter would know if any beast had broken from or taken to covert since he had harbored his stag in the morning. When the harborer went to move his stag with his limer,* he marked the track with twigs so the berners* with their hounds would know which way to go. See hunting; hunting terms. (Bibliog. 96)

bourbonnais, French denier (see denarius) issued under King Louis VIII (1137–1180) of which three varieties were minted: bourbonnais à la tête (with a head); bourbonnais à la tête barbur (with a bearded head); bourbonnais à la main bénissante (with a hand that blesses). (Bibliog. 150)

bourdonasse, long, elaborately painted lance* used in tournaments*; made with a hollow center so that it would splinter easily during the tourney* called "over the barriers," in which it was used most frequently. (Bibliog. 9)

bourgeois, 1. denier (see denarius) issued by Philip* le Hardi (1270–1285), called in full a bourgeois de la lange d'Oc; 2. several types of billon* currency issued under French King Philip le Bel (1285–1344). (Bibliog. 150)

bouvier, *bovarius,* ox-driver, an important man on the manor,* for by the 12th century the oxen had become so important that they were kept on the lord's demesne* and allocated for peasant (see villein) use in return for boon-days* and other payments. (Bibliog. 213)

Bouvines, battle of. See Battle of Bouvines.

bovarius. See bouvier.

bovate, oxgang, measure of land area that probably referred originally to the amount of land that an ox could plow in a year but which actually varied between seven and thirty-two acres* depending on the quality of the soil. This measure also was equal to the eighth part of a carucate,* the term coming from the eight oxen or boves of the standard plow team. (Bibliog. 394)

bow, weapon made of a strip of basil, wych elm, hazel, ash, or yew wood with a cord to connect the two ends which, when bent and released, propelled an arrow.* These shorter bows were used all over Europe until the 14th century when the English longbow,* reaching over six feet, came into use. Medieval war arrows* had broad, flat, triangular or lozenge-shaped heads and goose feathers for the fletches, but peacock feathers often were preferred for show. (Bibliog. 27)

bow shot, distance covered by an arrow* shot from a bow*; usual bow distance of 240 to 250 yards* was increased considerably by the longbow* arrow range of 400 yards. (Bibliog. 9)

bowe, bower, withdrawing room and sleeping apartment for the chief members of the family. On the first floor of the dwelling house of a castle* which also had a hall* or common room. Also known as the solar, this bower sometimes was called the great chamber, whose access was obtained through a doorway through the crosswall near the dais.* (Bibliog. 341)

bower, young hawk able to leave the nest but not ready to fly. (Bibliog. 226)

bowes. See boughs.

bowyers, bow* makers.

boy, servant, underling, attendant, churl, applied to cook's helper, butler's helper, messenger,* gatekeeper, and more often than not a young person. (Bibliog. 226)

Brabancons, French mercenaries.* (Bibliog. 159)

brabantine. See money, bad.

bracer, 1. leather wrist guard worn by longbow* archers; 2. generally used English word for the complete plate armor* for the arm, including the shoulder defenses. (Bibliog. 9, 27)

brachetti, ordinary "hounds for the hunt"* which hunted by scent. (Bibliog. 304)

bracket. See rache.

bracteate, peculiar species of money* with only one face, current in Germany, Switzerland, northern Netherlands, and Lombardy from unknown antiquity into the Middle Ages. Because this coin was as thin as foil, it had one side blank. Although gold and copper bracteates existed, silver was the most commonly used metal for such coinage.* (Bibliog. 150)

bragger. See corbel.

bragot, Welsh drink made of ale and honey. (Bibliog. 226)

braiel. See braies.

braies, wide linen underdrawers worn by sailors and workmen; fastened at the waist by a cloth belt studded with metal buttons, called a braiel. As these were not worn by women, they were the center of jokes about who wore the braies in the family, that is, who was the boss. (Bibliog. 161)

brail, soft leather thong used to confine a hawk's wing; it had a slit to admit the pinion joint, and its ends were tied together. See hawking. (Bibliog. 26)

brassarts, plate armor* protection for the entire upper arm; these were constructed either of one bent piece or of two plates riveted or hinged together. (Bibliog. 9)

brasses, monumental, engraved sepulchral memorials depicting knights and nobles in their armor,* surcoats,* and their armorial bearings (see charge) which were conspicuous in most great churches. Early in the 13th century these began to replace tombs and effigies carved in stone. Made of *latten* or sheet brass, they were embedded into the pavement of the churches and thereby formed no obstruction in the space required for church services as had the earlier effigies; they remained in popular use for 300 years. (Bibliog. 100)

brattice, wooden gallery* projecting over the outer walls of a castle.* Its joists for flooring passed through holes at the foot of the parapet* to support walkways for both the outer and inner galleries covering the rampart* walk; both galleries had a common roof. Holes in the floor of the outer gallery allowed missiles to be hurled at besiegers at the foot of the walls; slits in the outer face were used for straight firing. Being wooden, these were vulnerable to fire from arrows* tipped with any burning material or red-hot stones or coals flung by catapults.* (Bibliog. 341)

bread, three kinds of bread were served at supper: azimis, or ordinary raised bread; infungia, or unleavened bread; and placenta, or dumplings. (Bibliog. 161)

breaking. See boughs.

breastplate, metal plate molded to the shape of the body, and when joined with the backplate* it formed a cuirass* to protect the complete upper torso. Distinct from "plastron de fer,"* which had been worn for about a century, these came into general use around the middle of the 14th century. (Bibliog. 9)

brenage, brennage, bernage, feudal tenure in which land was held by the payment of bran and refuse from all grains for feeding hounds. (Bibliog. 96)

brene. See byrnie.

brenied. See brinied.

bretasche, breteche, covered wooden passage on top of a wall or tower, supported by a series of corbels* called machicoulis. This usually was removed during peacetime. See brattice. (Bibliog. 9)

bretessed, ordinary* which was embattled* on both sides, the inward and outward battlements lying opposite each other. (Bibliog. 43)

Breton lais, lays, short narrative poems in French whose subject matter frequently resembled episodes of Arthurian romances,* dealt with Arthurian characters, or were set at Arthur's court. See lai. (Bibliog. 41, 200)

breviary, book which contained the offices said by religious figures at each of the "canonical hours".* Coming from Latin, *breviarium*, this term first occurred in the 11th century; its English equivalent was portuary, portesse, or portuasse, from the Latin, *portiforium*. (Bibliog. 100)

brey. See barnacle.

brinied, brenied, wearing a coat of mail.* (Bibliog. 226)

brisees. See boughs.

Britton, title of the earliest summary of the law of England written in the French tongue; it purports to have been written by command of King Edward I. Although attributed to John le Breton, bishop of Hereford, references to statutes enacted after his death in 1275 made his authorship questionable. It may well have been a royal abridgment of the work of Henry De Bracton. (Bibliog. 100)

broad arrow, longbow* arrow* with feathers from a goose's wing, first used as a royal badge* by King Richard I.* (Bibliog. 71)

broches (Fr.), tines of deer's antlers. See brocket. (Bibliog. 96)

brocket, second-year hart. This term presumably signified *broches,** the French word for the tines of a deer's antlers, so that the diminutive of the word, brocket, by extension, meant a young stag bearing small tines. See hunting terms. (Bibliog. 96)

broigne. See byrnie.

brom bread, oaten bread made as food for "hunting dogs."* (Bibliog. 96)

brotherhood-in-arms, brothers-in-arms, a man's sworn companion. This involved not only the risks one ran as a soldier,* but in all that affected one's honor,* fortune, and emotional entanglements. Such a bond of brotherhood was a legal bond to which enforceable law gave reality. Under military law, the sworn companion genuinely was a brother, and as such he became heir to his companion's military fortune. Then when the companion died, he had a legal claim to any gains of war (prisoners, booty, and so on) which had been held at the time of the companion's death.

Sometimes the oath involved religious ceremony by which the brotherhood-in-arms was established. The two men heard mass together, and at the solemn moment of consecration during the service, the host was divided in two and administered to them. Sometimes it involved opening a vein and drinking together of their mingled blood. Described in the English metrical romance,* *Amis and Amiloun*, it detailed implicit trust in one's "brother." There Amiloun could demand from his brother any action and any sacrifice which did not involve dishonor. He allowed his sworn companion, Amis, to bed with his wife without a qualm for his own honor and reputation. Thus this association took precedence over every other, save those of blood and of "liege homage."* Three famous pairs were King Charles the Bald and Louis XI; the famous knight, du Guesclin, and Hugh Calverly; and Saladin* and the count* of Tripoli. (Bibliog. 179)

Brownsteel, King Arthur's sword (in *Arthur*). His sword also was known as Caliburn* and Excaliber.* (Bibliog. 2)

Bruiant, Charlemagne's horse* in the *chansons de geste,** *Maugis d'Aigremont;* the name meant fiery. (Bibliog. 191)

bruny. See byrnie.

bryman, 14th-century billon* coinage* of Brabant equivalent to a double gros.* (Bibliog. 150)

buccellarii (L.), private bands of soldiers who formed the bodyguards of prominent men in Gaul and other parts of the late Roman Empire. (Bibliog. 123)

Bucephalus, famous charger of Alexander the Great, the only person who could ride it. It always knelt to allow its master to mount. When it died at age thirty, Alexander built the city of Bucephala as a mausoleum for it. (Bibliog. 308)

buckler, small shield* carried by a footsoldier. Fitted with a crossbar for a grip, its curved front was equipped with a hollow spiked boss* in its center to serve as an additional stabbing weapon in close fighting. (Bibliog. 27)

bugue, small coin of the city of Metz in Lorraine during the late 14th and early 15th centuries. (Bibliog. 150)

bulbeggar, coat* worn when apprentices were to be corrected. Somewhat like a sack with holes for the eyes and arms, it was a garment worn over the head and body of the person appointed to flog an unruly apprentice, who thereby was prevented from identifying his castigator. (Bibliog. 392)

bull, seal of a public authority, both sovereign as well as ecclesiastical, who issued documents. These seals were made of metal according to certain classifications: lead seals for regular documents, silver for important acts, and gold for festive imperial and papal documents. Papal bulls were written on thick polished parchment in Latin and always began with the name of the pope but without any number: for example, Urban, not Urban II; then the terms *episcopus, servus servorum Dei*; and then either the phrase *ad perpetuum rei memoriam* or the greeting *in Domino salutem et apostolicam benedictionem*. It ended with the place and the date given as kalends, nones,* or ides of the month and year of the pope's reign. Popes used three kinds of seals: signet ring, a "bulla," and from the 13th century the *annulus piscatoris* (the ring of the fisherman). Over the years the word bull came to include both the documents and the seal, especially papal documents. (Bibliog. 139)

Bulle d'Or, edict promulgating the regulations concerning coronation* ceremonies established in Imperial Germany by Emperor Charles IV at the Imperial Diet at Nuremberg in 1356. As it had a gold seal attached, it was called the "*Bulle d'Or.*" See bull; or. (Bibliog. 178)

burdicia, term for tournaments* used in papal and royal prohibitions. (Bibliog. 78)

burg (Ger.), applied to the citadel of a town or to a castle,* equivalent to the French *bourg*. See burh.

Burghausen, Bavarian castle* built by the counts* of Burghausen, but in 1164 it passed to the dukes* of Bavaria, who maintained it as one of their most important strongholds. (Bibliog. 45)

burh, fortification built by the Saxons as a communally owned and fortified walled enclosure protecting a town; it encompassed a much larger area than a castle* and was defended by a much larger garrison. See borough. (Bibliog. 129)

burial practices. A dead body was turned over to men or women of a religious order, who washed it and then sewed it up in a deerskin. Then, attended by clergy and mourners, it was draped with a black* pall as it was carried on a bier consisting of two poles with wooden crosspieces.

The corpse of a prominent person, lay or clerical, would be laid to rest in a sarcophagus which was sealed with lead, covered with silken cloth, and surrounded by burning lamps and wax candles as respects were paid to it. Then it was placed under the floor stones or tiles of a church building, and its location often was marked by a large monumental brass (see brasses). People of lesser rank were buried in simple wooden coffins in a simple grave. (Bibliog. 161)

bushel, measure of capacity for dry products. In England the standard or Winchester grain bushel equalled four pecks, eight gallons,* sixteen pottles,* thirty-two quarts, sixty-four pints,* one-eighth seam,* or one-eightieth grain last.* (Bibliog. 394)

butler, king's, *pincerna,** servant in charge of wine* and dessert who had beneath him a staff of cellarers, cupbearers, and fruiterers. (Bibliog. 276)

butlery, body of servants charged with keeping and serving drink. (Bibliog. 226)

butsecarls, mercenaries* who were a combination of sailors and warriors, performing both sea and land duty; they probably were originally Viking warriors equally at home on land and the sea. (Bibliog. 158)

butt, 1. measure of quantity, used principally for wine*; 2. wine cask; 3. small strip of land. See pipe.

butte. See bitte.

buttery, room of a manor* house used for serving beverages; it stood off the main hall* and adjacent to another room, the pantry, used for serving the bread.* (Bibliog. 128)

button, ornamental knob or stud on armor,* knife, and so on. (Bibliog. 226)

buttress, masonry addition to strengthen a wall. (Bibliog. 280)

by-laws of a village, practices generally established by tradition governing village usage of the commons land. In general, the shareholders of a village had the right to pasture their beasts on what was left of the the waste* lands of a village and in the stubble of grain fields. As early sickles left long stubble, so the great fields of hundreds of acres, the roadsides, and patches of unplowable land became important sources of herbage; some pasture also was left after mowing. However, this stubble was not available for pasture until after the grain from all the acreage was removed and the beasts of plow given priority; horses* had to be tethered until others had eaten. (Bibliog. 13, 24)

byrnie, brene, broigne, bruny, battle-sark, main body covering of a coat* of thick leather tied at the waist. This garment was good for warding off sword* cuts and at mitigating arrow* and lance* hits. The Saxon leaders usually decorated their byrnies with rings of brass or iron, or with metal or horn scales and discs. (Bibliog. 9)

C

Cabal, King Arthur's dog, according to Nennius.

Caballeria, Libros de. Spanish books of chivalry.

caboshed, cabassed, an animal's head in blazon* when shown affronty* but cut off cleanly behind the ears so that no parts of the neck were visible. For the heads of lions* or leopards,* the word "face" was used instead. (Bibliog. 43)

cacothepas, catoblefas, slow-moving beast of Egypt with a small body and ungainly legs; it always let its heavy head hang low. It was so venemous that if any man looked into its face, he died instantly with no hope of being saved. (Bibliog. 21)

cade, small barrel* or keg holding 500 to 620 herring or 1,000 sprats. (Bibliog. 394)

cadency, system using marks of difference* to denote the line of inheritance in relation to the head of an arms-bearing family (see arms). The "one man, one coat of arms" rule made necessary a system whereby every cadet* in a family could differ his arms from the family head. Called cadency, this early was shown only by a change of charge* or tincture (see colors), but after the 15th century, small charges were added to the shield.* The Scots used a system of bordures,* but the English adopted a system in which a label of three points* was used by the eldest son during the father's lifetime; a crescent* was used by the second son; a molet* by the third son; a martlet* by the fourth; an annulet* by the fifth; a *fleur de lis** by the sixth. (Bibliog. 43)

cadet, youngest son or brother in a family.

cadge, wooden frame on which hawks were carried into the field by a cadger by straps across his shoulders. It was padded on its upper side as a perch for the hawks. See hawking. (Bibliog. 26)

Label

Crescent

Mollet

Martel

Annulet

Fleur-de-lis   Rose   Cross flory   Octofoil

Figure 4. Marks of Cadency

cadiere, 1. billon* coin struck under Charles VI of France (1380–1422); 2. gold currency in Brittany issued by Anne of Brittany as a cadiere d'or* on which she styled herself Queen of France and Dux Brittonum; it was the earliest French coinage* with a date. (Bibliog. 150)

Caen, French castle* built soon after 1047 by William* the Conqueror on the Orne river, nine miles from the seacoast of Normandy. Henry I added a great keep.* Philip* Augustus captured it from the English, but twice during the Hundred Years War, 1346 and 1417, it returned to English control. French control resumed in 1450. (Bibliog. 45)

Caerlaverock, Scottish triangular castle* which Edward I besieged and captured in 1300. In 1313 Sir Eustace Maxwell, its castellan,* declared for Robert Bruce instead of Edward II and dismantled the fortification to render it useless in accordance with the Scottish policy of destroying any castle which might be of help to the English. (Bibliog. 111)

Caerlon-on-Usk, location of King Arthur's second coronation* which the poet Wace* located in Glamorgan. On the right bank of the river Usk had been a colony and capital under Roman dominion; its name was a corruption of the Latin *Castrum Legionis*, which Nennius* named Cair Leon. (Bibliog. 341)

Caernarvon, Welsh castle* which King Edward I intended to be the finest of all his castles and the center of royal government in the north. This castle had two flanking towers and two gateways: the Queen's Gate at the east and the King's Gate at the North. He brought his wife Eleanor to Caernarvon to give birth to his son Edward, to be Edward of Caernarvon, later to be known as Edward II of England, and thus the first English "Prince of Wales."* See also castle building. (Bibliog. 45)

Caerphilly, concentric Welsh castle* begun by Gilbert de Clare in 1271. Later, Hugh le Despenser, companion and favorite of Edward II, became lord of Caerphilly by marrying into the Clare family. King Edward sought refuge here from his wife Isabella and other enemies, and then even after the king* had fled elsewhere, the queen persisted in its siege. When it finally surrendered some months later, Isabella was given its treasures and then, taking no chances on his returning to power, beheaded Despenser. (Bibliog. 45)

cagots, people in the Basque provinces of Bearn and Gascony who were looked on as cretins, lepers, heretics, and occasionally as cannibals. They had fair complexion, blue eyes, high cheekbones, prominent noses with large nostrils, straight lips, and no earlobes. They were excluded from all political and social rights, entered church only through a special door, were kept apart from the regular worshippers, and excluded from taking part in the regular mass. They had to wear a special garb to which was attached the foot of a goose or duck, and their touch was considered so pestilential that they could not walk barefoot along the common road and could work only as butchers, carpenters, and woodcutters. (Bibliog. 100)

Cahn, Kahu, Quahn, Caii, Saracen* god.

caladrius, also known as the plover, this bird as white as a gull was useful at the court* of kings* because it healed sick people if they were curable, merely by looking at them; incurable people, however, it turned its eyes away from and thus did not see. Additionally, marrow from its thigh bone restored sight to blind people. (Bibliog. 21)

Calatrava. See Knights of Calatrava.

Caledfwlch, King Arthur's sword in the Welsh mabinogian* story of "Culhwch and Olwen." See Excaliber.

Caliburn, sword* which Arthur drew from the stone in Arthurian legend and thereby became king.* See Excaliber. (Bibliog. 200)

caliph, kalif, sovereign dignitary of the Muslims, vested with almost absolute authority in all civil and religious matters. As the word in Arabic meant successor or vicar, the caliph bore the same relation to Mahomet* as did the pope to St. Peter. In Turkey, he was called *mufti;* in Persia, *sadne.* One of his chief functions was to begin public prayers every Friday in the chief mosque and to deliver the *khootba,* or sermon. The caliph always rode to the mosque on a mule while Seljuk sultans, though masters of Baghdad themselves, held its stirrups and led the mule by the bridle for some distance until the caliph gave them a sign to mount their own horses.* He was also obliged to lead pilgrims to Mecca in person and to march at the head of the armies of his empire.* At a window of the caliph's palace always hung a piece of black velvet twenty cubits* long which reached the ground and was called the "caliph's sleeve"; the grandees of the court kissed this daily with great respect. (Bibliog. 100)

calf, first-year hart. See hunting terms. (Bibliog. 364)

call off, to lure a hawk from the fist of an assistant from considerable distance and thus to confirm that the bird was approaching readiness for the hunt. See hawking. (Bibliog. 26)

caltrap, caltrop, calthrop, weapon used to maim a horse* in a charge. Usually it consisted of four short points of iron joined at their base and radiating from one another so that when thrown on the ground, one point always was uppermost to disable horses. Sometimes, rowel and prick spurs* were used for this purpose. Robert Bruce used them at Bannockburn, and among the stores at Dover Castle in 1343 was found a barrel* containing 2,900 calketrappes. (Bibliog. 9)

calygreyhound, heraldic monster* with the head of a wild cat, frond-like horns, tufted body, tail similar to a lion's,* and forelimbs which ended in claws. (Bibliog. 43)

camail, portion of armor* consisting of mail* fastened to the back of the basinet* by laces which passed through staples (*vervelles**) in the metal and falling loosely onto the shoulders to protect the neck. Such protection allowed the wearer to dispense with the *coif-de-mailles,** or hood of mail, and thereby to avoid its intolerable weight and heat upon the head. The term came from "cap [of] mail." (Bibliog. 7)

cameleopard, the giraffe, in heraldry.* (Bibliog. 251)

camerarius. See chamberlain.

camouflet, castle* defense consisting of a countermine so dug and charged that its detonation destroyed the enemy's galleries* being dug to undermine a castle wall; it destroyed both enemy and cavities without rupturing the surface of the ground. (Bibliog. 329)

candlesticks, holders made of wrought iron to provide light for the table at night. Candles were placed in small lanterns made of horn for use when moving about. One large type of candlestick was a candelabra, which stood high from the floor and had many small spikes on which many candles were impaled. (Bibliog. 161)

cannon, heavy metal tube used for firing projectiles. The first cannons were small, weighing only twenty to forty pounds,* and discharged a quarrel*—a heavy arrow.* Soon, however, metal balls were used instead, but by 1350 stone balls had replaced metal ones, being cheaper and easier to make. Although recipes for gunpowder* using saltpeter, sulphur, and charcoal were found in Europe for the first time about 1300, and the first records of their use in warfare in Europe followed soon thereafter, they were used on a large scale for the first time only in the third decade of the 14th century: at Metz in 1324, Florence c. 1326, and in England and Spain in 1331. Edward III used them at the siege of Calais in 1346, as did the Moorish defenders against King Alfonso XI of Castile at Algeciras. This new weapon produced no startling results for quite a while—merely alarm and annoyance. (Bibliog. 242)

canonical hours, times when church bells were rung eight times a day for all folk, church and lay, to know the time:

midnight—matins	midday—sext
3 A.M.—lauds	3 P.M.—nones
6 A.M.—prime	6 P.M.—vespers
9 A.M.—tierce	9 P.M.—compline

These were roughly three hours apart, but the actual times were vague because summer daylight made intervals longer and nights shorter. On trips, riders would begin at "*basse prime*" (daybreak) and ride until dinner at "*haute tierce*" when they would break for a midday meal; they would begin riding again after "*re-levée*" (after nones) and continue until vespers. (Bibliog. 161)

cantel, raised portion of the back section of a war saddle.* (Bibliog. 9)

canting arms, "allusive arms,"* those arms which arose from a pun or play upon the names of the bearer. For example, Barry (Ireland) bore "Barry of six, argent* and gules*"; Butler: "gules, three covered cups, or.*" (Bibliog. 43)

canton, square portion of the shield* in the dexter* chief*; smaller than the quarter,* it frequently carried augmentations.* (Bibliog. 43)

cap-a-pie, armed from head to toe in complete armor*; it came from the French, *cap à pied,* meaning head to toe. See arm and crown. (Bibliog. 27)

cap-mail. See *camail.*

cap of dignity, cap of maintenance, *chapeau,* originally a head covering generally of red velvet turned up with ermine* trim, formerly peculiar to dukes,* but later the hat which covered the top of the helm* before the mantling (see mantle) was introduced; as such it was frequently found on crests* rather than on wreaths.* (Bibliog. 43)

caparisoned, barded, horse* when it was bridled, saddled, and armored. Often the animal wore an additional embroidered covering which was charged with the arms* of the knight who owned it. See horse armor. (Bibliog. 251)

capellanus, clerk of the works at a castle.* See castle personnel.

capias (L.), writ ordering an individual's arrest and subsequent appearance in court.* (Bibliog. 171)

capias utlagatum (L.), writ of ordering the arrest and appearance in court* of an outlaw.* (Bibliog. 171)

capital, seat of government for a monarch. The early Anglo-Norman kings had no capital, no seat of government such as London or Westminster later became. Rather, the kings* moved ceaselessly from place to place about England or their continental dominions, holding court* at some royal castle,* abbey, or wherever they wished; they took with them all the materials of government: documents, treasurer,* chancellor,* clerks and their writing materials, and diverse members of the ''king's household.''* (Bibliog. 262)

captal. See baron; ranking of nobles.

capuchan, hood worn by civilians.

caput honoris (L.), fortified residence of a lord. (Bibliog. 330)

caritas (charity), measure of capacity for wine* of about the year 1300 representing the allotment of wine given to monks by their abbot over a certain period of time; it varied from three-fourths of a gallon* at Evesham to one and one-half gallons at Abingdon to two gallons at Worcester. (Bibliog. 394)

carlino, 1. gold and silver coins introduced by Charles II of Naples in 1287 containing the design of an angel greeting the Virgin on the obverse and a shield* on the reverse; 2. small silver coin of the Two Sicilies, and of Bologna under papal control; it was valued at five lire. See coinage. (Bibliog. 150)

Carnwennan, King Arthur's dagger in the mabinogian* story, "Culhwch and Olwen."

carpets, fancily woven mats hung on the walls for decoration and insulation, and on tables and benches; they were not placed on the floors of the upper stories of the keeps* in England and in northwestern Europe until the 14th century. (Bibliog. 129)

carry, a hawk was said to "carry" when she flew away with the quarry* as the falconer* approached. See hawking. (Bibliog. 96)

cart, two- or four-wheeled vehicles used to transport material when a king* or a lord moved from one castle* to another. Packhorses carried the household goods, that is, the dismantled bed,* sheets, rugs, furs, wardrobe*; another carried kitchen furniture, candles, a portable altar, chapel furnishings. These vehicles carried the heaviest goods: wine,* armor,* clothes, and to obtain added traction, had wooden wheels rimmed with iron strakes. (Bibliog. 129)

caruca, plow team of eight oxen as used in the *Domesday Book*; these eight-oxen teams were the key to the entire system of the carucate* and the bovate.* (Bibliog. 213)

carucage, tax imposed by King Richard I* on the plowlands (carucates*) of one hundred acres* as an emergency measure in 1194 and again in 1198; it resembled the earlier Danegeld,* which was last imposed in 1162. (Bibliog. 262)

carucarii. See *ackermanni.*

carucate, unit of land measure in Danish England before the Norman Conquest; it was equivalent to the land for one caruca,* or plow team of eight oxen, and was approximately 120 acres* or one hide,* but hide values differed markedly from place to place. (Bibliog. 109)

casque, defensive or ornamental helmet* with or without a visor.* (Bibliog. 9)

cast, pair of hawks in hawking.* (Bibliog. 26)

cast his chaule, actions of a deer when it drooped its head and closed its mouth— sure signs that it was ready to drop from exhaustion in the chase.* See hunting terms. (Bibliog. 96)

cast, the, the right to the first shot in an archery tournament* awarded by winning the last shot of the previous round. (Bibliog. 100)

cast, to, in archery, to become warped as a bow* or an arrow.* (Bibliog. 100)

castellan, person in charge of a castle* in the owner's absence. See constable. (Bibliog. 280)

castellaria, district organized feudally for the defense of a particular castle.* In its broadest sense, the term denoted a group of fees (see knighthood) owing service at the castle from which it took its name by finding knights or sergeants* or money* for its defense. For example, Earl Alan in Yorkshire had 199 manors* in his castellus, of which his men held 133, and apart from his castelry, he had forty-three manors of which his men held ten. This showed that the original castelry of Richmond was the large and compact fee known as Richmondshire, the "House of Richmond" in its narrowest sense; it excluded from castelry the fees which the earl's* men held of him elsewhere in England. As a castle was frequently the administrative seat of the barony* as well as its military nexus, it was understandable that the term castellaria occasionally was used as a synonym for barony or honour.* (Bibliog. 330)

castellum, vague 12th-century word thought to refer to a fortification whose defensive value was small. (Bibliog. 330)

casting, egg-shaped or oblong ball of feathers, bones, and other residue which all hawks threw up after digesting the nutritious part of their food. (Bibliog. 100)

castle, heraldic charge* of two crenellated* towers* joined by a crenellated wall which had a port or gateway. (Bibliog. 43)

castle, thoroughly fortified residence of a lord, but not necessarily of a prince* or king.* As such, it differed from other forms of fortification by its dual functions as a residence and as a fortress, and by its private as opposed to public or communal nature. Roman fortifications of camps or cities or the burhs* of the Anglo-Saxons were built to shelter the people, so they were not castles; the residences and palaces of the Carolingian kings and emperors* were not fortified, so they were not castles. Furthermore, as a castle was a sign and symbol of lordship, it became a prime objective in and an active base for waging warfare. Because a castle controlled the countryside around it, anyone wishing to control the land first had to hold or take the castles in it. Warfare, thus, came to center upon castles and the heavy cavalry of knights, so the castle and knight became the chief instruments of war.

The earliest type of castles, the motte* and bailey* type, had its origin in

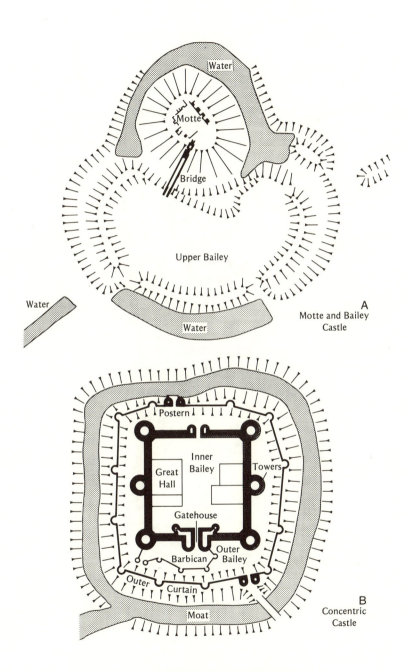

Figure 5. Types of Castles: Ground Plans

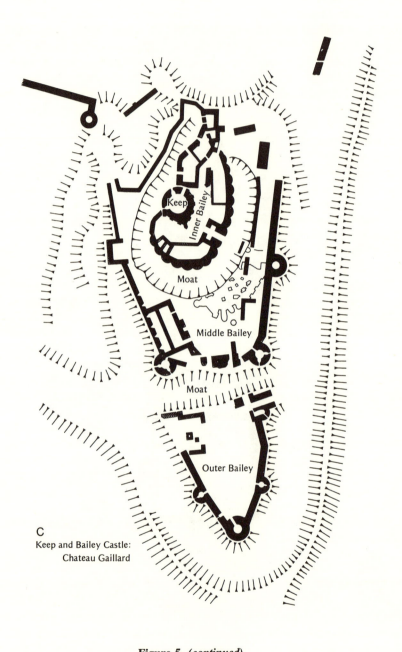

C
Keep and Bailey Castle:
Chateau Gaillard

Figure 5. *(continued)*

France and the Rhineland before the middle of the 11th century, and knowledge of its construction and utility must have been brought with William* in his invasion of England because no reference to castles was found in pre-Conquest English chronicles, laws, charters,* or writs. If King Edward the Confessor, Earl Godwine, or other magnates (see peer) had had castles, they would have been mentioned as were those in France and Normandy during the rebellions and crises there of 1051–1052 and as were William's demolishing castles there after 1047. These early motte and bailey castles were built as bases from which small bodies of mounted soldiers* under a single leader could range over a wide area of the countryside and to which they could retire if attacked. Basically this type had a bailey containing a hall,* well, kitchen, sleeping quarters, stables, storerooms, workshops for smiths and armorers, and chapel, all of which were surrounded by a ditch outside a steep bank and was entered by a drawbridge* across the ditch to a gap in the bank which would be further strengthened by a high timber fence called the palisade.* But such an area needed an overlooking watchtower to control it and to serve as a safeguard against treachery inside the gate. For added safety and height, then, a tower was built on a mound called a motte, generally on one side of the bailey, and was protected further by being ditched around. The top of the motte had its own fence and gate and was reached either by a flying bridge or gangway against its slope. Generally the size of the bailey and motte was dictated by the size and needs of the garrison it held and the nature of the site on which it was built. Usually the entire bailey was within bowshot of the motte. These were cheap and quick to build, but when this became the residence of a lord and a center of government, albeit local government, something more permanent was needed; the timber walls subsequently were built on stone sleeper walls to retard rotting in the damp ground or were replaced entirely by stone walls.

The tower was the first structure built in stone, and because the artificial mounds of the bailey often were unstable, it usually was built on the natural level. This main tower was called the keep* or *donjon** to distinguish it from lesser towers of the perimeter wall. In this keep the lord could be assured of safety and privacy for himself and his family, a prison (see jail) for his captives, and a strongroom for his treasure and documents. It could hold out after the rest of the castle had been overrun and usually could be captured or destroyed only by undermining (see mine gallery), by starvation or pestilence, or by treachery. This keep had three or four large rooms stacked vertically on top of each other with smaller rooms built within the thickness of the walls. Thus as the tower got higher to add more rooms, convenience was reduced because access to the upper rooms was obtained only by ladders or spiral staircases. Usually the lowest floor formed a storage hall with its own well independent of the main well within the bailey. Above this would be the entrance floor, reached by an outside staircase of stone or wood with a gap crossed by a drawbridge. The entrance door or series of doors would be strengthened by timber bars sliding into recesses within the walls, and by a portcullis* or iron grill that could be dropped to form an immovable grill in front of the door.

As everyone and everything went in and out through the one doorway, the first floor had a lobby or entrance hall and generally also had a hall for public business. Above it was the floor containing the private rooms for the owner or his resident agent, the constable.* Walls of the tower were built well above the roof of the top floor in order to protect the building against missiles and to provide a walkway behind the parapet* for the watch to patrol and to guard the castle below. Galleries* or turret* towers often projected out from the walls in front of the parapets, from which the defenders could protect the base of the keep.

A castle served both offensive and defensive roles. Offensively, it served as a heavily defended base for active operations by means of which the countryside surrounding it could be controlled. Thus it was prized highly and coveted, and thus the frequent sieges (see seige warfare) of castles. Defensively, it was built to be as impregnable as possible, and therefore its defense role dictated its design even though it also served other functions as a lordly and prestigious dwelling, a center of local government and administration, and as treasury, armory,* and perhaps as prison. In England, by the time William I had set up his knight quotas on his tenants-in-chief,* his barons,* English opposition to the Normans practically had ceased, and with its end also ended the need for building castles throughout the countryside; their role thereafter chiefly was administrative, for, serving as centers of regional government, they were useful in preserving law and order in the locality. However, they also became centers of baronial rebellion during periods of internal strife. During the reign of King Stephen,* for example, they contributed to the general chaos afflicting England (see adulterine castles). Thus the natural policy of later kings was anti-castle. Henry II confiscated and demolished dangerous baronial (see barony) strongholds and strengthened only royal castles. (Bibliog. 48, 263, 280, 291)

castle building. Freemasons, roughmasons, and quarriers; carpenters and smiths, plumbers, glaziers; carters, boatman, and a host of unskilled laborers were required to erect a castle.* Eight days were reported to have been the time needed to erect a castle within the existing fortifications at Dover in 1066 and for raising a second castle at York in 1069. Obviously such castles were wooden motte* and bailey* types (see also castle).

A masonry castle, on the contrary, required far more. Richard I* built Château Gailiard* in two years of feverish work (1196–1198) at the record cost of 11,500 pounds (see money). Henry II's* new castle at Orford on a previously unfortified site took eight years of seasonal work during spring, summer, and autumn to construct (1165–1173) at a cost of 1,400 pounds. Raising a new castle from its foundations in one continuous operation, such as that attempted at Orford, showed the cost of castle building. In 1165, 660 pounds were spent—the largest outlay of money on a single castle since the beginning of Henry II's reign, in 1166,

323 pounds; in 1167, when the building was in a well-advanced stage, the Pipe Roll* shows an entry for two pounds for stocking the castle and twenty marks* to Bartholomew de Glanville as custodian; in 1173, an entry for fifty-eight pounds, two shillings, eightpence* for the work to provide a great ditch around the castle along with palisades* and brattices* and the work on a stone bridge for some unnamed castle. At Dover Castle between 1180 and 1190 the work to build the great rectangular keep,* the towered inner bailey with its twin-tower gateways, and a section of the towered outer curtain to the northeast totalled 7,000 pounds. King Edward I employed as his master mason and engineer his "Master of the King's Works in Wales," Master James of St. George* from Savoy where he had built many castles similar to those which the English king had him build in Wales. At Harlech in the summer of 1286, this Master James employed 1,000 men per week; Conway Castle,* Harlech, and Caernarvon* among them employed 2,500 per week in the seasons of 1285–1287; and at Beaumaris* in the summer of 1295, 3,500 men were at work. These Edwardian Welsh castles took varying times to erect: Beaumaris, over thirty years, 1295–1330; Flint, eight and one-half years, 1277–1286; Harlech, seven and one-half years, 1283–1290, at a cost of 9,500 pounds; Builth, five and one-half years, 1277–1282; Rhuddlon, four and one-half years, 1278–1282; Conway, five years, 1283–1287, at a cost of 14,000 pounds; and Caernarvon, forty-seven years, 1283–1330, at a staggering cost of 27,000 pounds.

Obviously, castle building was the largest single and continuous expense of royal expenditure. Under Henry II, Richard I, and John,* annual expenditures for castle building, repair, and upkeep reached the formidable figures of between 1,000 and 4,000 pounds. At the same time, the king's average annual income under Henry II, for example, was only 10,000 pounds. Indeed, the regular annual income of one of the richest vassals* of the king in the early 13th century, Roger de Lacy, constable* of Chester, totalled only 800 pounds. Only seven members of the English baronage, who formed a small but immensely powerful ruling class, received more than 400 pounds per year in 1200. At the same time, a knight or country gentleman could live quite comfortably on ten to twenty pounds per year; wages for a knight on active service were eight pence per day (twelve pounds per year) in 1154, rising to two shillings per day (thirty-six pounds per year) by 1216. A constable at one of the royal castles could expect a stipend ten to twelve pounds to maintain himself in his office of considerable responsibility; the stipend of the chaplain, porter, or watchman at that same castle was likely to be one penny per day (one and one-half pounds per year). (Bibliog. 48, 70, 97, 263)

castle defense. A castle's* principal defense to resist and overcome sieges (see siege warfare) was the strength and ingenuity used in the design of its fortifications. Its answer to the pounding of the *petrarie** or "battering ram"* was the breadth of its masonry. Massive tower keeps* were almost impervious by reason of the plinth* on which the great tower stood, and the batters and spurs at the base of other towers and walls served to make bores and battering rams less effective and to make stones and other missiles shatter and ricochet among its attackers. Further, round and polygonal towers had no sharp angles for bores, no "dead angles"* for assailants to work on, and their shape tended to deflect missiles. Because of its inherent weakness, the gatehouse* drew much attention in its design and fortification, and its defense included such details as a turning or drawbridge,* a portcullis,* *meurtières*,* and machicolation.*Because much of the defensive strength consisted in preventing the enemy from coming close enough to use their siege weapons efficiently, castle architects used deep wet or dry ditches, or moats as deep and as wide as possible and built wherever possible on a solid rock base (see Château Gaillard). Further protection was provided by numerous well-placed "arrow loops,"* battlements,* and crenellations* to provide cover for the defenders atop the walls and towers; barbicans* in front of gateways; and hoarding (see brattice) or stone machicolation to protect the foot of walls, towers, and gatehouses. "Flanking towers"* also played an important role in castle defense. Thrust out over the wall toward the field to cover the base of the wall between it and its neighboring towers on either side against the enemy's use of ram or bore, these towers also overtopped the walls to protect them against escalade* and belfry*, and they divided the walls into defensible sections if the enemy gained a foothold or made a breach. (Bibliog. 48)

castle guard. The Norman Conquest of England resulted in a radically new type of fortification, the motte* and bailey* fortress (see also castle), which in turn resulted in a new concept in the administration and organization of the fortifications system: the private castle. Toward the end of the 11th century England had as many as 500 to 600 castles, and King Stephen* erected still more during his twenty-year reign; but these were hastily erected and equally as hastily demolished by Henry II* once he was on the throne (see castle). Nevertheless, as these castles needed men to staff them, castle guard duty soon became a "feudal obligation"* of many English fiefs.*

Long before it began in England, such service had been a characteristic feature of knight service on the continent but was not ordinarily demanded of a knight unless it was stipulated in his feudal contract. In Normandy, for example, castle guard service was a characteristic military obligation of vavasours.* Elsewhere in France host (see knighthood) and castle guard service frequently were joined in one tenure.* In Germany the services of host and castle guard were kept distinct, the latter being owned only by fiefs of an inferior order. By the 13th century the distinction was clearly made between continuous castle guard service (lasting from several months to several years) and simple castle guard service (lasting from a few days to a few months). At that time castle guard service was performed commonly for forty days at the vassal's* expense, but both shorter and longer terms were not unusual. Sometimes the lord paid for all service over forty days, and in time the tendency grew for all service to be stipendiary.

In the first English feudal feoffments,* a knight who received a fee (see

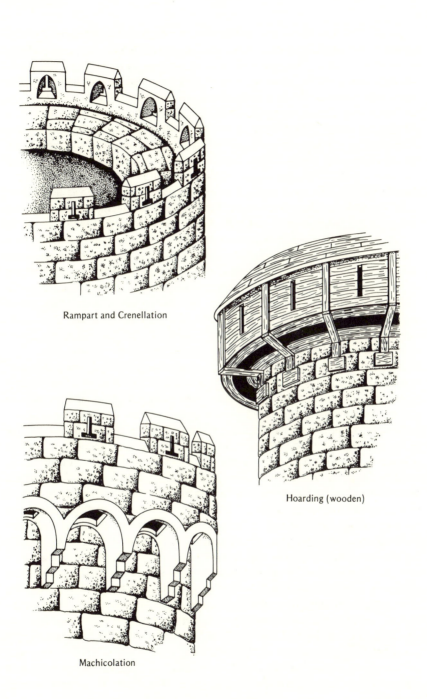

Rampart and Crenellation

Hoarding (wooden)

Machicolation

Figure 6. Castle Architecture

knighthood) was bound to personal service in a castle belonging to his lord and often also in a castle belonging to his king. Frequently this service was commuted for a money payment. England followed the Norman and French precedents but added unique features: some sergeanty* tenures owed nothing but ward (see bailey) duty at some English castle. Burghers (see *burg*) of Egremont Castle in Cumberland at the beginning of the 13th century were under the obligation to find twelve armed men in time of war to guard the castle. Others owed only local castle guard duty. In the court* of Eu's honour in the district of Hastings, for example, sixty knights were enfeoffed, each of whom owed a total of three months service at the count's castle at Hastings, but none was obligated to serve outside the district except at the count's expense. Thus there was no uniform pattern to this obligation but rather a maze of local arrangements adapted to the needs of particular castles in particular districts, a wide variety in the length and frequency of service and in the number and type of men required for duty. Large coastal and frontier castles generally required permanent garrisons; less important ones were guarded by a few sergeants or "household knights"* supplemented by larger contingents at times of unrest. Richmond Castle in Yorkshire, for instance, was held by forty-two knights in summer when the Scottish danger was greatest but by only twenty-six during the winter months. And often castle duty was demanded only in time of war.

In castle guard of the 12th century, knights often were outnumbered by sergeants, who in time grew to owe forty days castle duty in time of war, appearing with their arms and a horse* or two. At Richmond Castle in the 13th century, the knights enfeoffed within the honour* originally had been divided into six groups, each group owing service at the castle for two consecutive months in each year. Long before the details for such a system had been worked out, however, it was replaced by a system of money payments according to which a knight's fee was charged a definite sum by way of commutation. The fees lying in the northern portion of the honour, the original castlery of Richmond, were assessed at the low rate of one-half mark* each. At another castle, Dover, nine baronies* were responsible for providing the castle guard of more than 170 knights; and although the term of such service was only fifteen days, some owed it two or three times per year. The largest of these, the great honour at Haughly, Suffolk, which had fifty-six knight's fees, was called the "Constable's Honour."

At the royal castle of Windsor* during the reign of Henry II, the garrison was formed by a combination of four baronies: one owing the service of thirty knights, two owing a service of fifteen knights each, and one a service of ten. The addition of three single knight fees brought the total service for Windsor to seventy-three. As knights in the reign of Henry II could be hired to do castle duty for eight pence* a day, commutation of the service due from a knight's fee at the yearly rate of twenty shillings (one pound; see money) for each knight gave the king a round sum of seventy-three pounds per year. This could be apportioned into four shillings a day with which he could hire a permanent garrison of six knights at eight pence per day (forty-eight pence equals four shillings). Such commutation was particularly effective when a knight owed service at a castle far away from his home. Northampton knights, for example, owed service at Dover Castle, and payment at the rate of six or eight pence per day for commutation of this service was worth the cost.

In England, no knight could perform both host service and guard service concurrently. Wartime castle guard duty was not the same as wartime host service, for different types of warfare were involved. A feudal expedition was an offensive campaign which needed no garrisoning of castles. Wartime castle guard duty, on the other hand, was for civil war or unrest, and thus it was equivalent to host duty. On a campaign, a knight from the host might have to garrison a captured castle, or castle garrisons might have to take to the field in a battle. Often the relationship between a knight's host duty and castle guard duty was spelled out in the military obligations for his fee. He might owe guard duty at a baronial castle in peace time and host or castle guard duty in war time. Or he might owe guard duty at a royal or baronial castle for a set period every year and have to perform host service in addition, but requiring him to perform castle guard duty at both a royal and a baronial castle was too severe a requirement. By the reign of King John, barons were beginning to insist that both castle guard duty and host duty were mutually exclusive. This is implicit in Clause 29 of the *Magna Carta Libertatum*,* and the barons and king remained at odds over this issue during most of the 13th century. (Bibliog. 48, 111)

castle personnel. Usually in charge of the castle* was the constable,* for when a threat was imminent or a siege seemed likely, the lord would not remain to fight because his political and military value was too great and his ransom would be crippling if he were captured. Beneath the constable in the hierarchy of castle personnel were knights whose proficiency as horsemen made them leaders of the castle's strike force, which they formed with mounted sergeants* and mounted men-at-arms. Beneath the mounted forces were the archers and crossbowmen, and then the support forces consisting of smiths, farriers, carpenters, cooks, chaplain, porters, watchmen, and so on. Of the footsoldiers, the crossbowmen were the most valuable because of the penetration power and range of their quarrels (see crossbow). Castles frequently used their own siege engines to counteract similar engines brought by the besiegers. And the constable ensured that sufficient food, water, and supplies were on hand to wait out a siege (see seige warfare).

In addition to the military personnel needed for the castle's defense, other workers were needed to maintain it. Besides the "castle guard,"* a second group consisted of porters, watchmen, and a capellanus or clerk whose function was the supervision of the work done by the smiths, masons, and other workmen to keep the fabric of the castle in repair. Every castle had a chapel and a chaplain, who frequently performed both jobs of chaplain and capellanus. One or more porters were kept at every castle and were paid at the general rate of one penny* per day for a total annual salary of one pound (see money) ten shillings fivepence

(365 pence). Frequently a royal castle employed a *janitor civitatis* who (in the time of Henry II, for example) was paid twenty shillings per year for being the executioner of sentences of hanging or mutilation, for carrying out such other duties for the sheriff as escorting a counterfeiter who had "abjured the realm"* to the nearest port, or for conducting an ordeal.* Additional personnel included a staff of ushers who were employed to deliver writs or summons, and a group of watchmen (the vigil) who, besides patrolling the ramparts,* would guard treasure, prisoners, and the like. (Bibliog. 120)

Castle Sween, earliest stone castle* built in the Norman style (c. 1220) in Scotland; it had a large rectangular keep* with large pilaster and angle buttresses.* (Bibliog. 45)

castor, beaver whose testicles were used in a medicine called castoreum. When a hunter chased a castor to capture it, it would bite off its own testicles, hence the term, castor or castrated one. If the same beaver was pursued again by a hunter, it would lift itself up and expose its belly to show itself; the hunter, perceiving the testicles to be missing, would leave the animal alone. (Bibliog. 258)

castrum (L.), castle.*

cat, sow, penthouse sheltering warriors using a "battering ram"* or a bore in a siege; it was so named because of its stealthy approach. See sow. (Bibliog. 331)

catapult, class of siege machines used for throwing heavy darts* and spears* developed from the torneamentum* of Romans, so termed from the twisting of the ropes which supplied the propelling force. (Bibliog. 71)

catchpole, 1. police instrument consisting of a long staff with a U-shaped metal head, the open end of the U being closed by two hinged, spring-operated bars. When pushed against the back of someone's neck, the bars opened and then closed again around the throat. It was used in Germanic and Scandinavian countries for catching and holding criminals; 2. petty police official, usually serving under the sheriff* and mainly concerned with making arrests for debt. (Bibliog. 27, 171)

Catherine wheel, weapon ending with a wheel having eight spokes, each of which ended in a curved spike. It was supposed to represent the instrument of martyrdom of St. Catherine of Alexandria. (Bibliog. 27)

catoblefas. See cacothephas.

cells, small monastic houses generally found in the country, belonging to large convents, and intended as places for a change of air for monks and as places in which to reside as one looked after the lands, vassals,* and other holdings of one's lord. (Bibliog. 100)

cent egg. See basilisk.

centaur, monster* from Greek mythology having the body and legs of a horse* but with a man's trunk, arms, and head. As it usually was shown holding a bow* and arrow,* it was termed "sagittary" or "sagitterius." (Bibliog. 138)

centenary, officer equivalent to a captain who was in charge of one hundred men-on-foot in King Edward III's army at Calais in 1347. (Bibliog. 222)

centuriate. See hundred.

ceorl, old English freeman of the lowest class, opposed on one side to a thegn (thane*) or noble (see nobility), and on the other to the servile class. This was a common term before the Norman Conquest, but as it was replaced by the term villein,* it disappeared entirely, primarily because it was a designation of a freeman and had not quite lost that meaning just before the invasion. (Bibliog. 357)

ceraunius, stone of lightning, sometimes found in the shape of an arrow.* Formed in the upper regions of the sky where the winds battle, it was to be found stuck in the ground nine days after it fell. For chaste people it was a talisman* which brought good luck and pleasant dreams. (Bibliog. 258)

cerf. See stag.

ceronites, precious stone found in the eyes of a turtle of India. Those who put this incombustible stone on their tongues spoke only the truth, but its virtues revealed themselves between sunrise and the sixth hour during the new moon; when the moon was on the wane, the stone had its full powers only between dawn and sunrise. (Bibliog. 258)

cervellière, synonym for basinet* as an "arming cap"* and helmet* liner. However, it actually referred only to a small hemispherical metal skull cap, distinct from the basinet which was a characteristic conical helmet of the 14th century. (Bibliog. 27)

cetus, huge beast that lived in the sea. With its back covered by sand, it lay quietly at the surface, and sailors, believing it to be an island, disembarked and prepared to stay there. When they built a fire, however, the beast plunged to the bottom of the sea, drowning those it was carrying on its back. When it was hungry, it yawned, and small fish, drawn by the exquisite odor emerging from its mouth, swam into it and were swallowed. (Bibliog. 258)

chacechiens, grooms in attendance on the hounds during hunting.* (Bibliog. 96)

chaise, large French gold coin issued in the 14th century showing the monarch seated on his throne or chaise. (Bibliog. 150)

chalcedony, stone which when pierced and fastened to the mast ensured the safety of a ship on all occasions against the perils of the sea, fire, and so on. (Bibliog. 258)

chalder, measure of capacity for coal, coke, and grain in the British Isles. The standard chalder of coal in 1421 was thirty-two bushels* which equalled one ton of 2,000 pounds* and also one-twentieth of a keel of twenty tons. (Bibliog. 394)

chamberlain, *camerarius,* office of the royal household. Originally, the king's* chamberlain presided over the great chamber (*camera*) with his staff, which included the bearer of the king's bed, the king's tailor, and the ewerer* (*aquarius*) who dried the king's clothes and prepared his bath. He came to be an officer who superintended the arrangement of domestic affairs. He was to attend the royal person of the sovereign and regulate the etiquette of the palace. Specifically, he was entrusted with the privilege of keeping the king's signet ring. Under the Norman kings, the position was known as the master chamberlain. That office existed under William I, was vested in the family of Tancarville, and became an hereditary office.

Ralph the Chamberlain, son and heir of Ralph Fitzgerald, in 1066 attested charters* of Duke William* in Normandy, but he didn't cross the channel with the duke.* In the early years of Henry I,* Robert Malet's name appeared frequently as a witness of charters until he was banished and his lands confiscated some time before the battle of Tinchebrai* in 1106; Lord Tancarville still was serving as master chamberlain in Normandy. After Henry's conquest of Normandy, he became the king's master chamberlain automatically and remained in that position until 1129. Rabel de Tancarville succeeded his father as master chamberlain of England and Normandy, having narrowly escaped the wreck of the "White Ship disaster"* because there was too large a group of drunken and dissolute youths aboard. He was succeeded on his death in 1140 by his son, William de Tancarville, who transmitted the office to his descendants until early in the 14th century when an heiress carried the honours* and estates to the house of Melun. It ultimately became known as the office of the lord great chamberlain, similar to the offices of lord high chancellor,* lord high steward,* lord high constable,* and earl marshal* of England. In France the mayorality of the palace, which grew so powerful that it overthrew the Merovingian dynasty and began the Carolingian dynasty, grew out of the office equivalent to the chamberlain. (Bibliog. 75)

chamberlains of the Exchequer, knights who served in place of the chamberlains*; they carried the keys of the chests containing money.* See Exchequer. (Bibliog. 144)

champion for ordeals, professional fighter who substituted for an accuser or a defendant in judicial duels.* Usually an accused person fought for himself in a trial by ordeal* to prove the truth of his position. With only rare exceptions, the accusation (appeal*) of a felony* had to be conducted by the accuser and the accused in person. Clerics, up to 1176, had to fight. By virtue of their sex, women were excused, and their accusations were handled by a jury. Men over sixty were exempt if they so chose. Also excused were men who pled "mayhem,"* that is, the inability to fight by reason of a broken nose or the loss of a limb, ear, nose, or eye; even broken foreteeth could disqualify a man, for those teeth helped greatly in the victory. In civil cases, the defender or tenant fought in person or had an unobjectionable witness as his champion.

In accusations of felony, the accuser, in all cases but secret homicide, swore an oath as witness that he had seen and heard the deed. When substitute fighters began to replace the accuser or the accused, the person chosen actually to fight, the champion, had to have been a witness, for only as a witness could he intervene and swear his oath in contradiction and participate in the duel. In a plea of land, he swore to having seen the seisin*—that is, he or his father had seen such-and-such a person in possession of the disputed lands. Although that may well have been legal fiction, the practice was followed until 1275. Hiring champions was forbidden but also went on anyway; and championship became a regular occupation, notwithstanding its dangers. Objecting to a champion often occurred, but accusing him of being hired was not easy to prove. Nonetheless, when the same champions appeared in fight after fight, each time for a different master, questions did arise. The law watched these fighters closely. On the continent, a defeated champion had his hand cut off because he had sworn the claim he fought was true, defeat had proved it false, and so therefore he had perjured himself; in England such severity was not shown. See craven. (Bibliog. 121, 229)

chancellor, originally the keeper of the king's seal. The name derived from *cancelli,* or screen behind which the secretarial work of the royal household was carried on. Carolingian kings* had a *cancellarius* who was a royal notary and an *archi-cancellarius* who kept the king's seal, but Edward the Confessor was the first English king to have a seal and to have a chancellor to keep it. The chancellor was an ecclesiastic, chief of the royal chaplains, and charged with the administration of royal revenues from vacant benefices. As secretary of state for all departments, he was the king's first, or prime, minister. He drew up and sealed royal writs; he was a prominent member of the Exchequer* department of the *curia regis**; he acted as itinerant justice and justice for the Exchequer and the *curia regis*. His business required the employment of a staff of clerks, so he became the head of the department, the Chancery.* In 1199, the Chancery and the Exchequer separated, and the Chancery Rolls (see chancery fashion) began to be kept. (Bibliog. 156)

Chancery, secretarial bureau under Norman and Angevin kings,* and the chancellor* was the secretary of state for all departments. This connection between the chancellor and the Chancery with the *curia regis*,* the governing body of the kingdom, naturally was close; the chancellor thus was the king's natural prime minister. In 1238 Edward III dispensed with baronial chancellors holding office for life and took the office into his own hands. He established a system by which the king took the profits of the seal and paid the chancellor a fixed fee for maintaining a body of clerks. (Bibliog. 156)

chancery fashion, method of constructing a roll or record by sewing parchment members together head to foot, thus forming one long skin which was then rolled up; hence, chancery roll. See exchequer fashion. (Bibliog. 171)

Chandos, the Herald of, author of a metrical biography of the Black Prince of England written in 1386 in continental French rather than in Anglo-Norman. It was especially valuable for the account of the Black Prince's Castilian expedition, for the author probably was an eye-witness to the events he described. Five major elements of chivalry* appeared in this work: prowess, loyalty, compassion, largesse,* courtesy. Possession of prowess merited the term "bon chevalier" or "chivalrous," and the prowess referred to was based on skill at arms which commonly was illustrated by good swordsmanship and was held to be governed by a code of fair fighting. Loyalty, more intricate and more significant, was a quality of the soul and indicated a loyal heart. The Herald noted that the Black Prince undertook the Spanish campaign out of pity and concern, and he found his pleasure there in giving aid to him who asked it on a plea of mercy.* The Prince's largesse was illustrated amply by the rich gifts of gold, silver, and jewels he gave away freely and by the 400 men he entertained daily at his table at Bordeaux. His freedom and naturalness of manner were illustrated by his actions on meeting his wife and son, Richard, during his triumphal entry into Bordeaux: he dismounted and walked into the city holding their hands. His courtesy was amply shown by his conduct to the captured king of France to whom he tried to perform squires'* duties and by his humble manner of thanking his own knights. (Bibliog. 218)

chanfron, chamfron, armor covering a horse's* face, sometimes with hinged cheek plates. See horse armor. (Bibliog. 9)

change, substitution of one deer for another during the chase.* After the hounds had started chasing a stag, it often would find another stag or hind,* push it with its horns or feet to get it to rise, and take its place. Then lying down itself in the spot just vacated, with its antlers close over its back, it would keep quiet so that the hounds would go off in chase of the substitute. Sometimes stags ran into a herd of deer to try to shake off pursuers. Any hound that stayed with the scent of the first stag and refused to be satisfied with the scent of another was called a "staunch hound"*—one which would not take the change—which was one of the best qualities in a stag hound. See hunting terms; hunting dogs. (Bibliog. 96)

chansons de geste, Old French epic poetry, narrative poems of moderate length, averaging 4,000 lines, usually in ten-syllable verse with assonanced and rhymed laisses (stanzas of varying lengths); they were sung with an accompanying harp* or vielle.* Basically these centered on the themes of the glory of the Franks, the Christian religion, and the deeds of certain famous knights who owed allegiance to Charlemagne or to his son, Louis the Pious. Although most of the subject matter and characters were legendary, audiences believed them to be true history. Except for *Gormont et Isambar,* none pre-dated 1100. See *geste;* lai. (Bibliog. 162)

chanterres. See minstrels.

chape, metal tip at the bottom of a dagger or sword* sheath to reinforce it. (Bibliog. 27)

chapeau. See cap of dignity.

chapelle-de-fer, iron hat with a brim and a low crown long worn by men-at-arms. (Bibliog. 9)

chaplet, circular wreath* of leaves with four roses* in a cross,* in heraldry.* (Bibliog. 251)

char, measure of weight for lead equalling six score stone* (120 stone of fourteen pounds* each). See weights and measures. (Bibliog. 103)

charge, 1. measure of weight equivalent to and eventually supplanted by a fother*; 2. any design borne on a shield* or on another charge; the important geometrical charges generally were called "ordinaries"* (such as bend,* bar*) and the less important ones "subordinaries."* Exclusive of the subordinaries, charges generally came from one of the following categories:

1. Human figures (e.g., king,* child, savage)
2. Religious and ecclesiastical charges (e.g., crucifix, angel, chalice)

3. Mythological charges (e.g., Apollo, Neptune)

4. Beasts (e.g., lion,* elephant,* rabbit)

5. Birds (e.g., eagle,* swan, stork)

6. Reptiles (e.g., tortoise,* adder, frog)

7. Fish (e.g., perch, salmon, shark)

8. Invertebrate creatures (e.g., fly, snail)

9. Parts of men (e.g., head, arm, eye)

10. Parts of animals (e.g., head, horns, wing)

11. Monsters* (e.g., griffin,* unicorn,* sphinx)

12. Vegetable kingdom (e.g., trees, flowers)

13. Armor* (e.g., helmet,* hauberk,* gauntlet*)

14. Weapons (e.g., bow,* sword,* sling*)

15. Articles of attire and ornamentation (e.g., crown,* boot, ring)

16. Domestic use (e.g., chair, comb, cauldron)

17. Home (e.g., book, rebec,* flute)

18. Farm and home tools (e.g., pitchfork, adz)

19. Implements (e.g., knots, needles, wool comb)

20. Ships (e.g., mast, oars, anchor)

21. Heavens (e.g., sun, moon, rainbow)

22. Buildings (e.g., castles,* portcullis*)

(Bibliog. 43, 253)

chariot branlant, rocking chariot. Late in the 13th century, horseback travel for noble ladies was supplemented by a covered chariot; not until a century later, however, did the rocking chariot (chariot branlant) appear with strap and chain suspension. These were painted or gilded and covered with leather or fine woolen cloth in bright colors. Eleanor of Castile ordered a fancy cart* shortly before her coronation* as Edward I's queen: a bright red cart was hung with curtains of heavy silk, the nailheads and wheels were gilt, and the inside lined and padded with silk; it cost over seventeen pounds (see money). For his daughter, Margaret, duchess of Brabant, King Edward I ordered a cart costing over twenty-two pounds. (Bibliog. 291)

charm against spasm, a remedy which assured a knight that it was:

> most sovran by many who have used it at home and abroad. When a certain knight
> ... saw a gentleman so troubled with the spasm that his head was drawn backward
> nearly to his neck just like a crossbow, and he was almost dead from pain and anguish.
> ... He took the charm written on parchment and placed it in a purse and put it on
> the neck of the patient, whilst those who stood by said the Lord's prayer and one to
> our lady Mary; and, as he swore faithfully [that] within four hours or five he was

restored to health: "In nomine patris + et filii + et Spiritus sancti + Amen. + Thebal + Enthe + Enthanay + In nomine Patris + et Filii + et Spiritus sancti + Amen. + Ihesu Nazarenus + Maria + Iohannes + Michael + Gabriel + Raphael + Verbum caro factum est. +

(Bibliog. 76)

charnel house, repository for bones which were thrown up when digging graves. (Bibliog. 100)

charnels, hasps used to fasten the helm* to the cuirass* at the front and rear. (Bibliog. 27)

charter, coming from the Greek word *chartes* meaning a thick paper or parchment, this word came to be applied to a document granted by a prince* thereby conferring or acknowledging privileges to be enjoyed by the whole or a portion of the people under his rule. In England, from the Conquest onward, there was a struggle between those who sought to enforce the feudal exactions which the Normans had practiced in France and those who attempted to hold onto the ancient Anglo-Saxon customs which had prevailed for centuries. At first this was only a contest between William* and his Norman followers on the one side and the Saxon population on the other; but by the time of King John, 150 years later, conditions had changed markedly. By then the barons* were so frequently incensed by the oppressions and exactions of the overly ambitious and money-hungry monarchs, to whose power they had contributed so much, that they joined in the general demand for a return to old laws of King Edward the Confessor. One of the most famous of the charters issued by the kings of England was the *Magna Carta Libertatum*ature* issued by King John in 1215. Its main feature held that no freeman should be taken or imprisoned, or be disseised (see assise) of his freehold, his liberties, or his free customs, or be outlawed,* exiled, or otherwise damaged except by lawful judgment of his peers* or by the law of the land. (Bibliog. 262)

charter of liberties, the *Magna Carta Libertatum,** issued by King John of England in 1215. This most famous of charters,* was an expansion of an oath taken by early kings* of England at their coronation* which bound the king to his subjects by his promise that the church and the people should keep true peace, that he would forbid rapacity and iniquity, and that he would show mercy* and equity in all his judgments. Earlier charters issued by Henry I, Stephen,* and Henry II placed the king under the law; in them, the king pledged to abolish "evil customs" and to restore the law of King Edward the Confessor, the "good law of the past." Reciprocally, the subjects took an oath of allegiance, binding both king and people to mutual obligations. Actually, however, the king might do whatever he wished of his own free will, for there were few limitations on royal power; but it was customary and prudent for him to take into his confidence the magnates (see peer) of the kingdom on whose support he was really dependent and to consult with them and gain their consent on questions of policy and public interest. (Bibliog. 262)

charters of franchise, documents granting franchise* (liberty) in western Europe to a serf* whom the lord elevated, usually in administering justice.* From the 12th century on, the term applied to the freedom granted to the inhabitants of a town or borough* who were freed thereby from servitude to feudal lords. See feudalism. (Bibliog. 139)

chase, 1. hunting* of wild beasts on horseback, particularly the beasts of the chase: buck, doe, fox, marten, roe; 2. to hunt with a crossbow*; 3. French fief* held by one who had only a house and a little land; a type of "tenant" knight. (Bibliog. 96, 261)

chases, unenclosed park land; specifically a tract of unenclosed land outside of Bristol, England, reserved for breeding and hunting* wild animals.

chasse Royal, le, French term for hunting* the stag—the real sport of hunting wild deer. (Bibliog. 96)

chastons, clavones, fastenings for crests* worn by both men and horses* in tournaments* during the 13th century. (Bibliog. 331)

Château du Courdray. See Chinon.

Château du Milieu. See Chinon.

Château Gailiard, castle* built in Normandy by King Richard I* in two years, 1196–1198, on a promontory 300 feet* above the river Seine with a deep valley on either side. The north end of the promontory was so steep and rocky that there was little danger from an attack from that direction. Because the south end had a gradual slope, however, the fortifications had to be made exceedingly strong. There the outwork had five strong towers with walls eleven feet thick connected by "curtain walls"* from eight to twelve feet thick and thirty feet high. Surrounding these walls was a ditch forty feet wide and thirty feet thick, crossable by a wooden drawbridge* and a strong gate with a portcullis.* Between the two wards* was a middle ward, also protected by strong towers, curtain walls, and a moat; it contained the chapel and the well. Within the middle ward itself was an inner ward protected by walls thirty feet high and eight feet thick, strengthened by rounded buttresses and surmounted by battlements*; at its foot was a moat and a twenty-foot scarped wall of sheer rock before the base of the walls was reached. Entrance to the innermost ward was made by causeway protected by outer and inner portcullises, a gateway studded with iron, and a steep stairway cut into the rock. Within the inner ward was a second well and the keep* with walls eleven feet thick. It had only one window, no door in the basement, and only two small windows on the first floor. There a small and well-protected doorway provided entrance to the keep, a door many feet off the ground and reachable only by a ladder or movable stairway. To make the keep even stronger, Richard I had battered the lower part of the wall, that is, had sloped it outward at the base, while above the base rose machicolations* and brattices* through which the defenders could fire on the assailants. Joining the keep on the north was a building in which the castellan* lived. Stairs from this building descended to the postern* gate, a narrow door with heavy bars. To reach it from within, steps were cut in the rock for about thirty feet; to reach it from the outside would have been impossible, for it opened on the perpendicular face of the scarp. To send out a messenger or admit a friend during a siege, a ladder or movable bridge was let down.

France's King Philip* boasted to capture the castle even if its walls were made of iron. Calling it his "Saucy Castle" and "My fair child of one year old," King Richard answered, "And I could hold it if they were made of butter." Perhaps he could have done so, but within a year of its completion, he was dead at Chaluz. His brother, John, was not like him; and so when Philip laid siege to it in the autumn of 1203, after capturing many of the Norman castles held by the English, its defense was another story. He seized the neighboring villages and then, having cut off all supplies, waited for hunger to force the castle to surrender. After a few months, he got tired of waiting and captured the outer ward by undermining the wall. One of his followers noticed a small window and standing on the shoulders of his comrades was able to clamber through into the chapel or a storehouse. The defenders foolishly set fire to it, and as the flames spread out of control, the garrison escaped to the inner ward. The same man let down the drawbridge, and the besiegers poured into the middle ward. Philip's men then brought up a cat*; under its protection they undermined the wall to the inner ward and followed with a barrage of heavy stones. A breach was made in the heavy masonry, and after only six months of siege the "Saucy Castle" fell. (Bibliog. 336)

Châteaudun, 12th-century castle* dominated by the 148-foot-high cylindrical keep* dating from the time of Philip* Augustus; it overlooked the Loire River thirty miles northwest of Orleans. (Bibiliog. 45)

chatelet, outer gatehouse* or outer enclosure. Sometimes called a bastile,* all such defenses in advance of the gateway were classed under the heading of barbicans.* (Bibliog. 341)

chattels, any item of movable or immovable property except real estate. Personal chattels were movable such as goods, plate, money; real chattels were leases, growing crops, and so on. (Bibliog. 246)

chausses, mail, 1. strip of mail* down the front of the leg, laced across at the back and under the sole of the foot; 2. stocking of mail shaped like hose and fitted closely to the leg; sometimes a kind of garter was threaded through the mail below the knee to give additional support. (Bibliog. 27)

check, to fly at, to shift pursuit from one bird to another while in flight, in hawking.* (Bibliog. 26)

checky. See chequy.

chef of fustian. See weights and measures.

chelidoine, stone, either reddish brown or black, found in the gizzard of swallows. Placed in a cloth on the left arm, the reddish-brown stone healed langour, cured insane people, and made a sane person eloquent and amorous. The black stone assured one of success in the world and when wrapped in red ribbon was a specific against fever, but when powdered in water it was effective as an eye wash and was an aid to women in childbirth. For these stones to be effective, however, they had to be taken from swallows which were trapped while flying and had not been picked up from the ground. (Bibliog. 258)

chemise, high wall built to encircle a keep*; entry gates were built through it. (Bibliog. 70)

Chepstow. Also known as Striguil, this Welsh castle* was begun about 1070 by William fitz Osbern, a great marcher lord, and had two new enclosures of the barbican* and the lower bailey* added under the lordships of William Marshal* and then Hugh Bigod. (Bibliog. 45)

chequy, checky, field* or charge* divided into at least twenty small squares of two alternate tinctures (see heraldry) or of metal* and a tincture. (Bibliog. 43)

chevage, annual payment made to a lord by each of his unfree tenants. (Bibliog. 24)

cheval-trap. See caltrop.

chevalchia, mounted service performed by a vassal* to his immediate lord as distinct from the military service performed by the same vassal in connection with the general summons to the host (see knighthood) by the king* or duke.* This might mean summons to serve in a small local war, or it might mean escort or police duty of some kind. The crucial point of distinction between the two was the nature of the summons, not the service required. This theoretically peaceful obligation, however, could become warlike indeed at times of rebellion and civil strife if the rear vassals chose to ignore their reserved allegiance to the monarch and to follow the banners* of their lords in revolt against the crown. Additionally, the king might demand this of his vassals for a minor military or police expedition or for a tour of the countryside when a formal summons to the host would have been inappropriate. (Bibliog. 159)

chevauchee, cavalcade duty; one of the duties or aids* of a knight. It might range from a minor expedition with his overlord to a simple escort duty when his lord moved from one castle* to another. (Bibliog. 154)

chevron, ordinary* which issued from the base of the shield* shaped like an inverted V; the name was derived from French *chevron*, a rafter of a roof. (Bibliog. 43)

chevronny, field* divided into an equal number of chevrons.* (Bibliog. 39)

chief, ordinary* which consisted of the top third of the heraldic field*; a charge* in this top portion was said to be "in chief." (Bibliog. 43)

chief butler, one of the English great offices of state first conferred by Henry I on William d'Aubigny (de Albini) who henceforth was known as William de Albini, *Pincerna* (see butler), to distinguish him from William de Albini, *Brito* (Belvoir). William, *Pincerna*, was succeeded by his son, who became the first earl* of Arundel, and thenceforth the office descended with the earldom until 1243 when the last earl of this line died leaving co-heirs. Arundel itself passed to the second of these, as did the earldom, but this did not affect the office, for it was held by the family before they held either the earldom or Arundel. (Bibliog. 75)

Childermas, Holy Innocent's Day, December 28.

Chillon, castle* on an island in Lake Geneva. Its earliest portions, the Tower of Alinge and the Duke's Tower, were built in the 10th and 11th centuries and were modified and enlarged for Peter II of Savoy by the architect Pierre Mainier: he added "mural towers"* on the vulnerable land side. (Bibliog. 45)

chimedia, precious stone found in the head of fish. He who held it in his mouth became what he most desired and would never die before confessing his sins and receiving absolution. (Bibliog. 258)

chiminage, charge or fee levied on goods transported through a "royal forest."* (Bibliog. 163)

Chinon, three huge stone castles* in a row overlooking the town and valley of the Vienne. Each of these three castles—Château du Courdray, Château du

Milieu, and Fort St. Georges—was separated from its neighbor by a moat. The first two *châteaux* were begun in the 10th century and in 1044 passed to Geoffrey of Anjou. His son, Henry II of England, strengthened them and added Fort St.Georges; he died there in 1189. French kings* further strengthened the defenses after acquiring the castles in 1205; later the Knights Templar* were imprisoned there. (Bibliog. 45)

chivalry, the qualities of being a knight, of knighthood.* At its loftiest, and assuredly in its underlying theory, chivalry depicted the perfect gentleman*— gently born, gentle mannered, truthful, faithful, courteous to women, pure, brave and fearless, unsparing of self, filled with deep religious feeling, bowing before God and womankind, but haughty in the presence of all others. To these were added the elements of maintaining a high sense of honor, disdain for danger and death, love of adventure, compassion for the weak and oppressed, generosity, self-sacrifice, and altruism.

Often the term was used to connote a body of knights or horsemen equipped for battle, a body of cavalry. When Bevis of Hamton saw himself being pursued by Saracens,* he said, "They would after us with wonder-great chevalrie." Additionally, in the technical feudal sense it meant tenure* by knight service amplified into a tenure of service by which the tenant was bound to perform some noble or military office for the lord. In its broadest sense, however, it meant the entire knightly system of the medieval period with its peculiar religious, moral, and social codes and customs. At their best, the qualities of the chivalric knight were honor, piety, and love, and at their worst, ferocity, superstition, and lust. The virtues of chivalry were courage, faith, devotion, and its vices were murder, intolerance, and ferocity. (Bibliog. 125, 180, 274, 350)

choppin, measure of capacity in 14th-century Scotland equivalent to two mutchkins or one-half Scots pint.* A mutchkin equals one-quarter Scots pint or three-quarters English pint. (Bibliog. 394)

chough, small- to medium-sized bird of the crow family with red beak and legs and glossy black plumage. In Arthurian legend, bad luck would follow anyone who killed one in the neighborhood of Tintagel, King Arthur's stronghold, for Arthur was transformed into one of these birds, and because the color of its beak and talons—"all red with blood"—were said to mark the violent end to which Arthur came. (Bibliog. 177)

Christian knighthood, church-sponsored idea that knights should dedicate all their energies and activities to God. The church instituted several measures in the 10th and 11th centuries designed to secure some degree of peace and order in Europe. Interested in restraining warlike nobles in feudal Europe, the church introduced the "Truce of God"* (*Truga Dei*) and Peace of God (*Pax Dei*).* Then the crusades* in 1095 created a particularly effective means of subduing militaristic barons,* or at least of diverting their energies into channels sanctioned by the church. Ramon Lull's* work, *Le Libre del Orde de Cauayleria* [translated by William Caxton, *Book of the Ordre of Chyvalry**], proposed that the knightly order served as the arm of the church, and the ordination ritual became almost the eighth sacrament, for not only were knightings occasionally held inside a church, but to the secular ritual were added several acts symbolic of the dedication of a new knight to Christian purposes, and clergy frequently assisted in conferring the honor. (Bibliog. 1)

Christiana Religio, Latin legend on European coinage* which, with an accompanying temple, was introduced on the denarius* by the moneyers of Louis I, son of Charlemagne. Denari with this distinctive feature were copied extensively both in western and eastern Europe. (Bibliog. 150)

Christmas game, jollity and festivities during the Christmas season which ended at Twelfth Night. See gestum. (Bibliog. 24)

chrysal, archery term for a crack in a bow.* (Bibliog. 100)

cing. See king.

cingulum, narrow girdle or belt used to gather the folds of a cyclas.* (Bibliog. 9)

Cinque Ports, group of seaports (originally five) situated on the southeastern coast of England which had jurisdiction continuously along the coast from Seaford in Sussex to Birchington near Margate. In order of precedence, the five "ports" (see borough) were Hastings, Sandwich, Dover, Romney, and Hithe, to which later were added the towns of Rye and Winchelsea. In early times the Cinque Ports furnished the chief part of the English navy, in return for which they obtained many important privileges and franchises.* (Bibliog. 246)

cinquefoil, heraldic figure with five petals or leaves and usually with the center pierced. (Bibliog. 43)

civiliter mortuus, being declared civilly dead, as being an outlaw,* and hence one so declared could be killed with impunity. (Bibliog. 182)

Clarenceux. See king of arms.

clavones. See chastons.

clerk of the market, official of the "king's household"* in charge of the king's* measures, which were the standard measures for the entire kingdom. (Bibliog. 171)

clinckaert, gold coinage* struck in Antwerp by Emperor Louis IV (1314–1346); equivalent to the French chaise,* it also was minted in denominations of one-half and one-third. (Bibliog. 150)

clock. See horologium.

cloister (L. *claustrum*; Fr. *cloître*; It. *chiostro*; Sp. *claustro*; Ger, *kloster*), monastery. Originally meaning the enclosing wall of a religious house, the term then was extended to mean the whole building enclosed within that wall, that is, a four-sided enclosure surrounded by covered ambulatories usually attached to a convent or a cathedral. (Bibliog. 100)

close, marrows, small enclosure around individual homes for individual cultivation of such vegetables and fruits as were available. (Bibliog. 24)

cloth-yard. See measurements.

clouage, "nail money"*; payment to heralds* for nailing the knight's armorial shield* to the pavilion* at a tournament.* (Bibliog. 78)

clove, commonly called a half-stone, this was a weight of six and one-half, seven, or eight pounds* used for cheese, wool, metals, and other goods. See weights and measures. (Bibliog. 394)

cniht, Anglo-Saxon word for servant from whence came the word knight (see knighthood). The Anglo-Saxon cniht essentially was the retainer, the servant of some great man. His place was in his lord's household or by his side as he rode about the countryside. As such service might require him to fight beside his lord, he was mounted and otherwise equipped for war; but such fighting as he did was only an incidental part of his general duty to his lord, and the cnihts of the 11th and 12th centuries were servants rather than soldiers.* Although cnihts often received land from their lords, often making them important among the landed gentry, such land was reward for past service, for only a special duty drew the cniht from his lord's household. The cniht with whom the English in the 11th century identified the Norman *chevalier* was a retainer attached to personal service of a nobleman. (Bibliog. 330)

coat armor, "coat of arms."*

coat of arms, heraldic arms* borne on the surcoat* or tabard* worn over the armor* itself. Often shortened to "arms" or "coat armor," it came to refer to what was borne on the shield*; sometimes it was used erroneously to refer to the complete achievement.* (Bibliog. 43)

Cobbie Row's Castle, oldest Scottish stone castle,* built by a Norse chief, Kolbein Hruga, about 1145 on the Isle of Wyre in the Orkney Islands. The name for the castle was a corruption of its builder's name. (Bibliog. 45)

Cochem, German castle* built on a hill above the Moselle River about twenty-five miles southwest of Koblenz around 1020. Three hundred years later, it was enlarged by Archbishop Baldwin of Trier, and it became a toll station on the Moselle by means of a chain drawn across to bar the river. (Bibliog. 45)

cock-feather, uppermost and darkest feather of an arrow.* (Bibliog. 100)

cockatrice, monster like a wyvern* with a cock's head, feet, and legs, and a barbed tongue; it was called a basilisk* in Greek and Regulus (little king) in Latin because it was the king of serpents of whom all were afraid and fled when they saw him. It killed anything within sight by its smell and breath but was overcome by a weasel. It was so venomous and perilous that it would kill a man even at the length of a spear* away. When it died by weasel bite and was burned, its ashes were valuable in changing metals in alchemy. (Bibliog. 21)

cocket, coket, official seal for each port (see borough) used to attest the payment of customs; the controller kept one-half of it and the collector of customs the other. (Bibliog. 163)

cognizance, heraldic badge* or device* that identified its bearer. (Bibliog. 43)

coif-de-mailles, hood of mail* to protect the wearer's head and neck; heavy and hot to wear, it was replaced by the *camail*.* (Bibliog. 9)

coinage. The silver penny* or denier (see denarius) virtually was the sole coin in circulation in western Europe for over five centuries. Modeled on the triens or one-third solidus (see sol) gold coin introduced by Constantine in the late Roman Empire, the denarius began to be minted in the 7th-century Merovingian and Anglo-Saxon kingdoms. In England and Frisia, the contemporary pennies* were known as sceatta* or sceats and were closely related to the Merovingian denier. Minted in huge quantities during the latter part of the 7th and most of the 8th centuries, these sceats were used on both sides of the North Sea indiscriminantly because of the prosperous trade of the northern Netherlands. In Merovingian Gaul of the 7th century, one pound in silver equalled twenty solidi of Roman calculation; it also equalled 240 of the actual silver denarii coins. Then, after the gold triens coin stopped circulating, the relationship between the pound, solidus, and denier remained as a convenient means of counting coins: a solidus (later shilling; see sol) meant a dozen coins, and a pound meant a score of dozens. Pepin* reformed the coinage in 755 by increasing the weight of the denier; the new ones remained the same in appearance, but were struck on broad thinner flans* (blanks) of some three-fourths of an inch in diameter; in this way they resembled the silver dirhem* of Arab Spain which also was struck on a thin broad flan. These broader, thinner deniers were minted in all parts of the Merovingian empire: at Barcelona and Ampurias in Spain; at Lucca, Pisa, Milan, and Pavia in Italy; as well as in Gaul. New pennies, thinner and broader than the thick small sceatta, began to be minted in England around 775 at Canterbury and served as models for all later pennies in Anglo-Saxon kingdoms.

By the beginning of the 9th century, most of western Europe was using penny coinage. But as the Carolingian empire began to fragment in the 9th and 10th centuries, its strict control over the weight and fineness disappeared, and counts* began to issue money* of their own. Monasteries such as St. Martin of Tours and St. Martial also struck deniers. Some counts put their own names on the coins; others used both the king's name and their own. As new dies were copied slavishly from old ones, in time they became so worn and degenerated that the Carolingian monogram appeared in less and less recognizable form, and the head depicted on the obverse became grotesque from overcopying. Although the Capetian deniers were indistinguishable from those of their feudal neighbors, those issued by the counts of Champagne achieved international circulation by the great fairs of Troyes and Chalons, and those of Poivins even became the basis for money* of account by becoming the standard for Champagne and its fairs and extended even as far away as Lorraine.

The Anglo-Saxon denier was more closely controlled than any other denier in western Europe. The West Saxon conquest imposed a uniform coinage over the whole of England with only slight regional variations and exercised strict royal control by having the dies cut in regional workshops or in London. Furthermore, in 973, King Edgar ordered that every six years the complete coinage was to be reminted, and all outstanding issues were to be demonetized. This policy was followed and even tightened over the years; Edward the Confessor reduced the time for circulation from six to three years. Coming from a coinage system that had degenerated over the centuries, the Normans adopted and maintained the Anglo-Saxon system in its entirety until the reign of Stephen,* when it deteriorated into a continental type of feudal coinage and the monarchy no longer was able to validate its coins. Faced with that problem when he ascended the throne in 1154, Henry II abandoned the idea of a triennial coinage and began the coinage of a type to be fixed and known for many years because he recognized that if the coinage was based on the intrinsic value of the coin, it demanded a solid, well-recognized, and stable base. The only coin in circulation in England during the 12th century was the silver penny, and it was the sheriff's* responsibility to ensure that minters did not exceed the standard proportion of alloy. A sheriff could be dismissed from office for allowing the circulation of debased or clipped coins, and a portion of his farm* had to be paid in assayed* coins, a process which took place with much solemnity and anxiety on the part of the sheriff at Westminster (see Exchequer).

The sheriff's dismissal as his punishment, however, was a lesser punishment than that meted out to the false moneyer who had minted the spurious coinage; he was castrated and had his right hand cut off. By these strict controls Henry II ensured that the silver content and hence its value would remain constant for the next 200 years, and hence English coinage enjoyed a high reputation on the continent.

Louis VII made the first attempt to recreate a non-feudal coinage in France by issuing a denier parisis* and by taking to himself as king* the rights of control over the coinage. After regaining the Angevin lands from the English, his son Philip* Augustus ordered the mint at St. Martin at Tours to begin striking royal deniers tournois,* and he limited permissions for local coinages. Thus he allowed only deniers parisis and tournois to circulate. His grandson, Louis IX, controlled coinage even more strictly by insisting that these royal deniers be accepted freely throughout France and that local coinages be accepted only in the fiefs* issuing them. Until 1226 the only circulating coins in France were silver pennies and halfpennies* (oboles* or mailles*).

The coinage broke down in the Holy Roman Empire.* In the western areas of Frisia, the Rhineland, Lotharingia, Bavaria, and in parts of Franconia, silver deniers were issued. Along the Baltic to the east, and in Saxony and the rest of Franconia and Suabia, paper-thin pfennigs were minted. Called bracteates,* these pfennigs were struck on paper-thin pieces of silver; they were left blank on the concave side, but carried a design on the convex side; they had little intrinsic value. Efforts to stabilize the coinage led to imitations of the stable English penny, especially in the areas of the Low Countries along the North Sea coast. This interest carried into the 13th and early 14th centuries, particularly as interest flourished in the stable sterling* coinage of Edward I.

Coinage didn't change from border to border, nor did a different coinage for every minor seigneury mean a different currency for each. Only in England was there success in ensuring that local currency remained local coinage. Other areas were not successful at it, and the money circulating in any city or principality consisted of local coinage, coins from neighboring territories and cities, and a considerable number of pieces from distant areas. Included among them, between the 8th and 13th centuries certainly, were the gold nomisma* and dinar* from Byzantium and Islam, particularly in Italy.

As the penny was inconvenient for large sums, Venice, about 1202, issued a larger coin, the "grosso" (see gros) or "matapan," weighing 2.18 grams and valued at twenty-four of the old deniers. Other city-states soon followed. Verona issued a soldo veronese equal to twelve deniers; the duchy of Apulia issued a grosso known as a ducat*; the kingdom of Naples issued a grosso known as a gigliato* or carlino.* In France, Louis IX (St. Louis) issued a gros tournois weighing 4.22 grams, and though much larger than the matapan, it also was valued at twelve deniers just as in the Italian city-states. After 1290 the devalued successor to the gros, the blanc, at thirteen and one-eighth denier tournois, continued in France. Soon larger denominations were being issued elsewhere: the croat of Aragon; the maravedi de plata of Castile; the grooten in Holland,

Brabant, Liege and Namur; and in the 14th century, the Prague groat of Bohemia. England under Edward I struck its groat, but it was valued only at four old pennies because penny sterling had not deteriorated so much as the denier tournois; England did not issue a permanent large coinage until Edward III reintroduced the groat in 1351.

Gold trientes and solidi were minted in Sicily and southern Italy by Byzantium up to the end of the 9th century; during the Moorish occupation, the taro* or quarter-dinar was minted at Salerno and Amalfi up to the reign of Frederick II. Thus when he minted his augustale* in 1231 from Messina and Brindisi mints, the commerce into which it came was already familiar with gold coinage. This coinage inspired western European countries to issue gold coins during the 12th and 13th centuries when the declining standard of the dinar made it unacceptable for commercial purposes and so made necessary a replacement. In 1252 Genoa issued a genovino* and Florence a florin,* whose weight of 3.5 grams made them considerably more valuable than the dinar. In commercial transactions in the western Mediterranean, the genovino and its quarter, the quartarolo,* replaced the dinar and its quarter, the tari; to the north, the florin followed the trade routes in northern and western Europe and became the prototype for most of later European gold coinage. Venice in 1284 issued a zecchino* of weight equal to the genovino and florin. Some national gold coinages were tried but were not accepted; Henry III of England, for example, issued a gold penny in 1257, and Louis IX issued a gold ecu, but neither proved acceptable. Not until 1290 when Philip IV of France issued a gold coinage of three types—the massed'or,* the chaise,* and the agnel—did Europe accept new gold coinage. The chaise, or clinkaert as it was known in the Netherlands, weighed the same as two Florentine florins and depicted the king enthroned; it lasted into the 15th century. Similarly, the agnel or mouton* depicting the pascal lamb enjoyed success into the 15th century. A different type, the chevalier or franc à cheval, initially associated with the ransom* payable to England for the release of the captured French King John, was minted from 1360 and weighed one-half the English noble.* The French finally found an acceptable standard of gold coin in the ecu à la couronne or crown, which was valued at one livre tournois. Long after other countries had established their national gold currency, England issued from 1344 a gold noble which remained the same fineness and value for 120 years, even though its weight was reduced by a fifth during that period. It depicted the English king standing on a ship, reputed to represent the English naval victory at Sluys in 1340. It was much imitated by the counts of Flanders and by the house of Burgundy. See also Anglo-Gallic money; convention money. (Bibliog. 150, 324, 237, 187)

coket. See cocket.

Colchester, largest and oldest tower keep* in England. Built on Roman ruins by William* I, it was even larger than the White Tower of London. Both have a semi-circular projection at the southeast which housed the apse of the chapel serving the second and main residential floor within. Within the tower adjacent to the gateway was a spiral staircase which, in common with most castles,* spirals clockwise. It was made that way so that anyone climbing the staircase had his right or sword* arm on the same side as the central pillar, the newel. This inevitably cramped his movement while the defendant, presumably facing down toward the defendant, was far more advantageously placed. (Bibliog. 45)

colée (Fr.), the act of dubbing a new knight atop the shoulder with a flat side of a swordblade. See accolade.

collar of Lancaster, device* or cognizance* developed by the House of Lancaster to mark its adherents. See collar of SS.

collar of SS, collars studded with the letter *S* or consisting of many of that letter linked together, either alone or alternating with other figures, were worn at various times by "great officers of state,"* as well as gentry of various ranks from esquires* upward. These were worn by lords chief justice, lords chief baron of the Exchequer,* lords mayor of London, "kings of arms,"* and heralds.* Perhaps the device* was invented to represent the word "Soverayne," the favorite motto* of King Henry IV of England, which he bore when earl* of Derby and retained when he succeeded to the throne. Originally it was a badge* of the house of Lancaster to which Henry belonged, and he was the first sovereign who granted to the nobility* as a mark of royal favor the license to wear it. (Bibliog. 43)

collar of York, device* consisting of a collar of suns alternating with white* roses* and the pendant of a white lion* which the House of York adopted in its rivalry with the House of Lancaster (see collar of SS); the House of York also adopted a second version that had the roses placed *"en soleil"* [said of the sun when encompassed by its own rays and of other charges* when so encompassed]. (Bibliog. 251)

College of Arms, office having authority over all heraldic matters; it was composed of "kings of arms,*" heralds,* and "pursuivants of arms."* (Bibliog. 251)

colletin, armor* for the neck. See gorget.

collire, stone the color of the sea, resembling a sapphire. He who carried it around his neck was sheltered from the displeasure of his overlord. (Bibliog. 258)

colors, colours, principal metal* and color of the coat in a "coat of arms."* Generally the word "tincture" was used to refer to such colors. Colors used in heraldry* were gules* (red), azure* (blue), sable* (black), vert* (green), and purpure* (purple). Tenne* (orange), murrey* (reddish purple), and sanguine* (blood-red) occasionally were used but were referred to as stains.* (Bibliog. 43)

combat of chivalry, contest between two knights fought with weapons of war until one of the two was unable to fight any longer. At first, this was the judicial ordeal (see duel), but after being discarded by law it was an ordeal* to which chivalry* clung for the settlement of disputes between knights when their honor* was called into question. A knight supported his word not by swearing on his honor but on his readiness to fight. Even kings* proposed to settle a war by single combat: Henry II made such a proposition to Philip* Augustus in 1188. Combat of chivalry began hesitantly under Edward I in 1294, but only under Edward III (1327–1377) did it flourish. (Bibliog. 78)

comble, heaped measure which contained an amount of grain extending above the rim—the amount depending upon the proportions of the vessel. See weights and measures. (Bibliog. 394)

comitatus, group of free warriors of the early Franks (5th century) who took service of their own free will under a chieftain and fought with him and on his behalf as a band of close companions. When such freemen placed themselves under the personal service of the king,* they were the *antrustiones** which corresponded to the *comitatus.* (Bibliog. 123)

comite. See count.

commendation, contract of vassalage. When Duke Tassilo III of Bavaria, for example, became the vassal* of the Frankish King Pepin III in A.D. 757, he did so by commending himself into vassalage by his hands; he swore innumerable oaths, placing his hands on the relics* of saints, and he promised fealty* to King Pepin and to his sons Charles and Carloman "as by law a vassal ought to do with uprightness and devotion, assuming the position a vassal ought to have in relation to his lords." (Bibliog. 123)

commilitones, fellow soldiers,* a subclass of "household knights"* of the king's knights listed on the rolls of 1285, 1286, and 1290. They were paid at the same rate as the king's knights: eight marks* for a bachelor* and sixteen for a banneret.* The counts* of Hainault also used these household knights to accompany them to tournaments.* (Bibliog. 87)

commission of array. See *arrière-ban*; array, commission of.

compagnon, gros* blanc type of coinage* struck under Jean le Bon of France (1364–1380); its reverse bore a castle* surmounted by a lis.* (Bibliog. 150)

compline, 9 P.M.; the "canonical hour"* when the last service of the day was said.

compony, compone, gabony, charge* composed of a single row of equal divisions of two alternate tinctures (see colors); if of two rows, then it was "countercompony." (Bibliog. 43)

compurgation, method by which the oaths of a number of persons as to the character of an accused person in a criminal case, or a defendant in a civil case, were accepted as proof of his innocence in the one case or as proof in the other case that the claim made against him was not well founded. Those who swore such oaths were compurgators.* In London there were three forms of compurgations: the Great Law in respect of homicide which required the oath be supported by thirty-six compurgators; the Middle Law in respect of mayhem* which required the oath be supported by eighteen compurgators; and the Third Law which applied to torts and minor assaults which required an oath be supported by six compurgators. See also guilt, ascertaining. (Bibliog. 363)

compurgators, Anglo-Saxon oath-keepers, people who would swear to the truthfulness of an oath taken by a defendant in an Anglo-Saxon legal case. The validity of their oaths was credited not according to the believability of their words or the manner of swearing them but according to its weight assessed by the sum of their individual wergilds.* Such a society was hierarchical and valued the oath of an earl* at 1,200 shillings, six times more highly than a ceorl's* at 200 shillings (see money). (Bibliog. 163)

computatores, tellers who counted money in the Lower Exchequer* of England. (Bibliog. 102)

comtor. See titles of dignity.

concord, heavy fine* paid when the battle called for by a "writ of right"* did not occur. (Bibliog. 229)

condotierri, leaders of Italian military companies which were big enough to constitute a large army; they were hired out to carry on the wars of the Italian states, especially in the 14th and 15th centuries. (Bibliog. 45)

conflictus gallicus (L.), tournaments.* Legalized in England in 1194, these were run by rules which had come from France. Ralph of Dis, in a phrase attributed to Matthew Paris,* called them *"conflictus gallicus."* (Bibliog. 88)

congeners, peasants (see villein) who had descended from free but dependent ceorls* of Anglo-Saxon times. (Bibliog. 264)

Conisborough, castle* in Yorkshire built of stone by Hamelin Plantagenet,* half-brother of Henry II, to replace a wooden castle of his wife's ancestor, William de Warenne, companion to William* I and first earl* of Surrey. Its ashlar* keep* was a cylindrical tower with a splayed base and fitted with six large wedge-shaped buttresses. (Bibliog. 45)

conrois, units of varying strength under one leader's banner* participating in a tournament* or a war; the strength varied according to the power of the liege* lord. Between 1150 and 1200, some bannerets* commanded units of twenty knights; in the Welsh wars of Edward I, some had twenty knights and squires.* Their formation was three ranks of six to eight men in each rank in close formation, the horsemen side by side, horse* by horse. Their advance and charge in an orderly manner was so superior to units drawn up in a random manner that they were able to turn an obviously unfavorable balance of strength to their own advantage. One of the greatest acts of stupidity a knight could commit was to abandon the protection of the conroi and rush ahead into battle, for in so doing he destroyed the cohesion and integrity of the unit; a close-order attack pressed by a tightly unified group removed the risk of the enemy breaking through. A series of conrois next to each other formed a larger group of knights called a bataille* or battle. This gave a rectangular formation two to three men deep, with a front of fifty to sixty or more knights and squires. The French army marching to Cassel to crush the rebels from Flanders in 1328 was made up of ten battles with 177 banners which grew to 196 banners after all the reinforcements had joined with it. In a tournament in which units of Prince Henry (son of Henry II of England) fought the French, the French had overwhelming numerical superiority and knew it, but they overconfidently forgot about the unity of the conroi and charged about pell mell, recklessly and randomly, and consequently suffered a crushing defeat. (Bibliog. 351)

consanguinity, being related by blood or descended from a common ancestor. At the Lateran Council of 1215, Pope Innocent III defined as null and void all marriages within the fourth degree of consanguinity. Before that decree, the accepted doctrine in the west was that marriage within the seventh degree of canonical computation was not forbidden, but that kinship in the sixth or seventh degree was a cause which would render such a marriage sinful, but would not render it null. This seventh degree seems to have been a common rule among Germanic nations that for purposes of inheritance, kinship could not be traced beyond the seventh generation. Therefore, to prohibit marriages within seven degrees was to prohibit it among all persons who for any legal purpose could claim blood relationship with each other. The church's position was that sexual union in marriage made man and woman one flesh. Thus all the wife's blood kinswomen were connected with the husband as were all his own family members by way of affinity. A husband thereby was related to his wife's sister in the first degree; to her first cousin in the second degree; to her second cousin in the third degree. The church in the 12th century stated that a person may not marry in the seventh degree of this affinity; this was affinity of the first cause.

However, if man and wife really were one, then it followed that he was related by way of affinity to the wives of her kinsmen. This was affinity of the second genus: to the wife of his wife's brother, a man was related in the first degree of this second cause of affinity, and so on. General belief in the 12th century held that prohibition of marriage extended to the seventh degree of the first genus, but only to the fourth degree of the second genus and the second degree of the third genus. (Bibliog. 261)

conservator of the peace, English royal official probably created during the reign of Richard I* by Hubert Walter, the archbishop of Canterbury to whom Richard entrusted the reins of government while he was on the third crusade.* Chosen from among local knights, this forerunner of the justice of the peace was required to take an oath from all males over fifteen years of age that they keep the peace and would pursue malefactors in full "hue and cry,*" and having caught them would thereupon turn them over to the conservators who then would deliver them to the sheriff* to be guarded until they came up for trial. This curbed the sheriff's arbitrary power to make arrests, for conservators made the decision whether to deliver prisoners to the sheriff.* (Bibliog. 132)

constable, officer of peace in England. Under Edward I in 1285, the Statute of Winchester, which ordained every citizen to have armor* according to his condition to keep the peace, required that in every hundred* two constables should be chosen to view the armor twice a year and report to justices any defaults they found. Such were called high constables and were charged with keeping the peace of the hundred; petty constables, on the other hand, were charged with keeping the peace of the parish or township. They were appointed at the court* of the hundred, or if not there, then by justices at special sessions.

A constable also was any person in a position to command men, ranging from the "constable of England,*" one of the highest officers of the "king's household,"* to the village constable of the 13th-century peace ordinances. This title also referred to a ship's captain and to an officer in command of soldiers* in the field. Most commonly, however, it denoted a military officer in command of a castle,* including its garrison which, varying in size and importance, might be called the constabularia*; he also was in charge of a castle in the owner's absence.

When in the field, the constable commanded a contingent of knights constituting the *servitium debitum** of a great ecclesiastical person who abstained from leading his men in person. One such constable of Peterborough in 1294 had the responsibilities to summon the abbey's knights when their services were required by the king,* to "distrain"* them if they refused service, to bring them to the king, and to lead them while on service. (Bibliog. 264)

constable and marshal of England, chief military officers of the crown who acted jointly on almost every occasion, but the marshal was recognized as the lieutenant of the constable. Later these officers were known as the lord high constable and "earl marshal."* In time of war, their office was to punish all manner of men who broke the king's* statutes and ordinances to be obeyed by the host (see knighthood) at that time and to punish offenders by the means cited in the statutes. The constable and marshal were to have knowledge of all manner of crimes, contracts, pleas, quarrels, trespasses, injuries, and offenses committed beyond the sea in time of war between soldier* and soldier, between merchants, victuallers, leeches, barbers, launderers, shoemakers, labourers, and artificers necessary to the host. Their cognizance included all manner of deeds done on the land of England. Their high court also had jurisdiction over disputes related to armorial bearings (see charge). (Bibliog. 325)

constable's honour, largest of nine baronies* responsible for providing "castle guard"* at Dover Castle; the great honour* of Haughley (see knighthood) held this so-called constable's honour. (Bibliog. 159)

constabularia, military unit under a knight called a constable* which generally contained approximately 500 men. At Norwich Castle, however, the forty knights of Bury St. Edmonds, whose terms of "castle guard"* were three months a year, were divided into four groups of ten, each group called a constabulary including one man called a constable. These four provided a garrison of ten men the year round from Bury alone. (Bibliog. 159)

Constitutions of Clarendon. After an angry interview with Henry II at Northampton in 1164, Archbishop Thomas à Becket received letters from the pope and cardinals advising him to submit to the king's demand for the legal surrender of "criminous clerks" (criminal clergymen) to the king's officials. Many bishops joined in this plea, and Thomas reluctantly gave in. Accordingly, the king* summoned a council to meet at Clarendon in order that a solemn and public assent be given. This meeting, however, was far from calm. Heated debates stretched over three or four days, but finally the king ordered that a formal statement embodying the customs of his grandfather, Henry I, be drawn up and agreed to by all present. Its two most important provisions, numbers 3 and 4, read as follows:

> In the year 1164 . . . being the tenth of Henry II . . . in the presence of said king was made this record and declaration of a certain part of the customs, liberties, and privileges of his ancestors, that is, of King Henry his grandfather, and of other things which ought to be observed and maintained in the realm. And by reason of the dissensions and discords which had arisen between the clergy and the justices of the

lord king and the barons* of the realm concerning the customs and privileges of the realm, this declaration was made in the presence of the archbishop, bishops, and clergy and of the earls,* barons, and magnates [see peer] of the realm . . .

3. Clerks cited and accused of any matter shall, when summoned by the king's justice, come before the king's court* to answer there concerning matters which shall seem to the king's court to be answerable there, and before the ecclesiastical court for what shall seem to be answerable there, but in such a way that the justice of the king shall send to the court of holy Church to see how the case is there tried. And if the clerk shall be convicted or shall confess, the Church ought no longer to protect him.

4. It is not lawful for archbishops, bishops, and benefitted clergy of the realm to depart from the kingdom without the lord king's leave. And if they do so depart, they shall, if the king so please, give security that neither in going, nor in tarrying, nor in returning will they contrive evil or injury against the king or kingdom.

This "criminous clerk" clause (3) meant that a clerk (clergyman) accused of a grave offense such as murder was to answer before the king's justice for such a breach of the king's peace. Only then was he to go before the ecclesiastical court to answer there for the homicide. If convicted there, he was to be degraded and no longer protected by the church, and he was to be taken back to the king's court no longer as a clergyman but as a layman, to be sentenced without further trial to the penalties appropriate to a layman: death or mutilation. The presence of the royal witness in the ecclesiastical court prevented the accused from escaping. Purely ecclesiastical offenses were not involved in this clause, and the king had not proposed trying a clerk for such in a temporal court; that would have been a gross contradiction of canon law.
(Bibliog. 102)

conte, shorter form of story than and with the same general characteristics as a romance* but with three major differences: contes were shorter (under one hundred lines); all details led to one main scene—the climax; poetic style was subordinated to the action which sped toward the climax. It also was called in the 12th century by the name lai* (lay) or dit. (Bibliog. 162)

conteurs. See jestours; minstrels.

contoise, long flowing veil suspended from the top of the great heaume.* Usually this or the wearer's crest* was fastened to the top of the heaume. (Bibliog. 9)

convention money, principle by which currency was tolerated or recognized within a stipulated radius at a fixed standard. It occurred in the Low Countries in the 14th century. For example, the agreement among John I, count* of Namur (1297–1331), the count of Flanders, and the duke* of Gueldres; and the agreement among Edward III of England, Emperor Louis of Bavaria, and the duke of Brabant at a time when the extension of English commerce and coinage* rendered such facilities of peculiar importance to that country. (Bibliog. 150)

conveyancing, act of preparing writings to effect the conveyance (or transfer) of any piece of property or valuable right from one person to another. Occasionally it referred to the cumbersome forms which the feudal system (see feudalism) required for the transfer and tenure* of landed property. (Bibliog. 100)

Conway Castle, Welsh castle* built by Edward I between 1283 and 1287 on a plan similar to Caernarvon* with a series of mural drum-towers. See castle building. (Bibliog. 45)

coomb, measure of capacity for grain generally containing four bushels* or one-half seam.* (Bibliog. 394)

cope, hawking* term which meant to pare and so to shorten the beak and claws of a hawk. (Bibliog. 26)

copyhold, form of land tenure* legally defined as "holding at the will of the lord according to the custom of the manor." Originally, it meant the occupation by villeins* or non-freemen of portions of land belonging to the manor* of a feudal lord. In the *Domesday Book** survey, the manor was granted in part to the free tenants and in part reserved for the lord for his own uses. The estate of the free tenants was the freehold estate of English law; as tenants of the same manor, they assembled in the "manor court"* or "court baron"* of which they were the judges. The portion of the manor reserved for the lord, the domain or demesne,* was cultivated by laborers who were bound to the land: they could not leave the manor and their service was obligatory, but they were allowed by the lord to cultivate a portion of the land for their own use. (Bibliog. 100)

coquibus, silver coin of the bishops of Cambrai in the Netherlands and in the diocese of Metz in the 13th and 14th centuries; its name came from the eagle* on the coins being mistaken for a cock. (Bibliog. 150)

coral, cure for blindness and toothache,* according to Galen; when mixed with powder of cumin, it served well as a dentifrice and a lotion for the eyes. (Bibliog. 258)

corbel, piece of stone jutting out of a wall to carry any weight; a piece of timber projecting out in the same way was called a tasser* or a bragger. (Bibliog. 100)

corbie, raven.

corese (Ger.), simple bladed staff weapon with no projection at the back of the blade.

Corfe, castle* in the Dorset built first by William* I and considered one of his favorites; it was added to steadily over the next two centuries: William's wooden tower was replaced by a stone keep* by Henry I, and John built the elegant residence called "La Gloriette" next to the keep; its towered "curtain wall"* was added in the 13th century, and Edward I completed its outer gate late in the century. (Bibliog. 45)

corn, collective name for the seeds or grain of any of the cereal grasses used for food, such as wheat, rye, barley, oats, maize. (Bibliog. 246)

cornado, billon* coin of the ancient kingdom of Castile and Leon in the 13th century. (Bibliog. 150)

cornbole, the best sheaf of corn* levied at harvest time on each peasant by his lord.

cornu, horned beast, but used in the *chanson de geste,* * *Jerusalem,* as the name of the horse* of the Saracen* chief, Cornicas des Puis de Montribon, who was killed by Baudouin de Rohais, better known as Baldwin de Bouillon, successor to his brother Geoffrey de Bouillon on the throne of the kingdom of Jerusalem; Baldwin took the horse after killing its owner. (Bibliog. 191)

Corpus Christi, festival of the Catholic Church observed on the first Thursday after Trinity Sunday in honor of the doctrine of the Eucharist; it was instituted by Pope Urban IV in 1264. (Bibliog. 100)

coronal, crown-shaped tip applied to lances* to blunt or rebate them in *jousts à plaisance.* * (Bibliog. 9)

coronarius. See *custos placitorum corone.*

coronation, act of crowning a new monarch. From the coronation rites, especially the anointing,* the king* derived his divine authority; he ceased to be merely a layman but took on sacerdotal character: he was king *Dei Gratia*; he was God's vicar, *rex et sacerdos.* At the coronation of Clovis, first Christian king of France, on Christmas Eve, A.D. 496, in the church of St. Remi in Rheims, the ceremonies were conducted with much pomp. Remi led Clovis by the hand to the font and exhorted him to "Humble thyself, and burn what thou hast worshipped, and worship that which thou hast burnt!" Then Clovis professed his belief in one God and three persons, and Remi baptised him in the name of the Father, the Son, and the Holy Ghost while the bishops present immersed him in the laver. Then he entered the church for his confirmation, anointing, and coronation as a Christian king.

For his coronation in 1189, Richard I* of England ordered a ceremony which was followed closely at all subsequent English coronations. First, preceded by acolytes carrying a cross,* candles, and thuribles of incense, the clergy dressed in copes of purple silk processed to greet Richard in his chamber in Westminster and then with glorious song escorted him to the abbey over a linen cloth the entire way. This procession was led into the abbey by clerks carrying holy water, crosses, candles, and thuribles, followed by priors, abbots, and finally the bishops; in their midst walked four barons* carrying golden candelabra. Next came the king's regalia*: Godfrey de Luci carried the cap of state; John Marshall, the spurs*; William Marshall, the golden scepter* surmounted by a gold cross; William, earl* of Salisbury, the golden verge* with a golden dove at its end. Three earls carried swords* with golden scabbards (see sheath): David of Huntington, brother of the king of Scotland; John, Richard's brother; Robert, earl of Leicester. These were followed by six barons and earls carrying a chest bearing the royal insignia and containing Richard's regal garments; immediately behind them came William of Mandeville, earl of Essex, carrying a golden crown* studded with rich gems.

Richard himself came next walking under a silken canopy, held aloft over him by four lances* carried by four barons; Hugh, bishop of Durham, walked on his right, and Reginald, bishop of Bath, on his left. A crowd of earls, barons, knights, clergymen, and laymen brought up the rear of the procession. Later, the barons of the Cinque Ports* claimed the right to carry over the sovereign in the coronation procession a canopy of cloth of gold or purple silk, with a gilt silver bell at each corner, supported by four staves covered with silver, four barons to every staff, and to carry a canopy in like manner over the queen. As their fee, they claimed the canopies, bells, and staves and the privilege of dining at a table at the king's right hand. This was claimed as a reward for the readiness with which the Cinque Ports had assisted King John in his numerous voyages to and from Normandy. When this procession reached the high altar, everyone knelt. Richard then swore on the Gospels and the relics* of many saints that all the days of his life he would show peace and honor* and reverence to God, Holy Church, and the clergy; that he would exercise right justice* over people committed to his rule; and that he would blot out all evil laws and wrongful customs if any existed in his realm and would preserve good laws and customs.

At the throne, Richard was undressed except for his shirt, open at the shoulders, and his drawers. As slippers of gold were placed on his feet, Archbishop Baldwin placed the scepter in his right hand and the verge in his left and then anointed Richard's head, shoulders, and chest. As Richard handed the scepter and verge to the two bishops, Durham and Bath, a linen cloth and cap of state were placed on his head, and he was clothed in a tunic and a dalmatic [robe]. Then the archbishop handed him the sword of justice, two earls buckled the golden spurs on his feet, and the mantle was placed about his shoulders. He was led to the altar, and when the archbishop adjured him in the name of Almighty God not to take the kingship unless he intended to keep the oaths he had sworn, Richard replied that with God's grace, he intended to keep them; he took the crown from the altar, handed it to the archbishop, who in turn placed it on Richard's head. Thus crowned, and preceded by barons with the golden candelabra, three earls carrying swords, and the bishops of Durham and Bath on each side, Richard went to his throne and sat while the archbishop celebrated the mass. The crown was so heavy that two earls held it over his head during the mass. At the offertory, the two bishops led him to the altar where he made the customary offering of a mark* of gold. At the end of the mass, the procession led him back to his chamber where he laid aside the crown and vestments and donned lighter garb for the coronation feast. At the banquet, the clergy sat at the king's table in order of rank; earls and barons sat at separate tables. For this feast, 1,770 pitchers, 900 cups, and 5,000 dishes were bought specially. No women or Jews were allowed at this meal, and when several leading English Jews tried to enter the hall, the crowd at the gate protested their presence and killed several in a riot which spread through the city.

King Charles V of France wrote a description of his own coronation in 1365, headed by "This is the order of anointing and crowning the King," but the ritual he described followed the English ritual quite closely. (Bibliog. 178, 282, 308)

coronation chair, chair in St. Edward's chapel, Westminster, containing the stone, known as the Stone of Scone, reputed to have been Jacob's pillar, in which English kings* after Edward I were crowned. Although King Edward I brought the stone from Scone, originally it had been taken by a colony of Scythians to Ireland where it was known as the *"Liagh Fail,"* or Stone of Destiny, and from there to Scotland in A.D. 834 by King Kenneth. He had found it at Dunstaffnage, a royal castle,* enclosed it in a wooden chair, and removed it to the Abbey of Scone where for 450 years all kings of Scotland were crowned until the time of Robert I. During the reign of King Edward I (1272–1307) many cruelties were done by the English king, including the removal of the chair from Scone to London and its being placed at Westminster as an offering of conquest at the shrine of Edward the Confessor. The stone itself of dull red sandstone was oblong of irregular form, twenty-six inches* long, sixteen and three-fourths inches broad, and ten and one-half inches thick. At a coronation,* the chair was covered with a cloth of gold. (See Tanner and Davidson, *The Times* (London), May 1, 1937.) (Bibliog. 178)

Coronation Charter, statement of principles and intentions issued by King Henry I of England on August 5, 1100, at the beginning of his reign. This particularly informative evidence of feudal custom displayed the relationships between Anglo-Norman kings* and their tenants-in-chief.* Several of its more important provisions were:

1. Know that by the mercy of God and by the common counsel of the barons* of the whole kingdom of England, I have been crowned king of this realm. And because the kingdom has been oppressed by unjust exactions, I now, being moved by reverence toward God and by the love I bear you all, make free the church of God; so that I will neither sell nor lease its property; nor on the death of an archbishop or a bishop or an

abbot will I take anything from the demesne* of the church or from its vassals* during the period which elapses before a successor is installed. I abolish all the evil customs by which the kingdom of England has been unjustly oppressed. Some of those evil customs are here set forth.

2. If any of my barons or of my earls* or of my tenants shall die, his heir shall not redeem his land as he was wont to do in the time of my brother [William* II, Rufus], but he shall henceforth redeem it by means of a just and lawful 'relief.'* Similarly the men of my barons shall redeem their lands from their lords by means of a just and lawful 'relief.'

3. If any of my barons or my tenants shall wish to give in marriage his daughter or his sister or his niece or his cousin, he shall consult me about the matter; but I will neither seek payment for my consent, nor will I refuse my permission, unless he wishes to give her in marriage to one of my enemies. And if, on the death of one of my barons or of one of my tenants, a daughter should be his heir, I will dispose of her in marriage and of her lands according to the counsel given me by my barons. And if the wife of one of my tenants shall survive her husband and be without children, she shall have her dower* and her marriage portion, and I will not give her in marriage unless she herself consents. [See merchet; marriage, lord's right to control.]

9. I remit all murder-fines which were incurred before the day on which I was crowned king; and such murder-fines as shall now be incurred shall be paid justly according to the law of King Edward [the Confessor]. (See Englishry.)

12. I establish a firm peace in all my kingdom, and I order that this peace shall henceforth be kept.

(Bibliog. 102)

coronation holy oil. See anointing.

coronation oath, oath sworn at the time of coronation* by an Anglo-Saxon monarch, which the bishop, as representative of heaven, ratified by his benediction.

King Ethelred in 978 swore, as did Henry I in 1100: "In the name of Christ, I promise three things to the Christian people, my subjects: first, that the church of God under all our Christian people shall always preserve true peace under our auspices; second, that I will interdict rapacity, and all iniquities to every condition; third, that I will command equity and mercy in all judgments, that to me, and to you, the gracious and merciful god may extend his mercy."

King John swore in 1199: "to love the church and ordinances thereof; to keep and defend the same harmless from all invasions of evil-disposed persons; to disannul perverse laws, and erect good laws; and according to the same, to minister true judgment throughout the kingdom."

King Edward I swore in 1274: "I, Edward I, son and heir of King Henry, do profess, protect, and promise, before God and his holy angels, from this time forward, to maintain without partiality the law, justice, and peace, of the church of God, and the people subject to me; so far as we can devise by the counsel of our liege* and legal ministers; as, also, to exhibit due and canonical honor to the bishops of God's church; to preserve unto them, inviolably, whatsoever has been granted by former emperors and kings to the church of God; and to pay due honor to the abbots and the lord's ministers, according to the advice of our lieges, so help me God, and the Holy Gospels of the Lord.'' (Bibliog. 178, 283)

coronation regalia. See coronation; regalia of England.

coroner, officer of the crown. This position was established in September 1194 when justices in eyre* were required to see that three knights and a clerk were elected in every county* as "keepers of the pleas of the crown" (*custos placitorum corona**). The creation of this office came about because the English king,* Richard I,* was desperate for money.* His continental wars against the French and his ransom* had depleted his already meager treasury, and he could ill afford to lose any money involved in crown pleas. Therefore a full-time local official was needed to take care of the recently created general eyre. He was charged with making sure that all crown pleas were presented to the justices regardless of the length of time since their origins and of the potential financial loss they might impose on the jurors (see jury duty). The local sheriffs* could not be asked to perform these new duties, for they already were overburdened and tending to become corrupt as they grew ever more powerful. Thus in 1194, Justiciar* Hubert Walter in 1194 created this new official as a remedy for a difficult situation, and the duties set out for him were preserved almost intact for centuries in law books and statutes. Although these included holding inquests in connection with other felonies,* most notably a wounding, rape, housebreaking, and breaking out of prison (see jail), the coroner probably was concerned mainly with homicide and suicide.

Normally the coroner had to view the bodies and hold an inquest for all those who died unnaturally, suddenly, or in prison or about whose death any suspicious circumstances were involved, and he could hold such an inquest only if there was a body. When a body was found, the "first finder" had to raise the "hue and cry"* and to inform the four nearest neighbors who in turn informed the bailiff* of the hundred* who in turn informed the coroner. Because of a strong likelihood of having amercement* or other punishments* imposed because of the suspicions involved in being the first finder, many people who noticed a body hurried by it in silence. The "last finder" therefore raised the necessary hue and cry. When informed of a death, the coroner had to view the body immediately. Before setting out on that task, though, he would order the bailiff to summon a jury from four or more neighboring townships for a certain day; at first, every male over the age of twelve was required to attend from each township, but after 1300 only twelve to sixteen men represented the four townships at the inquest. Sometimes this representation consisted of the bailiff or reeve* and four men, its tithingmen or tithing,* or its constable* and other representatives.

Five main circumstances called for inquests into a natural death: if it was unexpected and sudden; if the body was found in the open and the cause of death was unknown; if there was any suspicion or possibility of a felony; if the hue and cry was raised maliciously; or if the death occurred in prison. At the inquest the facts had to be discovered, followed by the arrest of or attachment* by sureties of a number of people, and then the appraisal and commital to safe-keeping of anything which later might be forfeited. Everyone indicted at the inquest, whether of homicide or of aiding and abetting it, was to be arrested, for they should have been arrested in the hue and cry following the discovery of the body and have been brought to the inquest; this, however, was rarely done. Most of those who surrendered to the coroner had killed someone accidentally or in self-defense, so they had little to lose by surrender, for their pardon was almost assured. But they had much to lose by flight: the forfeiture of their chattels.

The jury listening to the evidence had to name the frankpledge,* tithings, or mainpast* of all those indicted so that they could be amerced at the eyre if the felon could not be found. The coroner had to inquire where the felons had gone and who had harbored them, for such people also had to be arrested. Furthermore, the coroner had to inquire into what weapon had caused the death in homicide and suicide. Most often, such weapons were staffs, stones, axes,* knives, or whatever else the felon might have had in hand or nearby in homicide in anger. Then the coroner's jury had to appraise the weapon (unless the felon had fled with it), and the coroner kept it and accounted for its value at the next eyre. Normal prices ranged from a halfpenny* to a shilling (see money). Baselards,* for example, were appraised at two or four shillings. After sealing the written inquest of the jurors, the coroner's duties in any case were practically over. In the rare inquests held after outlaws,* fugitives, or straying or returning "abjurers of the realm"* had been pursued and beheaded in the hue and cry as by law they should have been, the coroner had to send the head to the county jail. (Bibliog. 171)

coronet, small crown* worn by members of royalty other than the king* and queen. Members of the English blood royal who wore the coronet were the heir apparent, sons and daughters of the sovereign, the sovereign's brothers and sisters and their sons, and the sovereign's grandchildren. For the heir apparent, the coronet was the same as the royal crown except it had only one arch.* Other children of the sovereign wore the same coronet but without any arch; the surface of the circlet was decorated in simulation of containing the same jewels as the royal crown, but no jewels were set therein.

Male children of the sovereign's eldest son wore a coronet on which the two "crosses paty"* were replaced by strawberry leaves. Children of his younger sons and those of his brother wore a coronet with four strawberry leaves in place of the "fleur de lis"* and had four crosses paty alternating with the leaves.

Children of the sovereign's daughters wore a circlet with four fleur de lis and four strawberry leaves but no crosses paty.

The first peers* to wear coronets were dukes* and marquesses* in 1444, but these early coronets had no distinctive pattern to distinguish each rank; when the rank of baron* appeared, it carried with it specifics of design that followed into higher ranks:

duke: gilt circlet, embossed as jewelled but not jewelled; coronet heightened with eight strawberry leaves;

marquess: gilt circlet, heightened with four leaves, alternated with four pearls placed on small points;

earl*: gilt circlet with eight high rays, each topped with a pearl, alternating with a strawberry leaf;

viscount*: gilt circlet with sixteen pearls, each touching the next;

baron: unembossed circlet with six large pearls.

(Bibliog. 253)

corronat, coin struck at Marseilles in and after 1186 by the counts* of Provence, kings of Aragon, and the counts of Toulouse; its obverse contained a large crown* in the center of the field. (Bibliog. 150)

corseque (Fr.), weapon called a partizan*; it probably was derived from the lugged spear* and had a long triangular blade with a strong medial ridge radiating from its base or curving up like the prongs of a trident. (Bibliog. 27)

corsesca (It.), the partizan*. (Bibliog. 27)

Corsheuse, Ban's sword* with which he smote Rion, king* of Ireland in Arthurian legend. (Bibliog. 311)

corsnaed. See ordeal by bread and cheese.

cortes (Sp.), court*; referred to the Assembly of States of that kingdom.

costrel, measure of capacity for objects made of leather, wood, or earthenware; also used for wine.* (Bibliog. 394)

côte à plates. See hauberk of plates.

cottager, peasant living in a cottage; a rural laborer.

cottars, peasants who were descendants of the free but dependent Anglo-Saxon ceorls.* (Bibliog. 264) *cotteraux*, French mercenaries.* (Bibliog. 159)

couchant, heraldic beast when it is lying down with its head held up. See beasts, positions of. (Bibliog. 43)

coudieres, early reinforcements for the elbows in suits of mail,* frequently made of leather or metal. These later were close-fitting plates reinforced by splints to cover the elbow. Additionally, a small piece of plate was used to protect the inner part of the bend of the arm. (Bibliog. 9)

coule, glizade, sword thrust in a sliding motion along the blade of an adversary's weapon. (Bibliog. 331)

count, administrative officials of Merovingian and Carolingian France. Originally called *comites* and equivalent to the *civitas* of Roman Gaul, these men were chosen from all ranks of society and each given a *pagus*, that is, an administrative subdivision of the kingdom. In time, with the various partitions of the kingdom and the desire for more local functionaries, these officials grew more numerous and became similar to the ealdormen (see earl) of Anglo-Saxon England. Rollo, first duke* of the Normans, had *comites*, but these were "companions." "Comes" as a title was reserved for the dukes themselves until the end of the 10th century; even Duke Robert I (1027–1035) and William* the Conqueror sometimes were called counts of the Normans rather than dukes of the Normans. Normandy of 1066 had three counts: Richard, count of Evreux; Robert, count of Eu; Robert, count of Mortain. All three of these men were closely related to William: Mortain was his half-brother, and the other two were his cousins. Each county* had been created by Duke Richard II (996–1026); all were frontier districts: Evreux guarded the chief invasion route from Paris through the Vexin, Eu lay along the eastern border of the duchy, and Mortain guarded the line of invasion from Brittany. Roland,* Charlemagne's famous nephew and hero of the *Song of Roland,** was called Count Roland.
(Bibliog. 267)

counter, heraldic term which as a prefix meant the opposite or the reverse of a charge*: for example, counterrampant meant rampant* in the sinister.*

countercharged, heraldic term which meant that a shield* was divided by a partition* line and the colors* or metals* on one side were reversed on the other. (Bibliog. 43)

counterscarp, outer slope of a ditch, used particularly to refer to the outer slope of a motte.* (Bibliog. 280)

countess, title of the wife of an earl* or that of a woman who held an earldom in her own right. (Bibliog. 43)

county, territorial division made up of hundreds* in the same way that a hundred was made up of hides*: some of more, some of less than others, accordingly as the land was divided by men in the distant past. The county, then, was called after the count* or earl,* or alternatively, the count after the county name. He received the third penny* of the profits from jurisdiction of the county. (Bibliog. 102)

coup de grace, death blow with which a knight dispatched his mortally wounded adversary; frequently he used his misericorde* for this purpose.

couped, cut off cleanly, in heraldry.* Ordinaries* were couped if they were cut off before reaching the edge of the shield.* (Bibliog. 43)

couple, leash for "hunting dogs."* A child of age twelve was to be taught to care for dogs properly and to spin horse* hair to make couples for the hounds. These were made best from horse's or mare's tail, for they lasted longer than if they were made of hemp or wool. (Bibliog. 96)

courier. See cursores.

course, hunting* with a horse and hound by scent on the line of flight of the stag. See chase. (Bibliog. 96)

courser, cursar, swift horse* ridden in a hunt. (Bibliog. 96)

court, organ of government exercising political, juridical, and administrative powers. Coming from the Roman term *curia,* meaning originally one of the thirty parts into which Romulus divided the Roman people, this term was modified by the concepts brought into the West by the Germanic tribes. Their traditions were based on the concept that the ruler's primary duty was to administer justice* regardless of whether such administration be done at his estate or through leading his army. In time, the term grew to include assemblies of vassals* of various lords, not just the leader's court, the royal administration or *curia regis**; even the church had its *curia.* In England this concept of royal court was brought from France by William* the Conqueror. By the 13th century, the increased administrative and governmental activities increased the number of personnel at the court, and the work became more specialized. The four high offices of the feudal court became complex services:

1. the chamberlain* in charge of the treasury;
2. the constable* commanding the army;

3. the seneschal* responsible for the administration of justice on behalf of his sovereign;

4. the steward* responsible for the administration of the estates.

(Bibliog. 139)

court baron, 1. court* composed of free tenants who decided the fate of other free tenants—a concept introduced into the judicial structure of the English manor* by 13th-century jurists, along with the customary court in which the villein,* regarded as unfree, submitted to the judgment of the lord's steward*; 2. Thirteenth-century guidebook for stewards to hold court of the manor. Its full title was *Le cour de baron,* or *The Court Baron,* being precedents for use in seignorial and other local courts. See love-day; manor court. (Bibliog. 24, 381, 357)

Court of Attachment, court* held every forty days by verderers* to view the attachments by foresters for offenses against the vert* and the venison. It could take cognizance only of small trespasses to the vert; larger ones were heard by justices in eyre.* (Bibliog. 156)

Court of Chivalry, court* concerned with the conduct of soldiers,* convened before the constable and the marshal* or their lieutenants by virtue of their respective offices, from which an appeal could be made only to the crown* in Chancery.* Often referred to as proceedings "before the constable and the marshal," this was the same as the French *Court de Chivalrie* and Latin *curia militarius.* The Latin term was translated as "Court Military" by equating *militarius* with *miles** or "soldier," but *miles*meant "knight" so the *curia militarius* meant actually "Court of Knighthood." Thus it had not emerged from the disciplinary powers exercised by the constable and marshal over the army, powers which they derived from the "Ordinances of War" which the king* promulgated for the purposes of a particular expedition. Such ordinances provided detailed provisions for the conduct of the soldiers with general rules as to obedience. Henry V in 1419, for example, ordered "that all manner of men of whatever nation, estate, or condition soever he be, be obeisant to our sovereign lord the king, and to his constable and marshal, upon pain of as much as he may forfeit in body and goods." However, such ordinances were not enforced by the Court of Chivalry, for the constable and marshal referred to there were not necessarily the "earl marshal"* and the lord high constable but were military men necessary to every large unit of the army.

On August 23, 1348, King Edward III appointed two of his sergeants-at-arms to arrest William le Counte, whom William de Wynchelez had taken as prisoner of war in Normandy, and to bring him before the king's constable and marshal to answer for his broken faith and other things to be put forward against him. This clearly was an affair of honor,* not of military matters. During the siege of Calais, 1345–1348, a dispute arose between John de Warbeltone and Tibaud, son of Tibaud Russel, over the arms "lozenge* d'or* et d'azure.*" Such a dispute was heard by a special tribunal on July 19, 1347. It was the sort of subject that would have been brought before the Court of Chivalry, but such a court probably was not in existence then. Cases involving disputes over armorial bearings (see charge) brought about its creation. Other matters logically were brought before it: matters such as unjust detention of prisoners by their captors, payment of ransom,* exchange of prisoners. In 1389 the English Parliament* decreed the jurisdiction of the Court of Chivalry to be: "Cognizance of contracts touching deeds of arms and of war out of the realm, and also of things that touch [arms of] war within the realm, which cannot be determined nor discussed by the common law, with other usages and customs to the same matters pertaining, which other constables heretofore have duly and reasonably used in their time."

Jurisdiction over "contracts touching deeds of arms and of war out of the realm" may have been the reason of original necessity for such a court; such contracts must have been indentures* of war by means of which armies were raised late in the period. By such indentures, commanders who had contracted with the crown to provide a specified number of troops in turn subcontracted their obligations to lesser men. Thus by the early years of the 15th century, indentured troops had replaced feudal forces based on tenure* by knight service. So when disputes arose, lawyers must have appeared to handle the matters by the time the Court of Chivalry appeared.

The principal criminal jurisdiction of this court in its early life was an accusation (appeal*) which the accuser offered to support in single "combat of chivalry"* and which, in default of evidence, could result in trial by battle (see duel). In Courts of Chivalry, trial by battle was used primarily in cases of treasons and homicides committed abroad for which there was no remedy in common law. Such proceedings were begun by a petition and a detailed article of complaint sent to the king in Council who in turn would refer it to the Court of Chivalry where the parties met and had a date for combat assigned. There, if the accuser could prove his case by evidence to the court, he would do so without having to go to battle. If such an accusation involved treason, the vanquished party, if he still were alive (be he accuser or defendant), was disarmed in the lists,* drawn behind the horse* of the marshal to the place of execution* where he was beheaded or hanged. Because the common law courts recognized the jurisdiction of this Court of Chivalry, to kill a man in judicial combat was justifiable homicide. If the charge was for any other crime, however, the vanquished, or he who confessed to the charge, was not drawn behind a horse; and if the accusation referred only to a deed or action of arms, the penalty consisted of being disarmed and put out of the lists. The king could stop the proceedings any time he desired under a writ of privy seal directed to the marshal and constable. King Richard II, for example, forbade battle and banished both parties in the dispute between the dukes* of Norfolk and Hereford. (See Shakespeare's *Richard II*.)

Besides accusations of treason, the Court of Chivalry heard other charges such as that of attempted murder. One of the charges against King Richard II after his deposition was that he caused accusations to be brought in the Court of Chivalry against persons alleged to have spoken words which might have tended to the abuse, scandal, or disparagement of the king. (Bibliog. 171)

Court of Common Bench, Court of Common Pleas. See *curia regis.*

Court of Swanimote, English court* established by the Charter of the Forest to meet three times a year to handle business connected with agistment,* pannage,* and fawning.* (Bibliog. 261)

Courtain ("Short Sword"), one of the swords* of Ogier the Dane in the *chansons de geste**; it took the swordmaker Munifican three years to make this and Sauvagine for him. (Bibliog. 191)

courtesy title, title assumed by a person to which he had no legally valid claim. Peers* of England were of five ranks in the following precedence*: duke,* marquess,* earl,* viscount,* baron.* Their eldest sons were known by courtesy titles that were governed by certain practices. For an heir apparent to a rank of the peerage, his "style" [or phrase by which he was formally designated] was never higher than that of the secondary peerage vested in the actual peer, although his actual rank was always that of the next lowest grade in the peerage to that enjoyed by the actual peer. For example, although he ranked as Marquess of X, the "style" of the heir apparent of Duke of W would be Earl of Y; that of the heir apparent of the Marquess of A (though ranking as an Earl of B) would be Viscount C; that of the heir apparent of the Earl of L (though ranking as a Viscount M) would be Lord N.

Additionally, when the designation of the secondary peerage vested in the actual peer was the same as that of his principal title, the rank of the secondary title was, in many cases, prefixed to the family surname and thus formed the style of the heir apparent. For example, the earl of Belmore was a viscount (Viscount Belmore) of the same designation of his earldom, so his heir apparent was styled viscount—not Viscount Belmore, which would have lead to confusion, but Viscount Corry. (Bibliog. 75)

court-leet, court* held periodically in a lordship or manor* before the lord or his steward*; it exercised the jurisdiction of the sheriff's tourn* over petty offenses and the civil affairs of the district. To it was joined the right to hold the "Assize of Bread and Ale."* "Leet" was an East Anglian word originally meaning a division of the hundred* but later came to indicate a jurisdictional area. Generally the claim to hold a leet was accompanied by a long explanation of the kind of jurisdiction it claimed. At the end of the 13th century, to possess a leet was to have a court which had certain rights of petty criminal jurisdiction and police control within a defined geographical area and at specified times. See manor court. (Bibliog. 156)

Courtrai, battle of. See Battle of Courtrai.

coustel, coutelas, cultellus; a short sword* or long dagger.

coute, thin mattress. See bed.

couteau-de-breche, French fauchard*; a simple bladed staff weapon which had no projections at the rear of the blade. (Bibliog. 27)

couters, disc-shaped plates attached to the elbows of the hauberk* around the middle of the 13th century. (Bibliog. 27)

cove et keye, legal phrase used by Bracton* in reference to the functions and rights of the mistress of a house, from the age of fourteen or fifteen; the phrase meant literally a closet (or chamber) and key. It often was used with reference to the age of maturity for tenants by knight service. (Bibliog. 246)

coward, heraldic description of a charge* depicting a beast with its tail between its legs. See beasts, positions of. (Bibliog. 43)

crakanel, hard biscuit. See battlefield actions and conditions.

crannchur. See ordeal by lot.

crannock, measure of capacity used principally for grain in the British Isles; in Ireland, a crannock of wheat varied from eight pecks to eight bushels,* and of oats, from seven to fourteen bushels. (Bibliog. 394)

craven, cravent, cravant, referring to the losing champion in a duel* of "writ of right."* This meant that not only had he lost the case he fought, but he also was deprived of serious civil rights, for the loss of the duel proved him perjured. Hence he lost his law and, as an infamous person, never could be heard as a witness again. See also champion for ordeals. (Bibliog. 229)

creance, long line attached to a hawk or to a live lure; used in training the bird to hunt and return to the fist. See hawking. (Bibliog. 26)

crenel, crenelle, gap in a battlemented* parapet*; to crenellate was to equip a fortress with such a parapet. The term grew to include the whole system of defense because to fortify his residence, a lord needed a license to crenellate issued by the king.* See crenellated. (Bibliog. 280)

crenellated, embattled; fortress walls alternating in height for equal short distances to provide viewing apertures (crenels*) for archers and other men-at-arms between the high points (merlons*). See crenel. (Bibliog. 111)

crepons, bed* loops.

crescent, heraldic half-moon. This was the ancient ensign of the Turks and doubtless was introduced into heraldry* by the crusaders. If the horns of the moon pointed to the dexter,* it was said to be "increscent"; to the sinister,* "decrescent." With its horns pointing upward it was used as the mark of cadency* of a second son. (Bibliog. 43)

crest, heraldic object modeled on top of the helmet*; the object which crests the helmet. It was incorrect to use this term to refer to a "coat of arms."* In the complete achievement,* the base of the crest usually would be a coronet,* cap, or wreath* of twisted scarves, which probably originated in the favors bestowed by ladies upon knights of their choice in tournaments*: knights would bind their ladies' scarves around the base of their crests. Crests originally were affixed to the helmet of every commander for his distinction in the confusion of battle. King Edward III was the first to confer the right to use the crest in a family's arms* when he conferred on William Montacute, earl* of Salisbury, the right to bear an eagle.* (Bibliog. 43)

cric. See *arbalète à cric.*

Criminous Clerks controversy, basis for the dispute between King Henry II and Thomas à Becket, resolved in 1164 by the "Constitutions of Clarendon."* (Bibliog. 102)

crinet, armor protection for a horse's neck. See horse armor.

crisolite, stone which protected its bearer from nightmares and phantoms. One was assured of victory over demons if one carried it on the left arm, pierced and wrapped with the hair of an ass. (Bibliog. 258)

crockard, sterling* imitation of the penny* of King Edward I; it had a single thick cross* and pellets* on the reverse and a facing portrait of the king* bearing a garland of roses* on the obverse. These were minted after 1292 on the continent by Gui de Dampierre of Flanders and Namur, Jean d'Avesnes of Hainault, and Jean I of Brabant because of the stability and wide acceptance of the English coins they were imitating. King Edward ordered recoinage in 1300 to offset the impact of these and pollards* on English finances. See coinage. (Bibliog. 219)

crocodile. See hydra.

crocodile dung, substance providing an ointment with which old and wrinkled whores anointed their figures and were made beautiful until the flowing sweat of their efforts washed it away. (Bibliog. 140)

croft, piece of enclosed ground, generally adjacent to a peasant's (see villein) cottage, used for tillage and pasturage. (Bibliog. 24)

croquepois, weapon comprised of a stick armed with an iron hook. (Bibliog. 225)

cross, heraldic charge,* usually in the form of a Greek cross that had equal arms; its breadth was one-third the shield.* When plain, it was blazoned* only as a ''cross''; otherwise it was described in more exact terms. The cross of St. George was blazoned ''argent,* a cross gules,''* and the statute of the Templars* directed each knight to wear a red cross upon his *cotte d'arms* (coat of arms*), on breast and back. As a plain cross, it occurred six times in the ''roll of arms''* of Henry III and in varieties eleven times, but by the time of Edward II, the numbers had risen from seventeen to 102. Sixty different varieties of crosses were used on blazon. (Bibliog. 230)

cross paty, cross formy, this form of cross* appeared on the Hospitallers'* arms* and was the shape of the cross used on English crowns* and coronets.* It was a splayed linked cross with square ends; the wide ends of the arms of the cross tapered to one-half their width at the center. (Bibliog. 39)

crossbow, arbalest, weapon in which an ordinary bow* was fastened at right angles across the end of a stock called a tiller.* It was fitted with devices for holding the bow in the bent position by means of its string, for releasing the string when a trigger or lever was moved, and for supporting the arrow* or quarrel* in the correct position for discharge. Introduced into the west by the Romans who used a large siege engine called the arcubalista,* whence the medieval term arbalest,* the crossbow was outlawed as a weapon to be used against fellow Christians by the Second Lateran Council of 1139 and again by Pope Innocent III (1198–1211), but it continued to be a popular weapon. Richard I* found it particularly useful to defend fixed positions: castles,* towns, ships. At the battle of Crécy in 1346, the English longbowmen (see longbow) outshot the French and Genoese crossbowmen, particularly after a downpour made the crossbow stings useless.

Until early in the 13th century, they were spanned (cocked to get ready for shooting) by hand, but after that time they were fitted with stirrups. These allowed the bow to be placed on the ground, the left foot inserted into the stirrup at the fore end of the stock, and the string pulled back by both hands until it was engaged. To this basic weapon were added various mechanical devices to increase its projective power, but these also made the modified weapon harder to span and far more unwieldy. It fired projectiles called quarrels* or viretons* which were shorter and thicker than the longbow arrows but had greater penetration power. Its main value in castle defense lay in its range and its penetrative power, and even though it was heavy and cumbersome and its rate of fire was considerably slower than the bow and longbow, it needed less space and less exposure to be fired. (Bibliog. 27)

crossbow à jalet. See prodd.

croteys. See fumes.

crown, diadem or fillet worn by ancient chiefs to keep their long hair out of their eyes but with differing patterns of the diadem to distinguish themselves from fellow chiefs. The earliest form of crowns and coronets* used in Europe was a circlet of gold,* plain or jewelled, or ornamented with enamels. Queen Theodolinda gave to the Basilica of Monza the Iron Crown of Lombardy that had been used to crown Italian kings.* It was a jointed circlet of gold about three inches* wide and derived its name from the iron band on its interior, which was said to have been forged from *il sacro Chiodo*, one of the nails used at the Crucifixion. Edward the Confessor wore a diadem with four rays arched over, different from the early Saxon crowns which were simple gold circlets heightened at four intervals with plain uprights, each usually bearing a pearl at the top. Canute wore four trefoils* on his circlet. William* the Conqueror had a crown made of a gold circlet with three long rays with their points ending in crosses, a pearl or pellet* at each front of the crosses, and two fleurons* between the rays. His son, William II, used a crown similar to his father's but without fleurons. The Plantagenets* introduced strawberry leaves to the English crown, and Richard I's* was so heavy that two earls* had to support it after it was placed on his head. [See coronation.] Henry III's crown had eight leaves trefoil alternating large and small; Edward I used a plain gold circlet ornamented with jewels and leaves; Edward II used a far more ornate crown of four large and four small oak leaves rising with graceful curves from a jewelled gold circlet, with eight small flowers alternate with the leaves. Edward III used a coronet and cap with three strawberry leaves and three pearls alternately. He once pawned this crown to the bishop of Treves for 25,000 florins* to raise money* to continue his war with France. The royal crown of Scotland was a circle of gold set with stones and pearls and heightened with ten "fleur de lis,"* alternating with ten floriations resembling crosses fleury set with gems. For the French crown, see dauphin. (Bibliog. 178)

crown (monetary). See coinage.

crupper, metal covering for the rumps of horses* in armor; it often included a tail guard. See horse armor. (Bibliog. 9)

crusades, 200 years (1095–1291) of warfare by men and women from western Europe who sought to liberate the Holy Sepulcher and the Holy Land from the Muslims and to defend them once freed. Late in the 11th century the papacy had tried to help the Byzantine Empire fight off the invading Seljuk Turks. But internal dissension prevented any real assistance from the West, and Alexius Comnenus, emperor* of Byzantium in 1081, was too strong to accept the moves from Rome to reunite the two branches of the church. Although the Seljuks were inspired to great military advances by the idea of a jihad or holy war, they had not committed atrocities against the Christians in the Holy Land as the Western churchmen claimed they had. Christians in the Holy Land were treated as a subject minority population; they paid taxes but enjoyed the protection of Islamic law and were accorded some freedom of worship. Thus they had no need to appeal to the West for help.

When Odo de Lagery became Pope Urban II in 1088, he sent an embassy to restore relations between East and West and to lift Rome's excommunication from Alexius. Alexius was conciliatory, too, so friendly relations were reestablished. The Byzantine emperor, in trying to reorganize his army after its defeat by the Turks at Menzikert, asked Count Robert of Flanders if he would supply the needed troops. Robert conveyed the message to the pope at a council at Piacenza in 1095, and this was reinforced by envoys from Byzantium who had come to let the West know how welcome mercenaries* would be in the Byzantine cause. These envoys probably exaggerated the dangers facing the Eastern empire and left the impression that only drastic measures could save it. The envoys deliberately emphasized one word, the name Jerusalem, assuming that it would be a key propaganda word in Europe. Actually Alexius wanted only a few well-trained mercenaries to help him reconquer Anatolia, not the huge armies of knights who flocked across southern Europe. But the magic word had been uttered: "Jerusalem." And when at Clermont six months later on November 27, 1095, Urban called for the crusade, the crowd responded, *"Deus li volt!"* (God will it!), and tore up garments to make cloth crosses* to be sewn on the shoulders of the crusaders in imitation of Christ.

Enthusiasm spread far and wide, and the response was enormous. Urban continued to preach the crusade, as did bishops and other clergy, and men of peace joined warriors in far greater numbers than Urban dreamed of. Originally the crusade was to help the churches in the east, but soon this broad goal was narrowed to the specific target of freeing the Holy Land, above all Jerusalem, the Sepulcher of Christ, from the yoke of heathen dominion. St. Augustine's doctrine of the *bellum justum*, the just war,* was still considered authoritative: only when a war was fought to defend or recover a rightful possession was it a just war. And to whom did the Holy Sepulcher belong if not to the Christians. Popes Leo IV and John VIII had promised eternal life to all who fell in battle against Arabs and Vikings in the 9th century; crusaders received the same assurances from Urban II and later popes. The church had tried Peace of God (*pax Dei**) movements as one means of curbing the acts of brutal knights and forcing them to keep the peace. Another means was to organize and direct military companies and lead them in holy wars fought in service of the church. Thus the church took from kings* the responsibility for war and gave it to the knights, and by so doing, the church created ''Christian knighthood''* soldiers* of Christ. Furthermore, because the strictures of primogeniture* limited the futures of younger sons of nobles to the church or the military, the crusades offered them the chance to satisfy a love for adventure, a hunger for loot, and a chance to build a career and a future for themselves. Finally, to all men who went on a crusade and at their own expense, the Fourth Lateran Council in 1215 offered full forgiveness for all sins which they confessed truly and with a contrite heart. At the ceremony admitting all knights who swore to go on a crusade, cloth crosses were sewn on the shoulders of their surcoats.* These crosses were symbols of God's protection and of the privilege to bear arms as a pilgrim. They also were legal symbols vouching that the Peace of God and the church's protection extended to cover the crusader's belongings, a moratorium had been declared on his debts, and no taxes could be collected from his estate while he was gone. If after this ceremony a knight broke his oath to go on a crusade, he was excommunicated.

In reaction to the speech at Clermont, others also began to preach the crusade. Among them was a preacher from central France, Peter the Hermit, an unattractive man caked with dirt and mud and riding on a donkey. He was powerfully eloquent and distributed copies of a letter he claimed was from heaven saying that if only they dared, the Christians would drive the heathens from the holy places. He attracted a large following, including some poor knights, but they had little military organization and were forced to rob and steal provisions on their journey. By the time they reached Constantinople, their evil reputation had preceded them. So the emperor quickly transported them to Anatolia where they were badly beaten by the Seljuks and many were killed.

Under the barons,* however, the crusade was better planned. Godfrey of Bouillon led a force of German, Belgian, and Lorrainian knights; Raymon of Toulouse led a force from Provence; Bohemond of Taranto and Tancred led knights from southern Italy; other leaders were Robert of Flanders, Hugh of Vermandois, and Robert of Normandy. When this massive army arrived at Constantinople, Emperor Alexius I demanded they swear allegiance to help him regain territory in Anatolia. This they did reluctantly, and their victory over the Seljuks at Dorylaeum allowed Alexius to regain the western part of Anatolia. The crusaders went on and in 1098 conquered Antioch, which under Bohemond became the first crusader principality in the East. They conquered Edessa where Baldwin of Bologne, brother of Godfrey of Bouillon, founded an independent country. The major part of the crusading army, joined by the remnants of the earlier force under Peter the Hermit, continued on to Palestine. In 1099 they captured Ramlah and then advanced to conquer Jerusalem and establish a crusader state there. This officially ended the first crusade.

When in 1144 Pope Eugenius heard that Edessa had fallen to the Muslims, he preached a second crusade. He got strong support from Bernard of Clairvaux, who persuaded two kings to take the cross, Conrad III of Germany and Louis VII of France. They followed the alleged path of Charlemagne to Constantinople, marching down the Danube and through the Balkans. Manuel Comnenos, the Byzantine emperor, was afraid of the Germans, so he had Conrad's men taken across the Bosphorus to await the arrival of Louis and his men. There they were ambushed and defeated. Conrad blamed Manuel and the enmity began between the two. Conrad took a ship to Acre rather than accompany Louis and his forces along the coastal route, which was controlled by the Byzantines. At Cilicia, after they were attacked and cut to pieces by the Turks, Louis and his nobles left his army and sailed for Antioch, where they were lavishly received by Raymond of Poitiers, uncle of Eleanor of Aquitaine, Louis's wife. Louis insisted on pushing toward Jerusalem and left for Acre where he and Conrad called a great council to discuss strategy. All agreed Nureddin was too strong to be attacked, so in seeking a more likely target the barons of Jerusalem, interested only in making their position more secure, suggested Damascus. This city was an ally of Jerusalem against Nureddin, so its choice was peculiar, but the siege began. Poorly and foolishly organized, it began at one end of the city, and when it began to be effective, it suddenly shifted to another sector. Their supplies began to run out, so they abandoned the siege and Conrad returned to Europe, disgusted. Louis remained for a year but accomplished nothing. All this crusade accomplished was to verify to the Muslims that the Franks could be beaten and no longer were they to be feared.

In 1187, Saladin's* Moslem forces shattered the crusaders under Guy of Lusignan, king of Jerusalem, at the battle of Hattin. Because most of the Western knights were captured or killed, the kingdom of Jerusalem was left without defenders; it and its major port, Acre, fell to the forces of Saladin. News of this disaster prompted the leaders of the West to call for a crusade—the third crusade. Emperor Frederick Barbarossa,* King Philip II* of France, and King Richard I* of England left Europe in 1191 to restore the Latin kingdom of Jerusalem. Frederick, journeying overland, died in Anatolia on the trip. Richard and Philip sailed from Messina in Sicily for the Holy Land, continuing their rivalry for leadership of the forces along the way. Richard diverted from his trip long enough to capture Cyprus, and in 1192, created a new crusader kingdom under Guy of Lusignan, former king of Jerusalem. Once he arrived in Acre, he captured the city, but continuing quarrels between him and Philip divided the forces. After a lackluster performance, Philip on the pretext of suffering from the intense desert heat, returned home, leaving the crusader's forces under Richard severely weakened by the loss of the French forces. Richard stayed on to engage and defeat Saladin in several pitched battles, but never enough to destroy the Moslem resistance and to conquer the entire territory; Jerusalem eluded his grasp, for he recognized that supply lines necessary for an assault on that holy city would have been too thin and too exposed. News in 1192 that his brother, John, had been plotting with Philip of France to deprive Richard of the English throne forced him to conclude a truce with Saladin and to leave for England in disguise for a speedier trip. After his ship was wrecked along the Adriatic coast, he subsequently was captured by a vassal of Duke Leopold of Austria, an archenemy of the English crusader, and turned over to the Emperor Henry VI who held him captive at the castle of Triffels until ransom arrangements could be worked out.

Henry turned his attention to Byzantium when his brother betrothed the daughter of the Byzantine emperor, Isaac Angelus, in 1194. Shortly thereafter, when Isaac lost the throne to his weak brother, Alexius III, Henry began to exert political pressure on Byzantium under the guise of the right of inheritance for his brother. He took the cross in 1195, partly for his brother, and partly to help resolve his dispute with the pope. Henry then gave up plans to lead the crusade himself, and unexpectedly died in 1197. This plunged the west into a crisis, for the emperor had not had time to consolidate his achievements, and so the crusade plans were scrapped. Shortly thereafter in 1198 the pope died, and Innocent III, a man who believed that the pope should be a kind of priest-king, was elected to the papal throne. (Bibliog. 44, 297b, 310a)

In response to urgent pleas of some French knights, Pope Innocent III proclaimed the fourth crusade to strengthen the weakening kingdom of Acre, but his pleas for such an undertaking fell on disinterested ears. The French knights went ahead with their plans anyway and appointed Theobald of Champagne as their leader. His sudden and unexpected death in 1201 forced Boniface, marquess of Montferrat, to be appointed in his stead. Boniface was a close ally of the Hohenstaufen dynasty in Germany, who were enemies of the pope and of Byzantium, and he spent several months in Germany with Philip of Swabia, who lusted after the emperorship of the West. Philip's wife was the daughter of the blinded Isaac II of Byzantium, and Philip loved his wife deeply. While he was there the son of Isaac, Alexius, escaped from Constantinople and fled to his sister's court at Swabia. With such pressures on the leader of the crusaders, there were good and sufficient reasons why the crusaders should be misdirected and head for Constantinople. With the pope's permission, six French ambassadors went to Italy to seek ships to transport the crusaders to Alexandria in Egypt, and once Alexandria was taken, the crusaders could be supplied by sea; the overland route through Turkey was too dangerous. The Genoese refused to consider the job; the Pisans were unable to handle it. Enrico Dandolo,* the doge (see duke) of Venice, was delighted to undertake it for five marks* per horse, two marks per man, and fifty percent of whatever the crusaders won. What the crusaders did not know was that Venice and Egypt had signed a non-aggression pact providing that if the doge of Venice prevented the crusaders from attacking Egypt, the sultan of Egypt would give the Venetians considerable trading privileges in Alexandria. Thus the Venetians had much to gain by preventing the crusaders from ever reaching Egypt. And Boniface of Montferrat had agreed with Philip of Swabia to divert the crusaders to Constantinople to help his wife's family regain control of the throne there.

Because not enough men and horses arrived in Venice by the time agreed to in the contract, the doge was really in control of the situation. He had insisted that all the ships to be built for the crusaders should be constructed and manned by Venetians and would revert to Venice at the conclusion of the campaign. When the crusaders did not live up to their bargain, he then was in the position to keep both the money* already paid and the ships. He thus was able to impose his own terms and told them that winter was a bad time to cross the Mediterranean Sea: if they captured Zara on the Adriatic coast, they could winter there and depart in the spring, refreshed and refurbished with the loot from Zara. The crusaders knew that they had no choice but to accept his terms; if the crusade was to occur at all, Zara had to be sacrificed. So Zara was taken, but the crusaders spent all the money captured there on winter provisions. Hence when spring came they were just as badly off as before. This was what the doge had been waiting for. As the crusaders were entirely dependent on the Venetians for transport, they leapt at the chance, suggested by Boniface, to help restore Isaac to the Byzantine throne in exchange for 200,000 marks and 10,000 men. With that money they could pay the Venetians what they owed and have enough to proceed with their campaign. And so they sailed to Constantinople.

The Byzantines thought that the crusaders were there to restore the blinded Isaac to the throne. As the crusaders had been counting on putting Alexius IV on the throne and taking the promised money and leaving, they were dismayed when Isaac II entered the deliberations. However, Isaac had agreed to the terms and also that the Eastern church would accept the jurisdiction of Rome. That was asking the impossible. Emperor Alexius III fled the city, deserting his wife and all but one child, sailing south with 10,000 gold pieces and a collection of priceless gems.

Alexius IV, hated by his own people, had been placed on the throne by foreign intervention, so his position was not secure. A Byzantine named Alexius Ducas, nicknamed Murtzuphulus because his eyebrows met in the middle, plotted to get rid of the foreigners in his city, so he cultivated Alexius. When the ultimatum from the crusaders was delivered—to pay all that was owed or the city would be attacked—they could not comply. Ducas threw Alexius IV into a dungeon,* had him killed, and then usurped the emperorship; Isaac II died of grief. But with Alexius dead, no one would honor his debts. And so the war began.

The crusaders landed unopposed and captured the Castle of Galata, the only real defense at the north of the city. It contained one end of the huge chain stretched across the harbor. Once in the crusaders' hands, the chain was dropped quickly and the harbor was opened for Venetian ships to enter. Alexius III ignored the threat to his city. His nephew, Alexius IV, should have demanded his uncle's abdication to prevent the sacking and looting which was expected to occur, but he was an impotent weakling and did nothing. Meanwhile, the Venetians had covered the bows of their ships with hides to protect them from "greek fire,"* and had built long gangways from the spars of the lateen sails, some as long as 180 feet, to be suspended from the masts and to extend 120 feet at an angle to reach the top of the city walls. Mangons* on the bows of the vessels helped protect the crusaders who scrambled up these makeshift gangways to the city walls. Constantinople's main wall, the Theodosian wall, was fifteen feet thick, forty feet high, and had ninety-six "mural towers"* about fifty yards apart. A terrace forty feet wide separated this wall from the second wall, twenty-five feet high with towers one hundred yards apart; then open ground stretched to breast-works sheltering crossbowmen and archers on the outer side of which was a fifty-foot ditch which could be flooded in time of danger. On July 17, 1203, the attack began. When the Byzantines saw an enemy force landing with impunity underneath their walls, they became terrified and the army fled. Fire broke out and spread to a large part of the city. Soon the crusaders and Venetians were inside the city and began to sack and loot.

Baldwin of Flanders, and Boniface, marquis of Montferrat, as well as the doge of Venice, Enrico Dandalo, were candidates to assume the throne. Baldwin was chosen as the emperor of the Latin kingdom of Constantinople. When presented with the accomplished fact of a Latin church in the Byzantine empire, Innocent III forgave the crusaders for the diversion of the expedition and accepted the Latin empire as a client state of the papacy.

Such actions should have cooled the western European enthusiasm for crusading, but they did not. Five years later the twenty-year conflict against the Cathars in southern France began. (See Albigensian crusade.) That was followed in 1212 by crowds of children ranging in age from ten to eighteen who gathered in the Rhineland and Lower Lorraine to follow a boy from Cologne named Nicholas as they began to march "to God." Their goal was clear: to recapture the Holy Sepulcher and by so doing to accomplish what the rest of the world had been unable to do. They had no money, no organization, and only a few adults and clerics along for guidance. In France a twelve-year-old shepherd named Stephen told Philip* Augustus that Christ had appeared to him and told him to lead a children's crusade to the Holy Land. The French king refused, but the boy went to Marseilles with 20,000 young people following him. There the Mediterranean Sea was to open and allow them to walk to Jerusalem. Two shipowners promised to take them without charge in seven ships. A severe storm wrecked two of the ships off Sardinia; the others went to Egypt and Tunisia where the children were sold into slavery. When he heard about it, Frederick II ordered the shipowners hanged.

In 1213 Pope Innocent III opened his campaign for a new crusade. At that time England and France were fighting over the Angevin lands, and Frederick II and Otto IV were fighting over the German crown. So the pope appealed to the people of Christendom to hold processions monthly in order to intercede for the delivery of the Holy Land (that is to say, even the poor and weak could play a part in the war against Islam). He called for a council in 1215 to control and regulate the efforts to stimulate a new crusade and to curb the overly zealous. One priest, for example, was giving crosses to children, old men and women, the blind, and even to lepers. Thus as some sort of regulatory agency obviously was needed, each diocese set up a kind of propaganda office to provide preachers with papal letters and documents giving arguments that would make their work more effective. Supervisory control of crusade propaganda was handled by a new office in the *papal curia*, the penitentiary. Meeting in November 1215, the Fourth Lateran Council assembled 1,300 prelates in Rome. In addition to settling the fate of Toulouse territory conquered in the Albigensian crusade, this council formulated the doctrine of transubstantiation and established that an annual confession was required of all people; it also called for another crusade. Crusaders were to assemble in Brindisi and Messina in June of 1217 where the pope would bless the fleet; prelates would enforce crusaders' vows by means of excommunication or interdict.* Further provisions concerning this crusade included that any man who didn't go himself was to equip another for three years and by so doing would receive the same plenary indulgence* as the crusader himself. This led to the commutation of crusader vows for money. (See crusading vows, redemption of.) The *papal curia* promised 30,000 pounds of silver and a three-year tax on one-twentieth of the income from the clergy and one-tenth of the income from each cardinal. All crusaders were to be exempt from taxes and tolls, a moratorium was declared on all debts, and all Christendom was to remain at peace for four years.

When the young Hohenstaufen leader, Frederick II, suddenly took the cross in 1215, Innocent was unpleasantly surprised, for he feared the impetuous Frederick was challenging papal authority and would make the crusade into a secular expedition. Before the two could resolve this matter, however, Innocent died. In 1217 the new pope, Honorius III, renewed the call for a crusade to complete the work which the participants of the fourth crusade had left unfinished by returning home after sacking Constantinople. Forces from Germany, Austria, and Hungary journeyed to Egypt and reached Damietta at the head of the Nile. They besieged it for a year before it finally surrendered. Sultan Al-Kamil, the new sultan of Egypt and Syria, agreed to surrender most of Jerusalem, to free Christian prisoners held by the Muslims, and to return the True Cross to the Christians. He refused to pay the indemnity demanded by the crusaders, however, and the war resumed. No reinforcements came to support the crusaders. Frederick II, emperor of Germany and Italy, had taken the crusader's vow and thereby had promised to join the crusaders. When he did not do so, Pope Gregory IX excommunicated him. He departed on a crusade, however, in 1228, three years after he married Isabelle of Brienne, heiress of the crusader kingdom. After long diplomatic discussions between Frederick's court of Sicily and Al-Kamil's court in Egypt, Frederick journeyed to Jerusalem. He sent word to Al-Kamil that he would like to discuss the situation. Knowing Arabic, Frederick persuaded and negotiated the sultan to cede to the Christians the cities of Acre, Jaffa, Sidon, Nazareth, Bethlehem, and all of Jerusalem except the enclosure containing the Dome of the Rock, sacred to Islam. All prisoners on both sides were to be released, and peace was to be maintained for ten years and five months. Frederick crowned himself king of Jerusalem, for no churchman would crown him as an excommunicate. Ironically, the Holy City which he had liberated also fell under the ban of excommunication by having him as its king. The papacy felt Jerusalem should have been liberated by blood and not by diplomacy at the hands of one who was defiled.

By this treaty Frederick had succeeded where the rest of Christendom had failed for over one hundred years. However, because such a pact had been negotiated by an excommunicate, Pope Gregory IX denounced it as an insult and refused to ratify it. Frederick returned home to end this sixth crusade, and civil war among the nobility* in Jerusalem destroyed the peace which Frederick so carefully had negotiated. Internal strife in Germany occupied Frederick's mind for the next fifteen years, just as it occupied the Muslims. Finally by 1244, they had grown strong and united enough to retake Jerusalem, and Damascus a year later.

In 1245 Italy was ravaged by internal strife between the Guelphs* and the Ghibellines*; England's King Henry III was having troubles with his barons, so the only European monarch who harkened to Pope Innocent IV's call for a crusade was the French king, Louis IX. Mobilizing a huge army, Louis decided to attack Egypt to relieve the pressure on the sultans of Palestine. After initial successes along the coast, his army captured Damietta but were stranded there for six months by the spring flooding of the Nile. His army became soft because of the excesses of the city and the absence of the rigors of army life. Thus they were badly beaten at Mansurah, and Louis was captured. After paying a ransom of 210,000 livres, he was released and went to Acre to attempt to improve the fortifications of the cities of the kingdom of Jerusalem. His efforts proved futile, for between 1256 and 1268 the Egyptian sultanate recaptured all the towns in the Holy Land. Louis's brother, Charles of Anjou, king of Sicily, convinced him to make another attempt to rescue the holy places, and he took the cross again in 1267. Charles convinced him that the best plan would be to capture Tunis, convert the Bey of that country to Christianity, and then attack Egypt from the west. In that siege of Tunis, Louis became ill and died in 1270.

The final disaster in the Holy Land fell in 1291. Christian adventures robbed a Muslim caravan in Syria, hanged nineteen merchants, and sacked several Muslim towns. Sultan Kahlil demanded satisfaction for such an outrage, and when none was forthcoming, he marched on and captured Acre after a siege of forty-three days and then allowed his men to massacre its 60,000 inhabitants. A few feeble attempts were begun after that, but after too many years of blood-letting in the efforts, the crusades finally came to an end. (Bibliog. 44, 297 a, b, c, 310 a, b, c)

crusading vows, redemption of. A crusader's vow could be redeemed for a money* payment, especially after it became common for confessors to impose that vow on their penitents. Even Archbishop Giffard of York imposed it on numerous occasions between 1267 and 1276. For example, one John Ellerby appeared before the archbishop to explain not only why he had assaulted one Roger de Newton, priest, but also why the priest had absolved him for that action. As punishment,* the archbishop made him take the crusader's vow but then released him from it on his promise to give five shillings (see money) sterling* in succor of the Holy Land whenever it was demanded of him to send it. Usually for assaulting a priest, the culprit either had to go on a crusade* or pay one-third of his property, but sometimes a fine* amounting to two shillings was imposed instead. A knight assaulting a priest, however, was fined six pounds thirteen shillings fourpence* (or the sum of ten marks*). Sometimes this vow was imposed for other reasons. For committing adultery with the wife of another knight, one knight agreed to pay one hundred pounds in case of relapse, and then the archbishop, "pondering in our heart his contrition and mitigating the rigor of the penalty as best we may, have here given him the cross, that he may go to the Holy Land in his own person, or send a fit man of war at his own expense in atonement for this crime." (Bibliog. 297)

crusading warfare. See tactics.

cruzada, gold coin of Castile weighing ninety-two grains*; minted by Pedro I (1350–1368) its obverse had the bust of the king and its reverse the arms* of Castile and Leon. (Bibliog. 150)

cry of arms, method of signifying allegiance. See battle cry; signs of war. (Bibliog. 181)

cubit, measure of length, originally the distance from the elbow to the extremity of the middle finger; generally eighteen inches* or six palms* or two spans. (Bibliog. 394)

cubit arm, heraldic arm* couped below the elbow. (Bibliog. 43)

cuello. See barding.

cuir-bouilli, leather which had been boiled or soaked in hot water and, when soft, molded into the required form; on drying it became hard, retained the form given it, and offered considerable resistance to cuts, blows, and penetrations. Sometimes labelled "cuir-boli," it often was used as a lightweight substitution for metal armor.* Some authorities maintained that it was to be boiled in oil and not water; still others insisted that it had to be steeped in wax dissolved in certain essences. (Bibliog. 9, 78)

cuirass, metal plate consisting of backplates* and breastplates* covering the torso above the waist. (Bibliog. 9)

cuirie, defense worn over the hauberk* and beneath the surcoat* to protect the torso. Made of leather, probably cuir-bouilli,* it was sturdy enough to have

guard chains for the helmet* and sword* attached to it; sometimes it was reinforced with metal plates. (Bibliog. 27)

cuishes, metal protection attached to the saddle* to guard the knees and thighs
during tournaments.* (Bibliog. 9)

cuissarts, plates protecting the thigh which corresponded in leg armor* to brassarts* for the arm. These were fastened by straps and buckles passing around
the thighs. Although these often encircled the leg, frequently the rear portion
was omitted to allow the rider to get a better grip in the saddle.* When this
happened, the rider relied on mail chausses.* (Bibliog. 9)

cuisses, gamboised, quilted thigh defenses worn first under and then over the
chausses.* These pads were quilted vertically to protect the lower leg and shin
and were tied on or fastened by belt and buckle.
(Bibliog. 27)

culiere, part of a horse's* harness* passing under its tail and fastening to the
contour of the saddle.* (Bibliog. 161)

cultellus, coutelas, long Norman dagger or short sword,* used chiefly by infantry
dealing with fallen knights who were trying to get back into the saddle* or for
action in close quarters where a sword would be of little use. It was the progenitor
of the cutlass and was known by a variety of names: coutet-hache, coutel-axe,
curtle-axe, coutelace, and cutlass. (Bibliog. 9, 71)

culturae. See measurements.

curee, kyree, quyrreye, quarry, ceremony of giving the hounds their reward
after a successful deer* hunt, so called because originally this reward of neck,
bowels, and liver was given to the dogs on the hide or "cuir" of the stag.
Preceding this quarry came the ceremonial breaking up of the deer. The stag
was laid on its back with its feet in the air, slit open, and skinned by one of the
huntsmen* who took such pride in doing it according to the laws of woodcraft
that he didn't roll up his sleeves but instead performed things so daintily and
exactly that he got no blood on his garments. Princes* and noblemen alike took
pride in this accomplishment. After skinning the beast, the huntsman "undoing"
the deer was given a draught of wine*; he had to drink a hearty draft, for if he
should break up the deer before he drank, the venison would stink and putrify.
After they finished their main portion, the hounds were rewarded with the bowels
or guts which had been placed on large wooden forks for them. With cries of
"Tally ho!"* or "Tiel haut!" or "Lau lau!" the huntsman holloed them while
he held the fork high in the air. Then this treasure was tossed to them. This was

called the "forhu" from the word "forthuer," meaning to whoop or holloa loudly. See hunting calls; hunting dogs. (Bibliog. 96)

cures for mad-dog bite. See rabid-dog bite treatment.

curia regis, king's court* composed of the great officers of the state resident in the palace. Established by William* the Conqueror in his own behalf, this court followed the king* on all his expeditions. Thus any trial of common causes became burdensome to the people. Only in 1215 was this burden finally remedied by the fourteenth chapter of the *Magna Carta Libertatum**: "And to obtain the common counsel of the kingdom . . . we will cause to be summoned the arch-bishops, bishops, abbots, earls,* and greater barons,* individually by our letters . . . for a fixed date, . . . and to a fixed place."

This "fixed place" was established in Westminster Hall where it continued under the name of the court of common pleas or common bench. Basically feudal in character, this court was made up of the tenants-in-chief,* or barons (those who possessed "honours,"* or large estates), along with the principal officers of the crown: justiciar,* chancellor,* treasurer,* steward.* It exercised judicial, deliberative, financial, and administrative functions. Its members' advice could not be ignored, for without their support the king could not carry out his policies. The *Magna Carta* was proof of the successful resistance of the barons to a king who continually defied both them and custom. To resist the king, these barons could renounce homage* and fealty* and in the last resort could rebel.

Tenants-in-chief frequently had their own courts and households organized like a miniature king's court: they had courts and councils of honor without whose consent they hesitated to act; they had stewards who presided over the court and who directed affairs in their lord's absences. See manor court. (Bibliog. 261)

cursar. See courser.

cursores, couriers for the king*; foot messengers.* By the 12th century in England, the organization of departmental messengers was the normal part of the duties of the usher of the Exchequer,* and in due course a network of local messengers, serving as an obligation of tenure* in petty sergeanty,* covered all of England. By the beginning of the 13th century, there was a permanent, full-time staff of mounted messengers in the Chancery,* supplemented later by a body of footcouriers retained by the wardrobe.* These couriers never attained the status of mounted messengers who had secured an established position in the royal service by being formally appointed to office, by taking a solemn oath of faithfulness, and by receiving wages, robes, and food in court, maintenance during sickness, and a pension in retirement, and had developed an esprit de corps. (Bibliog. 153)

curtain walls, stone walls made of cut-stone courses* filled with a rubble core and crenellated*; these followed the line of the earthen bank surrounding the bailey* and replaced the timber stockade. The term was the general name for the wall enclosing a courtyard and thus was applied to the wall around a castle* enclosure. (Bibliog. 153)

Curtana, pointless sword* of mercy carried before the king in the English coronations* of Edward II and Richard II. It was borne in the front rank of the regalia,* supported to the right and left by two pointed swords of justice; all three were drawn. They were followed by the Garter* "king of arms,"* the lord great chamberlain,* the sword of state in its scabbard (see sheath), then the scepter,* the Edward crown* and the orb borne abreast, then the paten and chalice abreast, immediately in front of the sovereign.

This was a broad sword, thirty-two inches* long, twenty-three inches wide; its handle wrapped in fine gold wire was four inches long; its pommel* was one and three-fourths inches. Its scabbard was covered with rich brocade and had a gilt ferrule hook and chape.* The Curtana also was called the Sword of Edward the Confessor and was used also in the marriage ceremonies of Henry III in 1236. One of the privileges of the earl* of Chester was to bear this before the king. This reputedly was Roland's* sword, shortened when he broke its point by thrusting it into a block or perron* of steel to test it. (Bibliog. 91, 178)

Curthose. See Robert II.

curtilage, small court, yard, or piece of ground attached to a dwelling and forming one enclosure within it. (Bibliog. 24)

curtle-axe. See cultullus.

customal, written collection or abstract of the customs of a manor* which when coupled with the rental* provided a thorough list of the dues from all the land-holders on the manor. These embodied the many "by-laws" which gradually had evolved and which, therefore, made up the "custom of the manor." (Bibliog. 24)

customal of Dover. See execution.

customary court, concept introduced by 13th-century English jurists into the judicial structure of the manor* by which the villein,* regarded as unfree, submitted to the judgment of the lord's steward.* See manor court. (Bibliog. 28)

custos placitorum corona (L.), formal title of the coroner*; a shorter form, *coronarius,* was used at first, and then *coronator* was more widely used; the English form was crowner or coroner. (Bibliog. 171) *custos rotulorum,* one of the English justices of the peace and keeper of records for the county*; he nominated the clerk of the peace. (Bibliog. 100)

to cut the mark, an arrow* which flew straight toward the mark but fell short of it. (Bibliog. 100)

cutlass. See cultullus.

cyclas, cyclatoun, sleeveless tunic or surcoat* of linen, silk, or other pliable material, worn outside all other body defenses in the period 1325–1335. It was gathered at the waist by a narrow girdle or cingulum,* laced up at the sides, and reached the calf at the back; the front part was cut short for convenience when the knight was mounted and for freedom of movement to the armor* defenses beneath it and to the lower limbs. Silk was the most prevalent material and green the most frequent color. (Bibliog. 9)

cyng, cynig, cyning. See king.

cynophali, beast of the wilderness; a type of satyr* which had the head of a hound but which looked more like a beast than a man. (Bibliog. 21)

cynopodes, satyrs* in Ethiopia which had only one huge foot; they would shade themselves with it and were as swift as hounds when running. (Bibliog. 21)

D

dais, raised platform on which the lord of the mansion dined with his friends at the great table apart from the retainers and servants sitting at benches on the main floor. The lord and lady occupied a great chair, sometimes with a canopy to emphasize status. This platform was one step above the main floor at the end of the great hall,* opposite the entrance, and away from drafts and intrusions. Frequently at each end of the dais lay a deeply recessed bay window in which the lord or his guests could find greater privacy than the open hall afforded. (Bibliog. 128)

Dame John, corrupted form of the word *donjon** used at Canterbury to refer to its motte.* (Bibliog. 341)

Dame Nicolla de la Haye, sheriff* of Lincolnshire under King John in 1216. Born in 1150 during one of the worst excesses of King Stephen's* reign, as the eldest daughter of Sir Richard de la Haye she inherited his English estates sometime during the reign of Henry II. Included in this inheritance was the castellany (see castellan) of Lincoln Castle which was to be her home for almost eighty years; she resigned custody of it only in 1226 when she relinquished control to her grandson-in-law. She died four years later in 1230 at the age of eighty. (Bibliog. 132)

danaro, silver coin issued at Rhodes in the 14th century. See aspro.

dancetty, heraldic line of partition* showing only a few deep indentations. (Bibliog. 43)

Dandolo, Enrico, doge (or duke*) of Venice (c. 1120–1205) whose clever manipulations and shrewd financial dealings forced the crusaders on the fourth crusade* to divert from their original goal of Alexandria, Egypt, and to capture Zara and then Constantinople. (Bibliog. 297c)

Danegeld, two shillings (see money) of silver collected by Anglo-Saxon kings* from each hide* in the land to support the warriors who patrolled the shores to keep Danish marauders at bay. This became the most important source of military revenue for the Anglo-Saxon monarchs. It was regarded at the time as a tax to be used chiefly to pay mercenaries.* Collected frequently during the reign of Ethelred from 991 on to buy off Viking invaders, this was called logically the Danegeld. Edward the Confessor abolished it in 1052, but William* I restored it to enrich his royal revenues.

As it was an assessment by hides and carucates* rather than by knights fees (see knighthood), chattels, or revenues, this provided a convenient way for the king to raise money. For example, the 10,000 marks* loaned by William II to his older brother, Robert Curthose of Normandy (see Robert II) for his expenses on the first crusade,* and for which Robert gave Normandy as a pledge for repayment, was raised in part by a Danegeld of four shillings per hide. To get the money, William II summoned 20,000 footsoldiers for service overseas. When all had arrived at the assembly point of Hastings, however, the king's justiciar,* Ranulf Flambard, by royal order confiscated the money which each man had been given for provisions and ordered them all to return home; he then sent the money to William II in Normandy. As each soldier* had been told to have ten shillings with him, by this means William raised 10,000 pounds. Later, when Henry I's daughter Matilda was married to her first husband, Emperor Henry V, in 1110 (she later married Geoffrey of Anjou and bore Henry, later Henry II), the "aid"* was assessed at three shillings per hide. The term Danegeld disappeared after 1162, the last time it was invoked by Henry II, but the spirit behind it still was present, especially when the Angevins in England had to raise 100,000 marks of silver to ransom* Richard I* in 1194 (see carucage). (Bibliog. 163)

Danelaw, name of districts in eastern and northern Anglo-Saxon England including the kingdoms of Northumbria and East Anglia and five Danish boroughs* in which laws and customs of Danish origin prevailed, having been brought there by invaders from Scandinavia in the 9th century. (Bibliog. 139)

Danish axe. See battle axe.

dapifer. See steward.

dart, light throwing spear,* usually with a barbed* head and feathers, like a huge arrow*; it was used from about 1000 and favored by the Irish. (Bibliog. 27)

dauphin, title given to the eldest son of the king* of France. Originally it was the designation of the sovereign counts* of Vienne, rulers of a territorial principality east of the Rhone River known in common usage as the Dauphiné. But when this county* of Vienne was purchased in 1349 by the grandson of Philip* VI of France, later Charles V (1364–1380), it was transferred on his accession to his eldest son, thereby establishing that practice whereby the eldest son of the king of France was always known as the dauphin and either actually or theoretically was the sovereign dauphin of the Viennois. The first crown* of the dauphin was a jewelled circlet from which rose eight fleur de lis.* When the kings of France added arches* to their crowns in 1494, that of the dauphin was enclosed with four half-arches each in the form of a dolphin,* and a "fleur de lis"* was placed above the point of intersection; inside the crown was a cap of gold-embroidered crimson velvet. (Bibliog. 349)

Dauphiné, province in southeastern France bordering on Italy to the east and the Rhone River to the west and northwest whose rulers assumed the title of dauphin* from dolphins* on their arms.*

days of the week, named from the seven heavenly bodies known to the ancients: sun, moon, Mars, Mercury, Jupiter, Venus, and Saturn. In English and German the seven classical names were revered by their presumed equivalents in Teutonic mythology:

Latin	English	German
Dies Solis	Sunday	Sun's day
Dies Lunae	Monday	Moon's day
Dies Martis	Tuesday	Tiw's day
Dies Mercuri	Wednesday	Woden's day
Dies Jovis	Thursday	Thor's day
Dies Veneris	Friday	Friga's day
Dies Saturni	Saturday	Seterne's day

(Bibliog. 265)

de gestu et fama (L.), writ or inquisition issued by a coroner* concerning a person's behavior and reputation. (Bibliog. 171)

de malo lecti (L.), essoin* (excuse) for not appearing in court* when summoned; the only reason acceptable was being confined to bed by illness and having that illness witnessed by four knights appointed by the court. (Bibliog. 264)

dead angle, angle located at the foot of castle* walls. Besiegers along the length of "curtain wall"* of a castle lay safely within such an angle because vertical fire from the rampart* was impossible; only when wooden galleries* (hoarding) were extended over the walls was this area brought under fire from the defenders and the dead angle eliminated. (Bibliog. 341)

death of a knight. See knighthood.

decanummo. See nummi.

deck feathers, two center feathers of a hawk's tail. (Bibliog. 26)

decrescent, heraldic crescent* whose horns faced the sinister.* (Bibliog. 43)

deer, heraldic charge* which without qualification meant stag or red deer. Otherwise the genus and gender of the deer were indicated in the blazon*: buck, hart, hind, roebuck, stag. Its antlers were called attires*; its horns were called tines. A running deer was "in full chase," "full course," or "at speed." A passant* deer was "trippant"; statant* guardant was "at gaze"*; reclining was "lodged" and salient was "springing." See beasts, positions of. (Bibliog. 43)

defet, deffeten, opening a boar and removing its entrails. (Bibliog. 96)

degradation of a knight, ceremony of punishment for a dishonored knight. Because knighthood* was such a sacred honor,* betrayal of it became an unforgivable and irremediable horror. The culprit was regarded not only a traitor to his honor but also to his God. He was exposed on a scaffold in nothing but his shirt, after being stripped of his armor,* which was broken before his eyes and thrown at his feet; his spurs* were thrown on a dungheap, his shield* was fastened to the croup of a cart* horse* and dragged through the dirt; his charger's tail was cut off. Then after a herald-at-arms asked three times "Who is there?" three times the name of the knight being degraded was given and three times the herald* answered, "No, it is not so, for I see no knight here, but only a coward who has been false to his plighted oath." Then carried to a church on a litter like a corpse, the degraded knight was forced to lie and listen while a burial service was read over him, for he had lost his honor without which a knight could not live.

Sir Andrew Harclay was degraded on February 27, 1322, after serving his king* and country well for many years. He had been sheriff* or Cumberland from 1285 to 1298, from 1312 to 1315, and again from 1319 to 1322. He was warden of Carlisle in 1296, served in the Scottish wars between 1304 and 1311, and was member of Parliament* for Cumberland in 1312. He was made earl* of Carlisle in 1321 by the first patent of creation into honor to use a preamble importing the merits of the person so designated: "to him and the heirs of his body, with a grant of land to the value of 1,500 marks* a year because he routed the insurgents at Boroughbridge on 16 March 1321/2, and captured their leader, the earl of Lancaster."

However, because he was jealous of the favoritism shown to the Despenser family (see Caerphilly), he intrigued with the Scots and their king, Robert the Bruce, and aspired to marry the king's sister. After his treason was discovered, he was led to the bar as an earl, worthily attired with his sword girt on, horsed, booted, and spurred, and there accused of taking money* from James Douglas, a Scot, for not coming to the assistance of the king at the battle of Highland.

For this the king ordered his state to be undone, and so that lower knights might learn from this lesson his judge, Sir Anthony de Lucy, then said to him:

> Sir Andrew, the king . . . did unto you much honor, and made you earl of Carlisle, and thou, as a traitor to thy lord the king, led his people of this country, that should have helped him at the battle of Highland, away by the country of Copeland, and through the earldom of Lancaster, wherefore our lord the king was discomfited . . . by the Scots through thy treason and falseness; and if thou had come in time, he [would have] had the mastery. And all that treason thou did for the great sum of gold and silver that thou took from James Douglas, a Scot, the king's enemy. And our lord the king's will is that the order of knighthood by which thou undertook all thy worship and honor upon thy body, be all brought unto nought, and thy state undone so that other knights of lower degree may after thee beware.

After his spurs were removed, his sword broken over his head—the same sword which had been given to him by the king when creating him earl—he was stripped of his fur-edged tabard,* his hood, his "coat of arms,"* and his girdle. When thus shorn of all symbols of knighthood, Sir Anthony said to him, "Andrew, now thou art no knight, but a knave, and for thy treason the king's will is that thou be hanged." After he was hanged, he was beheaded, drawn, and quartered, his head set up on London Bridge and his four quarters sent to four towns of England as lessons to others. (Bibliog. 134, 225)

Dei Gratia (L. "By the grace of God"), legend that appeared on coins as early as the 9th century. Eudes, king* of France between 887 and 898, called himself, *Gratia Domini Rex*. (Bibliog. 150)

delf, square billet* in heraldry*; a delf in the center of the shield* was the abatement* for one who revoked a challenge. (Bibliog. 43)

dells. See fields.

demesne, central portion of a manor* that was set aside for the lord's own use and ministered to the wants of his own household. Sometimes in England it was called "board lands."* Bockyng in Essex, a manor belonging to the chapter of Christ Church, Canterbury, contained the following as an example of the distribution and relative value of demense land in 1309:

manor house and close* of 5 acres* (demense)

pigeon house

2 mills

fishery

2 wood lots containing 480 and 10 acres

arable land containing 510 acres

2 meadows containing 8 and 7 acres

30 acres for pature: 14 for cows and 16 for oxen and horses

(Bibliog. 357)

démesuré (Fr.), conduct or attitude of sinful pride which hich invited punishment. Roland* refused to sound his horn to summon Charlemagne's forces when he and the other *douzepeers** were outnumbered by pagan forces by forty to one. His threefold fear of disgracing his family, his country and king, and his God by such an action was classed as *démesuré*—pride in refusing to call for held. (Bibliog. 113)

demi-brassarts, armor* plates protecting the outer part of the arms. (Bibliog. 9)

demi-cuissarts, plates of armor* strapped over the chausses* to protect only the outer parts of the thighs. See cuissarts. (Bibliog. 9)

demi-greaves, shin guards of plate armor.* (Bibliog. 27)

demi-grevieres, leg defenses of armor* strapped over the chausses* covering only the shins. Also called demi-jambarts. (Bibliog. 9)

demi-poulaines, long-toed variety of solleret* from which the points had been removed so the wearer could fight on foot. (Bibliog. 9)

demi-vambraces, half-armor protecting the forearm. (Bibliog. 9)

denarius, denier, danaro, dinhero, dinero, dinar, standard silver coin of the Roman Republic. Under Charlemagne, it was reissued and became the standard coin of most of Europe for centuries. See coinage. (Bibliog. 150)

denierat. See librate.

Denis, St. See St. Denis.

deodand, anything animate or inanimate which caused the death of a human being. Such an object was to be handed over to the king* and devoted by his almoner* to pious uses "for the appeasing of God's wrath." The theory behind such actions stemmed from the belief that the object's sin for the death was expiated by its subsequent dedication to the church. The law on deodands stated: *omnia quae movent ad mortem, deodanda est* ("all which moves to the death of someone is a deodand"). Thus a mill wheel was a deodand but not the mill itself; a branch was a deodand but not the entire tree. In the 13th century, the deodand object was turned over to the townsmen in whose territory the death had occurred, and they had to answer to the royal officers for its value. A coroner's* jury could suffer amercement* for falsely appraising a deodand or for not presenting it to the coroner at all. For example, to avoid amercement, a jury decreed that a man who had drowned in the Severn River after falling from a cliff (which would have entailed no deodand) had indeed fallen from a boat which accordingly was adjudged deodand. Horses,* oxen, carts,* boats, mill wheels, and cauldrons were the commonest deodands. The English called the deodand the "bane," that is, the slayer. (Bibliog. 261)

descent. See law of descent.

Descriptio, official title of the great English survey undertaken in 1086 at the command of William* I, commonly known as the *Domesday Book.** (Bibliog. 213)

despotate (Gr.) prince* or ruler.

dessours. See jestours.

destrier, *dextrarius,* knight's battle horse.* To bear the weight of an armored knight and survive the shocks and impacts of battle, this steed had to be large and heavy-set and possess incredible endurance. It was an expensive beast which could not be bought for less than ten marks,* but the prices rose as high as one hundred pounds (see money) in the 14th century. See distraint of knighthood. (Bibliog. 264)

device, heraldic motto,* emblem, or other mark by which those who entered the lists* were distinguished at tournaments,* but the term applied especially to a motto affixed to the arms,* having some punning allusion to the name. It differed from a badge* or cognizance* only inasmuch as it was an arbitrary and generally temporary distinction, whereas a badge frequently was worn by successive members of the same family. (Bibliog. 43)

dexter, right side of the shield* when viewed from behind. It was the more important side of the shield, taking precedence over the sinister.* (Bibliog. 251)

dextrarius. See destrier.

dhimmis, Arabic term for a non-believer who, living in an Islamic state, was tolerated and accorded protection or hospitality in return for recognition of Islamic authority and payment of taxes. (Bibliog. 139)

diadocos, most powerful stone for divination; it resembled beryl.* Holding it in one's mouth gave one authority over devils, and those who were summoned up placed themselves in one's service without making the caller bad himself. Before one held it in one's mouth it first had to be cooled in water to prevent burns. Further, it made immortal all who carried it, but it did not stop from falling into a langour those to whom death was preferable. Bodies in contact with this stone rose up again suddenly without speech, sight, or movement but collapsed when it was withdrawn. This stone was holy among all others. (Bibliog. 258)

Dialogus de Scaccario, treatise written c. 1179 by Richard Fitz-Neale, bishop of London and treasurer* for Henry II, to explain in dialogue format the methods and detailed procedures used in operating the king's treasury; it was better known by its translation, *Dialogue of the Exchequer*. See Richard Fitz-Neale. (Bibliog. 102)

diapered, patterned heraldic field* and shield,* usually darker and lighter shades of the same tincture (see colors) to relieve the plain tinctures of the field. (Bibliog. 43)

dicker, measure of varying quantity for a variety of goods: 10 animal hides; 110 horseshoes; 10 pairs of gloves; 10 bundles of 10 necklaces each; 12 skins of tanned leather or parchment. (Bibliog. 394)

dienstmannen (Ger.), feudal vassals,* or liegemen, in the 12th century. These were the dependents of nobles or princes,* even of the emperor* himself, who in return for military service received fiefs* from their lords and frequently attained considerable position and influence. Often they acquired the status of free vassals, even though they might bear the family name of their overlord; on occasion, they even came to surpass in wealth and dignity the members of the older free nobility,* particularly if they were in service of the emperor. Such advantages induced some members of the free nobility to join their ranks. This new class of knights, *dienstmann*, furnished many of the chief poets of Germanic literature.

Coming from diverse backgrounds, these knights belonged to one privileged class: comrades-in-arms on equal footing with each other. Yet despite such levelling of all distinctions of birth or wealth among them, this privileged class was separated by a wide gulf from the common folk. It fit neatly into a society in which man had his place and his rights as a particular unit of society, but not as an individual human. Onto this society in which grace and elegance in social relationships never had been prominent, the courtly etiquette and social polish of French chivalry* were grafted. French names for tournament* and joust,* armor,* food, and dress became fashionable in the Germany of the 12th century.

Nonetheless, the Germans had their own ways of doing things. For example, their knighting ceremony used the *swertleite*, a ceremonial girding of the sword* in place of the French *colée.** Only later did the *ritterschlag* (*colée*) become the symbol of reception into knighthood.* This golden age of German chivalry occurred in the reign of Emperor Frederick I (Rotbart or Barbarossa, as he was called in Italy). (Bibliog. 274)

dies amoris. See love-day.

Dieu et mon Droit (Fr. "God and my right"), motto* used as the password given by King Richard I* to his army at the battle of Gisors in which he defeated the French. In remembrance of this victory, he made it the motto of the royal arms* of England. (Bibliog. 178)

Dieudonné, name given by the French to the son and heir to the throne, Philip* Augustus, born at long last to King Louis VII by his third wife, Adele of Blois.

difference, marks of, small marks added to arms* to distinguish the male members of a family one from another. See cadency. (Bibliog. 43)

digit, measure of length equal to a finger's breadth of three-fourths of an inch in the 11th century. Originally a unit of body measurement, this was equal to one-fourth palm,* one-twelfth span,* one-twenty-fourth cubit,* one-fortieth step, and one-eightieth pace.* (Bibliog. 394)

dimidiation, method of impalement* by which two coats* to be joined in the same arms* were bisected, and the dexter* (right) half of one was joined to the sinister* (left) half of the other. (Bibliog. 43)

dinar, Islamic or Muslim gold coinage.* The earliest ones dating from the late 7th century were imitations of the Byzantine sol.* From the beginning of the 8th century, however, the dinar had on both sides Arabic inscriptions giving the mint date and a religious formula; later the ruler's name was added. (Bibliog. 150)

dinher, gold coin of the Arabic emirs* of Sicily in the 11th century. (Bibliog. 150)

dionysia, black stone with reddish-brown spots; when powdered and added to wine,* it ameliorated and made harmless the effect of the wine. (Bibliog. 258)

dirhem, Islamic silver coin with designs similar to the dinar.* (Bibliog. 150)

dishonor, actions to. See degradation of a knight; ransom.

disparage, to degrade by an unequal marriage, that is, when women or men married someone who was not their equal, their "pare" or "peer".* (Bibliog. 264)

displayed, heraldic description of a bird whose outspread wings had their tips pointing upward. (Bibliog. 43)

distinction, marks of, marks of bastardy added to arms* to show the absence of a full blood relationship. (Bibliog. 43)

distraint, physical seizure of a person's goods and sometimes his lands in order to compel him to pay his rent, perform his services, appear in court,* accept knighthood,* and so on. (Bibliog. 246)

distraint of knighthood, general command issued by King Henry III in England in 1224 for all landholders holding knights' fees (see knighthood) but who were not themselves knights to be distrained to become knights. This was widened in 1242 to include holders of twenty librates* of land by military or socage* tenure* and further enlarged to forty librates as the regular figure by the end of the 13th century. Sheriffs* were ordered to coerce into knighthood those eligible by impounding their chattel and by holding inquests into the landed status of those who said that they were insufficiently landed. Such actions were taken not only to increase the number of men available for service in the king's army but also, and primarily, for money,* because by this action, the king* could gain money* from them for scutage,* reliefs,* wardships,* and marriages*—all incidental to military tenure.

King Edward I issued in 1278 an order for his sheriffs:

> to distrain without delay all those in your bailiwick who have lands worth twenty pounds a year, or one whole knight's fee worth twenty pounds a year, and hold us in chief and ought to be knights but are not, to receive from us before Christmas or on that feast the arms* of a knight; to distrain also without delay all those in your bailiwick who have lands worth twenty pounds per year, or one whole knight's fee worth twenty pounds, whoever they hold of, and ought to be knights but are not, to receive such arms on that feast or before; so that you can receive from them good and sufficient security for doing this, and cause the names of all of them to be entered under the supervision of two law-worthy knights of the aforesaid county on a certain roll, and sent to us under your seal and the seals of two knights without delay.

In January 1296, the same King Edward ordered an inquiry into the number of persons with forty pounds (see money) a year in land, as well as knights and others, to make certain that they had horses* and arms for the defense of the realm; in November of that same year, he ordered all freeholds worth twenty pounds in land to be distrained to become knights. Later he summoned 900 men by name, for he had recent information from an Assize of Arms* about those bound to arms, and from the Statute of Winchester (1285) to obey his summons. At Lincoln he pursued the distraint of knighthood to its logical end: all forty-pound freeholders were ordered to attend the king with horses and arms and accompany him to Scotland. (No evidence survived as to how many showed up.) The scarcity of knights was not due to distaste for military service but to economic and social conditions. In the time of Henry II (1154–1189), arms and equipment might have cost only five pounds or even twenty marks* (six and two-thirds pounds); but the developments in armor* for both man and horse, together with the cost for a good destrier* strong enough for his knightly actions in the field, had increased the cost five to ten times; a good destrier would cost between twenty and one hundred pounds. Added to this was the requirement to present the "earl marshal"* a palfrey* when a tenant-in-chief* was knighted or did homage.* Knighthood was a costly business. (Bibliog. 87, 271)

distringas (L.), writ ordering distraint.* (Bibliog. 171)

dit. See lai.

divorce, dissolution of marriage. Even though from early times the church maintained that a marriage could not be dissolved, it had to temporize Anglo-Saxon and Frankish penitentials to allow a divorce *ad vinculo matrimoni* (L. "from the bonds of matrimony") in various cases: if a wife was guilty of adultery, her husband could divorce her and marry another; she could remarry after five years of penance. Also, if a wife deserted her husband, he, after five years and with the bishop's consent, could marry another. And if a wife were carried into captivity, her husband could marry another, for "it was better to do so than to fornicate." (Bibliog. 261)

dobra, Portuguese gold coin equivalent to eighty-two sol* and one-fiftieth of a gold mark,* struck under Pedro I (1357–1367). (Bibliog. 150)

doge. See duke.

dogs of the chase. See hunting; hunting dogs.

Dolorous Garde. See Joyeuse Garde.

dolphin, chief among fish as a lion* was considered chief among beasts. As a charge* it always was shown embowed* and usually with a pronounced beak and fins. It appeared in the third and fourth quarters* of the arms* of the dauphin* of France. (Bibliog. 43)

Domesday Book, survey ordered in 1086 by King William* I of the whole country of England: its woods, pastures, and meadows, as well as its arable land, and all to be set down in a common language so that no man should try to usurp the rights of another. The prologue to the Ely Inquest revealed the scope of the survey, for the jurors at the inquest were asked in each instance:

> the name of the manor; who held it at the time of King Edward [the Confessor]; who holds it now; how many hides are there; how many ploughs in the demesne and how

many belong to the men; how many villeins; how many cottars; how many slaves; how many freemen; how many sokemen; how many woodland; how much meadow; how much pasture; how many mills; how many fisheries; how much has been added to or taken away from the estate; what did it used to be worth altogether; what is it worth now; how much has each sokeman and freeman. All this to be recorded thrice: to wit, as it was in the time of King Edward; as it was when King William gave the estate; and as it is now.

(Bibliog. 231)

By the completion of this survey the king* acquired an exact knowledge of the possessions of the crown. It gave him the names of landholders; it furnished him with the means of ascertaining the military strength of the country; and it pointed out the possibility of increasing the revenue in some cases and of lessening the demand of the tax collectors in others. Finally, it served as a register of appeal for those whose titles to their property might be disputed.

Originally known as the *Descriptio* or the *Liber de Wintonia*, the Book of Winchester, this work covered all the counties except those of northern England: Northumberland, Cumberland, Durham, Westmorland. It confirmed the introduction of feudalism* into England by the Normans because it was a formal written record of the introduction of feudal tenure* and therefore of feudal law. The massive amount of information gathered was rearranged into terms of tenure, royal demesne, and tenants-in-chief* by county.* Overwhelmingly obvious on every page of such a listing was the feudal concept of *nulle terre sans seigneur* (Fr. "no land without its lord") and the feudal principle that all the land was in the hands of the king who also was the feudal suzerain.

This work was called Domesday (Doomsday), that is, the day of judgment, for just as that Last Judgment could not be evaded by any subterfuge, so disputes in the realm could not evade the facts in undisputed writing. Thus it was called Domesday "not because it passes judgment on any doubtful points raised, but because it is not possible to contradict its decisions, any more than it will be those of the Last Judgment." (Bibliog. 102, 109, 213)

domgio. See *donjon.*

dominus (L.), title used by the English monarch after being elected but before being crowned as territorial lord and head of the feudal state; after being crowned by the entire coronation* ceremony, he became *rex* with all the attributes of royalty. Empress Matilda, daughter of King Henry I,* never was crowned but usually adopted the style *Anglorum domina,* and both Richard and John between their "election" to the throne and their coronations used the term *dominus Angliae.* See kingship. (Bibliog. 262)

dona, donum (L. "gifts"), aids* rendered to the king by the lords during the reign of King Henry II of England sometimes were termed gifts, or *dona,* a euphemism which implied compulsory contribution because this same money taken from villeins* was termed tallage.* (Bibliog. 262)

dondaine, early form of cannon* used for throwing stones or arrows* or an especially heavy weight for a short distance. (Bibliog. 225)

donjon (Fr.), great tower or tower keep* of a castle* which was the dominant feature of many castles; the word also referred to the motte* of certain early castles. A common word in medieval writing for motte was the Latin word, *dunio* or *domgio*, a debased form of *domino*from Latin *dominium* meaning lordship, which in turn became *donjon* in French and dungeon* in English. (Bibliog. 341)

dooms, judgments or decisions made formally by the jury of a "manor court."* (Bibliog. 24)

dorcon, goat.

dormant, position of a creature in heraldry* who was couchant,* that is, sleeping with its head down and eyes closed. See beasts, positions of. (Bibliog. 43)

double quatrefoil. See octofoil.

doubling. See ruses.

douze, dozen: for example, *douzepeers** meant twelve peers.*

douzepeers, dozepeers, dozepares (Fr.), twelve peers* or paladins* of Charlemagne attached to his person, said in the *chansons de geste** and the romances* to be the bravest of his knights. In history, the twelve great peers of France, spiritual and temporal, who were supposed to represent those attributed by the romances to Charlemagne, were:

Archbishop of Rheims	ranking as duke*
Bishop of Laon	ranking as duke
Bishop of Langres	ranking as duke
Bishop of Beauvais	ranking as count*
Bishop of Chalons	ranking as count
Bishop of Noyon	ranking as count
Duke of Normandy	
Duke of Burgundy	
Duke of Aquitaine	
Count of Toulouse	
Count of Flanders	
Count of Champagne	

Layamon wrote in 1205: "The French call them *douzepeers*." (Bibliog. 40, 246)

dower, marriage portion brought by a bride to a groom for which in return she received a dower amounting to one-third of her husband's estate; sometimes this meant naming specific lands at the church door on her wedding day which would become hers on her husband's death. Even without such a formal agreement, one-third of his land legally was hers; and if the heir was slow to relinquish it to her, she could bring legal action in royal courts* to secure it. However, if he added land to his holdings during the marriage, she could claim no part of it; if she accepted the dower at the church door, then she could claim no more. (Bibliog. 129)

draconitides, dragon stone, carbuncle, found in the head of dragons.* It had to be taken from the dragon when it was sleeping, for otherwise it lost its magical powers. Enchanters would put a dragon to sleep and then cut off its head to steal the carbuncle which they would sell for enormous profits. A riddle of Aldhelm described this stone:

> A bristling dragon's head contrived my birth,
> So men report; my crimson hue outshines
> Refulgent gems. But never could I get
> My proper strength and hardness, if death filled
> The snake's foul, scaly carcass ere some hand
> Wrenched me, all ruddy, from its hideous crest.

(Bibliog. 258)

dragon, 1. beast of the Middle Ages which seemed as much an actuality as elephant* and camel. Isidore of Seville in the 7th century said that it was the largest of living creatures, had a crest, an erectile tongue, and a powerful tail;

Vincent of Beauvais added that it had wings and a yellowish and black face. Some were said to have feet; others had no feet. The ancient poets of Greece and Rome introduced dragons into their fables to illustrate a combination of power and ferocity. Homer, for example, described the shield* of Hercules: "the scaly horror of a dragon coiled full in the central field,* unspeakable, with eyes oblique, retorted that askant shot gleaming fire." (Bibliog. 138) Ovid's *Metamorphoses* located the dragon slain by Cadmus in Boetia near the river Cephisus. It was blue colored and adorned with golden crests; its eyes sparkled with fire as it lay hidden in a cavern; it was terribly destructive because of its poisonous sting, long constricting folds, and venomous breath. Pliny described a dragon on Nysa, a mountain in India, as being twenty-four feet* long and colored yellow, purple, or azure* blue.

Several centuries later, Philostratus, around the year A.D. 200, classified these beasts into mountain dragons and marsh dragons. Mountain dragons, he said, had a moderate crest which increased with age as a saffron-colored beard grew from their chins; they were covered with gold-colored scales which shone brightly, they uttered a loud shrill cry, and had a protuberance on their heads the color of "burning coal." Marsh dragons had no crests and were silver colored instead of gold. Their length ranged between thirty and one hundred cubits.* One near Damascus was reported to have been 140 feet long and was of such bulk that two men on horseback with the monster* between could not see each other. An Ethiopian dragon was said to have had two feet with claws, two ears, and five conspicuous tubercles on its back; it was covered with green and dusky scales, had wings, a long flexible tail covered with yellow scales like those on its belly and throat, black pupils in the eyes, and flaring tawny nostrils. Middle English romances* added such different details as feet like those of a lion,* sometimes a span* long, a fiery head on its tail which ranged from seven yards* to five fathoms* long. Thus the description varied with location and century.

Fighting and slaying dragons was a famous accomplishment of many gods, saints, and heroes. Among these were Zeus, Phoebus, Theseus, Dionysius, Hercules, Cadmus, Jason, Perseus, Theseus, Thor, Siegmund, Siegfried, Beowulf, Frotho, Ragnar, Wigalois, Roland,* Lancelot, Tristram, Bevis, Guy of Hampton, Assipattle, St. George, St. Michael, and even St. Margaret. St. Marthe killed a terrible dragon named Tarasque at Aix la Chapelle,* St. Florent killed one haunting the Loire, and St. Romain of Rouen killed one called La Gargouille which was ravaging the Seine River. Besides carrying off the gold of the dragon's hoard as a prize, eating the dragon's heart gave the hero a knowledge of the beast's language, and painting himself with dragon's blood hardened the skin against all injuries. Some of the more famous dragon fights included that of Siegfried with Fafnir in the Siegfried epics and Tristan's fight with the Irish dragon in the various Tristan and Isolde stories.

Tristan spied the grisly beast belching smoke, flames, and wind from its jaws like the Devil's spawn it was. When the creature saw him, it charged; but Tristan lowered his spear* and, spurring his horse* to its full speed, he thrust his spear down the open mouth of the beast, tearing through its jaw and barely stopping at its heart. His horse was killed instantly by the shock of the impact. The badly wounded dragon attacked the dead horse and devoured everything as far as the saddle.* Realizing it had been badly wounded, the fiery beast turned and raced toward its lair in the rocky region behind it. Tristan raced in pursuit. Drawing his sword,* he faced the beast in its lair. Its fire and razor-sharp teeth and claws were turned furiously against the stalwart Tristan, who managed adroitly to evade close grips with the angry monster. Finally the spear did its work, and the beast sank to the ground, writhing in agony. Tristan raced to its side and plunged his sword into its heart beside the spear. At this the monster let out a roar as though the heavens themselves were falling, and fell over dead. Tristan then wrenched apart the awesome jaws, cut out the beast's tongue, which he tucked into the chest portion of his armor,* and he sank to the ground, exhausted.

Sir Degare, in the English romance of the same name, fought his dragon with different weapons:

> Then was there a dragon grim full of filth and venom, with wide throat and great teeth and wings to beat quickly. It had feet like a lion, and its tail was long and great; smoke came out of its nose like fire from a fireplace. Stoutly Degare lay on with his sword, and struck stout blows, but all his blows hurt it not, for its hide was as hard as wrought iron. Degare then took his cudgel, great and strong, and in the forehead, battered it and spattered it in pieces. Down it fell, and struck Degare with its tail, but Degare leaped up and smashed its head with his mace, and killed it.

(Bibliog. 119)

Yvain and Gawayn described Yvain's fight with a dragon in yet another way. To protect his face from the beast's fiery breath, Yvain held his shield in front of him as he thrust his lance* into the dragon's mouth so that it came out at its navel. Then he sliced off its adams's apple. Yvain's constant companion, the lion, still had its tail held by the ferocious beast, so to free the lion, Yvain cut off its tail. Then the dragon sank to the ground and died.

Two entries in an English chronicle, the *Annals of Winchester*, seemed to confirm that England was afflicted by dragons: "1177—In this year dragons were seen of many in England"; "1274—A fiery dragon frightened the English." (Bibliog. 138) Over forty sightings of dragons in Britain were recorded, and many dragon tales recounted both sightings and combats. For example, in Uffington, Berkshire, St. George slew a dragon on Dragon Hill. In Moston, Cheshire, a dragon living in Bache Pool was shot in the eye and then slain by Sir Thomas Venables, just as it was about to eat a child.

At Lambton Castle, Durham, young Lambton broke the Sabbath by fishing and swearing; he caught an ugly reptile and threw it into Worm Well. Later he repented his ways and became a crusader. The creature thrown into the well grew into a dragon which coiled around Worm Hill, devoured livestock, and could be pacified only with troughs of milk. If someone fought with it and severed legs, tail, or whatever, it rejoined its severed parts as though nothing had happened. When young Lambton returned, he donned spiked armor, and on the advice of a witch, fought the beast on a rock in the river so that the current would sweep away whatever limbs he managed to sever. Lambton overcame the wicked beast finally by that means.

The dragon of Linton was killed by a knight who, attacking while the beast was sleeping, thrust down its throat a piece of peat dipped in scalding pitch at the end of his lance. That peat served to protect the knight from the dragon's poisonous breath at the same time that it clogged the creature's jaws so it could not breath, and thus it died.

At Rhodes, in 1349, a knight named Gozione fought a monster which had the bulk of an ox, a long neck, a serpent's head topped with mule's ears, a gaping mouth with rows and rows of sharp teeth, four feet with claws like a bear, a tail like that of a crocodile, a body covered with hard scales, and two wings, blue on the top and yellow and blood-red on the bottom. It could move faster than a horse, partly by flying and partly by running. Gozione retired to the country, and to practice before confronting the beast, he built a model of the creature out of paper and burlap. He bought a charger and two English dogs, then told his servants to get inside the mock beast to snap its jaws and twist its tail around while he accustomed the dogs and his steed to the beast. Within two months, his horse had become accustomed to it, and his dogs were frenzied by the mere sight of the model. After hearing mass, Gozione went to the cave of the monster and positioned his servants to watch from a nearby rock, telling them that they should help him should he be overcome by the noxious breath of the dragon after he killed it, or to save themselves if it should kill him. Rousing the dragon, Gozione waited for its appearance. He shattered his lance on its horny scales at the first rush, but then he leapt from his horse and attacked it with his sword and shield. As it reared on its hind legs to grapple Gozione with its forelegs, it exposed the soft part of its neck. Gozione, close to exhaustion, plunged his sword into the beast, and both fell to the ground. His servants rushed in, dragged the beast off of him, and revived him with water. He was rewarded with high honors and was made magistrate of the province. (Bibliog. 138)

In Wales, the word dragon came to be used for chief* and pendragon for a leader created in times of emergency; knights slaying a leader in battle were said to have killed a dragon. In his *Historia*, Geoffrey of Monmouth recounted that after the appearance of a dragon-like star, which Merlin* interpreted favorably, Uther Pendragon had two golden dragon ensigns* made, one to be given to the church at Winchester and the other to be carried before him in battle. Harold Godwineson carried a similar ensign at the Battle of Hastings,* as depicted on the Bayeux tapestry; his dragon appeared as his vexillum or gonfanon.* Richard I* carried one in 1190 as he besieged Messina on his way to the Holy Land on the third crusade.* His brother, John, similarly used a dragon ensign. At the Battle of Bouvines* in 1214, the Emperor Othon IV had a golden dragon standard,* similar to that of the ancient Romans, made of cloth to swell out with the wind and with wings, tail, and gaping jaws; he had it set atop a standard surmounted* by an eagle.*

2. Heraldic charge* which usually portrayed a scaly monster with bat wings and eagle's claws. 3. In China, one of the gods of Buddhism. Dragons of the Four Seas were brothers named Yao who governed the North, South, East, and West seas. The fabulous dragon of China was a monster with scales like a crocodile's and had five claws on its feet; when it rose into the air, it was by the power it possessed to transform itself at whim: it could make itself large or small, visible or invisible, or rise and fall. It was the ruler of the clouds and sent rain and floods. (Bibliog. 43, 93, 138, 173)

drawbridge, movable section of bridge or causeway providing entrance to a castle* or manor* house. Keeps* frequently were built with an encircling wall called a chemise.* Entry was gained through a gateway in the chemise from which one climbed a flight of steps against the interior face of the wall and then crossed a wall walk connected to the keep by a bridge or causeway with a draw section. Such a drawbridge either was pulled back on a platform in front of the gate or was hinged on the inner side and raised by chains on the outer side so that when closed, it stood vertically against the gate, providing an additional barrier. It also might have revolved on a horizontal pivot, dropping the inner section into the pit while the outer section rose to block the gateway. By this means, any attacking group had to force the gate, climb the stairs, follow the wall walk and defile, and cross the causeway—all the while being exposed to attack from all directions. (Bibliog. 128)

drawing through the bow, drawing back the bowstring so far that the point of the arrow* came within the belly of the bow.* (Bibliog. 100)

dreng, threng, Scandinavian equivalent of the English cniht.* An Old Norse word, *drengr*, meaning "young man," was used in the late 12th century to refer to soldiers* who were the predecessors of the Norman *miles.** To serve with William* II (1087–1100) on his Welsh expedition, Archbishop Lanfranc sent a contingent of these young men who, although they had undergone the training for and had acquired the equipment needed to rank as knights, (see knighthood), proved to be totally unsatisfactory. They were, in the words of Anselm's biographer, "neither properly equipped nor were suitable persons for warfare of that character." (Bibliog. 330)

drit. See fumes.

droit de guerre. See law of arms.

dromon, dromion, dromond, dromedary, large, fast-sailing warship built for western European countries from the prototype of the supply ship of the Saracens.* This vessel had three masts, a high freeboard (that is, rode high in the water), and carried 1,500 men and their equipment. Roger de Hoveden, chronicler for Richard I,* described how Richard on his way to the Holy Land had encountered and captured a Saracen dromond on its way to relieve the beleaguered city of Acre. (See crusades). (Bibliog. 44, 100)

dub, word which came from "adoubements" and had four separate but related meanings: 1. to create a knight; 2. to give the accolade with a sword*; 3. to give the accolade with the hand or fist; 4. to invest with sword. (Bibliog. 2)

dubbing ceremony, ritual by which squires* became knights (see knighthood). One of the best examples was the ceremony by which King Henry I of England knighted his son-in-law, Geoffrey of Anjou, in 1128:

> When Geoffrey entered the inner chamber of the king's hall* at Rouen, surrounded by his knights and those of the king* and a crowd of people, the king went to meet him, affectionately embracing and kissing him, and taking him by the hand, led him to a seat. All that day was spent in joyful celebration. At the first dawn of the next day, a bath was prepared, according to the custom for the novice knights. After bathing, Geoffrey donned a linen undergarment, a tunic of cloth of gold,* a purple robe, silk stockings, and shoes ornamented with golden lions*; his attendants who were being initiated into knighthood with him, also put on gold and purple. With his train of nobles, Geoffrey left the chamber to appear in public. Horses* and arms* were brought and distributed. A Spanish horse of wondrous beauty was provided for Geoffrey, swifter than a flight of birds. He then was armed with a corselet of double-woven mail* which no lance* or javelin* could pierce, and shod with iron boots of the same double golden mesh; golden spurs* were gird on; a shield* with golden lions was hung around his neck; a helmet,* which no sword* could pierce or mar, and gleaming with many precious stones, was placed on his head; a spear* of ash topped with iron was provided; and finally from the royal treasury was brought an ancient sword. Thus the novice was armed, the future flower of knighthood, who despite his armor,* leapt with marvelous agility on his horse. What more can be said? Dedicated to the honor of the newly made knights, that day was spent entirely in warlike games and exercises. This celebration in honor of the new knights continued for seven days.

(Bibliog. 129)

ducat, gold coin issued by Roger II, Norman duke* of Apulia from 1134 to 1150, with the words "*DVX APVLIA*" on it; hence it was called ducat. This term also applied to the zecchino* of Venice, minted in the late 13th century, depicting the kneeling doge (see duke) of Venice receiving the standard* from St. Mark, because it also carried the Latin inscription *DVX*. (Bibliog. 150)

duchies, territorial sections of Alemannia or Swabia, of Bavaria, Saxony, Franconia, and Lorraine where between 905 and 915 the duke* was actually a diminished successor of a king.* (Bibliog. 28)

duel, single combat between two knights. Also known as judicial combat, judicial duel, trial by battle, trial by combat, "wager of battle."* Disputes could be settled in either of two ways: compurgation* or judicial duel. There was considerable difference between a duel of law and a duel of battle: the object of a duel of law was reparation; that of duel by battle was vengeance. For example, John Van Arkel, a knight of Holland, followed Godfrey de Bouillon on the first crusade.* When some German knights joined this army, a Tyrolese noble, seeing Van Arkel's banner* displayed before his tent and recognizing it as identical with his own, ordered it torn down. Although such an action was a flagrant insult, Van Arkle sought no satisfaction for his honor but rather laid the case before the chiefs* of the crusade as a judicial matter. In the ensuing investigation, both parties proved their ancestral right to the same bearing (see charge). To decide the conflicting and incompatible claims, the judges ordered a judicial combat in which Van Arkel deprived his antagonist of his life and quarterings* simultaneously, and vindicated his right to the "argent* two bars* gules*" which he bore for eight years in Palestine. This was not a quarrel about an insult but was an examination into a legal question for which there was no other solution according to the custom of the day.

Judicial combat, on the other hand, as an alternative to compurgation, required that an accuser and an accused or their designated representatives (see champion for ordeals) engage in battle, and the verdict would go to the victor because God would aid the combatant who represented the more just cause. As a general rule, the accuser would follow his appeal* (accusation) by offering to prove it with his body, that is, in a duel. One of the parties, however, could submit that he was maimed and could not fight or was past the age of fighting (the age of sixty), and both were allowable excuses. This duel was a violent and often mortal form of proof. If the combatants broke their weapons, they still had to go on fighting with hands, fists, nails, teeth, feet, and legs. Not surprisingly, men frequently withdrew accusations or sought permission to compromise their differences rather than endure such an experience.

Such a combat could be of two types: duel of law and the treason-duel of chivalry.* These two differed in the following ways:

Duel of Law:

1. Gloves were handed to the judge before being exchanged;
2. It could take place before any judge;
3. It began as a counterplea to perjury, and the defendant refuted the charge, waged his battle first, swore first;
4. The form of oath differed considerably;
5. It was not fought on horseback or in armor* of mail*
6. The weapon used always was a baton* and never a sword* or a spear*;
7. Usual positions of champions in this "writ of right"* were north and south;

8. Judge had no real authority to stop this duel of law, for the battle itself was the real judge; this was the direct tradition of 13th-century English law.

Treason-Duel of Chivalry:

1. Glove or gauntlet* was cast down;
2. Duel was fought only before the king,* the constable,* or the marshal*;
3. Appellant (accuser) waged* first, swore first, and was first on the field;
4. Form of the oaths differed considerably;
5. Always fought on horseback and in mail;
6. Always used sword and spear;
7. Invariable positions of duellists were east and west;
8. Frequently stopped and an arbitrary judgment delivered by the king.

King Philip* IV, the Fair, of France issued an edict in 1306 which allowed for strict rules to be followed in a case to be tried by combat:

1. The homicide, treason, or other serious crime must be notorious and certain;
2. The crime must be capital, not merely larceny;
3. The combat must be the only means of obtaining conviction and punishment*;
4. The accused must be notoriously suspected of the deed.

Once those four requirements were met, then other stipulations followed. A specific charge was necessary and the appellants (accusers) were to guard against saying about the accused anything villainous which did not bear on that particular quarrel. Once the appeal (accusation) was made, the accuser threw down his glove for a gage.* When the challenge was accepted, the glove was picked up by the defendant. Then pledges were found to ensure appearance of both parties in the lists* on the appointed day and hour set for the fight under pain of recreance,* and being vanquished.

With his visor raised and his arms carried in front of him, the accuser rode into the lists first on the appointed day. Then his opponent entered. Both men were advised to cross themselves, or to carry a cross* or banner* depicting Jesus, Mary, an angel, or a saint. In due course, the herald* signalled the crowd to be silent and keep order; he cautioned them not to bear sword or dagger into the stands or to enter the lists on horseback, but under threat of heavy penalty to sit and keep still. Then he summoned the combatants to enter the lists through separate gateways, crossing themselves as they did so, and to be escorted to their pavilions*: the accuser to the judge's right, the defendant to his left.

Then came the triple oaths. First the accuser approached the crucifix in front of the judge and kneeling, swore on the cross that his accusation was true, that his quarrel was holy and just, and ended by invoking the aid of God, Mary, and St. George. The accused knight then did likewise. Each then with his hands on the crucifix swore a second oath renouncing the joys of Paradise for the pains of Hell that upon his soul and honor* the quarrel was just, and again ended the oath with an appeal to God as his true judge, and the Virgin Mary and St. George. At that same time, each swore that he carried neither on his own person nor on his horse* any words, stones, herbs, charms, or conjurations of devils whereby he hoped for aid and that he placed his sole reliance on the justice of his cause, his body, his horse, and his arms; then he kissed the cross. Their third oaths were sworn while holding each other by their right hands. Each then called upon God, Mary, and St. George to witness the justice* of his cause. They kissed the crucifix once more, and thus, thrice sworn, returned to their pavilions as the cross was removed from the lists; to God and St. George their cause thus stood committed.

Three times the herald then cried, *"Faites vos devoirs"* (Fr. "Make ready"), and the knights prepared to mount. When both were firmly mounted, the marshal as master of ceremonies rode to the center of the lists carrying the glove which earlier had been the gage of battle. Three times he cried, *"Laissez les aller!"* (Fr. "Let them go!"), and then he flung down the glove as the signal to start. Both armored knights spurred their steeds, levelled their lances,* and began the fight. Splintered lances were followed by hand-to-hand battle on foot with sword and dagger. Finally, one lay bleeding; thrice he had invoked the aid of God, Mary, and St. George but in vain, for by his defeat he was a vanquished traitor and perjurer. See court of chivalry. (Bibliog. 121, 195, 229)

duke, highest order and rank of the English peerage (see peer) next to the princes* and princesses of the blood royal and the two archbishops of England. Originally the title came from the late Roman Empire, where it signified a military commander. The title of duke was introduced into England when, by charter* dated March 17, 1337, lordships, castles,* and lands were consolidated by King Edward III into the duchy* of Cornwall and were conferred upon his eldest son, Prince Edward of Woodstock, the Black Prince, making him duke of Cornwall. For more than two centuries, the ducal title was reserved primarily for those who were sons of the king* or his kinfolk, near or distant by blood or marriage.

England's second duke was Sir Henry of Grosmont, a knight of the Order of the Garter,* earl* of Lancaster, Derby, and Lincoln; he was of the blood, a crusader, a renowned warrior who repeatedly and successfully had fought for England in tournaments* at home and abroad, and was hereditary leader of an influential political faction; as he had no children, his dukedom became extinct at his death in 1361. Subsequent dukes were created by King Edward III. Lionel of Antwerp, earl of Ulster and second son of the king, became duke of Clarence on November 13, 1362, but his title also became extinct with his death in 1368. Then John of Gaunt, earl of Lancaster and Richmond and third son of the king, became duke of Lancaster on November 13, 1362; and his title merged with the crown when his son and heir became Henry IV in 1399. Richard of Bordeaux, son of the first duke of Cornwall, Edward the Black Prince, became the second duke of Cornwall on November 20, 1362, and his title merged with the crown when he became King Richard II on the death of his grandfather, Edward III.

Both Thomas of Woodstock and Edmund of Langley, uncles of Richard II, became dukes of Gloucester and of York, respectively, in 1385; and in the following year, Robert de Vere, ninth earl of Oxford, became duke of Ireland. Thirteen years later, the king created five new dukes: Edward of York, the king's cousin, became duke of Aumale; his half-brother, John Holand, became duke of Exeter; another cousin, Henry of Bolingbroke, son of John of Gaunt, became duke of Hereford; Thomas Mowbray, earl of Nottingham, became duke of Norfolk; and Thomas Holand, earl of Kent and half-nephew of the king, became duke of Surrey.

Although seemingly honorary titles, these men also commanded troops, and their special pay revealed the original military significance of the title: thirteen shillings fourpence* (one mark*) per day for a duke and one-half mark to eight shillings for an earl; bannerets* received four shillings a day; knights, two shillings per day.

In German territory, the duke (herzog; see titles of dignity) was regarded as the head of a people rather than the mere administrator of a provincial area, and the aristocracy* of the duchy frequently claimed the right to elect him; while drawing his power from his own honours,* the duke remained the supreme head of a much larger territory than that controlled by a French duke. In France, dukes, marquises,* and archcounts soon came to exercise real power only over the counties* which belonged to them personally or were held by them in fee. In Venice, the word for duke was doge. (Bibliog. 75)

dungeon, tower or keep* of a castle*; this English word derived from Latin *dominium*, which meant lordship, through French *donjon*; it came to refer mainly to the lower portions of the keep in which the lord kept his prisoners.

Durendal, sword given by Charlemagne to his nephew Roland* in the *chansons de geste*; its hilt was reputed to contain a tooth of St. Peter, blood of St. Basil, hairs of St. Denis,* and a bit of cloth worn by St. Mary. It was forged by Weyland and given to Charlemagne by Malakin d'Ivon as ransom* for his son Abraham. Charles subsequently gave it to Roland in the valley of the Maurienne the day on which God told Charles through an angel to present it to the best of his leaders. It was carried by Roland in his adventures for his emperor* (in *Roland*):

> With this I won him [Charles] Anjou and all Brittany,
> With this I won him Poitou and conquered Maine;
> With this I won him Normandy's fair terrain,
> And with it won Provence and Aquitaine,
> And Lombardy and all the land Roman,
> Bavaria, too, and the whole Flemish state,
> And Burgundy and all Apulia gained;
> Constantinople in the king's hand I laid; . . .
> With this I won Scotland, [Ireland and Wales]

And England where he set up his domain;
What lands and countries I've conquered by its aid
For Charles (vv. 2322–2334)

(Bibliog. 40)

dusty-feet. See piepowder court.

Dutch hood, head covering used to mask a hawk until she was ready to be flown (see hawking). Three pieces of leather were joined to form the body and two eye pieces so that no light would get through. It had a tuft of feathers fixed to the center of the crown of the hood, useful for steadying and holding the hood while it was being put on the bird. (Bibliog. 26)

E

eagle, king of birds that appeared as an heraldic charge* only on two or three "coats of arms"* during the reign of King Henry III (1216–1272); a century later, however, that number had grown to over forty. When an eagle's talons and beak differed in tincture (see colors) from the rest of its body, the eagle was said to be armed of them in whatever tincture was named. If the bird stood on the ground with folded wings, it was closed or trussed*; if he were atop some object, he was perched; if he was about to fly, he was rising or roussant. When poised in flight, his wings were:

1. displayed and inverted, that is, wings spread but with tips pointing down;
2. displayed and elevated, that is, wings spread and pointed upward;
3. elevated and addorsed, that is, wings raised but back to back with each other;
4. addorsed and inverted, that is, wings back to back but with their points down.

Once in flight, either he was soaring, that is, flying upward, or he was volant,* that is, flying horizontally; when the body was displayed affronty* with its wings and legs spread out to each side and its head turned generally to the dexter,* it was said to be displayed;* when the wings were displayed but the tips pointed downward, they were blazoned* as inverted. (Bibliog. 43)

ealdorman. See earl.

earl, holder of office under the early Anglo-Saxon crown. Some of the early earls (a word equivalent to the Scandinavian word *ealdorman*) may have belonged by birth to the ancient Germanic nobility* from which the kings* where chosen and may have been descendants of minor royal houses, but by the late 9th century earls had become men of power by reason of relationship to a higher authority and not by birth. This term frequently was used as an Anglo-Saxon translation of several Latin words: *optimas, patricius, princeps, subregulus, tribunus,* but always in the sense of a royal servant. Even though they were military leaders in command of the fyrd* or provincial governors with judicial powers or royal counsellors, earls always were officials and subordinate to the crown.

When King Alfred (A.D. 849–899) and his son, Edward the Elder, divided the country into shires,* the term ealdorman changed from anyone holding high office under the king to the chief lay officer of the shire with both military and civil functions: he commanded the fyrd of the shire; he headed its judicial system; with the bishop he presided over the shire court* which met twice yearly to ensure compliance with both ecclesiastical and secular law. For his judicial duties of calling special assemblies of notables of the shire and of resolving appeals* for redress of grievances, he was allowed one-third of the judicial profits and one-third of the revenues of certain boroughs* under his control; this was the famous "third penny."* He obtained additional revenues from some of the estates in his ealdormanry.

Alfred placed one ealdorman in each shire except those of Kent, which had two. This number gradually was reduced until under Athelstan (924–939) it reached only six, which his successor raised to eight. As these numbers decreased, each ealdorman found his responsibilities increasing so rapidly that he could not pay personal attention to shire business. Thus he appointed a deputy to preside at meetings of the shire court. Known first as the *gerefa*, or king's reeve,* this official soon became known as the *scirgerefa*, the shire-reeve; this in turn became better known as the sheriff.*

Under the Danish kings in the 11th century, the ealdorman's name changed to earl, from the Scandinavian *jarl*, and their numbers decreased even more. King Canute (Cnut) divided England into four parts: he kept Wessex, gave East Anglia to Thurkill, Mercia to Eadric, and Northumberland to Eric. As these were royal appointees, the king's authority over them never was questioned. In 1055 when Siward, earl of Northumbria, died, King Edward the Confessor ignored the hereditary claims of Siward's son Waltheof and placed Tostig, brother of Earl Harold Godwineson, in the position. Ten years later when the people of Northumbria deposed Tostig and replaced him with Morcar, brother of the earl of Mercia, they were careful first to obtain King Edward's approval. At one time or other, the sons of Earl Godwine held five earldoms: Sweyn, Harold, Tostig, Gyrth, and Leofwine. Some of these earldoms up to the time of the Conquest were regroupings of counties,* temporarily arranged for some royal expedient.

Earl served as the highest title and rank of English nobles between the Conquest and 1337, when Edward III supplanted it with duke* by creating the Black Prince as duke of Cornwall. The word earldom, however, still meant an office, contrasted with the word barony* which meant a tenure*; neither word conveyed a specific sense of honor.* So long as Norman French continued to be spoken in England, the English earls were styled as counts* or *comites* both in England and on the continent. Each of these earls or *comites* actually was an officer of the crown, having supreme authority in his own earldom or "county"; each derived from his earldom his fixed revenue, the possession of which was an apanage* of his official dignity as an earl, and as evidence of his lawful and recognized title to it.

William* I used these earls for the definite purposes of defending certain English territories against incursions from Wales, Scotland, and from across the Channel; all his earls were palatinate* or semi-palatinate. He created three earls;

Henry I created only two. When Stephen* came to the throne in 1135, there were but seven; however, by 1142 that number was increased to twenty-two: Stephen created nine; his opponent for the throne, Matilda, created six. In so doing, however, neither lowered the dignity of the rank, for both felt that such dignity must continue to be reserved for the highest in the land—for men whose personal distinction, territorial position, and signal services had earned for themselves a place in this exclusive society. These new earls were chosen from the most aristocratic Anglo-Norman baronial houses. (Bibliog. 262, 267, 360)

earl marshal, officer subordinate to the constable,* although they acted and sat together on the military Court of Arms and Honors which came to be known as the Earl Marshal's Court. The earl marshal represented the master marshal of the royal household under the later Norman kings* just as the lord great chamberlain* represented the master chamberlain. Probably there was one under the early Norman kings, but he was not particularly important. Even as late as 1135, the master marshal was an officer only of the third rank, for he received only two shillings (see coinage; money) per day if he ate *extra domum* or fourteen pence* a day if he ate *intra domum*, at a time when officers of the first rank were paid five shillings or three shillings six pence for meals. (See marshal.)

The constable always was listed first in documents naming them jointly; at coronations,* the constable ranked on the right and the earl marshal on the left of the sovereign. A chief marshal appeared as early as the reign of Henry I when a John, son of Gilbert, established his claim to the office. From it he took the name of Marshal,* a name also taken by his descendants. His most famous descendant was "William Marshal,"* earl of Pembroke in right of his wife, as well as earl marshal of England. On the extinction of this William's male issue, the king gave the marshal's rod to the eldest co-heir of the line, who brought the office to the Bigod family, earls of Norfolk. (Bibliog. 75)

ecu. See coinage.

edelinge. See nobility.

egrentyne, heraldic monster* with a dragon* head, long body, cloven hooves on its forefeet, webbed feet on its hind feet, a long hair tail, and considerable evidence of its masculine gender. (Bibliog. 43)

Eleanor of Aquitaine, wife of two kings and mother of two kings, she was the daughter of William X of Aquitaine, and grew up in the south of France. Born in 1122, when she married Louis VII of France at age 15 and became queen of France, she brought to him control of the vast area of the Aquitaine. After fifteen years of unhappy marriage, including a journey to the Holy Land with her husband on the second crusade,* Eleanor succeeded in having her marriage annulled in 1152. She returned to her court in Poitiers where she married Henry* of Anjou, heir to the English throne, and carried control of the Aquitaine to him, giving him control over a vast territory that stretched from the Pyrenees mountains in the south to the border of Scotland. She bore him eight children, two of whom became kings of England: Richard I,* and John.* At her court at Poitiers, she patronized poets and artists. On her death in 1204, the Angevin empire established by her husband began to disintegrate, for none of her descendants were strong enough to maintain it. (Bibliog. 139, 224, 235)

electors. See titles of dignity.

electrum, metal alloy compounded of gold and silver. Early coins of cities on the western coast of Asia Minor were made of this compound: three parts gold and one part silver, but gradually the percentage of silver increased. (Bibliog. 100)

electuary, lectuary, medicine* composed of powders or other ingredients mixed with honey or syrup to form a pasty concoction. (Bibliog. 335)

elephant, huge beast of the Far Indies and Africa which lived for 300 years. According to Isidore of Seville, elephants resembled huge oxen with ivory teeth; they carried houses on their backs; their intelligence and memory was strongly developed. Having legs of one piece with no joints, this beast was obliged to sleep standing up, leaning against a tree or wall; if he lay down, he could not arise. This fact helped people in the country inhabited by these beasts, however, for they would weaken the tree against which the elephant used to lean to sleep, and it would fall and be captured. When the time came for mating, these beasts, male and female, came to Paradise from the Orient. There they ate fruit of the mandragora* or mandrake tree. Afterward, the female conceived and would carry her unborn for two years; but for fear of dragons,* she would bear her offspring deep in water while the male stood guard. The odor of burnt elephant bone and hair was an effective repellent for vermin. (Bibliog. 21, 258)

elutropius, emerald veined with blood-red streaks found only in Egypt, Libya, and Cyprus. It was formed in the head of donkeys which were blinded as the stone grew. When placed in a silver basin and covered with water, it would cause the sunlight to turn blood-red, the water would bubble forth, and thunder and lightning would race across the sky. It was a specific against poison and jaundice, and it protected pregnant women. (Bibliog. 258)

ell, measure of length for cloth generally containing forty-five inches* or one and a quarter yards.* Ells contained fifty-four inches in Shropshire, forty-eight inches in Jersey, and thirty-seven and a half inches in Scotland. During the 12th to 14th centuries, the Latin term *ulna** was used amibiguously to refer to both an ell and a yard. (Bibliog. 394)

ematites, stone as black as iron and veined with purple that came from Ethiopia. When drunk in the milk from a woman whose firstborn was a male, it healed all maladies, notably gravel, and was particularly effective against snakebite. (Bibliog. 258)

embattled. See crenellated.

embowed, human arm flexed at the elbow, in heraldry*; frequently it referred to the posture of dolphins* in heraldry. (Bibliog. 43)

embrasure, opening in a wall: either the splay or inner opening of a window, or the openings between the merlons* and the crenels,* the solid pieces of a crenellated* parapet.* (Bibliog. 120)

emeer. See emir.

emerasse. See Order of the Bath.

emir, emeer, Saracen* military commander or independent chieftain. The term originally was an honorary one given to the descendants of Mohammed through his daughter Fatima. (Bibliog. 246)

emperor, imperator, title formerly borne by the sovereigns of the Roman Empire and then by a variety of other potentates. The term *imperator se imperator* seems to have belonged originally to every Roman magistrate who received the *imperium* (the power of the sword* and authority to command in war). It was, therefore, not strictly a title, but rather a descriptive epithet. Toward the end of the Roman Republic, however, it had become a special title of honor bestowed by the acclamations of the victorious army upon their general or by vote of the senate as a reward for distinguished services. Julius Caesar, however, assumed it under a vote of the senate in a different sense; he used it as a permanent title or rather as part of his name denoting the absolute military power which had come into his hands.

On the revival of the Roman Empire in the West by Charlemagne in 800, the title was taken by him and by his Frankish, Italian, and Germanic successors, as heads of the Holy Roman Empire.* The doctrine grew up about the time of Emperor Henry II (1002–1024) that although the emperor* was chosen in Germany—at first by the nation and then by a small body of electors—and entitled from the moment of his election to be crowned in Rome by the pope, he could not use the title of emperor until the coronation* had taken place. The German sovereign, though he exercised full imperial powers both in Germany and Italy as soon as he was chosen, called himself merely the king* of the Romans until he received the sacred crown* of the emperor in Rome. (Bibliog. 100)

empire, either the territories governed by a person bearing the title of emperor*
or, more generally, any extensive dominion. The territorial extent of the Romano-
Germanic empire (Holy Roman Empire*) varied greatly in different periods of
history. In the time of Charlemagne it included the northern half of Italy (except
the district around Venice), Gaul, western and southern Germany, and Spain
between the Pyrenees and the Ebro River. Under Otto the Great and his first
successors, it extended over the whole of Germany (including Holland and
Belgium), Burgundy, and had claims over the adjacent territories of the kingdoms
of Hungary, Poland, and Denmark.

The government of the Holy Roman Empire never was an absolute monarchy
in the sense that the Eastern Empire at Constantinople had been. Down to the
end of the Hohenstaufen line in 1254, it was a strong feudal monarchy in which
the sovereign enjoyed huge but limited powers. For example, he was obliged to
respect the rights of his vassals* and could obtain supplies and pass laws only
with the consent of the Diet, or supreme national assembly. From the time when
Rudolf of Hapsburg ascended the throne in 1272, its strength, which had been
broken in a long struggle against the pope and the Italian republics, was considerably lessened; its revenues had shrunk, and its greater nobles had become
practically independent princes* who not only were sovereign in their own
territories but sometimes were stronger than the emperor.

The imperial crown always was elective, at least in theory, but elective in the
sense that it required the consent of the nobles and people, and later of the nobles
alone, to elevate a sovereign to the throne. It became almost hereditary, that is,
the son or other near relative of the sovereign would be chosen to succeed him.
Partly owing to the extinction of several families in succession who had held
the throne, and partly to the influence of the pope and the idea that the imperial
office was more sacred than regal, the elective came to prevail over the hereditary
principle. From the 13th century onward, the Romano-Germanic throne was in
the hands of a small electoral college consisting of seven, then eight, and finally
nine princes. (Bibliog. 100)

emprise, adventure, undertaking, enterprise of a knight-errant.* Derived from
the word for device,* this referred to the actions of a young knight sometimes
for six months or even a year. While so involved, he would wear on his leg or
arm a bracelet, a chain, a star—whatever gave him a marked individuality.
Sometimes to procure an emprise, a young knight-errant would take up his abode
at the junction of four roads so that he could meet an adventure from any direction.
(Bibliog. 225)

enarmes, straps fastened inside a Norman shield* through which the left forearm
could be passed and rested on a pad to hold the shield in defensive position.
(Bibliog. 27)

enciente (Fr.), wall or fence surrounding a castle* or town and hence referring to the close* of a cathedral, castle, abbey, or town. (Bibliog. 100)

enfance (Fr.), story of a hero's youth from his conception to his early manhood. It detailed his training for knighthood.*

enfeoffed, invested with a fief* or fee*; given in vassalage.

enfield, heraldic monster* with the head, hindquarters, and tail of a fox, the body of a dog, and the claws of an eagle.* (Bibliog. 43)

English language, English tongue, national language of the people of Britain, even though French was the habitual language of the upper classes from the Conquest (1066) to the end of the 14th century. At the time of the Conquest, educated people (the clerics) of both countries could speak and write Latin; the Normans conversed in French and the natives in English. Not much before the beginning of the 14th century did the conquering race adopt the English language to any extent, and the division of the nation into the French-speaking upper class and the English-speaking lower classes began to disappear. A literary language common to all England did not appear until fifty years later with the writings of Geoffrey Chaucer in London. Not until the thirty-eighth year of the reign of King Edward III (1363) was it ordained in Parliament* that men of law, both temporal and church law, from that time onward had to plead in their mother tongue, English. (Bibliog. 150)

Englishry, establishment of the nationality of a dead body as being English rather than Norman. Following the Norman invasion in 1066, the native English used to lie in wait to kill the dreaded Normans in woods or secluded places and then flee. In retaliation, when the Norman kings* and their ministers found that the exquisite forms of torture they inflicted on the English did not stop the murders, they chose a new course of action: Englishry. Whenever a Norman was found slain, if the killer did not show himself or betray himself by flight, then the whole district or hundred* suffered amercement* between thirty-six and forty-four pounds sterling* on behalf of the royal treasury according to the district and the frequency of the murders, in order to secure the safety of wayfarers and to ensure that the men of the area would be induced to hand over the killers or punish the crime themselves. However, if the jury at the inquest could prove that the dead man was English, the hundred was freed from the fine.*

Although this probably was the original reason for establishing inquests in England, there also were sound financial reasons. Unless death had been caused by drowning in the sea, Enlishry had to be presented first at the coroner's* inquest, then at the following county* court,* and finally to the justices in eyre.* Failure to present it three times meant that the men of the neighborhood or hundred would incur the murdrum* fine. Murdrum was the secret death of a man whose slayer was unknown, for the word murdrum signified secret or hidden.

Even though requirements for Englishry varied from county to county, at least one or more relatives of the deceased always were required to appear before the coroner and prove the relationship. Such testimony varied from two paternal and two maternal relatives, to one paternal and one maternal, and even to just one relative on only one side of the family. These witnesses had to testify at all three courts—even though going to all three was expensive. Yet they were fined if they missed any of the hearings. However, if they did nothing, then the entire hundred was fined the murdrum. Remarkably, the number of defaults thus incurred probably meant little to the whole hundred because the individual amounts were relatively small, and the people must have seen the whole idea as little more than an elaborate system of further taxation. Therefore, even by presenting Englishry, the kinsmen would not have reduced the total amount of the fine appreciably but only would have inconvenienced and impoverished themselves.

In 1249 Englishry had been required by the testimony of three—namely, by two on the father's side and one on the mother's side. But a century later, by statute in 1340, Englishry had been abolished after the cessation of the general eyre not only made it unprofitable but the war with France made it anachronistic. (Bibliog. 104, 171)

engrail, in heraldry,* small semi-circular indentations cut into the edge of a border, bend,* or fesse* with the teeth or points extending outward into the field.* If the teeth turned inward, the term was "invected."* (Bibliog. 230)

enhanced, ordinary* when raised on an heraldic field* above its normal position. (Bibliog. 43)

enquiller. See aquiller.

enseame, to purge a hawk of superfluous fat and so to render it fit for flying. See hawking. (Bibliog. 26)

ensign, correct term for the armorial bearings (see charge) of a kingdom, an office, or a community. (Bibliog. 43)

entertainment, during dinner or even during routine days, entertainment included music, stories, jokes. Even though many households had their resident harpers and minstrels,* when a meal was over a guest might entertain with a song he had composed or had heard, accompanying himself by a vielle,* lute, or harp.* See scald. (Bibliog. 129)

eorl. See nobility.

epaulieres, overlapping lames of steel affixed to a larger plate covering the shoulders which were replaced in the 15th century by pauldrons.* (Bibliog. 9)

Epée aus Estranges Renges, sword* of David which Saleman placed on Solomon's ship and was the sword used for the Dolorous Stroke* (see Joyeuse Garde) which was destined to come into Galahad's possession. Its original hangings of hemp were replaced by Perceval's sister with hangings she had woven from her own hair. (Bibliog. 373)

eqitatio. See feudal levy.

erased, parts of living creatures rudely severed from their bodies and torn off roughly in blazon* to leave a jagged edge. (Bibliog. 43)

erbarmde (Ger.), chivalric-courtly virtue of mercy, drawn from Christian teaching.

ere (Ger.), chivalric honor. (Bibliog. 274)

ermine, heraldic device* consisting of black* ermine tails on a white* field.* (Bibliog. 43)

ermines, heraldic device* which was the reverse of ermine,* consisting of white* tails on black.* (Bibliog. 43)

erminois, heraldic device* consisting of black* ermine* spots on a gold* field.* (Bibliog. 43)

erw, standard acre* of land in Wales equal to 4,320 square yards.* See stang. (Bibliog. 394)

escalade, method of attack by sneaking into a besieged castle* by silently scaling with ladders the castle wall at an inadequately guarded point. Bohemund d'Hauteville captured Antioch (see crusades) by escalade using a bribe and a ruse. Corrupting one of the emirs* who commanded three towers by promising wealth, honor, and baptism, Bohemund had his own Frankish army feign withdrawal. That night, however, they returned stealthily, scaled the walls in the sector of the bribed emir, killed the resisting guards, and opened the city gates. (Bibliog. 129)

escallop, scallop shell used as heraldic charge,* normally showing the back of the shell with the point in chief.* As this was the badge* worn by pilgrims, it was often used in heraldry* to indicate that an ancestor had gone on a crusade.* (Bibliog. 43)

escarbuncle, heraldic charge* consisting of eight ornamental spokes, usually ending in a "fleur de lis,"* that radiated from a center boss.* (Bibliog. 43).

escheat, feudal incident whereby a fief* reverted to the lord or a tenant died without leaving a successor qualified to inherit under the original grant. When a tenant-in-chief* died, his land reverted to the king* until his heir proved his "age of majority,"* paid his relief,* and presented himself to do homage.* Sometimes the land was held longer by the king until the minor came of age, in which case the king would enjoy the wardship* and marriage* of the heir. If there was no heir at all, the estate would be absorbed permanently into the royal demesne* or until the king granted it to a new recipient. Sometimes it reverted to the king through forfeiture for treason. (Bibliog. 163)

escheator, shire* official who supervised the administration of land and appurtenances which had fallen into the king's hands by escheat* because no male heir was available, or through permanent or temporary forfeiture. The escheator took such lands into the royal administration, keeping them indefinitely or temporarily, and accounting for the materials and produce issued from them until he was instructed to release them to a new recipient—be he the original holder who had come of age or some new assignee. See feodary. (Bibliog. 163)

escutcheon, 1. shield* on which armorial bearings (see charge) were displayed; 2. shields used on a tomb which displayed arms* of the deceased; 3. ornamental plates from the center of which door rings and knockers were suspended. (Bibliog. 43, 100)

escutcheon of pretense, small shield* containing the arms* of an heraldic heiress which was placed in the center of her husband's arms in their marital achievement.* (Bibliog. 43)

escuyer. See esquire.

espadon, two-handed sword* used by footsoldiers. (Bibliog. 225)

espondes. See bed.

espringal, military engine or catapult* used for throwing stones, bolts, or other missiles. (Bibliog. 9)

esquire (L. *armiger*; Fr. *escuyer*), knight's attendant or shield* bearer, who ranked in one of five classes: 1. younger sons of peers* and their eldest sons; 2. eldest sons of knights and their eldest sons; 3. chiefs of ancient families who were esquires by prescription; 4. esquires by creation or office and allowed to wear a "collar of SS"*; 5. esquires of the knights of the Order of the Bath*;

each knight was appointed two esquires to attend upon him at his installation and at coronations.* See also knighthood. (Bibliog. 43, 116)

essoin, excuses for non-appearance in a court* of law at the appointed time granted for pilgrimage, king's service, illness, and so forth. Because serving on a jury was one of the many administrative obligations imposed on a knight, he could excuse (essoin) himself on the grounds of illness only if he were confined to bed by sickness (L. *essoin de malo lecti*), a condition which had to be verified by the visit of four knights who later testified in court as to the genuineness of his ailment. See jury duty. (Bibliog. 264)

essoin de malo lecti. See essoin.

estivals, metal coverings or casings for the legs of a war horse.* These were used only rarely, for basically they hindered the horse more than they helped protect it. See horse armor. (Bibliog. 9)

estoc, stabbing sword* with a long narrow blade designed for thrusting. (Bibliog. 9)

estoile, heraldic star with six points depicted as a charge* with wavy lines like a starfish arms. (Bibliog. 43)

ewerer, king's* servant who dried the king's clothes and prepared his bath under the supervision of the king's chamberlain.* (Bibliog. 14)

exact, to demand, require, enforce payment of fees, money, penalties; to require a person to appear in court* to answer a charge levied against him. (Bibliog. 163)

exactions, public demands made at four successive county* courts* that the person named in the action appear and surrender to justice.* (Bibliog. 171)

examen pedale. See ordeal of red-hot iron.

Excaliber, King Arthur's sword.* Called Caliburn* by Geoffrey of Monmouth and Caledfwlch* in the mabinogi,* this was the sword Arthur drew from the stone to establish his claim to the throne; its name was reputed to mean "cut steel." It had a varied romance* history. Arthur presented it to Gawain when he knighted him (in *Vulgate Merlin*); it was lent by Arthur to Meliadus (in *Guiron le Cortoise*) and by Gawain to Lancelot (in *Galehaut*). Morgan le Fee stole it for her lover, Accalon, but Arthur recovered it. Finally, as he lay dying, Arthur instructed Bedevere to throw it into a lake, at which time a hand mysteriously emerged from the water to grasp it in mid-air, twirl it, and then submerge with it. Historically, it was reputed to have been found in 1182 when Arthur's tomb at Glastonbury was exhumed by order of Henry II and last was heard of when Richard I* presented it to Tancred of Sicily on March 6, 1191, as a gesture of appreciation for his support. (Bibliog. 311, 373)

Exchequer, center for the administration of finances in Anglo-Norman England and Norman Sicily. Its origins lay in the practice of using a checkered table or board on which money* due the ruler would be placed by peasants (see villein), barons,* sheriffs* alike and counted. Such a board was called an "exchequer," but the term also applied to the court* which sat with the Exchequer. As a court, it had an Upper and a Lower Exchequer. In the lower court, money was counted at a table and recorded in writing as well as notched on tallies* so that later at the Upper Exchequer, an account could be rendered. In the lower chamber, one knight conducted the assays,* one was the melter or fusor,* one was the clerk of the treasurer* with his seal, two were knights of the chamberlains,* one was the silverer or argentarius,* and finally, four were tellers or computatores who actually counted the money.

Seated in the middle of the broad side of the Exchequer table was the chief officer, the justiciar.* On his left sat the chancellor,* the constable,* two chamberlains (the nearest being the older), and then a knight called the marshal.* To his right sat the bishop of Winchester by authority of his office under the constitution by which he was to give careful attention to the writing on the Pipe Roll.* Then came the treasurer to watch all and to account for the transactions; then the scribe of the roll of the Treasury, a second clerk, the scribe of the roll of the Chancery,* a clerk of the chancellor who checked to see that his roll corresponded with all the other rolls, and finally at the end of the bench sat a clerk of the constable. On the long side of the table sat the head clerk or other servant of the chamberlain with the "recauta."* Next to him, almost in the middle, was a man who recorded the amounts by placing the counters in their appropriate locations, and finally at the end of the bench sat the clerk who presided over the writing office. On the fourth bench sat a man chosen by the king* to keep his own account of the secrets and laws of the realm and the sheriff and his clerks who sat to render account with the tallies.

The table around which these people sat and on which the money was counted was quadrangular, about ten feet* long by five feet wide, and had a raised edge four fingers high running around its edge. It was covered with a dark, russet-colored cloth marked with chalk into squares and columns about a foot apart; in these spaces counters were placed. Each column on the table represented tens, hundreds, or thousands; a large pile of counters resembling gambling chips was stacked at the teller's right hand. These counters were unusual coins which had reached the Exchequer from foreign merchants: golden bezants* from Byzantium, Roman solidi (see sol), silver or bronze oboli (see obol) from Greece; all were used as counters instead of pennies* (the only English coin minted at the time) because their unusual size made them easily visible not only to all who sat around the table but also to the clerks who stood or sat in the background.

These tellers were to count newly minted money which had been sent to the Exchequer. One teller carefully mixed together the entire amount to be counted, the heavier with lighter coins. Then the chamberlain weighed as much as needed to balance a pound weight of the Exchequer. If the number of coins exceeded by more than six pence in the pound the twenty shillings in weight (a pound was calculated to contain 240 pence), then the coins were considered unfit to be received; if the excess was limited to six pence or less, then the money was carefully counted by the tellers, placed in wooden bowls at one hundred shillings at a time, lest there be an error in counting, and then put into the boxes. If any bowl was found to contain less than the required amount, its contents were dumped back into the pile of coins waiting to be counted.

When the money had been counted and placed in boxes containing one hundred pounds each, the clerk of the Treasury affixed his seal and recorded in writing on the Receipt Roll of the Exchequer the amount received, from whom, and for what reason. He also noted the amount on the tallies made by the chamberlains for a receipt* of the money and placed his seal on the chests and boxes which also held the rolls and the tallies. Knights served as assistants to the chamberlains and carried the keys of the chests. Each chest had two locks of different pattern, neither of which the key of the other would fit, and each was fastened by a fixed strap, on top of which, when the locks were closed, the seal of the treasurer was placed so that neither chamberlain nor assistant could have access except by joint consent. These chamberlains also made the tallies for receipts. The chamberlains in common with the treasurer also had the duty of disbursing the money received, either by order of the king's writ or at command of the justices of the Exchequer, but only after consultation with their superiors. These three officials (two chamberlains and the treasurer's clerk) accompanied the treasure when it was sent for.

If the coins to be tested were an account of the farm,* forty-four shillings were gathered from the pile and placed into a separate purse. On this the sheriff placed his mark so that the assay test commonly could be made of them afterward. Then the clerks of the treasurer and of the chamberlains put aside from the money received some lumps of tested silver, and the pence paid to the farm* in separate piles. Certain marks were then affixed on the bags containing them so that if the king desired silver vessels to be made for the service of the house of God, or for use in his own palace, or perhaps for money to be used overseas, they would be taken from that source.

The calculator, later the marshal, sat in the middle of his side of the table to be visible to all and to keep his working hand free. In the right-hand lower space of the table he kept a pile of pennies from eleven down; in the second space, a pile of shillings from nineteen down; and in the third space, pounds placed opposite and directly facing him. The fourth space held a pile of scores, the fifth a pile of hundreds, the sixth a pile of thousands, and the seventh a pile of ten-thousands—used only for receipts of the whole realm. Then he put a silver obol in place of each ten shillings and a gold obol in place of ten pounds.

The clerk who presided over the writing office was charged with providing suitable scribes for the roll of the Chancery, for the king's writs which were drawn up in the Exchequer, and for the proper writing and execution of summons. The knight silverer carried the purse of silver to be tested from the Lower Exchequer to the Upper Exchequer, and when he delivered it, removed the seal of the sheriff from it, shook onto the Exchequer table for all to see the forty-four shillings which he previously had marked when taken from the pile of coins. Mixing them all together, he put on one scale a one-pound weight and on the other as many coins as needed to balance. Then he counted to see if the proper number of coins made one pound. Whatever the weight was, he placed in a cup by itself twenty shillings to be tested and replaced in the purse the remaining twenty-four shillings; the melter then was paid two pence from the sheriff's money for his efforts. Then two other sheriffs were chosen by the justiciar, or the treasurer in his absence, to accompany to the melter the knight silverer and the sheriff whose money was to be tested in the fire of the assay. There again the coins carefully were counted in the presence of the melter and the representatives of the barons, and handed to the melter for the assay.

Taking the coins from the knight silverer, the melter counted them and arranged them in a bowl of burnt cinders in the furnace where they were reduced to a lump, melting and purifying the silver, making sure that the silver was not damaged but was thoroughly refined. When the test piece had been made, the silverer carried it to the barons, accompanied by the others who had witnessed the entire procedure, and then weighed it in the sight of all against a one-pound weight. Then he balanced the scale by replacing what the fire had consumed by adding coins out of the purse until the test piece balanced against the pound weight. This test piece then was marked with chalk, identifying its source, and noting that the pound had "lost in the fire so many pence"; then it was marked "assay." If the sheriff whose assay it was should challenge that too much was lost by melting or by heating, or if the melter admitted that the test failed, another twenty shillings were to be taken from the purse in the presence of the barons and the test repeated. According to the amount of money lost in the fire, the sheriff would know how much to subtract from every other pound. For example, if the test was twelve pence short, that is, five percent, he knew that only ninety-five pounds would be credited to him for the one hundred pounds he had brought in. Thus the amount lost in burning was subtracted from the sheriff's tally and was recorded on a separate tally "of combustion" that the "farm" of the sheriff was "blanched" (see blanching of farm rent).

Presiding in the Upper Exchequer sat the chief justiciar of the king, next in rank to the king by virtue of his judicial status, together with the greater magnates (see peer) of the realm who shared the king's innermost secrets. They sat there to interpret the law and to decide disputed points which arose from incidental questions. The chief officer of this Upper Exchequer could authorize a writ withdrawing any amount from the treasury. Additional members of this upper group included the chancellor, who represented the equitable power of the *curia regis** in the Exchequer. Nominally, he was the custodian of the great seal. The seal was locked in the Treasury by the treasurer for safekeeping and was brought out only by the treasurer or chamberlain when needed. Then it was returned to its case, sealed by the chancellor, and returned to the Treasury for safety. Each time it was brought forth, it was kept in its sealed case so all there could see that the seal was unbroken. Furthermore, the chancellor checked the accuracy of the treasurer's records in comparison to his own receipts; he had a scribe who copied the great roll, word for word, from the treasurer's clerk to form this autograph called the chancellor's roll, and he had a clerk who double-checked it to ensure additional accuracy. The constable was also a member. With his clerk, he paid stipends out of the receipts of the Exchequer to royal officers and other claimants after duly investigating their claims; he attested to writs along with the justiciar. The marshal kept writs and the returned tallies of the sheriffs' creditors in bundles for each county*; he took charge of offenders committed to custody for contempt of the court; he took accountants' oaths and paid salaries and allowances to the Exchequer officials. The chamberlain's sergeant* made the tallies.

The treasurer was the most important member, for he had to superintend every debt, receive accounts of the sheriffs, and take particular care of the matter and composition of the great roll written by his clerk on specially selected sheepskin. Each roll was made of two large membrances that had lines ruled on them and top-to-bottom headings; entries were made at regular intervals according to established form and order. No erasures were allowed for clerical error, but interlineations were used instead. Sheepskins were used because they were the most difficult to erase and therefore to change. His responsibility for the roll prevented him from leaving while the Exchequer was sitting; additionally, he had to dictate the words for his roll from which all other rolls were copied. So great was the power of his roll that no one was allowed to dispute or alter it unless the error was glaringly manifest to all, and then any changes could be made only with the common consent of the barons in their actual presence. The treasurer had an usher who watched all who entered the Exchequer and guarded everything carefully. He received two pence for each person he allowed in; he provided boxes for the money, the rolls, and the tallies. He furnished the Receipt office with wood suitable for tallies of receipt and account, and at Michaelmas (see Appendix A) each year, he received five shillings for wood for the year's tallies. He also provided, at the expense of the Treasury, the wooden bowls, knives, purses, straps, and other small necessaries for its operation.

Additional officers of the Exchequer were the remembrancer, a position established in the reign of Henry II. Before this appointment, barons used to reserve certain points of daily practice for consideration until the audit had been closed; these "memoranda," as they were called, were entered on a separate roll. In time, these grew as revenues of the kingdom grew, and they became more difficult to collect. Thus Henry appointed the new officer, the remembrancer, to keep this Memoranda Roll, to issue processes for recovery of the king's debts recorded thereon, and to act as a solicitor for the Treasury.

Salaries for the Exchequer personnel ranged widely:

Clerk of the treasurer (Lower Exchequer)—5d per day

Scribe of the treasurer (Upper Exchequer)—5d per day

Scribe of the chancellor—5d per day

Two knights who bore the keys—8d per day

Knight silverer—12d per day

Melter—5d per day

Usher of Exchequer—5d per day

Four tellers—3d per day when in London; 2d when in Winchester

Watchman—1d plus 1/2d for lights when guarding the treasure at night.

(Bibliog. 102, 144)

exchequer fashion, method of constructing a roll (or official document) by placing the parchment members on top of each other and sewing them together at one end, usually the head; then they were rolled up. See chancery fashion. (Bibliog. 171).

excommunication, depriving an individual of access to his religion in any form. Ecclesiastical courts* enforced obedience to their decrees by this means, for it was to spiritual courts what outlawry* was to temporal courts. If the excommunicant did not submit to the court within forty days, the ecclesiastical court notified the crown and a writ *de excommunicato capiendo* was issued to the sheriff.* He arrested the offender and kept him in prison (see jail) until he submitted. When that occurred, the bishop signified it by issuing a writ of *de excommunicato deliberando*.

An excommunicant could not perform any act which was required of any *probus et legis homo*: he could not perform any legal act, so that he could not sue anyone, although he himself could be sued. It was unlawful to speak to, pray with, or eat with an excommunicant either openly or privately. He was a man who had "leprosy of the soul." He could not serve on juries (see jury duty), be a witness in any court, nor bring any action either real or personal to recover lands or money due him; and if he obtained a writ, his excommunication made it invalid. (Bibliog. 156)

exebenius, white stone used by goldsmiths to purify gold. When drunk in wine,* it cured madness in women. (Bibliog. 258)

execution, besides death by hanging, people were executed by various other methods. The customal* of Dover stipulated, for example, that a man sentenced to death was to be led to a cliff called Sharpness, and there, if he had been convicted by the accusations of another man, his accuser executed him; if by the king,* the bailiff* executed him by throwing him from the cliff into the sea. Called *infalistatio*, this was perilous duty when the victim was obstinate, for he could grab his executioner and take them both to their deaths. Sometimes criminals were drowned in tubs or sewn in sacks if they were murderers of parents or relations. In one case of parricide, the offender was sewn in a skin with a dog, a snake, an ape, and a cock.

For execution by drowning, criminals were not thrown from the bank of the river but from a bridge because a long-lasting superstition among nations of classical antiquity was that Pontifex, the Roman bridge builder, also was the name of a priestly order, and hence the execution had priestly sanction. With the Franks, erection of bridges was one of the rights of royalty, and the structure had something of a holy character and stood in near relation to the priesthood. By the 14th century, however, execution by drowning was performed to avoid for the family the ignominy of public execution and usually was carried out at night. Crimes calling for this death penalty, regardless of the gender of the culprit, were murder, bigamy, robbery, sorcery, forgery, cheating at cards or dice. In Bohemia, John Nepomuk, canon of Prague and confessor to the queen, by order of King Wenceslas was thrown from the bridge of that city on April 28, 1383, for not revealing the secrets of the confessional. Five stars were said to have appeared in the water as he fell into it; he was beatified and canonized 350 years later.

In 1200 two women came to Southfleet with clothes they had stolen from Croydon. They were followed there by the owners of the clothes, and being taken and imprisoned, were adjudged by the court* of Southfleet to the "ordeal of red-hot iron."* One offender was acquitted; the other was forthwith drowned in a pond. For the preservation of order within his army, King Richard I* published an edict that he who killed another while the expedition was afloat was to be bound to the corpse and thrown into the sea. If on land, slayer and slain were to be bound together and buried in the same grave. (See law of King Richard about crusaders at sea.) This practice was followed as late as 1422 when, at the siege of Meaux by Henry V, a party of English soldiers was surprised and cut off from the rest of the force. Only one of that party survived by fleeing, and he was caught and condemned by the English to be buried alive with his slain comrades.

Under ancient Danish law, women convicted of theft were condemned to be buried alive, a punishment also known in France. In 1331 Marete Duflos, on suspicion of larceny, was scourged and then subjected to this cruel death at Abbeville. Another woman, Perette Mauger, a notorious thief and receiver of stolen goods, was, by order of the provost of Paris, buried alive in front of the gibbet of the city. This created a great sensation; it was, apparently, resorted to only on occasions when the authorities were desirous of inflicting the extreme penalty with every mark of ignominy. (Bibliog. 4) *exercitus.* See *expeditio.*

exigent, demand put on a person to appear to answer a charge levied against him; repeated failure to appear led to outlawry.* The exigent consisted of public demands made at four successive courts* that the man concerned should appear and surrender to justice.* A person so demanded was said to be "exacted."* This was the most solemn and awesome part of the medieval mesne* process; outlawry was its culmination. The whole process of exigent was concerned solely with the appearance of an appellee or defendant in court and his submission to justice. This could be used only in county* courts where, alone, outlawries could be pronounced. (Bibliog. 4)

exoculation, putting out the eyes in execution of a judicial sentence. William* the Conquerer did not hang felons (see felony); he ordered emasculation and exoculation to serve instead. See also punishments. (Bibliog. 261).

expeditio (L.), service in the king's* feudal host (see knighthood), performed on the occasion of a royal military summons. This word frequently was used interchangably with *exercitus* when referring to such military actions as feudal host, *arrière-ban,** or any kind of military expedition. Often used in Latin works from Anglo-Saxon England, they were used to describe the fyrd* or the obligation to serve in the fyrd. The three obligations that were always referred to in Anglo-Saxon charters* were bridge work, fortress work, and fyrd duty, and these were described in Latin charters of the period as *expeditio et pontis arcisque restauratio* or some variant thereof. A central and dominant obligation of military tenantcy was service described in these words *expeditio* or *exercitus.* He was expected to appear for service properly trained and equipped. Failure to perform such service could result in a forfeiture of the vassal's* chattels or even his lands. See Assize of Arms. (Bibliog. 159)

extent. See rental.

eyass, hawking* term for a nesting place. (Bibliog. 26)

eye on the string, in archery, that part of the bowstring which occupied the upper horn of the bow.* (Bibliog. 100)

eyre, journey. This was the highest commission of itinerant justices. Eyre justices dealt with assizes,* jail* delivery, civil pleas, and crown pleas. When the eyre was imminent, the sheriff* was instructed to summon archbishops, bishops, abbots, priors, earls,* barons,* knights, freeholders, four men, and the reeve* from townships; twelve men from boroughs*; and all others who should attend— at forty days notice to be present to hear and do the king's precepts. The sheriff was to have brought before the appointed justices all crown pleas arising since the last eyre. This court* of the justices itinerant, or justices in eyre, was regularly established, if not first appointed, by the Parliament* of Northampton in 1176, with delegated power from the king's court or *aula regis* (see *curia regis*) because they were looked upon as members thereof. Originally these justices were to make their circuit around the kingdom once every seven years, but in time they were directed to visit every county* at least once every year; however, as the power of the justices of the assize increased, these justices itinerant gradually disappeared. The greatest contribution of the eyre to the administration of justice* lay in the unifying influence exerted over the country at large by commissioners learned in the central courts of justice as they imposed standards of the common law on communities of the shires* in their travels. (Bibliog. 163, 363)

eyrie, eyry, nest or breeding place of hawks. See hawking. (Bibliog. 26)

F

Fabu, Fabur, Saracen* god. (Bibliog. 191)

fabulatores. See jestours.

Fadda, Mohammed's mule. (Bibliog. 308)

faggot, measure for firewood measuring three feet* long and two feet in circumference; it also was a weight for steel, equalling 120 pounds.* (Bibliog. 394)

faites vos devoirs, herald's* cry for the combatants to get ready, uttered three times at the start of a duel* of chivalry.* (Bibliog. 229)

falarica, machine used for throwing fiery darts.* With its shaft wrapped with tow steeped in oil and smeared with sulphur and resin, the dart then was ignited and launched against a *pluteus,* the prototype of the medieval sow* or cat.* (Bibliog. 9)

falchion, fauchon, broad-bladed sword* whose peculiar-shaped blade intended it for thrusting and not cutting; it was a kind of scimitar* described in the *Romance of Richard Coeur de Lion* as "broad and keen." Two varieties existed: one with its convexed-edge and concaved-back blade becoming wider toward the point, and the other with a straight-backed blade. (Bibliog. 44)

falcon, hawking* term referring specifically to the female peregrine but generally for all long-winged birds. (Bibliog. 26)

falcon-gentle, female peregrine falcon.

falconer, a person who cared for the hawks used in hawking.* In France the "grand faulconer" was an officer of great eminence: his annual salary was 4,000 florins,* he was attended by fifty gentlemen* and fifty assistant falconers, he was allowed to keep 300 hawks for his own use, he licensed every vender of hawks in the country, and received a tax on every bird he sold there, even within the verge* of the court.* The king* of France never rode out upon any great occasion of consequence without this officer attending upon him.

King Edward III of England had thirty falconers on horseback with him when he invaded France, and every day of that expedition saw the king out either hawking or hunting.* (Bibliog. 334)

falconer's glove, glove for the left hand, as most European falconers carried their birds on their left hand, reinforced to double thickness over the entire thumb and forefinger and reaching halfway up the forearm.

falconry. See hawking.

falconry birds, 1. long-winged "rameurs" or rowers as they moved their wings in flight. They had a short, wide, strongly-curved beak with a notch or tooth in the upper portion; long slender toes; closed wings which reached almost to the end of a broad, short, and stiff tail; and short, thick body. They hunted by wing power and endurance, flying at great altitudes and then dropping like a stone on their quarry,* delivering a violent and often lethal blow with their hind talon on the prey. The female was about a third larger than the male. These ranked in size as follows:

jer- or gyrfalcon:	male about 20 inches*; weight 3 pounds*
	female 2 feet* from beak to tail; about 3.5 pounds
peregrine falcon:	female about 21 inches; weight 2 pounds
lanner falcon:	same size as peregrine; ate small animals and reptiles
merlin falcon:	about 12 inches; resembled sparrowhawk; ate bugs
hobby falcon:	small peregrine with stumpy feet; ate birds and insects.

2. short-winged "voileurs" or sailors as they flew. They had a slender beak with a curve or "festoon," short powerful legs, and short thick thighs, a long tail, and a long slender body. They were birds of the woodland who hunted by stealth, sitting motionless on a tree branch and then gliding swiftly by a short, silent dash through the trees to snatch their quarry. These ranked in size as follows:

| goshawk: female | 26 inches long but weighed only 2 pounds; long head, long powerful legs, feet with short strong toes: first and third toe had immense claws |
| sparrowhawk: miniature | goshawk: female 17–20 inches long |

(Bibliog. 26, 118)

Falkirk, battle of. See Battle of Falkirk.

fallaro. See nummi.

family unity and solidarity, vital concept for the nobles in the medieval period, especially in the private wars which often resulted in heavy casualties. In 1127, for example, the Erembald family stood beside and supported its members who had murdered Count Charles the Good in Flanders. By that they had to endure with the guilty ones all acts of vengeance hurled against them. They sustained a lengthy siege in their castle* at Bruges under difficult conditions. After they surrendered, the surviving twenty-eight members of the castle, guilty or not of complicity in the murder of Count Charles, were hurled from the castle towers. One of them, Robert the Child, who had hastened only out of loyalty to stand beside the family in that crisis and who was considered innocent by the men of Bruges, nevertheless was beheaded by order of the king* of France. (Bibliog. 351)

fardel, measure of capacity for cloth and other items assembled as a ball or bundle of no standard dimension in the 14th century; it was also a measure of land equal to ten statute acres* or one-fourth virgate* of forty acres; it was equivalent to and superseded by the farthingale.* (Bibliog. 394)

farm, *firma,* fixed sum owed to the English crown by a single estate. In the earliest days, English monarchs wandered the countryside, consuming their dues in food on the estates where it was produced. Food rents, then, were the earliest form of royal revenue. However, foodstuffs did not keep, so to get cash, the food had to be sold at current market prices. Thus this commutation of food rents into a cash equivalent was a step in financial sophistication. The original fixed (*firma*) food rent of a single estate often was referred to as the farm, and that term continued to be used for the commuted rent due from single estates, boroughs,* hundreds,* and shires.* For example, the *Domesday Book** stated that Oxfordshire owed farm of three nights or 150 pounds (see money). A law enacted by the 7th-century West Saxon King Ine revealed that the food rent due from 10 hides* of land to its lord totalled 10 vats of honey, 300 loaves, 123 ambers* of Welsh ale, 30 ambers of clear ale, 2 full-grown cows or 10 wethers, 10 geese, 20 hens, 10 cheeses, a full amber of butter, 5 salmon, 20 pounds of fodder, and 100 eels.

The English Exchequer* used the term farm to refer to the moneys from manors* but used the term rents for income from woods: the produce of manors was justly called firm and immutable because although agriculture is renewed yearly, it constituted an assured revenue by perpetual law of custom; however, that which was due yearly from woods, which daily were cut down and perish, was not so fixed a demand but was subject to rise and fall frequently. (Bibliog. 102, 163)

farmery, monastic infirmary. (Bibliog. 385)

farthing, unit of monetary exchange which, by common practice of the Anglo-Saxons and Normans in England, was obtained for use as small change by cutting silver pennies* into halves or quarters. These quarters were known as farthings from the Anglo-Saxon word *feorthing*, meaning a fourth part. Round silver farthings were not introduced into England until the reign of King Edward I in 1279. See coinage. (Bibliog. 150)

farthingale, measure of area for land with two widely different dimensions, one forty times the other; in time it came to indicate ten statute acres.* This term superceded the term ferling* and then fardel.* (Bibliog. 394)

fathom, measure of length generally containing six feet* but occasionally stretched to mean seven feet in the 14th century. (Bibliog. 394)

fauchard, weapon resembling a scythe* which had a wide, flat, knife-like blade with a markedly convex cutting edge and an upturned hook at the end; this form of gisarme* inflicted such ghastly and deadly wounds that it was considered by some to be too dreadful to use. (Bibliog. 27)

fauchon. See falchion.

favel, chestnut color, a favorite color of a horse* and frequently used as the name of horses in the *chansons de gestes** (*Roland, Otinel, Gaidon, Raoul de Cambrai*, and others). From this word came the proverb, "to curry favel," from:

> He that will in Court dwell
> Must curry Favel,
> And he that will in Court abide
> Must curry Favelle back and side.

This meant to be subservient to the caprices of a patron in the hope of obtaining some advantage. That saying has been corrupted to "to curry favor" as people forgot what favel meant. The word also meant faun colored, "fauve." (Bibliog. 225)

fealty, obligation of fidelity on the part of a feudal tenant or vassal* to his lord. After the acts of homage* had been performed and he had become the "man" of another man, the vassal went through a second rite, basically religious. As he lay his hand on the Gospel or on relics,* the new vassal swore to be faithful to his master: "Hear this my lord: I will bear faith to you of life and member, goods, chattels and earthly worship, so help me God and these holy Gospels of God." Sometimes added was an express promise to perform the service due for some tenement or holding. This was called fealty: *foi* in French, *Treue, Triuwe,** in German. Homage was "done"; fealty was "sworn"; this oath was conceived as less solemn than the symbolic act and could be exacted in many cases in which homage was not applicable.

The second stage of this ceremony neither implied nor imposed anything specific; missing was the phrase, "I become your man," a significant omission. This did not bind one to another as did homage. Making clear this distinction is the fact that although the vassal swore fealty—faithfulness to his overlord— no reciprocal oath from the overlord was sworn. Homage established the dual aspect of dependence and protection; fealty did not. (Bibliog. 261)

Feast of the Swans, ceremony at which the ailing King Edward I of England knighted his son, Edward II, at Westminster on Whitsunday (May 22, 1306). It was the most splendid occasion of its kind since the king's father, Henry III, had knighted the young John of Brittany, who had died only recently, and Edward himself had knighted the two elder sons of Simon de Montfort. At this feast over 260 young men were knighted. The prince,* later Edward II, held his vigils in the abbey and was knighted privately by the king* and invested with the duchy* of Gascony; then he, in turn, knighted the rest of the men at the high altar of the abbey. At the subsequent feast, the king invoked the Feast of Swans. Two swans were brought in and laid on the table. Edward rose and swore "before God and the swans" to avenge the death of John Comyn of Badenock and the insult to the church and, that done, to fight only infidels in the Holy Land. (Comyn, a leader of the Scottish resistance on behalf of King John Baliol, was slain in Dumfrees by Robert Bruce in 1306.) The newly knighted Prince Edward, in the general enthusiasm, swore not to sleep more than one night in the same place until he had reached Scotland; he did not keep that vow.* See Vow of the Heron. (Bibliog. 87, 270)

fedus, gem from the Phase River in the land of the Saracens* which, when drunk with milk from a mother whose firstborn child was a male, served as a remedy against blindness. In the milk of an ewe that had borne a white male sheep, it was a remedy against gout; however, there it had to be drunk slowly and carefully to avoid damage to one's lungs. (Bibliog. 258)

fee, knight's. See knighthood.

felony, one of the two divisions of a crime in English law: felonies and mis-demeanors. The differences between them did not depend on the gravity of the offense, nor on the amount of punishment* attached to them, but were purely historical. Felonies were those crimes which at common law brought with them after conviction the forfeiture of goods, although they had nothing criminal about them. Every crime that could be prosecuted by appeal,* every crime that caused loss of both land and goods, every crime for which a man should lose life or limb, and every crime for which a fugitive could be outlawed* was a felony. For example, a breach of duty on the part of a vassal,* neglect of service, delaying in seeking investiture, and so forth were considered felonies, as were injuries by the lord against a vassal. In time, felonies came to mean capital crimes, although there were a few felonies not punishable by death. It became a principle of law that when a crime was declared by statute to be a felony, the punishment of death (see execution) with forfeiture of lands and goods necessarily was attached to it.

In the 13th century a felony was a crime which could be prosecuted by an appeal, that is, by an accusation in which the accuser as a general rule must offer battle. A convicted felon's lands reverted to his lord or to the king and his chattels were confiscated; the felon forfeited life or limb of his body; and if an accused felon fled, he could be outlawed. (Bibliog. 135)

fels, Islamic copper coin minted in imitation of Byzantine pieces, but from the beginning of the 8th century they were similar to the dirhem* and dinar.* (Bibliog. 150)

fence month, hunting* term meaning the month which began fifteen days before and ended fifteen days after midsummer (June 24) during which great care was taken so no men or stray dog should wander into the forest* and no swine or cattle allowed to feed within its bounds so that the deer should be absolutely undisturbed three to four weeks after fawning season. With men and weapons the "watch and ward"* served as a fence to defend the wild beasts, hence the term fence month. (Bibliog. 96)

feodary, franchisal official who had his duties under the lord in some franchises* similar to those of the escheator.* (Bibliog. 261)

feoffment, form of granting or conveying a freehold or fee. One of its essential elements was livery of seisin* (delivery of possession) which consisted of for-mally giving to the feofee of the land a clod or piece of turf or a growing twig as a symbol of the transfer of the land. This also was called livery in deed. (Bibliog. 100)

fer de glaive (Fr.), the sword* of chivalry* as well as the blade used by a headsman. (Bibliog. 71) *feria,* any weekday that was not a holiday or festival. See days of the week.

ferling, measure of land equal to ten statute acres* or one-fourth virgate* of forty acres. In the 13th century it was equal to and was superceded by the fardel* and farthingale.* (Bibliog. 394)

Ferrant d' Espagne, horse* owned by Oliver,* a hero in *chansons de geste.** (Bibliog. 308)

Ferrant, Ferant, epithet equal to "gris de fer" (steely-grey) which frequently referred to a battle horse.* This term also was used frequently as the name of horses in the *chansons de geste.** (Bibliog 191)

fert, small billon* coin of Savoy in the 14th century; it was equivalent to a Savoyard denier (see denarius), as well as four pites and two obols.* Originally twelve fert but later only eight fert made a grosso (see gros) and twelve gros were reckoned to equal a florin.* (Bibliog. 150)

fess, one of the ordinaries* which consisted of a broad horizontal band drawn across the center of the heraldic shield.* (Bibliog. 43)

fess point, center of a shield.*

fesse, originally referring to a cord used to bind the hay, this came to be used as a measure of quantity for hay, smaller than a truss* of fifty-six pounds* but larger than a bottle of hay of seven pounds. (Bibliog. 394)

Fête de l'Espinette, French tourney (or tournament*) in which a "king" was selected at Mardi Gras, jousts* were held, and the prize was a golden sparrow hawk.* This king was one of the challengers who had to meet all comers. (Bibliog. 47)

feu grégeois. See greek fire.

feudal army, never a huge army, probably ranging between 5,000 and 7,000 knights, and rarely mustered at full strength. The usual period of service was forty days for training during peacetime, but in wartime a knight (see knighthood) could be called on to serve for sixty days at his own expense; if the campaign lasted longer than sixty days, then the knights stayed on at the king's expense. Such service could be demanded of knights if the king* himself were present in the army. The hierarchy in this army seems to have constituted something of a military chain of command in time of war. The tenants-in-chief* (barons*) or their representatives were leaders of units within the feudal army, units which varied considerably in size, and these were combined into much larger units and groups which then were commanded by men chosen for their military skill as well as their importance in the entire feudal system. See conrois. (Bibliog. 262)

feudal levy, summoning, mustering, or calling into service of knights and other men-at-arms. Such military service demanding duty in the national host (see knighthood), "castle guard,"* and *equitatio* (riding service for one's immediate lord) was a matter of agreement between lord and tenant. Following the Norman invasion of England (1066), the English monarchs relied on two factors for their defense system: "feudal army"* and continental involvement. Such a levy must have shown its weak spots soon after its beginning, for the greater barons* with great retinues of trained knights in their households (see household knights) could field a good contingent of fighters. Smaller tenants, however, had difficulties meeting the summons; and no provisions were made for old or sick knights not fighting, and ecclesiastical tenants (bishops and abbots) who were called upon in 1066 to provide 750 knights had a difficult time fulfilling that summons.

The Anglo-Norman English used tenurial service to provide an army of about 5,000 knights. Specifically, the amount of service due from the honours* of tenants-in-chief was a new concept, and the specific military service owing from knights was established only after the rebellions under William* I had been suppressed. Under the subsequent Angevin kings* (Henry II,* Richard I,* John*) only a fraction of this quota was actually called up for service. In fact, Henry I and Stephen* did not use the militia. Henry II, though, with his Assize of Arms* of 1181 organized the militia to bear arms on a sliding scale conditioned by the wealth of the free men. Commutation of such service on a large scale occurred at the end of the 12th century when 4,000 knights secured exemption from service by scutage* or fine.* Obviously by that time, the feudal levy was no longer an effective fighting force; among other things, it was out of date and no longer could meet the requirements of warfare. It had been superseded by an army of mercenaries*—men paid to fight. See soldier. (Bibliog. 264)

feudal obligations, wardship* and marriage* were the most irksome of all feudal obligations applying to those who held tenancy by military service and by sergeanty (see sergeant) because the lord enjoyed the profits of an estate during the minority of the heir on the ground that by reason of his youth, the heir was incapable of rendering any service; that maintained until a boy became twenty-one and a girl reached the marriageable age of fourteen. The lord also controlled the marriage of his wards—both male and female—and disposed of widows. See also relief. (Bibliog. 264)

feudalism, organization of a society dominated by a secular class of knights who not only formed the military and social elite but who were bound to each other in a hierarchy culminating in the prince.* This organization was based on the holding of a fief,* usually a unit of land, in return for a stipulated honorable service, normally military, with a relationship of homage* and fealty* existing between grantee and grantor. All of the elements of feudalism—knights, vassal* commendation, fiefs, castles—were absent from pre-Conquest England but were increasingly manifest after the Norman invasion in 1066. Just as the Normans seemingly brought to England the concept of castle as fortified residence, so they also brought the concepts of feudal caste and vassal commendation. (Bibliog. 47, 114, 159)

fewmets. See fumes.

fewte, fuite, fute, hunting* term meaning trace, track, or foot; some beasts were called sweet fute and others stinking fute. (Bibliog. 96)

fewterer, servant that loosed greyhounds* during the hunt. See hunting; hunting dogs. (Bibliog. 96)

fief, normally a unit of land held by a vassal* of a lord in return for stipulated services, chiefly military. Sometimes unusual requirements were stipulated for transferring a fief. For example, Henry de la Wade held fifty-two acres* of land in Oxford by the service of carrying a gyrfalcon (see falconry birds) when King Edward I wished to go hawking.* In 1252 Roland de Sarcere held 110 acres of land in Suffolk by sergeanty (see sergeant) for which on Christmas Day every year before the king* (Edward I) himself, he was to perform "un Saut, un Pet, et un Suflet" (a leap, a fart, and a puff). Salamon de Campis held certain lands called Coperland and Atterton in Kent of King Edward I "in capite" by the sergeanty of holding the king's head between Dover and Whitford every time the king travelled that route by sea. In France one knight held his fief by beating the water of the moat of the lord's castle* to stop the noise of frogs during his lady's illness. (Bibliog. 114, 225)

fief de haubert, 11th-century French equivalent to the English term knight's fee (see knighthood) because of the coat (hauberk*) of mail* which it entitled and required every tenant to own and wear when his services were needed. This provided a definite estate in France, for only persons possessing this or a greater estate were allowed to wear hauberks. (Bibliog. 225)

fief-rente, money paid in annual installments by a lord to a vassal* in return for homage* and fealty,* military service (usually knight service), and various other "feudal obligations"*; it could consist of natural produce such as wine,* cheese, chickens, or wood paid in annual installments. By this tool, great lords could acquire vassals, convert simple homage to "liege homage,"* obtain rights to land, gain allies, and assure benevolent neutrality. It allowed the Capetian-kings* of France to acquire as vassals numerous lords, simple knights, and alleutiers (freeholders), thereby to expand their royal domains and to knit into a single, strong unit the loose conglomeration of petty feudal units. In most countries except England it provided the continuous service required for "castle guard."* The counts* of Hainault commonly granted fief-rentes to build up a large entourage of "household knights"* called commilitones* who were to follow their counts in their wars and in tournaments.* (Bibliog. 208)

field, 1. the surface of a shield* on which charges* were placed; it was plain, divided, or patterned; 2. the areas worked by peasants (see villeins) for their lord which could be divided into many compartments or large divisions, such as furlongs, shots, or dells, which in turn were subdivided into a number of strips or selions,* each separated from the others by raised balks of unplowed land. Such strips ran parallel to each other along the whole length of the furlong or shot and generally contained between one-half and one acre of land. At right angles to these strips ran the headlands, the unplowed portions that gave access to the strips in the furlong and to the other parts of the field. (Bibliog. 24, 116, 225)

fier, adjective describing a man's external appearance which complimented him as looking every inch a man of quality. (Bibliog. 161)

Finamonde, sword* of Aimeri de Narbonne in the *chansons de geste**; the name meant "perfect, ultra-fine" from the phrase which meant "end of the world." (Bibliog. 134, 191)

fine, alternative to the method of commutation of scutage* at the end of the 12th century. The tenant-in-chief* could offer a fine, a sum arbitrarily fixed by the king* which would relieve him of the whole burden of military service. Its acceptance by the king carried the authorization for the vassal* to collect scutage at the current rate from his subtenants. Frequently this amount was far in excess of the scutage, which implies that there was a substantial advantage in doing so. Possibly its distinction lay in the fact that while scutage relieved the baron* of recruiting and sending his knights into the army, it did not absolve him personally from service. This fine freed him from both obligations.

Such a solution seems to have required compromise. Barons did not want to serve abroad, a point which the king was willing to concede because he did not want so many knights as in earlier wars, for knights had ceased to form the rank and file of the army and the king needed only a few to act as officers in command of hired knights (see mercenaries) and to remain in arms for a long time. If the barons and their knights were going to get out of service abroad, they had to make substantial contributions to the costs of the war in return. Costs were huge for construction and maintenance of fortifications and the maintenance of a large army of hired knights and men-at-arms. Thus the king was in a good position to drive a hard bargain.

No fixed rules existed for setting these fines, and they varied wildly. For example, the abbot of St. Augustus, Canterbury, paid forty pounds (see money) for his fifteen fees in 1197 when the scutage which he could recover from his vassals was only fifteen pounds. Thus he paid only twenty-five pounds to escape going to war and to contribute to its expenses. Hugh of Bayeux, on the other hand, paid forty pounds for his twenty fees. (Bibliog. 264)

fiorino. See florin.

fire-bote, rights granted by a lord to his tenants to take firewood for use as fuel from his estate. (Bibliog. 24)

firkin, measure of capacity for ale, beer, butter, fish, and soap:

ale firkin equalled 8 gallons*

beer firkin equalled 9 gallons

butter and soap firkin equalled 8 gallons

fish firkin varied: for salmon it was 10.5 gallons, but for eels and herring it was 7.5 gallons.

(Bibliog. 394)

firma. See farm.

firmarius. See bailiff.

fitched, crosses* which are pointed at the foot, that is, whose lower limb ends in a point. (Bibliog. 43)

Fitz-Neale, Richard. Bishop of London and treasurer of England; author of the *Dialogus de Scaccario.** See Exchequer.

five-hide unit, used in the *Domesday Book** to assess a large number of manors* in the ''hideated'' (see hide assessment) portion of the realm. Apparently such a unit bore no relationship to the area or the value in a village and even less in a manor; such assessment was not objective, but was subjective. (Bibliog. 292)

flail, 1. agricultural tool used by peasant (see villein) levies, consisting of an iron-shod club hinged to a long staff; 2. military weapon resembling its agricultural namesake but had its head attached to the staff by a length of chain; frequently the head was formed into the shape of a ball studded with spikes. (Bibliog. 27)

flamberge, any large sword* with waved or undulating edges. One of Charlemagne's swords was so named. (Bibliog. 331)

flan, piece of metal or blank before it had been struck by the die to mint it into coinage.*

flanchards, two hanging plates of metal suspended below a war saddle* to protect the lower sides of a horse.* See horse armor. (Bibliog. 9)

flanking towers, projecting towers built at intervals along the outer walls of a castle* to command the field in which besiegers would have to work, especially the foot of the walls or tower on which the attack was being concentrated. (Bibliog. 45)

fleam, medieval lancet or scalpel which was depicted in the heraldic device* of the barber-surgeons.* (Bibliog. 392)

fletcher, arrow* maker.

fleur de lis, stylized form of lily used as the royal badge* of France which King Louis VII (1137–1170) adopted as an allusion to his name, "lois" of "lys." Legend states that Clotilde, pious wife of King Clovis of France, convinced her pagan husband to become a Christian after her prayers had secured a victory for him in a critical battle. He was baptized by St. Remigius and afterward had three lilies substituted in the "arms of France"* for the three toads or frogs (*crapaud*) which Clovis formerly had borne on his shield.* These reputedly were derived from the arms of a previous Salian king* of the Franks, Faramond (or Pharamond), who appeared much later as a king of Gaul in such French Arthurian verse romances* as *Giron le Courtois*. (Bibliog. 43, 178)

fleuron, heraldic "fleur de lis"* used by the French Kings Philip* II Augustus and Louis VIII on the crown* of their great seals. (Bibliog. 116)

florette, coin variety of the French gros* struck under Charles VI (1380–1422), having the equivalent value of twenty deniers (see denarius) tournois* or sixteen deniers parisis*; its name came from the three crowned "fleur de lis"* on its obverse. See coinage. (Bibliog. 150)

florin, 1. silver coin of Florence minted as early as the 12th century, depicting on the obverse the bust or the standing or seated figure of St. John the Baptist and on the reverse a lily (*fiorino*, Italian word for lily) and the arms* of Florence which also was called the "Lily of the Arno"; 2. an English gold coin depicting a king enthroned on the obverse with a value of six shillings (see coinage) struck briefly in 1344 by King Edward III (1327–1377); its unpopularity with the people caused it to be withdrawn and not issued again for several centuries. (Bibliog. 150)

flotant, floating in blazon* when referring to flags or ships. (Bibliog. 43)

foddercorn, grain (see corn) owed by a peasant (see villein) to feed his lord's horses.* (Bibliog. 24)

foi (Fr. "faith"). See fealty.

foiling down. See ruses.

follaro, copper coinage* issued by the Norman kings* of Sicily, and of Sicily and Naples in the 11th and 12th centuries; its weight and value varied from twenty to forty nummi.* Its name came from *follis*, meaning a wallet or purse. (Bibliog. 150)

follow the string, archery term which meant that by excessive use a bow* had lost its straightness and had obtained a forward curve. (Bibliog. 100)

folly. See rascal and folly.

foot, clutch the quarry*; a "good footer" was a hawk that was successful at killing, that was clever with its feet, because many hawks were good flyers without being "good footers." See hawking. (Bibliog. 26)

foot tournament, joust* using no leg armor.* Knights in this contest held lances* in both hands and splintered them across a low barrier, exchanging sword* blows on each other's helmets*; a blow below the belt meant a disqualification because of the absence of leg armor. See also *fussturnier*. (Bibliog. 53)

footings, lower portion of a wall including its foundations.

forest, certain territory of wooded grounds and fruitful pastures in which wild beasts and fowls of the forest, as well as those in the chase* and warren, could rest and abide in the safe protection of the king* and for his princely delight and pleasure. Such territory was bounded by unremovable marks either widely known or a matter of record. It was replenished with beasts of venery or chase and with great coverts of vert* for the succor and protection of wild beasts to have their abode. Certain laws, privileges, and offices that were fitting for such a place and for no other preserved, protected, and continued such a place, together with vert and venison.

However, the forest was protected by severe laws because it was so important to the king's economy by providing rents from pasturage, rents from assarts,* fines,* timber for ships and for castle-building* and repairs, sale of dead and fallen wood, venison for the king's larder, and for feeding the large court which followed the king up and down the countryside. The object of these forest laws was to preserve certain beasts "of the forest"—red and fallow deer, roe, and wild boar—and to preserve the vert, that is, the growing timber and undergrowth which gave them shelter. Under King Edward III, roe was struck from this list, for it drove away the other deer. No one except the king and foresters* could touch the red or fallow deer or the wild boar which was rapidly becoming extinct. Wolves, however, were pests to be exterminated, and King John placed a bounty of five shillings (see money) on every wolf's head.

Poachers, as one might expect, were fined heavily, imprisoned, mutilated, or hanged, but after the death of King John in 1216, the king's treasury was so depleted that they substituted fines for executions.* In 1176 one hundred men in Hampshire were fined for poaching, with the resultant fines ranging from one-half mark* to 500 marks totalling 2,093 pounds ten shillings.

Richard Fitz-Neale,* the author of the *Dialogue of the Exchequer* (c. 1190), described the forest as "the sanctuary and special delight of kings, where laying aside their cares, they withdrew to refresh themselves with a little hunting; there, away from the turmoils inherent in a court, they breathe the pleasures of natural freedom." For that freedom Richard I* built in Kinver forest in Staffordshire a hunting lodge with a fortified enclosure. It was sixteen perches* in length, sixteen perches in height, contained a hall* with accompanying offices, a kitchen, chamber, jail* for forest offenders, and a fish pond.

In the reign of Henry II (1154–1189) the forest embraced almost one-third of the English countryside. His sons Richard I* (1189–1199) and John (1199–1216) sold off the rights to certain forests to relieve financial pressures. For example, Cornwall forests were sold for 2,200 marks and 20 palfreys,* and Devon forests were sold for 5,000 marks. (Bibliog. 252, 262)

forest dweller, resident of the woods who, on payment of a fee to agisters,* could graze his pigs and cattle in the forest* except two weeks before and two weeks after Midsummer Day (that is, during the "fence month"*) when the deer were fawning. He also could take dead wood for fuel and repairs to his cottage; if he went beyond dead wood, however, and took a bough or cut down a bough, he was guilty of waste.* Further, he could not carry a bow* and arrows,* and his dogs had to be "lawed," that is, mutilated by having three claws cut from its forepaw so it could not run after the king's game (see mutilation of dogs). (Bibliog. 262)

forester, gamekeeper of the forest* paid by the wardens* but who also in actuality often paid to be appointed because of the splendid opportunities it offered to increase personal wealth. (Bibliog. 156)

forhu, to whoop loudly to call the "hunting dogs,"* from "forhuer," meaning to holloa. (Bibliog. 96)

fork, agricultural implement having two sharp tines and used as a weapon as early as the 12th century. (Bibliog. 27, 331)

"by fork and flail," technical phrase expressing the labor services of villeinage: the villein* was to work for his lord so many days and weeks in addition to boon-works* (*precariae**). (Bibliog. 264)

forlonge, signal blown on the hunting* horn by those who had been outdistanced by the deer and hounds. Hounds were said to be "hunting the forlonge" when the deer was some distance in front of them or when the hounds had gotten away with the deer and had outpaced the rest of the pack and hunters. See horn calls in hunting. (Bibliog. 96)

formy, cross* that had widely curving or splayed sides with straight ends. (Bibliog. 251)

Fort St-Georges. See Chinon.

fother, weight of lead, usually 2,100 pounds,* used interchangably with and eventually superseded the term charge* in the 14th century; reckoned in four ways: 30 fotmals* of 70 pounds each; 168 stone* of 12.5 pounds each; 175 stone of 12 pounds each; or 12 weys* of 175 pounds each. (Bibliog. 394)

fotmal, weight for lead in the 13th century equal to 70 pounds* and also equal to one-thirtieth of a fother* of 2,100 pounds. (Bibliog. 394)

fouaill, reward of the cooked bowels of a boar given to hounds after a boar hunt. See also curee. (Bibliog. 96)

fourche, forked, in heraldry,* as in a tail which was divided.

fourmi, Ethiopian ant as big as a dog which gathered grains of gold from a river but which protected this treasure strongly and killed any who approached. Greedy people, though, devised a ruse to obtain some of the gold: they sent mares with open empty chests strapped across their back near the ant colony. Thinking the chests would help them store the gold, the fourmi filled the chests, but then the Ethiopians had colts whinny to summon the mares who thereupon returned at a gallop, bringing the gold. (Bibliog. 258)

frail, woven reed basket which held between thirty and seventy-five pounds* of fruit and other small items and so became a measure of capacity in the 14th century. (Bibliog. 394)

franc à cheval. See coinage.

franchise, freedom or liberty from something; hence a special privilege or exemption from existing conditions, and so an immunity; franchise holders were often called immunists. This was the exercise of public jurisdiction in private hands, as the possession of a franchise gave the recipient the duty of administering the king's* law within certain limits in return for acknowledging his right to enjoy the profits of this jurisdiction and to keep the king's own officials out of his franchise, so long as it was properly administered.

Under a franchise, the normal functions of government were exercised by officials appointed by a private person or corporation, not by the crown. Such jurisdiction was quite different from that of honour* which the lords had over their baronial (see barony) tenants, and their jurisdiction of manor* which they had over villeins.* As such, this was independent of feudal structure, for it was a delegation of royal authority to a person or corporation within certain limits of power and territory. Common phraseology in the grants of franchise to lay and ecclesiastical lords from the late 10th century were such terms as "sac* and soc,"* "toll and team,"* and "infangentheof."* (Bibliog. 163)

francisca, special throwing axe* or hatchet used by the early Franks. See battle axe. (Bibliog. 71)

frankalmoign, one of the types of feudal tenure, ranking first in order above military or knight service (see knighthood), sergeanty,* socage,* and villeinage (see villein). It was a type of tenure granted to a church or a religious house with no strings attached; frequently given as a gift "in free alms" (*in elemo-siniam*) or more emphatically "in free, pure and perpetual alms" (*libera ele-mosina*). This was different, however, from an ecclesiastical benefice whereby land was given to a church in return for spiritual service, such as prayers. If the terms of the frankalmoign gift said nothing about service or merely stipulated in a general way for the donee's prayers, then no fealty* was due. (Bibliog. 264)

frankpledge, system to control the peace introduced into England by the Anglo-Norman kings* whereby every member of a tithing* was answerable for the good conduct of, or the damage done by, any one of the other members. All males over the age of twelve who were not under the personal pledge of a lord, that is, in his mainpast,* or themselves of sufficient rank and property to serve as surety, were obliged to be in frankpledge. These groups were predominantly villeins.* This frankpledge tithing originally was ten men under the direction of a head man known as the chief pledge. Entry into this tithing involved taking an oath of fealty,* and swearing not to steal or to consent to thievery. Obligations involved taking oaths to keep the peace, serving in arms, and joining in the "hue and cry."* The tithing was required to pledge for the appearance in court* of members of the group, to pursue and capture thieves and, if necessary, to pay the costs of their imprisonment, to present evidence of crimes at tourns* and eyres,* and to pay when the tithing failed in responsibility by letting men escape.

By the 13th century, the head man of the frankpledge had become virtually a constable* for the maintenance of peace, and he was elected at the renewal of frankplege. This ceremony was a court held annually for the production of the members of a tithing, in a hundred,* or in a manor.* If held in a borough,* usually the mayor or bailiffs* presided, unless the borough was divided into wards or leets,* each of which held its separate court at which the viewing of tithings and the presenting of offenses was conducted. As such, this was more of a royal police court than a communal assembly. (Bibliog. 261)

fraying post, tree against which a stag rubbed his antlers or frayed them (rubbed off their velvet). By examining this post, a hunstman* could judge whether the stag he wished to harbor* was a warrantable stag, for the greater the fraying post, the larger the deer. (Bibliog. 96)

free alms. See frankalmoign.

free course, course run in a joust* with no interposing barrier between the contesting knights. (Bibliog. 9)

freeman's duties, military obligations of the ordinary English freeman which were closely associated with his duties in the maintenance of the peace and with "watch and ward."* The distinctions between violations of the peace and insurrection, and between outlaws* and rebels, were so blurred that police duties shaded into military duties. As freemen were responsible for the security of the countryside against both marauding invaders and local bandits, they were accorded the right to bear arms. One of the central features of the 12th- and 13th-century manumission ceremonies was placing a lance* and sword* in the hands of a liberated serf.* Seemingly, the masses of unfree men had no military responsibilities until the reign of Henry III (1216–1272). (Bibliog. 159)

frigius, black-veined stone which, when drunk in wine* with the herb sabine, healed fistula and gout. See also asius. (Bibliog. 258)

frounce, disease in the mouth and throat of hawks. (Bibliog. 96)

frouwendienst (Ger.), knight's service to a lady emerging from the poetic transference to his lady of his obligation to his overlord whom he served in actuality in a military or some other capacity for his estate. Just as a knight endured toils and dangers for his lord, so he was expected to endure the pangs of unrequited love for his lady, hoping that someday she would reward him indeed. But such was always in the future, so that whatever small favors she accorded him until then were totally at her discretion. See also chivalry. (Bibliog. 124)

fues, deer's scent in its track or line of flight from hunters; ''not to find its fues'' meant a hunter could not find the deer's track or its line of flight. See hunting. (Bibliog. 96)

fuite, fute. See fewte.

full age. See majority.

full course, running deer* in blazon.* See beasts, positions of.

fumes, droppings of a hart, fallow, or roe deer; for other animals, the terms used were: for buck, roebuck, hares and conies: croties; wild boar, black beasts and wolves: lesses; fox: the wagging; gray or badger: the wardrobe; ''stinking beasts'' (see hunting): the drit; otter: spraintes. (Bibliog. 96)

funerals, obsequies displaying a knight's bearings (see charge). At the funeral of Louis de Male, count* of Flanders, in 1384, four knights bearing his arms* of war accompanied the body, preceded by four others bearing his tournament* devise* and his banners* of war and of tournament. At the funeral of Gerard de Montagne, lord of Espières and Caurines, two mounted squires* in black carried his pennons* of war and tournament to the door of the abbey. They were followed by two squires on warhorses wearing his arms of peace and of war, who in turn were followed by a long procession of nobles who donated shields,* helms,* horses,* pennons, and other regalia on behalf of the dead man and his family. These obsequies were attended by seventeen knights and twenty-four squires all dressed in mourning attire. (Bibliog. 350)

furca and fossa, gallows and pit. These were the two usual modes of capital punishment: being hanged or being buried alive. Because of feelings of delicacy, however, women were condemned to be drowned instead of being hanged as men, for such form of execution* was felt to be conducted in a manner least offensive to feminine delicacy. (Bibliog. 4)

furlongs. See fields.

furs, two furs used in heraldry* were ermine* and vair*; each had variants: ermine, ermines,* erminois,* and peau; and vair, vaire, vair potent,* and counter* potent. Fur could be placed on tincture (see colors) or on metal.* (Bibliog. 43)

fursten (Ger.), first men of German feudal society. See titles of dignity, French, German.

fusil, elongated lozenge* in blazon,* representing a spindle belonging to a distaff. (Bibliog. 253)

fusor, knight at the Exchequer* who melted metal to make into money* and who tested it for its content, under the watchful eye of the silverer (argentarius.*) (Bibliog. 102)

fusee. See grip.

fussturnier, (Ger.) form of tournament* used late in the 15th century, consisting of troop against troop. Each combatant had to exchange three charges with a lance* across a barrier and five strokes with a sword,* all directed toward his opponent's head, not only against just one but against every opponent on the opposite side. No prize was awarded if the lance did not splinter, if the combatant stepped back or had been driven back in any way, or if someone struck a blow below the belt, because no leg armor* was worn. See also foot tournament. (Bibliog. 71)

fustibal, sling on a four-foot staff which had one end of the sling fastened near the end and the other end contrived to slip off the staff easily in the act of throwing. Both large and small stones could be hurled great distances with this weapon. (Bibliog. 9)

fylfot, swastika, gammadion, type of cross* used as a symbol by Buddhists but found on coinage* of Ethelred, king of Northumbria, in the 9th century. (Bibliog. 253)

fyrd, army based on the personal obligations of freemen to defend their homeland and not on a contract. Service in this army called the ''great fyrd'' was local and defensive and corresponded to the continental *arrière-ban** which was summoned only in the time of invasion or to be the continental militia of various *burgs** which served only within half a day's march of their town. It was based on the obligations of territorial units normally of five hides* to produce and support financially one warrior representative to fight on land or sea when the royal army was summoned. Such an army of free farmers of Anglo-Saxon England performed so well at the battle of Hastings (1066) that William* the Conqueror retained it for his own uses. (Bibliog. 159)

fyrdwite, fine* for default of fyrd* service in Saxon England. (Bibliog. 159)

G

gab, to boast or brag about one's abilities. In *Pélerinage de Charlemagne*, Roland* gabbed that he could blow his horn, Olifant,* so loudly that all the doors of Constantinople would fall in; Oliver,* in the same poem, gabbed that if the emperor* of Constantinople would let him sleep with his bright-haired daughter, he would "know her an hundred times ere morning." (Bibliog. 162)

gabelle, any direct tax levied by the French monarchs on their populace but frequently referring to the tax on salt and its consumption imposed by the French King Charles V, the Wise (1337–1380), in his efforts to restore stability to French finances to counter the disastrous expenditures in the Hundred Years War against England. (Bibliog. 139)

gabony. See compony.

gadlings, spikes on gauntlets* to protect the knuckles. Often projecting a considerable distance from the gauntlet, these were added to both offensive and defensive armor.* Both gauntlets of the Black Prince over his tomb in the cathedral at Canterbury contain not only gadlings on the first joints of the fingers but also small brass figures of lions* or leopards* in erect positions as pseudo-gadlings on the knuckles. (Bibliog. 9)

gage, challenge, pledge of a person's appearance to do battle in support of his claim. Usually a glove or a cap was cast to the ground and was taken up by an opponent to accept the challenge. See duel.

galgate. See pyrites.

gallery, long room or passageway in a manor.* (Bibliog. 385)

gallon, measure of capacity for both liquid and dry products containing four quarts or eight pints.* (Bibliog. 394)

Galway sparth. See sparth.

gambeson, thick garment, padded or quilted in vertical lines, worn under the cyclas.* Although it was the sole garment of defense for many soldiers* at Hastings, men who could wore hauberk* of mail* beneath this garment. Sometimes this was referred to as a garment made of silk or other rich fabric, decorated with embroidery and "coats of arms."* See aketon. (Bibliog. 9, 27)

gamboised. See cuisses.

gammadion, type of cross.* See fylfot.

Ganelon, arch traitor in the *chansons de geste.** He betrayed Roland* to his death in *Song of Roland.** (Bibliog. 162)

gaol, jail* (English).

gaol delivery, writ of King Edward I (1272–1307) which commissioned judges, assisted by local knights and burghers of the shires,* to return to freedom captives who had been unjustly imprisoned. (Bibliog. 139)

garb, unit of weight for thirty pieces of steel in the 13th century. (Bibliog. 394)

garde de bras (Fr.), armor* for the arm. See brassard.

garde de cuisses (Fr.), armor* for the thighs. See cuisses.

garde de queue (Fr.). See horse armor.

garderobes, privies or latrines* in English castles*; not to be confused with the wardrobe* (Fr. *garderobe*). The French used the term *longaigne* for privy. (Bibliog. 385)

garrison duty. See castle defense.

Garter, Order of. See Order of the Garter.

gatehouse, building forming the entrance to a town or the enciente* of a castle.* Generally it contained a large gateway protected by a gate and also by a portcullis* over which were battlemented* parapets* with machicolations* through which the defenders could throw darts,* melted lead, and hot sand on attackers. A gatehouse had a lodge with apartments for the porter and guardrooms for the soldiers* with rooms for officers above them and for prisoners beneath. (Bibliog. 100)

gathercorn, grain gathered from several peasants' (see villein) homesteads by a manorial servant for use by the lord of the manor.* (Bibliog. 24)

gauntlets, gloves of mail.* At first these were just continuations of the mail sleeves without divisions for the fingers, but in time they became leather or cuir-bouilli* gloves, which then became gauntlets of steel plates with articulated fingers and thumbs. One or more plates covered the back of the hand, and a single plate formed the cuff. Frequently gadlings* were added. For tournaments,* special gauntlets were worn; on his left hand, the bridle gauntlet, the knight wore a large and heavy mitten; on his right, he wore a glove with long finger plates that overlapped the wrist plate and thus securely locked the weapon (sword* or lance*) in the hand. (Bibliog. 9, 331)

gavelkind, system of tenure* by payment of "gavel," that is, rent or fixed services other than military prevailing in the county* of Kent, England. Frequently identified with socage,* it had unique characteristics: the tenant could alien (see alienated) his lands by enfeoffment (see feoffment) at fifteen years of age; he could dispose of the land by will; and in case of intestacy, the estate descended to all sons in equal shares and not solely to the oldest son as in primogeniture.* And there was no escheat* for attainder for felony.* These gavelkinders were not knights, nor gentle folk; they were freemen: they paid rent to their lords, their tenure was protected by law, and they were not burdened with week-work.* (Bibliog. 24)

gavelock, 13th-century weapon variously described as a javelin* or a double-bladed axe.*

gavelseed, corn* paid by peasants (see villein) to their lord in addition to money rent.

gefolgschaft (Ger.), *comitatus** as described in Tacitus, *Germania*. (Bibliog. 123)

gelaticum. See niger.

geldable, land subject to normal taxation and administration. (Bibliog. 171)

gemot, shire* court* in Anglo-Saxon England. In King Edgar's reign (944–975), this court met twice a year under the presidency of the lay official, the ealdorman (see earl), and under the ecclesiastical official, the bishop, who expounded both the secular law and the law of God. As cases were taken beyond this court to the king* only if justice* had not been obtained locally, this court had general competence to hear both ecclesiastical and civil matters. (Bibliog. 163)

genouillieres, knee pieces of armor* plate, frequently little more than a plain cap of metal on the outside of the armor; early ones were cuir-bouilli* strapped over mail.* (Bibliog. 9)

genovino, gold coinage* of Genoa bearing a gateway and a cross* and issued during the 13th and 14th centuries; it also was issued in one-half and one-quarter denominations and corresponded in value and weight to the Venetian and Florentine gold currency of the same period. (Bibliog. 150)

gentle, peregrine falcon (see falconry birds) caught after it had left the nest but before it had migrated. (Bibliog. 118)

gentleman, one who bore arms* by inheritance or grant or was eligible for a grant of arms. Two qualitative terms, ''gentle'' and ''simple,'' were applied to the upper and lower classes respectively. ''Gentle'' came from Latin *gens* (*gentilis*) meaning man, because these were *men* who were not serfs.* The word ''gentleman'' was derived from ''gentle,'' and gentle qualities were so named because they were the qualities supposed to belong to the upper class. A man was not a gentleman because he possessed those qualities; he was a gentleman only if he belonged to the upper class and not otherwise. (Bibliog. 116)

gentry. See gentleman; nobility.

Geoffrey de Preuilli, reputed inventor of tournaments*; he was said to have been killed in a tournament in 1062. (Bibliog. 71)

Geoffroi de Villehardouin, marshal* of Champagne (1150–1213?) who took part in the fourth crusade* and subsequently was made marshal of Romania, never returning to France. As one of the leaders of this crusade, he wrote *Conquêt de Constantinople*, written after 1207, to justify the capture and sacking of Constantinople from the point of view of the noble leaders. (Bibliog. 162)

Geoffrey of Anjou, count of Anjou (1113–1151). After his marriage to Mathilda, daughter and heiress of Henry I of England, he received the French counties of Anjou and Maine. He claimed the throne of England for his wife after Henry I died in 1135, but when Stephen of Blois seized the crown Geoffrey left his wife to fight for her patrimony alone until their son, Henry (born 1133), was old enough to join the fray. Meanwhile Geoffrey concentrated all his energies on conquering Normandy. That done, he assumed authority as its duke, and imposed his rule over its nobility. From his custom of wearing a sprig of *planta genesta* in his helmet, his family assumed the name of Plantagenet.* (Bibliog. 139, 235)

ger, gyr, jer, falconer's* term for the larger of the ''falconry birds.''* (Bibliog. 26) *gerefa.* See earl.

German chivalry. By the *Constitutio de pace tuenda* of the Emperor Frederick I (Barbarossa) in 1152, no German could be knighted unless he had four knightly ancestors. Only after Frederick I's sons were knighted at Mainz in 1184 was chivalry* recognized in the German lands as a socially acceptable institution. (Bibliog. 124)

German duchies, powerful political units within Germany. With the decline by 843 of the system of *missi dominici** established by Charlemagne, the defense of the eastern areas was left to the counts* of those areas. Under Charlemagne, these counts had been royal officials who were replaceable at least in theory by the emperor.* As royal prestige and power declined, their status and power increased, and by the 10th century these counts were ruling Germany often as dukes.* Within each territory each duke had far more power than the king*; his office had become hereditary, and only an extraordinarily strong king was powerful enough to replace him. Different tribal customs and traditions further strengthened the independence of these duchies.* By 911, there were four such duchies: the great duchy of Saxony protected the eastern frontier on the north, Bavaria protected against the Magyars and Slavs in the south, Suabia in the south protected the Alpine passes, and Franconia lay in the center. (Bibliog. 139)

gersuma, fine* paid to the lord when one entered a holding. Upon the death of the head of a family, not only was his family deprived of some of its goods through the demands of heriot* and mortuary,* it also left them facing the problem of succession to his unfree holdings. In theory, as the land belonged to the lord, it reverted to him on the death of its tenant, at which time he could reallocate it at will. In rare cases he would evict the old tenants to give the holdings to a new family, but generally he would leave the same family in possession, ceremonially admitting them at the "manor court"* after they had paid the gersuma and had sworn an oath of loyalty. (Bibliog. 24)

geste (Fr.), metrical record of seemingly historical deeds and events that gradually incorporated the entire lineage of the family of those who accomplished the deeds. As most of these accounts were related in verse and generally sung to the accompaniment of lute, rebec,* or viol, the entire unit came to be known as a song of deeds, or *chanson de geste.** (Bibliog. 162)

gestech (Ger.), jousts* of peace (see *jousts à plaisance*), even though the German root word, *stechen,* meant to pierce. This event depended more on adroitness and skill than the Italian joust in which knights tilted* with a barrier between them. In the *gestech*, lances* were capped with coronals* and were aimed by each participant at his opponent's *stechtarsche,* a small ribbed shield tied to the left shoulder by laces. Each horse* had only a straw cushion tied over its breast as protection. (Bibliog. 71)

gestum, allowance of meat and drink set aside at a meal as a guest's portion. In Wells, England, for example, a villein* had the right of gestum and medale,* but he had to bring to the gestum his own cloth, cup, and trencher,* and to take away all that was left on his cloth; in addition, at Christmas tide, he was allowed for himself and his neighbors one wastel (loaf) of bread* cut in three for the ancient "Christmas game."* (Bibliog. 24)

Ghibelline, Italian political faction in the 12th through 14th centuries in northern and central Italy which strongly supported the Hohenstaufen dynasty on the throne of the Holy Roman Empire,* especially Frederick (Barbarossa) I (1123–1190) and Frederick II (1194–1250). They were vigorously opposed by the Guelphs.* (Bibliog. 139)

gigliato, silver coin, and its one-half denomination, equal in weight and dimension to the gros* and half-gros of Sicily and issued by the Knights of St. John of Jerusalem (see Hospitallers) at Rhodes; its name comes from *giglio* meaning lily. See also coinage. (Bibliog. 150)

Gilbert of the Haye, author of *Boke of the Law of Armys* (edited by J. J. Stevenson, London, 1901), a 15th-century handbook for knights.

gill. See pint.

gimmel, gimbal, heraldic device* consisting of two or more rings interlaced. See also annulet.

gisarme, guisarme, long-handled staff weapon used by French and English footsoldiers from the 12th century onward. Its blade was shaped like a scythe* coupled with a pronged fork, and it usually ended in a sharp point with both sides of the blade razor sharp. It may also have been a long-handled axe,* bill,* or glaive,* for the term was used to refer to various weapons. (Bibliog. 27, 331)

gite, special tallage* in France to welcome a new lord. (Bibliog. 24)

gladius, short stabbing sword* used by the Roman legions.

gladness, glade, smooth bare place, or bright clearing in the wood in which one caught a clear, sharp, and distinct view of the deer being chased. (Bibliog. 96)

glaive, sharp-pointed, long-handled staff weapon sometimes called a scythe-knife* and often confused with the gisarme*; it had a sharp edge on the convex side and sharp edge on the other side down to a hook projecting forward that was used by infantrymen to drag horsemen from their saddles.* (Bibliog. 9)

glancing knobs, raised projections on the peytral* of horse armor* to fend off spear* blows. (Bibliog. 9)

Glanville. See Rannulf de Glanville.

Glastonbury, abbey in Somersetshire supposedly where Joseph of Arimathea was buried; a tomb there also has been identified as the burial place of King Arthur. (Bibliog. 10, 200)

glatissaunt beest. See questing beast.

glebe, land that belonged to the church and was tilled sometimes by tenants and sometimes by the priest himself. This partly supported the parish along with mortuary,* offerings on feast days (see Appendix A) and the tithing* produce of every tenth sheaf or the crop of every tenth acre.* (Bibliog. 129)

gleeman, poetical musician in Anglo-Saxon Britain; he was a court favorite and was offered asylum by the courts of kings* and by residences of the rich. Basically a gleeman was a merrymaker and did mimicry, dancing, tumbling, sleight of hand, as well as singing and storytelling. See minstrel. (Bibliog. 334)

glizade. See coule.

Glorious, Oliver's* sword* which easily hacked to pieces the swords forged by pagan smiths. See Haltelere. (Bibliog. 308)

glory, halo which was depicted in heraldry* as a roundle,* an annulet,* or an irradiated cloud. (Bibliog. 43)

goat's-foot crossbow, weapon which was discharged by a lever made of two pieces joined. The smaller of the two divided into branches, each of which ended with a catch: one to grasp the bowstring and the other to engage lugs or projections on each side of the stock. To charge the bow,* the larger arm of the lever was drawn back, and the smaller fork which grasped the bowstring followed it until the string became engaged in the notch. See crossbow. (Bibliog. 9)

godendag, goudendar, mace* with a spike at the end and frequently with a fluke or spikes around the side of the head. This weapon came into popular use about the time of the Battle of Courtrai* (1302); the name came from the brutal jest of the soldier's* "pleasantries" when using it: as they struck with the weapon, they would grunt out the word "Godendag" or "Good-day." Some references to this describe a staff weapon over six feet* long, ending with a seven-inch spike, and having twelve short spikes projecting slightly over an inch* arranged in four rows around the head. (Bibliog. 9)

going to soil. See ruses.

gold, noblest of colors* in the achievements* of arms* because of its bright, shining, and virtuous nature. It was so comforting that a physician would give it as a sovereign cordial to any man who was sick unto death. It represented the sun which was a very noble body, for the law said that there was nothing more noble than light; the Scriptures related that holy persons shine like the sun; ancient laws ordered that none but a prince* should bear the color; hence it truly was the noblest color. (Bibliog. 31)

gone, arrow* which was judged to have fallen wide of or far from its mark. (Bibliog. 100)

gonfanon, gonfannon, gonfano, gunfanto, banner* or long flag having several tails or streamers borne near the leader of an army and affixed by its top to a frame or staff so it would turn in the wind like a ship's vane. William* I's gonfannon had a gold* cross* on a white* background with a blue border and ended in three tails. (Bibliog. 331)

gonne. See cannon.

gorge, hawk that had eaten to repletion, hence it had "a full gorge." (Bibliog. 26)

gorged, said of a beast in heraldry* when it was collared. (Bibliog. 43)

gorget, colletin, plate defense (see armor) for the chin and neck, introduced in the last quarter of the 13th century. (Bibliog. 9)

goshawk, See falconry birds.

Goswhit, King Arthur's helm,* earlier the property of Uther Pendragon. (Bibliog. 311)

goudendar. See godendag.

goupil, fox; wily animal who bloodied the earth and killed with its open mouth and hanging tongue.

gout, disease stemming from an inflammation of the joints. (Bibliog. 364)

goutty, field* of a shield* strewn with drops, as argent* in gutte d'eau, representing drops of water; or in gutte d'or,* representing drops of gold*; azure* in gutte de larmes, representing drops of tears; sable* in gutte de poix, representing drops of pitch; gules* in gutte de sange, representing drops of blood; vert* in gutte d'huile, representing drops of oil. (Bibliog. 43)

graf (Ger.), count.* See titles of dignity.

graffle, belthook by which early crossbows* were charged for firing. (Bibliog. 331)

Grail, Graal, Holy, cup of the Last Supper in which Joseph of Arimathea caught the blood of the crucified Christ. Later he carried it to Britain where in Castle Corbenic it was entrusted to Joseph's descendants, ending with Galahad. (For interpretation in Christian legend, see Bibliog. 50; in Pagan fertility legend, see Bibliog. 374; in Celtic tradition, see Bibliog. 201.) (Bibliog. 117)

grain, smallest unit of weight, equal to 2/875 avoirdupois* ounce,* 1/450 mercantile and tower ounce, and 2/951 of a Scottish troy ounce, 1/480 apothecary and English troy ounce; it also was the basis for standardization of the inch* in the 13th-century at three medium-sized barleycorn* grains placed end to end. (Bibliog. 394)

Gram, one of Siegfried's swords.* (Bibliog. 308)

Grand Assize, assize* of twelve knights during the reign of King Henry II of England (1154–1189) at which a land tenant might demand to settle his claim to ownership of the land to prevent the matter from being settled by a duel* or trial by battle. This protected the possessors of tenements. A claimant had to offer battle, but the possessor could refuse and put himself in the hands of the grand assize. Four knights from the county* of the dispute acted as a committee to elect twelve others as a jury (see jury duty) to hear the arguments of who had the right to ownership of the land. This was a long and tedious action, subject to continual postponements before it ended usually by agreement between parties. As the number of knights in any county was not large, some men were called repeatedly to serve. Robert of Holdenby, for example, served on eleven juries between 1200 and 1204.

The three new assizes created by King Henry II—Assize Utrum,* Assize of Novel Disseisin,* and Grand—revealed royal protection of possessions, for they ensured that no one was to be disseised (dispossessed) of his free tenement unjustly and without judgment, or even with judgment unless he had been summoned by royal writ to answer the claim, and that no one was forced to defend his seisin* of a free tenement by duel or trial by battle. (Bibliog. 261, 264)

Grand Ordonnance. See Rights of the King of France.

Grani, Siegfried's horse,* famous for its marvelous swiftness; its name meant grey colored.

graper. See grate.

grate, bracket fastened to the breast of a suit of armor* which allowed the shock of a blow of the lance* to be absorbed by more than just the hand of the knight. (Bibliog. 27)

grave, Portuguese silver coin of the 14th century equivalent to three dinheros.* (Bibliog. 150)

grease, fat of hunted game. It played an important role in the economy of all households by helping to replenish the larder. Fat of red deer was called suet, occasionally tallow; that of roe-buck was called bevy-grease; that of hare, boar, wolf, fox, marten, otter, badger, coney, or any other beast was called grease. A ''deer of high grease'' indicated the time of year when the deer was fattest. (Bibliog. 96)

grease time, that time of year when hart or buck were the fattest and thus the fittest for killing; it did not mean the entire season when hart or buck could be hunted. See hunting seasons. (Bibliog. 96)

great fyrd. See fyrd.

great helm. See helm.

great officers of state (England), king's butler,* chamberlain,* constable,* marshal,* and steward.*

Great Roll. See Exchequer.

greave (Fr.), armor* protection for the lower leg which by 1400 had replaced the English word jamber.* (Bibliog. 27, 107)

greek fire, inflammable and destructive compound used in warfare. Also known as wildfire, wet fire, fire rain, *feu grégeois* (Fr.), and *grieches Feuer* (Ger.), this compound was used chiefly in naval engagements and sieges when it was poured from cauldrons and ladles onto besiegers or through tubes projecting from the prows of vessels onto enemy ships. Sometimes it was put in earthen jars and hurled against attackers by *petraria.** It was a thick, viscous liquid of sulphur, pitch, dissolved niter, and petroleum boiled together. It burned so hotly and so fiercely that it was impossible to extinguish except with a mixture of sand, vinegar, and wine*; water seemed to have intensified the blaze. The Byzantine garrison of Dyrrhachium used it against the Normans in 1108; Saracen* defenders of Acre used it to burn the siege towers of the crusaders; French King Philip* Augustus (1180–1223) brought back the secret of its composition from the third crusade* and used it against the English ships in the siege of Dieppe. Richard I* used it at the siege of Nottingham in 1194, and Edward I used it at Stirling in 1294. (Bibliog. 71, 241)

gregois, grigois, gregeois, grezois, grecois, term in the *chansons de geste** used variously to mean a bishop, an emir,* a palace, a destrier,* a mantlet,* a spy, a helmet,* a hauberk,* gold,* but most frequently to mean "greek fire."* (Bibliog. 191)

gresche. See gros.

grevieres, armor* coverings for the lower part of the legs. (Bibliog. 9)

greyhound, generic term for the whole group of "hunting dogs"* used to chase both big and small game. Basically they were swift hounds which hunted by sight only. Every gentleman* was expected to have one; according to a Welsh proverb, "a gentleman might be known by his hawk, his horse,* and his greyhound." These dogs were used by the limers (see hunting dogs) who began the hunt and then let them run as relays to a pack of scenting or running hounds. They could be used by themselves for coursing game in open countryside, placed at passes where game was likely to run in order to turn back the game to the archer, or to chase and pull down a wounded deer. They always were used in couples* when on the hunt.

Lévrier, the French word for greyhound, covered such dogs as the Irish wolfhound, the Scottish deerhound, and the smaller Italian greyhound. In France, the powerful hound that chased stag, wolf, and wild boar was called *lévrier d'attache*; the smaller, nervous harehound was known as the *petit lévrier pour lièvre* (hare). (Bibliog. 96)

grieches Feuer. See greek fire.

griffin, monster* with head, claws, and wings of an eagle,* the ears, body, and hind parts of a lion,* and a short beard. It lived in the Hyperborean hills at the extreme north of the world and kept in its nest a stone called Smaragdus as protection against venomous beasts of the mountain. Its wings were reputed to be twelve paces* long and when spread out extended thirty paces. Sir John Mandeville (died c. 1372) described how a griffin could carry off two oxen yoked together, clutching them with its talons as great as the horns of oxen. From these talons men made drinking cups, and from its ribs and wing feathers men made bows.* Marco Polo (1254–1324), however, claimed that the creature wasn't as described but actually resembled an eagle, though so much larger that it could pick up an elephant* and soar into the air with it, drop it, and then pounce on its carcass. (Bibliog. 177)

grip, fusee, part of a weapon meant to be grasped by the hand. (Bibliog. 331)

groat, English silver coinage* of the value of four pence (see penny), issued first by Edward I in 1279. Its name derived from its French counterpart, gros* tournois, which had been minted twenty years earlier at Tours. It was not popular in England because it represented too large a sum for the poorer classes. Because the English economy changed, it was reissued in 1351 and regularly thereafter. (Bibliog. 150, 237)

groot. See gros.

gros, groot, grosch, gresche, grosz, grosso, grote, coinage* apparently of Italian origin, equal to four denarii (see denarius), the highest denomination of coin previously available. Under Doge [duke*] Enrico Dandolo (1192–1205) the Venetians struck the grosso or matapan* as the first coin of this type, and this was followed in many other parts of Europe from the 12th century onward, especially in France by the popular gros tournois.* (Bibliog. 150)

groschen, German silver coin valued at 60 to the mark,* and struck in imitation of the French gros tournois.* (Bibliog. 324)

grossetto, copper coin of Venice equal to four sol,* introduced under Doge [duke*] Antonio Veniero (1383–1400); it weighed thirty-eight grains,* nine carats. (Bibliog. 150)

grossmutigkeit (Ger.), chivalric word for largesse.*

grosz, grote. See gros.

guardant, with face looking outward toward the viewer, said of beasts and figures in heraldry,* as in lion* passant* guardant. (Bibliog. 43)

Guelpho grosso, variety of silver fiorino (see florin) of Florence with the standing figure of St. John. Struck in 1363, one type had a fox under the feet of the saint signifying Pietro Farnese, general-in-chief of the Florentine forces. (Bibliog. 150)

Guelphs, Italian political faction of the 12th through 14th centuries which opposed the Hohenstaufen (Ghibelline*) emperors,* especially Frederick I, Barbarossa (1123–1190) and Frederick II (1194–1250). (Bibliog. 139)

guidon, lance* flag of a "knight bachelor"*; also known as a pennon.*

Guienne, Guyenne, corruption of the name of the French province, Aquitaine.

Guiennois, large gold coin issued in the English possessions in Guienne* by Edward III of England and his son, Edward, the Black Prince; it showed the prince in armor* on the obverse and an elaborate cross* on the reverse. (Bibliog. 295)

guige, looped strap at the top of a Norman shield* by means of which the shield could be suspended from the neck. (Bibliog. 27)

guilt, ascertaining, rather than placing the burden of proof on the accuser, who had to produce witnesses to testify as to the veracity of his claim in Roman times, barbarian law relied basically on negative proof by which the accused sought to prove his innocence. The most widely used method was compurgation,* by which the parties involved swore an oath several times at several places that what they said was true. More often they found the requisite number of compurgators to swear with them, not as to their actual knowledge of the case but as to their willingness to believe the oath of one or the other of the parties. Merovingian Queen Fredegunda, for example, established the disputed legacy of her son by persuading three noblemen to support her oath that the child actually had sprung from the loins of her dead husband. And in Anglo-Saxon England, an accuser could substantiate his claim by swearing an oath in four churches, but to rebut the charge, the defendant had to swear his oaths in twelve churches. (Bibliog. 220)

guisarme. See gisarme.

gules, tincture (see colors) red in heraldry.* The term derived possibly from the crusaders bringing back the Arabic word *gule,* meaning a red rose, but it also may have come from the Latin *gula* and Old French *gueule,* meaning a red throat of an animal. (Bibliog. 43)

gun, gonne, gunne. See cannon.

gunfanto. See gonfannon.

gunpowder, inflammable mixture of saltpeter and charcoal to which sulphur later was added. Known as early as the 13th century, this substance was used for explosions of considerable strength only after grains of it could be formed by "corning." (Bibliog. 331)

gunstone. See roundel.

gusset, 1. charge* resembling either side of a pall* without the top opening; when borne sinister,* it was an abatement* for adultery; 2. metal piece fastened to the body to protect joints. (Bibliog. 116, 331)

Guyenne. See Guienne.

guze. See roundel.

gwyde. See stick.

gypciere, leather bag suspended from the belt, often with the misericorde* going through its top. (Bibliog. 9)

gyr. See ger.

gyron, lower half of a quarter* on a shield* but divided by a line bendwise (see bend). (Bibliog. 43)

gyronny, shield* divided into at least six wedge-shaped sections by three or more intersecting lines radiating from the center. (Bibliog. 230)

H

hache, "battle axe"* which along with sword,* baselard,* and dagger, by Ordinance of 1386, strangers and foreign visitors to England were forbidden to carry. (Bibliog. 9)

hack, state of partial liberty in which young hawks were kept. Fed early in the day and again later by food fastened to a board so that it could not be carried off, they were kept close so they would not seek food for themselves. To eat this tied food, they were trained to stand on the falconer's* hand, to wear a hood, and to eat from this board called a lure.* See hawking. (Bibliog. 118)

hacketon. See aketon.

hackney, horse for ordinary riding as distinguished from a destrier,* or a hunter.

haft, handle of a weapon.

haggard, wild hawk that has molted for the first time, as distinguished from an eyass,* the younger, and a "passage hawk,"* the older bird. (Bibliog. 118)

halbard, halberd, staff weapon generally five to six feet* long used only by the infantry or footsoldiers between 1300 and 1500. It had a square or crescent-shaped axe* blade at the front and a sharp hook-like projection at the back; it always had a spear* at the top of the staff. Its head extended a considerable distance down the staff to protect it from axe or sword* cuts. (Bibliog. 9)

halfpenny, silver coinage* minted by a few of the Viking and Saxon kings* of Britain but not issued as a regular English coin until 1279 during the reign of Edward I. However, as the price of silver rose over the centuries, the halfpennies grew so small that they became more of a nuisance than a means of exchange; at one time they were only ten millimeters in diameter. (Bibliog. 295)

half-stone. See clove.

halimot, hallmote, English "manor court,"* a moot* in a hall,* which met normally every three weeks but could be summoned more frequently at the pleasure of the lord. Usually the suitors were peasants (see villein) living within the manor,* but sometimes when they were more important freemen, or when a thief was to be hanged, outsiders were summoned into court by royal writ. As this "jury duty"* imposed considerable time, cost, and hardship upon the jurors, many tried to obtain exemption from that duty. Tenants of the manor had to appear on the day following receipt of a summons. (Bibliog. 357)

hall, salle, salon, sale, salone, saal, principal apartment in the large manor* dwelling used for receptions, feasts, and other important gatherings. In Norman castles* the hall generally was in the keep* above the ground floor where retainers lived, the basement being devoted to stores and prison (see jail) cells. (Bibliog. 100)

hallmote. See halimot.

Halteclare, Hauteclaire, Hauteclere, Oliver's* sword.* Originally it had belonged to a Roman emperor* who dropped it into the grass of the battlefield on which he was killed. A mower found it when his scythe* hit it. It was then given to the pope, who deciphered its name from the lettering on its blade and kept it as one of the treasures of St. Peter's in Rome until King Pepin the Short* of France took possession of it. He gave it to Duke Beuve as a feudal gift, and Beuve sold it to a Jew who kept it carefully hidden for a hundred years until it was given to Oliver, the son of Renier de Gennes. See Glorious. (Bibliog. 162)

hammer, weapon used continuously as a war hammer since the 12th century. Types of hammers included the long-handled footman's hammer; the English maul* used by common soldiers*; and the knightly hammer which had a thick, beak-like fluke balanced by a small but heavy head channelled into four or more pyramidal points. The last type was called a polaxe* by the English and *marteau** and *martel* by the French. Others were the 14th-century short-handled horseman's hammer which resembled a pick-axe and the throwing hammer which resembled a throwing hatchet but simply was an iron cross with sharply pointed arms, some having six or eight arms. (Bibliog. 27)

hand, when depicted in heradlry,* the dexter* human hand usually was depicted couped* at the wrist or apaume.*

hand palisado, hog's bristle, sweyne feather, stake five to six feet* long, four fingers thick, ending in a piece of sharp iron; it was buried in the ground at an angle so that the iron point was at the height of the breast of a charging horse.* (Bibliog. 331)

handbook for knights,
Boucicaut (Jean le Maingre). *Le livre de faicts du bon messire Jean le Maingre, dit*

Boucicaut. In Michaud et Poujoulat, *Nouvelle collection des mémoires pour servir à l'histoire de France.* vol. 2. Paris, 1881, 205–332.

Chandos Herald. *Life of the Black Prince.* Ed. M. K. Pope and E. C. Lodge, Oxford, 1910.

Christine de Pisan. *Book of the Fayttes of Armes and of Chyvalry.* Tr. William Caxton, ed. A. T. P. Byles. London: EETS OS #189, 1932, repr. 1971.

Etienne de Fougeres. *Livre des maniéres.* Ed. F. Talbert. Angers, 1877.

Geoffrey de Charny. *Le Livre de chevalérie.* Ed. Arthur Piaget, *Romania,* vol. 26, 1897, 394–411.

Knyghthode and Bataile (15th-century verse paraphrase of Flavius Vegetius Renatus' *De re militari*). Ed. R. Dyboski and Z. Arendt. London, EETS, 1935.

Luce, Simeon. *The right joyous and pleasant history of the feats, gestes, and prowess of the chevalier Bayart.* Tr. Sara Coleridge. London, 1906.

Lull, Raymon. *Book of the Order of Chyvalry.* Tr. William Caxton. London: EETS OS #168, 1926, repr. 1971.

Ordene de Chevalérie. In E. Barbazan, ed. *Fabliaux et contes des poètes français des 11e, 12e, 13e, 14e, et 15e siècles.* Paris, 1808, vol. I.

Painter, Sidney. *William Marshal, Knight Errant, Baron, and Regent of England.* Baltimore: Johns Hopkins, 1933; repr. 1967.

Thomas of Zirclaire, *Die wälsche Gast.* Ed D. Rocher. Paris, 1977.

Tieck, Ludwig. *Frauendienst, oder Geschichte und Liebe des Ritters und Sängers Ulrich von Liechtenstein.* Stuttgart, 1812.

haqueton, aketon, thick, padded garment to cover a person from neck to knees worn under a hauberk* of mail* to relieve the pressure of the hauberk and cuirass,* if worn, and to prevent chafing. See aketon. (Bibliog. 9)

harbor, harbour, to track a hart* to his lair. See boughs; hunting.

hardel, 1. leash to tie couples* of hounds together by passing a small flexible branch like that of a willow through the couplings of the hounds and bending it back on itself so both couples of hounds could be held by one hand; 2. to bind together the four legs of a roe-buck after its head was placed between its forelegs and thus to carry it whole into the kitchen. (Bibliog. 96)

hardi, gold coinage* struck in the French possessions by Edward, the Black Prince of England; it bore a half-length portrait of the prince* and an elaborate cross.* (Bibliog. 150)

hare, animal of the chase* which in the 11th century was thought to be valueless because in one month it was thought to be a male and in the next a female. (Bibliog. 96)

harness, 1. knight's armor,* including weapons; 2. paraphernalia by which animals could be caught and taken. (Bibliog. 96, 251)

Harold Godwineson, last Anglo-Saxon king of England (1066). Made Earl of East Anglia in 1046, Harold proved his strength and military abilities to King Edward the Confessor. For the first five years of his earldom, Harold joined his four brothers in supporting their father, Godwine, in his power struggle with the king. King Edward finally exiled all of them in 1051, but a year later, after Godwine died, Harold returned to England to assume his father's earldom of Wessex, and became the most influential person in England during the remaining years of Edward's reign. After Edward died in January 1066, Harold was proclaimed king by the Anglo-Saxon earls, who opposed the claims of William,* duke of Normandy. He defeated a Norse invasion in northern England, but was then defeated by William and killed at the Battle of Hastings.* (Bibliog. 139, 327)

harp, 1. musical instrument on which minstrels* accompanied their performances; 2. heraldic insignia of Ireland. (Bibliog. 122)

harrier, small running hound resembling a foxhound that was used to hunt all kinds of game. See hunting dogs. (Bibliog. 96)

hart, animal of the deer family which royalty chased while hunting.* (Bibliog. 96)

Hart Royal, any stag ten years of age or older if hunted by the king*; if it was pursued and not taken, and ultimately was driven out of the protection of the forest,* the master of the hunt issued a proclamation to warn anyone against chasing or killing that particular animal, for by that proclamation, it became a "Hart Royal Proclaimed." (Bibliog. 96, 304)

hastilude, spear* play; a diversion in a tournament* in which only lances* were used. (Bibliog. 72)

hastiludium (L.), word for tournament* used in papal or royal proclamations. See *behourd*; burdicia.

hatchment. See achievement.

haubergeon, hauberk* which after 1300 was shortened along its sides and curved down in front just below the knees. (Bibliog. 27)

hauberk, long "coat of mail"* worn over the gambeson* as the principal defense of knights in the 11th, 12th, and 13th centuries. Early types were made of scales of various materials sewn to a textile base similar to the armor* worn by Romans, the loricam, which had bronze scales overlapping with their points downward; these scales could be made of horn, leather, cuir-bouilli,* iron, bronze. Other types included iron rings sewn on a leather or other heavy garment, with bands of leather sewn between the rings, possibly jazerant* work, and ordinary quilted armor with a variety of materials used for padding: tow, wool, shredded cloth. This helped prevent a cleaving wound, a sweeping cut by a sword,* or a penetration from an arrow.* Its upper part often extended upward to form protection for the head, leaving a small opening for the face; its sleeves ended at the elbow; and its skirt opened in the front for ease in riding and for protection of the thighs. (Bibliog. 9)

hauberk of plates, garment of cloth or leather lined with metal plates and worn between the surcoat* and the hauberk* as the most widely used form of body defense throughout most of the 14th century. (Bibliog. 27)

haussepied, snare. See anceps.

haute tierce, hour in the afternoon (usually after 3 P.M.) at which most travellers would stop for dinner, having begun their riding day at "basse prime"* (daybreak). See canonical hours. (Bibliog. 161)

Hauteclaire, Hauteclere. See Halteclaire.

hawking, falconry, art of training and flying hawks for the purpose of catching other birds and all sorts of small game including grouse, pheasant, partridge, quail, duck, woodcock, snipe, heron, crows, gulls, magpies, jays, blackbirds, thrush, larks, hares, and rabbits. In training a hawk, a person kept the bird on his fist as much as possible, taking her wherever he went—into law courts,* into church, into the streets—so that the bird would become accustomed to men, horses,* carts,* dogs, and all other objects and beings around her. Not only was hawking held in such high esteem that a lack of interest or skill in it was held to be a slur on one's breeding, but also severe laws were enacted to protect hawks and falcons* and to safeguard the interests of their owners.

Persons of high rank rarely appeared without their hawks, frequently carrying them from one country to another, sometimes even into battle, and refusing to part with them when captured, even to procure their liberty. Persons of nobility* considered hawks as ensigns* of their rank and thus deemed as dishonorable the act of a man giving up his bird. Persons of different rank used different birds: emperor*—an eagle,* vulture, or merlin*; king*—gerfalcon (see falconry birds) or tercel* or gerfalcon; prince*—falcon gentle* or tercel gentle; duke*—falcon of the rock; earl*—peregrine falcon; baron*—bastard; knight—sacre and sacret; esquire*—laner and laneret; lady—marylon; young man—hobby*; yeoman—goshawk; poor man—tercel; priest—sparrowhawk; holy water clerk—musket*; knave or servant—kestrel.

Hawks were treasured so highly that when the king of Scotland presented King Edward III with a gentle falcon in 1334, it was so valuable that Edward rewarded the falconer* who carried it from Scotland to London with a gift of forty shillings (see money). Later that same King Edward ordered a statute enacted in 1361 by which a person who found a lost falcon, tercelet, laner, laneret, or any species of hawk was commanded to turn it over to the sheriff* of the county* in which it was found. The finder was to proclaim throughout the county that it had been found and that its noble owner or falconer* might claim it by identifying it and by repaying the sheriff for any costs incurred in his search for the rightful owner. However, if the owner did not claim the bird within four months, the finder could keep the bird if he were a person of rank, or else the sheriff would keep it and reward the finder. On the other hand, if the finder kept the bird for himself, he had to pay a fine* of the price of the bird to the owner and suffer two years imprisonment, or longer if he were unable to pay the fine. This confirmed that stealing a hawk was a felony.*

A falconer was to keep his birds keen and to assure that their appetites in the field were sharp enough to make them put forth full powers to obtain food. Thus, they had to be trained carefully. When first caught, a hawk had a "rufter hood"* placed on her head and was furnished with jesses,* swivel,* leash,* and bell. Moreover, she had to be carried by humans as frequently as possible, both day and night, and to be stroked constantly with a bird's feather or wing, gently. At night she was tied on a perch in a darkened room and fed while tied. She was induced to eat by having a piece of beef drawn across her feet while brushing her legs with a feather, so that whenever she snapped at the sensation, a piece of beef was slipped into her mouth. Furthermore, while she was swallowing, the falconer would whistle a low note so that by associating that sound with eating, she would bend to feel for food every time she heard it. That trained her to come to him at the sound of that note. After that, she would become accustomed gradually to more and more light, and more and more people, and to being carried on the gloved fist of her trainer. Finally, she was taken into the field and taught to attack her particular quarry*—bird or small game—by having it released near her, gradually moved farther and farther away, and to feed on a lure* as it was moved gradually as far as 1,000 yards from the falconer. Then she was ready for a hunt in the field. (Bibliog. 26, 118)

haye-bote, peasant's (see villein) right granted by the lord to take wood or thorns from the forest* for the repair of his fences. See also fire-bote. (Bibliog. 24)

hayward, messor, manor* officer in charge of the enclosures, especially at harvest or haymaking time. Appointed to oversee the manorial reapers and mowers, he watched over the pastures to ensure that no one infringed on customary rights and remained in the field after all had left to see that no one carried off the lord's grain. He also measured sheaves to make sure they were the correct size. At the end of the year he tallied* with the reeve* for all the materials under his responsibility. For pay, he often was excused from rent or had it lowered, received a piece of the meadow called the beadle-mead,* and a measure of seed-corn for his own use. (Bibliog. 24)

head, unless otherwise specified in the blazon,* a head in heraldry* was drawn in profile facing dexter* and couped* at the neck. (Bibliog. 43)

headland. See fields.

health, code of health from the School of Salernum (Salerno) dedicated to the king* of the English and containing a compilation of popular maxims of health which opened with these lines of sound advice:

If thou to health and vigor wouldst attain,
Shun weighty cares—all anger deem profane,
From heavy suppers and much wine abstain.
Nor trivial count it, after pompous fare
To rise from table and take the air.
Shun idle, noonday slumber, nor delay
The urgent calls of nature to obey.
These rules if thou will follow to the end,
Thy life to greater length thou mayst extend.

(Bibliog. 364)

heartbone, hard red cartilage found in a deer's heart, to which medicinal qualities were ascribed. As the most cowardly of beasts, the deer relied on this bone not to perish from fright, and so its "bone" comforted the frightened heart of someone, especially a woman expecting a baby. (Bibliog. 340)

heater, shield* in the shape of a flat iron and of moderate size that evolved around 1270. (Bibliog. 27)

heaume, metal head covering which evolved between 1180 and 1250 from the pot-de-fer or iron skull cap which transmitted every blow directly to the head of the wearer. Because removing the covering from direct contact with the head gave the wearer greater protection, the pot heaume was developed by adding ear flaps to the conical helmet,* and these gradually were enlarged to meet the nasal (see helmet) and absorb it. This created a barrel heaume with a flat top and a slit called an occularium.* In time, the top became pointed, creating the sugar-loaf heaume which rested on a padded cap on the head, but as these were not fastened to the body, they were knocked off in battle occasionally. With his face thus covered, a knight needed means for identifying himself. Thus heraldry* began. King Richard I,* Coeur de Lion (1189–1199), used a lion* passant* on his heaume, a fan-shaped ornament above it, and three lions passant guardant* on his shield.* With openings for vision and breathing, his heaume was a single piece of metal riveted to cross pieces in front and on top which greatly strengthened it. To a lance,* javelin,* or arrow,* this presented a glancing surface and partially distributed or parried a blow from a mace or a sword*; its enemy, however, was the "battle axe."* (Bibliog. 9, 71)

Heerschilde (Ger.), knighthood.* See titles of dignity.

helbelin, halfpenny* of Strassbourg in the 14th century. (Bibliog. 150)

heliens, deniers (see denarius) circulating in Perigord, France, in the 11th century. (Bibliog. 150)

heller, billon* or copper coin equally half of a pfennig (see coinage) introduced in the 12th and 13th centuries into the currencies of Hesse, Treves, and other areas; the earliest was the bracteate*; eight hellers equalled one kreutzer.* (Bibliog. 150)

helm, 1. helmet*; 2. gold* quarter-florin (see florin) minted by English King Edward III with obverse depicting a helmet surmounted by a lion.* (Bibliog. 240)

helm, frog-mouthed, helmet* which came into use at the end of the 14th century and was so named because it had a low skull area and curved up and out at the front to form a flattened point along the line of sight which was formed by a gap between the bevor* and the skull. When leaning forward in the correct position for couching his lance,* a knight could obtain proper vision, but when he straightened just at the moment of impact with his opponent, its lower edge protected his eyes because they were completely concealed. (Bibliog. 27)

helmet, protection for a warrior's head. Early ones consisted of an iron or bronze framework formed by a headband supporting two vertical bands converging at the apex of the helmet and having a separate band called a nasal riveted to the lower edge and protecting the nose of the wearer. The entire unit was lined with iron, bronze, or horn. Used until the mid-13th century, this was followed by a round-topped version without a nasal. Then a cylindrical model appeared, tapering slightly from top to bottom but with a slightly rounded or domed top. These were followed by a small hemispherical skull cap called a cervelliere* or basinet,* frequently worn beneath a *coif-de-mailles.* * See heaume. (Bibliog. 9, 27)

helmet decoration, adornments on warrior's headpieces, worn since the earliest times as marks of identification. Included among such decorations were horns of honor worn by the Vikings. In an early Italian tournament,* the horns or trumpets heralded the combatants; horns again adorned the helmets of victorious knights. The defeated knight was deprived of them and non-combatants could not wear them. From the comb on a cock's head came the feathered decorations called the panache.* (Bibliog. 78)

Henry II, king of England (1154–1189). The son of Geoffrey Plantagenet,* count of Anjou, and Mathilda, heiress of Henry I, he inherited Normandy, Maine, and Anjou on the death of his father in 1151. In 1152 he married the divorced queen of France, Eleanor of Aquitaine,* and assumed control of her duchy. When Stephen of England died in 1154, Henry assumed the crown, founding the Angevin empire. He was one of the greatest kings of England. Because his reign was marked by his continuous movements between England and his domains in France and by a continuing struggle with the French kings—first Louis VII* and then his son, Philip II,* Augustus—Henry was forced to organize the government of his possessions so he could obtain the resources necessary to maintain his empire. As king of England he created a system of government based on an administration dependent on the king and governing according to common law of the country. To impose respect for these new legal practices he issued a series of constitutions (see Constitutions of Clarendon) and assizes (see Assize of Novel Disseisin) based on the superiority of the royal authority and its administration. Such a government was based upon local communities, governed by sheriffs* representing the crown. The central government controlled the sheriffs and the courts of the shires by itinerant justices (see eyre) and by justiciars who became powerful royal officials. He imposed trial by jury as a means of imposing peace and respect for the law in the country. He attempted to control the church by appointing his friend and former chancellor, Thomas à Becket,* as Archbishop of Canterbury, but Thomas refused to be Henry's pawn. He gave his sons, Henry, Richard,* and Geoffrey* power in Normandy, Aquitaine, and Brittany under his control, but they revolted against him and obtained support from the French kings, Louis VII and then Philip II. He was planning to accompany the emperor Frederick Barbarossa* and Philip II on the third crusade* when he fell ill and died in 1189. (Bibliog. 235, 262)

Henry I, laws of, compilation of a general statement of principles of English law dated about 1118 and called the laws of Henry because they begin with his Coronation Charter.* (Bibliog. 363)

herald, servant of the king* sent on military and diplomatic missions and who, because of dedication to and knowledge of the chivalric profession, became immune from the ravages of war (see safe-conduct). A herald's allegiance was not to his masters alone, but also to the order of knighthood* at large. All French and English heralds belonged to one special fellowship with its own rules, ranks, and ceremonies. For example, at the battle of Agincourt (1415), heralds of both sides stood together on a hilltop away from the fighting because their order had no part in it. After that battle the French herald, the Mountjoy "king of arms,"* informed the English King Henry V that his side unquestionably had won the day. Their immunity was observed far better than any other because soldiers* recognized that heralds were an essential part of their own chivalric profession; they were attached to every major body of troops.

Heralds carried out special and essential duties during war: they brought summons of captains to towns before seiges; they brought challenges of princes* to pitched battles; they obtained safe-conducts for ambassadors; they obtained safe-conducts for soldiers to parley or to joust* with the enemy; they helped negotiate ransoms* for prisoners with relatives at home. They were forbidden by strict rules to reveal any secret information. Thus they were too useful to be plundered, and savage reprisals would accrue to anyone who did violence to any herald. They were treated with respect on all sides.

Peacetime also saw them busy, for they were known for their associations with tournaments* which they proclaimed or prohibited and regulated under the marshal.* They drew up tournament rolls to record who participated in each tourney. To do this required them to master the ability of recognizing "coats of arms"* and descriptions; this, in turn, necessitated their presence to help the marshals with identification at tournaments, sieges, battles, "round tables,"* or wherever organized forces were used. Such work provided them with certain prerequisites. In early times, for example, they took as theirs the armor* that fell to the ground during tournaments; the armor of anyone who entered the lists* without having the right to do so; the helmet* of a knight at his first tourney, but not his first joust if he already had fought in a tourney; and clouage* or "nail money,"* the payment for nailing to the pavilion* the knight's armorial shield.*

Shields of arms* appeared in England from about 1130 and increased dramatically during the reign of King Stephen* (1135–1154) in close association with the unorganized mass-tournament (see *mélée*) of which King Stephen was inordinately fond. When King Richard I* imposed strict controls in 1194, greater opportunities were provided for the emergence of heralds who travelled throughout the countryside and abroad to proclaim forthcoming events. They made arrangements, announced the competitors, kept the score, declared the victors, and marshalled the processions to and from the lists. Heralds, however, were not spoken of until the rules for tournaments emerged in the *Statum Armorum in Torniamentis*,* c. 1265, ten years after the first "roll of arms."*

These rolls were not sacrosanct. Heralds had to support themselves, and so they found that a convenient way to keep a patron happy was to keep the heraldry information up to date, to glorify a person or family by the "discovery" of a noble ancestor or two, and by the introduction into their genealogy and arms rolls of Arthurian heroes and other fabulous persons.

Throughout the reign of King Edward I (1272–1307) and well into the 14th century, minstrels* and heralds were lumped by household clerks under the term "menestrali"; everything pertaining to heraldry or to minstrelsy came under their charge, for the two careers were not clearly distinguished: if not referred to as the "king of arms,"* they might be called harpers or minstrels. At the king's

Feast of the Swans,* for example, the heralds were listed as minstrels, and each was paid five marks.* Such an association was readily understandable, for heralds were drawn at first from the ranks of minstrels and served as heralds only if they could find a patron. In these early days, heraldry was essential, but not everyone was fond of or needed minstrelsy. Simon de Montfort (1208–1265), who seemingly had no minstrels, had to have someone at the battle of Evesham to identify who was who, and so he paid his barber Nicholas to serve in this capacity.

In time their military and diplomatic duties changed to granting and regulating armorial bearings (see charge), investigating genealogies, and superintending public ceremonies. England's six heralds ranked according to seniority, and although their titles were derived from certain districts, they had little connection with those areas: Chester herald was created in Edward III's reign; Lancaster herald was created by Edward III (1361) when the king created John of Gaunt as duke* of Lancaster; Windsor herald was created by Edward III in 1365; Richmond herald was created by Edward IV; Somerset herald was created by Henry VII in 1494; and for the York herald no records survived. By the time of King Henry III (1216–1272), three ranks of heralds existed: king of arms, herald, "pursuivant of arms."* Their costume consisted of an embroidered satin surcoat* of the royal arms and a "collar of SS."* (Bibliog. 43, 87, 116, 259, 361)

heraldic heiress, woman whose father left no living male issue, nor children of dead sons at his demise. If a man died leaving four daughters, those four were regarded as co-heirs of their father and were treated as heraldic heiresses. When they married, they placed their arms* in a shield of pretense over those of their husband, and on their deaths their children inherited the arms as a quartering.* (Bibliog. 43)

heraldic helmet, important appendage to the shield* with a crest* affixed to it. The sovereign's helmet was gold* affronty* with six bars* or grills and lined with crimson; dukes* and other peers* had silver* helmets* with five gold bars and lined with crimson, but not profile or affronty, rather half-way between; baronets'* and knights' helmets were affronty and open; squires* and gentlemen* were in profile with visor closed. (Bibliog. 43)

heraldry, system of personal symbolism following certain rules. Such devices* for recognition were essential to knights who owed feudal service to their lords; they needed symbols by which they could be recognized and seals by which the authenticity of documents could be established. These were hereditary; it was considered an honor to bear them. The principal vehicle for displaying them was the shield.* Heraldry and everything that went with it was part of the climate in which medieval kings* like Henry III and Edward I lived: shields of arms* were a natural form of decoration for the king's palaces at Westminster, including the abbey, and Winchester. Even armorial glass for Rochester Castle in 1247

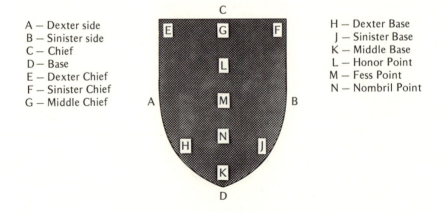

A — Dexter side
B — Sinister side
C — Chief
D — Base
E — Dexter Chief
F — Sinister Chief
G — Middle Chief

H — Dexter Base
J — Sinister Base
K — Middle Base
L — Honor Point
M — Fess Point
N — Nombril Point

Figure 7. Points and Parts of Shield

was ordered with King Henry III's shield on it. By the end of the 14th century royal heralds were asserting their armorial authority, and the senior heralds were called kings of heralds of arms. Further, as sons succeeded to their fathers' arms, they conveniently and proudly bore those arms, but they made small additions to distinguish themselves from the head of the family. One's arms were one's ensigns* of honor,* for they were painted on a shield which was itself an object of honor; respect for the profession of arms was honorable and noble, and hence a man's armor* and weapons were regarded with respect. The only people who needed to use arms were the nobility,* that is, those who were worth recognizing in battle, those who were invited to tournaments,* and those who needed a seal. Because arms and the right to bear them was conferred by the crown, the king had to exercise some control. Thus when a dispute arose over a "coat of arms,"* it was settled in the Court of Chivalry,* also known as the High Court Military, or the Court of the Constable* and Marshal.*

Around the death of Edward I (1307), heraldry entered most emphatically into the lives of the king and his knights. The king ordered lists of earls,* barons,* and knights drawn up in no particular order, with their armorial bearings on painted shields or banners,* or in blazon,* the technical language of the heralds, and then later copied "in trick"* by which the arms were sketched and their colors indicated by conventional symbols. The first "roll of arms"* of this period, 1307–1319, generally was known as the Parliamentary Roll of Arms.* In time, custom dictated that these representations displayed a banner for a banneret* and a shield for a simple knight. From such displays and rolls emerged heraldry.

Elements for decorating the surface of the shield called the field* involved color,* divisions, and objects. Six tinctures were used: or* (gold*), argent* (silver*), gules* (red*), azure* (blue), sable* (black*), vert* (green), purpure* (purple); three "stains" also were used occasionally: tenne* (orange), sanguine* (blood color), and murrey* (purple-red or mulberry). When an object was shown in its natural coloration, it was said to be "proper." Certain rules pertained to the use of tinctures: metal* could not be used on metal, nor color on color. Heraldic tinctures in black and white drawings followed certain practices. Or was represented by dots, argent was left plain, gules by perpendicular lines, azure by horizontal lines, sable by conjunction of both horizontal and vertical lines, vert by diagonal lines from dexter* chief* to sinister* base,* and purpure by diagonal from sinister to dexter.

If the field were divided vertically, horizontally, or diagonally by a single straight line, and single or contrasting tinctures applied to each side, then the simplest heraldic insignia called a "party field," from the word "partitioned" (see partition, lines of), would have been formed. If such a line went horizontally through the center of the field called the "fess point,"* the field was "party per fess"; if vertically through the same point, "party per pale"; if diagonally from the upper left or dexter side of the field to the lower right or sinister side, then the field was "party per bend"; its opposite was "party per bend sinister." Four other lines join with these main lines to form eight basic divisions. Complexities were added by using various types of lines: wavy, serrated, zigzag, and so forth. Further changes occurred by using multiple divisions of the field by those lines. For example, a field divided by an odd number of horizontal lines, or bars,* made it "barry"; vertical lines, "paly"; diagnonally, "bendy." Adding circles, squares, lozenges,* triangles, and other geometric figures made even more variations in design.

Added to these were the charges, the most frequent of which were called "ordinaries"*: chief, fess, bar, pale,* bend,* bend sinister, chevron,* pall, saltire,* and the most prominent one, the cross.* To these could be added subordinaries,* such small subdivisions of the main ordinaries as the bordure,* inescutcheon, orle,* gyron,* label,* and lozenge. Beyond these geometric shapes and divisions, the field was decorated by the addition of figures from the world, called charges. That choice was limitless: animals, real and imaginary, natural objects, inanimate objects, divine and human beings.

To read an achievement* of arms, one had to put oneself behind the field as if wearing the helm,* so that the left side as one looked at the shield became the right side or dexter, and the right observed side became the left or sinister side. (Bibliog. 43, 87, 253, 361)

herald's roll, pictorial representation to serve for the identification of the arms* of knights associated with his lord or those he came in contact with. The original "Herald's Roll" was a 13th-century document containing much extraneous material so that it extended to seventeen membranes containing 697 shields* painted in color. In it, heroes of romance* were assigned "coats of arms"* side by side

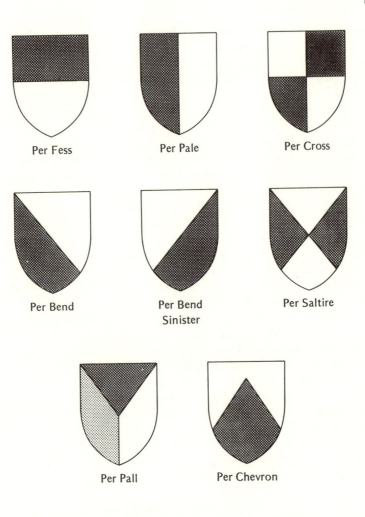

Figure 8. Eight Principal Divisions of Shield

with actual Edwardian knights; it included ladies, foreign princes,* and such legendary heroes as Prester John,* Roland,* and Sir Gawain. (Bibliog. 87)

here, originally the Danish army but later used interchangeably with the word fyrd.* (Bibliog. 158)

heregeld, annual tax levied by English King Cnut for the upkeep of the armed forces. (Bibliog. 327)

hergeat, war gear consisting of horse,* harness,* and weapons which the lord supplied to a knight. In strict theory, it remained the property of the lord, and thus it was only right that he should take possession of it again on his man's death. See heriot. (Bibliog. 24)

heriot, surrender of the best beast or chattel of a deceased tenant due by custom to the lord who held the tenant's property. When a peasant (see villein) died, one of the claims made by his lord arose from the old custom whereby all inhabitants, both bond and free, were obligated to return on their death the hergeat* because in theory it was the lord's property and should revert to him on the death of his man. In time, many freemen escaped this, for they were neither equipped by the lord nor obligated to pay a heriot on their death. A serf,* though, was not so fortunate. Although he served only limited military duties, he still was considered to have received hergeat, so he had to pay the heriot, usually in the form of the best beast or chattel. In the early laws of King Cnut of Denmark (1018–1035), of England (1016–1035), and of Norway (1028–1035), heriot ranged from eight horses* (four saddled and four unsaddled), four helmets,* four coats of mail,* eight spears* and shields,* four swords,* and 200 mancuses* of gold* for an earl* to the two pounds (see money) due for a lesser man. This contrasted with an example in which, on the death of a serf in March 1347, the lord seized his horse, cart,* and two pigs totalling twelve shillings (see money) in value but allowed the widow to buy them back for that sum and gave her five months to raise the cash. Villeins of St. Albans had to give the best head of cattle and all their house furniture. In most cases only the best beast was taken, and if the peasant had no cattle, then a money payment was exacted instead. (Bibliog. 24, 357)

herisson, hedgehog which at harvest time climbed up vines, knocked down grapes, rolled among the downed fruit, and then carried off to its young the grapes stuck on its spines. (Bibliog. 258)

herse, pikemen (see pike) or archers arrayed in a harrow-like battle formation and used as a secondary line of defense. (Bibliog. 246)

herzog (Ger.), duke.* See titles of dignity.

hide, measure of land which, though never accurately defined, seemingly was the amount of land reckoned capable of maintaining the average household based on 120 units, each of which represented a forenoon's plowing; on it was based the responsibility for taxation and public service proportional to the number of hides held. It frequently was divided into four quarters known as virgates,* from the Latin *virga*, rood* or rod. In its primitive form it consisted of one hundred acres,* but in the *Domesday Book*,* one virgate was equivalent to thirty acres, so a Domesday hide equalled 120 acres. (Bibliog. 109, 157, 213)

hide assessment, money due from a holding of hides*; at the normal Danegeld* rate of two shillings (see money) on the hide, an assessment of fifty hides would represent one hundred shillings, or five pounds (see money). (Bibliog. 109)

high reeve. See wic reeve.

hind, female red deer of which the male is a stag.

hind's-foot crossbow. See goat's-foot crossbow.

hip-belt. See baldric.

hippe, form of halbard* with a short, broad point, used in the 14th century. (Bibliog. 331)

hippogriff, heraldic monster* formed by uniting the top hand of a female griffin* with the hind portion of a horse.* (Bibliog. 43)

Histoire de Guillaume le Marechal, Anglo-Norman poetic biography of one of the most important figures in the late 12th century, William Marshal* (c. 1140–1219), a knight who rose from humble origins to become the regent of England during Richard I's* absences. This work contained valuable documents on the history and customs of the 12th and early 13th centuries and served as a "handbook for knights."* (Bibliog. 249)

hoarding. See brattice.

hobbies, hoby, hobyn, small ambling horse* used by King Edward's light cavalry at the battle of Calais in 1347. (Bibliog. 246)

hobby falcon. See falconry birds.

hobelars, hobilers, light cavalry who wore steel caps, a haqueton* or mail,* iron gauntlets,* and carried a sword* and a lance* or bows* and arrows.* Mounted archers frequently were called hobelar archers. King Edward III used them at the battle of Calais in 1347. (Bibliog. 104)

hoby, hobyn. See hobbies.

Hock Day, date connected to the movable feast of Easter, frequently used in England as a time for paying rent or collecting dues. It fell on the Tuesday after the octave* of Easter, that is, the third Tuesday after Easter, and included the preceding Monday. It was taken as a convenient time for spring payments when autumn payments were collected at Michaelmas (September 29) because these two dates divided the rural year into winter and summer halves. Rents usually fell due at the four customary quarter days which were all feasts but also twice a year on the Conversion of St. Paul (January 25) and the feast day of St. James (July 25). (Bibliog. 265)

hofisch (Ger.), courtly, the highest term of praise for knights in the era of the *minnesingers.** (Bibliog. 274)

hog's bristle. See hand palisado.

hogshead, measure of capacity for many products: 48 ale gallons* or 1.5 barrels* of ale; 54 beer gallons or 1.5 barrels of beer; 60 gallons of cider (Guernsey, Jersey); 110 gallons of cider (Worcestershire); 63 gallons or 0.5 pipe* of honey, oil, vinegar; 100 gallons of molasses. (Bibliog. 394)

Hohenzeuggestech (Ger.), late-14th-century joust.* As its object was to splinter lances,* a distinctive saddle* was required, one with the seat raised some ten inches* above the horse's back so that the mounted knight was in a standing posture. Its front was shaped to form a large wooden shield forked over the horse's back to protect the rider from slightly above his waist to his feet. Although the two wooden bars that extended backward from this shield and curved around his thighs protected him from being thrown out, they caused many broken thighs and backs. (Bibliog. 27)

Hoher muot (Ger.), chivalric term meaning the characteristics of the true knight: stout heart and high emprise.* The church in Germany saw this as an undesirable feature of the effect of chivalry* in the new courtliness in that country, for such elevation of spirits closely resembled the cardinal sin of excessive pride. (Bibliog. 124)

hoist, portion of a flag or banner* next to the staff. (Bibliog. 331)

Hoke Day. See Hock Day.

Hola, word cried to stop a tourney.* (Bibliog. 78)

holmgang, old Norse custom of duelling (see duel) on a small island; the practice was used frequently in the *chansons de geste.** (Bibliog. 161)

Holy Days, Saint's Days (see Appendix A) used as commemorations, found in the Roman Calendar. Unless otherwise distinguished (for example, *Nativity* of St. John the Baptist), this day was understood to be that of the saint's burial (*depositio*). Sometimes, however, the saint's burial place was moved or "translated" to a different location and celebrated at a time of year more suitable for great popular commemoration: for instance, the Feast of St. Martin was November 11, but his Translation was July 4. Not all feasts were celebrated uniformly on the same day, and confusion was rampant whent the saint's title was omitted: for example, St. Stephen the Martyr was celebrated on December 26; St. Stephen the Pope on August 2.

Chief feasts had a subsidiary observance a week later, called the octave,* also known in English as the utas; a fortnight later it was called the quindene or quinzaine. Such dates were used commonly to summon councils, parliaments,* and the like as a convenient date for attendance when the great festival was over. In the 13th century it became usual to date letters and other documents by the Holy Days and convenient for specifying the dates on which rents should be paid. (Bibliog. 265)

Holy Grail. See Grail, Holy.

Holy oil. See anointing.

holy oil of St. Thomas à Becket. See coronation; anointing.

Holy Roman Empire, another name for ''Holy Roman Empire of the German Nation,'' a political organization created in A.D. 962 when Otto I, king* of Germany, was crowned emperor.* It established the perpetual union of Germany and northern Italy, which under Otto III was elaborated into an empire of the four ''nations'' of Germany, Italy, Gaul, and the Slavs with the idea of protection of the Catholic Church by the emperors, an idea which gave them special prerogative of interdependence with the papacy under one sovereign rule. (Bibliog. 139)

holy water sprinkler, long, spiked club with a fancied sardonic resemblance to an ecclesiastical sprinkler, the *aspergillum*. Mistakenly used to refer to a staff weapon, a type of flail* consisting of a chain linked to a plain or spiked ball attached to the head of a staff. (Bibliog. 9, 27)

homage, formal and public acknowledgment of allegiance by which a tenant vassal* declared himself to be the man of the king* or lord from whom he held his fief,* and bound himself to his service. Likewise the law held that homage was a legal bond whereby a lord was holden and bound to warrant, defend, and acquit the tenant in his seisin* against all men in return for certain named service expressed in the gift. In such homage the lord owed as much to the tenant as the tenant owed to the lord, saving only reverence.

The ceremony of homage was much the same all over Europe. Two men faced each other. The one agreeing to serve knelt, put his hands together, palm to palm, and then in an unmistakable gesture of submission, placed them between the hands of the man who agreed to be served and publicly announced that henceforth he was the "man" of the person before whom he stood. Then kneeling on both knees, without his sword,* mantle,* spurs,* or cap, he said simply, "I become your man of the tenement I hold of you, and to you faithfully will bear body, chattels, and earthly worship, will support you against all folk saving the faith that I owe to our lord the king." The chief then raised the kneeling man, and as a symbol of accord and friendship, they kissed each other on the mouth, by which the vassal became the overlord's "man of mouth and hands." Initially this rite had no connection with Christianity or the church, but early in the Carolingian period (c. A.D. 785) a second rite, basically religious, filled that gap: the rite of fealty.*

This tie of homage lasted as long as the two lives were bound together; the death of one party automatically ended the homage obligation. In time, however, homage became hereditary, and it mattered little that the son of a deceased vassal usually performed this homage to the lord who had accepted his father's, or that the heir of the previous lord almost invariably accepted the homage of his father's vassals; this ceremony had to be repeated with every change of the individual persons concerned, and it could not be accepted or offered by proxy. (Bibliog. 28, 129, 261)

home, arrow* that had been drawn back in the bow* as far as it ought to be. (Bibliog. 100)

"Honi soit qui mal y pence" (Fr. "Shame to him who thinks it shameful" or "Evil to him who evil thinks"), motto of the Order of the Garter.* (Bibliog. 253)

honor point, area of a shield* located between the "fess point"* and the top of the shield. (Bibliog. 43)

honor, sense of, controlling factor of a knight in battle which forbade flight before the enemy. An ideal knight was Roland* in the *chansons de geste.** There he accepted battle against overwhelming odds when he might have avoided combat, but being a proud knight, he chose to fight, refused to flee, overcame his fear, and died. He gave his life for the cause he was defending and never would do anything that might taint his honor. A knight's honor preoccupied the writers of the *chansons de geste*, for to them knights feared most of all being denounced as cowards. Practical experience, though, coupled with human weakness, dictated that not everyone should allow himself to be killed once it became obvious that the army was defeated; lost battles do not mean lost wars, which would have been the case had they let themselves be killed. In such cases, honor had to be reconciled with the interests of society and of human safety and prudence.

Flight was regarded as a disgrace; knightly honor in theory allowed only two possibilities: death or capture. For example, during the third crusade,* the master of the Templars,* who regarded flight as a terrible scandal that would dishonor not only him personally but the entire order, refused to flee from a battle while he still could, and as a result he was slain. Distinction, however, must be made between the escape of an individual during a battle while the outcome was still undecided and the retreat or collective flight of an army facing defeat. A rule of the Templars provided the generally accepted practice for just such a case of defeat and its consequences: once Christians were so near defeat that there were no banners* left flying anywhere on the battlefield, a knight then might escape to wherever he pleased.

However, battlefield deaths were not so certain because effective armor* made killing fellow knights difficult, and a captured knight could be more profitable than a dead one by being held for ransom.* At Bremule in 1119, for example, only three knights were killed but 140 were taken prisoner. Furthermore, an enemy was less likely to resist so feverishly when he knew that he probably would be taken prisoner and not killed during pursuit by the victor; if they knew that no quarter was going to be given and that no prisoners would be taken, they would fight more stubbornly and more fiercely. (Bibliog. 351)

honorus. See knighthood.

honour, great expanses of land held of the king* by one of his mightier tenants. Sometimes the term barony* was used to refer to the same holding, but there was a slight distinction between them: honour was reserved for the largest complexes of land—every honour could be deemed a barony, but not every barony could be deemed an honour. The term barony usually was given to lands which a bishop held by military service, even though they were large enough to have been classed as an honour. (Bibliog. 330)

honours, ceremonials of the lord's court. See knighthood.

by hook or by crook, tenants, particularly in the "royal demesne"* of Pickering in Yorkshire, could take for their own use all the dry wood lying on the ground as well as any wood they could knock from trees by hook or by crook. A hook was a sickle, an instrument for cutting grass or grain; a crook was a shepherd's staff. (Bibliog. 24)

horn armor, a body protection made of a gambeson* covered with plates of horn, leather, or wood in the 13th to 15th centuries. (Bibliog. 331)

horn calls in hunting, notes blown on a hunting horn* to signify the various points of a chase* to the rest of the "hunting party."* These different signals were made by varying the length of the notes and the intervals between them, as represented by the words "trout, trout, trourourout": the first two blown as single notes by a separate breath with an interval between them, and the third as three notes blown without interval and with a single breath. The difference calls were:

moot or mote—a single note sounded long or short.

apel—three long notes sounded when the pack was released to pursue the stag.

recheat—a four-syllable sound blown three times with an interval between them, as in trourourourout, trourourourout, trourourourout; when the limer* moved the stag and the huntsman* saw him run, the huntsman blew a moot and a recheat. If the stag moved but was not seen and the huntsman knew it had moved only by its slot,* he blew the recheat without the moot.

forlonge*—signal that the stag had gotten far ahead of the hounds, which in turn had far outdistanced some or all of the huntsmen.

perfect or parfit—signal blown only when the hounds were on the right line; this consisted of moot, then trourourout, trout, trout, trourourout, trourourout, trourourout, trout, trout, trourourout, and then a second moot; this was blown three times.

prise—four moots blown by the chief person on the hunt only after the quarry*; it was blown only when the deer had been slain by strength, not when it had been shot.

menée*—blown at manor* door after the return of the huntsmen.

mort or death—a long single note blown as the huntsman pierced the downed animal's neck with a knife or sword* to ensure the death of the animal before the quarry.

(Bibliog. 96, 340)

horn, hunting, instrument to signal progress or stages of a hunt.* This was to be two spans long (eighteen inches*), slightly curved, the wider end being as wide as possible, and the smaller big enough for a mouthpiece; the horn was waxed heavily or thinly as the huntsman* dictated to produce the best sound. It was made from horns of cattle or of rarer animals such as an ibex, or of ivory or precious metal. But regardless of its material, it was decorated with gold or silver ferrules, rings, and mouthpieces; some were provided with a stopper so they could also serve as drinking horns. (Bibliog. 96)

horn work, two bastions* connected by a "curtain wall"* in front of a fortification to which it was connected by wings. (Bibliog. 331)

horns of a bow, ends of a bow* which had been tipped with horn. (Bibliog. 100)

horologium, clock. One such device was sent by the sultan of Egypt to Emperor Frederick II in 1232. It resembled a celestial globe in which the sun, moon, and planets moved, being impelled by weights and wheels so that they pointed out the hour, day, and night with certainty. Another clock with great bells was placed in the tower of Westminster, being paid for by a fine* on a corrupt chief justice; it had the motto *Discite justiciam, moniti* inscribed on it. (Bibliog. 100)

hors de combat, out of the fighting; disabled from continuing a fight.

horse, beast of burden used for riding and for carrying heavy loads. Several types of horses were available: destrier,* a knight's war horse which to and from battlefield and tourneys (see tournament) carried his helmet* and armor* and was ridden by a squire (see knighthood); palfrey, his usual mount when he was not in war or a tourney; courser, mount for the hunt (see hunting); rouncey, roncey, or roncin, the horse ridden by his servant or mesnie*; sumpter or sommier, a packhorse carrying baggage; hackney, a gentle horse reserved for ladies. Knights rode only stallions because it was degrading for a knight to ride a mare.

Most of the best horses came from France, Spain, Gascony, Castile, Aragon, and Outremer*: Turkey, Greece, and Barbary. These had to have massive quarters, be able to carry great weights, and have stamina, for if a knight's mount failed him in battle, he would be on foot and at the mercy* of the footsoldiers who could move with much greater speed and agility on the ground than he. Westerners' contacts with Arabs and Moors in Spain had brought back the true appreciation of the destrier. A knight's faithful steed was a closer friend than his sword.* Such animals were known to have sorrowed at their master's biers and to grieve visibly over their loss. (See Bucephalus.) Naturally, such mounts were valuable and were a great expense. When a knight lost a horse in a campaign for his lord, the lord was expected to replace it, so each horse had a value placed upon it. In 1297, for example, Geraard de Moor, lord of Wessengen, had the following horses valued as his prized possessions: best horse called Mouton—300 "livres tournois"*; black horse from Louis of Bethune—250 livres*; black horse from French king*—125 livres; horse from count* of Flanders—225 livres; horse from William of Dendermonde—120 livres; horse from John of Namur—140 livres; horse for the march (courser)—40 livres. Thus he had horses worth a total of 1,200 livres tournois or 960 "livres parisis"*; his six squires who already were mounted had horses worth sixty, fifty, forty, forty, forty, and twelve livres parisis respectively.

Although William* I introduced into England the knightly fief* requiring a vassal* with a hauberk* to serve, not until over a century later, in 1181, was the horse mentioned. The first clause of Henry II's "Assize of Arms"* stipulated that in addition to a hauberk, helmet, shield, and a lance,* every holder of a knight's fee (see knighthood) had to possess a horse to ride as well. In 1187 the count of Hainault aided King Philip* Augustus II of France with a unit of 190 horsemen, of whom 189 had barded,* or armored, horses. By the 13th century, squires had to have barded* horses to earn higher pay: King Edward I paid a squire with an armored horse in his Welsh wars (1277–1295) one shilling (see money) a day, but those with unprotected horses only half of that, six pence (see penny) a day.

Equipping himself was expensive for a cavalryman. It was not easy for a knight to buy and maintain expensive war horses, especially considering that he also had to buy expensive equipment for himself, including such items as armor, weapons (sword, lance, and pennon*), tent, kitchen* untensils (pots, pans, kettles), plus a beast to carry it all. In the 8th century, for example, Ripuarian law listed comparative prices:

helmet	6 solidi
brunia (byrnie*)	12 solidi
sword and scabbard	7 solidi
sword alone	3 solidi
leggings	6 solidi
lance and shield	2 solidi
horse	12 solidi

for a total of forty-eight solidi (see sol). At that same time, a sound ox with horns cost two solidi, a cow with horns cost from one to three solidi, a sound mare three solidi; thus the equipment for a cavalryman cost as much as fifteen mares or twenty-three oxen. In contrast, a destrier cost twenty pounds (see money) in England in 1375, whereas seventy-five years earlier, a palfrey cost twelve pounds and twelve shillings for the queen of Edward I, and a sumpter or mule at the same time cost between four and eight pounds. (Bibliog. 130, 225, 351)

horse armor, plates of cuir-bouilli*; bardings* of mail* and quilted material used to protect a horse* in battle and tournament.* Early in the 1400s this changed as plate armor* began to appear, supplemented by reinforced chain mail and quilting and cuir-bouilli. Parts of horse armor incuded: a chanfron* (chamfron) to protect the face, often having a spike protruding from the forehead; a crinet to protect the neck; a peytral* of projecting plate to protect the horse's chest, having two projections to carry away a lance* thrust without injury should that weapon strike it; flanchards* of cuir-bouilli and later of plate hanging on each side of the saddle* to protect the lower sides of the horse; a crupper (*garde de queue*) to cover the rump portion of the horse; and estivals* to encase the legs (rarely used). (Bibliog. 9)

horses, famous, owned by famous personages both real and fictional:

Aarvak*—(Norse myth) drew the sun's chariot

Alborak—Mohammed

Alfana—Grandasso

Aquiline—Raymond of Toulouse

Arion*—Hercules

Arundel—Bevis of Hampton

Bavieca—El Cid

Bayard,* Baiart*—Renaud de Montauban

Bayardo—Rinaldo

Brigliadoro—Orlando

Broiefort—Ogier the Dane

Bruiant*—Charlemagne

Bucephalus*—Alexander the Great

Capalu—Godfrey de Bouillon

Cornu—Baldwin de Rohais

Facebelle—Foucher

Fadda—Mohammed's white mule

Favel—Richard I* and many others

Ferrant d'Espagne—Oliver*

Florentin—Aimer de Narbonne

Flori—in many *chansons de geste*

Grani*—Siegfried

Lamri—King Arthur's mare

Liart—Richard I

Marchegai—Elie, and then Aiol

Marchepalu—Ogier's father, Gaufrey

Margaris—Renouart

Morel—in many *chansons de geste*

Pliemont—Guibert d'Andrenas

Prinsart—in many *chansons de geste*

Regibaut—Doon de Mayence

Ruffin—Foucon de Candie

Sautperdu—in many *chansons de geste*

Trachebrune—Ogier the Dane

Vegliantino—Orlando

Veillantif—Roland

(Bibliog. 191, 266)

horseman's hammer, war hammer* with either a short or long handle and a plain or dentated head. (Bibliog. 331)

Hospitallers, military order whose full and official name was the Knights Hospitallers of St. John of Jerusalem. About 1048, when pilgrimages were frequent to that Holy City, before Jerusalem fell into the hands of the Seljuk Turks, some merchants of Amalfi in the kingdom of Naples obtained permission from the sultan of Egypt who ruled Palestine to build three religious edifices in Jerusalem for the shelter and comfort of pilgrims from Catholic Europe: a church, St. Mary ad Latinos; a convent for women dedicated to St. Mary Magdelene; and a hospital dedicated to St. John the Baptist. That hospital grew to become one of the most celebrated orders of knighthood* ever created. The Seljuk conquest of Jerusalem in 1076 slowed but did not stop pilgrimages, and it tested the faith of the Hospitallers. These brethren of the Hospital of St. John materially assisted the 11th-century crusaders (see crusades) responding to Pope Urban II's plea by providing relief to the sick and wounded. In gratitude for these services, many European princes* gave the Hospitallers, as they were known, considerable property in their respective states. Additionally, Jerusalem's return to Christian control in 1099 opened a new era of importance and prosperity for the order's members because they were almost overwhelmed by the number of sick and wounded among the pilgrims who flooded Jersualem. Wealth flowed in. For example, Godfrey of Bouillon endowed them with his estates in Brabant. As a result, branch hospitals were set up in the Holy Land and in seaports of Europe for pilgrims leaving for the Holy Land.

Those who served were bound by monastic vows, and they wore a distinguished costume of a long black* robe with an eight-point Maltese cross* of white* cloth on their left breast. Pope Pascal II in 1113 ratified their adoption of the rule of St. Augustine. Five years later, its master, Raymond Dupuy, added militance to the male section of the order by assuming the task of defending the Christian kingdom of Jerusalem. Such a decision soon took precedence, and the order segregated itself: knights were required to be of noble and gentle* birth; serving brethren who were not men of rank were to serve as squires (see knighthood) and attendants; chaplains added care of the sick to their usual clerical duties. As it was joined by persons of high rank, the order rapidly increased in power and influence. When Christian influence in Jerusalem fell in 1187, the Hospitallers moved to Acre until it fell in 1291, and thence to Cyprus. But finally in 1310 they besieged and conquered Rhodes; as a result sometimes they were called the Knights of Rhodes. Their ensign* was gules,* a cross argent*; their badge* a Maltese cross enamelled white* and edged with gold.* (Bibliog. 253, 274, 287)

host service. See knighthood.

hosting harness, armor* for war as distinct from that for tournaments.* (Bibliog. 331)

hôtel de ville (Fr.), town hall in France, Germany, and northern Italy which served as the center for the local administration of justice,* receipt of town revenues, regulations of markets, prisons (see jail), police barracks, and so on.

hôtel Dieu (Fr.), hospital.

hour-glass gauntlet, single plate shaped to fit the knuckles and base of the thumb to protect the back and side of the hand, then narrowing at the wrist before flaring out to form a short almost-bell-shaped cuff. Small overlapping plates riveted to leather and fastened to the main plate protected the fingers and thumb. An ordinary leather glove was fastened inside this gauntlet* to hold it to the hand. (Bibliog. 27)

hourds. See brattice.

hourt, straw-filled, crescent-shaped bag worn to protect a horse's* breast in tournaments.* (Bibliog. 331)

hous-bote, right of a tenant to take wood from his lord's estate to repair his house. (Bibliog. 24)

House of Commons. See Parliament.

House of Lords, one house of the British Parliament* consisting of the lords temporal and lords spiritual. The lords temporal were peers* who held their seats by hereditary right; the lords spiritual were the two archbishops (Canterbury and York) and the twenty-four bishops. The phrase, "the King in his council in Parliament to hear cases coming before it," came to mean not a joint session of the council and Parliament but simply a session of the House of Lords to which judges and certain other officials of the crown were summoned merely as assistants. Such a separation emerged from the idea that the magnates (see peer) summoned to Parliament and sitting together in the House of Lords were peers and that being a member of the peerage conferred special status. One clause in the *Magna Carta Libertatum** (clause 39) called for trial by peers; in the 14th century that meant peers in the House of Lords who were charged with treason or a felony* had the right to be tried by their peers in that house. Such a privilege made the class of peers a particularly distinct class and separated it from the royal officials who were summoned to the King's Council in Parliament. (Bibliog. 156, 267)

house servants, sergeants* and servants (servientes) in a lord's residence especially to keep accounts, wait on the lord personally, take charge of the wardrobe,* of the kitchen, and so on. Both the military system and the lack of safety of early leaders confirmed the need for a numerous retinue of armed followers and guards. See castle guard. (Bibliog. 357)

housecarle, any household warrior or retainer in Anglo-Saxon Britain from the time of King Cnut (1016–1035) onward. Sometimes they were the same as thanes,* sometimes just retainers in the retinues of important lords. The term also referred to a closely knit organization of professional warriors who served the kings* of Anglo-Saxon Britain from Cnut to Harold (1066) and became the spearhead of the army. Just as thanes and peasants (see villein) fought on foot, so too did the housecarles, and they excelled in it; they were a professional military elite and were the most formidable infantrymen in Europe. Their famous and characteristic weapon was a two-handed "battle axe."* Of necessity it was an infantry weapon because it could not be wielded from a saddle.* Thus these housecarles were not knights; but neither were the thanes nor the peasants, for the Anglo-Saxon army had no cavalry, and without cavalry one could not have knights, and without knights one could not have feudalism.* The Anglo-Norman knight may have dismounted to fight in such battles as Bremule, Tinchebrai,* Lincoln, but he was a cavalryman fighting on foot—an infantryman could not fight on horseback—but he primarily was a cavalryman. See tactics; battlefield. (Bibliog. 47)

household knights, large entourage, also called commilitones,* who began as followers of the counts* of Hainault in their wars and to tournaments.* At first they were given food and housing, then paid salaries in money,* and then, toward the end of the 12th century, granted most commonly, fief-rente.* By the 13th and 14th centuries, the household knight was different. No longer was he a continuous resident of the household; no longer was the fief-rente his only benefice. By this time, he had become a highly qualified warrior serving as an officer on his lord's military staff. When needed he was always at his lord's side and completely provided for; when not, he often lived elsewhere, usually on a landed benefice, partially supported by his fief-rente. In England he held no land after participating in the Norman conquest. Not having provided fully for the knight service by feoffments* in land for the service owed the king,* many barons* made up the difference either by maintaining the knights in their own households or by hiring them. By the 13th century practically all such household service had disappeared. (Bibliog. 208)

household warriors, group of powerful fighters with which every powerful figure, even the king* himself, surrounded himself. (Bibliog. 28)

how to measure the correct size for sheafs of hay: "if any sheaf appears less than is right, it ought to be put in the mud, and the hayward* should grasp his own hair above his ear, and the sheaf drawn midway through his arm; and if this can be done without defiling his garments or his hair, then it is adjudged to be less than right; but otherwise it is judged sufficient." (Bibliog. 24)

howett, usual cry to encourage a hawk when the quarry* she had chased into a hedge or bush had been routed out. (Bibliog. 96)

Hoxtide, feast fifteen days after Easter. (Bibliog. 246)

hue and cry, riding against or summoning assistance in pursuing peace breakers. When a felony* was committed, the hue and cry (*hutseum et clamor*) was to be raised. For example, if a man came across a dead body, he was to cry "Out! Out!" (Normans cried "Haro! Haro!" meaning "Hither!") to summon the neighbors. If he omitted to raise the hue, he was fined* and opened himself to ugly suspicion of complicity in the deed. Those summoned were to appear with bows,* arrows,* knives—the weapons they were bound by the Writ of 1252 to keep—and take up the shouting and blow horns to "horn" this hue from vill* to vill. If a man were overtaken by the hue and cry while he still had about him the evidence of his crime, he had short shrift. If he resisted, he was cut down instantly. Even if he surrendered, his fate was already decided: he would be bound with the stolen goods on his back, brought before a court* hastily summoned for the purpose, and without being allowed to utter a single word in his own defense, would be hanged, beheaded, or thrown off a cliff; the owner of the goods he stole could act as executioner. (See execution.) Behind that action was the idea that a criminal taken in the act was *ipso facto* an outlaw*: he was not entitled to any "law." If there was talk of proof, it centered on the proof that he was caught red-handed by the hue and cry and not whether he was guilty of murder.

In the 13th and 14th centuries, the *posse comitatus* could be called out by the sheriff* to take vagabonds and malefactors. That term derived from the demand of the 1195 oath that men over the age of fifteen should aid the sheriff to their utmost power (L. *posse*) for keeping the peace. All able-bodied men except ecclesiastics and peers* were expected to turn out at the sheriff's summons. The pursuit of the trail of lost cattle developed into the pursuit of robbers, and the hue and cry was still raised and followed with authorized sanction in the 13th century. Should one of the group of frankpledge* be suspected of a crime, it was the duty of the rest of the group to produce him in court; if he fled they were to raise the hue and cry by shouting and blowing horns, to follow and capture him if they could, for should they fail to do so they were "in mercy"* and liable to be fined themselves. (Bibliog. 163, 261, 264)

huese, heavy shoes with a high top of soft leather, worn by travellers. (Bibliog. 161)

humble pie, humbles. See numbles.

humors, four fluids or juices—blood, phlegm, choler (yellow bile), and melancholy (black bile)—which entered into the constitution of the body and determined a person's health and temperament by their relative proportions. Each of these was located in a different part of the body and had a different color, quality, affect on the spirit, variation of the mood, and affect of superabundance. Blood was located in the arteries and veins; was ruddy in color; was moist and warm; made a person wild; caused the mood to become benevolent, simple, moderate, bland, sleepy; and when overabundant caused alienation of the mind as was shown by laughter and singing. Phlegm was located in the brain; was white; was moist and cold; made a person sluggish; caused the mood to become vigilant, thoughtful, prudent; and when overabundant caused loss of appetite. Choler, or yellow bile, was located in the liver; was reddish; was dry and warm; made a person bolder; caused the mood to bcome unperturbed; gave good digestion; in excess it caused great tribulations of the mind. Melancholy, or black bile, was located in the spleen; was black; was dry and cold; made the spirit firmer; caused the mood to become wrathful, envious, sad, sleepy, critical; and overabundance caused one to become taciturn and sad. (Bibliog. 286)

hundred, 1. administrative unit in the British Isles. Appearing in the law of Edmund (939–946) as a fiscal, police, and judicial unit, this may have originated as a convenient assessment of land into areas of approximately one hundred hides,* or from an early association of one hundred heads of families in a group for police purposes, or from the necessary units on which defense burdens could be imposed. In Cnut's time (1016–1035), its judicial position was more clearly defined: no one could apply to the king* unless he was not entitled to justice* within his hundred (see hundred court), and no man was to make any distress, that is, seize someone's goods, before he had demanded his right in the hundred three times. If he received no justice after this third demand, he could proceed to the "shire moot"*; if that failed, he might seize what he could with either court's permission.

When justices came on eyre* to a county,* juries of twelve men from each hundred were summoned to declare on oath answers to certain questions (see jury duty). These juries thereby informed the government about malpractices of officials, misuse of franchises,* and so on. Between the Norman Conquest (1066) and the 14th century, a hundred was a fineable unit if it failed to identify and produce the murderers of a Norman in it (murdrum* fine*), and its jury could be fined for false presentment or other mistakes in court. Militarily, this unit was used in the 13th century for the array* of troops.
2. measure of quantity (the cent—C) and a weight (the Cwt) for many products. The C generally numbered 100, but not always; a hundred of other things varied: 106 lambs and sheep in Roxburyshire and Selkirkshire; 120, the long hundred, for canvas, eggs, faggots, herring, linen cloth, nails, oars, pins, reeds, spars, stockfish, stoves, and tile; 124 for cod, ling, haberdine, and saltfish; 132 for herring and fifefish; and 225 for onions and garlic. The Cwt generally weighed 112 pounds* or one-twentieth of a ton of 2,240 pounds (see weights and measures), but it also had variations: 100 pounds for aloes, asafedita, cotton, ginseng, gunpowder, tobacco; 104 pounds for filberts in Kent; 108 pounds for almonds, cinnamon, nutmegs, pepper, sugar, and wax; 120 pounds at the king's scales at Cornwall. (Bibliog. 213, 394)

hundred bailiff, official who stood on a par with the sheriff,* sometimes an undersheriff, and sometimes the executive officer of a hundredal franchise.* See bailiff; hundred. (Bibliog. 213)

hundred court, judicial proceedings in the hundreds,* preserved by royal order to serve for civil and limited criminal business. By 1270 over 200 of these were in lay hands completely and 139 in ecclesiastical. Gradually this court* came to have jurisdiction in two spheres: the frankpledge* sessions and the representation of the hundred by a jury in eyre* before itinerant justices. The twice-yearly sessions of the court to handle criminal cases emerging from frankpledge met in the spring and autumn. As these were attended by the sheriff or his deputy, they often were called sheriff's "tourn."* (Bibliog. 213)

hundredman, earliest official of the hundred* who was assisted by the officers of the frankpledge* tithings*; later the hundredal officials were called bailiffs.* (Bibliog. 213)

hunt, royal, whenever the king* thought it proper to hunt hart* in the parks or forests* either with bow* or greyhounds,* the master of the game and park-keeper were to see that everything was provided for him. The sheriff* of the county* where the hunt was to occur had to see that there was fit stabling for the king's horses* and carts* to carry off the dead game. Hunters and officers under the forester,* and assistants, erected temporary buildings called trystes* for the royal family and its train and covered them with green boughs* to protect them from sun or rain. Early on the hunting* day, the master of the hunt was to see to proper placing of the greyhounds and of the man to blow the horn signalling the game was turned out. Others placed at appropriate places in the enclosure were to keep the general populace at a distance. A yeoman, or king's bow, and grooms of his greyhounds had to prevent anyone from disturbing the game before the arrival of the king. When the royal "hunting party"* had taken their places, the master of the game blew three long notes on his horn for the uncoupling of the hounds (see horn calls in hunting). The game then was driven from its cover, turned by the huntsmen* and hounds to pass by the stands where the king and queen either could shoot it or pursue it with greyhounds, whichever they preferred. A hart chased but not killed by the king became a Hart Royal.* (See also hunting terms.) All game, except that killed by the royal party, was controlled by the master of the game, and by tradition certain portions of the fallen game were given to the huntsmen and other attendants. (Bibliog. 334)

hunting, popular sport among all levels of society, the most popular among the kings* and aristocracy* being the chase.* Beasts were grouped into three classes: beasts for hunting—hare,* hart,* wolf, wild boar; beasts for chase—buck, doe, fox, marten, roe; beasts for great disport—gray or badger, wildcat, otter. These frequently were subdivided into beasts of sweet flight—buck, roe, bear, reindeer, elk, and speytard (one-hundred-year-old hart); and beasts of stinking flight— fulimart, fitchat or fitch, cat, gray (badger), fox, weasel, martin, squirrel, white rat, otter, stoat, and polecat. Wolves were so prevalent in Britain that King

Edgar (A.D. 944–975) accepted 300 wolf hides instead of gold or silver as payment from Constantine of Wales. Other kings put bounties on wolves' heads, but that action did not eliminate them, for as late as 1370, Thomas Engaine held lands in Northampton by his service of finding at his own cost certain dogs for the destruction of wolves, foxes, and the like in the counties* of Northampton, Rutland, Oxford, Essex, and Buckingham. Hunting wild boar was considered a highly dangerous exercise, and although the boar was considered as a beast of venery chaseable by "hounds for the hunt,"* it should not have been so classed, for, as a heavy beast that would not flee or make chase before hounds, it was proper prey of mastiffs and similar huge dogs. Yet it was such a popular beast for hunting that King Edward the Confessor (1042–1066) rewarded his hunts-man* Nigell for slaying a fierce boar in the "royal forest"* of Bernwood in Buckinghamshire by granting him an estate and the custody of that forest.*

When a lord hunted he was accompanied by a sizable number of servants, for there had to be crowds to shout and make noise as well as to perform chores. When a hunt was planned for several days, the whole court might move to the woods. Official huntsmen and falconers* were there, as were cooks, "house servants,"* scribes, the chamberlain,* the chaplain. Every kind of comfort was provided: mosquito netting for the tents and a chapel in a tent with a portable altar.

All means of pursuing and capturing game were thought to have merit: stalking on foot; approaching in a camouflaged cart;* preparing traps, pits or enclosures; driving animals into a net; hunting with falcons (see hawking); or the most popular, coursing: chasing a stag with horse* and hounds. This noblest of the hunts had ten stages: (1) unharboring of the game, (2) gathering, (3) posting the relays,* (4) departure and laying on the pack, (5) change,* (6) recheat (see horn calls in hunting), (7) game exhausted, (8) bay, (9) death, (10) quarry.

To unharbor (1) or dislodge a deer was to make it get up from its lair and to start it running, normally early in the morning. A harborer set out on foot with his scenting dog, or limer,* a dog trained to make no noise. As he went his way, he dropped branches or boughs* to mark the places the deer had passed and to leave broken boughs dangling from trees to show its probable route. The gathering (2) occurred when the harborer returned to the gathered "hunting party"* to report and show his fewmets (see fumes), generally at a meal. Before the party set out, the relays (3) were posted. The entire pack did not run at once, but six to twelve dogs would be led by valets to three or four various relay posts along the company's expected route. The valets had to know by the tone of the running dogs' barking just when to release their hounds to join the chase. By this time, the company was mounted and ready to start, including the harborer. Huntsmen carried with them all the materials necessary for the completion of the hunt: cord, axes,* scissors, grindstone, files, flints, and so on. Until the harborer had led the party to the location of his branches or to where he had last seen the deer, the dogs remained leashed. Tying his scenting dog to a tree, the harborer then would show the party the direction he thought they should take; and once that was settled, he would release the pack (4) and sound the apel, three long notes on the horn (see horn calls in hunting).

Dogs sometimes lost the scent through error, bad weather, or such ruses of the deer as rousing another animal and pushing it into the path of the onrushing pack of dogs. Sometimes the deer would retrace its steps for some distance toward the hunters, then leap in a wide arc and escape in another direction. The hounds would pursue the original scent and bypass the point at which the deer escaped. Pursuing the scent of a different animal was the change (5). To urge the dogs back on the scent the recheat (6) would be sounded and the dogs encouraged with appropriate cries such as "tally ho"* to find the original scent. When the deer showed signs of exhaustion, malmene, recognizable by the huntsmen, it might make short rusing runs, it would run with its mouth and toes tightly closed whereas it had run earlier with mouth open and toes spread apart, and it might leave the woods and run through a village. The real sign was the bristling of hair along its spine and rump. At that point it often would take to water, and the huntsmen would cry, "*l'eau! fuit l'eau*" to signify that the end was near, and the whole party would plunge into the water after the beast. This was dangerous for the dogs because the terrified beast might try to drown them by pushing them under the water.

Once it realized that its ruses were useless, and it was near the end of its strength, the stag turned at bay (8), and the dogs would surround it. It would seek shelter under a tree or in a thicket, and the huntsman pursued it and by throwing stones forced it to seek a place where he could render it helpless by hamstringing it and then finish it off by piercing its neck with sword* or knife. This assured the death before the quarry; the blowing of the death or mort (9) was a single long note. Finally the quarry (10) was performed immediately after the beast was slain. Laid on its back, its feet in the air, and its antlers bent into the ground, it was then cut up according to precise instructions. First the testicles were removed and placed on a forked stick to be carried home in the procession at the end of the hunt. Then the huntsmen slit the animal from throat to tail, then made lateral incisions between the forelegs and the hind legs, and then cut the hide around the legs to remove them in a certain and established order: right forefoot, left forefoot, right hindfoot, left hindfoot. Following incisions behind the ears, the huntsmen then would skin the animal, leaving a layer of red flesh on the hide. Next came the shoulders, right and left, and then the entrails in a definite order. Then they cut the breast, broke the joints, cut the haunches, and finally removed the head and tail, making sure that no blood touched the ground but all remained on the hide. All this time, the hounds were encouraged to bay constantly. Finally the heart, lungs, liver, and windpipe were washed, cut into pieces, mixed with blood and bread, and spread on the hide for the dogs to feed on (see curee).

After the Norman Conquest, the Normans extended the royal forests and confined the privileges of hunting in them to the king and his favorites. King

John was especially fond of hunting and was partial to receiving fine horses, hounds, and hawks by way of payment for renewal of grants, fines,* and forfeitures belonging to the crown. King Edward III was so fond of hunting that he took sixty couple* of stag hounds and sixty couple of hare hounds with him on his invasion of France. Even though these kings imposed severe forest laws, they began to be relaxed. Under King John the Forest Charter stated that no man should forfeit life or limb for stealing the king's deer; but if taken in the act of stealing venison of the king, he would be subject to a heavy fine, and in default of payment be imprisoned for one year and one day and then find surety for good behavior or be banished. An archbishop, bishop, earl,* or baron* could kill a deer or two when travelling through a royal forest if a forester* were on hand; if one were not available, they were to blow a horn so that they would not appear to be stealing game. One additional reason for the popularity of the hunt lay in the fact that because it developed the capacity for endurance, it was esteemed as a means of keeping fit in body and in use of arms between campaigns. (Bibliog. 96, 334, 340, 304)

hunting cries, commands to ''hunting dogs.''* Many were brought into England by the Normans as was apparent from their French words:

"ho moy, ho moy, hole, hole, hole": to encourage the limer* when it was drawing scent from a stag;

"cy va, cy va, cy va": to call the hounds when any sign of the stag was seen;

"le douce, mon ami, le douce" ("softly, my friend, softly"): to the hounds when on couple* near the expected location of the stag;

"so arere, so howe, so howe" ("harken back"): if hounds were on the wrong track;

"hoo sto, hoo sto": to harriers* drawing away from the stag;

"oyez a X [dog's name], oyez, assembe X" ["harken to X"]—said to the hound that picked up the right scent, to bring the others to him;

"hoo arere" ("back there"): to hounds when they charged from the kennel too lustily;

"hors de couple, avaunt, sy vaunt, so howe, so howe, so howe": when hounds were uncoupled;

"sa sa cy avaunt, cy sa avaunt, sa cy avaunt": forward, forward.

"here howe, mon ami, howe ami": when hounds drew away from huntsman* too rapidly;

"illoeque,* illoeque" ("here, here"): if hounds were on the right line;

"tally ho,* tally ho": to encourage hounds to find the original scent after they had lost it. (See curee.)

(Bibliog. 96, 340)

hunting dogs, for deer chase,* there were three kinds of dogs: limers*—bloodhounds kept on a leash to finish by scent alone the stag at bay; brachetti*— smaller hounds; greyhounds* or *lévrier*—a large dog capable of killing a deer by itself. Other dogs included raches,* or scent hounds; harriers* or running hounds which chased hares*; alands* used chiefly for hunting boar; mastiff* for hunting boar; and spaniel for hawking.* (Bibliog. 334)

hunting music. See horn calls in hunting.

hunting party, group to manage and organize the hunt included the huntsmen,* kennelmen, foresters* and woodwards,* verderers* (who had the special duty of attending the forest* court*), regarders* who made periodic inspections of the forest, and justices who held a forest eyre every three (later seven) years to try offernders. See hunting. (Bibliog. 340)

hunting seasons, times for hunting* were determined more by the condition of the larder than by any other reason: to hunt when the beasts were in the best condition. These times varied from beast to beast:

red deer stag: nativity of St. John the Baptist (June 24) to Holyrood Day (September 14)

red deer hind*: Holyrood to Candlemas (February 2)

fallow deer buck: Nativity of John to Holyrood

fallow doe: Holyrood to Candlemas

roe deer buck: Easter to Michaelmas (September 29)

roe deer doe: Michaelmas to Candlemas

hare*: Michaelmas to Midsummer (June 24)

wild boar: Christmas Day to Candlemas

wolf: Christmas Day to Annunciation (March 25)

fox: Christmas Day to Annunciation

otter: Shrovetide (February 22) to Midsummer

martin, badger, rabbit: all seasons of the year.

(Bibliog. 96)

hunting terms, when retired in its lair, a hart* was said to be harbored*; a buck lodged; a roe-buck bedded; a hare* formed; rabbit set. When beasts were together in company, they were assigned collective terms, such as a herd of deer, a bevy of roes, a sloth of boars, a sownder of wild swine, a route of wolves, a harras of horses,* a rag of colts, a stud of mares, a drove of kine,* a skulk of foxes, and a cite of badgers. Huntsmen* spoke of a stag's blenches* and ruses* when referring to the tricks the beast used to rid itself of the hounds; of doubling and rusing to and fro upon himself when it retraced its steps; of its beating up the river when swimming upstream; of foiling down when it swam downstream; of its going to soil when it stood in water. When a deer lay down it was quat; when it stood, it was stalling; when it was tired, it was casting its chaule, that is, dropping its head when it was done in. It was meved when started from its resting place, quested when hunted for, sued or chased when pursued; its resting place was its ligging or lair; its fues were its scent of the line of flight. It was in herd with rascal and folly if keeping company with other deer; young and lean stags and hind* were classed as folly and rascal. Special terms referred to its age: in its first year it was a calf; second, brocket* (tines); third, spayard; fourth, staggart; fifth, hart; a stag of ten years or older if hunted by the king* became a Hart Royal. If such a stag were hunted and not taken but was driven out of the forest,* a proclamation was made to warn everyone that no one should chase or kill that hart, for it was then a Hart Royal Proclaimed. (Bibliog. 96, 334)

huntsman, man in charge of a hunt who had to know the different signs of a stag so as to be able to judge well the slot,* the gait, the "fraying post,"* the rack or entryplace where it entered its covert, the fumes* or droppings; by recognizing the differences in these signs made by a young stag, a hind,* a stag, he was able to find where each was harbored,* and by the slot* and gait he recognized when the stag was approaching its end. (Bibliog. 96)

hutseum et clamor. See hue and cry.

hydra, 1. heraldic monster* with seven heads; 2. creature resembling a snake and archenemy of the crocodile. This crocodile was a vile beast as long as twenty cubits,* with four feet and a skin as hard as a rock, which lived in the waters of the Nile River and cried as it ate a man. As it slept with its mouth open, the hydra would crawl into the open mouth to let itself be swallowed and thereafter be healthy, secure, and safe as it caused so much devastation to the crocodile's insides that the beast would die. (Bibliog. 253, 258)

hyena, lynx, a foul animal which man is forbidden to eat but which has in its eye a stone, hyenia, by which a man might see the future if he placed it under his tongue. (Bibliog. 258)

hyenia. See hyena.

hypocras, red or white wine* to which ginger, cinnamon, pomegranate, sugar, and sunflower seeds were added; popular with nobility.* Sometimes called claret. (Bibliog. 246)

hyacinth. See jacinthe.

I

ikta. See *iqta*.

Île de France, political center of old France; historical region of northcentral France bounded by Picardy, Champagne, Orleanais, and Normandy. Originally comprising the duchy* of France or Francia as early as the 10th century, this became the nucleus of an evergrowing crownland when Hugh Capet, duke* of France and count* of Paris, became king* in A.D. 987, and the Île grew by 1483 to comprise most of modern France. (Bibliog. 105)

illegitimacy, marks of, "bar sinister"* supposedly borne on one's arms.* Such was an impossibility, however, for the bar* was a horizontal charge,* and that term was a literal English translation of the French *barre sinistre*. As the French word *barre* meant "bend"* and not the English "bar," the term should have been "bend sinister." But this was not required on one's shield,* either, for an illegitimate person was required to distinguish his shield only enough so that his heirship would never accrue but never to reveal his own lack of birthright. Sons of Richard, earl of Cornwall,* son of King Henry III of England (1217–1272), for example, bore their father's lion* of Poitou on their shields but inverted the colors* to show their heritage. (Bibliog. 116)

illoeques, "hunting cry"* meaning "here! here!" used to reveal that the hounds were on the correct line of flight of the deer; it may well have been the origin of the hunting cry "Yoicks!" (Bibliog. 96)

immunists. See franchise.

immunity from war, privilege granted to individuals to avoid capture or to be released immediately from capture for several reasons: his standing or profession, his possession of a safe-conduct,* or his being captured in time of peace. Individuals covered by such immunity included churchmen and their goods, pilgrims, hermits, ox drivers, plowmen, husbandmen (those who raised the food, tilled the fields, and so on), heralds,* ambassadors, prisoners of war. Heralds were granted an immunity similar to churchmen because their allegiance was not to their masters alone but to the order of knighthood* at large, and their "coats of arms"* usually were sufficient safe-conduct in all places. Generally ambassadors, too, were protected by the same rules as heralds, as were prisoners of war, but these two groups also required a safe-conduct to guarantee their safety. See ransom. (Bibliog. 181)

imp, to mend a broken feather in a hawk's wing. An imping needle was a triangular needle filed out of soft iron wire about one and a half inches* long and wide enough to allow it to be inserted halfway up the shaft of a feather without splitting it. The base of the broken feather in the wing was cut at an angle; and a previously molted feather of the same size was cut at the same angle and inserted on the imping pin to replace the broken feather effectively. Shortly thereafter, the pin would rust to hold the feather firmly in place. (Bibliog. 26)

impale, to divide a shield* per pale* and place one coat on the dexter* and another on the sinister* sides. When showing his marital coat, a husband impaled his wife's arms* unless she was an "heraldic heiress,"* in which case he placed them on an escutcheon* of pretense.* (Bibliog. 43)

imperator. See emperor.

impost, wall bracket which supported an arch.* (Bibliog. 280)

in elemosiniam. See frankalmoign.

in full chase, blazon* term for a running deer.* See beasts, positions of.

in herd with rascal and folly, stag that was keeping company with other deer and was not "soule" or alone. See hunting; rascal; folly. (Bibliog. 96)

in mercy, someone who had gotten into trouble with the authorities, often quite innocently, was adjudged *in misericordium,* that is, in the king's* mercy; he was punished by amercement.* Such a situation had a sinister meaning and could easily spell ruin before it was mitigated by Clause 20 of the *Magna Carta Libertatum,* for to be at the king's mercy was a terrible plight as rich and poor alike were amerced ruthlessly and fined heavily. Fortunately the honest men of the districts who levied the amercements frequently took into account the circumstances of the men at their mercy. Even before this was eased by the *Magna Carta,* fines* frequently were remitted altogether. The civil disruptions which surrounded the *Magna Carta* brought much additional misery and destitution to the country, and after peace was restored, the justices were temperate and pardoned case after case because the person was poor and had nothing.

Yet thousands of amercements were imposed by courts* of all kinds. If at a royal court, an alleged criminal was in the king's mercy; if at a county* court, the sheriff's mercy; if seignorial court, in the lord's mercy. The process required that the court declare the offender to be in mercy, *in misericordia*, as soon as his guilt was proved. Thereupon the offender "waged an amercement," that is, he found pledge for the payment of whatever sum might be set upon him when he was to have been amerced; as yet, however, he was not amerced. Only at the end of the session were good and lawful men, peers* of the offender (two were enough), sworn to affeer* the amercements, and it was they who set on him some amount of money* he was to pay. (Bibliog. 264)

in misericordium. See in mercy.

in trick, rendering armorial bearings (see charge) in sketches which indicated colors* and designs by conventional symbols. The name of the field* tincture (see colors) normally was written on the field itself while most of the tinctures of overlayed charges were designated by terms written outside the field and connected to the charges alluded to by means of short straight lines. See herald. (Bibliog. 87)

inch, measure of length introduced originally as a unit of body measurement commonly associated with a thumb's breadth. As part of the Roman duodecimal system in which it equalled one-twelfth of a foot,* it became a part of the British system of "weights and measures"* and was defined as three medium-sized barleycorns.* (Bibliog. 394)

increscent, crescent* with horns facing dexter.* (Bibliog. 43)

incubus demones, evil spirit or demon in male form who was supposed to descend upon persons in their sleep, especially to seek carnal intercourse with women. Their existence was recognized by both ecclesiastical and civil law. See *succubus.* (Bibliog. 311)

indenture, one of the three methods of raising troops: indenture, commission of array,* and voluntary enlistment. Indenture was a contract either written or oral which guaranteed pay to the upper ranks of the army. Edward I contracted with his barons* by oral agreements, but by the time of the Hundred Years War of his grandson, Edward III, these had become written and formal affairs. For example, Maurice de Berkeley agreed to remain with the king* for life, supplying fourteen men-at-arms in time of war. In 1341 Captain Edward Montagu agreed to serve in Brittany for forty days with six knights, twenty men-at-arms, twelve armed men, and twelve archers. His wages of seventy-six pounds (see money) for this period were met by assessments on the wool subsidy in Suffolk. As a method for raising troops, indenture was superior to the other two, for its agreements were for short terms and it freed military tenants from the burden of paying and the Exchequer* from the labor of collecting scutage.* Furthermore, problems connected with fragmentation of knights' fees (see knighthood) were ignored, and it substituted discipline and a proper chain of command for the unruly individualism of feudal masters. The nucleus of the troops under indenture would come from "household knights"* and life-retainers, and the majority would have been enlisted under subcontracts. To raise the rank and file of the main body of troops for an expeditionary force, however, the king had to rely on the ancient obligation of free and unfree men to the shires* and boroughs* for the national defense, that is, the commission of array. (Bibliog. 222)

indulgence, granting the forgiveness of sins. Up to the 11th century, these were given by the church to the faithful who made penance before going to fight for the church against infidels. By so doing, the church assured salvation for their souls if they should fall in battle. During the crusades,* however, indulgences were extended automatically to those who participated in a crusade. By the 13th century, this practice had become extended to include all who, because of illness or age, donated funds to the church instead of participating directly in a crusade. (Bibliog. 139)

infalistatio, hurling a convicted person to his death into the sea from a cliff. See execution. (Bibliog. 4)

infamous, public disgrace. A person who had cried craven* or one who had been convicted of perjury or other offenses and against whom judgment had been pronounced was considered to have totally lost his character under common law and was deemed incompetent to give evidence. See duel. (Bibliog. 163)

infangentheof, jurisdiction over a thief apprehended within a lord's manor* which gave the lord the right to try and to amerce (see amercement) such a person. As part of the privileges which belonged to a higher aristocracy* and great churches long before the Norman Conquest, this was part of the mnemonic: " 'sake and soke,'* 'toll and team,'* and infangentheof." Such rights were taken over by the Norman kings* as applicable to the rights which their barons* would expect to possess. These three privileges were felt to cover the rights of tenure* by barony* even as late as the 13th century. However, infangentheof by no means was confined to the higher aristocracy. Rannulf II, earl* of Chester, granted it impartially to a fellow earl, to the lord of a great castlery in the north, to a military tenant of no particular distinction, and to men who served him in the routine of his castle,* for example, the butler and the cook, as evidence of their standing at his court rather than as a delegation of his rights of justice.* (Bibliog. 330)

infant, person between birth and his or her twenty-first birthday. See youth, terms for. (Bibliog. 261) *ingenui in obsequio,* freeman in dependence. This term from Ripuarian law referred to a freeman who placed himself under both the protection of and the service of another freeman at the same time while maintaining his own free status. (Bibliog. 123)

Inquest of Sheriffs, King Henry II's grand inquiry (1170) by a band of itinerant barons* into the conduct of sheriffs* whom he just had removed from office as a result of complaints made against their conduct; it served as an example by which the entire machinery of government was subjected to examination and amendment. (Bibliog. 261)

inquisition post mortem, inquiry held on the death of a tenant-in-chief* to establish who was the next heir and to ensure that the king* obtained all the feudal incidents due him. Sometimes this was held on the death of a subtenant for the benefit of his immediate lord. (Bibliog. 171)

interdict, edict authoritatively cutting off a group of people or a locale from any religious offices or privilege. During the eighteen years of his pontificate, Innocent III (1198–1216) placed fifty-seven interdicts, and threatened twenty-seven more. (Bibliog. 186)

intermewed, hawk that had been molted* in confinement. (Bibliog. 96)

intrinsic service, granting away a portion of one's land by a contract with a tenant for the performance of some service, such as a portion of knight service (see knighthood), spiritual service, or rent; it was called intrinsic because it was inherent in the bargain. (Bibliog. 264)

invect, reverse of engrail* but with the points on the margin of the bend* or bar* being turned inward instead of outward as in engrailed. (Bibliog. 43)

iqta, ikta (Arabic), land or revenue assigned by the ruler of Islam to an individual as a form of reward for service to the state. Its forms ranged from the governorship of a province with powers bordering on total independence from the central government, to the right to collect the taxes in an area named and to return to the government only a specified amount while keeping the remainder for himself, to the right to retain all the revenues collected in an area in return only for personal service in the army. (Bibliog. 322)

Isma'ilites, sect in Syria better known as the Assassins.* (Bibliog. 139)

J

jacinthe, hyacinth, gem whose three varieties—granular, veined, and smooth— were remedies against sadness and hemorrhage of the blood. The first one turned red and purified itself in fire; the other two did not, being respectively cold and moderate by their natures. (Bibliog. 258)

jack, male merlin* in hawking.* (Bibliog. 26)

jacque, padded leather coat that frequently was thickly quilted and sometimes studded with metal defenses when worn by men-at-arms. (Bibliog. 9)

jail, gaol, secure enclosure primarily used to hold suspects awaiting trial rather than convicts sentenced to confinement. From jail, prisoners usually were either hanged or released; if hanged, their chattels, having been evaluated previously as a part of the judicial procedure, usually were forfeit to the king.* Beginning in the 13th century punishments* were exacted in jails, and precise terms were rarely laid down but usually began at forty days and rarely lasted beyond three years. Jails varied from makeshift village lockups to specially built jails and to the verminous and dreary dungeons* of some fortresses. Most medieval prisoners were expected to pay their own costs, that is, they had to find money* to get enough to eat, to be released, and to pay any other "fees" exacted by the jailer. To keep people from escaping, jailers used stocks, chains, fetters, manacles, and/or rings and collars fastened to walls. (Bibliog. 163, 220)

jambarts, leg defenses from the knee to the ankle. See grevieres. (Bibliog. 9)

jamber, English term of about 1300 for the protection for the lower leg; after 1400 it was replaced by the French word, *greave.** (Bibliog. 27)

janitor civitatis. See castle personnel.

jar, measure of capacity for liquid and dry products: green ginger = 100 pounds*; oil = 12 to 26 gallons*; green vinegar = 100 pounds; wheat = 52 pounds. (Bibliog. 394)

jasper, gemstone known in many countries by sixteen different species in diverse colors; once held sacred, it was carried faithfully by some as protection against fever; others carried green jasper called chalcedony* as protection against phantoms and drowning. (Bibliog. 258)

javelin, light horseman's spear* used for throwing; ranging in length from three to four feet,* it usually had a broad, barbed,* leaf-shaped head and was carried in pairs. (Bibliog. 9, 27)

jazerant, jazeraint, jesserant, body defense consisting of plates or splints held between two layers of a pliable material by a quiltwork type of sewing. The term came from the Arabic word *kazaghand* described by the 12th-century Arabian-Syrian warrior, Usumah, as consisting of a mail* shirt between two thicknesses of padded fabric. (Bibliog. 9, 27)

jeddart staff, long-shafted axe* that was more halbard* than axe because it had a half-circular blade and a side spike. (Bibliog. 71)

jer. See ger.

jesse, leather strap eight to nine inches* long fastened to each leg of a hawk just below her bells by which falconers* held on to her. (Bibliog. 26)

jesserant. See jazerant.

jestours, entertainers, also known as conteurs, dessours, and seggers (sayers), and in Latin as *fabulatores* and *naratores*; these literally were the storytellers who recited either their own compositions or those of others, consisting of popular tales and romances* for the entertainment* of any audience on any festive occasion. See minstrels. (Bibliog. 334)

jihad. See Crusades.

John, king of England (1199–1216). He was the fourth son of Henry II* and Eleanor of Aquitaine.* Because he was the only son not granted a duchy he was often called Lackland. His father's attempts to bestow land upon him were foiled by the revolts of his brothers. He was his father's favorite son, but turned against him and sided with his brother, Richard I,* just before his father's death in 1189. When Richard was on the third crusade* and in captivity John conspired unsuccessfully to usurp the English throne with the help of the French monarch, but these schemes made him unpopular with the English nobility. At Richard's death he was proclaimed king of England, duke of Normandy and Aquitaine, and count of Anjou. His continual scheming aroused the anger of the nobility in the French fiefs,* so Philip II had little opposition in conquering them in

1204–1206. John allied with his nephew, the Emperor Otto IV, in an attempt to defeat Philip and regain the lost French domains, but at the Battle of Bouvines* he was badly defeated and fled to England. That defeat and its economic impact made him even more unpopular in England and led to a general uprising in London. As a result the barons forced him to sign the *Magna Carta Libertatum** that ensured liberties of the communities of the realm and became the basis of the English parliamentary system. (Bibliog. 139, 199, 245)

jongleurs, jougleurs. See minstrels.

jour d'amour. See love-day.

joust, just, single combat or series of single combats for prize or prizes, but not a tournament,* which was combat between a presumably equal number of armed knights on each side. In a joust a knight's equipment had to be in good shape so he could show off effectively before his lady-love and protect himself against possible injury or defeat, because knights vanquished in jousts lost their armor* and horses* to the victors, generally to be ransomed later for money.* See just; ransom. (Bibliog. 9)

jousts à outrance (Fr. "jousts to the death"), combat that simulated war between two knights on horseback using lances* without coronals* on their tips. These battles were fought until one of the combatants was killed or wounded severely enough to yield to his opponent. Later called jousts of war, these often were linked with the trial by combat (see duel). (Bibliog. 27)

jousts à plaisance (Fr. "jousts of peace"), combat between two knights on horseback using lances of courtesy—lances* rebated with coronals* on their tips to reduce the possibility of fatalities. These battles were fought with the object of splintering lances or of unhorsing an opponent. An early 14th-century form of this combat, a German exercise called *gestech,** owed its name to furnishing lances with blunt points to distinguish it from the exercise of "sharp-lance running,"* *sharfrennen.* In such an exercise each horse's* chanfron* had no eye holes, the horse's ears were plugged with wool, its breast was padded with a well-stuffed cushion, and the saddle* had no upright plate at its back so that unhorsing was not hindered in any way. To the vambrace* of the jouster's right arm was fastened the polder-mitten,* a lance rest fitted to the breastplate,* and a huge circular besagew* with a bouche* cut out for the lance protected the knight's right shoulder. (Bibliog. 9, 27)

jousts of peace. See *gestech*; *jousts à plaisance*.

jousts of war. See *jousts à outrance*.

joutes plénières (Fr.), tournaments* open to all comers in the 14th century.

jowk, to sleep, said of a hawk. (Bibliog. 331)

Joyeuse, Charlemagne's sword which bore the inscription, *decem praeceptorum custos Carolus*, and was buried with him. In its pommel* Charles was said to have placed the point of the lance* which pierced Christ's side, still carrying traces of the blood of Jesus. When he raised it in battle, light flashing from its blade terrified the enemy. (Bibliog. 126, 308)

Joyeuse Garde, castle* of Lancelot, said to have been either Alnwick* Castle in Northumberland or Bamburgh Castle, sixteen miles north of Alnwick. It was renamed Dolorous Garde after Lancelot was forced to surrender Guinevere to Arthur. Tristan was reputed to have kept Isolde there for three years. (Bibliog. 311)

Judica Civitatis Lundoniae. See tithing.

judicial combat. See duel.

judicial ordeal. See duel.

judicium. See ordeal of red-hot iron.

jugum, unit of land measure equivalent to an acre* or the amount of land plowed in one day by a yoke of oxen. See sulung. (Bibliog. 24)

juise. See ordeal of red-hot iron.

jupon, sleeveless garment fitted tightly to the body, reaching to mid-thigh, and laced up the back or side. Usually it was made of two or three thicknesses of material, the outermost being silk, velvet, or some such rich material, or leather faced with a rich material. Its elaborately embroidered hem was scalloped or dagged. (Bibliog. 9)

jury duty, obligation of every freeman and knight; it was so a heavy burden that favored subjects obtained charters* granting them exemptions from serving, thus making the burden heavier on the rest. By 1258 this situation had become so serious that in several counties* the Grand Assize* could not be convened because of the lack of knights to serve on it. (Bibliog. 264)

jus belli, just war. See law of arms; war, just.

just, accurate spelling of the word joust* from the 13th century. Under the French influence the word juster or joster became jouster and the form joust began to be used, but the accurate pronunciation remained as with the original spelling: just. (Bibliog. 78)

justice. Once the Fourth Lateran Council (1215) banned the use of ordeals,* the justices in eyre* meted out justice. Those accused of the crimes of robbery, arson, murder, and similar heinous acts, and whom public suspicion held to be guilty, and who even if allowed "abjuration of the realm"* still probably would do evil—all those were kept in prison (see jail) and safely guarded. Those accused of medium crimes and of whom there was no suspicion of their doing harm if they were allowed to abjure the realm were allowed to do so. Those of lesser crimes with no suspicion of evil attached to them were allowed to find pledges of their keeping the peace and then were released. Other sentences and punishments exacted by these justices, by the coroner's* court,* and by "manor courts"* revealed the extent to which justice was meted out. In one instance a sheriff* in 1344 received what seemed to be a bribe for supplying a warden* of Merton College, Cambridge, with a "good" panel of jurors in an action brought by William de Saint George. The officials and the jury were feasted well on the first day of Lent, and members of the inquisition received spurs* and shoes; men who had come to stand by the warden also were given presents for their efforts. In the following year the sheriff received similar payment, and the men of the panel received fees ranging from one shilling sixpence to four shillings (see money). In the coroner's court in Cambridge in 1348, an official was paid one-quarter of a mark* (three shillings sixpence) for sitting on a case of a boy who drowned by a sudden opening of a mill dam. One of the sworn witnesses was paid a shilling for his testimony.

Manor court proceedings throw considerably more light on the business of justice in ordinary life. The seneschal* or steward* presiding over this court often had jurisdiction over more than simple policing or discipline of the manor*; sometimes he was involved in the right of pit and gallows, of hanging male and drowning female criminals. (See execution.) Usually, though, he exercised police powers over breaches of the peace, violations of the custom of frankpledge,* evasions of the Assize of Bread and Ale,* and others. Records of Holywell Manor in Oxfordshire reveal some interesting examples of such justice and manorial jurisdiction. For example, the chattels of a fugitive valued at three shillings fivepence and his black horse* were said by a court held in 1349 to be in the hands of the bailiff,* and he was answerable for them to his lords. In 1371 John de Hankelon was summoned to answer for spreading a scandalous rumor about his own mother. In 1337 Walter Slene, shepherd to the abbey of Godstowe, demanded to be admitted before the court to prove his ownership of twelve sheep which had strayed from Walton field and had been driven by dogs into the liberty of Holywell. The bailiff under oath testified that these sheep had been stolen from Walton field by some unknown thief who feloniously had broken the sheepfold of the abbess at early dawn and had driven the sheep to the liberty within Holywell. The bailiff testified that he had seen and pursued the thief and sheep and tried to apprehend them, but the thief, seeing his pursuer, scattered the sheep and fled to the church of the Austin friars where he was helped to escape from his pursuer. Thus the bailiff lawfully attached the sheep as having been waived.* He asked the shepherd whether he could swear that these sheep had strayed from his keep and had not been stolen, driven, and waived. When the shepherd refused to take that oath, it was decided that the sheep should remain in the possession of the lords of the liberty as waifs, be valued at ten shillings, and laid to the debit of the bailiff; the shepherd was declared not to have a case for them. Other examples from manor courts included Johanna, wife of William the Smith, who struck Agnes Janakyn so hard that she drew blood and was fined fourpence. Nicholas Harcourt paid two shillings for license to make his son a monk. Agnes Godyer was fined for harboring a stranger. William the Miller was fined sixpence for having false measure and threepence for taking excessive toll. Robert Heyne complained that he had not been paid for work done for Nicholas Brown and Isold his wife, and he wanted permission to enter their house to distrain* them for said work. Thus the manor court was competent to secure to its suitors the payment of debts. But it did not have cognizance of real actions because by infeudation, the mesne* or manor lords lost to the crown the feudal contingencies of escheat,* wardship,* marriage (lord's right to control),* and fines.* (Bibliog. 289)

justiciar, originally the lieutenant or viceroy of the king* during his absence from England. This position as the king's alter ego met the need for an extension of the king's person and power that emerged from two facts of English politics. First, the king ruled personally and was the center of government, and his court or household was the center of power; second, he was regularly and frequently abroad because England was part of the continental empire* whose other dominions required the royal presence for the government just as England did. When William* I left England, William Fitz-Osbern, steward* of Normandy, and Odo of Bayeux acted as justiciars in 1067: Fitz-Osbern to govern the north of England and Odo to hold Kent. These powers ceased on the king's return. His son, William II, however, made it a permanent office whose duties included the direction of the whole judicial and financial arrangements of the kingdom. Largely through the actions of Ranulf Flambard, this office became the first minister of the kingdom. Up to his time, (c. 1060–1126), this office had been held by one of the great nobles (see nobility). But the subsequent treason of Odo of Bayeux and the bishop of Durham showed that it was dangerous to entrust so important an office to such persons. Flambard was a royal official who gained his fame as a financier. After him, the office was filled by royal officials who similarly had made their careers in the king's service. Under Henry I (1100–1135), the most famous was Roger of Salisbury,* who remodelled the administrative system of the country, especially the Exchequer.* Under Henry II (1154–

1189), the most famous was Rannulf de Glanville,* whose nephew, Hubert Walter, author of the treatise bearing Glanville's name, was Richard I's* ablest justiciar. He separated the Chancery* from the Exchequer and began to keep the records or rolls of the Chancery. (Bibliog. 156, 371)

juvenis, juventis. See youth, terms for.

K

Kahu. See Cahn.

kalends. See month, days of.

kalif. See caliph.

keep, innermost and strongest part of a castle.* A Norman keep, called a *donjon*,* was a massive square tower with its basement or stories partly below ground used for stores and prisons (see jail). Its main story used for the guard room generally was built a considerable distance above ground level with a projecting entrance approached by a flight of steps and a drawbridge*; above it were the hall,* which usually extended over the whole area of the building, and then the apartments for the residents on the top floor. Winding staircases in the angles of the building provided access between the levels. An ingeniously concealed well and small chambers and other passages frequently were set into the thicknesses of the walls. See castle. (Bibliog. 45, 100, 111)

keeping a length, shooting an arrow* the exact distance to the target, not necessarily in straight line of flight. (Bibliog. 100)

keeping the peace, English statute of 1242 that required the sheriff* to station at each gate of each city six to twelve armed men in a borough* and four to six in a vill* to keep watch from sunset to sunrise and to arrest all strangers until dawn. Sheriffs accompanied by two knights were also required to visit each hundred* and borough to assemble all citizens, burgesses, freeholds, villeins,* and others between the ages of fifteen and sixty in order to have them sworn to the following arms according to the annual worth of their lands and chattel:

15 pounds (see money)—hauberk,* helmet* of iron, sword,* knife, horse*

10 pounds—haubergeon,* helmet, sword, knife

100 shillings (see money)—doublet, helmet, sword, lance,* knife

40 to 100 shillings—sword, bow,* arrows,* knife

under 40 shillings—scythes,* gisarmes,* knives, and other small weapons

60 marks* of chattel—hauberk, helmet, sword, knife, horse

40 marks of chattel—haubergeon, helmet, sword, knife

20 marks of chattel—doublet, helmet, sword, knife

10 marks of chattel—sword, knife, bow, arrows

40 shillings to 10 marks—scythe, knives, gisarmes, and other small weapons

In a city or borough, those bearing arms were to swear to keep the peace and to obey the mayors, reeves,* and bailiffs*; in vills they were to appoint a constable* or two; and in each hundred they were to appoint a chief constable who was to obey the sheriff and the two knights. Further, the sheriff was to journey around his jurisdiction to proclaim that no tourneys or jousts* or any other kind of knightly adventure whatever (see tournament) was to take place and that no one was to be armed unless he was deputized, for anyone found armed was to have the "hue and cry"* raised and to be arrested. (Bibliog. 103)

kenettes, small hounds. (Bibliog. 96)

Kerbogha, leader of the Muslim forces from Mosul who gained fame among the crusaders through the disastrous campaign in 1098; he was badly defeated in the battle of Antioch (see crusades) in 1098 and died a broken man in 1102. (Bibliog. 310a)

kettle hat, *chapelle-de-fer,* iron hat with a wide brim introduced in the 12th century as the headpiece for the common footsoldier. It had a cross-shaped domed plate with spaces filled in with separate riveted plates and a separate brim riveted to the lower edge. The lower margin of the skullpiece was pierced with a series of holes through which stitching attached the lining; a chin strap held the hat on the head. See *chapelle-de-fer.* (Bibliog. 27)

khootba, sermon delivered by a caliph* at public prayers in the chief mosque every Friday. (Bibliog. 100)

kilderkin, measure of capacity for ale, butter, fish, and soap: ale kilderkin = 16 gallons* or 2 ale firkins* or 0.5 ale barrel*; beer kilderkin = 18 gallons or 2 beer firkins or 0.5 beer barrel; butter and soap = 16 gallons; fish (salmon) = 21 gallons or 2 firkins of 10.5 gallons each; all other fish = ale kilderkin of 16 gallons. (Bibliog. 394)

kinebairn, English royal child, king's* son, prince.*

kinehelm, English crown,* diadem.

kinekin, English royal family.

kinelord, English liege* lord, royal lord.

kinemede, English royal reward, great reward.

kinemot, English royal council.

kinering, English royal ring, the king's* signet ring.

kinestol, English royal throne.

king, crowned ruler of a country or territory. Derived from the Germanic word *können*, "to be able," this word in Anglo-Saxon occurred as cyning, cynig, cyng, cing, and others; in Swedish, *konung*; Danish, *konge*; Finnish, *kuningas*. The Tatar word *khan* meant king; the Latin *rex* came from the Hebrew *rosch* meaning a chief, and from that came *rajah*. See kingship. (Bibliog. 178)

king of arms, principal herald* of England. Originally called the king of heralds, the king of arms had become established as a specialist in heraldry* by the end of the reign of Edward I (1307); and under the marshal* he prohibited or proclaimed and officiated at tournaments,* assisted the marshal at coronations,* acted as ambassador or the king's messenger,* and assisted at the creation of new knights. But he did not entertain the king* with story and dance as did the lesser minstrels* listed on the records with him. Under King Henry IV (1399–1415), the king of arms became the Garter king of arms to serve the Order of the Garter* and was made chief of heralds with assigned apartments in Windsor Castle.* His official costume as principal king of arms of the English was a surcoat* of velvet, richly embroidered with the arms* of the sovereign, a crown,* and a "collar of SS."*

The second-ranking king of arms, Clarenceux, originally was titled Roy des Armes des Clarenceux, that is, of the people of Clarence, a district encompassing the castle* and town of Clare in Suffolk, but his province was all of England south of the Trent River. His costume was similar to that of the Garter king of arms: crown, collar of SS, and an embroidered surcoat. Older but ranking lowest of these three was the Norroy king of arms who was in charge of England north of the Trent River. His official title was Roy des Armes des Norreys, a word used by the chronicler Peter Langtoft in the sense of "northmen." His outfit was just like the other two: crown, collar, and surcoat. For Scotland the chief heraldic officer was the Lord Lyon king of arms, the title coming from the insignia of Scotland; for Ireland, he was the Ulster king of arms. (Bibliog. 43)

kingmark, distinctive mark, usually a glowing cross* on the right shoulder of a prince,* indicating his royalty, especially French royalty. Havelock the Dane, a hero of English romance,* bore one, as did the hero of *Richars li Biaus* and *Lion of Bourges* in English stories and of *Emare*, *Macaire*, and *Parise le Duchesse* in French. (Bibliog. 152)

king's bannerets. See king's knights and bannerets.

King's Bench. See Marshalsea of the King's Bench.

king's champion, armed and mounted knight who immediately after the coronation* ceremony of a new king* flung down his gauntlet* and proclaimed that he was ready to do battle with anyone challenging the new monarch's right to the crown.* (Bibliog. 195)

king's constable, military right-hand man of the king,* whose duties during a conflict were to assist the king's marshal* by dividing the forces available to the king according to the exigencies of command, tactics,* and morale. (Bibliog. 272)

king's friendship, foreign locations at peace with the king.*

king's grith. See king's peace.

king's household, servants listed as attending King Edward I on November 13, 1279, included: two stewards,* two marshals,* two submarshals, two ushers of the hall,* two assessors,* three panters, two butlers,* two buyers, two cooks of the king's kitchen,* two cooks of the kitchen of the household, one naperer, one porter, three kitchen helpers, one assessor before the king, one salser, five ushers of the king's chamber, one his tailor; six clerks, king's wardrobe*: comprising treasurer,* controller, clerk under the treasurer, three helpers; four clerks of the wardrobe,* one surgeon, one physician, one usher of the wardrobe, one chandler, four chaplains, one clerk of the chapel. (Bibliog. 103)

king's keys, crowbars and hammers* used by the king's* men to force entry in pursuance of a writ. (Bibliog. 156)

king's knights and bannerets, leaders of the household cavalry who, as a class apart, received robes or a fee from the "king's household."* Some were the king's* personal bodyguard, the constables* of his castles,* and the trusted officials at the king's sites that needed soldiers* rather than clerks. Of the twenty-three named as king's bannerets in the wardrobe* rolls of 1285, seventeen were barons.* (Bibliog. 87)

king's mund. See king's peace.

king's peace, Anglo-Saxon concept of peace of the land which all offenses broke; it also was known as king's grith or mund. Any such breach was considered to be an act of personal disobedience and far more serious than an ordinary breach of public order, for it made the wrong-doer the enemy of the king.* After the Norman Conquest (1066) this extension of the king's peace, peculiarly English, became the normal safeguard of public order. Earlier, on the continent, the king had been recognized as the protector of the general peace in addition to having the power to grant special protection or peace of a higher order. (Bibliog. 135, 261)

king's reeve. See wic reeve.

king's standard, official English measure of length.

king's writ, private documents sent by a king* to his shire* courts* and authenticated by impressions of his seal hanging from one corner. These were not ordinary instruments of government but were private documents of his reign. (Bibliog. 330)

kingship, state, office, or dignity of a king.* In the early Middle Ages a leader needed "kin-right," that is, the necessary membership of the royal stock, although it was not absolutely mandatory, for there was no right of primogeniture* or strict order of succession to the throne. In its absence, the king was "elected." The most suitable member of the royal family was chosen, usually the eldest son if he was an adult, was deemed worthy, and was recognized or accepted by the magnates (see peer) of the realm individually rather than by a formal election. Once chosen, or self-chosen, the candidate would seek the best way to gain the "recognition" of the magnates. In such circumstances, the selection by the preceding king was of primary importance. The reigning monarch usually nominated and received the recognition of his successor, normally his eldest son, in his own lifetime to ensure continuity and to avoid the perils of a disputed succession. It was in this context that English King Edward the Confessor (1042–1066) nominated William,* duke* of Normandy, to be his heir. However, this king's alleged dying bequest of the kingdom to Harold Godwineson* became suspect if for no other reason than that it was unwise to leave until the last moment so important a matter as succession because of the chaos and turmoil that could result from a disputed throne.

Under William I (1066–1087) the English throne and succession were governed by no specific rule but were influenced by such considerations as kinship with the royal house, popular election to confirm the established fact, designation by the late king, and personal fitness. Over a century later Richard I* (1189–1199) was the first English king to ascend the throne in accordance with the strict rule of hereditary succession.

Until the chosen was crowned and anointed,* he was known only as *dominus**—the territorial lord and head of the feudal state. Note that because the Empress Matilda, disputant with Stephen* (1135–1154) for the English throne, never was crowned, she called herself *Anglorum domina*. Between their elections to the throne and their coronations,* both Richard I and John used the term *dominus Angliae*. From the coronation rites, however, the king derived divine authority and ceased to be just a lay lord, but he took on a sacerdotal character from the anointing*: he became king *dei gratia*; he was God's vicar, *rex et sacerdos*, with all the attributes of royalty.

William I wore his crown* at three festivals a year: Easter at Winchester, Whitsuntide at Westminster, and Midwinter at Gloucester. At these three occasions of ritual and pageantry, festivity and frivolity, the king exhibited himself in all his glory to impress on the minds of his subjects the dignity of the crowned monarch. Henry I additionally claimed and exercised the power to heal scrofula merely by touching the afflicted person. Such power was said to have come from the time of Edward the Confessor, who was reputed to have learned and practiced the art in Normandy. Half a century later, Henry II persuaded Pope Alexander III to canonize Edward the Confessor because of such powers and to have his life rewritten by hagiographers to give solidity and prestige to the Anglo-Norman monarchy.

By the oath taken at his coronation, the king bound himself to his subjects. He promised that the church and the people should keep true peace, that he would forbid rapacity and iniquity, and that he would show equity and mercy* in all his judgments. For example, in his "coronation oath"* of August 5, 1100, Henry I of England swore not only to free the Church of God but also to abolish all the evil customs by which the kingdom of England had been unjustly oppressed. He referred specially to such customs as merchet*; he remitted murder fines,* and he ended with, "I establish a firm peace in all my kingdom, and I order that this peace shall henceforth be kept."

A king didn't just reign, he governed. He appointed his own officers of church and state, conducted his own foreign policy, declared war, and generally led his own army and made his own peace. He was expected to support himself and conduct the affairs of state on his own independent income derived from feudal dues, from crown lands, and from taxes called tallages* arbitrarily imposed on towns in the "royal demesne,"* on villeins,* and on Jews. He obtained additional money* from the profits of justice*: the peace was the "king's peace"* and he had to take notice of any breach of that peace and to reap whatever profits he could from it.

He usually had no capital* or fixed seat of government but moved about restlessly from castle* to castle, from abbey to hunting* lodge, seldom staying anywhere for longer than a few days or a week, holding court* wherever he happened to be. He took with him all the necessary materials for government: treasurer,* business documents, chancellor,* clerks with writing materials, and the numerous members of the "king's household."* Such wanderings were a cause for serious concern by the barons*: William II and his entourage often were unruly, undisciplined, and terrifying to any on whom they descended. Frequently the inhabitants of an area would flee and hide when the court approached. (Bibliog. 49, 264)

kinking, small barrel,* keg.

kippers, squires* or non-knightly men who would use any means—clubs, knocking opponent off his horse,* and so forth—to protect their master in German tournaments.* (Bibliog. 149)

kitchen, castle* room for preparing food; usually built of timber with a central hearth or several fireplaces where meat could be spitted or stewed in a cauldron. Utensils used in cooking were washed later outside the kitchen in a room called a scullery. Near the kitchen the cook usually planted a garden with fruit trees and vines at one end, herbs and flowers at the other, and a pond stocked with pike and trout frequently located nearby. (Bibliog. 128)

kiusche, virtue of self-control in the Germanic chivalric courtly culture; it included sexual continence as well as modesty and restraint. See chivalry; German chivalry. (Bibliog. 124)

knee-cop, reinforcing plate protection for the knee. See armor.

knight bachelor, oldest and lowest rank of knighthood.* An esquire* at age twenty-one was eligible for knighthood; after being knighted, he usually began his career by following the standard* of another. Every holder of a knight's fee (see knighthood)—certain amount of land that varied at different periods and localities—was capable of receiving knighthood; his arms* were distinguished from those of an esquire only by the full-faced and open helmet.* As a young knight he was a novice in arms and was not allowed to lead a body of his retainers onto the field, that is, was not allowed to *lever bannière* (raise his banner*); he was too young or had too few vassals* to display his own banner but carried instead pennons* ending in a point* or points and followed the banner of another. If on the field of battle or otherwise he distinguished himself, the tails of his pennon were cut off, ideally by the king* himself who had witnessed the heroism, and he became a knight banneret.* For his duties as a knight bachelor, see knighthood. (Bibliog. 253)

knight banneret, knight whose pennon* was rendered square by having the points* of his "knight bachelor's"* pennon cut off in immediate recognition of extraordinary gallantry on the battlefield. This process of converting a pennon into a banner* usually was performed by the English king* himself standing beneath his own royal standard* on the field of battle, and the knight so honored ranking above all other knights except those of the Garter.* By accepting this honor the banneret was expected to provide and support fifty or more men-at-arms for his sovereign, but because of this great expense poorer knights often declined the honor. Although this banner bore the blazon* of the banneret himself and served as an ensign* for his followers and retainers, it was a dignity that died with the person who had earned it. Heralds* recorded such awards among the blazons of all the knights in the kingdom. This distinction began under the reign of King Edward I as shown on the roll of Caerlaverock,* for example, which contained the blazons of nearly one hundred bannerets (including the king, eleven earls,* and the bishop of Durham) who were present with King Edward I on his campaign against Scotland in 1300. (Bibliog. 253)

knight-errant, knight wandering in search of adventures in which to demonstrate prowess, military skill, and generosity. This term was used first by William Marshal* to refer to knights who frequented tournaments.* In the earliest times knights-errant wore and caparisoned* their horses* with green when appearing in a tournament abroad. Such a color presumably was chosen to show that the knight was in the springtime of his life, to serve as protective coloration when passing through forested areas, and to cover his own heraldic bearings (see charge) so that as an unknown knight he could win a prize for the sake of his far-off lady. (Bibliog. 88, 225)

Knight Hospitaller. See Hospitallers.

knighthood, rank, dignity, and profession of a knight. Although no references to knights or knighthood occurred in England before the Norman Conquest, French and Norman knights accompanying William,* duke* of Normandy, dominated the scene at Hastings in 1066 and the whole of England afterward. Because the defeated Anglo-Saxons saw these newcomers riding throughout the countryside mainly in the train of the new Norman and French masters, the natives called them by their own word for retainer or servant, cniht.* The Latin word *miles** frequently was used to refer to an armed man, a soldier,* but did not change its meaning in England to refer to a feudal knight until early in the 1100s, a century later than that change of meaning in France and Normandy. By late in the 11th century, William needed experienced warriors to garrison the castles* he had erected throughout the English countryside to control the populace. Thus he created a small number of knights to be ready to serve for short periods as needed. Within 150 years, however, this need had expanded. Later, as Richard I* (1189–1199) had to prepare for lengthy campaigns during his almost-continuous wars, the king* had to rely on some organization more than the simple "feudal levy"*; thus the concepts of knight service changed.

Knighthood emerged from the formal investiture of arms* that marked the end of a young man's training. His being knighted originally had no connection with birth but signified only that he successfully had mastered the art of fighting while mounted. But within a century, knighthood had ceased to be a matter of social custom and had become involved in an elaborate military tenure.* Thus knights formed the core, the rank and file, of the "feudal army."* A precise definition of knightly service emerged from the concept of society of the times. Pre-Conquest thegns (see thane) of 11th-century England were familiar with the services due their lords and acknowledged the strength of the bonds of homage.* They recognized that failure in duty to their lord was so serious that they could forfeit their power and rights, but they did not regard this obligation as specialized service. Their inherited rank of thegn required from them a variety of duties to be performed in reward for the land obtained from their lord. As a result, when William's militant Norman aristocracy* replaced King Edward's conservative Anglo-Saxon aristocracy, the effect on the land was catastrophic. The knight suddenly became the central figure of a society in which knight service was the most valuable return a man could make for a grant of land. Such service basically amounted to attending a lord in war, mounted and equipped as a knight. In one of his first orders, for example, King William I (1066–1087) ordered his followers to be ready to serve the crown whenever the need arose. That article was revised and clarified a century and a half later in 1199 when King John (1199–1216) made it more specific:

> The king orders that all earls,* barons,* knights, sergeants,* and all freemen throughout the realm shall keep themselves well supplied with arms and horses,* and shall always be prepared to fulfill the whole of their service to the crown whenever the need arises in accordance with their legal duty to the crown by virtue of their fiefs* and tenements, and in accordance with what the crown has ordained for them. (Bibliog. 103)

In the field, knights were associated usually with a unit called the constabularia.* Records reveal that knights sometimes were punished by fine* for not being in their constabulary. They frequently were employed as officers in command of bodies of troops composed chiefly of infantrymen but occasionally containing some cavalry. As such they were called indiscriminately constable* or master,* and the unit under their command, the constabularia, contained approximately 500 men.

Aside from their military duties, knights were involved in the administration of their counties,* including judicial duties. The "Grand Assize"* was largely their responsibility. Four knights acted as a committee to appoint twelve other knights to serve on the jury of the assize.* Such a burden was heavy, for the number of knights in any county never was large. In Northumberland in the reign of John, as fewer than one hundred knights were available for such duty, some men had to act repeatedly. Robert of Holdenby, for example, served on eleven juries in the five years between 1200 and 1204. Such "jury duty"* was only one of their many duties. If a knight excused himself from such duty on the grounds of illness, his *essoin de malo lecti* (see essoin) had to be confirmed by a visit of four knights who then swore in court* that the absent man was indeed sick in bed. In pleas involving land, the knights were called upon to inspect the ground—tenement, wood, marsh, whatever was being disputed— and walk out its boundaries thoroughly. They had to make assignments of dowers* and marriage portions, to evaluate land in settlement by a final agreement, and to audit the accounts of an estate in wardship.* In a case being transferred from a lower to a higher court, a knight had to carry the records of the proceedings between the two courts.

In criminal cases their burdens were no less arduous. Some had to act as coroners,* which occupied most if not all of their time. They had to take an oath to keep the peace under Hubert Walter's (see Rannulf de Glanville) Ordinance of 1195, and such duties were increased by later ordinances in the 13th century. All offenders were delivered unto them for safekeeping until they could be turned over to the sheriff,* who on occasion turned them over to yet other knights for safety. Knights had to inspect the scene of the crime, view and measure any wounds of victims of assault, and then testify about them in court. Such an inspection had to be made while the wounds were fresh, and measurements had to be precise about a wound's length and depth, for if it was only a slight wound, no appeal could be made concerning it. In judicial duels,* knights acted as seconds and kept a record of the fight and its outcome. Despite these onerous responsibilities, their power was limited. If a king's sergeant was not with them to arrest suspected robbers, they were powerless to act on their own. However, if they were negligent in the performance of their own duties, they were liable to punishment.* They were fined if they issued a bad record at a higher court; if they gave a wrong verdict as jurors, had sworn falsely in an assize, even in the Grand Assize, they could suffer an attaint.* Many, however, relished the power and authority accorded them and trained themselves to act well in carrying out their responsibilities.

As explained above, early in its existence in the 11th and 12th centuries, knighthood simply denoted proficiency in the art of fighting on horseback. Although the infantry was important in many battles, what gave the knight his superiority in a battle was not his being mounted but his professional training and experience with better arms and equipment than the footsoldiers. Such training and position accorded to the knight certain privileges. He had the power of jurisdiction over his retainers, could assemble them for service in any war in which he was to participate, and could discipline them as needed. Corresponding obligations accompanied those privileges, however. He was expected to have largesse* and pity, he was to aid the suffering and the poor and weak, and he had to be courteous. Above all he was expected to possess and exercise two virtues: prowess and loyalty. Prowess was the acquired skill at arms, the ability to defeat another knight in battle, to which two attributes were added: indomitability and rashness, or magnanimity and audacity. Loyalty relied on a loyal heart and implied fidelity to his pledged word or to an individual because of friendship or even some transient relationship. Such a quality abounded in the romances* of the period. For example, Gawain sought out the Green Knight to be beheaded rather than betray his loyalty to King Arthur by breaking his promise; Amis killed his two small sons to use their blood to heal the leprosy afflicting his friend Amiloun. He was expected to show compassion for the oppressed, to punish a wrong-doer, to be generous with gifts and money in his largesse, and to be courteous, that is to demonstrate freedom and naturalness in manner and conduct, especially with women.

Many of those qualities applied only to peacetime conditions and circumstances, for during war he was expected to defeat his enemies with the smallest possible losses. To do that required certain tactics. He had to overcome the natural fear in his own men of death, mutilation, wounds, and pains to ensure they carry out the orders of their superiors. He had to allay those natural fears in his men while trying to instill panic in his enemies if possible. Flight from battle was a natural reaction among men far from home, but the knight had to convince his men that such flight was far more dangerous than the battle itself. Robert de Clari reported that after the Byzantine usurper, Murzuphlus, had ambushed crusader troops in Constantinople in 1203 (see crusades), the crusaders were terror-stricken, but they realized that if they fled they were sure to be killed, so they might as well die fighting rather than trying to escape. King Richard I was a skilled tactician who also had personal concern for the welfare of his men. He took care to provide for them properly, allowing no unreasonably long marches, imposing strict discipline to protect the entire column of march, personally supervising the execution of his orders, all the while maintaining his own readiness for any unforeseen eventuality. On a march, a leader had to be prepared to reach his destination with the last of his knights, and if the enemy ambushed them, to stay and fight with his troops. If flight or retreat was indicated, he was expected to remain with the rearguard to keep the pursuing enemy at bay.

Roland,* Charlemagne's nephew and hero of the French *chanson de geste,** the *Song of Roland,** served as an ideal: he accepted battle against overwhelming odds when he might easily have avoided conflict; because he was a knight, he chose to fight, refused to flee, overcame his fear of death, and died on the field of battle. He gave his life for the cause he was defending and did nothing in the struggle which would stain his honor.* One of a knight's greatest fears was of being called a coward and of disgracing himself by flight from battle. In theory his honor allowed him only two courses of action: death in action or capture. The grand master of the Templars* regarded flight as such an unbearable scandal— not only for himself personally but also for the entire order—that during the third crusade he refused to flee during the battle of Acre while he could do so safely, and as a result he perished.

Chivalry* was designed essentially to ameliorate the horrors and brutality of war, to provide a means whereby men were encouraged to view their enemies as fellow humans whose misfortunes in war were to be considered with pity rather than with revenge. Thus the concepts of knighthood and its rules which directed that the men who took such vows were brothers-in-arms should have exerted the same effect. Knights should have demonstrated unceasing courtesy, generosity, bravery, selfless devotion to one's lord's ladies and knightly comrades, and unflagging religious zeal. Yet such lofty goals were not followed in the real world. For example, following those goals, knights would never attack a fortress governed only by women. History, however, revealed that such attacks did occur. King David of Scotland assailed the fortress of the countess of Salisbury, and King Stephen* besieged the castle of Lincoln held by Dame Nicolla de la Haye,* to name just two examples. Some women had the courage of lions and the hearts of men. The countess of Montfort, for instance, wore armor* and rode a huge courser.* She encouraged her women defenders of Hennebaut to cut short their kirtles so they could move more easily as they carried stones and pots of chalk to be hurled on the besiegers from the ramparts.* Then she led 300 men in a foray against the enemy camp and destroyed their tents and supplies by fire.

Furthermore, a knight was expected to be valorous. So claimed the *chansons de gestes* and romances, for he had to be ready to overcome giants, to show a friendly, encouraging visage to his own men and a fierce, terrifying one to his enemy. These literary works also required that opponents be of equal strength and number and fight one against one or against only a few, for by that means a knight could achieve greater glory by overcoming a force larger than his own. An uninjured knight was not to attack an injured, weaponless, sleeping, or unhorsed opponent. If he unhorsed an opponent, he was expected to dismount to continue the fight on foot or to help the opponent remount to keep the contest between them a fair fight. In warfare, however, these niceties were totally ignored, for there the goal was to win by overcoming one's opponent by any means. Brutality was commonplace. Enemies were beheaded and their heads thrown into beleaguered cities, bodies were dug up in search for booty (see spoils of war), and crusaders impaled heads of fallen enemies on their lances* to terrorize the enemy. Life was brutal and fighting was reckless.

Greed, however, ameliorated one form of battlefield brutality. A live knight could be ransomed for a handsome profit; a dead one could not. This also reflected partly on the knightly code of sparing a fellow brother in arms, particularly if that fellow could raise a considerable sum to ransom* himself. Further, an enemy was less likely to resist so fiercely if he knew that he was more likely to be taken prisoner than killed. As for his being captured, a knight had to solve his own dilemma. He could save his honor by staying to fight back, but this increased the danger of his being killed. Or he could flee from the field to battle and suffer the accompanying shame, but by so doing he freed himself from the worry of having to ransom himself for an enormous sum or of exposing himself to further danger. His choice, then, came down to honor or self-interest.

Not all knights were paragons of these chivalric virtues, and a knight could be stripped of his knighthood (see degradation of a knight) for such crimes as holding and practicing heretical religious beliefs, committing treason or *lèse-majesté** against the king, or fleeing from battle or an encounter in which banners* had been unfurled (see banners displayed). Beyond that he could be executed for striking the provost of an army with the intent to harm him, for disobedience of the governor of the army, for fleeing the battlefield while others were standing their ground, for revealing his lord's secrets to the enemy while scouting the enemy terrain, for feigning illness as the reason for not joining his lord in battle, for spreading dissension and deadly rumor, or for riding out to challenge the foe to single combat.

English knights were never numerous in this period. Most men could not become knights until they became of age (twenty-one) and had been dubbed by a formal ceremony (see below). Men of full age who held a full knight's fee (see below) or more were required by the king to "take up arms and cause himself to be made a knight." Even though some holding even one-half a knight's fee were knighted, many who were duly qualified sought to escape the duties and responsibilities which knighthood demanded by paying a fine and remaining a country gentleman.* Some men who held land by knight service and paid scutage* belonged to that ill-defined class, tenants in free socage.* With all this, the total number of knights in England lay somewhere between 6,000 and 7,000 in a country with a population of around 3 million people, that is, roughly one knight for every 500 people. Other countries placed similar restrictions on membership in knighthood. Emperor Frederick Barbarossa in 1152, for example, forbade peasants (see villein) to carry the usual knightly weapons of lance and sword* and recognized as knights only men whose ancestors had been knights before them; thirty-five years later he expressly forbade the sons of peasants from being knighted. In 1140 Roger II of Sicily decreed that only the descendants of knights could be admitted to knighthood; this was followed by similar decrees in 1234 by James I of Aragon and in 1294 by Count Charles II of Provence. Even though no such law existed in France, judgments of the court of Louis IX were quite explicit on this point. Only with special dispensation from the king himself could knighthood be conferred lawfully on someone whose father or grandfather in the male line had not been a knight. A man could be knighted at any age but was discouraged before the age of fifteen; generally the age for most knights was twenty-one. However, the higher his social standing, the more likely he was to be made a knight while still a boy: Henry III was knighted at age nine, Edward I at fifteen; even French and English romances frequently cited fifteen as the best age for knighting.

A man usually was knighted with elaborate ceremony at which his lord gave him rich and expensive clothes and equipment. When the king was involved with such a ceremony, the knight-to-be could expect particularly luxurious gifts. For example, King John of England instructed the sheriff of Hampshire to provide Thomas Esturmy, his valet, with a robe of scarlet with doeskin hood and a robe of green or brown, a saddle, a pair of bridles, a rain cloak, a mattress, and a pair of sheets when he became a knight. When King Henry III's daughter Margaret married the king of Scots at York in 1251, twenty young men were knighted in honor of that occasion. The cloth for their robes for that knighting came from the king's great wardrobe,* and these garments varied according to whether the candidate was to be a "knight bachelor"* or a "knight banneret."* More than just a simple garment, this robe included a tunic, supertunic, pallium, and capa, and its squirrel-fur trim instead of rabbit was chosen according to his rank.

The right of creating a knight was so widely exercised in the 12th century that one knight could knight another. Long past was the time when only the king or one of his barons or some other high official could bestow knighthood. When he was chancellor,* Thomas à Becket knighted a young nobleman whom he had brought up in his household. William Marshal* was knighted by the chamberlain of Tancarville, and he in turn knighted young Henry, eldest son of Henry II.* Yet it was a special honor to be knighted by the king.

One aspect of the "dubbing ceremony"* which is missing from English romances but which played a large role in French romances was the ceremonial bath. Geoffrey of Brittany, third son of Henry II, was said to have bathed before he was knighted in 1180. Before the all-night vigil of prayer and fasting which preceded the main ceremony, the aspirant donned clean white* garments and presented himself in church. Guy of Warwick, hero of a lengthy English romance, chose twenty squires* who were to be dubbed. They put on white silk kirtels, purple mantles, and stockings but no shoes; each wore a garland of precious jewels and pearls. Thus apparelled, they were led into the room where the earl awaited them. Then a squire gave each man a new sword to hold by its point, and he hung new gilt spurs on the hilt of each sword. Then each man knelt before the altar and prayed until midnight. Such a vigil, although varying in detail, was a well-established custom in reality as well as in story. It was a part of the dubbing ceremony of Geoffrey Plantagenet* by his father-in-law, Henry I, in 1128, and a part of the dubbing of the duke of Lancaster, soon to become Henry IV, in 1399. Placing the sword on the altar was a self-evident religious act. Some authorities claim it was done after the dubbing; others before. Regardless, it seems to have been an integral part of the ceremony. Then the candidate had the sword girded on him—either hung around his neck by a baldric* or belt or girded around his waist. This act emphasized the significance of the event: a knight was belted with the sword of knighthood. Additionally, but appearing less frequently in romances than the investment with the sword, was the investment of spurs.* The king or the investing noble fastened the right spur on the candidate's heel, and the candidate himself fastened the left one. Manuals of chivalry such as that of Raimon Lull* stressed the great allegorical value of bestowing the spur on the candidate, but the event frequently was omitted from battlefield ceremonies. Instead, the act which served as the culmination of the ceremony was the accolade, the neck blow or *colée*,* which the officiating lord bestowed on the candidate with either his hand or a drawn sword. Occasionally a kiss was used instead of the accolade. As he did so, the lord uttered some admonitory words. Although no such historical speeches have survived, it is safe to assume some were spoken, for the official would have to declare the candidate to be a knight to end the ceremony. Quite possibly words were similar to those uttered by Huon of Bordeaux, the hero of the romance bearing his name: "remember this order, that which you have received this day, and I pray to God that it may be to the increase of your honor, and ever beware that your thoughts be not light or wavering, but be wise and discreet and temperate, and be hardy in battle." (Bibliog. 1) This ceremony ended with a feast at which largesse was distributed. Froissart described how the dubbing of the duke of Lancaster and forty-six additional knights in 1399 was followed by a feast and a tournament* in which the new knights were expected to display their strength and skill; tournaments were a part of this ceremony only when a nobleman was dubbed.

Sometimes obstacles stood in the way of knighting. A squire could be prevented from being knighted by reason of his previous licentious life, his unreadiness to command, or his or his family's poverty. Poverty was the major reason because largesse was expected of knights, and the additional expenses connected with entering a tournament and providing all the necessary accoutrements, travel and living expenses, or of holding a tournament and hosting a large number of knights and their attendants, or of feeding daily his large mesnie,* and buying and maintaining destriers,* palfreys,* squires, and paying periodic taxes, all these made the costs prohibitive for some. Despite those costs, occasionally the king would need additional knights and by ordering the distraint* of knighthood would force potentially eligible men to become knights and thus serve him or pay scutage in lieu of service. This distraint involved seizing and detaining a person's goods or chattel to force him to perform some obligation or to punish him by seizure and detention for non-performance of some obligation.

The knight's fee was set at the income from land owned by a follower of the king, which set the rate at which he could discharge his duty. Customarily set at the service of one armed man for each five hides,* this amount frequently was determined by rent and valuation rather than acreage and varied not only from place to place but also from king to king. For example, the knight's fee for the abbey of St. Albans varied from five and one-half to eight and one-half hides; in Dorset it was two hides, and in Cambridgeshire one was as high as twenty-seven hides; in Yorkshire, fees of ten or twelve carucates* were common, but instances there record fees of seven, eight, fourteen, fifteen, and even twenty carucates. Such valuations were made even more difficult by the varying sizes of the hide or carucate: the *Domesday Book* recorded them at 120 acres,* and the assessment of carucage* in 1198 recorded them at 100 acres. Land values in terms of the mark* or pound (see money) provided a more satisfactory idea of the knight's fee. In the 13th century, when distraint* of knighthood (see below) began, possession of land worth twenty pounds a year was considered proper for a knight; yet evidence abounds that a unit of ten pounds perhaps was more common. And by Rannulf de Glanville's* time it was definitely recognized that a just and legitimate relief* was one hundred shillings (five pounds) for a knight's fee, calculated as a year's rent for a socager. Before 1160 the knight was paid six pence (see penny) per day, but Henry II* raised that to eight pence, and by 1210 that amount had risen to two shillings—high wages but necessarily so, for the knight had to buy his own equipment, and the costs of living had risen as had the costs of bodily defense. At the same time, cavalrymen received four to six pence and an infantryman two or three pence per day. His destrier could not be gotten for less than ten marks; his armor and mail* was equally expensive.

The equipment required of a knight usually consisted of a shield,* helmet,* hauberk,* sword,* and lance.* Raimon Lull assigned symbolic attributes to these and other pieces of knightly equipment. The sword, for example, was in the form of the cross* in token of the cause in which it was to be used always in defense of justice*; the shield represented the knight standing between the prince* and his people or as protector standing between the prince and his enemies. The spear* was straight and even just as truth was; its iron head served as a symbol of strength, and its pennon* was seen from afar as a sign of courage which was not to be hidden. The helmet symbolized modesty, the hauberk fortification for the body against the powers of evil, and the spurs were tokens of diligence and swiftness in all honorable designs.

Knights fought on foot as well as mounted. Frequently they were obligated to attack a fortress as footsoldiers. In 1122, for example, Louis VI (the Fat) and his knights attacked the castle of LePuiset on foot, as did Richard I's knights when they attacked the castle of Milli near Beauvais; William Marshal directed part of that attack and even scaled a ladder to capture the wall. Frequently knights dismounted to stiffen the ranks of the footsoldiers, to encourage them, and to stay and fight until the final victory or defeat. At Tinchebrai,* which won Normandy for England in 1106, for example, Henry I dismounted with his retinue and fought in the middle of his footsoldiers as did his opponent, his brother, Robert of Normandy; and he did so again at Bremûle. Despite these numerous examples of knights on foot, mounted knights led by the king or one of his greater barons played a prominent role in medieval warfare.

With the introduction into Europe of the stirrup in the eighth century, the mounted warrior had a far greater stability in the saddle than theretofore and could be more effective charging his opponent with his lance couched under his right arm. Without the stirrup, such a charge would not have been possible. The saddle and the spear also were highly important. By the 12th century the saddle consisted of a central "tree" with two arches, the head or saddlebow in front and the raised cantle in back. Gradually the upper external part of the cantle and pommel* were raised and widened, with the pommel ending in a high rim in front and the cantle forming a raised back support which gave the rider even greater security in his seat. That security allowed him to develop four ways to use the lance more effectively. Using a lightweight spear and grasping it at the point of balance with his right arm extended, he could deliver a blow as an underarm or overarm thrust, or he could hurl it at his foe from close quarters. He also could tuck a heavier one under his right armpit, grasp it farther out with his right hand, level it at his opponent, and handling both his reins and shield in his left hand, he could become a deadly weapon increasing in might by the weight and speed of the charging horse. In massed attacks the effort would carry the day. Additionally, with foot support from the stirrup, he could deliver greater blows with his sword by standing up to strike downward on his opponents on foot, and he could lean sideways safely to deliver a sweeping blow as he rode past. Facing footsoldiers, he could spear them, knock them aside, and cut them down with sword blows whether they stood or fled. He could strike them from their mounts and kill them as they lay helpless on the ground.

Training for knighthood began at birth. Between the first moments of life and the first armed encounters on a field of battle some twenty-one years later, a man had to learn to withstand fatigue, to endure hunger, thirst, cold, heat, and to master the art of fighting a fellow man. As a young boy, the son of a knight, he would be entrusted to the care of another knight, a relative or close friend, or perhaps the monarch himself if the boy were lucky, to learn the profession of arms. He would be trained in riding, fencing, and javelin* throwing to develop his physical strength to endure the heavy equipment of later life when wearing all the accoutrements of his profession while controlling an excited horse amid the extreme conditions of noise and confusion of the battlefield. King Henry II's sons were trained just that way. Their youth was described by Hoveden's *Chronicle*:

> They strove to outdo the others in handling weapons. They realized that without practice the art of war did not come naturally when it was needed. No athlete can fight tenaciously who has never received any blows: he must see his blood flow and hear his teeth crack under the fist of his adversary, and when he is thrown to the ground, he must fight on with all his might and not lose courage. The more often he falls, the more determinedly he must spring to his feet again. Anyone who can do that can engage in battle confidently. Strength gained by practice is invaluable: a soul subject to terror has fleeting glory. He who is too weak to bear this burden, through no fault of his own, will be overcome by its weight, no matter how eagerly he may rush to the task. The price of sweat is well paid where the temples of victory stand. (Bibliog. 296)

At birth a knight's son was bathed immediately under his father's guidance because it reminded him of the ceremonial oath he had taken long before as a candidate for knighthood. Then the lad was bound tightly with his arms at his sides, his feet together, and swaddled, and then covered with a rich robe. Next he was made a Christian by being baptized, for until he was immersed in that font, he was considered an evil object; when lifted from that holy font, he had become not only a Christian but had in his heart the making of a Christian knight. After the baptism a celebration including singing, dancing, feasting, entertainment,* and frequently a tournament was held to welcome the new son. Guests to this party left gifts for the infant as they departed; the godfather gave gold or silver; the godmother gave furred robes, frocks, and shoes, gifts which often were given to the poor later. After that the child was given to a wet nurse to suckle, for ladies rarely suckled their own children. Alexander Neckham's* mother suckled both her own son and Richard, later Richard I; Edward II was suckled by Alice de Lethegrew, who later was awarded the wardship* of Geoffrey de Scotland in 1284 for her services. Giving infants to other women to be suckled was not unusual when one considered the life of a woman in a castle. Often she was quite young, hardly more than a child herself, and had married to satisfy policy for her parents rather than for love of her husband. Life in a drafty castle was hardly suited to maternal duties, for the halls, rooms, entrances were constantly filled with armed men or pages who scorned her except when through some courtly love she gave them favors for a tournament or incentives for emprises.*

Before the age of seven a boy learned to walk on stilts, play rackets, fly kites, play bowls, marbles, and to play chess, backgammon (tables), and dice. At seven he left female tutorship and childhood things and became a page, damoiseau, or valet in the household of some important lord or knight to learn the disciplines and spirit of knighthood. Such an education began at seven with learning hawking* and hunting* under the falconer* and chief huntsman.* He mastered the first four rules of hawking: how to fly a hawk, how to feed her in her mews,* how to call her back when on the wing, and how to keep her when she returned. Hawks became so important to the young page that he would do almost anything to protect her. For example, Roland and Oliver,* famous heroes of the *chansons de gestes* who were the closest of friends, quarreled bitterly about a hawk under the walls of Vienne. Becket* nearly drowned as a youth when he dove into a mill-race to save his downed hawk. Further, he became familiar with his lord's destrier as he exercised it on a tether in the castle yard. His education was added to by his lord's private chaplain who taught him religion and courtesy in words and deeds and actions. He was taught, for example, not to sit until asked to do so, not to claw at his body or to lean against a post in his master's presence, to be obedient to his lord, and to do instantly whatever was asked of him by his lord. He did not necessarily learn to read and write, for more important things awaited him: to be brave on the field, to endure hardship, and to be expert on the chase, because the next phase of his training built on these.

That next phase was, at age fourteen, becoming a squire (French, *écuyer*). As a squire he was allowed greater intimacy with his lord and lady than as a page. At a solemn, formal, religious ceremony, he was presented to a priest before the altar by his parents, each holding a blessed taper which they later donated to the church. Prayers and blessings then were said over a sword and belt which were to be his alone, and then he was girded with his new symbols. Then he took up additional duties while still maintaining rigorous practice in the martial arts. Squires in a lord's household were divided into different classes, the first two of which were considered most honorable: Squire of the Body and Squire of the Honors (*Honorus**). As Squire of the Body, he rendered personal service to the knight and his lady: he took part in courts and assemblies, learned conversation and conduct by first-hand observation, and became skilled enough in elegant speech and manners, modesty, learning, and witty conversation to accompany his lord and lady frequently on visits. As Squire of the Honor (Honorus meant ceremonies of the court), he took part in the marshaling of ceremonies of the court: he carried his lord's sword of honor, stood by his chair or the throne of state, carried his lord's helmet of honor, led the destrier with all its glittering caparison,* carried his lord's mantle of state when it was being worn. He also had the duty of carrying his lord's banner and of raising the "battle cry"*; sometimes he was dispatched in place of heralds* and often assumed the office of herald to cast down the gage* of battle before his master's adversary. The remaining squires' duties were onerous: as Squire of Table, he carved, served and carried water for guests to wash their hands; as Squire of Wines he served wines*: hypocras,* a claret mixed with honey, and piment, a claret with more wine than honey; he made sure that his lord and guests had refreshments before retiring at night by taking them their sleeping cups; as Squire of Pantry he served from the pantry.

Besides these household duties, the squire attended his lord when he was preparing for a joust* or battle. He armed him before a fight, especially after plate armor had replaced mail and an armorer was needed to replace a rivet. He and his fellow squires carried his lord's armor on a journey: one carrying the gauntlets and armpieces; another the lance and sword, pennon and banner; another led the destrier on which from the saddlebow hung the helmet; but the most coveted duty was to carry the shield. As soon as these squires were through attending their lord in the field, they would return to the castle or manor* to resume their practice of putting on armor or mail and thus accustom themselves to its weight; they would wear heavy gauntlets and practice holding lance or "battle axe."* Naturally a squire had to be a skillful rider, so during his whole training from page through squire he practiced riding; one of the feats of horsemanship he sought to master was to leap into the saddle in full armor. He learned to use a shield in practice for warfare, to ride a destrier fully armed and at full tilt as against an adversary in a tourney,* to endure cold and exposure in open countryside, to scale walls, to leap and do those other exercises required later when he would besiege a town or castle. In sum, by the time he became twenty-one, he was a knight in miniature, trained in all the arts he would need to know to serve his lord well as a knight. See also Christian Knighthood. (Bibliog. 1, 33, 54, 87, 121, 225, 262, 264, 274, 296, 330, 343, 351)

Knights of Calatrava, oldest and greatest of the Spanish military orders of chivalry dedicated to the crusade in their homeland. An order of the Cistercians founded in 1158 by Sancho III of Castile to hold the city of Calatrava, captured from the Moors in 1146 by Alfonso VII and granted by him to the Cistercian Order, they were confirmed as a military order in 1164. Their insignia was a green cross* with a "fleur de lis"* on the end of the arms.* (Bibliog. 17)

Knights of Rhodes. See Hospitallers.

Knights of St. James (Santiago) of Campostella, Cistercian religious order which tradition claimed was founded by Ramiro II of Leon (931–950) but actually was confirmed as a military order by Pope Alexander III in 1175. Their badge* was a red cross* of St. James. (Bibliog. 17)

Knights of St. John of Jerusalem. See Hospitallers.

Knights of St. Julian del Pereyo, Cistercian order founded in Spain in 1156 by two brothers of the de Barrientos family and dedicated to the crusade* in their homeland. They received confirmation from Pope Alexander III in 1177. Because they were entrusted with the defense of Alcantara* in 1213, they became known as the Order of Alcantara. Their badge* was a red cross* with "fleur de lis"* on the ends of its arms.* (Bibliog. 180)

Knights of the Round Table, in echo of the legendary group of knights from King Arthur's time, King Edward III on January 1, 1344, ordered a great festival held in a great round tower 200 feet in diameter at Windsor Castle.* (Bibliog. 253)

Knights of the Temple. See Templars.

Knights Templar. See Templars.

komture. See Teutonic knights.

Krak des Chevaliers, one of the greatest fortresses of the crusades* in the Holy Land. Situated on the western bank of the Orentes River in Tripoli, it was begun in 1142 when the Hospitallers* built on the site of an ancient Muslim castle.* Typical of the Eastern castles, it had a double line of walls and an ingenious arrangement of towers, bastions,* and bulwarks from which the defenders could shower rocks and other missiles on attackers. Instead of having the plain "curtain walls"* of the Western castle, this had walls strengthened by projecting towers at regular intervals all along their length. In addition to being able to defend the area below the walls on each of its flanks, each of these towers could be entered only by staircases within the tower itself. Thus if an enemy captured one tower, he would find himself stranded high above the ground, for the other towers would be shut to him. Additionally, it had cisterns that held a five-year's supply of water, a windmill to grind grain, and a stable to quarter 400 chargers behind a wall that was eighty feet* thick. It housed 2,000 Knights Hospitaller. (Bibliog. 139, 273, 296)

kreutzer, *kraicjar,* billon* or copper coin widely spread throughout northern Germany and Hungary valued at four pfennig (see bracteate; coinage) or eight heller.* (Bibliog. 150)

kreuzlied. See *minnesang.*

kyree. See curee.

L

label, horizontal band beneath which three vertical wedges were attached in blazon*; it was placed on the shield* of the eldest son as a mark of cadency* during the lifetime of his father. (Bibliog. 43)

labor, prices of. See money.

lagen, measure of capacity equal to one gallon* for both liquid and dry products in the 13th century. (Bibliog. 394)

lai, lay, short form of French romance* in octosyllabic couplets. Also called conte,* contoise,* or dit, this story form differed from the romance in that it was much shorter, usually being under 1,000 lines; its details converged on one main scene or climax; and its poetic style was subordinate to the action which sped towards the climax. The term lai came from the Celtic word *laed*, song. (Bibliog. 162)

laisse, stanzaic division of French epic *chansons de geste** and romances.* Ranging anywhere from five to eighty or more lines, it marked a unit of action or of the poet's thought and allowed him to emphasize action and thus avoid tediousness in his recital. (Bibliog. 162)

laissez les aller (Fr. "Let them go"), words used to begin a tournament.* (Bibliog. 78)

lambrequin, protective scarf or covering to protect a helmet* from heat and dampness. See mantle. (Bibliog. 43)

Lammas, church festival on August 1.

Lammasse of Peter Apostle, church festival on June 29.

lance, common shafted weapon of varying lengths. Saxon cavalry used one with a shaft of ten feet,* but a footman carried one of only six feet. As the Saxon shaft always was referred to as made of ash, the footsoldier frequently was called "aesc-born"* or ash-bearer. Despite the varying shape and size of the spear-heads, ranging from three to eighteen inches* with the commonest being ten inches, rarely were they barbed because the barb* would impede the quick withdrawal of the weapon from an enemy's body. The butt end of the spear* usually was fitted with a spiked iron shoe so it also could be used as a stabbing weapon.

Contrasted with this heavy Saxon weapon, the Norman lance served as a javelin* by being hurled at the foe by mounted cavalrymen. It had a twelve-foot slender shaft of uniform thickness and a fairly broad blade, sometimes barbed, and usually was carried erect with its end resting on the stirrup when not in use. As this war lance grew to fourteen feet in length with a small steel leaf- or lozenge-shaped head, a small circular steel vamplate* to protect the hand was fitted over the shaft from early in the 14th century.

One of the difficulties in managing this weapon in battle arose from the impact of a successful thrust, which was liable to drive it backward under the arm. After 1300 such an impact was countered by fastening over the shaft behind the hand a small disc-shaped stop which would rest against the armpit and thereby assume some of the shock previously taken by the hand alone. From 1400 on, however, a bracket called a grate* or a graper was fastened against the breast of the armor* which stopped the backward movement of an opponent's lance.

In tourneys (see tournaments) after 1200 the heavy war lance was replaced by a thinner, lighter weapon of sycamore or fir that was rebated with a crown-shaped coronel* over the point to reduce the possibility of fatalities. (Bibliog. 9, 27, 71)

lance of courtesy. See *jousts à plaisance*.

land tenure, five means by which a person could be granted land under Norman and Angevin rule in England: frankalmoign,* knight service (see knighthood), sergeanty (see sergeant), socage,* and villeinage (see villein). (Bibliog. 264)

langedebeve. See partisan.

landgrave, landgraviate, German count* having jurisdiction over a territory and having beneath him several inferior counts. (Bibliog. 246)

langue-de-boeuf. See partisan.

langue d'oc (Fr.), dialect predominant in the south of France, especially around Provence, where the word *oui* was pronounced *oc*, thereby giving its name to a large region there. (Bibliog. 162)

langue d'oïl (Fr.), dialect predominant in the north of France where the word *oui* was pronounced *oïl*. (Bibliog. 162) *langue de si* (Fr.), dialect in northern Italy where the word for yes was pronounced *si*. (Bibliog. 246)

lanner. See falconry birds.

lapis-lazuli, Frisian stone which, when drunk with the tips of roses in wine,* was expected to heal quartan ague or fever. (Bibliog. 335)

largesse, granting lavish gifts as part of a feudal contract as payment for military or other service or as the price of one's adherence to a cause. The largesse of chivalry* was little concerned with the material welfare, lawful claims, or personal rewards of the recipients but was, in fact, more involved with meritorious conduct when it was bestowed on the undeserving. "It is not only to the good and deserving that one should give, for the valor in them, but also to the bad for the valor which is in the act of giving" (*Lancelot du Lak*). Thus indiscriminately and freely giving of one's possessions of money,* jewels, horses,* gold* objects, fighting gear, or clothing became an essential feature of the chivalric world. Clothing especially was suitable largesse for it was recognized as a token of wealth, rank, mental poise, decorum, and social acceptability; a gift of clothing enhanced both the giver and the receiver. For the giver it was tangible proof of his willingness to carry out obligations of his knightly honor*; for the recipient it signified a recognition and confirmation of his social worth; thus, if the garment was removed and bestowed on the spot, it became a doubly honorific gesture.

However, where lavishness on a grand scale was sought, a mere garment was hardly an adequate gesture. On the contrary, such a person would have to have had a large stock of clothing brought from storage and distributed at random for everyone present. For example, when Thomas à Becket* travelled to Paris in 1157 to negotiate the marriage* of King Louis VII's daughter Marguerite to Henry the Young King, oldest son of the English King Henry II*, he took with him a huge retinue described by Giraldus Cambrensis. First came 250 male servitors on foot singing English songs, followed by huntsmen* with fine dogs on double leashes walking just in front of eight fully loaded carts* drawn by five horses* with each driver walking beside his wagon leading a dog. The next two carts carried beer or ale in iron-bound casks, furniture for a chapel, fittings for a bedchamber, kitchen* utensils, clothing room hangings, and the like. Behind them walked twelve pack animals loaded with boxes of linen, silver, golden utensils, cups, bowls, plates, clothing, and books, each with a rider carrying a monkey. These were followed by knights on palfreys* leading their destriers,* accompanied by squires* with birds on their fists, by officers of the household, by more knights and clergy riding two by two, and finally by the Archbishop Becket himself and his associates. All these great quantities of furs, clothing, plate, horses, and so on he gave as largesse to knights and poor scholars alike in France, thereby increasing both his own and King Henry II's reputation. Two other examples show the extremes to which some nobles went to prove their largesse. On his way to marry Beatrix, daughter of the duke* of Lower Lorraine in 1045, Boniface of Tuscany had his horses shod loosely with precious metal so that these shoes would be cast along the road and picked up by the natives as tangible proof of his wealth. Betrans Raiembaus at Beaucaire in 1174 had the ground plowed and then sown with deniers (see denarius) valued at 30,000 solidi (see sol) which the assembled guests were invited to search for and keep.

One means of spreading the reputation of one's largesse lay with the minstrels* and jongleurs who could proclaim and celebrate far and wide the exploits, virtues, and generous acts of knights who were generous with them. Similarly, such errant entertainers could hold up to scorn, ridicule, derision, and shame far and wide any knight or master who treated him in a niggardly or penurious fashion. (Bibliog. 149, 161)

last, commercial denomination of weight for dry and liquid products, most frequently was equivalent to 2 tons or 4,000 pounds.* In wool weight it was 4,368 pounds or 12 sacks*; of gunpowder it was 2,400 pounds or 24 barrels*; it also equalled 12 barrels of ashes, 12 barrels of beer, 600 bowstaves, 12 barrels of butter, 1,700 pounds of feathers, 600 bonds of flax, 20 dickers* of 10 hides each or sometimes 12 dozen dozen, and 12,000 herring. See weights and measures. (Bibliog. 394)

latch crossbow. See *arbalète à cric*.

lathes, administrative units in Kent, England, larger than hundreds* or wapentakes,* which seemed to have originated as regions administered from royal vills.* (Bibliog. 163)

latrine, privy, toilet in a castle* or manor* house. Often called garderobe* and thus confused with wardrobe,* this room was placed at the end of a short right-angled passageway in the thickness of the wall as close to the bedchamber as possible and was supplemented by the universally used chamberpot. Often it was built to be cleansed by rainwater from the gutters or from a cistern or from kitchen* drainage diverted down the shaft. When the walls were not thick enough to hold this room, it was built on corbels* projecting out from the walls over the moat or river or with a long shaft reaching to the ground. Such a shaft could be dangerous, however, for at Château Gailiard* besiegers climbed up the latrine shaft and gained access to the castle. (Bibliog. 128, 385)

latten, form of brass used by armorers in their experiments on plate armor* late in the 13th century. (Bibliog. 27)

Laudabiliter, bull* issued in 1155 by Pope Adrian IV, the English pope, at the request of King Henry II of England which sanctioned the privilege sought by

Henry to conquer Ireland. This pope also gave to Henry an emerald ring by which investiture the right to rule over Ireland was granted. (Bibliog. 264)

lauds, "canonical hour"* representing roughly three o'clock in the morning; this was the first of the day-hours of the church, the Psalms of which always ended with Psalms 148–150, sung as one psalm, and technically called "lauds." (Bibliog. 246)

law of arms, unofficial but generally agreed upon rules of conduct during warfare concerning "spoils of war,"* ransoms,* and "signs of war."* Additionally, it became a specific right accorded by English King Edward III (1327–1377) to the Court of Chivalry* to judge matters arising out of war within the realm. Apart from cases of treason, the most important cases heard by this court* concerned ransoms, safe-conducts,* and the rights of armorial bearings (see charge). See also siege warfare; war, just. (Bibliog. 381)

law of descent, English rules of inheritance established at the end of the reign of King Henry III (1217–1272). The first class of persons called to the inheritance comprised the dead person's descendants; if he left an "heir of his body," no one else would inherit. Among descendants, six rules set precedence:

1. a living descendant excluded his or her own descendants; that is, a son inherited rather than that son's children

2. a dead descendant was represented by his or her own desendants; that is, if a son was dead, then precedence went to the grandchildren: children of the dead son

3. males excluded females of equal degree: sons inherited; daughters were excluded if sons lived

4. among males of equal degree, only the eldest surviving son inherited all, and his younger brothers were excluded

5. females of equal degrees inherited as co-heirs; all daughters shared alike in the inheritance if no sons survived

6. a dead descendant was represented by his or her own descendants; this overrode the preference for the male sex: a granddaughter by the eldest son excluded a younger son. For example, when King Edward III died in 1377, the crown* went to Richard, son of his eldest son, Edward the Black Prince, and not to King Edward's second son, Lionel.

(Bibliog. 261)

law of King Richard about crusaders at sea, regulations issued by King Richard I* concerning conduct aboard his ships en route to the Holy Land on the third crusade.* Anyone who killed a man on shipboard was to be bound to the dead man and thrown into the sea; if he killed a man on land, he was to be bound to the dead man and buried with the corpse. If anyone was seen drawing a knife to strike another man or drawing blood, he was to lose his hand; if however, he struck with fist without drawing blood, he was dipped three times into the sea. Anyone who taunted a man, insulted him, or charged him with hating God was to pay as many ounces* of silver as the number of hurled insults. A convicted thief was to have boiling tar poured over his shaved head and feathers shaken over the tar so that he would be known publicly as a thief, and then he was to be put ashore at the next port of call. (Bibliog. 151)

laws of William [the Conqueror], *Leis Willelmi,* ten old laws which King Edward the Confessor (1042–1066) held and which the new Norman monarch, William* I, carried over for the people of England. Set in writing possibly as early as 1090, but no later than 1135 (during the reign of Henry I), these were a combination of old English laws, King Canute's code, and Norman additions. The first law requested belief in one God, faith in Christ, and peace between English and Normans. The second one called for all English freemen to swear oaths of loyalty and fidelity to the new Norman king.* The third required the English not to harm the Normans, and the lord of any English murderer was to yield the killer to the Norman authorities within five days or to pay forty-six marks* of silver if he was able to, and if not, then his hundred* was to pay what remained of the fine* (see Englishry). The fourth required the French who owned English land to pay ''scot and lot.''* The fifth forbade the sale of live cattle outside cities. The sixth called for any Englishman accused of murder, theft, or rape of a Norman to defend himself either by the ''ordeal of red-hot iron''* or by ''wager of battle,''* the loser to pay forty shillings (see money) to the king; if a Frenchman was accused by an Englishman who was unwilling to defend his charge by either ordeal or battle, the Frenchman could clear himself by swearing an oath of innocence. The seventh called for all to abide by the previous laws of King Edward with respect to their land and possessions. The eighth required every freeman to be in frankpledge.* The ninth prevented sale of any man by another outside the country. The tenth forbade anyone from being hanged or executed in any fashion (see execution) but instead called for him to be blinded and castrated as the only form of capital punishment. (Bibliog. 102)

lay. See lai.

layes. See stankes.

league, measure of length generally equal to 15,840 feet* or three miles* of 5,280 feet each; however, two other distances also were referred to as leagues: 7,500 feet; 7,680 feet or 12 linear farthingales* of 40 perches.* (Bibliog. 394)

leash, leather thong about a yard* long and half an inch* wide with a button on one end and tapering to a point at the other, by which a hawk was confined. (Bibliog. 26)

lecours. See minstrels.

lectuary. See electuary.

leet court. See manor court.

leet jurisdiction. See tourn.

leets, wards into which a borough* was divided. (Bibliog. 261)

Leis Willelmi. See laws of William [the Conqueror].

lemona, lemocia, altered type of barbarin coinage* issued by Gui VI, vicomte (see viscount) of Limoges (1230–1263), just prior to his death. Because it had his name on its obverse, his vassals* rejected it and made a treaty with his representatives to withdraw it. (Bibliog. 150)

leopard, 1. any lion* depicted in armorial bearings (see charge) that was not in a rampant* position was, in strict accuracy, termed a leopard; common usage, however, changed it to become synonymous with lion. To the French, the heraldic lion was the English lion rampant; the leopard was the English lion passant* guardant*; the leopard-lion was the English lion passant; and the lion-leopard was the English lion rampant guardant. King Richard I's* shield* bore three leopards, that is, three lions passant guardant. 2. gold half-florin (see florin) of King Edward III whose obverse showed a lion guardant. (Bibliog. 116, 150)

leporaii. See hounds for the hunt.

lèse-majesté, hurt or violated majesty; any offense against the sovereign, such as treason. See spoils of war; ransom. (Bibliog. 181, 246)

lesses. See fumes.

letites, vitreous stone which when hung about the neck prevented sadness; when placed outside a woman's dress, it prevented hemorrhage. It also killed vermin and extinguished fires. (Bibliog. 258)

letters of marque, reprisals in the form of authorizations to vessels owned, manned, and officered by private persons. These letters commissioned the privateers to prey upon the commerce of a hostile opponent and keep the plunder they obtained as reward for their services. By this means men could obtain compensation by force for injuries or hostile acts done by aliens who could not be brought to justice* without breaking a truce and plunging a whole people into the horrors of a general war. These letters licensed a sort of limited war to recover goods, chattels, or persons to the value of the loss originally sustained. Reprisals, then, permitted taking "spoils of war"* but only in payment of a specific debt and not as gains in a general war.

These reprisals could be granted only by a prince* who had no superior and who laid down careful procedures to be followed. First the injured person had to seek justice from a judge with authority over the man who had injured him. If he failed to get it, then he could have recourse to his own sovereign lord. This sovereign then inspected the evidence and, if satisfied, demanded redress in a legal manner. The accused then had to be given the chance to express his side of the case. If and only if after all this, justice still was desired, the sovereign licensed reprisals on behalf of his subject. (Bibliog. 181)

letters patent, open document announcing an honor, or granting power and authority to a person to do some act or enjoy some right, and containing a seal or seals attached at the end. See safe-conduct. (Bibliog. 43)

leudes, special inner circle of close personal retainers around a king*; a group chosen from among the group of freemen he chose to surround himself with; his mainbour.* (Bibliog. 28)

levée en masse. See *arrière-ban.*

lévrier, French greyhound.* See hunting; hunting dogs. (Bibliog. 96)

lévrier d'attache. See greyhound; hunting; hunting dogs. (Bibliog. 96)

leyr, fine* imposed by a "manor court"* for the incontinence of bondwomen, whereby according to legal theory, the value of the lord's property was depreciated. In 1378 three women were fined eighteen pence (see penny). (Bibliog. 104)

Liagh Fail, Stone of Destiny, better known as the Stone of Scone. See coronation chair. (Bibliog. 178)

liam, lyome, lyame, rope of silk or well-tanned horsehide by which "hounds for the hunt"* were led. It was fastened to the collar by a swivel, and both the collar and the liam were gorgeously decorated. Derived from the old French word *liamen,* meaning strap or line, this rope used by the limer* (see hunting dogs) was three and one-half fathoms* long. (Bibliog. 96)

liart, common horse's* name in the *chansons de geste,* meaning a color between white and gray, often a mixture of the two colors. (Bibliog. 134, 191)

liber de Wintonia. See *Domesday Book.*

libera elemosina. See frankalmoign.

librate, measurement of land by its annual value in pounds sterling* used by English King Henry II (1154–1189); forty librates of land was land bringing in forty pounds per annum. From 1200 on, the total acreage of the librate depended on local soil conditions and on the value of the pound, varying from several bovates* or oxgangs* to as much as half of a knight's fee (see knighthood). Even later, however, the values were set to correspond to the relative value of the different moneys*: an oblate worth half an acre* corresponded to an obol* or halfpenny*; a denierat per acre to one denier (see denarius) or penny*; a solidat at twelve acres to one sol* or shilling; and a librate at 240 acres to a libre or pound (240 pence). (Bibliog. 163, 394)

liege, the feudal superior to a vassal* to whom primary allegiance and service were due. See also homage. (Bibliog. 246)

liege homage, simple unconditional homage.* A man who had but one lord did unconditional homage. If he acquired a fee from another lord, his homage to this second lord was to be conditional, for he had to honor the faith he owed his first lord. If tenements held of several lords descended to one heir, his liege homage was due either to the lord from whom he claimed his principal dwelling place or to that lord who made the oldest feoffments* under which he claimed. This person to whom liege homage was done was by no means necessarily the king.* However, the king insisted that in every expression of homage or fealty* to another there should be a saving for the faith due to him as king, and so he insisted that every male of the age of twelve onward take an oath of fealty to him and his heirs "to bear faith and loyalty of life and limb, of body and chattels and of earthly honor" which made no reference to any tenement. Such an oath promised a fealty so unconditional that it became known as the oath of liegance or allegiance. Should enmity arise between his different lords, the tenant properly stood with him to whom he had sworn liegance—his liege lord. (Bibliog. 28)

ligging, deer's resting place or lair. See hunting terms. (Bibliog. 96)

limbs, those parts of a bow* both above and below the handle. (Bibliog. 96, 100)

limer, scenting hound which was held on leash or liam* while tracking game. Although no particular breed of dog was specified, such a dog had to be keen of scent, staunch on line, not too fast, and taught to run mute, for if the exact whereabouts of game were to be discovered, the dog must not be allowed to challenge while on scent. As soon as the stag was "moved," that is, flushed from cover, the limer's work was over, and other hounds were uncoupled to take up the chase. The harborer with his limer nearby, though, mounted and followed the hunters closely, ready to use the limer again if the stag ran in company with other deer, or gave the hounds the change.* See hunting dogs; hunting terms. (Bibliog. 96)

lincis, compound made from the urine of a lynx that was effective in healing stomach complaints. (Bibliog. 258)

lingua franca, common language consisting of Italian mixed with French, Spanish, Greek, and Arabic spoken in the ports of the Mediterranean. (Bibliog. 246)

lion, 1. oldest, most popular, and most frequently used heraldic charge.* Early heraldic artists, eager to fill as much space on the field* as possible with the charge, depicted the lion in an upright position, that is, rampant.* Until perhaps the second half of the 13th century the body of the lion appeared straight upright so that its head, trunk, and left hind paw fell into the angle of the shield.* Its left forepaw was held horizontally, its right fore and hind paws placed diagonally upward. Each paw ended in three knobs from which extended the claws. When placed in any other position on a shield, the beast depicted was called a leopard.* The lion rampant usually was depicted in heraldry* as "armed and langed," that is, with its tongue and claws of a different color* from the animal, usually gules* unless the lion was on a field of gules, in which case they were represented azure.* Additionally, there could be no more than one lion on a shield; when more than one beast like it was depicted, again the beasts were called leopards or lioncels. For example, King Richard I's* shield had three leopards passant* guardant.* 2. king of beasts; when he wished to hunt he drew a circle in the dust with his tail, and any beasts he wished to prey on could not leave that circle once they had entered it. When he was pursued by hunters he would wipe out his tracks in the dust with his tail as he ran. He trembled the first time he saw a man, and he slept always with open eyes, alert to the world about him. (Bibliog. 43, 116, 258)

lion of England, lion* passant* guardant* or on a field* of gules.* (Bibliog. 116)

lioncel, little lion,* used to describe groupings of two or more lions on one field.* It was used first as a device* by Geoffrey of Anjou whose shield* depicted six lioncels. (Bibliog. 251)

lions of England, two lions* (leopards*) borne on the arms* of the kings* of England since William* I (1066–1087); Henry II (1154–1189) added a third. (Bibliog. 253)

lis, gold coin issued by Raymond IV, prince* of Orange, 1340–1393. (Bibliog. 150)

lists, barriers surrounding places of refuge to which a knight could retreat to rest or repair his armor* during a tournament.* As no boundaries were set in the early tournaments, fighting could range over several square miles,* and the tiring combatants needed places of safety. Later the term came to refer to the enclosures like the center ring of a circus in which knights fought each other surrounded by gaily colored tents and stands filled with spectators. (Bibliog. 17, 263)

lithsmen, pre-Conquest (1066) term for mercenaries* who originally were Viking warriors equally at home on land or sea. Such men marched north from London with King Harold Godwineson to fight and defeat the invading Harold Hardrada in 1066 at Stamford Bridge* and returned south with him to face the invading Normans under William* at Hastings. (Bibliog. 158)

livery in deed. See feoffment.

livra, bronze monetary or weight unit current in the south of France around Toulouse and Bordeaux from the middle of the 13th century. (Bibliog. 150)

livre, French money of account which in the time of Charlemagne (768–814) equalled one pound* of silver, but in time its value lessened. (Bibliog. 324)

Livre de Chasse. See *Master of Game.*

livre parisis, livre* of Paris, a French silver unit equalling twenty-five sous of twelve deniers (see denarius) each. (Bibliog. 324)

livre tournois, livre* of Tours, a French silver unit equalling twenty sous of twelve deniers (see denarius) each. This had the same value as the Italian lira and equalled one-sixth of a silver ecu (see coinage). (Bibliog. 324)

Lochaber axe, weapon with a long, thin, shafted blade resembling a vouge* with a hook at the top of the staff. The blade's top had a wavy edge, but its lower end was curved. (Bibliog. 71)

lockets, two metal bands around the mouth of a sword* sheath* to which metal terminals on the belt were linked by rings. (Bibliog. 27)

London bushel. See London weights and measures.

London pound. See London weights and measures.

London quarter. See London weights and measures.

London stone. See London weights and measures.

London weights and measures, twelve ounces* equalled one London pound; eight London pounds equalled one wine* gallon*; eight wine gallons equalled one London bushel; eight London bushels equalled one London quarter; twelve and one-half pounds* equalled one London stone; six score stone* equalled one char* of lead; one char of lead equalled thirty footmals of six stones each but two pounds less when each stone weighed twelve pounds and each pound contained twenty-five shillings (see coinage; money). (Bibliog. 103, 394)

longbow, powerful weapon which came to the fore in English battles during the wars of King Edward I (1272–1307) against the Welsh who had developed it. Its proper length was the archer's height, between sixty-six and seventy-two inches,* and its arrow* could penetrate an oaken door four inches thick. Bows* of yew were preferred, but as yew was scarce an act of Parliament ordered bowmakers (bowyers*) to make four bows of witch hazel, ash, or elm to every one of yew. The bowstring was twisted or plaited hemp or silk, always made round at the "nocking point"* where the notch of the arrow was placed. This weapon was to be held perpendicular, as the archer kept both eyes open and looked only at the target as he drew back the string with two or three fingers toward the ear when shooting at short marks and toward the breast when shooting at long ranges. Its bowman carried a sheaf of twenty-four arrows in his quiver, each one a clothyard shaft or about thirty-two inches long. Arrows of ash were preferred and feathered or plain at their base, tipped with a sharp, sometimes barbed, head of iron or pointed with steel. Although arrows with goose feathers called "broad arrows"* were so popular that King Henry V of England ordered the sheriffs* throughout the land to take six wing feathers from every goose to feather arrows for his bowmen, plain, featherless arrows were considered to have better penetration power.

These archers wore a leather wrist-guard called a bracer* to protect their arms from injury by the recoil of the string. Additionally, they carried an axe* or short sword,* one or two stakes, and a hammer* with a leaden head to drive the stakes into the ground in front of their positions as protection against a cavalry charge, as well as for giving a *coup de grâce** to a fallen enemy. An archer's first duty in battle was to send clouds of arrows against the cavalry to disorganize their formation by killing or disabling as many horses* as possible, causing their riders to become "hors de combat."* From the 13th century onward, England had large numbers of mounted archers in the ranks of the army, mounting between 3,000 and 5,000 bowmen for every 1,500 fully equipped lancers. Each lancer's entourage was five or six mounted soldiers, at least two of whom were bowmen. Archers were so vital to the English armed forces that King Edward III decreed in 1337 that throughout all the realm of England every man must practice only with the longbow and arrows on pain of death and that every bowyer and fletcher* should be freed from all his debts. This weapon remained popular throughout

England until it was replaced by guns. It was popular on the continent also because it was much easier to use than a crossbow,* requiring less physical power to use and discharging twelve arrows in the time that a crossbow fired only three. Its range and effectiveness was about the same as that of the crossbow, about 250 yards,* at which range an ordinary English archer would rarely miss a target as big as a man; continental bowmen were not so accurate. The longbow's extreme range went from sixteen to twenty score yards, that is, a bow shot of 400 yards. (Bibliog. 71, 146, 241)

long-cross penny, English coinage* issued in 1247 to replace the "short-cross penny"* in order to deter unscrupulous people from clipping slivers of metal from the edges of earlier silver pennies.* King Henry III (1216–1272) ordered the arms* of the cross* on the reverse of these new coins to be extended to the edge of the designs so that if more than one end of the arms was missing, the coin no longer would be acceptable as legal tender. (Bibliog. 150, 240)

loop holes, openings in the outer wall of a building made narrow on the outside so they were difficult targets for enemy arrows and splayed on the inside to provide wide range of coverage through which arrows* and darts* could be discharged on an enemy. Often in the form of a cross,* these openings had round holes at the end. (Bibliog. 100)

Lord Prince, title of the eldest son of the king* of England before the reign of King Edward I. In 1301 Edward I changed that by conferring the title of Prince of Wales* on his son, Edward, who was born in Wales after Edward I had conquered it; subsequent monarchs carried on the tradition with their eldest sons. (Bibliog. 178)

Lords Appellant, title assumed in 1388 by the heads of the baronial opposition to King Richard II of England. Led by the king's uncle, the duke* of Gloucester, these lords seized control of the government and impeached the king's ministers, but in the following year they were dismissed by the king* with the help of his uncle, John of Gaunt, duke of Lancaster. (Bibliog. 8, 186)

lords temporal. See House of Lords.

lords spiritual. See House of Lords.

loricam. See hauberk.

lose one's law, to be deprived of one's privileges under the law. After a champion lost a fight in a duel* of law, he was declared a craven* and was deprived of most of his civil rights because the duel proved him a perjurer; thus he lost his law and became an infamous person, so he never again could be heard as a witness. (Bibliog. 229)

Louis VII, king of France (1137–1180). He was proclaimed king in 1131 on the death of his older brother but did not ascend the throne until the death of his father, Louis VI, the Fat, in 1137. He married Eleanor of Aquitaine* in 1137, and began his reign as king of France and duke of Aquitaine. Under the influence of his wife, he began a series of conflicts with the papacy and some of his feudal lords, but changed his attitudes when his army began a series of retaliatory raids on French villages in 1143. He was one of the leaders of the second crusade,* and proved himself to be a good knight. On his return to France, his continuing government based on justice and a good relationship with the clergy won him the respect of the nobility. For many reasons, among them because she bore him only two daughters, he agreed to divorce his wife in 1152. By that separation, he lost a major portion of France, from the Pyrenees to the English Channel, to his most powerful vassal, Henry II* of England. In the protracted series of conflicts between the two rulers, Louis had the support of his other vassals as well as the papacy. His support of Pope Alexander III against the emperor, Frederick Barbarossa,* earned him the title of "The Most Christian King," which became a hereditary title of French kings. During his reign, the schools of Paris developed into a prestigious university, making Paris the center of west European culture. (Bibliog. 139, 186)

Louis IX, "Saint Louis," king of France (1226–1270). Becoming king when only twelve, the first years of his reign were under the regency of his mother, Blanche of Castile, who educated him to be a pious Christian. His suppression of baronial revolt in central France in 1241 enlarged the royal domain, and gave appanages* to his brothers. His court extended the system whereby Philip II had made personal agreements with individuals, placing them under the royal protection; Louis granted his mercy and justice to great and small alike. In 1244 he embarked on the seventh crusade as a religious and military expedition to save the Christian kingdom of the East. His first assault was against Egypt, where after initial successes, he was defeated and captured at Mansura in 1249. Released for the huge ransom of 400,000 livres, he went to Acre and fortified the Christian cities before being recalled to France in 1254. Under his reign the Parlement* of Paris was organized as the high court of justice. His reputation as an equitable ruler led him to become the arbiter of disputes in Europe that did not necessarily involve France. For example, he was asked to arbitrate a dispute between the English king, Henry III, and his barons. He authorized the crusade against the Cathars in southern France, the Albigensian crusade,* and subsequently proclaimed the ninth crusade against Tunis in 1270. He died on that expedition, and was canonized in 1298. (Bibliog. 139, 297c, 355)

love-day, *dies amoris, jour d'amour,* day appointed for a meeting between enemies, rivals, parties in a lawsuit, and so forth to reconcile or arbitrate differences. Such a meeting was far from a settlement by arbitration arranged by the court* but instead granted permission for people to settle out of court and provided a recess in a case so such a settlement could be attempted. (Bibliog. 381)

Lower Exchequer. See Exchequer.

lozenge, diamond-shaped heraldic charge* of a square set on its corner; if it was long and narrow, it was called a fusil.* Spinsters and widows frequently bore their arms* on a lozenge rather than on a shield.* (Bibliog. 43)

ludus trojae. See tournament.

lug. See measurements.

Lull, Raimon, seneschal* at the court of James II of Aragon and author of *Book of the Order of Chivalry,** in which he attempted to modify chivalry* to become an established pattern of Christian society. His object was stated in the prologue, "May the knight through this book return to the devotion, loyalty, and obedience which he owes to his order." He divided the work into eight sections: "The Hermit and the Squire"; "The Origin of Chivalry"; "The Office of a Knight"; "The Examination of a Squire"; "The Ordination of a Knight"; "The Significance of a Knight's Arms"; "The Custom of a Knight"; and "The Honour Due to a Knight." (Bibliog. 207)

lure, implement used to bring a hawk down from the air to the falconer.* It was a leather pad in the shape and size of a horseshoe with wings of a pigeon or some other bird sewn on both sides and pieces of meat tied in its center. A long piece of line allowed it to be swung or thrown into the air to attract the hawk. See hack. (Bibliog. 26)

lyame, lyome. See liam.

lymphad, ancient galley with one mast used as an heraldic charge*; the blazon* stated whether in full sail or with sails furled and whether flags or pennon* were flying. (Bibliog. 43)

M

mabinogi, Welsh story which corresponded to the French enfance* that detailed a hero's youth from his conception and birth to his early manhood. (Bibliog. 200)

mace, oldest of all weapons, which, in its simplest form, was a wooden club. By the 12th century metal heads had been added: simple metal cylinders either grooved lengthwise or covered with bosses.* By the early 14th century, most had a squat head that was divided into a series of deep longitudinal flanges and were frequently topped with a short spike. (Bibliog. 27)

machicolation, opening between a fortification's wall and parapet* formed by a corbel* over the parapet so that the defenders could throw darts,* hot sand, stones, and oil on assailants below through *meurtrières** or could fire arrows* through "arrow loops."* This served the same function as hoarding* in a castle* building, except that hoarding and brattice* work was built out of wood and therefore was in danger from fire. (Bibliog. 280)

machicoulis. See bretasche.

madness, sickness in "hunting dogs"* that ranged through seven types: furious or hot-burning madness; running madness; dumb madness; lank (drooping); rheumatic or slavering; falling; sleeping. (Bibliog. 96)

magistri. See master.

Magna Carta Libertatum, great "charter of liberties"* issued by King John of England in 1215. His barons,* angered by the arbitrary rulings by the king* and his officers, had compelled him to accept their conditions by threatening to depose him and to incite a general revolt. As a result, at Runnymede on June 15, 1215, they forced the king to concede on many privileges of feudal tradition and therefore to limit the power of his monarchy. What made this charter* unique was its provision (Clause 61) that gave to the barons the power to deal with their grievances against the king. (Not only was this an innovation in medieval law, but also it laid the foundation for the English Parliament* a half-century later.)

To resolve the discord between the king and his barons, this Clause 61 required the barons to choose twenty-five barons of the kingdom to maintain the peace and liberties so that if the king, justiciar,* or any of his bailiffs* or servants violated the articles of peace, notice was sent to at least four of the twenty-five barons, who were to present their grievance before the king in person. If he did not correct the injustice within forty days, these four were to refer the matter to the remaining barons who then were to subject the king to distraint* and distress in every way they could, including the seizure of castles,* lands, possessions, and any other items, except the persons of the king, queen, and royal children, until, in their opinion, amends had been made. (Bibliog. 163)

magnate. See peer.

magnet, iron-colored compound that attracted iron, found in the River Jordan. To test a woman's faithfulness it was to be placed on her head as she slept: she would turn on her stomach if chaste but on her back if wanton. Furthermore, it cured dropsy, rendered impotent any man or woman who drank it three times, and aided thieves, for if placed on glowing coals in a house they wished to rob, it gave off such fumes that all who breathed them fled in terror believing that the house was about to collapse. (Bibliog. 258)

Mahomet, heathen idol worshipped by Saxons. (Bibliog. 311)

mail, banded, type of armor* whose existence has been challenged. One authority claimed that it was made of rows of leather washers threaded with strips of leather and flattened alternately in direction, row by row. As such it would have been light and pliable and as effective as other mail in deflecting or protecting against sword,* lance,* javelin,* mace* or shafted weapons. If every other or every third ring was of metal, the mail would have had a metallic appearance. However, a separate authority claimed that such mail existed only in art, devised by artists to avoid the monotony of their illustrations of regular chain mail. (Bibliog. 9, 331)

mail, chain, body protection formed by iron links joined together and shaped to fit a warrior's body. It consisted of a knee-length shirt of interlocking iron rings called a hauberk,* split up the front and back almost to the waist to allow its wearer to sit in a saddle.* It usually had a mail hood made in one piece with the shirt. (Bibliog. 331)

maille, small silver coin equal to half an obol* in Antwerp, Brussels, Ghent, Alost, Bruges, Courtrai, and other such places on the continent. See coinage. (Bibliog. 150)

maille blanche, bourgeoise, noir, parisis, poitevine, tournois, different varieties of small silver coinage* issued under Philip* Le Bel of France (1285–1314) and his successors. (Bibliog. 150)

maille tierce. See tournois.

mainbour, medieval French term equivalent to the Latin term *mundeburdum**that described the protection extended by a powerful man to his weaker neighbor. As leader of all the people, the king* owed his support to all his subjects without discrimination and thereby was entitled to their allegiance. To a number of them, however, he granted his personal protection so that any wrong done to one of them was considered as an offense against the king himself and was treated with especial severity. Within this select group was a distinguished body of retainers called the leudes* of the prince*—his ''men.'' (Bibliog. 28)

mainmorte, serf's* land which, when he died and left no direct descendants, reverted to the lord. (Bibliog. 123)

mainour, stolen goods found in a thief's possession on his arrest. (Bibliog. 261)

mainpast, legal aspect of a lord's household; virtually a private tithing* so that the lord was responsible for all his servants. (Bibliog. 171, 261)

mainpernor, manucaptor, one who gave his mainprise* or who assumed responsibility for another person's appearance in court* on a specified day. (Bibliog. 171, 261)

mainport, loaves of bread* or comparable items given to a church in lieu of tithes.* (Bibliog. 246)

mainprise, finding mainpernors* or sureties to be responsible for a man's appearance in court* or for his future good behavior. If a man was arrested, he usually was mainprised or replevied (see replevin), that is, was set free as soon as some sureties agreed to be bound for his appearance in court. As imprisonment was costly and troublesome, a mainprise of substantial men was considered to be as good a security as any jail.* (Bibliog. 171, 261)

majority, age of, age at which a person achieved legal status. A tenant by knight's service was of age when he became twenty-one, a young sokeman when he became fifteen, a young burgess when he could count money* and measure cloth. (Bibliog. 261)

make hawk, old hawk flown with a young one to assist and teach her. (Bibliog. 26)

make point, hawk's perpendicular rise in the air over the place where her quarry* has "put in."* (Bibliog. 26)

Malet, William, most famous of King William* I's sheriffs.* His rise to power and influence served as example for many to follow him. In the forefront of the Norman troops at the battle of Hastings, he had his horse* killed beneath him but was saved by prompt action by two companions and their followers. Remounted on a fresh steed, he carried on vigorously. When the battle was over and the forces of Harold had been defeated, Harold's mother offered William I the weight of her son's body in gold if he would let her remove it for burial in consecrated ground. Fearing the location might become a shrine for local insurrection, William refused and ordered Malet to bury the body in an unmarked grave. Malet had to get the help of Edith Swannehals, Harold's mistress, to find the body, and the two of them had it buried somewhere near the seashore.

Two years later, remembering that deed of unquestioning loyalty and ruthless efficiency, William chose Malet to become sheriff of Yorkshire and sent him north to suppress a rebellion in Scotland. To obtain money* for his forces, Malet looted wagons loaded with goods for the Easter feast belonging to the archbishop of York. Even though the archbishop complained to the king* and was recompensed for his loss, Malet continued to rank high in the king's favor. He obtained thirty-two manors* during his tenure as sheriff. (Bibliog. 132)

malmene. See hunting.

Maltese cross, cross* with semi-forked endings that come to sharp points. See Hospitallers. (Bibliog. 43)

maltote, maletote, toll levied in 1275 at the rate of half of a mark* for each sack,* half of a mark on each 300 woolfells (which make one sack), and one mark on each last* of hides leaving the realm. It was renewed between July 29, 1294, and November 23, 1297, at the rate of three marks for ordinary wool and more for dressed wool. (Bibliog. 103)

malvoisin (Fr. "bad neighbor"), 1. wooden towers built to shelter a besieging force. This term emerged from a siege of Robert Mowbray in Bamburgh Castle by William* II of England in 1095. Built on a great rock girdled by marsh and sea, this castle* was not easily besieged by a frontal attack. William, however, compelled its surrender by building nearby a timber castle of the motte* and bailey* type which was given the name *malvoisin*, or "bad neighbor." 2. *petraria** or siege engines that Prince Louis of France used at Dover in 1216. (Bibliog. 48, 341)

man, to train a hawk to become accustomed to the presence of strangers. (Bibliog. 26)

man of mouth and hands, precise descriptor of one who has performed the act of homage* to his overlord by placing his clasped hands between those of his lord and then following this act by exchanging a kiss on the mouth. (Bibliog. 28)

mancuse, Anglo-Saxon gold coin worth thirty pence (see penny). (Bibliog. 305)

mandragora, mandrake, tree whose root cured all ailments except death. When soaked in wine* its bark caused sleep or at least so benumbed a man that if he were cut he felt nothing. Men who dug up this root had to be careful not to touch it while they dug but to make three circles around the tree with a sword* and to dig only until the sun went down. A safer way to gather it was to tie a starving dog to it and then show the beast a bit of meat. The dog would pull the cord so strongly that it pulled up the roots, but the poor beast would drop dead from the cry the tree made as it was uprooted, for nothing could live after hearing the cry of an uprooted mandragora. (Bibliog. 258)

mangon, mangonel, siege engine which used the sling principle on a projectile arm pivoted against a fixed stop to hurl the object. The word "gun," originally "gon," was derived from this term. See also siege warfare. (Bibliog. 71, 280)

manifer, large rigid gauntlet* for the bridle hand worn with jousting (see joust) armor* from the 14th century. (Bibliog. 246)

mannesmuot (Ger.), virtue of bravery, stressed in the epics. (Bibliog. 274)

manor, feudal estate in England after the Conquest (1066). Such an estate contained lands worked by peasants (see villein) and the lord's demesne* that contained the lord's building surrounded by his own outbuildings to keep all the necessary equipment and working animals. Frequently this manor was controlled by a seneschal,* bailiff,* or reeve* who ran it in the lord's absence. Other servants of the manor, besides the bailiff and/or reeve, included the plow-driver, shepherds, baker, hayward,* carter, and dairymaids. (Bibliog. 139)

manor court, court* held on a manor* by a lord or one of his officials. Its powers varied from dealing with villeins* and the economic matters on the manor to matters of villeins and freemen and thereby considered more than just economic affairs. It investigated criminal charges, assessed fines* and levies, and set measures to keep the "king's peace."* Early manorial courts had the powers of sac* and soc,* "toll and team,"* and infangentheof,* which still were being exercised, and the serf* on many manors still was liable to seizure and punishment under quasi-legal rights in the 13th century. For example, in the matter of hanging someone for theft, the law stated that he had to be prosecuted by the loser of the goods and the coroner* had to be present; frequently, however, the manor court did not bother about such details and hanged him. A thief was a thief, and because he had been captured with the goods in his possession, he was hanged, despite the fact that only the king* had the power to erect a gallows and hang a man. (See execution.)

Three kinds of seignorial court were held on a manor: "leet court,"* "court baron,"* and "customary court."* Leet had the power to keep the peace of the king. It had police and criminal jurisdiction up to a point and was similar to the "sheriff's tourn"* in the hundred.* Additionally, it was held twice a year to register all the male population over the age of twelve and to present those who had not joined the tithings.* As such, an arrangement was set up to ensure the maintenance of peace: everyone on entering the tithing swore not only to keep the peace but also to conceal nothing that might concern the peace. Court baron was a court of free tenants under the presidency of a steward* who had been entrusted with the exercise of minor franchises.* Customary court was in charge of the unfree population of the manor. At it the steward was the only judge, and tenants and villeins around him were called merely as presenters of fact. (Bibliog. 24, 357, 381)

manse, quantity of land deemed sufficient to support a family; originally the basis of the Anglo-Saxon military obligation based on hides,* this was parallel to the subfeudal obligation based on acres.* As a recruitment measure, the five-hide unit paralleled similar structures elsewhere in Europe. During the time of Charlemagne and his immediate successors, all freemen owed military service by tradition (see freeman's duties). However, to raise an army with reasonable skill and manageable size, those monarchs recruited normally on the basis of land units of four manses. A tenant holding three manses served in the army and was supported by an adjacent holder of a single manse. If two neighboring tenants each held two manses, one served in the army and the other contributed to his support. Tenants who held a single manse owed and supported a single footsoldier to the Frankish host just as Anglo-Saxon hide-holders supported their representatives in the military. (Bibliog. 158, 246)

manticora, heraldic monster* with a tiger's body, an old man's face with a flowing beard and hair, and two spiral horns. (Bibliog. 43)

mantle, mantling, lambrequin, originally a short cloak attached to a helmet* which not only helped deflect a sword* blow aimed at the neck but also to reduce the ferocity of the sun's rays on the back of the metal helmet. It grew to become an ornamental design in achievements* which hung down from the helmet and fell away on either side of the escutcheon.* The royal mantling was gold* and ermine*; that of the peers* was crimson lined with ermine. (Bibliog. 43, 253)

mantle children, ancient custom to allow parents on the occasion of their marriage to legitimize the already existing children of their union by the device of placing the children under a cloak which was spread over their parents during the marriage ceremony; the children thereby became "mantle children." This practice was followed in Germany, France, and Normandy but actually was an act of adoption rather than legitimization; Henry II's English courts* rejected the practice. (Bibliog. 261)

mantle over food, hawk spreading her wings and tail over her food to hide it from view as a sign of her greed and jealousy. (Bibliog. 26)

mantlet, inclined barrier or protective shield* of timber and wickerwork held in a position by a prop behind which two or three men could operate as sappers or pick-men in comparative safety as they hacked at stones in castle* walls during a siege. See pavise. (Bibliog. 9)

mantlet wall, low outer wall of a castle.* (Bibliog. 280)

manucaptor. See mainpernor.

manumission. See freeman's duties.

manuum imixitio (L. "joining the hands"), one of the symbolic acts performed in the ceremony of homage* in which the vassal* would place his hands in those of his liege.* By this act he symbolized his submission to as well as his need for the protection and defense of his lord. (Bibliog. 123)

La Mappemonde de Pierre, written by a prolific French writer in the early years of the 13th century, this view of the world provided an explanation of some of the wonders found in it. In Asia lay Paradise, circled by a wall of red flames which reached to the sky. There grew the tree of life whose fruit rendered man immortal and whose fruit Adam did not taste, preferring the fruit of knowledge. There also was a fountain from which flowed the four great rivers—Phison, Geon (Nile), Tigris, and Euphrates—which flowed under the earth. Geon circled Egypt and emptied into the sea in seven mouths near Alexandria. Around Paradise lay huge deserts peopled only by vermin and serpents. Then lay India, a huge country with more than ten huge cities. In it resided people who were huge and lived a long time and who spoke a language which no one else understood, nor did they understand anyone else. To trade with strangers they spread their wares on the shore and exchanged with traders in wordless barter. Its year had two winters and two summers, but the plants always remained green. Trees there grew almost to the clouds. Its mountains were made of gold, but no one ever saw them because of the great number of serpents there. It contained forty-four distinct countries where lived great varieties of people, among them the Gara-mantes. There also lived a race of men who were only two cubits* high, who begot children at age three, and were old at the age of seven. Next to India and adjacent to the Caspian Sea to which it had given its name lay Mount Caspius, where lived a race of felons, Gog and Magog. No one ever entered or left their country, for Alexander the Great had enclosed it thoroughly. (Bibliog. 217)

maravedi, gold coinage* of Sancho I of Portugal (1185–1212). (Bibliog. 150)

marc (Fr. and Ital.), money* of account. The French under Philip* I in 1060 had substituted the marc for the livre* as money of account, and in 1093 nine marcs of silver were given to the king* to rebuild a burned church. (Bibliog. 150)

marche, mark, frontier counties* established by Charlemagne and his successors along the borders of the Frankish empire.* These were military districts in which the chief official, the count* of the marche or the markgrave, then margrave, known later in England as marquis,* exercised palatine* or independent jurisdiction with wide authority in military and administrative affairs, including the responsibility for defending the frontier against the attacks of barbarians. Later, because of the threats of the vikings, marches were established even in such interior regions as the Île de France.* England also established them along its borders with Wales and Scotland. (Bibliog. 23)

marchio. See marquess.

mark, money* of account in England equivalent to two-thirds of a pound, that is, thirteen shillings four pence (see penny). See also marc. (Bibliog. 324)

markgrave. See marche.

marquis, marquess, title given originally to officers in charge of English marches* along the border with Wales and Scotland. Under Edward III the French form of the word, *marchio*, was used. As an hereditary rank of the peerage (see peer) of England, marquess, the preferred English spelling of the word, ranked below duke* and above earl.* Its first holders were created by "letters patent"* of King Richard II elevating Robert de Vere, earl of Oxford, to become marquess of Dublin in 1386 and a year later John Beaufort, earl of Somerset, to become marquess of Dorset. (Bibliog. 75)

marriage, age of, age of rational consent. If two people had not reached the age at which they were considered capable of rational decision, they could not marry. On the other hand, if they had reached that age, then a marriage between them would be valid even though the consent of their parents or guardians had not been asked or had been refused. At the age of seven a child was considered to be capable of consent, but any marriage remained voidable so long as either party was below the age at which it could be consummated: fourteen for boys and twelve for girls. If only one party was below that age, the marriage could be voided by that party but was binding on the other.

Thomas of Saleby, an aged and childless knight in Lincolnshire, not wanting his estate to pass to his brother William, instructed his wife to take to her bed and produce a child. She did, but the daughter she claimed was actually the daughter of a villager's wife. Hearing of that birth and disbelieving it, the bishop threatened Thomas with excommunication* if he kept that child as his own. Fearing his wife's wrath more than God's, Thomas said nothing, and he died shortly thereafter. Because his widow stayed with her story about the girl being Thomas's daughter, the king* gave the supposed heiress to Adam Neville, the brother of his chief forester,* to be raised. When she was only four, Adam proposed to marry her, and even though the bishop forbade it, he did so when the bishop was in Normandy. Furious at this disobedient action, the bishop excommunicated all who had taken part in the ceremony and suspended the priest from office and benefices. Then the widow confessed the fraud, but when the bishop tried to annul the marriage, Adam refused and appealed to English law claiming that Thomas had received the baby, Grace, as legitimate, and so she was legitimate. The bishop was powerful enough to block Adam for a while, but when he once again went to Normandy, Adam pressed his suit and was close to winning, when he died suddenly. King John then stepped in and sold Grace to his chamberlain,* Norman, for 200 marks,* and after Norman's death, the king sold her again for 300 marks to her third and worst husband, Brian de Lisle. In the end she died childless, and her inheritance finally fell to its rightful heir, William, brother of her supposed father, Thomas of Saleby. (Bibliog. 261)

marriage, lord's right to control, one of the "feudal obligations"* which a lord could impose on his vassals* and serfs.* Aristocracy* was more severely limited in this choice than the peasantry. For a small sum called merchet* paid to his lord, a villein* could give his daughter in marriage; this was the supreme test of his servility as a villein. A baron's* widow on the other hand, on payment of a hundred or even a thousand pounds (see money), could marry whomever she chose; this was normal and expected of persons of exalted birth. In his Coronation Charter* of 1100, King Henry I promised to reform this custom by agreeing to take no more money for a license to marry, nor to refuse a marriage unless it was to one of his enemies. He did not keep his promise, however, and soon widows and orphans were being sold for huge sums, and the practice continued for decades. Geoffrey de Mandeville, for example, in 1214 paid 20,000 marks* (over 13,000 pounds) to marry Isabelle, countess of Gloucester, with all her lands, tenements, and knight's fees (see knighthood), except the castle* of Bristol and the chases* outside of Bristol. As the divorced wife of King John, she brought an earldom (see earl) and considerable wealth to her new husband. This was at a time when the entire revenue of the English crown was only 42,000 pounds. Other knights bought wives for their sons for over 1,000 pounds. Gereard de Camville bought for 1,000 pounds the widow of Thomas of Verdun for his son.

Disobedience to the king's* orders in respect to marriage was severely punished. For example, the marriage agreement might contain a statement such as "if the widow refuse him, he [the proposed husband] shall have all her land." Women, however, could remain unmarried and not disparaged* if they chose but only for a price. In 1205 Mabel, widow of Hugh Bardolf, offered 2,000 marks and five palfreys* so that she could remain a widow and not remarry. Even though this point was included as the eighth clause in the *Magna Carta Libertatum*—"No widow shall be compelled to marry so long as she wishes to live without a husband"—nothing was said there about not paying for this right to remain unmarried. (Bibliog. 264)

marrows. See close.

marshal, court* official of rank lower than a constable* to whom was entrusted the duty of maintaining discipline at court. He also was charged with supplying receipts or tallies* for payments made out of the treasury and other disbursements as well as gifts and liveries made from the king's chambers. In time of war he joined the constable in exercising military functions: constables as quartermasters-general and marshals as their assistants. Under his control came all servants connected with the royal sports: the keepers of the "hounds for the hunt,"* keeper of the king's* mews,* such hunt servants as the stag-hunter, wolf-hunter, and cat-hunter. He also controlled the king's bodyguard of archers and was in immediate charge of the horses.* Both the marshal and constable were required to witness writs.

The king's marshal was referred to as the Great Marshal of England. Usually the holder was referred to as the earl marshal,* not because the office was called that of earl marshal but because the holder happened to be an earl.* He also played an important role in coronations.* For Richard I's* coronation, he carried the gold spurs,* but for the coronation of Queen Eleanor in 1236, his role was considerably enlarged. By then the man holding the office was Gilbert Marshal, earl of Striguil (Pembroke). Although the records did not mention gold spurs, it stated that his duty was to appease disturbances in the king's palace, assign billets,* and guard the doors of the king's hall.* Moreover, he received from every baron* knighted by the king and from every earl that day a palfrey* with a saddle.* He bore his baton* before the king, clearing the way both in the church and the hall, and arranged guests at the banquet that followed. This baton was the recognized symbol of his office, for when King Henry III had restored the marshalship to Gilbert two years earlier in 1234, he handed him the baton "as the custom is as his predecessors had had it." (Bibliog. 75)

Marshal, William (1146–1219), fourth son of a minor baron* possessing neither fief* nor land. Becoming a knight-errant* for fifteen years, he made a name for himself in tournaments* and was appointed tutor for Henry, son of Henry II. Through his physical strength and his military and administrative qualities, he rose to become earl* of Pembroke and regent of England. (Bibliog. 249)

marshaling, art of arranging several "coats of arms"* on one shield* for the purpose of denoting alliances of a family. (Bibliog. 43)

marshalsea, court* or seat of the marshal* of the "king's household."* (Bibliog. 171)

Marshalsea of the King's Bench, prison (see jail) in which were kept prisoners awaiting trial in the King's Bench, so called because such prisoners were in the custody of the marshal* of the King's Bench. (Bibliog. 171)

marteau, martel, long-handled hammer* used by knights.

martel-de-fer, also known as a pole hammer, this weapon had either a simple hammer* head or a small halberd-shaped (see halbard) blade with a plain or toothed hammer head at the opposite side. (Bibliog. 71)

martial law. See constable and marshal of England.

martlet, common bird resembling a marten but in heraldry* was depicted with tufts of feathers for legs; it was used as the mark of cadency* for the fourth son. (Bibliog. 43)

Mary Magdalene Day, June 22.

mascle, heraldic ordinary* in the shape of a hollow lozenge* resembling a square chain link; it was supposed to depict the links of chain mail.* (Bibliog. 43)

masse d'or, French gold coinage* first introduced under Philip* III (1220–1285) owing its designation to the mace* the king* held in his right hand; it was continued only by Philip V (1294–1322). (Bibliog. 150)

master (L. *magistri*), knight's role as leader of a group of armed men. Occasionally it referred to non-commissioned officers. In 1195 a Hampshire account listed the transport of 1,300 footsoldiers and three knights as masters. (Bibliog. 264)

master chamberlain. See chamberlain.

Master James of St. George, master mason whom King Edward I brought from Savoy to become the "master of the king's works in Wales" for the construction of the eight castles* there between 1277 and c. 1330. See castle building. (Bibliog. 45)

Master of Game, oldest book on the chase* in English. Written between 1406 and 1413 by King Edward III's grandson, Edward, second duke* of York, this work was a translation of Count Gaston de Foix's *Livre de Chasse.* Edward, earl* of Rutland before becoming duke of York, was better known as the duke of Aumarle (Albemarle) and was killed leading a vanguard at the battle of Agincourt. (Bibliog. 96)

mastiff, powerful mongrel dog used to tackle a wild boar when it had run by other hounds, thus saving the more valuable "hunting dogs"* for use when the boar had been brought to bay. Such a dog also was useful in protecting the master's flocks from wolves. To safeguard the mastiff from wolf bite, it had fastened around its neck a huge, iron spiked collar eight inches* in diameter with forty-eight spikes each an inch long and weighing two pounds.* (Bibliog. 96)

matapan, late 12th-century silver grosso (see gros) of Venice containing a design similar to a ducat.* (Bibliog. 150)

matins, "canonical hour"*; the first church service said in a day, properly sung at midnight but sometimes recited at daybreak followed immediately by lauds.*

maul, long-handled hammer* used by footsoldiers in England. This crude weapon had a head of lead or iron shaped like a croquet mallet and sometimes included a spike on top. (Bibliog. 9)

Maundy money, small silver coins distributed by the king* to elderly men and women at a service on Maundy Thursday, the day before Good Friday in Easter week. This ceremony commemorated Christ's act of humility in washing the feet of his disciples before the Last Supper and his order, *mandatum,* for them to do likewise. King John was the first English monarch recorded as having participated in a Maundy ceremony when he distributed silver pennies* to thirteen poor men at Rochester in 1213. (Bibliog. 150)

mayhem, plea of men against fighting in a trial by battle (see duel). One could plea mayhem by reason of broken bones, loss of a limb, ear, nose, or eye, or even broken or missing front teeth (which frequently were of great help to victory). (Bibliog. 229) *diu maze* (Ger.), maintaining the golden mean of harmonious self-control, the font of all social virtues in the German romances* of chivalry.* This tempered the strict epic quality of *triuwe** or loyalty with the observance of due measure, moderation, and good form. See German chivalry. (Bibliog. 124, 274)

mease, measure of quantity of herrings varying from 520 to 630 and equal to one-twentieth of a last.* (Bibliog. 394)

measurements. Despite repeated efforts of numerous monarchs to standardize measurements, no uniformity existed. An old Scot law, for example, stated that the ell* ought to contain thirty-seven inches* meted by the thumbs of three men: a mickle (great, huge) man, a man of measurable stature, and a little man. In Germany, if a perch* or rod of fifteen feet* needed to be made, the first fifteen people who chanced to emerge from a church each contributed the length of his or her foot toward the construction of the standard.* Men, trying to find something that was fairly invariable in length, found the barleycorn.* Before the Conquest in 1066, an Anglo-Saxon inch was set at three barleycorns ''good and chosen without tails.'' A century and a half was to pass before a uniform measure for cloth was established by Richard I* ordering guardians of ''weights and measures''* to be appointed in every county,* city, and borough.* These officials were to use and preserve the iron ulna* which a royal official delivered to their custody. These standards were an ell or a cloth-yard long, and five and one-half ulnae made a royal perch.

Three units normally measured land: the human foot, a day's plowing, and a measuring stick that indicated between feet and acres*—a stick that had many names: rod, perch, pole, gad, goad, lug. In the *Domesday Book** one acre of land generally was considered to be the amount of land that could be plowed in the forenoon of a day, for the oxen had to go to pasture in the afternoon. This usually was equal to a piece of land four perches by forty perches; forty perches equalled one furlong or *quarentina* which was set by the natural endurance of the oxen. Fields were broken into shots or *culturae*, sets of contiguous parallel acre strips with two sides being a furlong (furrow-long) but of varying width. An acre was an acre, and to tell a man that one of the acre strips was not an acre because it was too narrow was like telling him that his foot was not a foot because it was not twelve inches long. Further land units included a virgate,* also called a rood* or a yard* of land that equalled one-fourth of an acre and a furlong in length. A virgate also stood for a much larger quantity of land, frequently as much as thirty acres. Such doubling of terminology stemmed from the typical tenement equalling a hide.* If a lord wanted to bestow a quarter of a hide on a tenant, he gave a quarter of every acre in the hide, that is, a virgate in every acre, so therefore he gave a virgate as a typical tenement. In Kent a sulung, which in most other counties* was called a carucate,* equalled eight bovates* or oxgangs.* See also London weights and measures; weights and measures. (Bibliog. 213)

medale, meadow-ale, a drinking festivity for the villeins* after the lord's meadows had been mowed. (Bibliog. 24)

medicine. The works of Isidore of Seville served to provide most of the information on medicine to physicians, surgeons, and barber-surgeons* in Europe. In Outremer,* works by Hippocrates along with Persian, Hebrew, and Indian sources on anatomy and diseases were translated into Arabic to form the bases of study and practice of medicine. With the establishment of the medical school at Salerno about 1030, medicine moved beyond simple surgery and treatment of wounds to the study of Arabic treatises translated into Latin and the study of anatomy. In the 13th century medicine became a part of university curricula in the west, and medical schools began to be established in Italy and southern France a century later. Despite these advances, popular medicine and its connections with superstition and magic continued to flourish and to remain popular with all classes. It was practiced by hermits and village women known as *bella donna*. Concerned for the health of his people, Emperor Frederick II (1194–1250) promulgated a detailed law about the practice of medicine which included among its provisions strict requirements for physicians, surgeons, and apothecaries.* No one could call himself a physician, for example, unless he had studied at the University of Salerno, been given a certificate which attested to his trustworthiness of character and sufficiency of medical knowledge, and obtained a license from the king* himself to practice medicine. In his studies he had to have pursued logic (generally the seven liberal arts) for three years before turning to the study of medicine, including surgery, for at least five years, and then worked under an experienced physician for a year. Every physician given a license to practice had to take an oath that he would obey the law and would report apothecaries selling weakened drugs. He further was to visit his patient at least twice a day, and once at night if the patient requested it. If he did not have to leave the village, he could charge no more than one-half tarrene in gold for each visit; if he had to leave the village or the town wall, he could charge three tarrenes plus expenses but no more than four tarrenes total. Further, he could not enter into any arrangements with apothecaries, nor keep an apothecary shop for himself.

Practitioners of the 12th century tried repeatedly to simplify medicine. They introduced myriad wonder salves colored green and red and black to be applied with sure-cure results. They proposed certain regimens to improve health, cautioned that resting after meals would aid the digestion, and advised drinking water at mealtime rather than wine* because being heavier, water was better for the digestion. Fever was classed into tertian, quartan, daily, and hectic according to the interval of its recurrence: every third day, fourth day, daily, or the severity of its onset—hectic. See also bloodletting; wound treatment. (Bibliog. 286, 364)

medkniche, haymaker's fee calculated at as much hay as he could lift with his little finger to his knees. Other fees he could collect included the serf's* right to take from the abbot's courtyard a bundle of as much straw as he could carry, but if the band broke before he passed through the yard door, he lost his straw and paid a fine.* (Bibliog. 24)

mêlée (Fr. "free–for–all"), early form of tourney (see tournament) in which an indefinite number of knights met on a meadow and charged one another in mass confusion. No rules applied, fighting was rough, crude, and bloody, and several knights could gang up against one or two, for the losers had to ransom* their horses* and armor* from the winners. (Bibliog. 72)

Memoranda Roll. See Exchequer.

menée, hunting* term with three meanings: (1) line of flight a stag had taken; *chacier la menée* meant pursuing game with a hunting horn* and "hunting dogs"* by scent along a line of flight in contrast to chase* with bow* and arrow*; (2) challenge of the hounds when on the line of flight, for they would make more noise when they had found the scent of line of flight of the stag they were chasing; (3) note sounded on a horn (see horn calls in hunting) as a signal that the stag was in full flight. (Bibliog. 96)

menestrali. See herald.

mercenaries, bands of foreign troops who fought for wages. These were quite different from those men in the national army who also were paid regular wages but who not only owed military service as a consequence of their tenures but who also carried a sense of patriotic identification with their country. Mercenaries were divided into three groups. The first group were the household retainers of royal or baronial familia. These were knights hired on a permanent basis by royal vassals* who did not possess enough knight's fees (see knighthood) to fill their contracts when summoned by the king.* They might act as bodyguard while their lord travelled from one estate to another, serve in his court,* accompany him on a hunt (see hunting), carry messages, and help maintain law and order in his barony.* Frequently they would become enfeoffed (see feoffment) and would settle down as landed feudal knights. They had their counterparts in earlier times as the Germanic *comitatus** and *buccellarii** and then the *antrustio** and *gasindi.*

The second group were the professional warriors, chiefly from outside England, who were hired individually or in groups for service on a particular campaign and dismissed when it was over. They were recruited for long campaigns at fixed wages. Chroniclers referred to them as *stipendarii*. Also called *solidarii* ("men who served for pay"), which evolved into the word soldier,* these men fought in the continental manner as heavy and light cavalry, as archers, and as footsoldiers. When the English fought on the continent, they recruited soldiers from Flanders, Brabant, and Brittany rather than summon up the feudal host (see knighthood) and transport it across the Channel. Although kings also needed money* to build and strengthen castles,* to oil the wheels of diplomacy, to reward a victorious army, and to bribe wavering barons,* payment of these wages was the biggest expense among war finances. These *stipendarii* played a major role at the battle of Hastings (1066) and in the subsequent battles of consolidation. No one used them more lavishly than William Rufus (William* II), who began collecting soldiers at the beginning of his reign. His famed generosity was known far and wide, and soldiers flocked from all over Europe to serve in his army because he denied them nothing and promised them much. He got money to pay them by ruthless taxation and ironically was killed by one of his own mercenaries, Walter Tirel.*

The third group were soldiers of neighboring lands (such as Brittany and Maine) who fought for the Norman kings under the leadership of the lords of their respective provinces. Some of these lords were vassals of the Anglo-Norman crown* and thus should have been allies, but their support was obtained only by money. (Bibliog. 159, 241)

merchet, fine* paid to the lord by a villein* when his daughter married. When a woman married outside of the power of the lord, a new element entered the feudal relationship because the lord was losing a subject and her offspring and thereby became entitled to a special compensation. This most odious of all exactions had to be paid for every one of the daughters and even the grand-daughters of a villein. This payment had nothing to do with succession, however, and sprang from personal subjection; it was considered as one of the basest notes of servile descent. (Bibliog. 357)

mercy, *misericordia* (L.), clemency or forbearance of an absolute lord which he had the power to withhold or extend as he saw fit. The king* had the absolute power of pardon, and when persons forfeited the king's grace, they had to do things not otherwise required by law to regain it. When one was put in the mercy of someone, he was subject to amercement* (fine*). In ecclesiastical circles the term had a technical meaning. It was the mercy of God that permitted penance to wipe away sins. And it was mercy which permitted the redemption of penances in money*; and the monetary commutation of penances sometimes was referred to as alms, and sometimes mercy and alms were used interchangeably. See in mercy. (Bibliog. 103)

merker (Ger.), person who sought to frustrate the union of a knight and his beloved or to detect and betray them, a role often played in German poetry by a false steward* or seneschal.* (Bibliog. 124)

Merlin, sorcerer and counsellor to Uther Pendragon and his son, Arthur. (Bibliog. 311)

merlin falcon. See falconry birds.

merlon, solid portion of a wall's crenellation.* In the beginning, these were quite broad and frequently pierced with "arrow loops"* or slits; the openings between them called crenels* were narrow. (Bibliog. 280)

mermaid, siren, heraldic charge* depicting a creature with long flowing hair who was a woman to her waist and fish below. These creatures sang in the sea when it stormed and cried when the weather was good, and mariners who heard them forgot their ships and families. (Bibliog. 43, 258)

mesne tenure, relationship of every person who stood between the king* and him who held in demesne*; he was both tenant and lord: tenant of the king above him and lord to those who stood beneath. (Bibliog. 261)

mesnie, military personnel attached to a castle,* including "household knights"* and outside knights who performed "castle guard"* duties, squires,* men-at-arms, porters who kept the outside door of the castle, and watchmen. (Bibliog. 128)

messengers, carriers of messages. General custom guaranteed the rights of these men regardless of their arrogance, because a good messenger capable of fulfilling his task and of escaping alive was extraordinarily valuable. He needed certain characteristics: he had to be sage, prudent, fearless, and complete, never omitting anything from his message. Such a responsibility was both delicate and dangerous, for no messenger could be guaranteed immunity; even if his manner was innocuous, his message might be resented, and hot heads hearing it might act suddenly and violently. In such cases he had to protect himself either by strategy or force or to submit to the denial of his rights. Not surprisingly, death frequently was his fate. (Bibliog. 131)

messor, man who took charge of the harvest and collected agricultural fines* imposed for the benefit of the lord. See hayward. (Bibliog. 357)

messuage, portion of land occupied as a site for a dwelling and its appurtenances. (Bibliog. 24)

mesure (Fr.), moderation, prudence, level-headedness; opposite of *demesure,** Roland's* flaw. See *Song of Roland.* (Bibliog. 113)

met, measure of capacity for grain and other dry products in the 13th century, generally containing two bushels* but varying from one-half to two bushels. (Bibliog. 394)

metals, heraldic, only two metals were used as tinctures (see colors) in heraldry*: gold* (Fr. *or*) and silver* (Fr. *argent*).

meurtrières (Fr. "murder holes"), holes in hoarding* through which stones, boiling water, oil, or lead could be hurled on besiegers at the foot of the walls below. Above gates or in gateway passages, these holes were used more often to quench fires than to slaughter enemies. (Bibliog. 45)

meute, mute, number of hounds; a pack, cry, or kennel of hounds. (Bibliog. 96)

meved, a deer started from his ligging* or resting place. See hunting terms. (Bibliog. 96)

mew, mue, 1. to molt or to shed her feathers, said of a falcon; 2. to shed, cast, or change, as a deer casts his head to shed his antlers: "the hart* mewed his horns." (Bibliog. 96)

mews, house or room where hawks were kept to breed and molt. (Bibliog. 96)

mezzanino, silver coinage* of Venice first struck under Francesco Dandelo (1328–1354). (Bibliog. 150)

mickletorn, frankpledge* used in Nottingham. (Bibliog. 261)

Midsummer, June 24.

mile (Fr. *mille* = "one thousand"), unstandardized measure of length varying from 5,000 feet* or 1,000 paces* of five feet, or eight furlongs (see measurements) of 125 paces of five feet, to 6,600 feet or ten furlongs of 220 feet each. The earlier English mile had 1,500 paces which varied in size from region to region. (Bibliog. 394)

miles (L. "soldier"), warrior who, protected by mail* shirt, steel cap, and shield,* fought on horseback with sword* and lance* up to the end of the 11th century. Late in that century, two important developments changed its meaning into knighthood.* By then knighthood had become a social distinction synonymous with nobility,* and these *milites* were a class, almost a caste of society into which men were received with an elaborate ceremony of knighting. Secondly, as defensive armor became more elaborate and heavier, it and a good horse* became more expensive to obtain. (Bibliog. 159, 322)

military duties, one of the *trimoda necessitas*,* the three duties of Anglo Saxon thanes*: service in the king's* army for two months, burh* repair, bridge work.

Service in the army was enforced only in time of war or serious threats to the realm, but the thanes could be recalled in case of emergency, as happened in 1016 when the fyrd* was summoned five times. After the Conquest, the *Domesday Book* elevated such *expeditio* as a duty of a *miles* from each five hides* of land, each hide contributing four shillings (see money) for two months' expenses. Norman knights had to serve in the host of a Norman duke* or the French king for forty days a year at their own expense and perhaps an additional term of forty days for ''castle guard''* in time of war. Service beyond this forty-day annual obligation was to be at the duke's expense. German knights, on the other hand, were summoned to serve only for six weeks but could be recalled after an additional six weeks had passed. (Bibliog. 158, 159, 272)

militia Christi, knights, crusaders generally who fought for the Christian church but more specifically the orders of the Hospitallers,* Templars,* and Teutonic knights.* See Christian knighthood. (Bibliog. 54, 139)

milk brother, two children born of different mothers but suckled by only one. Richard I* and Alexander Neckham* were so nursed. (Bibliog. 44, 161)

milte (Ger.), chivalric generosity, a quality highly praised in noble lords by the *minnesingers** who were refreshed by the ''golden rain'' of money* and support that such praise produced. (Bibliog. 124)

mine gallery, undercutting the wall of a fortress to make it collapse, as a method of ''siege warfare.''* Such tunnels were filled with trees and brush, old timbers— anything combustible—and then ignited to speed the collapse of the wall above. (Bibliog. 280)

minne (Ger.), respectful love, one of the chivalric virtues embodied in Middle High German courtly poetry of the 12th and 13th centuries. (Bibliog. 124)

minnedienst (Ger.), service of a German chivalric knight to his lady. (Bibliog. 124)

minnesang (Ger.), formal German love poetry of the chivalric age between 1180 and 1220, deriving its inspiration from the poetry of the troubadours and *trouvères* (see minstrels). It was based on the standard situation of a knight adoring in secret a lady who was of a higher degree than he; without expecting any gratification, he sang her praises and expressed his longing and gratitude for any token of favor. Because such a tenuous relationship was secret, it was endangered by watchers, spies, and envious rivals. Two variations occurred: *kreuzlied*, a lament for separation when the knight left for or was on a crusade, and *tagelied*, a dawn song in which the lovers actually met privately and lamented the coming of dawn that compelled them to part. (Bibliog. 124) *minnesinger* (Ger.), poet who wrote formal German chivalric love poetry between 1180 and 1220. (Bibliog. 124)

minstrels, entertainers. After the Conquest in both England and France gleemen* were called minstrels, but their ancient art continued. They also were called jongleurs (jougleurs) or jugglers, rimours or rhymers, chanterres or singers, jestours* or tellers of heroic tales, lecours or buffoons, troubadours or poets. Of these entertainers, some composed the works they sang or recited: *trouvères* used rhyme in their recitations, but conteurs (see jestours) told prose stories. Some used the compositions of others: jougleurs accompanied the songs of the *trouvères* on the vielle,* a stringed instrument sounded by turning a wheel within it, and chanteurs. The terms jongleur and minstrel seemed to have been used interchangeably for the professional storyteller, though minstrel was considered a more general term covering the arts of both music and poetry. Although sometimes the name *trouvère* was applied to someone who recited a story, it more frequently was reserved for the creator of the romances* and other stories which the minstrels and jongleurs recited. Thus the *trouvère* was considered the author and the jongleur and minstrel the editors of stories. (Bibliog. 42, 80, 334)

misericorde, dagger of mercy*; a poniard* with a fine point intended to penetrate the joints of armor* in order to give the *coup de grace** to a fallen adversary. Normally this weapon had a triangular-shaped blade and an open hilt without a guard. It usually was worn at the right side and was hooked to one of the taces.* A knight always wore one in *jousts à outrance.** (Bibliog. 71)

misercordia. See mercy.

missi dominici (L.), royal emissaries whom Charlemagne sent out to reorganize the system of local government by curtailing the powers of the counts and dukes, and by checking closely on the activities of his local governors. (Bibliog. 186)

Model Parliament. In 1295 King Edward I summoned the earls,* barons,* knights* and burgesses,* bishops* and abbots,* cathedral and parochial clergy to meet and hear the royal message, then to divide into separate sections for debate, and then come together again as a single body to return their answer to the king. These representatives of the counties, cities, and boroughs and of the lower clergy met with secular and ecclesiastical lords. Although termed a model, this parliament did not in fact serve as a model for future parliaments because members of the lower clergy ceased to attend. See Parliament. (Bibliog. 186)

molet. See cadency.

moline, heraldic cross* whose endings each had short twin curls going in opposite directions.

molt, to shed or to cast off feathers, which were replaced by new growth. (Bibliog. 26)

money. Two types of money existed: money of account and actual coinage.* Money of account was the measure of value as distinct from the actual coin which reflected the medium of exchange and the store of wealth; it was used almost exclusively for accounting purposes. Most financial transactions were determined first in money of account, and then arrangements were made for subsequent payment in coin. The relationship between them fluctuated as a result of the alterations made by public authorities of the times. As the denier (see denarius) declined at different rates in different places in the 11th and 12th centuries, a standard of reference was needed for the variety of deniers circulating. With the introduction of the fine silver groat* and the gold florin* in addition to the denier, a common denominator became necessary to express varying values of gold, silver, and billon* coins, as well as other commodities. Money of account supplied both these needs.

Such an amount in both England and France long had been expressed in pounds or livres* of twenty shillings or sous which in turn were made up of twelve pennies* or deniers. "Livre tournois"* was the most common unit of money of account in France although others existed, such as the "livre parisis"*; the pound sterling* was used in England and the livre bordelaise in Guyenne, and the exchange rate between them varied according to alterations made from time to time by the kings* of England and France. During most of the 14th and 15th centuries, the rate was five livre bordelaise to one pound sterling and six livre tournois to one pound sterling. A second money of account was the mark.* In England it was always worth two-thirds of a pound or thirteen shillings fourpence.

Difficulties arise in attempts to provide a present-day value of this early money. One basis for comparison lay in the average wages earned by the lower classes in the 12th century with present wages. The normal wage for the 12th-century worker was one penny a day or thirty shillings fivepence (365 pence) per year; every footsoldier, porter, carter, and chaplain, for example, earned such wages. By the end of the 12th century, however, because of the difficulty of recruiting and the cost of equipment, soldiers' wages had risen to one and one-half pence per day, even though one penny per day was the average worker's wage. Furthermore, assets that were confiscated from convicted and outlawed felons (see outlaw; felony) at their trials and sold by the crown* in 1175 showed only a total of 312 pounds, which averaged only ten shillings per individual. A second calculation of people amerced (see amercement) provided an average of slightly more than nine shillings. These amounts occurred at a time when the ordinary revenues of the English crown were about 30,000 pounds per year. Fewer than half a dozen earls* enjoyed incomes of around 3,000 pounds from their holdings, and most received only sixty to seventy pounds income. In contrast, the daily pay of a knight in the king's army at this time was only two shillings, yet this was a substantial sum, for from it the knight had to keep two or three horses* and a page or valet. Assuming that the sixty to seventy pound annual income equates with $60,000 to $70,000 by 1984 standards, that pound was worth a modern $1,000 and breaks down to roughly one penny being worth four dollars of modern buying power. A comparison with other 12th- and 13th-century prices reveals that such a figure is fairly accurate. A knight receiving two shillings or twenty-four pence translates into ninety-six dollars per day to pay for horses and servants; eggs, however, sold in 1320 at fivepence for ten dozen (or twenty dollars for five dozen at today's prices); butter for half a penny for a pound (two dollars per pound). Early wages of one penny per day also do not fit this equation; for those to be equivalent, the penny would have to be worth ten to fifteen dollars. See tithe. (Bibliog. 161, 289, 324)

money, bad, debased and bad metal coinage* such as crockards,* pollards, scaldings, brabantines, lions dormant, and various other types of coins brought into England by foreign merchants. These were all white money* that imitated silver but were compounded of silver, copper, and sulphur; rarely could a pennyworth of silver be found in four of them. In 1299 King Edward I issued the Statute of Stepney which forbade anyone from bringing into England any such money on pain of forfeiture of life, goods, and whatever else he could forfeit, or taking from England any good English money. To enforce this, he appointed wardens* for each port (see borough) of entry and exit to set up tables for travellers in each direction to exchange currency. Then he prohibited these spurious coins entirely and ordered them exchanged for English coins at the rate of five or six for one sterling* of his own mint. (Bibliog. 103)

money of necessity. See siege money.

monocerous. See unicorn.

monster, any fabulous creature used in heraldry.* Among them were: amphisbene,* apres,* argasil,* bagwyn,* basilisk,* bonacon,* boreyne,* calopus, centaur,* cockatrice,* dragon,* egrentyne,* enfield,* griffin,* harpy, hippogriff,* hydra,* lion dragon, manticora,* mermaid,* nebek,* opinicus,* satyr,* satyral,* theow,* unicorn,* wyvern,* yale,* and ypotryll.* (Bibliog. 116)

monstrant regibus astra viam (L. "The stars show the way to kings"), motto of the French *Ordre de l'Etoile* (Order of the Star*). (Bibliog. 17)

monstraverunt. See writ monstraverunt.

Mont-joie Saint Denis (Fr.), "battle cry"* which originally summoned the vassals* of the St. Denis* abbey to battle in the 12th century but from the 13th century onward was adopted by the royal French army and was used as a proclamation of war. Mont-joie was the banner* borne by Charlemagne. (Bibliog. 40, 139)

month, days of, method of calculating days of the month from three fixed points: counting backwards from the kalends or first of the following month, from the ides or the thirteenth of every month, and from the nones or the fifth of every month. In March, May, July, and October, the nones and ides were placed two days later: on the seventh and the fifteenth respectively. (Bibliog. 265)

moot, mote. 1. horn calls in hunting. See horn calls. 2. an assembly for legal purposes or for settling accounts, a judicial council. (Bibliog. 226)

morning star, spiked mace,* also called "holy water sprinkler,"* similar to a godendag* used by both cavalry and infantry but with a shorter shaft; these were easily produced by any village smithy. (Bibliog. 9)

mort. See horn calls in hunting.

mort d'ancestor. See assize of *mort d'ancestor*.

Mortimer, Roger (1287–1330), earl* of March; lover of Queen Isabelle, wife of Edward II, after she became widowed. He was executed by Edward III to wrest control of the throne from his mother, Isabelle, and him. (Bibliog. 186)

mortuary, severe death duties imposed on villeins* consisting usually of the second-best animal paid as a customary gift to the parish priest from the estate of a deceased parishioner. Accompanying heriot,* this was exacted by the church on the convenient theory that during his lifetime, a man would be unlikely to pay in full all his tithes* and other charges to the church, and so it was necessary for the church to exert this final claim by exacting mortuary. It was done after the lord had the first choice of the best beast or chattel as his heriot; the church then was given second choice but only if there were at least three beasts. (Bibliog. 24)

mote. See horn calls in hunting.

motte, raised portion of a motte and bailey* castle.* The term came from the French word *motte* meaning mound or actually the turf of which it was composed. This artificial or part-natural mound, usually with a ditch about its base, was the prominent feature of early castles. It usually was confined and needed some sort of enclosure. As the symbol of dominion of the feudal lord and the center of his dominium or demesne,* this mound bore his strong tower and to it the name of the mound was transferred. A common name for motte used by writers was Latin *dunio* or *domgio*, a debased form of *dominio* which became *donjon** in French and dungeon* in English. (Bibliog. 280)

motte and bailey castle. See castle.

motto, war or "battle cry"* used by early barbarian nations to instill panic in their enemies, to invoke the protection of their gods, or to rouse patriotic fervor in their own troops. From this oral use, these cries soon became a part of the banner* and badge* and were written on a scroll placed beneath the heraldic arms* or over the crest* when used to signify a war cry. They were not hereditary in England, for no one was compelled to bear one, nor was any authority needed to adopt one; such choice was left completely to the personal pleasure of the individual, as was the manner of displaying it. (Bibliog. 116, 251)

moulinet and pulleys crossbow, *arbalète à cranequin,* crossbow* with a system of pulleys affixed at the butt end over which cords were led. A small windlass set these cords in motion, and the pulleys attached to the bowstring pulled it back until it engaged a nut. Then the archer removed the tackle and hung it from his belt, ready for use to engage the next bolt. (Bibliog. 9)

mouse, fanciful name for a bore used to pick holes in masonry during "siege warfare."*

mouton, gold coinage* containing a lamb of God, a cross,* and a standard* on the obverse and a florette* cross on the reverse, in 14th-century France. (Bibliog. 324)

movable feast, Holy Day* of the church, the date of which varied as much as five weeks according to the date of Easter, for Easter could fall on any Sunday between March 22 and April 25. The earliest of these feasts was Septuagesima Sunday which could occur as early as January 18. See also Appendix A. (Bibliog. 265)

mue. See mew.

mufti. See caliph.

mullet, heraldic charge* which originally depicted the rowel of a spur* but was stylized as a star with five points. (Bibliog. 43)

multure, portion claimed by the lord from all the grain ground at his mill. Peasants (see villein) had to grind the grain at their lord's mill, and he took as his portion amounts varying from one-twenty-fourth to one-sixteenth. (Bibliog. 24)

mund, protectorship over women, a wife's honorable position as her husband's consort which was assured by the marriage contract. See wergild. (Bibliog. 261)

mundeburdum (L.), protection extended by a powerful man to his weaker neighbor in early Germany. It came into French as _mainbour.*_ (Bibliog. 28)

murage tax, tax paid to the borough* bailiff* by a stranger for permission to enter through the wall of a city, particularly London. (Bibliog. 161)

murdrum, concealed death of a man whose slayer was unknown. See Englishry. (Bibliog. 102)

murrey, reddish-purple or mulberry tincture, a color* between gules* and purpure* in heraldry.* (Bibliog. 43)

musket, male of the sparrowhawk (see falconry birds) in hawking.* (Bibliog. 26)

mustelle, weasel.

mute. See meute.

mutchkin, a Scots quarter of a pint measure.

mutilation notice, official pronouncement on May 20, 1302, that in Roxburgh, William, son of John le Noble, had his right ear torn off in his minority by the bite of a pig. That notice was issued to prevent him from being accused of having been mutilated as punishment* for some crime (see torture). (Bibliog. 103)

mutilation of dogs, clipping the claws from dogs to prevent their being used for hunting.* See Assize of the Forest. (Bibliog. 102)

N

naifty, state of being born in bondage or serfdom (see serf). (Bibliog. 24)

nail money, fee paid to a herald* for nailing the armorial shield* of a knight to the pavilion* at a tournament*; it also was known as clouage.* (Bibliog. 78)

naratores. See jestours.

narcotic, when henbane, darnel, black poppy, and bryony root were broken together in a brass mortar and ground to a fine powder, and then given to someone in pottage or wheatcake or in a drink, he would sleep at once all day or longer, depending on the amount used, whether he wanted to or not. (Bibliog. 286)

nasal. See helmet.

nebek, heraldic monster* that resembled an unusually hairy tiger. (Bibliog. 43)

Neckham, Alexander (1157–1217), abbot of Cirencester, teacher at University of Paris, and "milk brother"* to Richard I* of England. (Bibliog. 44, 161)

nef, saltcellar in the form of a ship. This item was the chief article on the table at meals, for no salt was used in cooking. It also served as a social demarcation line, the gradation of rank, for the lord and his relatives and guests sat above it, and the ordinary mesnie* sat below it. (Bibliog. 225)

Nennius, author of a 9th-century Latin work, *Historia Brittonum*, containing two tales about King Arthur in a section on Mirabilia. One described a cairn in Breconshire called Cairn Cabal which bore the footprint of Arthur's dog, Cabal,* while it hunted the pig Troit. The second tale told of the marvellous tomb of Arthur's son, Amr, beside the river Amr in Herefordshire. This work also included a historical reference to Arthur fighting against the Saxons and listed his twelve victories. (Bibliog. 200)

niger, a powerful stone also called gelaticum. If put in one's mouth a long time after rinsing the mouth with wax and honey, one could foresee the projects of adversaries. Moreover, it was a powerful aphrodisiac. (Bibliog. 258)

Nine Worthies, nine personages rated as being the most worthy, the choice showing a remarkably close connection to the romances* of chivalry*: three Gentiles (Hector, son of Priam; Julius Caesar; and Alexander the Great); three Jews, (Joshua, conqueror of Canaan; David, king* of Israel; and Judas Maccabaeus); three Christians, (Arthur, king of Britian; Charlemagne; and Godfrey de Bouillon). (Bibliog. 169)

nithing, vile coward, abject wretch, villain of the lowest type, a man without honor.* King Edward the Confessor (1042–1066) declared Harold Godwineson's* elder brother, Swein, a nithing in 1050 after Swein had treacherously murdered his cousin, Earl Beorn. So heavy was this pronouncement that six of Swein's eight ship crews deserted, and he was considered an outcast in most of the northern world. For simple murder, Swein would have been declared an outlaw,* but his treachery was so atrocious that he was condemned as a nithing. In 1088 William* II (Rufus) called out the English militia with a proclamation that anyone who disobeyed the summons would be declared nithing. It remained a term of opprobrium for centuries. (Bibliog. 330)

nobility, quality or state of persons possessing an acknowledged preeminence founded on hereditary succession. Not every dominant class was noble. To deserve such a title a class had to possess legal status of its own which confirmed and made effectual and hereditary the superiority it claimed, and its social position and hereditary succession had to be recognized by law. The ancient idea of family pride based on ancestry from the aristocracy* of the Roman Empire long had disappeared in the new kingdoms where the bases of superiority were power, wealth, and service to the king.* Although such power often was passed from father to son, still it left room for sudden rises and falls in power and prestige.

A noble's total commitment to his service as a warrior explained his role as a military vassal* in medieval aristocracy. Such warriors did not constitute the entire aristocracy, for owners of allodial (see allodium) manors* could not have been excluded. Ancient Anglo-Saxon laws had contrasted eorl, a noble in the Germanic sense, and ceorl,* an ordinary freeman. Later laws retained the concepts but changed the word eorl to thegn (see thane) or thegnborn, meaning a companion or vassal or a descendant of a vassal. Whether he was a vassal or an allodial lord, the noble of early feudal times contrasted with the temporary soldiers* by being a better armed and professional warrior. He was a mounted fighter, and though he might dismount during a battle, he always moved about on horseback. His head and body were covered partly or wholly with metal. He fought fully equipped with lance,* sword,* and occasionally a mace,* and he carried a round or triangular shield.* Even though both his squire* and sergeant* rode, the combination of horse* and complete equipment distinguished the noble as the highest class fighting man.

In time, however, in these days when so many men agreed to hold their lands of a lord, mere possession of an allod usually was enough for a man to be a noble. From the end of the 11th century onward, however, such nobles became scarce as the idea behind nobility was changing. In Frankish lands, for example, many slaves who had received their freedom were not accepted as equals by those whose families had never been slaves. Therefore, an unblemished ancestral line became a sign of genuine nobility: "To be noble is to count among one's ancestors no one who has been subject to slavery."

By a highly significant restriction in use of the concept in England from the 9th century onward, only relatives of the king retained the right to the name aethling (see atheling), a title harkening back to the German edelinge or noble. About that same time, the word noble found frequently in documents had no legal meaning but merely indicated an actual or accepted preeminence by various criteria, including distinction by birth and a measure of wealth. And the term referred to peers* who in "letters patent"* were "ennobled" by the crown,* for lesser nobility were called gentry. A grant of arms* from the king recognized gentility (see gentleman) but did not create a nobleman.

On the continent, the word noble had different connotations. Not until noble families broke away from the royal household in France and acquired autonomous authority and private lordship did they organize themselves into dynasties. The house of a noble became a noble house by serving as the central point around which an independent and lasting race crystallized and to which it owed its power. This male line grew stronger by reserving for itself the hereditary transmission of authority, landed wealth, ancestral glory and as a result, nobility. Such autonomy was achieved first by the houses of counts,* the heads of houses, then by masters of castles,* and last by knights (see knighthood) in their own homes which by the end of the 12th and 13th centuries had become fortified houses. Appropriation of power to command and to punish, exercised only by a male and transmitted to his son, together with the purely masculine heritages of honor, fief,* title, family surname and "coat of arms,"* and the gradual exclusion of married daughters from the paternal inheritance, all without a doubt helped confer dynastic features on noble families.

Yet despite such pretensions to antiquity, one of the dominant features of these early families was the shortness of their pedigrees. For example, the earliest ancestor of the Guelfs* (Welfs) who played such large roles in West Francia and wore the crown of Burgundy from 888 to 1032 was a Bavarian count whose daughter had married Louis the Pious, Charlemagne's son and successor. The Bourbons descended from the Capetians were probably the oldest dynasty of Europe, but even they went back only to Robert the Strong who was killed in 866. (Bibliog. 28, 94, 221, 248)

noble, large gold coinage* issued by Edward III in 1344 with the value of six shillings eightpence, that is, one-third of a pound (see money); its obverse depicted the king* standing on a ship; its reverse had an ornate cross.* (Bibliog. 150)

nock, notch in both a bow* and an arrow.* (Bibliog. 100)

nocking point, that portion of the bowstring on which an arrow's* nock* was placed. (Bibliog. 100)

nombril point, point on a shield* located between the fess* point and the base of the shield. (Bibliog. 43)

nomisma, large gold solidus (see sol) of the late Byzantine Empire. See coinage. (Bibliog. 324)

nones, "canonical hour"*; daily canonical office usually said at the ninth hour, usually about 3 P.M. See also month, days of.

Northallerton, battle of. See Battle of the Standard.

novel disseisin. See Assize of Novel Disseisin.

nowed, tied in a knot, as in heraldic serpents and tails of beasts. (Bibliog. 43)

nulle terre sans seigneur (Fr. "no land without its lord"), pure feudal principal of requiring everyone to have an overlord. (Bibliog. 47)

numbles, parts of a deer between the thighs: liver, kidneys, entrails. These were considered the right of the huntsman,* but sometimes he received only the kidneys, the remainder reserved for the king* or chief personage of the hunt. Loss of the initial letter led this term to become known as umbles, often written as humbles, whence came "humble pie"—a pie made of the umbles of the deer and at hunting* feasts set before the huntsman and his followers. (Bibliog. 96)

nummi, presumed nominal unit of the Byzantine bronze coinage* which circulated in Greece, Asia minor, southern Italy, and Sicily from the 7th to the 10th century. These were also minted in multiples of five (pentanummo), ten (decanummo), twenty, thirty, and forty, the last being equal to a fallaro. (Bibliog. 150)

O

oath, an invocation of some deity or supernatural power to grant or withhold his favor in accordance with the veracity of the swearer, but commonly rendered more impressive by interposing material objects such as holy relics or taking an oath on a church altar. In certain cases the Anglo-Saxons allowed the reduplication of oaths by having the swearer repeat his assertion in four separate churches, while the defendant could rebut the charge by taking an oath of negation in twelve. The intense veneration of relics caused them to be adopted as the most effective means of adding security to oaths; because the simple oath was given such little respect these adjuncts came to be regarded as an essential feature of the oath and the oath was divested of its binding force without them. Canon law under Pope Gregory III (A.D. 731-741) provided one year's penance for perjury committed on an unconsecrated cross, but three years' penance for perjury on a consecrated one or the hand of a bishop. And in court cases prosecution and defense both required relics to give validity to the oaths of all parties on each side. If a plaintiff came into court without relics on which to take his oath, he was fined nine-score pence.

Another rule stipulated that a man who suspected another of theft could go to him with a relic and in the presence of witnesses demand an oath of negation. If the accused failed to swear such an oath, he was considered convicted without further trial. Even so, the ecclesiastical authorities agreed that a powerful motive might extenuate the sin of such a perjury. If committed voluntarily, seven years of penance were demanded for its absolution; if involuntarily, sixteen months; but if sworn to preserve one's safety, the offense could be atoned for in only four months.

Because people who were clamoring for the return of stolen cattle or for a share of wergild* refused to be deprived of their rights by a simple perjury, this practice gave way, however, to the ancestral custom of oaths from compurgator,* which long remained as part of English law under the name of the Wager of Law.* (Bibliog. 195)

oaths, Norse, Norsemen swore "by board of ship, by rim of warrior shield,* by shoulder of steel, and by edge of sword.*" (Bibliog. 200)

obligations, feudal. See feudal obligations.

obligations, military. See *servitium debitum.*

obol, small silver coinage,* originally equal to one-sixth of a Greek drachma but in later issues in England it equalled a halfpenny.* (Bibliog. 150)

obolus argenteus, silver counter used at the counting tables at the Exchequer* to represent ten shillings (see money). (Bibliog. 102, 144)

obolus aureus, gold counter used at the counting tables at the Exchequer* to represent ten pounds (see money). (Bibliog. 102, 144)

obstacles to knighthood. See knighthood.

obulus, silver coinage* of Hungary under Bela I (1235–1270) on which the word obulus appeared between two lions'* heads. (Bibliog. 150)

occularia, eye holes in heaumes.* (Bibliog. 9)

ocrea, baggy cloth draped around the legs of peasants (see villein) and bound with leather thongs. (Bibliog. 161)

octave, utas, subsidiary observance of a feast day (see Appendix A) one week later. This date was used commonly in summons to councils, parliaments,* and the like as a convenient date for attendance when the great festival was over. For this purpose, the quindene or quinzaine, a fortnight after the feast, sometimes was used. See Holy Days. (Bibliog. 265)

octofoil, heraldic flower like the cinquefoil* but with eight petals. Illogically, it was the mark of cadency* for the ninth son. (Bibliog. 43)

oenophorum, measure of capacity for wine* equal to one gallon* from the year 1275 on. (Bibliog. 394)

offices of state, England had five great offices of state: the steward,* the constable,* the marshal,* the chamberlain,* and the butler.* The steward of the Norman kings* in time became the lord high steward who was appointed only for coronations* or for the trial of peers.* His place at court* was occupied by the lord steward, who was his deputy. The constable was essentially a military officer, commanding a garrison in the castle* or an army in the field. The marshal originally was an officer subordinate to the constable, although so long as the constable existed, they sat and acted together in that military court of arms* and honours* which came to be known later as the "earl marshal's"* court. The chamberlain served the king in his chambers, and the butler was in charge of the wines.* (Bibliog. 75)

official titles. See titles of dignity, official.

ogress. See pellets.

Olifant, Roland's* horn with which he summoned Charlemagne's troops to come to his aid after he already had lost the battle against Marsile's pagan forces at Roncevaux* in the Pyrenees on August 15, 778. See demesure; *Song of Roland.* (Bibliog. 40)

olim (L. "once"), French judicial record kept on parchment scrolls by the clerks of the Parlement of Paris; it contained judgments and charters. See Parliament. (Bibliog. 139)

Oliver, Roland's* friend and close companion who died with him at Roncevaux.*

onager, 1. wild ass of central Asia and Africa. Large and untameable, these beasts wandered in the desert. One male presided over a herd of females, and when little males were born their fathers became jealous of them and bit off their testicles, for fear of which their mothers hid their young in secret places. This animal brayed twelve times at night and twelve times during the day at the spring equinox (March 25) because day and night were of equal length on that day and it preferred night to day. 2. machine for hurling rocks by means of a sling. It was named after the onager or wild ass because like its namesake when it "kicked" in anger, it flung stones a great distance. (Bibliog. 71, 246)

onyx, stone that brought bad luck when carried in battle. (Bibliog. 258)

opinicus, heraldic monster* with lion's body, griffin's* or dragon's* neck and head, eagle's* or dragon's wings, and a camel's tail. (Bibliog. 43)

or, gold; metal* or tincture (see colors) in heraldry* represented frequently by the color yellow. (Bibliog. 43)

ordainers, group of twenty-one magnates (see peer) of England who forced King Edward II (1307-1327) to reform his realm and his household, especially to stop his showering Piers Gaveston with money,* estates, titles, and power. These powerful men agreed that such actions were essential to remedy the situation of their times but were not to be considered as establishing a precedent for future monarchs. They were: the archbishop of Canterbury, the bishops of Lincoln, Salisbury, Chichester, Norwich, St. David's, and Llandaff; the earls* of Lincoln, Pembroke, Gloucester, Lancaster, Hereford, Richmond, Warwick, and Arundel; Hugh de Vere, Robert Clifford, Hugh Courtney, William Marshal,* and William Martin. (Bibliog. 222)

ordeal, judicial process ordained by law for certain cases to learn the judgment of God and carried out by tribunals as a regular form of ordinary procedure. Generally the absence of satisfactory testimony rendered the case one not to be solved by human means alone. From the earliest times, the accused was compelled to submit to the ordeal as to any other decree of the court.* If he refused to do so, he was summoned before the king's court where, if he still refused, he was declared an outlaw* and his property was confiscated. Directions for these tests were precise and allowed no variations or alternatives. These were held inside or just outside a church until the Fourth Lateran Council in 1215 forbade any priest from performing the religious ceremonies which were their basic ingredients, primarily of the ordeals of fire and water. These tests were used for both the free and the unfree for criminal offenses. The free usually had to carry hot iron; the unfree had to endure the ordeal of water. The aristocracy,* however, rarely had to endure either, for apparently there was no need for divine proof in the cases of persons of quality. Most often the ordeal of water was used for peasant (see villein) men, and peasant women had to carry hot iron. For example, in Cornwall in 1201, six men and one woman were implicated in a burglary. The verdict of the court was that the men were to purge themselves by water and the woman by the ordeal of iron.

There were eleven varieties of ordeal (see "ordeal by" or "ordeal of"): bier right,* bread and cheese,* cold water,* cross,* Eucharist,* fire,* hot or boiling water,* lot,* oaths on relics,* poison,* red-hot iron.* In England these were used universally as late as the end of the 12th century. The Assize of Clarendon* (1166) directed the ordeal to be used to determine at an inquest in each shire* if all who were indicted for murder, robbery, and other felonies* were guilty or innocent. Usually the ordeals of hot or cold water were used for peasants and of hot iron for the nobility,* but this rule was not universal.

This frequently was considered as a form of punishment* because it was inflicted upon those whose guilt was so generally accepted that they could find none to stand up at the altar with them to support their oath of denial. Its misuse to extort confessions or unwilling testimony was the main reason in the 13th century that the ordeal fell into disuse and disappeared because it had fulfilled its mission, being replaced by torture such as the *peine forte et dure.** (Bibliog. 196)

ordeal by bier right, belief that the corpse of the slain would bleed afresh or give some other sign at the approach of its murderer. When Richard I* hastened to the funeral of his father, Henry II, and met the procession at Fontevrault, blood poured from the nostrils of the dead king.* Witnesses credited that event as evidence of Richard's disobedience and rebellion in causing his father's death. In the *Nibelungenlied*, when Hagen was called upon to prove his innocence of the murder of Siegfried by approaching the corpse, the body's wounds bled afresh. (Bibliog. 196)

ordeal by bread and cheese, accused was handed a piece of bread* (generally barley) or one ounce* of cheese over which prayers had been said. Then after an appropriate religious ceremony including communion, the morsel was eaten, and the innocence of the accused was determined by his ability to swallow the morsel; if he could not do so, he was judged guilty. This ordeal* was used primarily by people allied to the Saxon race who called it corsnaed. Its psychological power was evident when Godwine, duke* of Kent and father of King Harold Godwineson, dined with King Edward the Confessor. Some trivial disagreement between them caused Edward to hurl the old accusation that his brother Alfred had met death at the hands of Godwine. At this the old but fiery duke cried, "May God cause this morsel to choke me if I am guilty in thought or deed of this crime." Then the king took the bread and blessed it, and Godwine, putting it into his mouth, suffocated on it and fell dead. (Bibliog. 196)

ordeal by fire, test based on the belief that humans could withstand normal physiological effects of fire, as did Shadrach, Meshach, and Abednego, if the gods desired it. Its preliminaries were the same as for the "ordeal of cold water"*: fasting, prayer, taking the sacraments, exorcism of the fire, and blessing of the various pieces of paraphernalia needed. Sometimes this ordeal* called for one to put his hand directly into the fire, have the wound bound, and after three days unwrap it to be examined. Sometimes it was enlarged by having someone walk through a huge pyre and emerge unscathed. A famous example occurred when Peter "Igneus" gained his surname and reputation at such an occasion. In 1063 Godfrey, duke* of Tuscany, was protecting the unpopular bishop of Florence against charges of simony and heresy, and despite the challenge of his accusers to prove his guilt by the ordeal of the fire and his being acquitted of those charges by the Council of Rome, the bishop continued his tyrannical oppression. After four years, the monks of Vallombrosso could take no more, and they denounced him publicly. Supported by 3,000 enthusiastic Florentines who had assembled for the purpose, these determined monks decided to use the ordeal by fire to prove the guilt of the bishop. One of the monks, Pietro Aldobrandini, offered to undergo the trial for his brother monks. After the usual preliminary rites, he slowly walked barefooted on two inches* of glowing coals covering the six-foot-wide passageway between two piles of blazing wood ten feet* long, five feet wide, and four and one-half feet high. The violence of the flames whipped his hair and his clothing, but he emerged unharmed; even the hair on his legs remained unsinged. The wild crowd pressed in so reverently around him to embrace and kiss him that only then was he in danger. In response to the formal report of this event, the pope deposed the bishop and elevated Peter "Igneus." He eventually died as Cardinal Albano. Despite the efforts of Pope Innocent III to abolish this ordeal, especially at the Fourth Lateran Council in 1215, St. Francis of Assisi offered to go through it for the propagation of the faith. He told the sultan of Turkey that he would do it if the sultan would agree to convert if Francis were successful; the sultan, however, declined. (Bibliog. 196)

ordeal by hot or boiling water, oldest form of test in Europe using the judicial application of fire as a mode of proof. Bishop Hinomar (806–882) particularly recommended it because it combined the elements of water that represented the deluge which was God's judgment inflicted on the wicked of old and the fire that represented the fiery doom of the future day of judgment. Before the ordeal* the accused had to spend three days in fasting and prayer. On the day itself, at mass and communion the priest said to the accused, "this body and blood of Jesus Christ be to thee this day a manifestation." Then the various utensils were blessed, the fire lit, the water exorcised and brought to a boil. For a minor offense, a single ordeal was required. Into it the accused would plunge his hand to the wrist and withdraw it or retrieve a stone or ring from the required depth. For a felony* a triple ordeal required the accused to plunge in his whole forearm up to the elbow. Then his hand or arm was bandaged with cloth and sealed with the signet of the judge so that the wound could not be tampered with during the required three days before the bandages could be removed to determine guilt or innocence. A blister half the size of a walnut was considered sufficient proof of guilt to warrant the suspect's execution.* (Bibliog. 196)

ordeal by poison, test for truth used mainly in the East. Seven grains of a susbtance growing in the Himalayas, when mixed with clarified butter, was given to the accused. If no evil symptoms appeared during the day, then the accused was declared innocent. (Bibliog. 196)

ordeal of cold water, (L. *judicium aquae frigidae*), different from other ordeals* in that it required a miracle to convict the accused. Here, after the usual preliminary of fasting, prayers, and religious rites as in other ordeals, the accused was bound hand and foot and lowered into cold water at the end of a rope in which a knot was tied somewhere between a long hair's breadth and a half a yard* from where it was fastened around the middle of the body. If the accused pulled the knot down with him as he sank so that it broke the surface of the water, he was cleared; but if both the accused and knot floated, he was guilty. Such a test was based on the belief that the pure element of water would not receive into its bosom anyone stained with a crime of false oath. This ordeal spread throughout Europe on equal footing with other ordeals. In 1083 during the intense struggle between Henry VI, the Roman emperor,* and Pope Hildebrand, Henry's imperialists circulated reports that supporters of the pope had tested his cause by this ordeal. After three-days feast and proper benediction of the water, they had placed it in a boy to represent the emperor, and to their horror he sank like a stone. When he heard about this experiment, Hildebrand ordered the ordeal repeated, but the result was the same: the boy sank. Then, throwing the same boy into the water on two separate trials but this time as a representative of the pope, he obstinately floated despite all their efforts to force him under the surface. All who witnessed this unexpected result were sworn to inviolable secrecy by the embarrassed pope.

This test maintained its hold on popular faith for one class of cases: accusations of witchcraft and sorcery. Drowning was the punishment inflicted by custom of the Franks for such crimes. Added to the widespread belief that pure water would refuse to receive anyone tainted with crime was the idea that people adept in sorcery and magic lost their specific gravity, so it was only fitting that their guilt should be determined by the cold water ordeal. (Bibliog. 197)

ordeal of oaths on relics, rendering an oath as to the truth of a matter at issue when swearing on relics* of a particular sanctity. In Milan, according to St. Augustine, a thief who swore upon some holy relics with the intention of bearing false witness was forced irresistibly to confess himself guilty of the offense which he was attempting to fasten upon another. In another case, a perjurer was afflicted by an epileptic fit, or was made rigid at the moment when, in the shrine of a saint, he called upon the holy shrine to witness his oath. (Bibliog. 196)

ordeal of red-hot iron (L. *judicium ferri juise*), one of the earliest forms of determining disputed questions. The term *judicium* grew to mean an ordeal* and generally the ordeal of hot iron; the corruption of that word, juise, probably meant the same ordeal. Used widely throughout Europe from Spain to Byzantium and Scandinavia to Naples, it was believed to be an unfailing means of ascertaining the will of Heaven. This ordeal was administered in two forms. One, the *vomeres igniti* or *examen pedale*, consisted of laying on the ground at certain distances six, nine, or twelve red-hot plowshares among which the accused walked barefooted and sometimes blindfolded. Sometimes to test her chastity, a lady was required to press each iron with her naked foot. The other form required the accused to carry a piece of red-hot iron in his hand for a certain distance, usually nine feet,* the weight of the iron being determined by law and varying with the importance of the question at issue or the magnitude of the alleged crime. In England under Henry I (1100–1135) the iron for a simple ordeal weighed one pound,* but for a triple ordeal in cases of accusations of plotting against the king's life, counterfeiting, secret murder, arson, robbery, and felonies* in general, the iron weighed three pounds. In both cases the accused's hand was wrapped for three days before being examined to render the decision in accordance with its condition. As with other ordeals, the same solemn observances were followed, the iron was exorcised, and the intervention of God was invoked in the name of Divine clemency.

In early times this test was used for crimes of particular atrocity. Charlemagne, for example, ordered it for parricide; the Council of Prisbach in 799 directed its use in cases of witchcraft and sorcery; the Thuringians ordered it for women suspected of poisoning or otherwise murdering their husbands. By the time of King Edward II in England (1307–1327) it was reserved for the aristocracy.* Edward the Confessor disliked his mother, so he listened eagerly to accusations of her criminal intimacy with Alwyn, bishop of Winchester. She was condemned to undergo the ordeal of the red-hot plowshares; she walked over them barefooted and unharmed and proved the falsity of the charges against her. Because it was easy to arrange collusion by paying off someone—an accuser or a cleric—the pope abolished this practice in 1215. (Bibliog. 196)

ordeal of the cross, test of truth by simple endurance. After the appropriate religious ceremonies, both plaintiff and defendant stood with uplifted arms before a cross* while the divine service was performed. Victory was judged to the one who was able to hold his position for the longest time. Charlemagne liked this test so much that he directed in A.D. 806 that all territorial disputes emerging between his sons as he divided his empire* among them should be settled in this manner. (Bibliog. 196)

ordeal of the Eucharist, simplification of the "ordeal of bread and cheese.*" Its administration invariably was a portion of the preparatory ceremony with the awesome admonition, "May this body and blood of our Lord Jesus Christ be a judgment to thee this day." Because the pious priests of that time believed literally that admonition of the apostle who said, "he that eateth and drinketh unworthily eateth and drinketh damnation to himself," this ordeal was effective. For example, a dissolute priest of Turgau near Zurich in the 14th century was a habitual drunkard, fornicator, and gambler, yet he said daily mass with exemplary regularity. Warned of the dangers to which he was exposing himself by partaking of the Eucharist, he shrugged off the warnings until he finally confessed that in mass he never consecrated the host, but instead he carried with him a small round piece of wood resembling the holy wafer which he exhibited and passed off as the body of Christ. The angry peasants (see villein) drove him off unceremoniously when they learned of his subterfuge. (Bibliog. 196)

ordeal of the lot, decision of guilt or innocence left to pure chance based on the belief that Heaven would interpose to save the innocent and punish the guilty. In Frisian law, for example, when a man was killed in a chance brawl and the murderer remained unknown, friends of the dead man had the right to accuse seven of the participants in the brawl. Each of these defendants had to take an oath of denial with twelve compurgators,* after which they were admitted to the ordeal.* One of two identical pieces of twig was marked with a cross,* and both were wrapped in white wool and laid on the altar. Prayers invoked God to reveal the guilt or innocence of the party, and then the priest or an innocent youth chose one of the bundles. If it contained the marked fragment, the defendants were absolved, but if the unmarked one, then the guilty party was among them. Each of them then took a similar piece of wood and made a secret mark on it. These then were rolled up as the first two had been and placed on the altar, taken one by one and unwrapped, each man claiming his own. The one whose piece was chosen last was considered guilty and had to pay the wergild* of the murder. In Ireland the lot or *crannchur* was employed by mingling white and black stones; if the accused drew a black stone he was judged guilty. (Bibliog. 196)

Order of Alcantara. See Alcantara.

Order of Calatrava. See Calatrava.

Order of Ermine. See orders of chivalry and knighthood.

Order of St. Michael. See orders of chivalry and knighthood.

Order of Santiago, military order founded in Spain in 1164. At the height of the Moorish threat, and when various kings in Spain persisted in fighting each other instead of the common pagan enemy, thirteen knights adopted the badge* of the sword* with a cross* at the hilt and swore to fight no one but pagans and never to injure a Christian. Renouncing earthly vanities and governing their lives by Holy Writ, they grew to be influential in western Spain by holding frontier castles.* They ultimately were integrated into the Spanish government by King Ferdinand and Queen Isabella in 1482. See orders of chivalry and knighthood. (Bibliog. 17)

Order of the Bath, English order which King Henry IV created at his coronation* in 1399 when he bestowed membership on forty-six squires.* Although the dignity was conferred at coronations and other national ceremonies, it was not really one of the "orders of chivalry and knighthood"* but an honor. Its members were distinguished by their emerasse, an escutcheon* of azure* silk upon the left shoulder charged with three crowns* proper and the motto "Trois en un" ("Three in one"). (Bibliog. 87, 253)

Order of the Garter, highest of the "orders of chivalry and knighthood"* in England founded in 1348 by King Edward III to bring to reality an idea he had expressed in 1344 to found an Order of the Round Table at Windsor Castle.* In the course of a Round Table tournament,* he vowed to create an order with that name for 300 members. The Garter was the result. Because he only recently had assumed the title of king* of France, he may have wanted to reward some of the distinguished people without whose assistance he never would had gotten the French crown.* Hence the choice of the colors* of the royal French livery, blue and gold, and the motto* *"Honi soit qui mal y pense*"* (Fr. "Evil to him who thinks it evil"). Its emblem,* the garter, was worn by knights buckled below the left knee, but by women on their left arms. Originally it consisted of twenty-five companions and the king; the Prince of Wales* was first in rank.

Legend related that at a feast at Calais in August 1347 to celebrate the recent capture of that town, King Edward danced with the young countess of Salisbury, Joan of Kent. As they danced one of her garters fell to the floor, and as she blushed at this mishap, the king picked it up and buckled it below his own knee. His reaction to the whispered astonishments of the bystanders was his rebuke which became the motto "*Honi soit qui mal y pense*" and his declaration that soon the garter would be held in highest esteem. (Bibliog. 87, 253)

Order of the Golden Fleece, one of the "orders of chivalry and knighthood."* Founded by Philip the Good of Burgundy on the occasion of his marriage to Isabella of Portugal in 1430, this order was modeled closely on the Order of the Garter* and had a similar number of knights (twenty-four excluding the duke*). Its goals were to do reverence to God, uphold the Christian faith, and to honor and increase the noble order of chivalry.* The fleece was chosen, a later legend explained, because Philip admired the golden hair of a lady at Bruges. (Bibliog. 17)

Order of the Golden Shield. See orders of chivalry and knighthood.

Order of the Passion of Jesus Christ, chivalric order founded by King Richard II of England and Charles VI of France in 1380 for the recovery of the Holy Land. It was to have consisted of 1,000 knights, each attended by a squire* and three men-at-arms; its officers were to be a grand justiciary (see justiciar) and a grand bailiff,* but it survived only briefly. See orders of chivalry and knighthood. (Bibliog. 253)

Order of the Porcupine. See orders of chivalry and knighthood.

Order of the Round Table. See Order of the Garter.

Order of the Star, French chivalric counterpart to the Order of the Garter.* Created in 1351–1352, it was much larger than the Garter; its original 200 knights proposed in 1344 had increased to 500 by 1352, and the Blessed Virgin had ejected St. George to become the order's sole protector. Its emblem* was a star bearing the motto* "*Monstrant regibus astra viam*" (L. "Stars show the way to kings"). Although its goals were the furtherance of chivalry* and increase of honor, it added a military purpose in 1352 when it decided to work for the unity and accord of the knights of the realm and to stimulate them to ensure its security and peace. It was virtually eliminated at the battle of Poitiers* only four years after its being founded, however, when the French were badly defeated by the Englsih and their king,* John the Good, was captured. (Bibliog. 17)

Order of the Sword, military order founded in 1200 by the Bishop of Riga to convert the people of Livonia (Southern Estonia and northern Lithuania); it was absorbed by the Teutonic Knights* in 1237. See orders of chivalry and knighthood. (Bibliog. 253)

Order, Teutonic. See Teutonic Knights.

orders of chivalry and knighthood, military orders of knights in monastic-type organizations who fought against Islam first in the Holy Land and then in Spain. The most famous of these in the Holy Land were the Knights of the Hospital of St. John or the Hospitallers,* the Knights Templar,* the Teutonic Knights,* and in Spain, the Alcantara,* Calatrava,* and the Order of Santiago.* The term later was applied to the 14th-century chivalric secular associations founded to imitate the social mores of the higher nobility* and the chivalric ideals of that later period. The most famous of these were the Order of the Garter* (English), Ordre de l'Étoile (French; see Order of the Star), Ordre de l'Escu d'Or (Golden Shield) of Bourbon, Ordre de le Porc-Epic (Porcupine) of Orleans, Ordre d'Hermine (Ermine) of Brittany, Order of the Golden Fleece* of Burgundy, and Order of St. Michael (French). (Bibliog. 17)

ordinaries, basic geometric charges* used in blazon*: bend,* chevron,* chief,* fess,* pale,* pile,* and saltire.* See heraldry.

ordines (L.), prayers and wordings used in the ceremony of investiture of a king and recorded to serve as precedents for future use. See coronation. (Bibliog. 308)

ordo (L), coronation* ritual. See anointing.

Ordre de l'Étoile. See Order of the Star.

oriel, small room serving as a secluded area for the lord and his family. Projecting off the upper end of the hall* and accessible from the great chamber, it might have been only the landing at the top of an external set of stairs built over a small room above the ground floor. In time it expanded into a great upper-floor bay window and sometimes had a fireplace. (Bibliog. 128)

oriflamme of France, fork-tongued military banner* of the French army derived from a banner belonging to the abbey of St. Denis* near Paris. Made of crimson silk with green fringe and tassels and charged (see charge) with a saltire* wavy, it had rays or golden flames issuing from the center crossways from which the name auriflamme was said to have been derived. Preserved at the treasury of St. Denis, it was taken from the altar of the king* himself in time of war and flown beside the king's standard* at Crecy in 1346 and again at Poitiers* in 1356. It was unfurled only at moments of dire necessity and when no quarter was to be given, when the fight was to the death. Legend credited this banner as being a gift of St. Peter to Charlemagne. Originally it was named *Romaine*, but on the battlefield of the fight between Charlemagne and the pagan Baligant in retaliation for the debacle at Rancevaux,* its name was changed to *Mont-joie* (Montjoy). See *Mont-joie Saint Denis*. (Bibliog. 40, 181)

oristes, black or green incombustible stone which served as protection against the bite of animals and against fear. It also made men sterile and caused women to abort. (Bibliog. 258)

orle, 1. band worn around the basinet* by knights to fill up the space between the interior of the heaume* and the headpiece and to deaden the shock when the heaume was struck in an encounter; 2. charge* in blazon* which was like a bordure* but did not reach the edge of the shield.* (Bibliog. 9, 43)

ornest, earlier name than "wager of battle"* for judicial combat (see duel), this was not practiced in England before the Conquest. It originated in the Scandinavian kingdoms where it was practiced under the name of *holmgang,** from the custom of fighting duels on a small island or *holm*. (Bibliog. 229)

ounce, 1. leopard* in heraldry*; 2. unit of weight in apothecary,* avoirdupois,* mercantile, tower, English troy, and Scots troy systems. In the apothecary system it equalled 24 scruples,* 8 drams or 4,880 troy grains* and was equal to one-twelfth apothecary pound* of 5,760 grains; in avoirdupois it equalled 437.5 grains or one-sixteenth pound of 7,000 grains. In mercantile and tower systems it equalled 450 grains or one-fifteenth of mercantile pound of 6,750 grains but one-twelfth of tower pound of 5,400 grains. A Scots troy ounce equalled 475.5 grains or one-sixteenth Scots troy pound of 7,609 grains; an English troy ounce equalled 480 grains or one-twelfth troy pound of 5,760 grains. (Bibliog. 43, 394)

outfangentheof, lord's right to pursue a thief outside his own jurisdiction, to bring him back to his own court* for trial, and to keep his forfeited chattels on conviction. See infangentheof. (Bibliog. 24)

outlaw, outlawry, putting an individual outside the protection of the law of the land by a legal decision of the king* or his courts.* By that sentence a man was denied henceforth his ancient inherited privileges at law which were every man's birthright. He who had broken the law was deemed to have gone to war with the community, so the community went to war with him. It was the right and duty of every man to pursue him, to ravage his land, to burn his house, to hunt him down like a wild beast, and to slay him. He thus became an outcast from society, having no more rights than a hunted beast. In fact, the judgment of the court against him contained the words *caput gerat lupinum,* ("with the head of a wolf"). The price on his head originally was the same as that upon a wolf, whence the phrase for an outlaw, "he had a wolf's head." Another phrase for an outlaw was that he was civilly dead (L. *civiliter mortuus**), and thus he could be killed with impunity. As "wolves' heads," outlaws under Richard I* carried a bounty of five shillings (see money) on their heads, paid by royal writ to sergeants.* This attitude softened with time, however, and by the 13th century the outlaw in Bracton's day forfeited his chattels and his rights to law, and his revenues were taken for the time being into the crown's hands. But he did not lose all his claim to his inheritance, nor was the man who killed him free of the charge of homicide as in earlier times. Nevertheless, he remained an outcast, a man with no defense except by force against those who trespassed against his goods or his person. His only hope of survival was by his own skill in eluding the authorities; his only hope of restoration lay in suing for pardon from the same man who had condemned him. He was a fugitive whom his fellows aided at their own peril. He was a man who had to live solely by his own wits. Outlawry was the law's ultimate weapon, for if an outlaw was captured and brought before justices, he could be sent to the gallows as soon as the mere fact of his outlawry was proved.

An exigent* could demand at four successive county* courts that the person accused appear and surrender to justice.* If the accused still absented himself after the fourth exaction,* he was outlawed unless one or two men pledged themselves to secure his appearance at a fifth county court. If he still did not appear after being called loudly three times well spaced to appear, his outlawry would be delayed no longer, and his sureties could look forward to being amerced (see amercement) at the next eyre.* When the sheriff* returned the writ of exigent and certified the outlawry, the court issued a writ of *capias utlagatum,** whereupon one of three things would occur: (1) the outlaw would flee or would be arrested; or (2) if outlawed for civil offenses and trespasses, he would surrender, buy his pardon or work it off by serving a term in the king's service, and thereby clear the books both of the outlawry and the original felony,* or (3) stay in the community to continue his prefelony existence. Women and children under twelve could not be outlawed because technically they were not under the law, never having sworn to it and not being in frankpledge* tithing.* Women, however, could be exacted and waived,* which amounted to outlawry, and could elect abjuration of the realm,* but children could not. (Bibliog. 171, 182, 261)

Outremer, collective name given to the four crusading states of Antioch, Edessa, Jerusalem, and Tripoli established in the Holy Land by the European leaders after the first crusade. See crusades. (Bibliog. 310a)

over the barriers, joust* across a barrier five feet* high which separated the riders who charged on each side of it and directed their lances* over it. Its original idea was to unhorse the opponent, but because the saddle* used was the war saddle built to prevent the rider from being unhorsed, unhorsing became rare and splintering lances became the test of endurance and dexterity. Tipped with a coronal,* the lance was held to the left of the horse's head at a thirty-degree angle from the path of the horse,* and the course was run with the left side next to the barrier. When splintering lances was the chief object, the bourdonasse* was used. (Bibliog. 9)

overbowed, power of an archer's bow* greater than his ability or strength to command it. (Bibliog. 100)

oxgang, as much land as an ox could plow in a year. As a plow team contained eight oxen, and the land they could plow in a year was a carucate* or 100 to 120 acres,* so an oxgang was calculated roughly at one-eighth of a carucate, or twelve to fifteen acres. Like acreage of other measures, the total acreage depended upon local soil conditions, but oxgangs of seven, eight, ten, twelve, thirteen, fifteen, sixteen, twenty, thirty, and even fifty acres were common. See bovate. (Bibliog. 363)

Oxydracca, fabled land of the East, filled with marvels. See Prester John.

oyer and determiner, commission of, commission issued to royal judges, sergeants,* and others empowering them to hear and determine treasons, felonies,* and misdemeanors at the assizes* or on special occasions. The term literally meant "to hear and determine." (Bibliog. 246)

oylets, oiletts, round holes at the ends of arrow* slits in towers. (Bibliog. 9)

P

pace, measure of length equal to two steps or approximately five feet.* (Bibliog. 246)

pack, measure of capacity and quantity for a variety of items: cloth—10 pieces; flax—240 pounds*; teasels—9,000 heads; wool—240 pounds. (Bibliog. 394)

pagus, administrative subdivision of the Carolingian kingdom placed beneath a *comite* or count.*

pair of arrows, in archery, three arrows,* because of the liability of any one of them to break. (Bibliog. 100)

pair of plates. See hauberk of plates.

paladin, in the modern forms of the Charlemagne romances, one of the douzepeers* of Charlemagne's court (see Roland, Oliver), and by extension, one of the Arthurian Knights of the Round Table; a medieval champion; a knight errant. (Bibliog. 246)

palatinate, territory under the rule or jurisdiction of a palatine.* This was an independent principality of the continental type within which the "king's writ"* did not apply. England had three politically unsettled areas where the king* could expect to benefit from granting unusual powers to a local figurehead in the interest of keeping the peace and in meeting the needs of defense—Durham, Chester, and Lancaster, two of them bordering on Scotland and Wales. Even though their judicial systems copied common law and they were bound by acts of the English Parliament,* their distinguishing traits lay in the exercise of local sovereignty as a kind of limited royalty. As English law had no word to describe their great franchises,* it adopted the foreign word *palatinate* from the word palace to imply royal powers of jurisdiction similar to those in areas on the Rhine and in Champagne. Those who had counties* palatinate had king-like power and authority; they could pardon treason, murders, felonies,* and outlawries*; they could appoint justices of eyre* and of assize*; and could issue writs and indictments of treason and felony in their own name as having the county palatinate, and not the king's. As it began in the 13th century, in Durham the power was in the hands of the bishop, in Chester of the earl,* and in Lancaster of the duke.* (Bibliog. 156, 163)

palatine, officer of the imperial or royal palace—the chamberlain,* mayor of the palace, chief minister of the empire*—but in time it changed to mean a lord having sovereign power over a province or dependency of the empire. In England he was the lord of a palatinate.* (Bibliog. 246)

pale, ordinary* in blazon* consisting of a broad vertical band drawn down the center of the shield.* It was considered as one of the honorable ordinaries and could occupy as much as one-third of the field.* Arms* ascribed to Hugh de Grandmesnil, lord high steward* of England under King Henry I (1100–1135), were blazoned "gules,* a pale or.*" (Bibliog. 43)

palette, roundel, plate disks used to protect the armpits and elbow bends. See roundel. (Bibliog. 9)

palfrey, horse* used by a knight for ordinary occasions but not in war or tournaments.* See destrier.

palisade, timber fence or wall embedded along the outer edges of a bailey.* See castle. (Bibliog. 280)

palm, measure of length. Originally a unit of body measurement referring to a hand's breadth equal to one-third of a span or one-sixth of a cubit*; based on a foot of twelve inches,* it equalled three inches. (Bibliog. 394)

palmer's staff, pilgrim's staff, long stick used by a traveler to identify himself as a pilgrim. It ended in a knob which usually had a hook at the top from which a script, purse, or wallet could be hung. (Bibliog. 43)

panache, plume or bunch of feathers, usually ostrich feathers, worn on the heaume* or helmet.* (Bibliog. 43)

pannage, payment made to the lord for the privilege of pasturing beasts in the lord's woods about the village. See Assize of the Forest. (Bibliog. 24)

panther, gentle beast loved by all except the dragon.* It slept for three days after eating and awakened itself by crying out. Then a sweet odor spread out, drawing all the animals in the area except the dragon, which fled in fear to its underground lair. (Bibliog. 258)

Papal States, political authority exerted by the papacy based on the Donation of Pepin, A.D. 754, by which the king* of the Franks promised to the pope lands formerly belonging to Byzantium but conquered from the Lombards in central Italy. This area was enlarged by acquiring Benevento in 1052 and was strengthened and enlarged by Innocent III (d. 1216) to include Ravenna, Romagna, Spoleto, and much of Tuscany. (Bibliog. 185)

parados, low wall of fortification placed on the inner side of a wider wall. (Bibliog. 280)

parapet, second wall of a fortification placed on the outer side of a wider one and made low enough for a warrior to shoot over but high enough to protect him from answering fire while he reloaded his weapon. (Bibliog. 280)

parfit, perfect, "horn call in hunting"* blown to indicate that the hounds were on the line of the right stag. (Bibliog. 96)

parfitiers, perfecters, last relay* of "hounds for the hunt"* uncoupled (see couple) during the chase* of the stag. First came the vaunt chase, then the midel, and finally these parfitiers that completed or perfected the pack. Generally these were the slowest and staunchest hounds used when the stag rused and foiled (see ruses) as it neared the end of its strength and sought by every means to elude its pursuers. (Bibliog. 96)

Paris, Matthew, England's greatest medieval historian (d. 1259). He became a monk of St. Albans in 1212 and succeeded Roger Wendover as historian there after 1236. He used such primary sources as papal bulls* and royal documents. (Bibliog. 141)

parisis, French coins of the Paris standard fixed under Philip* Augustus (Philip II) at one-fourth above that of Tours. See coinage. (Bibliog. 150)

Parlement. See Parliament.

Parliament, representative assemblies from the 13th century onward. The word meant a colloquy rather than a body of persons. Slowly it came to refer to colloquies which the king* had with the estates of his realm and then to the body of men he summoned. Originally these groups were the king's council made up of those among his great "offices of state"* and the judges, and they heard important cases and answered petitions. In England during the reign of Edward I (1308–1307), it grew beyond the prelates and barons* to include knights of the shires* and boroughs* who had been summoned by the sheriff.* No rules existed to determine who was to be summoned, how they would be summoned, how long they would meet, or what they would discuss; its main role was to deal with royal demands for taxes, and the king alone determined who, when, and under what circumstances he wished to consult with such a group. In the 14th century it divided into two separate assemblies: the House of Lords,* made up of the prelates and barons, and the House of Commoners, made up of knights of the shires and boroughs. The king presided over the House of Lords, and the Commoners were allowed to elect a chairman who would serve as their speaker before the king and his council.

The French Parlement, however, was an organ of royal authority, emerging out of the feudal high court of justice where during the reign of King Louis IX (St. Louis; 1214–1270), professional lawyers introduced legal procedures to replace judgment by equity. In time the king and his nobility* left the court because it had become too specialized and professional, and they let their interests be handled by proctors. Its judgments and sentences were recorded in a special collection, the *olim.** (Bibliog. 147, 156, 267)

Parliamentary Roll of Arms, roll listing armorial bearings, (see charge) of knights around the time of the death of King Edward I (1307) of England and for several years afterward. See herald. (Bibliog. 87)

partisan, staff weapon of the pole type with a two-edged straight blade introduced during the reign of Edward III (1327–1377); it had two small upturned projections at the base of its blade. It also was known in England as the langedebeuve and in France as the *langue-de-boeuf.* (Bibliog. 9)

partition, lines of, lines used to divide a shield* or charges* in blazon.* When a shield was so divided, the word "per" preceded the name of the ordinary* whose direction the line followed, as in "party* per fess*" meaning partitioned through the center or "party per pale*" meaning partitioned vertically. These lines were capable of a number of variations: engrailed,* embattled,* invected,* and so forth. (Bibliog. 43)

party, blazoning term meaning "partitioned by." See blazon; partition, lines of.

pas d'armes, chief event of a tourney* or tournament.* (Bibliog. 78)

pas de Saladin, tournament* involving spear* play said to represent the half-legendary exploits of English King Richard I* (1189–1199) against the Muslim leader Saladin.* (Bibliog. 78)

passage hawk, bird caught on migration in immature plumage. (Bibliog. 96)

passage of arms, combat between several knights on each side, some on horseback and some on foot, using harmless weapons, or if using lethal weapons,

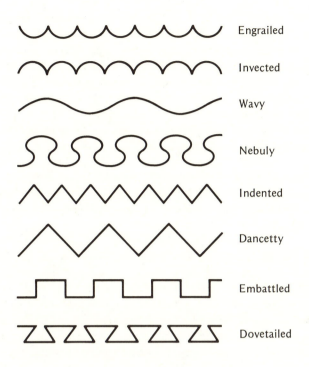

Engrailed

Invected

Wavy

Nebuly

Indented

Dancetty

Embattled

Dovetailed

Figure 9. Lines Used to Form Divisions

wielding them in such a way as to cause minimum injury. Such swords* might be made of whalebone or wood and would be blunted; if actual swords were used, no thrusting or stabbing was allowed. (Bibliog. 9, 71)

passant, heraldic description of a beast walking with dexter* forepaw raised. See beasts, positions of. (Bibliog. 43)

passus, tournament* exercise simulating attacks on temporarily erected fortresses, or at bridges or defiles to reenact incidents from the crusaders' sieges, or in imitation of incidents that occurred on open ground or at other places similar to the locations of early tournaments. It was from these exercises that the combats at the barriers of later times were derived. (Bibliog. 78)

pater sancte (L. "holy father"), secret password between King Edward III and Pope John XXII in 1330. Secret envoys sent by Edward III to the pope in September 1329 returned with a verbal message that the pope wanted a private sign to identify the genuine thoughts and wishes of the king,* especially at the dangerous time that Edward was trying to rid himself of the control of his mother,

Queen Isabelle, and her lover, Roger Mortimer.* After the queen and Roger had ordered the execution* of the earl* of Kent in March of that year for complicity, the young king realized that he would have to be extremely cautious and wary. Thus he sent to the pope a message saying that all requests he wished to have granted would bear the words *pater sancte* in the king's own hand. (Bibliog. 20, 104)

paunce, armor* for the body, probably the taces*; the word derived from the French *panse*, meaning abdomen. (Bibliog. 9)

pauncenars, men selected for their bodily vigor who were capable of marching on foot in full armor.* They were held in reserve by Edward III at the battle of Calais in 1347 for such difficult enterprises as storming castles* and fortresses. (Bibliog. 104)

pavage, dues collected by the borough* bailiff.* (Bibliog. 163)

pavilion, 1. large square or round tent with a peaked or rounded top and made of rich cloth with curtains of wide stripes usually of bright red, blue, green, or gold. Frequently heraldic bearings (see charge) were woven into the tent's fabric. Its center pole extending through the roof frequently was highly ornamented and displayed the lord's banner.* 2. gold coinage* issued by Philip* VI of France (1328–1350) depicting on its obverse a king* seated under a canopy and imitated by Edward the Black Prince for his possessions in France. (Bibliog. 150, 247)

pavise, large shield* used as protection by archers and arbalestiers* in the field, especially during "siege warfare."* Nearly the height of a man, this platform of wooden planks strengthened with leather was propped upright by a wooden pole. See mantlet. (Bibliog. 9)

pavon, single pointed pennon* with a straight bottom side rather than tapered, displaying the personal badge* or shield* device of a "knight bachelor."* (Bibliog. 251)

pax Dei (L. "Peace of God"), attempts by the church to enforce peace. Emerging from the *pax ecclesiae*, a peace which a person forfeited upon the commission of a sin but which was restored to him upon penance, this movement began at the end of the 10th century when three Synods announced it in the sense of general protection, particularly of church property. Subsequent efforts sought to safeguard people like rustics, women, merchants, clerks, and to sanctify special occasions like going to church. Its basic sanction was the oath,* and so the man who violated the truce not only violated his oath but also became a self-confessed liar. Later Emperor Frederick Barbarossa between 1152 and 1157 promulgated a Peace-of-God edict in an effort to exclude from warfare the persons and lands of churchmen and the poor and to maintain peace between fractious knights in his realm. Among its provisions, this document provided that anyone killing another should lose his own life unless he could prove in a judicial duel* that he had killed his victim in self-defense; that anyone wounding another should have his hand amputated unless he could prove self-defense; and that anyone who beat another with rods without shedding blood, or pulled out his hair or beard, should pay a fine* of ten pounds (see money) to the injured party and thirty pounds to the judge. See Truce of God. (Bibliog. 135, 151)

pean, heraldic charge* of black fur strewn with gold ermine* spots. (Bibliog. 43)

peasant. See villein.

Peasants' Revolt, armed uprising of the English serfs* in 1381. After the Black Death* swept across Europe several times killing millions, the resultant shortage of labor forced wages to rise. In an effort to force them down to their pre-plague level, the English Parliament* in 1351 enacted the Statute of Laborers.* It succeeded to a point, but after thirty years of smoldering resentment for this gross economic injustice, the peasants (see villein) rose in an attempt to force change. Although the peasants were defeated, their working conditions never returned to the pre-plague level, and the lower classes began to have a voice in their own destinies. (Bibliog. 154)

pectoral, square or oblong piece of stiff material worn on the chest in addition to the hauberk* to serve as a reinforcement for the neck and chest. (Bibliog. 9)

pecuels. See bed.

peer, term almost synonymous with baron* but carrying a more exact legal significance. One of a vassal's* most cherished privileges was being tried in his lord's court* by his lord's other vassals. Such a common tie of vassalage made for equality because equal decided the fate of equal and peer tried peer. Yet not all vassals were the equals of all others: a "banneret knight"* was not to be judged by a mere knight. Thus the leading vassals reserved the right to sit in judgment on cases involving their equals in rank, as well as to offer advice on other serious issues. Such a circle of the highest peers was restricted to a small number that became traditional, like the twelve apostles or Charlemagne's *douze-peers.** Writers used other terms like magnate or poestatz to refer to these highest of the aristocracy* who dominated the mass of knights from great heights.

By the 13th century the English aristocracy had built an instrument of government called Parliament* out of the "feudal obligations"* of court service. There the term baron was used to describe the principal feudatories of the king* who, by virtue of a monopoly that gradually became an established hereditary right, were summoned to his great council called Parliament. This closely knit group finally was allowed officially to call themselves the Peers of the Realm.

These men were the members of the various degrees of nobility* in England. The first duke* was Edward the Black Prince, son of Edward III. Earl* from the first was a dignified official, and the title always denoted a name of dignity. Marquis (or marquess*) and viscount* were foreign words introduced at a later period. Baron was not an official title but was used only to designate the tenure* by which certain estates rated as baronies were held. Up to the middle of the 14th century, barons were summoned to Parliament capriciously and not until John de Beauchamp was created Baron Kidderminster in 1387 by "letters patent"* was barony* regarded as a dignity. With the abolition of military service as a requirement for tenure of a barony, the term baron became a title of dignity simply as a matter of course, and the baron ranked as a peer.

In France the terms vavasour* and baron diverged widely due to simple differences in wealth and prestige. To make the distinction clearer, lawyers devised a criterion based on gradation of feudal authority: high justice* for barons and low or middle justice for the fief* of a vavasour. France had few peers. As epic legend favored the number twelve, six of the most important vassals of the Capetian monarchy and six of the most powerful bishops and archbishops of churches directly dependent on the crown obtained for themselves the exclusive right to the title of peer; but because their numbers were so small, they gained little practical advantage from it. Three of these original six vassals became extinct within the first century, and their fiefs reverted to the crown. Thus after 1297 the French king began creating new peers in their own account, thereby controlling the formation of the French nobility from top to bottom. See titles of dignity. (Bibliog. 28, 156)

peeter, pietre, gold coinage* minted in Louvain, Brabant, in the 14th century with an effigy of St. Peter on it; it was imitated by the bishop of Liege during 1364–1378. (Bibliog. 150)

Pegasus, winged horse* from Greek mythology used as a charge* in English heraldry.* (Bibliog. 43)

Peggin, Elias, exemplary figure used by Bracton as a practical illustration of English law. In the early 13th century, Peggin swore to the validity of a warrant concerning a stolen horse* but was challenged as being a hired champion paid to undertake the testimony. During the inquiry, Elias admitted that in fact he was a teacher of swordsmanship. Taking his job into consideration, the jury found him guilty of fraud and sentenced him to lose a foot, telling him at the same time that he should consider himself lucky to get off so easily. (Bibliog. 229)

peine forte et dure (Fr. "pain strong and hard"), torture of men who refused trial by jury. In it the prisoner, dressed only in a thin shirt, sat on a cold bare floor and was pressed by as great a weight of iron as his wretched body could bear. His only food was rotten bread, and his drink was cloudy and stinking water. On the days when he ate he could not drink, nor eat when he drank. Only one of superhuman strength survived to the fifth or sixth day. If a notorious felon (see felony) confessed to a charge, he could be expected to be convicted and hanged (see execution), his lands would escheat* to his lord, and his goods and chattels would be forfeit to the crown. If he died under strong torture, however, he died untried and unconvicted, and thus his possessions would revert to his heirs. Such practice was carried out in England as late as 1322. See ordeal. (Bibliog. 103)

pel, post quintain.* A post six feet* high was embedded in the ground so firmly that it would not be moved by sword* strokes. A trainee for knighthood* would attack the pel with sword and shield* held as though he were attacking an adversary, aiming his blows as if at head, face, arms, legs, thighs, and sides, taking care at the same time to keep himself completely covered with his shield so as to give no advantage to any real enemy opposing him. (Bibliog. 334)

pele, head of an arrow* made of iron. (Bibliog. 100)

pencel, pencil. See banderolle; pennoncelle.

pendragon. See dragon.

penitentiary. See crusades.

pennon, guidon, small tapering flag attached to a lance*; it bore the arms* of the "knight bachelor"* who carried it; some triangular ones could not be converted into a banner* without mutilating the arms. See guidon; signs of war. (Bibliog. 87)

pennoncelle, pencel, pencil, tapering lance* flag shorter than a pennon.*

penny, silver coin introduced into England during the 8th century by two little-known Anglo-Saxon kings* of Kent, Heahbert and Ecgbehrt, and popularized about A.D. 783 by the powerful King Offa of Mercia. It gradually was reduced in size because of the rising price of silver and the need for a larger number of coins as trade and commerce grew. See coinage. (Bibliog. 150)

pennyweight, weight in both the troy and tower systems, originally the weight of a silver penny* equal to 1/240 of a pound of tower silver and in currency called either a denarius* or a sterling.* Troy pennyweight contained 24 grains* of barley and equalled 1/20 troy ounce of 480 grains; tower pennyweight contained 32 wheat grains or 22.5 troy grains and equalled 1/20 tower ounce of 450 grains from about A.D. 1200 onward. (Bibliog. 394)

pensarius, pesarius. See ponderator.

Pepin the Short, the Dwarf, *le Nain,* father of Charlemagne.

per loricam (L. ''by reason of mail''), in return for undertaking military duties, barons* held land by the sword* and the coat of mail.* (Bibliog. 262)

perch, land measure generally equal to 16.5 feet* or 5.5 yards* but varying to such lengths as 9, 10, 11, 11.5, 15, and even 26 feet. Perches of 16.5 feet and less generally were used as agricultural land measurements*; larger ones were used by woodsmen in forest regions and by town craftsmen engaged in draining, fencing, hedging, and walling operations. (Bibliog. 394)

peregozi, pierregordin, variety of denarius* used in Perigord in the late 13th century. (Bibliog. 150)

peregrine. See falconry birds.

perfect. See parfit; horn calls in hunting.

perfecters. See parfitiers.

perriere, *petraria,** trebuchet.*

perron, grand flight of external stairs leading to the entrance of the manor* of nobility* or high officials and itself considered as a mark of jurisdiction. Sometimes criminals were executed (see execution) at the foot of the steps, as at the Grand Steps of Venice. (Bibliog. 100)

Peter Bartholomew, ignorant peasant (see villein) follower of Raymond VI* in besieged Antioch in 1098 on the first crusade* who declared that in a series of visions, Jesus had revealed to him that the lance* which had pierced His side at the Crucifixion was buried in the church of St. Peter there in Antioch. After several men found nothing in the spot he indicated, Peter Bartholomew leapt into the trench and after two strokes of his pick unearthed the priceless relic* which he gave to Raymond. Revived by this priceless treasure, the hard-pressed crusaders turned back the besieging infidels and routed them with great slaughter. Possession of this lance so enhanced Raymond's importance that rivals jealously claimed that the relic was nothing more than a rusty Arabian spearhead especially hidden for Raymond's devious purpose. To silence that criticism, Peter agreed to vindicate the relic by the ''ordeal by fire''* after being allowed to fast and pray for three days. Dry olive branches were placed in a piles fourteen feet long and four feet wide with a one-foot-wide passage down the middle, and ignited. Clothed only in a tunic and bearing high the lance, Peter rushed through the flaming pile as 40,000 men eagerly watched. Accounts of that event differed considerably. Foes of Raymond claimed that Peter sustained mortal injury in the fire; supporters said that Peter emerged safely with only one or two slight burns, but the crowd enthusiastically pressing around him in triumph knocked him down, trampled him, and injured him so severely that he died in a few days, swearing with his dying breath the genuineness of the relic. It was subsequently lost. (Bibliog. 297a, 310a)

Peter Igneus. See ordeal by fire.

Peter the Hermit. See crusades.

Peter's pence, Peter-penny, annual tribute or tax of one penny* paid to the papal See of Rome by each household of England having land of a certain value. It was established before King Alfred's reign (849–899) and continued until 1534. (Bibliog. 246)

petit lévrier pour lièvre. See greyhound.

petraria **(L.), perriere,** any stone-throwing engine of "siege warfare"*: mangon,* trebuchet.* (Bibliog. 71)

petticoat, spoon, background of an archery target outside the color white. (Bibliog. 100)

petty assizes, assizes* comprised of ordinary freeman instead of knights. These formed the juries (see jury duty) for the Assize of Novel Disseisin,* "assize of *mort d'ancestor*,"* and Assize Utrum.* (Bibliog. 261)

peytral, projecting plate of steel to protect a horse's chest. See horse armor. (Bibliog. 9)

pfennig. See bracteate; coinage.

Philip, kings* of France: Philip I, 1060–1108; Philip II, Augustus, 1180–1223; Philip III, the Bold, 1270–1285; Philip IV, the Fair (*le Bel*), 1285–1314; Philip V, the Tall, 1316–1322; Philip VI, of Valois, 1328–1350.

phoenix, purple swan or eagle* of Arabia that lived for 500 years. When it sensed its approaching end, it gathered branches of fragrant bushes in a funeral pyre, lay on the pyre until the sun ignited it, and on the third day, emerged from its own ashes to begin life for another 500 years. When depicted in blazon,* it was shown as an eagle arising from flames. (Bibliog. 258)

phlebotomy. See bloodletting.

pick, military, weapon whose heavy metal head had a point at one end and the head of a hammer* at the other. Mail* was defenseless against the point, and the hammerhead would inflict wounds like a mace.* A pick with points at each end was called a bipennis. See also axe. (Bibliog. 9)

piece, measure of capacity, length, quantity, and weight. Of cheese it indicated uncertain weight; of fruit, four quarterns* or one-third of a sort; of lead, 126 pounds.* Most often it was used for cloth goods although the term frequently was replaced by cloth, chef, cheef, chiffe, sheet, caput, or the name of the fabric. Its length was measured by the yard* or ell* and its breadth by the quarteryard, but that varied with the quality of the fabric, its construction, its monetary value, and its place of manufacture. The standard was twenty-four yards long and seven quarters* broad. (Bibliog. 394)

Piepowder court, *piepoudreux* (Fr. "dusty-feet"), court* for summary jurisdiction licensed by the crown for offenses committed during a fair. In these courts the suitors were all of the same class and appeared informally in their travel-stained condition; a jury of merchants rendered the judgments or declared the law. For example, at the St. Ives Fair in 1300, six men had been appointed to watch in Cross Lane near the canvas booth on the night of Thursday before the feast of St. Dunstan; but they withdrew from their vigil so that the booth was robbed of the greater part of its canvas, and they were judged "in mercy"* for three shillings (see money) for the contempt. (Bibliog. 261)

pierregordin. See peregozi.

pietre. See peeter.

pike, shafted weapon with a variety of heads, but generally it referred to a long, small-headed, sharply-pointed spear* sixteen to twenty-two feet* in length used chiefly as defense against cavalry by disciplined bodies of infantry moving in unison. Usually the metal-head socket extended down the shaft for a considerable length as a guard against sword* or axe* cuts. (Bibliog. 27, 71)

pile, 1. ordinary* consisting of a triangular wedge issuing from the top of a shield*; it was supposed to represent the stake used in the construction of a military bridge but may have derived from the construction of the shield itself. 2. head of an arrow.* (Bibliog. 9, 43)

pilgrim's staff. See palmer's staff.

Pinabel, Ganelon's* champion in the trial by combat (see duel) at Aix-la-Chapelle* fighting against Thierry, the king's* champion, to determine Ganelon's guilt or innocence of treason (See *Song of Roland*). (Bibliog. 40)

pincerna (L.), butler.*

pinfold, place for confining stray or impounded cattle, horses* and other animals; a pound. (Bibliog. 24)

pint, measure of capacity for dry materials equal to one-eighth gallon* and for liquids equal to four gills or one-half quart or one-fourth pottle.* A Scot's pint equalled a jug or a stoup* or two choppins* or four mutchkins*. (Bibliog. 394)

pipe, measure of capacity for dry and liquid materials, generally synonymous with butt.* For cider it equalled 120 gallons*; for salmon, 84 gallons; for wine,* oil, honey, 126 gallons or one-half tun*; for peas, 12 bushels*; for salt, 16 bushels. (Bibliog. 394)

Pipe Rolls, Rolls of the Exchequer, records which began in 1131 in the reign of Henry I and were kept in a scattered fashion, but beginning in the second year (1155–1156) of Henry II's reign they provided an almost unbroken sequence of annual expenditures. Compiled annually, two copies of these rolls kept by the Exchequer,* the financial office of the king's government, contained the annual accounts of the sheriffs* and certain other royal officials, and detailed most of the king's receipts and expenditures. They were called pipe rolls because the parchment or sheepskin on which they were kept was rolled up to resemble a pipe. (Bibliog. 48)

pitch, height to which a hawk rose in the air when she was "waiting on"* her prey. (Bibliog. 26)

pittancer, officer of a religious house who distributed charitable gifts or allowances of food. (Bibliog. 24)

pizaine, stiff mail* collar made by thickening rings of a hauberk's* collar so that they became semi-rigid. (Bibliog. 27)

pizane. See pysan.

placitum (L. "pleasing or agreeable"), general council or assembly held for consultation upon affairs of state and presided over by the king.* (Bibliog. 246) *plançon-à-picot* (Fr.), long wooden club having at the top an iron ferrule, often with a projecting flange and a vertical spike; used in Flanders from the late 13th century. (Bibliog. 27, 71)

planta genesta, broom plant growing in profusion in Anjou and chosen by Geoffrey of Anjou, father of King Henry II of England, as his badge*; a sprig of it showing leaves and open pods was chosen as the badge of the royal house of Plantagenet.* (Bibliog. 235)

Plantagenet, English royal dynasty begun when Count Geoffrey of Anjou married Mathilda, daughter of King Henry I, in 1128. It reigned continuously from the accession of Henry II to the throne in 1154, through the reigns of Richard I*, John, Henry III, Edward I, Edward II, and Edward III, until the deposition and murder of Richard II in 1399; it was continued by the two collateral branches of the houses of Lancaster and York who fought each other continuously for the throne in the War of the Roses, 1399–1485, and it ended with the battle of Bosworth Field in 1485. (Bibliog. 185, 235)

plastron de fer, flat plates of iron suspended from the shoulders by straps and worn under the surcoat* to protect the front and back of the body. Often the great heaume* was fastened by a chain to a staple in the front of these plates. (Bibliog. 9)

plates. See hauberk of plates.

plinth, splayed-out base on which rectangular stone keeps* were built in the 11th and 12th centuries to increase the strength of the keeps. These projections made more difficult the work of attacking miners and borers to undermine the wall. (Bibliog. 45, 70)

plommee, short-shafted club. See holy water sprinkler.

plover. See caladrius.

plume, bunch of five ostrich feathers. See panache.

pluteus. See sow.

poestatz. See peer.

point, making her, hawk rising perpendicularly in the air over the place where she has "put in,"* that is, traced her quarry.* (Bibliog. 26, 118)

points of the shield, areas of a shield* named to help with the blazon*: honor,* fess,* nombril.*

Poitiers, Battle of. See Battle of Poitiers.

poke, large sack or bag whose size varied with the quality and weight of the product it enclosed; it became a measure of capacity for a variety of products, but generally was used to ship raw wool. (Bibliog. 394)

polder-mitten, brace fastened to the vambrace* of the right arm as added support for the lance,* used in jousts.* (Bibliog. 9)

pole hammer. See martel-de-fer.

poleaxe, long-handled axe* used by the English footsoldiers at the battles of Stamford Bridge* (1066) and Hastings (1066) with fearful effect; few could survive its blow. It resembled a long-handled hatchet with a curved, single-edged blade. (Bibliog. 9, 71)

poleyns, small plates attached to the knees of the chausses* or to the gamboised cuisses,* but after 1270 they grew larger and hemispherical to cover the front and sides of the knees completely. (Bibliog. 27, 251)

pollards. See money, bad.

pomeled, spotted, like the young roe-buck at birth with its reddish-brown coat dotted with white spots; it also referred in a pejorative sense to a flea-bitten or dappled old horse.* (Bibliog. 96)

pomme, cross* whose limbs ended in roundels* or balls. (Bibliog. 251)

pommel, horn of a saddle.*

ponderator, pensarius, pesarius, locally appointed weigher of agricultural and non-agricultural goods in a village market or in a town weighing station. (Bibliog. 394)

pone, writ whereby an action could be moved from the county* court* to the royal court at Westminster. (Bibliog. 171)

poniard, small dagger similar to the misericorde* but with a sharper blade, worn by both civilian men and ladies. (Bibliog. 71)

Poor Knights of Christ, name used by the Templars* to refer to themselves. (Bibliog. 17)

popinjay, wooden bird used as an archery mark of target, particularly in Scotland. (Bibliog. 100)

port. See borough.

portcullis, 1. heavy wooden or metal grating or screen housed in a castle* room immediately above the entrance passage and dropped vertically in grooves in the wall to block a passageway or gateway; 2. one of England's "pursuivant of arms."* (Bibliog. 45, 116)

portesse, portuary. See breviary.

postern, sally port, small gateway in the enceinte* of a castle,* abbey, town, or other enclosed area from which a person could enter and leave unobserved. (Bibliog. 329)

potcarrier. See botdragers.

pot–de–fer, small metal skull cap worn under coif* of mail.* See armor.

potent, cross* whose four limb endings each form a T. (Bibliog. 251)

potin, base metal of lead, copper, tin, zinc, and silver from which some ancient coinage* of Rome, Greece, and early Gaul were made. (Bibliog. 324)

pottle, measure of capacity containing two quarts used primarily for liquids. (Bibliog. 394)

poulaine, long-toed solleret* or shoe; in the late 15th century it attained a length of twenty-four to twenty-six inches.* (Bibliog. 9)

pound, measure of weight in various systems: in the apothecary* system it equalled 5,760 grains* or 288 scruples* of 20 grains each, or 12 troy ounces* of 480 grains each; in the avoirdupois* system it equalled 7,000 grains or 256 drams of 27.344 grains each or 16 ounces of 437.5 grains each; in the mercantile system it equalled 6,750 troy grains or 15 mercantile ounces of 450 troy grains and equalled 1.25 tower pound of 5,400 troy grains; a tower pound, the Saxon or moneyer's pound, equalled 5,400 troy grains or 12 tower ounces of 450 troy grains each and generally was used for English money* and spices until 1527 when Henry VIII declared it illegal and replaced it with the troy pound; English troy pound equalled 5,760 troy grains or 240 pennyweight* of 24 troy grains each and was used in England for gold, silver, electuaries,* and precious stones; the "London pound"* equalled 12 ounces. (Bibliog. 394)

pourpointerie, body defense made up of thickly quilted material sometimes studded with metal defenses. English footsoldiers in the time of Richard I,* late 12th century, wore a coat of mail* over a garment of many folds of linen called pourpoint, thus providing a protection that was extremely difficult to penetrate. (Bibliog. 9)

praecipe. See writ of praecipe.

precariae (L.), boon-work.*

precedence, act or state of going or being before in rank or dignity, that is, of superior order. The ancient order of precedence of the sovereigns of Europe was as follows:

1. Holy Roman Emperor*
2. king* of Rome
3. king of France
4. king of Spain
5. king of Aragon
6. king of Portugal
7. king of England
8. king of Sicily
9. king of Scotland
10. king of Hungary
11. king of Navarre
12. king of Cyprus
13. king of Bohemia
14. king of Poland
15. king of the Danes
16. doge (see duke) of Venice

The order of precedence for England was as follows:

sovereign

his children

his grandchildren

his consort

his uncles

his nephews

archbishop of Canterbury

lord high chancellor* (if a baron*)

archbishop of York

lord treasurer* (baron)

lord president of the Council

lord privy seal

lord chamberlain*

lord constable*

lord marshal*

lord admiral

lord steward*

lord chamberlain of household

dukes*

marquesses*

dukes' eldest sons

earls*

marquesses' eldest sons

dukes' younger sons

viscounts*

earls' eldest sons

marquesses' younger sons

secretary of state (if a bishop)

bishop of London

bishop of Durham

bishop of Winchester

bishops

secretary of state (if a baron)

barons

speaker of House of Commons (see Parliament)

viscounts' eldest sons

earls' younger sons

barons' eldest sons

knights of the Order of the Garter*

privy councillors

chancellor of the Exchequer

chancellor of the duchy* of Lancaster

lord chief justice of England

master of the rolls

knights banneret* royal

viscounts' younger sons

barons' younger sons

baronets*

knights banneret

knights of the Bath*

attorney general

solicitor general

sovereign's attorney general

sergeants* at law

knights bachelor*

country* court* judges

baronets' eldest sons

knights' eldest sons

baronets' younger sons

knights' younger sons

colonels

doctors and barristers

esquires*

gentlemen*.

(Bibliog. 294, 363)

Prester John, supposed ruler of India who in 1165 sent a letter to the Byzantine emperor,* Manuel Comnenos, who in turn forwarded it to the Roman emperor, Frederick Barbarossa.* This letter described John as a Christian sovereign of a land in the east and in patronizing and condescending tones described the power, wealth, vastness, and diversity of his empire* with its botanical, zoological, and anthropological marvels. For example, in the seas off its shores lay great rocks of adamant stones which drew iron to them so that if ships with outer bonds or nails of iron should try to pass them, the adamants (or magnets) drew them so that they may not pass. As no wheat or barley grew there, the people ate only rice and honey, milk and cheese, and fruit. Prester John's empire contained seventy-two provinces, each ruled by a king,* all tributary to him. Whenever he went into battle, three great high crosses* of gold filled with precious stones were borne before him like banners,* with 10,000 men-at-arms and 100,000 men on foot assigned to keep each cross safe. And it would take four months to cross his lands, so extensive were they. (Bibliog. 19, 104)

preudhomme (L. *probus homo*: "worthy man"), man of prowess. To call a man preudhomme was to pay him the highest compliment, for prowess enabled a knight to fulfill his function in society without which he was an object of scorn to his contemporaries. "Be *preux*" was a usual admonition given to a young man as he was dubbed knight. See knighthood. (Bibliog. 248)

prevot, 12th-century French official entrusted with administering estates belonging to the "royal demesne"*; by extension the term came to refer to royal agents administering a district. (Bibliog. 139)

Pridwen, "Blessed form," the name of King Arthur's shield.* (Bibliog. 311)

prime, first "canonical hour"* of daylight, usually around 6 A.M. or break of day. (Bibliog. 161)

primogeniture, rule of inheritance which gave the whole of a dead man's land and estate to the eldest of several sons because the great fief* as both property and office must descend as an integral whole if it was to be inherited at all. With regard to the English crown Henry II strove in vain to establish this principal. Before his reign succession was governed by no particular rule but was influenced by four considerations: kinship with the royal house, popular election, designation by the late king,* and personal fitness. (Bibliog. 261, 262)

prince, ruler. Singular of the Latin word *princeps* ("first in rank"), its use transferred from the late antiquity to the new kings* of the west and from these to the non-royal rulers as well. It was distinct from the plural of the word *principes* which meant the great men who surrounded the ruler. Pope Gregory VII recorded forty-five kings and eighty princes under his jurisdiction, and for him, kings were members of a group of all those who as *princeps* or rulers determined the fate of their subjects and hence of the church in their territories. French kings, especially, were conscious of the role of princes because the legal basis of their kingship was election by princes from among one of their number. Under the Capetians most princes left the kingship untouched so long as the king did not intrude on their princely independence. Earlier the *duces*, or dukes,* of the 10th-century Frankish empire* had become viceroys of the king in complete small subkingdoms. Officially as such they were called the *marchio* (see marquess), but gradually the title of *dux* or *dux regni* became their normal titles, and their rise in political power to almost autonomous positions was expressed in the use of the singular term *princeps*. This meant that *dux* was *princeps* over a *regum* in place of the king, and had the highest power and the right to delegate its high officials, the counts.* Gradually after the 10th century the use of the term spread from these dukes to less important men. (Bibliog. 370)

Prince of Wales, heir to the English throne. Up to the time of Edward I, the eldest son of the king* was called the lord prince, and the title of Prince of Wales originally distinguished the native princes* of that country. King Henry

III gave to his son Edward, the heir apparent, the principality of Wales and the earldom of Chester as an office of government rather than as a special title. After he became king, Edward, as Edward I, conquered in 1277 both Llewellyn and David, the last native princes of Wales, and by so doing united Wales with England. Then as he presented his infant son, Edward, who had been born in Caernarvon* in 1284, to the Welsh as their prince to satisfy their national feelings, Edward promised them a prince without blemish on his honor, a Welshman by birth, and one who could not speak a word of English. To fulfill that promise literally, he sent his queen, Eleanor, to be confined in Caernarvon Castle for the birth of her son, and only later, on February 7, 1301, invested the seventeen-year-old prince with the principality, by creating him Prince of Wales. Henceforth the title was borne by the heir apparent to the English crown, who bore from birth the title of duke* of Cornwall but was created Prince of Wales only by special investiture. The rites used at the investiture of this prince with the coronet,* ring of gold, rod of silver, mantle,* and sword* were detailed in the Charter of Creation of Edward of Cornwall, son of Edward III, in 1343. (Bibliog. 178, 349)

princips. See prince.

prisage, duty levied on imported wine.* (Bibliog. 171)

prise. See horn calls in hunting.

prison. See jail.

private wars. Despite the efforts of such clergy as Pope Urban II to stop private wars and to divert the energy of the participants to such beneficial pursuits as a crusade to fight Moslems, these disputes were too deeply rooted in custom and even were celebrated in songs which exalted knightly passions to heroic proportions. For example, the *chanson de geste,* *Raoul de Cambrai*, was devoted to a war between Raoul's family and that of Herbert of Vermandois. See Truce of God. (Bibliog. 351)

privy. See latrine.

probator regis. See approver.

proclaim, declare someone an outlaw* or rebel.

prodd, *arbalète à jalet,* crossbow* used on the chase* for shooting small rocks and lead balls. It was bent by means either of a lever fixed to the stock or by the hand alone; its cord was doubled for better support for the missile. (Bibliog. 9)

proofs of age, relatives and friends swore an oath about someone's birthdate to prove its validity. For example, in 1335 William, son of William le Marchal of Kyngestanleye, Gloucester, sought to prove that he was over twenty-one years of age, having been born in the town of Kyngestanleye and baptized at the church there on Thursday in the feast of Rogation in the second year of the reign of Edward II [1309]. John Potelyn swore he knew this to be true because on that Thursday, Alice, his daughter, died at Gloucester and was buried at the church of St. Oswald. John Clavyle swore he knew it to be true because on the previous Wednesday, William de Tyderynton espoused Margery de Heygrove, his kinswoman, at Staverton by Gloucester. Thomas de Bacar said that on the following Friday, Agnes, his wife, while on her way to Gloucester had fallen and broken her right leg. (Bibliog. 261)

proper, heraldic charge* portrayed in its natural color.* (Bibliog. 43)

proscribe, put outside the protection of the law, to outlaw*; write up or publish the name of a person condemned to death and property to be confiscated. (Bibliog. 246)

punishment, kinds of. When punishment was due, it was severe. Amercements* of money* generally were imposed only on minor misdemeanors such as selling wine* or cloth contrary to regulations or for sins of omission such as the failure or neglect of public duties or of mistakes. Serious crimes, however, were punished by death, mutilation, or outlawry. Death was imposed by hanging, beheading, burning, drowning, stoning, and *infalistatio*,* (See execution.) Other death penalties included such diverse approaches as the sentence imposed on those who allowed sea walls and banks to decay; they were staked in the breach of the wall to remain forever as part of the new wall. Non-capital punishment included castration, flogging, sale into slavery, dunking, exile, "abjuration of the realm,"* or mutilation, that is, loss of ears, nose, upper lip, hands, feet. (Bibliog. 4, 261)

purpesture, building a house or homestead within the forest bonds, that is, encroachment on royal land without permission. Through negligence of the sheriff* or his officials, or the prolongation of a war, some dwellings encroached on some portion of crown land and the dwellers treated it as their own property; then justices in eyre* seized it, valued it separately from the "farm"* of the county,* and turned it over to the royal treasury. If the dweller had built the building, he was punished by a heavy fine*; if the heir of the builder, then loss of the land was enough punishment. (Bibliog. 102)

purpure, heraldic tincture (see colors) purple.

pursuivant of arms, follower or messenger* attendant on a superior of arms*; a junior rank of herald*; a novitiate and candidate for the superior office of herald and "king of arms."* England had four: rouge croix, the eldest whose title derived from the cross* of St. George; blue mantle, created by Edward III and whose name derived from the robes of the Order of the Garter*; rouge dragon, created by Henry VII on the day before his coronation* and whose name was derived from the supposed ensign* of Cadwaladyr; portcullis, created by Henry VII and named for a badge* of the king.* The pursuivant's costume consisted of a tabard* of damask silk and a surcoat* with the royal arms embroidered on it worn sideways with one sleeve hanging down before and one behind, but no "collar of SS.*" His duties were similar to those of a herald, assisting for a fee at such public occasions or ceremonies as royal weddings, funerals, installations, and the creations of peers,* baronets,* and knights, and donations for attending court upon the principal festivals of Christmas, Easter, Whitsunday, All Saints, and St. George's Day; he also received a small salary from the Exchequer.* (Bibliog. 116)

purveyance, feudal right of the lord to stay in his vassal's* home at the latter's expense for a stipulated number of days per year. As one of the most unpopular of feudal privileges, it was commuted into a money* payment from the 12th century onward, after the king* decided on a capital in which to hold his court.* (Bibliog. 139)

pusan. See pysan.

put in, to seek refuge, as a quarry* fleeing from a hawk. (Bibliog. 118)

put out, to drive a quarry* out of the cover in which it had taken refuge from a hawk. (Bibliog. 118)

pyrites, galgate, stone good for diseases of the eye and diarrhea. (Bibliog. 258)

pysan, pusan, pizane, breastplate* like "plastron de fer.*" (Bibliog. 9)

Q

Quahn. See Cahn.

quarentina (L.), unit of measurement* used in the *Domesday Book** for one furlong or forty perches.* (Bibliog. 213)

quarrel, vireton, arrow* or bolt* for a crossbow* that was shorter and thicker than a longbow* arrow. (Bibliog. 9)

quarry, game pursued by a hawk, hounds, or men. See also curee; hunting. (Bibliog. 96)

quartarolo, Venetian bronze or copper coinage* of the 13th century introduced by Doge Pietro Ziani (1205–1228) and its double by Lorenzo Tiepolo (1268–1274). (Bibliog. 150)

quarter, measure equal to a seam.* (Bibliog. 394)

quartering, division of a shield* into four quarters to accommodate more than one "coat of arms."* Each quartering represented arms* inherited from a different branch of the armiger's* family. Such a shield was read left to right: the first quartering was the patronymical coat; the next was the first quartering acquired; in the third quarter was the second quartering acquired, and so on. If a blank remained at the end of the shield, the first coat was repeated for symmetry. Sometimes six or eight or even more positions needed to be included, each one containing a coat of arms inherited from an heiress and each called a quartering. (Bibliog. 43)

quartern, weight of twenty-eight pounds* of fruit equal to one-fourth of a piece* or one-twelfth of a sort. (Bibliog. 394)

quat, term for a deer lying at rest. (Bibliog. 96)

quayage, dues collected by a borough* bailiff* for space allotted on a quay or wharf. (Bibliog. 394)

queen's gold, money* paid to the queen in addition to that promised to and paid to the king.* For example, when one promised money to the king, he was under an unstated obligation to pay the queen one mark of gold for each one hundred marks of silver paid to the king. (Bibliog. 102)

quested, hunting* term for a deer being sought. (Bibliog. 246)

questing beast, animal in Arthurian legend with the feet of a stag, thighs and tail of a lion,* body of a leopard,* head of a serpent, and with thirty whelps howling in its belly. It also was known as the glatissaunt (howling) beest. It was born after the daughter of King Ypomenes lay with the Devil. After her brother with whom she was in love had repulsed her advances, she had accused him of rape. After he had been condemned to be torn asunder by starving dogs for that crime, he prophesied that she would bear a monster with whelps constantly yelping in its belly. She confessed her crimes after the beast was born and was executed. This beast was pursued by Pellinore and later by Palomedes. (Bibliog. 100, 234)

queue, tail of an animal in blazon.* (Bibliog. 43)

quickevil, disease of "hunting dogs."* (Bibliog. 96)

quillons, cross-guards below the handle of a sword* to protect the hand from cutting blows of an opponent's blade sliding down his own blade. (Bibliog. 9)

quindene, quinzaine, subsidiary religious observance a fortnight after the chief feast. It sometimes was used in summons to Parliament* and councils as a convenient date for attendance when the festival was over. See Holy Days. (Bibliog. 265)

quintain, pel, training device for aspirants to knighthood* to learn to master the use of spear* and sword.* Originally nothing more than the trunk of a tree embedded in the ground at which beginners with swords learned various sword strokes, it changed to a shaft stuck in the ground from which a shield* was suspended. That change allowed the dexterity of the performer to be displayed as he charged with levelled lance* to smite the shield properly and break its fastenings so that it fell to the ground. This in turn gave way to a device resembling a human figure carved in wood, often resembling a Turk or Saracen "armed at all points,"* bearing a shield in its left arm and brandishing a club or saber with its right. This new figure was placed on a pivot to move freely and quickly. In running at this figure, the horseman had to aim his lance with great skill to strike the figure between the eyes or nose, for if he struck anywhere else, especially on the shield, the figure whirled so quickly that it would give the rider a heavy blow on his back with the wooden club or saber in its right hand. That blow disgraced the rider to the amusement of spectators.

When many "ran at the Saracen" in a contest, the winner was declared by the number of his strokes and their value. If he struck the figure on top of the nose between the eyes, he got three points; below the eyes on the nose, two; under the nose to the point of the chin, one. All other blows were not counted. If he struck the figure so that it pivoted, he forfeited all his remaining turns that day as punishment for his lack of skill. (Bibliog. 334)

quintal, hundredweight of iron.

quire, measure of quantity for paper consisting of either twenty-four or twenty-five sheets and equal to one-twentieth of a ream. Originally this was a set of four sheets of parchment folded to form eight leaves and was the unit most commonly used for manuscripts. (Bibliog. 394)

Quo Warranto (L. "by what warrant"), statute issued by King Edward I in 1290 requiring a baron* to show by what authority he held a private court.* Created to prevent the extension of private feudal justice,* this statute invalidated the barons' right to hold courts unless they could show either royal permission or the precedence of holding such a court prior to the accession of King Richard I* in 1189. (Bibliog. 139)

quota system, method by which only a portion of the feudal host would be called to serve during a year. As King Richard I* (1189–1199) kept an army in the field in France almost continuously during the later years of his reign, his barons* and other tenants proposed the quota system because they were reluctant to spend so much time abroad. Additionally, by a new method of commutation first offered in 1196, many barons freed themselves and their knights of the entire burden of service by paying a lump sum arbitrarily fixed and generally larger than the normal scutage* assessment. On payment of such fines,* they received an authorization from the Exchequer* to recover their payments by levying scutage on their undertenants. (Bibliog. 262)

quyrreye. See curee.

R

rabid-dog bite treatment. If a person was bitten by a mad dog, several remedies were available. He could go to sea and let nine waves pass over him. He could take an old cock, pull all the feathers from above his vent, hang him by the legs and by the wings and set the cock's vent on the hole made by the dogbite, stroke the cock along the neck and shoulders, and then the cock's vent should have sucked all the venom from the bite wound. If the hound was mad, that cock would swell and die, and he that was bitten by the hound would be healed. Alternatively he could make a sauce of salt, vinegar, strong garlic, and nettles and twice every day lay it upon the bite as hot as it could be endured until he was made well or else in nine days he would die. More effective remedies were proposed including a large cupping glass applied over the wound to draw out as much blood as possible, after which the wound was to be dilated and cauterized as thoroughly and deeply as the wound went and then covered with substances to draw out the poison. That was the treatment recommended by Lanfranc of Milan, a cleric, physician, and surgeon of the latter part of the 13th century in Lyons and Paris. (Bibliog. 96, 364)

rache, ratche, "hunting dog"* that hunted by scent. Scenting hounds hunted in a pack later called running hounds and then simply hounds. The usual cost to keep such a hound was a halfpenny* per day, a greyhound* three farthings,* and a limer* a penny* per day. Dogs were fed bran bread* and received the curee* (quarry) at the end of the hunt. (Bibliog. 96)

rack. See huntsman.

rag. See hunting terms.

raising troops. See troops, raising.

rake away, action by a hawk that flew too wide or that left the falconer* to pursue a distant quarry.* (Bibliog. 26)

ram, assault weapon made of largest tree nearby, fitted with an iron cap and swung by ropes from a frame. By swinging it back and releasing it repeatedly

against a wooden gate or a section of wall, besiegers could breach a defense
through which they would gain entrance into the besieged castle* or town.
(Bibliog. 341)

rameurs. See falconry birds.

rampant, blazon* description of a beast with its left hind leg on the ground
while its other three were raised, and the beast faced dexter.* It was the most
common position for the lion* in blazon, rearing with its forepaws in the air.
When blazon for a lion did not specify a position, it was assumed to be rampant.
See beasts, positions of. (Bibliog. 230)

rampart, broad embankment around a fortification on which a parapet* was
raised. (Bibliog. 246)

ranking of nobles, French. At the lowest end of the scale was the vavasour*
who was lord only over rustics, but, as soon as he became chief of other nobles,
he increased in dignity. The various indemnities due to a knight who had been
struck, imprisoned, or otherwise maltreated increased as his importance increased. If he had two other knights on the lands of his fief* and maintained
another in his household, his compensation was doubled. If he assembled under
his banner* a large number of armed retainers, he was called a banneret,* and
if no further step separated him from the king* or territorial prince* to whom
he paid homage* directly, he was also called tenant-in-chief,* captal, or baron.*
(Bibliog. 28)

Rannulf de Glanville, justiciar* of England from 1180 to 1189 and the reputed
author of the oldest English legal classic, *Treatise on the Laws and Customs of
England* (c. 1190), although his nephew, Hubert Walter, probably wrote the
work. He was instrumental in implementing the great legal reforms and inno-
vations by which King Henry II welded the heterogeneous mass of laws and
customs derived from a variety of sources into a living, growing body of law.
Glanville's book dealt with initiations and procedures of litigation and trial both
in civil and criminal law. Even though he was wise, eloquent, and proud of his
role in the justice* of the royal courts,* he himself was not a paragon of virtue
or honesty. As sheriff* of Yorkshire for the year 1170, for example, he took
from that shire* twice the revenue of Lincolnshire, the king's richest shire: 1,644
pounds, sixteen shillings, fourpence cash (see money); two silver dishes, four
gold rings, two chargers, sixteen palfreys,* three greyhounds,* thirty-six horses,*
six falcons,* seven mewed* hawks, seventy-five head of cattle, eight pigs, 120
sheep, forty-nine seams* of oats, and 140 carloads of timber. With his charm
and persuasive ability, however, he convinced the king* to let him keep what
he had taken without any recompense at all. (Bibliog. 132)

ranseur, staff weapon similar to the partisan* with a long broad blade and two projecting short blades at each side. (Bibliog. 71)

ransom, act of redeeming oneself from capture for an agreed upon amount. This practice was governed by rules ensuring the rights of both captor and prisoner. The captor's right was based on the oath given by the prisoner when taken and imposed a natural obligation to pay, guaranteed by the universal agreement that all natural contracts must be obeyed. Because of his lawful interest in his captive, the captor could do whatever seemed reasonably necessary to ensure payment, even keeping the captive under lock and key or in irons; but he could not threaten him with death or demand from him any actions contrary to his honor or the the law because such demands would free the prisoner from his obligation. The prisoner's obligation was a private one because he made it to his captor and no one else.

Basically this promise emerged from battlefield actions in which the prisoner said, ''I yield myself your prisoner,'' and the captor, to establish his rights of ransom against other claimants, had to take two more actions. He had to be the first to seize the prisoner's right gauntlet* and put the prisoner's bare right hand into his own; the gauntlet served as the token of the captor's claim. Second, to protect his prisoner's life he had to put his captive into someone's custody and escort him to a safe place behind the lines. By taking these two steps the captor ensured that the verbal promise was legally binding. If he did not do this, the prisoner remained a free man. (Bibliog. 181)

Once captured, a prisoner was protected by law. He became a non-combatant, his lands from which he had to derive the revenue to pay his ransom became technically immune from the war, and he had the right of safe-conduct.* In his own country, he was a free man and could defend himself in his lord's court*; in his captor's country, though, he had no legal voice. Although he could appear as a witness, he could not make contracts because he was not free, nor could he challenge anyone to a duel.*

His captor also had rights, and these overrode bonds of allegiance, for the liege* lord could not forbid the prisoner to obey his master's (captor's) summons. Should the captor order the prisoner to fight against his own side, however, that was treason and automatically freed the prisoner from his obligations.

Once the battle had ended, the captor wrote out a solemn deed in which the captive agreed to three points: (1) to promise to be a good and loyal prisoner and to obey all reasonable things; (2) to renounce any right to dispute the master's title to the ransom; (3) to invoke savage condemnations against himself if he failed in his obligations of the ransom, that is, he was to hold himself to be a traitor to his faith, a perjurer, and one dishonored in any court in Christendom. Further, he was to accept any actions which his master could take against him, such as displaying his arms* reversed or humiliating him in any way he wished. Other items usually included in this charter* were the detailed arrangements for the amount, terms, and places for paying the ransom; the penalties for defaulting;

sureties and pledges of his faith; an acknowledgment that the captive was responsible for his own keep and expenses; and conditions of his captivity. It was signed with the captive's seal.

The amount of the ransom had to be fair by not being beyond the resources of the man's patrimony. Such a debt was inheritable because it was as absolute as a fief,* and so was the obligation to pay it. Tradition usually set it at a sum equal to one year's revenue of the knight's estate:

> and if he does not wish to let him go free, let him ask reasonable and knightly ransom, such as is possible for the prisoner to pay and according to the usage of arms and of his country, and not such as to disinherit his wife, children, relations, and friends; for justice demands that they should have the resources to live after the ransom has been paid.

(Bibliog. 31)

About the conditions of captivity, two major points nearly always were mentioned: (1) a prisoner was to remain a prisoner whether rescued or not rescued until the obligation had been met, for that obligation was between the two of them; and (2) so long as he was a prisoner, he could not arm himself against his master or his master's party. Rescue did not release him from these personal obligations. Often, if the prisoner was freed on parole in order to return home to negotiate ransom, the captor demanded a second letter from him detailing the terms of the parole and the date for his return. Once the ransom had been paid, the freed prisoner had to retrieve these two letters of obligation to prove that the ransom had indeed been paid, for an unscrupulous master would easily question the quittance given for the ransom and therefore get more ransom money.

If the ransom was being gathered too slowly, the captor could make conditions harsher in prison (see jail) for the sureties, and if that did not speed up payment, the captor could proceed with either the "voie de fait" or the "voie de justice." The first of these invoked reprisals against the land and goods of the prisoner or pledges, but because such actions would damage any possible later case in court (voie de justice), they were used only as a last resort. A more effective way was to initiate actions to dishonor the captive or his pledges. Such actions might involve exhibiting in a public place a painting of the captive's arms reversed or of a prisoner hanging by his heels or in some other undignified pose. For example, La Hire rode on a campaign with the reversed arms of Robert de Commercy, one of the pledges of his prisoner, Monsard d'Aisne, hanging at his horse's tail. Such a deadly insult was effective, for only a highly self-confident prisoner would not respond to such an action. This was particularly effective when used to insult a pledge, as La Hire did, because it stimulated them to take actions in their own courts to make the prisoner pay. However, a very real danger in those actions lay in the fact that such acts of dishonor were acts of war, and because only a prince* could levy public war, only he could confer public honor.* Therefore, one needed the license of his prince or his prince's constable* to dishonor a man publicly. However, this was much more advantageous than reprisal or war, for its risks and expenses were far less, and it probably was the captor's most effective weapon against a defaulting prisoner. It was not material injury, but it showed how people regarded honor: it was similar to treason to a sovereign lord because the captive, by giving his oath, stood in relation to his captor as his lord.

However, once the prisoner had been released on parole to gather the ransom and had defaulted on the payment despite repeated summons and threat of sanctions cited in the ransom agreement, to whom did the captor turn? He turned to his prisoner's sovereign as the only one who had authority over the man and who was capable of independent actions with external people and powers. Even then, the sovereign had to have a special court. England possessed such a court in the Court of Chivalry,* presided over by the lord high constable and the "earl marshal"* in the White Chamber at Westminster. France had a corresponding court at the Table de Marbre in Paris. See also spoils of war. (Bibliog. 31, 181)

rape, one of the six administrative districts of Sussex, each of which contained several hundreds.* (Bibliog. 246)

rascal, any lean deer, and any deer under ten years of age. (Bibliog. 96)

rascal and folly, young and lean stags and hinds*; folly meant a lesser deer, not a hart or buck. See hunting. (Bibliog. 96)

Raymond VI, wealthiest and oldest of crusading leaders of the first crusade.* His army was biggest and his wealth allowed him to maintain it in strength. As count* of Toulouse (d. 1105), he was the greatest lord in southern France: count of Rodez, Nîmes, Narbonne, and Toulouse, as well as marquis (see marquess) of Provence. Doubtless he was expected as one of the leaders of the Christian forces to become a prince* in the Latin east. (Bibliog. 186)

real, silver coinage of the gros* type crowned with the royal initial and the arms* of Castile and Leon, issued in Spain from the 14th century on. (Bibliog. 150)

rebatements. See abatements.

rebec, rebeck, musical instrument having three strings and played with a bow. (Bibliog. 15)

recauta, stock from which the tally* was split and which served as evidence if the tally was lost. (Bibliog. 144)

Receipt, early name for the Lower Exchequer.* (Bibliog. 102)

recheat. See horn calls in hunting.

Récits d'un ménestrel de Reims, collection of anecdotes about England, France, and the Holy Land since the early 12th century; compiled about 1260, it contained such interesting legends as that of the minstrel* Blondel's locating Richard I* in the Austrian prison in 1192. (Bibliog. 44, 162)

reclaim, to tame a hawk and make her familiar with and accustomed to humans. See hawking. (Bibliog. 26)

Reconquista, name given to the wars waged by Christian realms in Spain against the Muslims aiming to reconquer territories lost early in the 8th century. (Bibliog. 139)

recreance, recreancy, heavy fine* on a champion who failed to appear to fight or who lost a duel,* for it meant confessing himself to be defeated, overcome, or vanquished. As the loser, he was fined sixty shillings (see money) in the name of recreance. In a duel, one or the other champions necessarily was beaten and forced to yield, thereby incurring the implication that he was a craven,* not only losing the case in which he fought but also incurring serious deprivation of his civil rights. The duel was held to have proved him perjured, so he "lost his law," and as an infamous person never again could he be heard as a witness. (Bibliog. 229)

red, tincture (see colors) in blazon* normally termed gules.* As red was the color signifying cruelty and ferocity of a prince* against his enemies, that was the reason offered for its being chosen as the color of the banner* flown to signify no mercy* shown to combatants. See banners displayed. (Bibliog. 181)

Red Beard. See Barbarossa.

red hawk, peregrine (see falconry birds) in her red or immature plumage. (Bibliog. 26)

reeve, administrative official whose duties included maintaining order on his estate, collecting rents and other dues from his lord's dependents, and ensuring that they performed their various duties. At the side of the bailiff,* this man was chosen from among the peasants (see villein) of a manor* and generally by them. He was chosen by various means: an autocratic choice by the lord, a democratic election by the peasants, or a primary selection by the peasants with final selection by the lord. As a man of the manor, he knew every field* and had seen since boyhood the habits and eccentricities of everyone on the manor. Frequently the lord insisted that no one could refuse to serve in this capacity, and thus it was often treated as one of the characteristic marks of serfdom (see serf). This election to office usually took place at the "manor court"* at Michaelmas* with a term of office for the coming year, although customarily if he had any aptitude at all, he would be kept in office for a longer period of time. As he was a manor official constantly among the peasants for 365 days, he was best qualified to present the yearly manorial account to the auditors.

His duties included basically every aspect of the manorial economy. He had to make sure that the peasants arose and got to work quickly; he oversaw the plowing, carting, seeding; he watched the threshers to be certain that they didn't waste or steal food; he supervised the livestock; he kept the manor house and other buildings in good shape. He could take men away from the fields and use them at pleasure in his own service. He witnessed all buying and selling transactions so that disputes could not arise over rightful ownership of the goods concerned. As the chief peasant, he had double duties of equal importance in guarding the interests of his lord and the customs of the community.

In Anglo-Saxon England the reeve of a royal estate was responsible for raising the farm* due from that estate, and providing it when required. By the 10th century, one particularly important reeve emerged, the shire-reeve, *scir-gerefa*, in charge of a shire* when the ealdorman* in control had more than one shire in his jurisdiction. That *scir-gerefa* became the sheriff.* After the Conquest (1066) the word reeve continued to refer to lesser officials of vill* and manor or to the public official who was required to come with four men to the eyres* or to a manorial officer whose duties were bound up with the agricultural routine of a private estate; the shirereeve continued to be the main financial officer of the shire. (Bibliog. 24, 163, 357)

regalia of England, emblems of sovereignty. Edward the Confessor (1042–1066) ordered this regalia and other state treasurers stored in the Chapel of the Pyx, a new room he had built in Westminster Abbey, behind a double door with seven locks to prevent its being opened by any but officers of the government or their successors. There he stored the emblems of the Saxon kings* and other valuable treasures. Besides the regalia, these treasures grew to include the black rood of St. Margaret (the holy cross* of Holyrood) from Scotland; the cross of St. Neot from Wales deposited there by Edward I; the scepter* of Moses; the sword* with which King Athelstan cut through the rock at Dunbar; the sword made supposedly by Weyland the Smith with which Henry II was knighted; the sword of Tristan given to John by the Holy Roman Emperor and later lost in the Wash*; the dagger which wounded Edward I at Acre (see crusades); the iron gauntlet worn by King John of France when taken prisoner at the Battle of Poitiers* in 1356.

At the coronation* of Norman kings, the regalia connected with King Edward the Confessor was used: the crown* of Alfred or of St. Edward for the king and the crown of Edith, wife of William* the Conqueror, for the queen; the scepter with a dove was reminiscent of King Edward the Confessor's peaceful days, after the expulsion of the Danes; gloves were a reminder of the abolition of the

Danegeld* as a token that the king's hands should be moderate in taxing; the ring with which the king was wedded to his people; and the great stone chalice prized highly since King Edward's days, out of which the abbot of Westminster administered the sacramental wine* at the coronation. In the reign of Henry III (1216–1272) a small Jewel House was built in the Tower of London to house the royal treasure and regalia, where it has remained since. Currently that includes the imperial crown, St. Edward's crown, the Prince of Wales's* coronet,* the queen consort's crown, the queen's diadem, St. Edward's Staff, the royal scepter or scepter with the cross, the rod of equity or scepter with the dove, the queen's scepter, and the ivory scepter. Swords include the Curtana* or pointless sword of mercy*; swords of justice,* Temporal and Ecclesiastical; bracelets and spurs*; Ampulla* and spoon; golden salt cellar used at coronation banquets; and other items used at the coronations. (Bibliog. 178, 308)

regard, inquiry begun by King Henry III (1216–1272) into the purpresture,* and waste,* held every three years by twelve knights chosen specially for the purpose. Persons who were guilty of making purpresture or waste were dealt with by justices in eyre.* Other articles dealt with hawks and "falconry birds"*; mines; harbors in the forest suitable for timber, honey, underbrush; the possessors of arrows*; greyhounds* or other things likely to harm the deer of the "royal forest."* (Bibliog. 156)

regardor, official concerned primarily with offenses committed within the "royal forest."* (Bibliog. 171)

regnal years, actual time a particular monarch reigned, from the date of his coronation* to the date of his death. A particular year is indicated by a numeral preceding the monarch's name; for example, 6 Richard I would indicate the sixth year of his reign that is from September 14, 1195, to September 13, 1196.

regulus (L.), cockatrice.*

rei, reis, unit of Portuguese monetary system and money* of account; it was equated with the French centime, Spanish centimo, English penny,* and German pfennig (see bracteate; coinage). (Bibliog. 150)

relays, groups of "hounds for the hunt,"* usually three, used in a chase*: vaunt chase, midel, parfitiers.* In the early days of venery, the whole pack of hounds was not used from the start of the chase. After the stag had been "started" (see hunting) from its lair by the limer,* some hounds were uncoupled and laid on (see couple), and the rest were divided into relays or groups which were stationed in charge of one or more berners* along the probable line of flight of the stag and then uncoupled when the hunted stag and the hounds already chasing it had passed. (Bibliog. 96)

relevée, time of day in the afternoon shortly after nones* when travellers usually resumed their journey to continue riding until vespers.* See canonical hours. (Bibliog. 161)

relics, mortal remains of a saint which were revered by the faithful. Originally relics were the tombs of the martyrs and saints worshipped in the chapels and monasteries erected over their tombs, because the spirits of the saints were thought to hover near their tombs or shrines. With the spread of Christianity in the West and pilgrimages to the Holy Land, however, the worship of relics spread to include parts of clothes worn or said to have been worn by saints, as well as other objects associated with them by transference of reverence for the martyr's body to anything that had been in contact with him. These included portions of the saint's body or remains (skull, finger bone), napkins or pieces of fabric saturated with a martyr's blood, and earth and dust from graves and coffins. These relics were placed at the doors of churches where the faithful kissed them or in rich reliquaries in other parts of the building. They were carried in processions, thereby exhibited to the people who were blessed by them; pilgrims flocked to shrines of famous relics. The Fourth Lateran Council (1215) forbade showing relics outside their reliquaries or admission of new relics without the express sanction of the papacy, but the edict had little effect. (Bibliog. 212)

relief, succession duty; money* paid to a lord when an heir entered into possession of his inheritance. This "feudal obligation"* was similar to heriot,* but heriot referred to chattels and relief to tenement; one was payment in kind, and the other in money. When a baron* was faced with this problem of paying a large relief, he obtained the money for it by exacting an aid* from his under-tenants. In his "Coronation Charter,"* King Henry I (1100–1135) promised that these reliefs would be just and lawful, and he gave the example of the type of relief he would expect from a vassal* to his liege* lord: his father's horse,* breastplate,* helmet,* lance,* shield,* and sword.* But if he did not have these, then payment of one hundred shillings (see money) would acquit the man of the items. Relief of a man who held land by annual rent was to be a year's rent. By the time of Henry II (1154–1189), that figure of one hundred shillings for each knight's fee (see knighthood) was firmly fixed so that if a knight possessed only one-half of a knight's fee, he paid only fifty shillings. From his barons,* however, the king* could exact greater sums, for those were not fixed. If his tenant held by barony,* the king exacted an arbitrary relief of up to 200 pounds (see money). For example, Walter Brito was charged 200 pounds for his fifteen knight's fees, but William Beretram was charged the same amount for only three fees; had they held by knight service, these fees would have dropped to seventy-five pounds and fifteen pounds respectively (one hundred shillings or five pounds per fee). (Bibliog. 264)

remembrancer. See Exchequer.

Rencesvals. See Roncevaux.

rental, extent, document that detailed minutely just what was demanded of every landholder on a manor.* (Bibliog. 24)

rents. See farm.

replevin, release on bail of either goods or men. (Bibliog. 163)

rerebraces, metal defenses for the upper arm in early 14th century, but after the end of that century the term referred to shoulder defenses. Vambrace* was used to refer to all the rest of the arm defense, including the couter.* (Bibliog. 9)

reremouse, bat when depicted in blazon.* (Bibliog. 43)

reseeyuour, greyhounds* who pulled down game after it had been chased. Teasers* were light, swift greyhounds who were released first; reseeyuours, big, heavy greyhounds capable of pulling down a large stag, were released last. (Bibliog. 96)

rest, bracket on the breastplate* which "arrested" the backward movement of the lance* on impact. See grate. (Bibliog. 27)

Rhodes, Knights of. See Hospitallers.

rhymed chronicles, vernacular chronicles of the Anglo-Normans in the early 12th century composed in rhymed octosyllables. Their heroes were more or less contemporary historical figures and not fictional as were many of the heroes of the *chansons de geste.** Emphasis in these works centered on events and genealogies, not on battle descriptions or exaltation of Christian versus pagan religion or the prowess of an individual hero. They were written in reaction to the exploitation of Charlemagne, hero of the French *chansons de geste.* Examples included Wace's *Brut,* written before 1155 at the request of Queen Eleanor of England, and Ambroise's *Estoire de la Guerre Sainte* which described much of what he had seen accomanying Richard I* on the third crusade.* (Bibliog. 162)

rhymers. See minstrels.

Richard, kings* of England: Richard I, Coeur de Lion (1157–1199; king: 1189–1199); Richard II (1367–1400; king: 1377–1400).

Richard I, Coeur de Lion, king* of England (1189–1199), duke* of Aquitaine; able leader and endowed with attributes of a skillful tactician. Although he had qualities of a brave knight who would rush resolutely at the ranks of the enemy (see knighthood), he also was concerned with the welfare of his men, taking care to provide for them, allowing no unreasonably long marches, imposing strict discipline to protect the entire body of troops (see laws of King Richard about crusaders at sea), supervising the execution of his orders personally, and at the same time remaining ready for any sudden and unforeseen occurrence.

His opinion of England, however, was not usual. Hardly had he been crowned when he revealed his true feelings. England to him was the source of revenue by which he could pursue his passion for a crusade* and foreign wars. Three weeks after his coronation,* he sold earldoms, honours,* wardships,* justiciarships,* public offices, rights, privileges, castles,* towns, and manors* to the highest bidders; he even said he would have sold London if he could have found a buyer. (Bibliog. 44, 132, 236, 351)

Richard, earl of Cornwall (1209–1272). As younger brother of Henry III of England, he was reared on the ideals of chivalry* and Arthurian legends. He led a crusade* in the Holy Land in 1240–1241, and on the death of the Emperor Conrad IV he became a candidate for the imperial crown,* using money provided by his brother for the purpose, much to the anger of the English barons.* He was elected emperor* but never reigned in Germany (see Holy Roman Empire). (Bibliog. 139)

Richard Fitz-Neale. See Fitz-Neale, Richard.

riding, division of the counties* of Lincolnshire and Yorkshire into administrative units larger than hundreds* or wapentakes*; called riding from the Old Norse word *thridjunger*, or third. (Bibliog. 163)

Rights of the King of France, *Grande Ordonnance* of King Louis IX (1254) which was the clearest title-deed to the French king's rights by which the king* endowed that monarchy with great moral dignity. It ranked with the Coronation Charter* (1100) of Henry I of England. The French document stated:

> The seneschals* and other royal officers shall swear and observe the oath under pain of punishment* by the King himself, to give justice* without distinction of persons, according to the approved customs and uses; to protect the rights of the King without encroaching on those of private persons; to receive no gift, neither they, nor their wives, nor their children, and to give back any they may have taken; never to borrow from those under their jurisdiction a sum over twenty livres,* and to repay within two months; not to take any share in the proceeds of sale or appointment to subordinate posts, of rents due to the King, etc.; not to protect their subordinates who may be guilty of peculations or abuse of power . . . but on the contrary to punish them. . . . They shall not buy any house within the area of their jurisdiction without the King's consent, under pain of confiscation. . . . They shall not make the monasteries admit their relations or their servants, or procure for them ecclesiastical benefices. . . . They

shall take neither bed nor board in monastic houses without the King's authorization. ... They shall only have a small number of beadles* and sergeants* to execute their judgments. ... The seneschals and their bailiffs* and their servants shall cause no man to be arrested for debt, unless the money be due to the King. They shall not be able to detain a man accused of a crime who may be in a position to clear himself. ... Persons of good reputation, however poor, shall not be put into question on the evidence of a single witness. ... The royal officers, after their term has expired, shall remain for fifty days on the spot to answer any complaints which may be laid against them.

(Bibliog. 105)

rights to castles, some lords acquired castles* by substituting fief-rentes* for them, an arrangement with obvious military advantages. More often, however, a lord would grant a fief-rente to a man who in return would take his castle in fief* and promise either to make it accessible to the lord during hostilities or to hold and defend it against all enemies of the lord. Thus many lords developed strategic defense of their lands. For example, upon receiving a fief from Blanche of Navarre, regent of Champagne, in 1217, John de Toul took his castle in liege* homage* and swore that it would be put at the disposal of the counts* of Champagne whenever they so ordered. (Bibliog. 208)

rimours. See minstrels.

ring, movement of a hawk as she rose spirally into the air. (Bibliog. 26)

ring work, roughly circular earthenwork or ditch around a fortification. (Bibliog. 280)

ritterschlag (Ger. of Fr. *colée*), act of dubbing a new knight in Germany; this replaced the earlier *swertliete*, or ceremonial girding on of the sword* which was the first symbolic gesture of knighthood.* (Bibliog. 274)

Robert II, Curthose, duke* of Normandy (c. 1054–1134), oldest son of William* I, the Conqueror. Dubbed Curthose—*brevis ocrea* or short leggings—because he was short, he was markedly different from his brothers. He was courageous and honorable, serving with distinction on the first crusade,* but not harsh or cruel. He was good-natured, easy-going, affable; and because he could refuse nothing to anyone, he went through his inheritance in a few weeks as he granted castles* and lands freely to lawless barons.* As a result, he constantly needed money* and therefore was easily manipulated. (Bibliog. 264)

Robin Hood, legendary English outlaw* operating in and around Nottingham and Nottingham Forest. He was the subject of many verses, especially ballads: "A Geste of Robyn Hode," "Robin Hood and the Monk," "Robin Hood and Guy of Gisborne," "Robin Hood and Maid Marian" to name but a few. He also was a reputed historical figure outlawed in the 13th century. Robert was one of the five or six commonest male Christian names in post-Conquest England, and its diminutive was more popular in the 13th century than the name itself. Hood meant a head covering and was used to indicate a person's profession, hood-maker or hooder, as John the Miller became John Miller. Many figures named Robert Hood—and the diminutive of Robert was Robin—appeared in English records of the 13th and 14th centuries. One was arrested for theft in London in 1263; six others were found in the records between 1302 (during reign of Edward I) and 1337 (reign of Edward III). (Bibliog. 92, 164)

Robinet, name given to the mangon* used by Richard I* on his crusade.* (Bibliog. 71)

Roger Mortimer. See Mortimer, Roger.

Roger of Salisbury, chief justiciar* under Henry I in 1101 and the first to bear that title, for Henry created the position because he needed someone to act as his vice-regent, to issue writs, and to preside over his court* known as the Exchequer* while he was ensuring his hold over Normandy. (Bibliog. 284)

Roland, count* of the marches,* nephew of Charlemagne, formidable fighter, and leader of the *douzepeers.** After he and the other *douzepeers* had been betrayed by Ganelon* and ambushed by the outnumbering forces of the pagan Marsile at Roncevaux* on August 15, 778, his refusal to blow his horn Olifant* to summon Charlemagne's aid was a classic example of *demesure.** The entire story was related in the most famous and best of the *chansons de geste,** the *Chanson de Roland,* (*Song of Roland**). (Bibliog. 40)

roll of arms, manuscript rolls or books that contained listings of armorial bearings (see charge) either in blazon* or depicted ''in trick.''*

romances, works written in the French vernacular during the 12th century and in English during the following centuries. Using between 8,000 and 30,000 eight-syllable verses, their authors generally developed histories of chivalry* and love. (Bibliog. 162)

Romanie, Charlemagne's banner* or oriflamme,* the name later being changed to Mont-joie* or Montjoy. (Bibliog. 126)

Roncevaux, Rencesvals, pass in the Pyrenees mountains between Pamplona, Spain, and St. Jean-Pied-de-Port, France, where on August 15, 778, Basques attacked and slaughtered the rear guard of Charlemagne's troops on his return from his first expedition into Spain. That battle was detailed in heroic proportions of treachery, defeat, and revenge in the *Song of Roland.** This location was a

site along the "via franca," the pilgrim route to the tomb of St. James at
Campostella, Spain. Along it moved fourteen expeditions of northern Frenchmen
into Spain to fight the infidel during the 11th century, fifteen more in the 12th,
and five in the 13th century. (Bibliog. 40, 162)

roncey, roncin. See horse.

rondel dagger, 14th-century dagger with its guard formed by a solid disc with
the tang of the blade passing through its center. (Bibliog. 27)

rood, measure of length equal to 660 feet or one-eighth of a mile 5,280 feet;
also a measure of area equal to 40 square perches* or one-fourth statute acre*
in the 12th century. (Bibliog. 394)

rose, five-petalled flower of the common sweetbriar or dogrose when used in
heraldry.* (Bibliog. 43)

Rotbart, Redbeard, Emperor Frederick I of Germany (1122–1190) called Barbarossa in Italy.

rouge croix. See pursuivant of arms.

rouge dragon. See pursuivant of arms.

rouncey. See horse.

round tables, type of tourney* or joust* in which the bohort* used a short
lance* not headed with steel in order to avoid fatalities. The event was run
supposedly in imitation of the adventures of Lancelot, Tristan, and Palamedes
while they were knights of King Arthur's Round Table. One of the earliest took
place in 1223 when Jean d'Ibelin, lord of Baruth, knighted his eldest sons with
a grand festivity at which the bohort was used to imitate adventures of Britain.
In 1235 knights from Flanders and elsewhere convened at Hesdin and after
participating in a round table, pledged themselves to a crusade.* The count* of
Flanders, Philip (d. 1190), as patron of Chretien de Troyes, had commanded
him to write the *Perceval* story and had furnished him with the source. In 1240
Ulrich von Liechtenstein, a minstrel* knight from Bavaria, instituted a different
sort of round table. Travelling through Styria and Austria in the role of King
Arthur, he challenged all knights whom he met to a joust and admitted to the
"Order of the Round Table" all those who broke three spears* on him without
missing. Even though Henry III of England (1216–1272) forbade nobles in 1242
from taking part in these, they continued as popular entertainment.* In 1279
Roger Mortimer,* a close friend of Edward I, held one at Kenilworth to which

he invited one hundred knights and ladies and where Roger himself won the prize of a golden lion for being the bravest knight.

These were popular exercises all over Europe and seemed to reach their zenith at Windsor Castle* in 1344 when King Edward III undertook to imitate chivalry* as he believed it existed in the time of Arthur and his knights. He wished to rebuild the great castle* of Windsor where he believed Arthur had founded his Round Table and from which so many valiant knights had gone forth to deeds of prowess. For this celebration he sent heralds* with invitations into Burgundy, Hainault, Scotland, Flanders, Brabant, and Germany. Two kings,* two queens, the Prince of Wales,* ten earls,* nine countesses, and many other people of importance attended. After the tournament* was over, he began to build at Windsor a house 200 feet* in diameter which he called the Round Table, and for this building he ordered a circular table built out of fifty-two oak trees. See Order of the Garter. (Bibliog. 73, 202, 203)

roundel, 1. heraldic disc known by different names according to its tincture (see colors): gold* roundel was a bezant*; silver* was a plate; gules* was a torteau; azure* was a hurt; vert* was a pomeis; sable* was a pellet, ogress, or gunstone; purpure* was a golpe; tenne* was an orange; and sanguine* was a guze; 2. plate disk used as a defense for armpits and elbow bends, also called a palette.* (Bibliog. 9, 116)

roussant. See eagle.

route. See hunting terms.

routiers, French mercenaries* who were nothing more than cruel and bloodthirsty plunderers. (Bibliog. 159)

roving, shooting arrows* at casual marks (rovers) of uncertain distances. (Bibliog. 100)

Roy des Armes. See king of arms.

royal demesne lands, estates which the king held *de dominio*, that is, in his own lordship and not enfeoffed (see feoffment) to others. This was not a solid block of land, however, for individual estates in it were granted out on various terms for various political or other reasons, and other estates had come into this demesne* through escheat* and forfeiture. Royal manors* were removed from the sheriff's* care, and justice* on them was administered by the central government alone through special custodians answering only to the royal Exchequer.* (Bibliog. 163)

royal forest, legal entity of the land reserved for the king* for hunting* and subject to special laws administered by special officers. See forest; hunt, royal. (Bibliog. 163)

royal houses of Europe, historical order of precedence* of the antiquity for the royal houses of Europe was:

France (Clovis, A.D. 481)

Spain (Kingdom of Asturias, A.D. 781)

England (Egbert, A.D. 828)

Poland (Mieczyslaw, A.D. 963)

Hungary (kingdom, A.D. 1001)

Denmark (Knud, A.D. 1015)

Bohemia (kingdom, A.D. 1088)

Two Sicilies (Norman kingdom, A.D. 1130)

Sweden (union of kingdom with the Goths, A.D. 1132)

Portugal (Alphonsus I, 1139)

(Bibliog. 294)

royal standard, banner* of the royal arms* always was referred to as the royal standard even though it was technically not a standard.* (Bibliog. 43)

royal touch. Supposedly the king* of England could heal by the royal touch. A legend emerging from the early days credited King Edward the Confessor with healing a woman with a badly pustulated face by washing it and continuously touching it, thereby drawing from "out of the kernels little worms whereof they were full with corrupt matter and blood" until he had brought forth all the corruption; she was in perfect health in a week. (Bibliog. 178)

royal "we". Although King Richard I* in a charter* was actually the first English king* to use the royal "we," King John was the first to speak in the plural in his grants. His son, Henry III, in his *Magna Carta Libertatum,** used the singular "ego," but John and those after him used "nos." (Bibliog. 178)

ruaille, amount to be paid to the victor in a judicial duel* beyond the fourth sou (see money) required of the loser in the time of Edward II; this was in addition to the loss of the suit. (Bibliog. 197)

rubble, unsquared stone used to fill in portions of the walls of a keep* between the inner and outer ashlar* to give it thickness for protection against missiles during "siege warfare."* (Bibliog. 280)

rufter hood, hawk's head covering with the back cut away, put on a newly caught hawk so she could be fed easily. It was not removed from her head until she was ready to be fitted with the hood proper. (Bibliog. 26)

rumors, news of the birth of a child in England. The person who arrived first with the news received a large fee according to the pleasure of the queen. King Edward I gave fifty marks* for the rumors of the birth of his grandaughter, Margaret de Bohun, in 1303. Even though he reduced the amount to ten marks for her sister in 1304, he was more generous to the extent of forty marks with the news of the birth of his grandson, Edward, later Edward III. (Bibliog. 225)

rundlet, measure of capacity for wine* containing eighteen or eighteen and one-half gallons,* generally equal to one-fourth of a tun.* When used for products other than wine, it was synonymous with kilderkin.* (Bibliog. 394)

ruses, tricks of a deer to rid itself of hounds: "doubling,"* "rusing to and fro upon itself" when it retraced its steps, "beating up the river" when it swam upstream, "foiling down" when it went downstream, and "going to soil" when it stood in water. See hunting. (Bibliog. 96)

S

saal. See hall.

sabaton, plate defenses for the foot consisting of overlapping horizontal lames shaped to the pointed shoe of the time; worn during the 14th century. (Bibliog. 27)

sable, heraldic color* of black. (Bibliog. 116)

sac, matter or cause in a dispute between litigants. (Bibliog. 246)

sack, measure of capacity for dry products: three and one-half bushels* of apples in Kent but four bushels in Worcestershire; five bushels of ashes; eight pecks of charcoal; four heaps of bushels of coal; five bushels of flour weighing 280 pounds*; and 364 pounds of wool. (Bibliog. 394)

sacrabar, sakeber (O. Scand. *sakaraberi*, "bearer of a suit"), public prosecutor in a shire* or hundred.* In the 13th century, thieves caught with the stolen goods still in their possession were prosecuted by an official called the sakeber. With the prisoner's guilt proved, the local court* sentenced him to be decapitated or to be thrown off a cliff into the sea, giving him no opportunity to deny the theft. In some cases, the duty of beheading him fell to the sakeber. See execution; punishment. (Bibliog. 261)

sadne. See caliph.

safe-conduct, permission to travel through hostile or enemy territory in relative safety. As public war did not mean total war (see war, just), certain people were expected to pass through hostile territory in safety: merchants, students, knights going to tournaments,* pilgrims, palmers and diplomatic envoys, all on special business. These permissions were of two kinds: safe-conduct of grace and safe-conduct of war. Giving wider protection by securing the holder not only against acts of war but against any prosecution and arrest, the first type could be given only by a prince* and bound all his subjects to honor it. Its disadvantage lay in the fact that only his subjects were bound; another prince's subjects did not have to honor it. Safe-conducts in war gave greater ordinary protection, although as a sealed document which one purchased, it too, bound only those under the authority of he who issued it. Safest security was derived from one issued by a king* or his constable,* but even that wasn't totally effective because in areas where free companies operated, a traveler needed safe-conducts from all the independent captains.

Every safe-conduct detailed the name of the bearer, the number of persons he was allowed to have in his company, the arms and goods he could carry, the route he was to follow, and the places he could or could not enter. Any goods not expressly listed on it were subject to instant confiscation. For example, the Navarese in 1350 always plundered "hats of beaver, ostrich feathers" and "spearheads" because they never listed those items on their safe-conducts and so could confiscate them. Certain general conditions governed the security given by these documents. For example, security was given for protection against open war and "letters of marque"*; safe-conduct to travel to a place in enemy territory automatically gave security for the return trip provided it was within the time period for which security was given; and the bearer's security could not be forfeited for a breach of local regulations about which he reasonably could not have known. If the bearer of the safe-conduct infringed on any of the conditions listed, he could be taken lawful prisoner, for he was expected to conform to his supposed good intentions. He had to show the document to any who had a legitimate right to see it. He could not add to his group anyone of greater importance than himself, because then he would not be the principal of the party. He could not bring outlaws* or personal enemies of the grantor into his country under its cover, as the safe-conduct was given only to him and his party. Before entering any town or fortress, he had to obtain the permission of its captain or lieutenant or else he could be taken prisoner. (Bibliog. 181)

sails, wings of a hawk. (Bibliog. 26)

St. Ampoule. See anointing.

St. Denis, 1. bishop of Paris and patron saint of France. Gregory of Tours wrote in the 6th century that Denis was one of the seven bishops sent to Christianize Gaul under the Emperor Decius, and after becoming the first bishop of Paris, he was martyred in A.D 258. His relics* were taken to the Benedictine abbey at St. Denis near Paris which Dagobert had founded. As his grave became a revered shrine, his name was used as a "battle cry"* for French knights, and the oriflamme* banner* of the abbey was adopted by the kings of France. 2. A monastery near Paris founded in the 6th century over his tomb began to gather legends connected with Charlemagne's supposed pilgrimage to the Holy Land, and by the 11th century, these stories were being cited as the sources for the relics* held there. Under the patronage of the kings* of France, it became not only the place of royal worship but also the royal burial place. (Bibliog. 139)

St. James of Campostella. See Santiago de Campostella.

"saint sepulchre" ("Holy sepulchre"), rallying cry for the crusaders. See crusades. (Bibliog. 191)

sake and soke, right of a vassal* to hold a court* and keep its profits. The term came from the formula by which both the English king* and his barons* granted jurisdictional powers for their recipient to hold with sake and soke, toll and team,* and infangentheof.* (Bibliog. 330)

sakeber. See sacrabar.

Saladin (Salah Al-Din Yussuf, 1139–1193), sultan of Egypt and Syria, 1173–1193; Muslim leader against the forces of the crusades* led by Richard I* of England. (Bibliog. 236)

Saladin tithe, tax imposed in 1188 by both kings Henry II of England and Philip* II of France to raise money* to finance the third crusade.* Arrangements for its collection in England were placed in the hands of the local priest and dean, who in each parish using a local jury obtained support from a Templar,* a Hospitaller,* a sergeant,* clerks of the king,* the local baron,* and the bishop. The religious figures were to confirm the religious use of the tithe,* and the Templar and Hospitaller were to confirm its use for a crusade. These were to collect a tenth of every man's revenues and movables with the "exception of the arms, horses,* garments of the knights, and of horses, books, garments, and vestments, and all appurtenances of whatever sort used by clerks in divine service, and all the precious stones belonging to both clerks and laymen." (Bibliog. 102)

salamander, species of lizard which lived unhurt in fire but which poisoned apples and any wells into which it fell. (Bibliog. 258)

sale. See hall.

Salic law, compilation of the legal traditions of the Salian Franks living northeast of the Rhine River during the 6th to 8th centuries. Samples of its provisions revealed the breadth of its coverage. For example, anyone stealing a bull that had never been yoked was fined 1,800 denari (see denarius) or 45 sol (shillings; see money), but if he stole the bull used for cows in the village, he was fined 2,700 denari. The fine* for rape was 2,500 denari; for marrying an alien spouse, 2,500 denari; for striking a blow so that blood flowed, 600 denari, but if no blood flowed, the fine for each blow—up to three— was 120 denari. Anyone killing a pregnant woman was fined 28,000 denari, but anyone killing a woman who could have no more children was fined 8,000 denari. Anyone calling another a "fox" or "hare" was fined 120 denari. (Bibliog. 151)

salient. See beasts, positions of.

Salisbury, Roger of. See Roger of Salisbury.

salle. See hall.

sally port. See postern.

salon, salone. See hall.

saltire, ordinary* consisting of a cross* placed diagonally on a shield* in heraldry*; it was assumed to represent the cross on which St. Andrew was crucified. (Bibliog. 116)

salung. See carucate; measurements.

salute, gold coinage* of Charles VI of France (1380–1422); it also was issued by Henry V and Henry VI of England for use in the English possessions in France. (Bibliog. 150)

sanctuary, sacred and inviolable place of traditional refuge and protection in which one was guaranteed immunity from the law. A few English abbeys and ministers had a special right of sanctuary which extended for some distance, often a league* around the building, so that anyone who took refuge there could remain for life. All other monasteries, chapels, churches, and graveyards, however, provided sanctuary only for a limited period. Most who sought sanctuary were robbers or murderers who took refuge when pursued by the "hue and cry"* immediately after committing a felony* or after breaking out of prison (see jail). They could stay there unharmed for forty days measured from the first day of sanctuary and could exercise their right of "abjuration of the realm"* in front of the coroner* any time during the forty days. Sanctuary was denied only to men who had committed a sacrilege such as a felony in a sanctuary. For example, a Buckinghamshire thief was pursued to a church where he stole the vestry keys in order to try to escape; he was dragged from the church and executed promptly.

Even though infamous, habitual, or convicted felons could be dragged from sanctuary, their forcible removal was rare because not only was it a serious offense and resulted in excommunication, but it allowed the felon to be restored to sanctuary. Enemies of those in sanctuary, however, often hid in cemeteries of the churches to waylay fugitives who emerged to get food or to relieve themselves. (Bibliog. 171)

sangraal. See Grail, Holy.

sanguine, heraldic stain* or "tinge" of deep blood red. (Bibliog. 116) *sans* (Fr. ''without''), used in blazon* to describe a creature with missing parts or limbs, as ''lion* sans tail.'' (Bibliog. 116)

Santiago de Campostella, popular shrine of St. James of Campostella on the coast of Spain. Roland* and the *douzepeers** were ambushed and slaughtered at Roncevaux* on the route through the Pyrenees from France to this shrine. (Bibliog. 40)

sapphire, precious stone thrown upon the coasts of Libya by the waves; it had the property to bestow the gift of prophecy and to remove the chains of prisoners. (Bibliog. 258)

saracen, generic term in many early works to refer to any non-Christian, generally Arabs and Muslims, but in actuality referred to a Bedouin tribe of Sinai, the Banu Sara. (Bibliog. 162)

saracen arrows, inferior arrows* protected against by the coats of mail* of the crusaders (see crusades). (Bibliog. 9)

sarpler, large, coarse, canvas bag that served as a measure of capacity for wool, generally equalling two sacks* totalling 728 pounds* or one-sixth of a last.* (Bibliog. 394)

satyrs, strange creatures of various shapes and features, some of whom resembled man but had horns in their forehead and goat feet; others, the cynophali,* had heads of dogs; others were headless and noseless but had eyes in their shoulders; others of Styria had ears so large that they covered their bodies with them; others called cynopodes* in Ethiopia had only one foot but that one so large that they shadowed themselves from the hot sun with it, but yet were so swift that they raced like greyhounds.* (Bibliog. 21)

satyral, heraldic monster* with old man's face, lion's* body, and antelope's tail and horns. (Bibliog. 43)

sax, early weapon. See scramasax.

sayers. See jestours.

scabbard, sword's. See sheath.

Scaccario, Dialogus de. See *Dialogues of the Exchequer.*

scald, skald, poet and musician of ancient northern nations. These resembled the bards of the Britons and were held in equal veneration by their countrymen.

They were considered necessary by royalty, and even lower chieftains hired them to record their actions and indulge their vanity. (Bibliog. 334)

scaldings, See money, bad.

scantilon, mason's rule or measure used by huntsmen* to measure the slot* of a deer to be able to show with its droppings to the Master of Game* that the deer in question was a warrantable deer. (Bibliog. 96)

scarp, inner slope of a ditch. (Bibliog. 280)

sceatta, 1. small silver coin issued in the 7th and 8th centuries in the southern kingdoms of Anglo-Saxon England; it was copied from a late Roman Empire coin. 2. Kentish unit of account: twenty made one shilling equal to one grain* of gold. See coinage; money. (Bibliog. 150, 305)

scepter, emblem of dignity carried by a monarch on state occasions. See coronation; regalia.

schilling, silver coinage* struck in the dukedom of Prussia as the currency of the Teutonic Knights* in the 14th and 15th centuries. (Bibliog. 150)

schynbalds, English term for demi-greaves* or shinguards. (Bibliog. 27)

scimitar, sword* with a long curving blade used for cutting blows, not thrusting blows. (Bibliog. 9)

scirgerefa. See sheriff.

Scone, Stone of. See coronation chair.

scorpion, siege engine resembling a huge crossbow* that cast missiles in the 11th and 12th centuries; it was named from its shape. (Bibliog. 71)

scramasax, sax, seaxe, characteristic sheath knife of the Germans, Norsemen, and Anglo-Saxons, often big enough to be called a short sword.* Its blade was shaped like a flattened triangle with its base forming the single, straight, cutting edge; its hilt normally had no guard. (Bibliog. 27)

script, palmer's wallet, purse, or pouch, often hung from the knob at the end of his staff (see palmer's staff).

scruple, weight of the apothecary* system equalling twenty grains,* one-third dram of sixty grains, or one-twenty-fourth apothecary ounce* of 480 grains. (Bibliog. 394)

scudo, Italian counterpart of the gold and silver French coin, the ecu,* with a shield* of arms* on its reverse. (Bibliog. 150)

scutage, shield* money*; commutation of military service by money payment established early and in widespread use by 1100. In its broadest sense, scutage simply was a tax apportioned on knight's fees (see knighthood) rather than by hides,* carucates,* librates,* or chattels. The *Dialogues of the Exchequer** described it this way:

> It happens sometimes when the realm is threatened or attacked by enemies that the king* ordains that a certain sum, usually one mark* or one pound [see money], shall be paid from each knight's fee, and from this source are derived the soldier's wages and gratuities. For the king prefers to expose foreign mercenaries* rather than his native knights to the fortunes of war. And so this sum, which is paid in the name of shields, is called "scutage."

(Bibliog. 102)

Thus through scutage the military obligations of enfeoffed knights (see feoffment) could be translated into money with which mercenaries could be hired. In the beginning it was levied at the rate of a mark or a pound on the knight's fee in lieu of actual service in the field. As each knight's fee owed forty days of military service to the king, scutage was computed not on the basis of the week or month owed but on the mark and the pound, because forty days of service at fourpence (see penny) a day equalled thirteen shillings fourpence (one mark) and at sixpence a day equalled twenty shillings (one pound). Late in the 12th century the monarchy found it difficult to collect in full such a monetary equivalent of forty days of military service. The one-mark scutages of 1162, 1165, and 1168 gave money enough only to replace each commutating fee with a mounted man-at-arms. The scutage of two marks, raised for the expedition of Toulouse in 1159, represented eightpence a day for forty days of feudal service, or exactly a knight's pay. In the 1170s, angered by the increase in the knight's wages from eightpence to one shilling per day, the king increased the scutage rate from one mark to twenty shillings through the scutages of 1172, 1187, 1194, 1195, and 1196. Each of the nine scutages between 1162 and 1196 was set at the rate to replace each fee with a mounted sergeant,* because assessing at the rate of the full forty shillings needed to hire a knight for forty days not only would have been unprecedented but virtually impossible to collect. King John's attempt to duplicate the rate in 1215 was one of the barons'* chief grievances against him in the *Magna Carta Libertatum.**

In Normandy, scutage was called the *auxilium exercitus** as early as 1172, levied at a rate varying from four to ten pounds per fee in the reign of Richard I* or John but normally five pounds in the reign of Philip* Augustus.

Scutage was not confined just to payments to royalty; tenants-in-chief collected it from their mesne* tenants, who in turn passed it down through the hierarchy to the rest of the rear vassals* and even to the peasants (see villein). Some tenants-in-chief turned a profit from this by enfeoffing more knights than were required to carry out their *servitium debitum*,* by collecting scutage from all of them, and then by pocketing the excess money. However, compared to all the other sources of revenue available to the king (dona,* auxilia, [see aids], tallage) the importance of scutage was overrated. (Bibliog. 102, 159, 261, 262, 264)

scutiferi, squires* to knights (see knighthood) and barons* in the time of Edward I. (Bibliog. 87)

scytale, serpent, a speckled slow-moving animal, one view of which immobilized people to the spot. (Bibliog. 193)

scythe, weapon of men-at-arms made from the blade of the agricultural scythe mounted vertically on a shaft. (Bibliog. 27)

scythe-knife. See glaive.

seam, measure of capacity and weight equal to a quarter* for dry products: nine heaped bushels* of chopped bark (Yorkshire); 120 pounds* of glass; and generally eight level bushels of eight gallons* each of grain. (Bibliog. 394)

season for hunting. See hunting seasons.

seasons, four divisions of the year, the middle of each fixed at the time of the equinoxes or solstices. Bede's calendar had spring begin on February 7, summer on May 9, autumn on August 7, and winter on November 7, that is, on the seventh of the ides of the month. However, Isidore of Seville put the dates more than a fortnight later: spring on February 22 (Feast of cathedri Peter); summer on May 24 (Feast of St. Urban); autumn on August 23 (Feast of St. Bartholomew); winter on November 23 (Feast of St. Clement). See Appendix A. (Bibliog. 265)

seat of government. See capital.

seaxe. See scramasax.

seel, to sew closed the eyelids of a newly caught hawk, a practice common to Persian falconers* but rarely used in the West. (Bibliog. 26)

seggers. See jestours.

seisin, possession of land or chattels that arose from the completion of the investiture of livery of seisin; possession of a freehold estate in land by having title to it. (Bibliog. 24, 246)

sejant, blazon* description of beast sitting facing dexter* with its forepaws on the ground. See beasts, positions of. (Bibliog. 116)

selion, measure of an area for the strip of land or pathway between two parallel furrows of the open field.* (Bibliog. 394)

semé, poudre, blazon* description of a field strewn with several of the charges named, drawn small and without reference to any number depicted. (Bibliog. 116)

seneschal, steward, lord's representative for all purposes in the general super-vision of an estate: to preside at "manor courts,"* to audit accounts, to conduct sworn inquests, and to decide the general husbandry arrangements. See steward. (Bibliog. 357)

sense of honor, See honor, sense of.

serf (L. *servus,* "slave"), peasant; lowest class of persons referred to in the *Domesday Book,** ranking below cottars*; any person belonging to a group bound to the soil and subject to the will of the owner of the soil, and gradually becoming synonymous with the English villein* in the 12th and 13th centuries. (Bibliog. 47, 246)

sergeant, serviens, broadly used term to include a rank in all infantry and light cavalry troops. Every military sergeant was a serviens, but not every serviens was a military sergeant. Sergeanty tenure* was created by royal officials late in the 12th century to categorize a considerable variety of broader services. Its tenure implied some special service connected with the "king's household,"* government, sport, or army, often approximating military tenure or socage.* His pay was two or three pence (see money) a day; mounted sergeants were paid four or six pence per day, less than knights because their equipment was less elaborate than the demands of chivalry* would allow. (Bibliog. 264)

sergeant's armor, heavy canvas hauberk* with rings or leather plates sewn on it; often he wore no helmet* but only a *coif-de-mailles** and ventail* instead. He bore a gisarme,* perhaps a Danish axe,* darts,* javelins,* and lances.* (Bibliog. 161)

serra, winged marine beast with the head of a lion* and tail of a fish. When it saw a ship on the high seas, it rose from the water, spread its wings to block the wind, and thus becalmed the ship. Then it quietly folded its wings and sank back beneath the water to resume feeding. (Bibliog. 258)

services, feudal. See aids.

servitium debitum, military service owed by knights to their overlords, the baronial tenants-in-chief, for their knight's fee (see knighthood); they reported with their men-at arms for duty in the "feudal army"* in response to a summons issued by the king.* (Bibliog. 272)

sester, measure of capacity for dry or liquid products: twelve gallons* of beer or ale, one seam* or eight bushels* of grain, three to four seams of lime, and four gallons of honey, oil and wine.* (Bibliog. 394)

setions. See fields.

sext, third "canonical hour"*; originally it referred to the sixth hour of the day—midday.

sextary, six gallons* of wine.*

shaftment, part of the arrow* shaft occupied by feathers. (Bibliog. 100)

sharp-lance running (Ger. *sharfrennen*), tourney* encounter whose object was to unhorse an opponent with war lances.* The knight used a saddle* with a high back guard and large steel projections fastened to the saddle to protect his legs and thighs. His arm and hand supporting a large and heavy steel-pointed lance were protected by a large vamplate* through which the lance passed. Later an oblong block of iron called a queue* was screwed to the right side of the breastplate* where it formed a lance rest, and a piece of plate called the grande-garde covering the breast and left shoulder was screwed to the breastplate and formed additional protection over armor* for the left side of the body. A volante added to the grande-garde protected the face and eyes. At the moment of impact, each combatant dropped his lance to avoid injury to his arm from splintering. Usually one rider was unhorsed, and unless he had been knocked unconscious, he could remount with help from his valets. (Bibliog. 9, 71, 78)

sheaf of steel. See weights and measures.

sheath, scabbard, sword's, protection for a sword* blade made of thin slats of wood covered with leather, parchment, or rich material with its tip reinforced by a metal ferrule called a chape.* As this was made to form snugly around a specific blade, no other blade was likely to fit in it. Until the mid-13th century this sheath was attached to the belt with laces, but after 1250 the belt usually was made in two pieces so that the ends laced around the sheath at different points causing the sword to tip toward the front; sometimes a diagonal thong united these two parts to prevent them from sliding apart. Shortly after 1300 this sheath began to be fitted near the mouth with two or more metal bands called lockets* to which metal pieces on the belt were fastened by metal rings, but after 1350 the belt generally was worn horizontally with the sword sheath attached by a loop or hook at the back of the top locket. (Bibliog. 27)

shell keep, ring wall encircling the summit of the motte* which frequently just replaced the wooden palisade* with a stone wall. Sometimes because of insecure foundations of the motte, this shell stood alone with no great tower within it. By the 12th century this frequently was crenellated* and had a parapet* with hoarding* for better defense. Such a keep* would be joined to the curtain walls* of the bailey,* and the whole castle* would be united by wing walls up the sides of the motte. (Bibliog. 280)

sheriff, shire-reeve, royal official whose title, *scirgerefa*, combined two Anglo-Saxon words—*scir* (shire) and *gerefa* (reeve or guardian)—and was abbreviated into sheriff. His powers were best shown by the example of Godric, sheriff of Berkshire and Buckinghamshire under Edward the Confessor. As sheriffs greedily tended to "confuse" the king's* manors* with their own, Godric's "confusion" became considerable. When William* the Conqueror sent around the *Domesday Book** suyrveyors to learn accurately who had held what lands in Edward's rule, they found that Godric had held forty-three acres* of the king's manor of Kintbury as pasture for his own horses,* had plowed 120 acres of the king's manor of Sutton for his own use, had taken twelve acres of the king's manor of Sperolt, had appropriated half of a hide* of the king's manor of Shalbourne even though he already rented tax free four manors from the king, and also took land from the abbey of Abingdon which totalled many hundreds of acres of plowland, meadow, and woodland, two churches, and a fishery. Naturally, for making so free with the king's land, he lost his shire-reevedom. After his death his widow was granted one small hide of land by King William I in return for feeding his "hunting dogs,"* but even this was taken away from her in 1086 by an even greedier sheriff, Henry de Ferrers.

Early on, William I stripped English sheriffs of their lands and possessions and replaced the English officials with Normans by 1076, for he recognized that such an action was one of the best ways to reward the help given him by men-at-arms who joined him on the invasion. With this appointment he changed their title to vicomte (see viscount) because of the similarity between the vicomte's office in Normandy and that of the sheriff in England. (A century later Henry II changed the title back to sheriff.) To these newly appointed sheriffs William entrusted many of the new motte* and bailey* castles* built at his command in Kent and through the midlands to York and west to the Welsh marches. He had handpicked these men for their loyalty, ability, and ruthless military efficiency to crush the English revolts against his reign. They became indispensable servants of the crown*; they performed their major function of tax gatherers efficiently to the king's satisfaction because he left them to act on their own initiative during those violent times.

By the time of William's death in 1087 the Norman sheriff had become a well-established local magnate (see peer). He was marrying his sons and daughters to the children of other sheriffs to build up his family's territorial influence, he was building adulterine* castles, he was obtaining charters* to hold markets and fairs, and he was considering his office as hereditary. In short, he was becoming an independent feudal unit. To control these sheriffs the new king, William II (1087–1100), and his justiciar,* Flambard, created a new royal servant, a local justice to hear pleas of the crown, and thus deprive the sheriff of that right. William II's successor, Henry I (1100–1135), went one step further and created a new itinerant justice to visit the shires* at the king's command in order to stop the drain of royal revenues by the thefts of clever sheriffs. By this means and others, this new monarch began to control the sheriffs. He demanded of them many new and arduous duties: inspections of royal castles and bridges, visits to royal manors to confer with reeves,* inspections of crops and boundaries, and twice a year a tour of every hundred* in the shire to take the view of frankpledge* and the "tourn.*" Additionally the sheriff summoned suitors to the shire court,* which he was empowered to convene, fined those who didn't appear, and increased arbitrarily the judicial fines* he was empowered to levy. By the end of Henry I's reign, however, the new itinerant justices had curbed this misuse of power by these sheriffs.

Henry II (1154–1189) instituted judicial reforms, making the position of justice more attractive and creating a more uniform and swifter justice* than was possible in the "manor courts,"* thereby increasing royal revenues and decreasing the power of the local lords. As members of the *curia regis*,* his itinerant justices joined with local justices and sheriffs during his reign to impose one system of law for all residents of England: Norman, Dane, Saxon, Angle. All the king's subjects now were Englishmen and subject to one common law. Under this revision, the processes of compurgation* and oath-swearing were replaced by sworn juries (see jury duty) of twelve worthy men known as juries of presentment nominated by the sheriff; knowing the facts of the criminal matters being investigated, these men answered questions put to them by the justices or the sheriff. Later, sheriffs lost this power to interrogate, and juries became answerable only to the justices. Henry II also replaced the "writ of right"* with the "writ of praecipe,"* which ordered the sheriff to act on a matter and report what he had done. By 1170, however, the people were so angry at the misconduct of the sheriffs that the king dismissed them all and ordered a nationwide investigation: the Inquest of Sheriffs.* His Articles of Commission ordered investigation into all possibilities for bribery, corruption, and extortion regarding land rents, sale of chattels of fugitives, receipts of feudal aids,* restocking royal manors, forest* trespasses, and so on. Twenty-two of the twenty-nine sheriffs were removed permanently from office and were replaced by professional administrators chosen from the Exchequer.* As a result, as the sheriffs' thefts disappeared, the king's annual income doubled. Rannulf de Glanville* was one of those removed because he, too, had taken from one area more than twice the annual revenue of the richest shire in England; however, he bought his way back into the king's good graces by presenting him with two Norwegian falcons.

Richard I's* reign was a different matter entirely. As he was absent from the country most of the time, he had turned control of the government over to the chancellor* and justiciar, William Longchamp, and a great malaise fell over the countryside. The king's insistent demands for money for his crusade* and ransom* made easier the treason of Prince John, political intrigues, outrages against the Jews, and corruption in the government to make life miserable for the common Englishman. On ascending the throne in 1199, his successor, John, realized the value of the sheriffs to himself personally and stretched their potential to its limit; he drew on the entire range of the sheriff's duties—financial, military, judicial, police, executive, advisory, administrative—and demanded personal service from them and intimacy with the crown. With all that power went corresponding corruption and wickedness. In fact, of the sixty-three clauses in the *Magna Carta Libertatum*,* twenty-seven relate directly to the sheriff and his office: some to correct an abuse, some about the kind of man hired as sheriff, some about specific abuses of power. Even so, King John hired about one hundred of them in the years of his reign (1199–1216), including Dame Nicolla de la Haye.* (Bibliog. 132, 227, 228)

sheriff's aid. See sheriff's tourn.

sheriff's tourn, circuit of the county* made by a sheriff* twice a year (spring and fall) on which he presided at the hundred* court* in each hundred in the county. These proceedings were known as the view of frankpledge* at which offenses were presented by the tithings* and the sheriff ascertained that every male over the age of twelve was in a tithing or a mainpast.* These were so useful in handling cases of petty crime that they passed into private hands as one of the common franchises* in the 13th century and were called leet* jurisdiction. In contrast to the shire* courts where the local justice or itinerant justice watched the proceedings, the sheriff's only watchdog was a local reeve* or bailiff* who was himself the sheriff's assistant or servant, so this court, or tourn as it came to be called under Angevin kings of England, provided the sheriff with his greatest opportunity to fleece the peasants (see villein). During the reign of Henry I (1100–1135), the sheriffs began to levy on the shires a small tax called the sheriff's aid* which they justified putting into their own pocket on the grounds that it was their just payment for all their troubles in carrying out their official duties and services to the crown. The barons* united to stop these injustices (see *Magna Carta Libertatum*). (Bibliog. 24, 132, 163, 171)

shield, broad piece of defensive armor* carried on the arm. Usually made of wood and covered with leather, these frequently had reinforcing strips of metal or horn. Early ones were either large oval or circular-shaped shields concave toward the body, which the Saxons used, or large kite-shaped shields also concave toward the body, as carried by the Normans. The circular Saxon shield was made of limewood covered with leather and further strengthened by an iron boss,* or the umbo,* that projected from the center cover of a hole through which the soldier's hand grasped the handle stretching across the shield. Its convex surface was painted with a design and ornamented with studs of bronze or iron. Used chiefly by footsoldiers, these circular shields in time became the targe,* a large shield fitted with enarmes,* and the buckler,* a small shield fitted with a crossbar as a grip. The kite-shaped Norman shield, by contrast, offered more protection than its Saxon counterpart. Held close to the eyes by the left hand, its broad upper part protected the body while the long tail protected the left thigh. Simple designs painted on it developed into armorial bearings (see charge) by the end of the 12th century when Richard I* bore three leopards* passant* guardant.* Two straps, enarmes, inside the shield allowed the left forearm to pass through and rest against a large pad to hold the shield securely. In addition it had a large looped strap, the guige,* at the top to suspend it from the neck or upon the back. This Norman type remained in general use until around 1200, and its curving top became flat by the early 13th century. Within fifty years it had become smaller and its sides more convex, until after 1270 it became moderately sized and shaped like the bottom of a flat iron, called a heater.* From the end of the 14th century, its right-hand top corner had a notch cut into it, a bouche,* which served to support a couched lance.*

For heraldic designations, a shield had nine main areas: chief,* fess,* base,* dexter* chief, dexter fess, dexter base, sinister* chief, sinister fess, and sinister base for use in blazon.* Thus a bend* traversed the shield diagonally from sinister base to dexter chief. (Bibliog. 9, 27, 251)

shield wall, fortification created by embedding shields* in the ground adjacent to each other. Behind this the soldiers could fight off cavalry charges just as King Harold's forces did twice at the Battle of Hastings.* Only when his soldiers were deceived by William* the Conqueror's forces into thinking they had routed the attacking Normans did the Anglo-Saxon soldiers destroy the integrity of the shield wall by racing onto the battlefield to retrieve loot from fallen foe. When William saw the wall had been broken, he signalled his forces to reassemble and to charge the weakened Anglo-Saxon position, which they did successfully. (Bibliog. 49, 158,)

shields of knighthood. See titles of dignity.

shilling, See coinage; money.

shiltron, formation used by the Scots, most notably at Falkirk where footsoldiers armed with pikes* were grouped in a circular formation of three ranks: the front row crouched, the second row knelt, and the third row stood, thus presenting three levels of pikes directed toward the enemy. (Bibliog. 296)

ship scot, tax collected for one's obligation in time of war to build and keep a ship manned by sixty armed oarsmen; the term came from ship-soke* paid for its upkeep. (Bibliog. 159)

ship-soke, districts of 300 hides* comprising sixty five-hide units, each of which had an obligation of producing one warrior-seaman for the fleet. This ship-soke also was charged to pay for the construction and maintenance of a warship which its warrior-seamen were expected to man. (Bibliog. 159)

shires, administrative unit consisting of a number of smaller districts (hundreds* or wapentakes*) united for the purposes of local government and ruled jointly by an ealdorman* and a sheriff.* A few (such as Lincolnshire and Yorkshire) had larger administrative divisions called ridings* from the Old Norse word *thridjunger*, meaning third, which in turn were divided into hundreds; in Sussex they were called rapes*; in Kent they were called lathes.* In Anglo-Saxon times the leading official in the county* had been the ealdorman who presided over the shire court,* led its forces, and executed its financial business. Early in the 11th century several shires were combined under a single earl,* and a subordinate shire-reeve (see sheriff) was in charge of individual counties. Under King Canute, (1016–1035) England was divided into four earldoms, but his successor, Edward the Confessor, felt threatened because he believed they had too much power. Under Norman rule, the division of England into shires continued but adopted the Anglo-French word *counte* as the equivalent term for shire. William* replaced the Anglo-Saxon earls with Normans, but their rebellions caused him to reduce their power and number. The Anglo-Saxon earldoms gave rise to shire-reeves (sheriff) who after the Conquest became important figures as the main points of contact between the county and central administrations. (Bibliog. 163)

shire moot, judicial assembly or court* of the shire* in Anglo-Saxon times.

short-cross penny, English silver coinage* whose name was derived from the small cross* within a beaded circle on its reverse. Introduced in 1180 by Henry II, it was replaced in 1247 by the "long-cross penny"* of Henry III. (Bibliog. 150)

shots. See fields; measurements.

Shrovetide, three days before Ash Wednesday.

Sicilian Vespers, uprising on Easter Monday 1282 in which the Sicilians, smoldering under the corrupt and ruthless occupation of the French forces of Charles of Anjou, rose in opposition to the hated intruders and slaughtered 3,000 to 4,000 men, women, and children who spoke French. This violence caused the French forces of Charles to withdraw permanently from the island of Sicily and the papacy to become involved in the conflict between Charles of Anjou and Peter I of Sicily. It was called vespers because the revolt erupted at the time of vespers.* (Bibliog. 186)

siege money, money of necessity, pieces of money* struck in all metals—gold, silver, copper, lead, tin—and even in leather and paper or vellum by the besieged for their use, and also by the besiegers for their use. Germans called it *feldklippe*. One of the doges (see duke) of Venice issued leather tokens to pay his fleet during an expedition in the Levant. (Bibliog. 150)

Siege Perilous, seat at King Arthur's Round Table assumed by Galahad as a symbol of his undertaking the Grail* quest. Originally commemorating the treason of Judas, the seat remained unfilled until it was taken by the purest of the descendants of Joseph of Arimathea. Siege is an ancient English word for seat. (Bibliog. 311)

siege warfare, military blockade of a city or fortified place to force it to surrender. Two methods were used by the besiegers: bombardment and close assault. Bombardment involved the use of siege engines to soften up the target area and to batter a breach in the defenses through which an assault could be made. Three types of weapons were used for this end: mangon,* trebuchet,* and balista* or springald.* Working on the principle of torsion, a mangon had a long arm with a sling or basket at its end passing through a skein of ropes stretched between two upright posts. These ropes were twisted toward the target by a windlass so that when the arm was pulled down against the torsion, any large rock or other projectile placed in the holder at the end would be hauled up and over by the torsion of the ropes acting on its lower end and hurled toward the target. The second type, the trebuchet, introduced in the 12th century, was a new device that used the principle of counterweight for its propulsion. This machine hurled its projectile toward the enemy from the longer end of a long beam pivoted between two upright posts using motive power of a great counterweight at the shorter end of the beam. More powerful than the mangon, it was more consistent because it was not affected by the weather and could vary its range by moving the counterweight along the beam or by adjusting the weights used. As both of these weapons fired any handy objects including stones, dead animals, and "Greek fire"* to batter down defenses, the Latin word *petraria** often was used indistinguishably to refer to both. The balista or springald operated on the principle of tension and resembled a huge crowssbow.* Because its flatter trajectory made it far more accurate than either of the other two, it was used to fire iron shafts or javelins* to pick off enemies who showed themselves at battlements* or other openings along a rampart.*

Close assault techniques, by contrast, required different types of machines including the "battering ram,"* bore, "mine gallery,"* scaling ladders, assault tower or belfry,* and penthouses. The battering ram was a huge tree trunk with an iron cap at its battering end. Suspended by ropes from strong supports, it was crashed repeatedly against a wall or gate until it crashed through. Sometimes to counter its effect the defenders would drop a forked apparatus to catch and pinion the head or some buffer padding between the head and the point of impact. That buffer, however, frequently was turned against the defenders, particularly if a gate were the target, for the attackers would set it aflame. The bore was a smaller instrument with an iron head used on sharp angles to work away the stones of the masonry; sometimes crowbars and picks were used as well. As the most effective method of destroying a section of wall was to undermine it, the mine was considered the most dreaded device of sieges. Professional miners would tunnel their way under the foundations of a target, shoring up the tunnel walls and roof with timbers as they dug. Then they would fill the chamber with brush, debris, and anything else combustible and ignite it to burn the props. As the props collapsed so would the wall of their target, and waiting forces would rush through the breach in the wall. Only castles* built primarily on rock or with a broad water defense were safe from this form of attack. The only protection against it was a countermine dug to meet the first tunnel and combat the miners in close hand-to-hand combat in the dark confining area of the mine. Scaling ladders, also called the escalade,* were a common method of forcible entry and were used most effectively when a diversionary attack drew defenders from a relatively isolated section of the wall, allowing the besiegers to clamber up to the ramparts in relative ease. A variation of the escalade was the great movable tower or belfry. This apparatus would be pushed up to the walls of the castle on rollers or wheels and let down a drawbridge* from the tower across which attackers would race onto the castle walls. It also served well as a lookout tower and a firing platform which overlooked the interior of the target. Its drawback stemmed from its need for a level surface, for even the slightest ditch or depression would cause it to stop, and ditches and moats had to be completely filled in before it could be used; that task often proved to be too enormous to tackle. Men working the ram and the bore could be protected by a movable shed on wheels called a sow* or a cat under cover of which the men could move close to the walls of the target. This was little more than a portable roof to protect the men from weapons being fired above them. It, the belfry, and the missile engines frequently were covered with raw hides to protect them from fire.

There were two ways to capture a castle or city: by assault after its defenses had been breached or by surrender. The rules differed for each method. Protocol demanded that the attacking captain send a messenger,* usually a herald,* under security, with a summons to surrender. This gave the garrison and town the opportunity to surrender on the spot. In his message the herald included warnings of the consequences of refusing the summons. If the summons was then refused, the besiegers could invoke all the sanctions permitted by the "law of arms"*

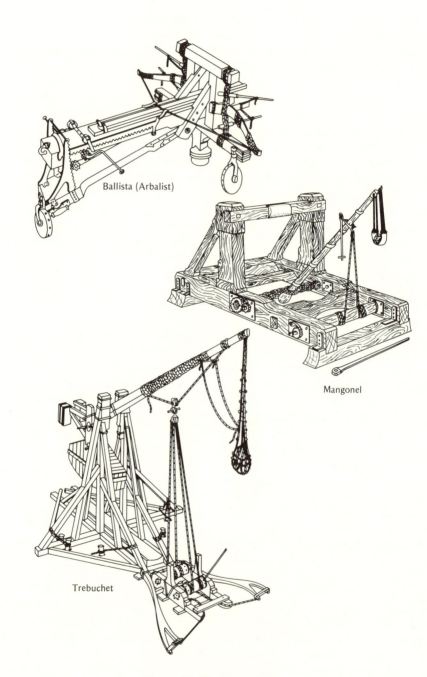

Ballista (Arbalist)

Mangonel

Trebuchet

Figure 10. Siege Weapons

in a town taken by assault. Such rigorous sanctions were enforced from the moment the siege began. First the suburbs were destroyed, then the town itself was attacked, and if it was reduced to rubble then the citadel was attacked. A sign that the siege formally had begun was the firing of the besiegers' cannons* or siege engines. Once that shot was fired, the captain had sole discretion to accept surrender or to offer terms. Unless he chose to offer terms, the war was to the death with no quarter given on either side. Rich prisoners worth high ransom* naturally would be spared. Even messengers attempting to enter or leave could be executed. In a city taken by assault (the word assault meant that surrender was unconditional), anything was allowed; women could be raped, men killed out of hand, all goods forfeit; even the churches and churchmen, though technically secure, often were not spared. If any lives were spared, it was done only by the captain's leniency. Prospects of this blood, "spoils of war,"* and lust kept soldiers on lengthy sieges.

This seeming harshness of an unconditional surrender was based on the inhabitants' disregard of a prince's* summons to surrender; by doing so, both their goods and lives were forfeit. Note the difference between the conquest of a town by force and arms and a victory on the field of battle. To accept a challenge of a battle was to accept judgment from God; He would determine who was in the right in such a contest between two adversaries of approximately equal standing. Furthermore, no stigma was attached to surrendering on the battlefield, and the law of arms protected the life of a captain who had given his word to his enemy. In contrast, to refuse to surrender on a summons of a prince who claimed the town as a right was an insult to his majesty and was punishable as such, even though refusing one prince's summons was supporting another's. In a siege there were no safeguards either for the life or honor* of the besieged. A captain who surrendered a town without siege was guilty of treason, for he broke his oath to his lord that he would not yield the town to anyone but the king* or his representative; thus he was false to his word and was dishonored; if he held out he likely was condemning his men and the townsfolk to death. One form of surrender commonly was followed. In it the besiegers and the besieged agreed to cease all hostilities for a given period at the end of which the town would be surrendered unless a relieving force had arrived in the meantime. The rules which allowed plunder and rapine in a conquered town would not apply under these circumstances. This was a sealed agreement that guaranteed the lives of the inhabitants and the garrison and saved not only the town from plunder but the besiegers from the expenses of a lengthy and costly siege. On the fixed date—a few days, six months, sometimes even a year—the town would yield unless relieved, and the nature of the relief meant that a force had arrived and was ready to give battle at a given spot. During the period of the truce neither the attackers nor the town garrison could resupply except for current needs, nor build new engines nor defenses, nor repair old ones; all had to remain exactly as it had been when the agreement was made. And if battle did ensue, the garrison had to stay out of it. Then hostages were exchanged, and if the guarantee was not kept, the hostages could be executed with impunity (see execution). (Bibliog. 159, 181, 351)

signs of war, indicators of the type of conflict to be waged: the usual sign of a war to the death was displaying a red flag, banner,* or oriflamme.* To declare an open, just (or public) war (see war, just), the banner of the prince* in whose name it was being fought was displayed. By showing a banner unfurled, he was issuing a challenge to combat and announcing that a state of war existed. Any opponent who was not a subject, however, was free to shun the conflict if he so chose. As a banner or pennon* was a man's personal emblem, by displaying it he was committing himself on his honor* to do battle. Moreover, as a banner also was a sign of a higher personal status than a mere pennon, any battle in which banners were displayed was a much more serious one than one in which only pennons were shown. In contrast, a private war was one which a man armed in his own coat armor* and using his own "battle cry"* conducted on his own. Provided he had a lawful cause and had defied his enemy, he could fight and kill in his own name, but he could not burn and ravage and ride about with banners unfurled, however, because his was not an open war, but a covert one. See truce. (Bibliog. 181)

silica, siliqua, silver coin and its half denomination of the Gothic and Lombard kings* of Italy between the 5th and 8th centuries. The Gothic coinage* bore the names of the Roman emperors* on the obverse and the monogram of the Gothic sovereign on the reverse in order to inform the people of changes of monarch. (Bibliog. 150)

siren. See mermaid.

skald. See scald.

skep, measure of capacity for grain and other dry products varying from one or two bushels* to one or two seams.* (Bibliog. 394)

skulk. See hunting terms.

slaying adder. See asp.

Sleipnir, Odin's eight-footed gray horse* that traveled over both land and sea.

sling, oldest projectile weapon used for millennia by peasants (see villein) and yeomen. It consisted of a length of leather, plaited cord, or other suitable material with a loop on one end and a widened section of a pouch in the middle. A pebble or specially suited sling-stone was placed in the pouch, one finger passed through the loop, the free end was held between the fingers, and the sling was swung around rapidly. When the end was released, the stone was hurled at its target with incredible speed. Some sling-stones were two and one-third inches* in diameter and covered with lead. The Spaniards used this weapon with great effect at the battle of Navarete where they broke skulls and helmets* and unhorsed a great many of their opponents. (Bibliog. 27, 71)

slot, trace or footprint of a deer by means of which an experienced huntsman* could recognize the age, size, and sex of the deer. An old stag left a blunter print with a wider heel than did a hind.* Any slot into which four fingers could be placed with ease belonged to a warrantable stag. See hunting. (Bibliog. 96)

sloth. See hunting terms.

smaragdus. See griffin.

soc, right to hold court,* to do justice* and to receive fees and fines* that arose from it. See sac. (Bibliog. 246)

socage, tenure* of land by specific services other than knight-service (see knight-hood); it included the main incidents of fealty,* relief,* and escheat,* but without scutage,* wardship,* and marriage.* Originally this tenure was held by service fixed in amount, generally agricultural, but with later commutation it came to include any tenure having money* rent only. (Bibliog. 24, 246)

social status. See status, importance of.

soile. See soule.

sol, solidus, Latin word for shilling (see coinage) and a copper coin of France corresponding to the German solidus, Italian soldo, and the Spanish sueldo. (Bibliog. 324)

solar. See bower.

soldier (L. *solidarus,* "man who served for pay"). The Latin word for shilling (see coinage) was *solidus,* and the receipt of the king's* shilling or a day's pay was the final and irrevocable act which changed a civilian into a soldier. A shilling was the normal day's pay for a knight in the 12th century. In 1162 a *milites solidari* was paid eightpence (see penny) per day; by 1210 it had risen to two shillings per day because the knight had to buy his own equipment. (Bibliog. 264)

soldo veronese. See coinage.

solidarii. See mercenaries; soldier.

solidat. See librate.

solidus. See sol.

sollerets, solerets, metal defenses for the feet formed by long, narrow, overlapping plates similar in outline to civilian fashion in shoes. (Bibliog. 9)

sommier. See horse.

Song of Roland (Chanson de Roland), oldest extant *chanson de geste,** dating from 1135. Based on a historical event of August 15, 778, it described the treachery of Ganelon,* Roland's stepfather, against Roland, one of Charlemagne's *douzepeers**; of their ambush and death at Roncevaux*; of Charlemagne's retaliation against the pagan Moors; and of Ganelon's subsequent trial for treason and execution. Roland was depicted as the personification of chivalry* and knighthood*; he was brave, fearless, and true to his word. He refused to summon help at the last battle because it would bring disgrace on his God, his country, his king,* and his family. (Bibliog. 3, 40)

sou. See money.

soule, soile, single deer in hunting.* (Bibliog. 96)

soutiens (Fr.), trees and other inanimate objects used as armorial supporters* by the French. (Bibliog. 116)

sovereign's role in battle. The king* occasionally took an active part in a battle but usually led the reserve forces. Sometimes he led his forces as did William* II at Thielt in 1128, Guy of Lusignan at Acre in 1189, Richard I* on the third crusade,* and the count* of Artois at Courtrai.* Generally, though, the king kept a reserve in order to force a decision, and he led that group himself. As medieval armies were quite small, their leaders could not afford the luxury of staying out of the battle with their bodyguards because the absence from the fighting troops of even that small a group would have weakened the forces seriously. The commander thus felt obligated to take an active part. Geoffrey Martel of Anjou, for example, led the reserves at Noit in 1044, as did Bohemond on the first crusade, Baldwin I at Ramleh in 1101, Henry I of England at Tinchebrai* in 1106 and Bremule in 1119, and Louis VII of France on the second crusade in 1147–1148. The list of such participation is long. (Bibliog. 351)

sow, cat, shed on wheels covered with raw hides as protection from fire and used as a cover for a "battering ram,"* bore, or for men working to prepare the way to use the belfry* and other siege engines. See siege warfare; cat. (Bibliog. 71)

sownder. See hunting terms.

sparrowhawk. See falconry birds.

sparth, long-handled axe* or Danish axe (see battle axe) used in England from the 14th century on; the Irish favored it and called it a Galway sparth. (Bibliog. 27)

spatha, long sword* used by cavalry auxiliaries of Roman, Gaulish, and German troops. (Bibliog. 239)

spayard, hart in its third year. See hunting terms. (Bibliog. 96)

spear, any staff weapon designed primarily for thrusting. The infantry war spear of about 1000 had a long leaf-shaped blade with two small lugs or wings set on each side of the socket to prevent the spear from penetrating too deeply and thus hindering its quick withdrawal; they also were helpful in parrying blows. After the 12th century these lugs disappeared except for use in hunting,* and the spear maintained just the simple leaf- or lozenge-shaped head. See lance. (Bibliog. 27)

speytard, hundred-year-old hart, classed as a "beast of sweet flight."* See hunting. (Bibliog. 96)

spoils of war. The right to take spoil (booty) and to hold prisoners for ransom* by "law of arms"* applied only in a "just" or public war (see wars, just), which legally meant a war declared by a prince.* In other kinds of war, for example, private war, such rights were severely limited. Pillaging and taking prisoners in a war other than that declared by a prince was therefore not only public robbery but also *lèse-majesté** since the commander of the troops in question was arrogating royal power to himself. Spoil came from three main sources: plundered goods, ransom of prisoners, and appatis* paid by villagers and peasants (see villein) for immunity from hostilities. In a just war, prisoners could be made slaves and goods taken could become the property of the captors, but in wars between Christian princes, prisoners were ransomed. Important prisoners, such as great captains or princes of the adversary's blood, were completely at the disposal of the head of the war; he could reserve any prisoner for himself for reasons of state, provided he was prepared to compensate his lord for the loss of that prisoner's ransom.

In the person of his prisoner a captor acquired a property but not absolute property which slavery and servitude implied. Captured goods were movable;

land and tenements did not become the property of the prince for whom the captor fought, and people remaining in conquered territory became the subjects of the prince but not slaves or prisoners. Thus movable goods interested the soldier.* These goods had to be taken in a just war or else restitution could be demanded. Even so, the term was broad enough for pillage because such goods were not restricted to the battlefield; soldiers could plunder civilians because they had given aid to the enemy. Thus any goods taken were lawful prey. The owner of goods taken in unlawful spoliation could ask for them back if the enemy kept them for only a short time. The courts* ruled in the 1400s that the owner lost title to his goods which remained in enemy hands for over twenty-four hours; in the interval they were not lost, and the owner could demand them back from those who had recovered them.

A captor was obligated to hand over his spoil to the leader of the battle, for after the victory all goods taken were gathered together and called booty and then were sold and the profits shared. Anyone attempting to conceal spoils or a prisoner for his own profit forfeited his right thereto. In England the royal portion of the booty was one-third; in Spain, one-fifth; in France, any portion over 10,000 francs. The captain's share was one-third in England, one-seventh or one-tenth in Spain (depending on the captain's standing), and one-tenth in France. After that, the soldiers divided the remainder according to rank. Certain other rules controlled the distribution of spoil. The marshal* of England, for example, claimed all gelded beasts taken as prey on a royal expedition, and the constable* of France claimed all the horses* and harnesses taken. Battlefield division of spoils gathered by foragers was regulated by cries. These were readily understood and often were necessary in the heat of pursuit when all were in search of spoil: "*à butin*"* meant that the spoil was to be shared according to rank as normally was done; "*à bonne usance*"* meant that what each man took he could keep for himself; and "*à prix d'une esquilette*" meant shares would be strictly equal. (Bibliog. 181)

spontoon, cross between a pike* and a partizan,* carried by infantry officers. (Bibliog. 71)

spoon. See petticoat.

spraintes. See fumes.

springald, balista,* siege engine designed to shoot javelins* and iron shafts. It resembled an arbalest* on wheels. Basically it was a huge bow* of steel which threw javelins, spears,* darts,* and sometimes two or more stones in a single discharge. To discharge the stones required two vertical springs of steel which were pulled back by ropes and pulleys and when released would hurl one missile from a sling attached to the tip and another from a cup attached to the steel spring itself. See siege warfare. (Bibliog. 71, 225)

spurs, pointed device attached to a rider's heel and used to urge on a horse.* One, called a prick spur, had a single spike instead of rowels. The rowel was a wheel with blunted spikes on it. These were so important to a knight's equipment that the "earl marshal"* carried the Great Golden Spurs in the coronation* of Richard I* in 1189. (Bibliog. 9)

squire, knight's attendant and novice for knighthood.*

SS, collar of. See collar of SS.

stables, huntsmen* and kennelmen with hounds on leash whose duty it was to take up a post or station assigned during the chase.* (Bibliog. 96)

staete (Ger.), constancy, a quality of noble ladies which knightly poets and singers praised extravagantly. (Bibliog. 274)

staff, "battle axe,*" Danish axe, double-edged weapon with a total length of about four feet.* Its head in profile resembled a trumpet with a convex edge and a flat back. From 13th century onward its flat back gave way to a spiked or fluked back. (Bibliog. 27)

staff sling, two-handed weapon consisting of a four-foot pole with a sling in the middle, used to hurl large stones at the enemy. See fustibal, sling. (Bibliog. 71)

staggart, hart in its fourth year. See hunting terms. (Bibliog. 96)

stains, tinctures (see colors) used in abatements* to stain the nobility of arms*: murrey,* sanguine,* and tenne.*

stalling, deer standing still in its covert.* (Bibliog. 96)

Stamford Bridge, last battle fought on English soil in the Teutonic and Viking manner of hand to hand, axe* to axe. It was fought between Harold Godwineson's Anglo-Saxon housecarles* and the Norse invasion fighters of Harold Hardrata on September 24, 1066. After his victory over the Norse, Harold Godwineson learned of William's* invasion at Hastings and force-marched his men south to combat and lose to the Norman invaders. (Bibliog. 327)

standard, long tapering flag or banner* under which an overlord mustered his forces in battle. A rule of the Templars* held that the banner was a tactical and useful assembly point around which the troops regrouped and also a symbol of resistance, for troops fought as long as a banner was flying. At the battle of Hattin (1187), for example, twice the Franks attacked the Muslims and were beaten back, but only after the banner of the king* of Jerusalem fell did they acknowledge that they had lost the battle. If a Templar was cut off from returning to his own banner, he was to fight under the first Christian banner he came to; if a pagan army was defeating a Christian army, no Templar could leave the battlefield while a single Christian banner flew. Thus this valuable item had to be protected as diligently as possible. The Templars detailed ten knights to guard it, and every deputy commander had a spare banner ready to unfurl the moment the primary one fell. The Templar assigned to carry the lance* with the standard attached was expressly forbidden to use the lance as a weapon; violation of that action meant loss of the Templar's habit, but if the banner was harmed by such use in any way, the knight not only was dismissed from the order but even was chained and thrown into prison (see jail). King Edward III introduced the concept of a standard as different from the banner and other knightly pennons* by its size, which varied according to the rank of the knightly person using it. The king's great standard, for example, was eleven yards* wide. His ordinary standard, the one carried in battle, was nine yards wide. Others varied in width: a prince's* or duke's* was seven yards, marquess's* six and one-half, earl's* six, vicount's* or baron's* five, knight banneret's* four and one-half, and a baronet's* four. (Bibliog. 116, 251, 351)

stang, measure of land in Wales commonly identified with a customary acre* of 3,240 square yards,* but in certain regions it was smaller and was considered the equivalent of one-fourth of an erw* or standard acre of 4,320 square yards. (Bibliog. 394)

stankes, layes tanks, pools, or large ponds; a stank house was a moated house. (Bibliog. 96)

statant, blazon* term for animal with all four feet on the ground. See beasts, positions of. (Bibliog. 116)

Statum Armorum in Torniamentis, promulgation of the rules for tournaments* about 1265 which referred to heralds* and their duties; it appeared about ten years after the first "roll of arms."* It stipulated that any knight going to a tournament should have no more than three squires (see knighthood) as assistants, should not carry a pointed sword* or dagger, a mace* or staff, but should carry only a broad sword. If any knight violated that provision, he was to lose his horse* and harness and be imprisoned, and a squire who violated them also would lose horse and harness and be imprisoned for three years, while a groom or footman would be imprisoned for seven years. (Bibliog. 71)

status, importance of. A person's social status affected the burdens to which he was subjected. A knight's relief* was different from that of a sergeant* or a baron*; the marriages* of a knight's widow and children were controlled by their lord, but a socager's (see socage) widow and children were not so controlled. Different rules on wardship* applied, as did the disposition of property. The widow of a freeman was entitled to a dower* consisting usually of one-third of the property, but the widow of a villein* was not. A socager came of age at fourteen, but a tenant holding by military tenure* was not a man until he was twenty-one. Special customs in certain areas affected townsmen: in Coventry in 1221, for example, he who could count up to twelve pennies* and measure cloth was considered to be of age. (Bibliog. 264)

Statute of Laborers, attempt by the English Parliament* and king* in 1351 to return working conditions of peasants (see villein) and laborers to their status before the Black Death* swept across Europe in the 1340s, reducing the work force considerably. Throughout Europe this sudden reduction in the work force was used as an excellent opportunity to demand and get increased wages. English lords, however, were unwilling to pay the extra money,* and King Edward III sided with them by issuing this statute. It provided that every man under sixty was to go to work or go to jail*; that if a man left a job before his employer agreed, he was to be jailed; that the old wages (before the plague) be reestablished and that if some employer paid more than those wages, he would be fined three times the amount paid and the worker would yield to the town any excess wages received. (Bibliog. 154)

Statute of Stepney. See money, bad.

staunch hound, dog that stuck to the scent of the first stag hunted and which refused to be lured by or satisfied with the scent of another deer if the first one changed.* This was considered to be one of the most valuable and desirable qualities in a stag hound. See hunting dogs. (Bibliog. 96)

staynaude colors. See abatements.

stechtarsche (Ger.), small ribbed shield* tied to a knight's left shoulder by laces. It served as the target for opponents in jousts of peace (see *gestech*). Its ribbing served to grip the coronal* of the opponent's lance.* As there was no rear plate to the saddle,* nothing impeded the knight's fall from his horse* if struck squarely on this shield. (Bibliog. 71)

stele, arrow* shaft without feathers or head. (Bibliog. 100)

Stephen, king* of England, 1135–1154.

sterling, English silver penny* of Norman and subsequent dynasties. It often was used in the phrase "a pound of sterlings" to mean a pound* weight of silver pennies, afterward as the name for the English pound of 240 pence as a money* of account. Presumably the word derived from the Old English "steorling," meaning a coin with a star, referring to some of the early Norman pennies having a star on them, and not from the four birds, martlets,* or starlings on some coins of the reign of Edward the Confessor (1145–1066), for the word then would have been starling. (Bibliog. 246)

steward, chief of a lord's officials and a man of rank and standing higher than the manorial reeve.* Originally he was a servant of the Norman kings,* having charge of the hall* (*aula*) and all that pertained to it, including the kitchen, pantry, and larder, each of which had a master dispenser at hand. He was the voice and representative of the lord on the manor* and was in charge of the management of the agriculture of the land. From time to time he would preside over the "manor court"* and would hold the frankpledge.* He summoned once a year all those whom he had placed in charge of the daily conduct of manorial affairs and received from them a detailed account of the affairs of the manor. He had to know the size and needs of every manor, how many acres* should be plowed and the amount of seed needed, how the bailiffs* and reeves conducted the lord's business and how they treated the peasants (see villein)—he had to control all the manorial business. Among his ceremonial duties was to place the dishes on the lord's table at solemn feasts. His office was identical with the seneschal* and appeared alternately in Latin as *dapifer* and *senescallus*. His position at court later was changed to become the lord high steward, an officer appointed only for coronations* or for trials of his peers.* (Bibliog. 24, 262)

stick, measure of quantity for twenty-five eels which equalled one-tenth of a bind* or one-tenth of a gwyde. (Bibliog. 394)

stinking flight, beasts of. See hunting.

stinting, limiting the rights of pasture. (Bibliog. 24)

stipendarii. See mercenaries.

stone, weight for dry products equalling fourteen pounds,* but important exceptions ranged from five pounds to thirty-two pounds: five pounds for glass; eight pounds for almonds, alum, pepper, sugar, wax, and London beef; twelve pounds for Herefordshire beef and lead; fourteen to sixteen pounds for flax; and sixteen, twenty, and even thirty-two pounds for hemp. (Bibliog. 394)

Stone of Destiny. See coronation chair.

Stone of Scone. See coronation chair.

stoop, rapid descent of a falcon from a height upon her quarry.* (Bibliog. 26)

storyteller. See minstrel.

stoup, measure of capacity for liquids, generally wine* and honey, and varying in size from one pint to one or more gallons.* (Bibliog. 394)

Strasbourg Oaths, pact sworn in 840 by Louis, king* of the Germans, and Charles the Bald, king of the Gallo-Franks, both grandsons of Charlemagne, to support each other in their efforts to drive out their third brother, Lothair, king of Italy and Lotharingia (Lorraine). Each man swore in the language of the other. (Bibliog. 186)

Striguil. See Chepstow.

strike the hood, pull the braces that opened the hood so that it was ready to be removed from a hawk's head. (Bibliog. 26)

striking point, optimal point at which, when the edge of a sword* blade met the object struck, the blade vibrated the least and the most effective weight was delivered by the blow. It varied according to the balance of the sword. (Bibliog. 239)

styca, small coin of debased silver, then of copper, which circulated along with the sceat* in Northumbria. (Bibliog. 150)

subordinary, subordinate, diminutive of the ordinary* or geometrical charges of less significance, such as orle,* canton,* gyron,* fusil,* label,* roundel,* in escutcheon* in heraldry.* (Bibliog. 116)

succession to the throne. See *dominus*; kingship.

sued, deer being chased or pursued. See hunting. (Bibliog. 96)

suet, fat or grease.*

sulung, unit of land measure in Kent, implying plowland, the fourth part of which was the yoke or jugum* derived from the pair of oxen which made up a quarter of the normal plow team, just as the bovate* derived from eight oxen. (Bibliog. 109)

summed, hawk with fully grown plumage. (Bibliog. 26)

sumpter. See horse.

supporters, figures of living creatures placed on the sides of an armorial shield* and appearing to support it; the French used the word *support* for real or imaginary animals, the word *tenants* for human figures or angels, and *soutiens* for trees and other inanimate objects. (Bibliog. 116)

surcoat, sleeveless garment reaching the heels and worn over armor* to reduce the effect of the scorching sun; it was slit up the front and back for convenience in riding. (Bibliog. 9)

swanimote, court* held three times per year to deal with agistments* and pannage.* (Bibliog. 163)

swastika, type of cross*; fylfot.*

sweet flight, beasts of. See hunting.

Swein, Earl Godwineson's eldest son, a soldier of fortune who was utterly ruthless. After he treacherously killed Earl Beorn, who had come to help him, King Edward the Confessor declared him "nithing."* (Bibliog. 327)

swertliete. See *ritterschlag*; *dienstmannen.*

sweyne feather. See hand palisado.

swivel, metal connection between a hawk's jesses* and leash.* (Bibliog. 26)

sword, weapon with a long blade for cutting or thrusting; often used as a symbol of honor or authority, it was the knight's most treasured possession. (See knighthood; dub.) Usually it had a two-edged blade thirty inches* long that narrowed to a point. Its parts were the blade, hilt, tang—piece of wrought iron welded to the shoulder of the blade and inserted into the grip—the short grip or handle without a swell, the knob-shaped pommel* at the end of the grip, and the quillons*—pieces or guards which passed between the hilt and the blade. Normally a sword was the work of five people: a cutler or bladesmith, the hiltmaker, the sheather, the girdler, and the furbisher who assembled all the parts and usually sold the completed weapon. Towns famous for swords included Cologne, Pavia, Poitou, Bordeaux, Valencia, Passau, Solingen, Milan, and Augsburg. Once assembled, the sword needed to be tested or proved by striking a heavy blow against a block of iron, first flat and then on the edge and then on the back; then the blade was twisted flatwise; then it was given the Toledo test, driving its point through a thin iron plate.

Early on, the cavalry auxiliaries of Rome, generally Gaulish or German troops, used the long sword, the spatha*; the legionary used the short stabbing sword, the gladius.* The early Scandinavian sword carried by no one under the rank of thegn (see thane) had been longer (thirty-six inches) and had a straight double-edged blade rounded at the end. About A.D. 900, a new type of blade came into use, one that had better balance and a more graceful form. Its blade was thirty inches from hilt to point, two inches wide at the hilt but tapered more sharply than its predecessors, and its point of balance was nearer the hilt so it could be wielded with greater agility and speed. This was the basic sword developed to oppose chain mail.* It saw no major changes until the last quarter of the 14th century when changes in armor* required a change its design. The new sword had a strongly tapering, acutely pointed blade of a four-sided, flattened diamond section in order to serve the dual purposes of cutting and thrusting: the upper portion was stiff enough for a cutting blow, the lower section sharp and stiff enough to thrust effectively, and its point was sharp enough to penetrate plate armor. Thus it was useful against both types of armor, chain and plate, or combinations of mail and plate.

A knight obtained his sword in various ways. He could buy it from a traveller from the great weapon-making towns: Milan, Augsburg, and others where the blade might have been forged, but the rest assembled in such places as Paris, London, Salisbury, Chester, or Norwich. Or he could get it as a gift from a feudal lord who might have been a baron* of Normandy who won the sword in a personal fight with a Spanish knight who had gotten it from Seville. Or he might obtain it on a battlefield in Aquitaine or in a tournament* in Saxony. He might lose his sword by dropping it in battle, or in a river, or have been overcome in a joust* in Provence by a knight from Prussia who took it home for his tomb, or have given it to his brother-in-arms* in the Holy Land. If he didn't lose it and died with it in his possession, it was placed on his tomb. (Bibliog. 9, 56, 71, 239)

swords, famous, names of famous swords included: Almace of Archbishop Turpin; Anguravadel of Frithiof; Arondight of Sir Launcelot du Lac; Balmung* of Siegfried; Curtana* of King Edward the Confessor; Durendal* of Roland*; Excaliber,* Caliburn, or Caledfwlch of King Arthur; Flamberge, Floberge, or Joyeuse* of Charlemagne; Glorious* of Oliver*; Mimung, borrowed by Siegfried; Nagelring of Theoderic the Great or Dietrich von Bern; Tizon* of El Cid. (Bibliog. 308)

sword of Sir Tristram, one of the treasures of the English throne given to King John by the Holy Roman Emperor. It was lost along with King John's jewels in the Wash* in 1216. See Curtana. (Bibliog. 169)

T

tabard, simple tunic, generally without sleeves and open at the sides, worn over the armor* and commonly emblazoned front and back with the arms* of the wearer; the name later was given to the garment worn by heralds*; it superseded the jupon* in the first half of the 15th century. (Bibliog. 9)

taces, lames* of plate metal which overlapped upward and replaced the skirt of mail.* (Bibliog. 27)

tactics, battlefield. Kings* considered war a sport to be entered during the spring as they embarked with their armies, their minstrels* and troubadours, and their hounds and hawks (see hunting; hawking) until the autumn when they made truces to last until the following spring. Winter warfare was far too uncomfortable to be endured in the open countryside of battlefields on foreign soil. Like tournaments,* battles often were held at places and at times agreed upon between leaders of opposing armies, and their outcomes were affected by the code of chivalry.* Leaders frequently adapted tactics from tourneys,* and knights in battle often imitated knights in romances,* as in the battle of Crécy.* A hardened warrior in the enemy ranks could turn such actions to his own advantage, and a clever leader who knew enough to retreat when common sense dictated such a move nearly always emerged victorious. For example, a letter sent by King Peter of Aragon to his mistress, declaring that he had undertaken the enterprise for "her sweet sake," was intercepted by Simon de Montfort, who recognized that it would be easy to overcome such a knight who declared war on God's cause to please a sinful woman. At the resultant battle of Muret on September 12, 1213, Montfort's 500 horsemen overcame an enemy of 15,000 footsoldiers and 600 to 700 horsemen. The first encounter between the forces was a hard cavalry fight, followed by a massacre of footsoldiers by the victors.

However, methods of attack varied as weapons and armor* varied. Early armies generally were armed alike and used the same weapons: sword,* spear,* and axe.* Battles were begun by an exchange of missiles, followed by the shock of hand-to-hand combat. Although horses* transported men to the site of battle, and some armed men fought from horseback, only on the continent had mounted combat become normal for gentlemen.* It was this lack of armed horsemen that contributed markedly to the defeat of the Anglo-Saxon forces under Harold at

Hastings. Harold had fought and defeated the Norse invaders under Harold Hardrata at the battle of Stamford Bridge* late in September 1066, only to learn of the Normans' invasion in the south. He marched south as quickly as he could, but the speed took its toll of the men who couldn't keep up with the pace. When he finally faced the Normans, he had only a fraction of the military potential of England. Thus his forces numbered between 6,000 and 7,000 men, as did the Normans. With his housecarles,* thanes,* and villeins* recruited from the immediate neighborhood, Harold arranged his forces in a strictly defensive formation of a "shield wall"* atop the crest of a hill, with its flanks protected by steep slopes. Among William's* troops were mounted warriors to whom the Latin word *miles** was applied, men who, armed in mail* shirt, iron cap, and long kite-shaped shield,* and weaponed with lance* and sword, constituted the most effective fighters of the day. Norman footsoldiers backed by mounted men attacked the shield wall but were repulsed by spears, axes, and stones hurled by the defenders. Only when the English followed fleeing Normans was the integrity of the wall broken. This was followed by a mounted assault by William's forces, and the battle was lost; Harold lay dead.

Later, in the 12th and 13th centuries, infantry was used frequently to form defensive lines of protection for the cavalry and to turn back charges of enemy knights, as in the battles of Arsouf and Jaffa in the Holy Land and Legano, Bouvines,* Steppes, Warringen, and so forth on the continent. Leaders at those battles were better off than Harold because they were backed by numerous archers, including crossbowmen, and a heavy cavalry. Frequently, however, the infantry's role in a battle equalled that of the cavalry. For example, after the conquest of England, in every important Anglo-Norman battle, the Norman kings of England strengthened their infantry by having their knights dismount and fight as footsoldiers, ignoring the lesson of the supremacy of the horseback fighter that had been established at Hastings. At Tinchebrai* in 1106, for example, ninety-six percent of King Henry's army fought on foot, including the king himself, and the knights dismounted and fought behind a shield wall just as at Hastings.

Mounted knights found considerable improvement in offensive technique by the use of two-handed lance because penetration would be farther and deadlier than a one-hand lance. However, that deep penetration meant difficulty in withdrawal of the lance head, and without the lance, the knight's fighting strength was dangerously weakened. Not only to prevent the lance from going in too far but also to make withdrawal easier, knights attached a pennon* below the blade of the lance. This use of the two-handed lance required the warrior to drop the reins and to control his horse solely by voice and pressure of his knees at a crucial and heated part of a battle. If the horse were wounded, this could be extremely dangerous. To overcome this potential danger, a knight held the reins in the left hand during the charge and exerted maximum control over his beast by the use of a cruel and powerful bit. Additionally, the use of a two-handed lance prevented the use of a shield; so that weapon may have been effective against footsoldiers, but against another cavalryman it would have been fool-hardy. The knight of western Europe needed a shield on his left arm and lance under his right one to provide a balance of offense and defense in the shock of combat.

During the first crusade* (1095–1098) early Byzantine leaders followed certain tactics against the Turks. They took a large force into the field, maintained an elaborate screen of pickets and guards around their forces to prevent surprise attacks, avoided fighting on broken ground where the enemy forces and for-mations could not be seen, and kept large reserves and flank guards. They fought with their rears protected by such natural defenses as rivers or cliffs to prevent being encircled by the enemy, fortified their encampments, and never separated their infantry from their cavalry to pursue a fleeing enemy. Such common-sense tactics were adopted by the western crusaders after the battle of Dorylaeum showed their practical value. To these tactics the Christian forces of the third crusade a century later added the practice of surrounding the cavalry with a shield wall of infantry reinforced by lances and crossbowmen while on a march. During an attack, the infantry opened a corridor at the appropriate moment through which the cavalry would charge the enemy. These knights would ride out in closely packed units of serried ranks to lessen the danger to any individual, to instill confidence for an effective charge during the heat of battle, and to attack as a unit rather than as a collection of individuals. Should such an attack be unsuccessful, the returning knights would ride through openings in the infantry ranks, which would close behind them to protect them from attack while they regrouped for another charge. To the typical cavalry charge thus was added the shield wall and the advancing infantry formation.

To counter the Christian forces, the Muslims developed tactics of their own. Warfare in the Outremer* became seasonal when winter rains made mass move-ments extremely difficult. During those months the emirs* would return home and allow their men the chance to see families, for if they were denied such opportunities by being kept in the field for lengthy stretches, their fighting enthusiasm dropped sharply. Saladin,* the Muslim leader, needing to capture Tyre in 1187, could not mount his offensive until late in November, but by that time the approach of winter and its accompanying restlessness among his forces made the proposed siege impossible. Leaders like Saladin relied on plunder (see spoils of war) as an additional powerful incentive to keep troops in the field, but this was not readily controlled. For example, Saladin lost the battle at Mont Gisard because his forces were so preoccupied with loot that they lost their cohesiveness as a fighting unit, and Richard I* won a tactical success at Jaffa because his skill as a leader was aided by the low spirits of Saladin's troops. Earlier, Saladin had negotiated with the garrison at Jaffa instead of turning loose his troops to take it by storm. Because they felt deprived of plunder, their effectiveness as soldiers* was considerably reduced.

Crusading Franks admired and feared the tactics of the Seljuk Turks' horse archers. The pace and agility of their mounts, and the lightness of their bow,* shield, lance, sword, and club made them more flexible and faster than the Franks. Their lances, for example, were lighter because they were reedlike with metal points and not made of solid ash or oak as were those of the Franks; their shields also were lighter because they were round and small and not like the long kite-shaped ones carried by the Franks. Most importantly, their steeds were more mobile because they had to carry less weight, an advantage which they were quick to press in several ways. For example, they could remain at a distance, just waiting for the best moment to attack. When they did so, and were charged by the Franks, they would retreat rather than face the massive charge of the crusaders; and like flies beaten off but not driven away, they would attack again and again after the Franks abandoned their charge. Moreover, they would feign a retreat lasting for several days to tire the Franks and draw them far from their bases or to lure them into well-prepared ambushes. This ingenious mobility allowed them to attack the rear and flanks of the Frankish forces while making a simultaneous frontal assault just to keep the Christian soldiers constantly edgy as to just where the enemy would appear next. Furthermore, they attacked and forced the Franks to react while on the march and thereby prevented them from forming units in good order prior to a charge. These tactics were used with considerable success by the Turks against the western forces on the second crusade.

To their speed and agility the Turkish horse archers combined archery. They could fire from the saddle* without halting and dismounting, and thereby maintained a high rate of fire even while retreating. Their weapons were light and would not inflict necessarily mortal wounds on the mail-coated Franks, but they shattered their enemy's cohesion by inflicting more damage on horses than on men. Forage for mounts was scarce in Asia Minor, and knowing the reliance of the Franks on the mounted charge, the Turks destroyed enemy horses whenever possible. Additionally, a rain of arrows* caused an incredible nervous strain on the Franks. However, the Turks were well aware that neither their mobility nor archery was enough; they recognized that victory would come only after they had demoralized and weakened the enemy forces, and then they could be defeated by close hand-to-hand combat with lance, sword, and club. When they saw an opportunity, such as at the battles of Hattin (1187) and Arsouf (1192), the Turks would sling their bows* across their shoulders and attack with other weapons. The opposing Arabs, however, did not fight in the same way. Quite the contrary, they had massed bowmen on foot and horsemen ready to resist a mounted attack. As a result they presented a solid target and thus were usually defeated easily by the most powerful tactical weapons of the Franks—the charge of mailed and mounted knights. (Bibliog. 158, 159, 339, 351)

tagelied. See *minnesang*.

talbot, heraldic dog composed of mastiff's body, hound's head, and bloodhound's long drooping ears. (Bibliog. 116)

talisman, stone or piece of metal on which was engraved a figure or inscription and which when worn on one's person, was useful to cure ailments or to prevent illness. See bezoar. (Bibliog. 336)

tallage, tax levied by a manor* lord on his unfree tenants. At first, a lord could assess the peasants (see villein) whenever and in whatever amount he wished, but from the 12th century on, this right to collect "tallage at will" began to be modified and controlled because the lords were destroying the peasants by such demands. On a Norfolk village, for example, the tallage varied from one pound (see money) to ten pounds from year to year, and the peasants rarely knew the reason for the money being collected. Essential for the manorial income, these taxes had to be paid. Usually they were collected at Michaelmas, sometimes from individuals but usually from the vill* or the manor as a whole. Sometimes the serf* had to pay according to the amount of his land, or the number and value of his animals, or sometimes in common with all, but each had to work out individual payments. In France a special tallage called *gîte* was collected to welcome a new lord. Payment of such a tax was held to imply servile status. Frequently, in deference to the sensitiveness of the boroughs* to this concept, the Latin word *donum* (see *dona*) and *auxilium* were used. (Bibliog. 24, 262, 357)

tallow. See grease.

tally (L. *talea*, a cutting), stick of elm or hazelwood as long as the distance between the tip of the forefinger and thumb when fully extended and bored at one end so that it could be filed on a rod. It was used as a form of wooden money* and as a receipt for money received. Split lengthwise, it bore the names of the recipient on the stock and the consignee on the foil. It was used extensively by sheriffs* as a receipt for payment of debts due the king* or for debts incurred by the king when the sheriff bought goods on his behalf. It was of great value to the sheriff when he came to claim his allowance for moneys he had spent, as well as to the king's debtors who felt that they needed some tangible proof that they had paid money to the sheriff, who otherwise conveniently might forget and slip the money into his own purse. These were of two kinds: tally and memorandum tally. The memorandum tally was shorter because as record of payments that were blanched after the assay* by which the farm* was blanched, the original tally was broken into pieces, and then for the first time, a full-sized tally was issued when the tally of combustion (see Exchequer) had been tied to it. (See blanching of farm rent.)

At the top of the tally a cut was made the thickness of the palm of the hand to represent 1,000 pounds; then the breadth of the thumb to represent one hundred pounds; then the breadth of the little finger for twenty pounds; the width of a swollen barleycorn* for one pound; a rather narrower cut that removed some of the wood and left a furrow for a shilling (see money); and a single cut without removing any wood for a penny.* On the edge where the 1,000 notch was cut, no other cut was to be made. If no thousand amount was involved, the one hundred cut was placed there, and so on for twenty and one pound so that on the more exposed edge of the same tally, that is, the edge which was placed uppermost when the tally was inscribed, the larger amount was to be cut and on the other edge the smaller. No special notch was cut for a mark,* but the amount was recorded in shillings. After the notches had been made in the stock, it was split in two, one half being kept by the recipient and the other by the consignee.

This was impossible to forge, and at a time when monks and clerks had achieved considerable skill in altering records and charters* to suit the needs and desires of their clients, this aspect weighed heavily in its favor. It was more convenient to handle than bulky rolls of parchment, was extremely durable, was in unlimited supply, and was a visible record for those who could not count beyond ten. It also saved the crown considerable expense of shipping heavy loads of pennies from place to place, for if the king wished to make a purchase of wine,* cups, or cloth, his sheriff armed with the king's writ authorizing the purchase would present the tally to the merchant showing the cost of the goods, and the merchant could recover the money either from the local collector of customs or from the Exchequer* in Westminster. During a year, a sheriff would acquire many bundles of these tallies, which he carefully tied together and stored to await the summons to Westminster and the accounting day. (Bibliog. 24, 102, 132, 144)

tally ho, ''hunting cry''* to encourage ''hounds for the hunt''* to find the original scent of a stag after they had lost it. Presumably it came from a French word, *taiaut*, used solely in the chase of the red, fallow, or roe deer. French King Henry IV sent three of his best huntsmen* to the court of the English monarch James I (1603–1625) to teach the English how to hunt stag in the French way because the English hunting* had degenerated into coursing (see course) of stags within the enclosures of a park. (Bibliog. 96)

tang, piece of wrought iron welded onto the shoulder of a sword* blade and inserted into the grip or handle. (Bibliog. 71)

targe, target, fairly large, round wooden shield* fitted with enarmes* for attachment to the arm used by early Saxons and which remained in popular use by footsoldiers between 1000 and 1400. (Bibliog. 9)

taro, gold coinage* equal to quarter of a dinar,* similar to those issued in north Africa, struck by the Arab emirs* of Sicily during the Muslim occupations in the 10th and 11th centuries, and by the dukes* of the Two Sicilies and Amalfi under the Norman rule in the 11th century; it was reissued as a silver coin in multiples of eight, twelve, sixteen, and thirty by the Knights of St. John in Malta (see Hospitallers) and contained on its obverse the bust of the master of the order and on its reverse a shield* or the St. John's cross.* (Bibliog. 150)

tasser, piece of timber jutting out of a wall to support or to carry weight; it also was called a bragger. If made of stone, it was called a corbel.* (Bibliog. 100)

taw, process of changing hide into leather; a tawer was a maker of white leather. (Bibliog. 96)

teaser, teazer, mongrel greyhound* who hunted game to be shot with bow* and arrow.* Sportsmen standing in their trysts* would shoot at game which these dogs would rouse in the park and drive in front of the royal marksmen standing in the trysts. (Bibliog. 96)

tegulated armor, armor* made of overlapping square, scale-shaped, or foliated plates fixed to flexible material by studs. (Bibliog. 9)

Templars, military and religious order officially known as Knights of the Temple. It was founded in the Holy Land about 1119 to guard the supposed site of the Temple of Solomon and to protect the pilgrims who came to visit it. Such a need arose in the years following the capture of Jerusalem in 1099 when the Franks, gradually consolidating their holdings, always were short of men because most on the first crusade* had returned home, and the new states that had emerged in the East never had attracted enough settlers to provide an adequate defense. As a result, the unprotected pilgrims who journeyed to the shrines of Palestine constantly were being attacked by brigands and Muslim raiders. To their defense came a group of men, among them Hugh de Payns and Godefroi de Saint-Omer, who had sworn an oath to protect pilgrims on the roads and routes in the Holy Land to the best of their ability against thieves and ambushers. Before the patriarch of Jersualem they took a vow of poverty, chastity, and obedience. This idea of monks living by the sword* was possible only in Palestine where there was a holy war to recover Jersualem. Although they soon gained the support of King Baldwin III of Jerusalem and others, not until they commissioned Bernard of Clairvaux in 1130 to draw up the rules for their order did they receive widespread fame.

His work, *In Praise of the New Knighthood*, written to sell a new type of knighthood*—the fighting monk—to Western Christendom, contained seventy-two articles which created the order's basic structure. It had two main classes of membership: knights and sergeants* or serving brothers. Entrants had to be old enough to bear arms. It had no associated houses for women because women drove men from the right path to Paradise, and thus the order wore white* as a symbol of the total rejection of women. With Pope Eugenius III's approval they added a red cross* to this garment. Sergeants or serving brothers wore a black or brown mantle to show their lower status. Married men were admitted but only as sergeants, and on their deaths their property went to the order; a widow received only a portion of the estate and had to move off the property because men who had sworn to chastity could not remain in the same house with a woman. With such bequests and gifts of land and money from rich princes,* they grew so strong that in 1308, King Philip* IV, fearing their incredible power, ordered their leader arrested and charged with witchcraft and other heinous crimes, executed, and the order abolished and its money confiscated by the royal treasuries. (Bibliog. 16, 174, 317)

tenants-in-chief, barons* of the king,* holders of great honours.* A military tenant-in-chief generally had to provide his proper contingent of armed men and to pay scutage* or to go himself. His only choices were either to obey the king's summons or to bear whatever fine* the barons of the Exchequer* imposed upon him for disobedience. If he held his honour by service of fifty knights, he was bound to appear in person with forty-nine; if he was too old or too ill to fight, he had to send a substitute and an excuse. Women and ecclesiastics might send substitutes. (Bibliog. 261)

tenants in free socage, men who held land by knight service (see knighthood) and who paid scutage* but who themselves were not knights. (Bibliog. 264)

tenant's obligations, requirements due the lord for more than just the service due for a fief,* the *servitium debitum** of tenants. The lord could demand a succession duty called relief* when an heir entered into the possession of his holding; from tenants on such special occasions he could demand money* called aids* or *auxilia*; he could enjoy the profits of an estate when the heir was a minor; and as no woman could be married lawfully without the consent of her lord, he could control the marriages* of widows and daughters of his tenantcy. (Bibliog. 262)

Tencendur, Charlemagne's horse.* (Bibliog. 126)

tenebra, ''battering ram''* of the Romans made of a heavy oaken beam tapering toward the head and shod with an iron cap having a point at its end. (Bibliog. 71)

tenne, heraldic tinge or stain of orange. See heraldry; colors.

tenure, act or right of holding property of a superior, usually the sovereign from whom all land ultimately was held, and embracing all forms of proprietorship of property. (Bibliog. 176, 246)

tercel, tiercel, male of the falcon,* so named because it was only one-third of the size of the female. (Bibliog. 26)

terebra, bore, heavy pole with a sharp iron head used to pry stones from masonry and thereby to breach the wall of a castle* or town. (Bibliog. 341)

Tervagant, Saracen or pagan god.

testoon, teston, testone, tostao, in various languages a coin originally bearing a head or portrait, apart from its strict denomination; subsquently it was assigned in Europe to a coin of the dimensions of the English florin* with the weight and value of a quadruple groat.* (Bibliog. 150)

testudo, covering or shed made of shields,* the edge of one shield overlapping the edge of another like the scales of a tortoise shell, and used to protect the soldiers* who operated a "battering ram"* against a fortress. See siege warfare. (Bibliog. 71)

Teutonic Knights, military-religious order originally titled Teutonic Knights of the Hospital of the Blessed Virgin, to which only Germans could belong. This order began when a group of German knights associated with the Hospitallers* in Jerusalem in 1198 separated from that order and under Hermann von Salza began to wear a distinctive garb of a white* cloak with a black* cross* on the left shoulder. As the Hospitallers, so these, too, combined care of the sick and poor with the profession of arms. When Acre fell (see crusades) and the kingdom of Jerusalem disappeared in 1291, however, they were left homeless, so they went to Venice where Emperor Frederick II commissioned them with the pope's approval to convert and civilize the "heathens" in Prussia, Lithuania, and Estonia. By 1309 they had made Marienburg in Prussia their headquarters, where they remained for over 200 years. Supported by some thirty komture or commanders, their grand master administered his own district from his own headquarters. (Bibliog. 274)

tey. See weights and measures.

thane, thegn, official term of rank used in Anglo-Saxon England after King Alfred's time. Originally a household officer of some great man, especially the king,* this man was attached to the king's person and his service was especially distinguished. He was a warrior from a five-hide unit who would serve his king when the fyrd* was summoned. Each hide* would be charged four shillings (see money) toward his maintenance and wages for a term of two months, so he would receive twenty shillings or the equivalent of twopence (see penny) per day, the sum roughly comparable to knights under the Norman kings of England. As the kings rewarded thanes by granting them land for their own support, they gradually became a land-owning aristocracy.* Such grants generally were made in recognition of three specific obligations owed by the thane to the king, or the *trimoda necessitas* of landholders before the Conquest: building bridges, maintaining fortifications, and most importantly, serving in the military forces when the fyrd was summoned. He also was called upon for such other services as work on the deer fence at the king's residence, equipping a guard ship, seaward, guarding the lord, alms-giving, and church dues. The word thane not only indicated a definite legal rank and a social condition above a ceorl,* but it carried with it both privileges and customary duties. A thane's wergild* was six times that of a common man, and his oath correspondingly was weightier. (Bibliog. 261, 267)

theft punishment. Courts* made sharp distinctions between great and petty theft. Great and manifest or red-handed theft was dealt with in summary fashion: punishments* fluctuated between death and mutilation. One of King Henry I's sheriffs,* for example, hanged forty-four red-handed thieves in Leicestershire in one day. In the 13th century, manifest grand larceny also was a capital crime whose sentence was pronounced frequently in local courts and was carried out by the pursuer or sakeber* who struck off the thief's head or threw him into the sea. At some seaports, such a felon was tied to a stake below the high-water mark and left to drown. Generally, though, a non-manifest thief was tried by a local court and hanged; a manifest thief was tried by a king's justice and then hanged. By the 13th century, leniency began to appear when people who had stolen an item worth more than a shilling (twelve pence; see money) were allowed ''abjuration of the realm''* or could choose to suffer the loss of a thumb instead of the usual punishment of being hanged; petty thieves were punished by whipping, by pillory or tumbrel, or occasionally by the loss of an ear. One ear was taken for the first offense, the second ear for a second offense; the gallows awaited he who stole a third time. Sometimes, however, local conditions forced a second-offense thief to do the executioner's work when his ear was nailed to a post and he could free himself only by the use of a knife. (Bibliog. 261)

thegn. See thane.

Theoderic the Great (c. 454–526), king* of the Ostrogoths (c. 473); he also was known as Dietrich von Bern. (Bibliog. 124)

theow, heraldic monster* with a wolf's body and head but with cloven hoofs and a cow's tail. (Bibliog. 116)

therscol, Anglo-Saxon name for a weapon similar to an agricultural flail* but with a spiked ball at the end of the chain instead of a bar as on a flail. (Bibliog. 71)

third penny, one-third of the profits of a shire* which many of the earls* appointed by William* I took for their financial support; this soon was commuted to a definite sum. By Henry II's reign (1154–1189), these all were fixed sums:

the earl of Essex, for example, received forty pounds, ten shillings, tenpence (see money); the earl of Arundel (Sussex), twenty marks*; the earl of Devon, eighteen pounds, six shillings, eightpence. (Bibliog. 264)

thistle, Scottish emblem that emerged from a Danish invasion of Scotland. Tradition stated that during the early days, warriors considered it unwarlike to attack an enemy at night rather than await a pitched battle by day; the Danish invaders, however, resolved to use the darkness of night to cover their approach and marched barefooted to prevent their footsteps from being heard. Nearing the unsuspecting Scottish forces undetected, the Danes were ready to begin their assault when the cry of pain of one soldier* who unluckily had stepped on a thistle revealed their presence to the Scots. In the battle that followed, the Danes were defeated with great slaughter. As a result, the grateful Scots adopted the thistle as the insignia of their country. (Bibliog. 178)

thrave, measure of capacity for grain and thatching straw generally containing twelve to twenty-four sheaves. (Bibliog. 394)

three-day's tournament, literary device used in romances* to allow a hero to appear at a tournament* on three successive days dressed in different disguises: red, white, and black armor* with horses* to match. At the end of each day's tourneying, even though he disappeared from the field, he was declared the winner of that day's events. It was used in such romances as *Ipomedon, Cliges, Sir Gowther, Richard Coeur de Lion,* and *Partenopeus.* (Bibliog. 152, 375)

threng. See *dreng.*

thridjunger. See shires.

throwing axe. Although most axes* were used as missiles by armies through the centuries when the occasion demanded, special throwing axes frequently were developed. In the second half of the 14th century, for example, the Germans had developed a weapon made from a single piece of iron in the shape of a cross* with one arm longer than the others to serve as a handle and with one of the two horizontal arms widening into an axe blade. Each of the arms, including the handle, was so sharply pointed that however it struck when thrown with a spinning motion, it was certain to inflict serious damage. (Bibliog. 27)

thrymsa, Anglo-Saxon 8th-century copies in gold of Merovingian and Byzantine coinage*; the obverse contained a portrait and the reverse a cross*; continual minting with no change in design made its original Latin legend so illegible that it was replaced by one in the Runic alphabet. (Bibliog. 150)

tiel haut. See curee; hunting cries.

tierce, third "canonical hour"* indicated by ringing of church bells at approximately 9 A.M. (Bibliog. 265)

tiller, stock of a crossbow.* (Bibliog. 27)

tilt, barrier erected down the center of the lists* as a safety measure to prevent tournament* contestants from colliding. Originally of cloth, this wall later was built of wood. When such a barrier was used, jousting (see joust) was called tilting, and thus in time the word transferred to include the military exercise in which two combatants charged each other with lances* or spears* as they tried to unhorse each other. (Bibliog. 27)

timber, measure of quantity for forty fur skins of beaver, squirrel, cony, ermine,* ferret, badger, jennet, miniver, mink, otter, sable; so called because skins were packed and shipped between two boards; most other furs were measured by the hundred* and shipped in bales. (Bibliog. 394)

Tinchebrai, decisive battle in 1106 in which King Henry I of England defeated his brother, Count Robert II* (Curthose), and took control of Normandy from him. (Bibliog. 241)

tinctures, heraldic colors.* See heraldry.

Tirel, Walter, mercenary* who had entered the service of William* II (1087–1100) to get the gifts and wages which that English monarch was so lavishly providing his soldiers.* Subsequently he had married into the illustrious English Clare family and had been granted the fief* of Langham in Essex. On a fatal hunting* expedition, he was the hunter who fired the arrow* which killed William II in the New Forest in 1100. (Bibliog. 159)

tithe, tenth part of every Englishman's yearly wages, arising from the profits of land, stock, or personal work, paid to the church in kind or money. At times this demand on all people exerted considerable pressure, particularly when there were too few animals to make cheese or when there were too few calves, lambs, kids, chickens, piglets, geese, or fleeces to be divided by ten. In those cases the church ruled that one farthing* should be given as tithe for each lamb, kid, or piglet; but if there were seven or more, one was to be given for the tithe. For the milk of a cow, one penny* was due; of each milk-ewe, one farthing; and of each she-goat, one halfpenny.* Because some took the milk to church instead of money* as payment and found no one there to receive it, they would pour it onto the altar in defiance. (Bibliog. 77)

tithing, small administrative division, the tenth part of the hundred,* which consisted of a group of ten men and their families—ten households—bound for the good behavior of each other in the system of frankpledge.* (Bibliog. 261)

titles of dignity, French, German. For England, see peer; precedence. In France, three ranks of dignitaries existed: duke,* marquess,* and count.* Dukes, from the Latin *dux*, were military leaders who became heads of districts comprised of several counties*; marquesses were officers in charge of marches* or frontier regions of the kingdom; and counts were officials in charge of smaller subdivisions of the kingdom. All three were in the first ranks of magnates (see peer), as were their descendants known as comtors. Originally counts had been the heirs of the great honours* of the Carolingian period and had been public officers, but they grew to become fiefs.* As the rights accompanying these titles shrank and varied from area to area, the title of count became merely an indicator of one with great power and prestige, not necessarily a successor of a provisional governor. By 1338 the kings* had begun to create counts, thereby establishing a formal classification of nobility.

In Germany the first titles were controlled by a rule peculiar to German feudalism*: on pain of forfeiture of rank, a person could not hold a fief of someone who was considered an inferior. Thus vassalage (see vassal) was not allowed to interfere with hierarchic beliefs. This rigidly ordered the shields* of knighthood,* the *Heerschilde*. At the top stood the *Fürsten*, the first men, which in Latin was *principes* and in French *princes*. Under this term were grouped all who held the office of count even when not figured among the king's immediate vassals. After the mid-12th century, a shift altered the divisions between ranks. First, the word prince* was reserved for the direct feudatories of the king, especially those whose authority spanned several counties. Such men and their ecclesiastical counterparts were the only ones empowered to elect a sovereign. A second segregation occurred shortly thereafter when an even more select and restricted group called electors was placed over the first group. Eventually a new class of lay princes including the electors formed the third level of shields ranking after the king and princes of the church—the bishops and greater abbots directly dependent on the crown. This lowest class of knights, the *dienstmannen*,* in French were called the sergeants,* or the *ministeriales*. German words for the English and French ranks include *herzog* for duke; *marquis* for marquis; *graf* for both earl* and count; *vicomte* for viscount*; and *baron* for baron.* (Bibliog. 28)

Tizon, Tizana, one of El Cid's swords.*

toft, homestead, site of a house and its outbuildings. Often used in the phrase "toft and croft," it denoted the entire holding consisting of a homestead with an attached arable piece of land. (Bibliog. 246)

toise. See weights and measures.

Toledo test, testing or proving a sword* by driving its point through a thin iron plate. (Bibliog. 71)

toll and team, one of the privileges belonging to the higher aristocracy* before the Conquest and carried over by the Norman kings* as a right of their barons.* Toll empowered a lord to take a portion of the money* from the sale of cattle or other goods within his land and certainly included the more ancient right to take payment for cattle passing through his estate. Team empowered him to hear in his court* testimony from a person suspected of wrongful possession of cattle or other goods, who would support any pleas by producing good witnesses of his purchase of the disputed materials. See infangentheof; sac and soc. (Bibliog. 330)

tolleno, siege machine used to lift soldiers* up to the ramparts* of a wall. See siege warfare. (Bibliog. 71)

toothache, painful ailment, the cures for which varied considerably. One suggested that the patient should take a candle of mutton fat mingled with seed of sea holly and burn it as closely as possible to the ailing tooth while holding a basin of water beneath it, for the worms which were gnawing the tooth would fall into the water to escape the heat of the candle. Other remedies included holding in one's mouth a frog boiled in water and vinegar or a dog's tooth that had been burned, pulverized, and boiled in vinegar; or touching the ailing tooth with a tooth from a corpse. Cavities were to be filled with such a variety of substances as toasted earthworms, spider's eggs mixed with unguent of nard, or cow dung. (Bibliog. 286)

tourneamentum, collective term for knightly field sports all of the same nature which involved fighting in groups or singly and generally mounted; some were held on foot or on water. In the early days, the chief features of such an encounter were mimic battles between two opposing groups of knights, the *mêlée,** and often preceded by single contests between two knights. Later exercises included attacks on temporarily erected fortresses to imitate sieges of the crusades,* or at bridges or passes to recreate incidents in open countryside. These were called passus* and led to combats at barriers. (Bibliog. 78)

torteau, roundel* tinctured gules.*

tortoise, fanciful name for a movable penthouse sheltering besiegers who were using a "battering ram"* or a bore; it was so named because of its slow steady approach. See siege warfare. (Bibliog. 48, 241)

torture. After Pope Innocent III (1198–1216) banned priests from administering the ordeal,* making it impractical, the papacy tolerated the inquisitorial use of torture to get evidence in the exercise of royal justice.* Pope Gregory IX (1227–1241) maintained that confessions dragged from people under torture were invalid, yet Pope Innocent IV in 1252 directed torture be used in cases of suspected heresy. An accused person was tortured until he confessed and then was invited to make a free confession. If he refused, he again was tortured and again was asked to make a free confession until he finally succumbed. Some of the tortures used included the rack, in which arms and legs were tied to separate wheels which then were slowly rotated, stretching the arms and legs until they popped from their sockets; the pulley also known as squassation; the iron boot in which wooden or metal wedges were hammered between the naked flesh of the leg and the boot itself; various forms of water torture such as forcing the victim to inhale in water or to swallow so much that he almost drowned or suffocated.

Authorities were convinced that the spectacle of a criminal undergoing punishment* deterred his fellow men from following or committing similar offenses, and so the horror value was increased by new methods. Victims were tortured by red-hot pincers or iron plates before execution.* They were boiled to death, flayed to death, racked to death, pulled limb from limb, or broken on the wheel. For misdemeanors, the stocks, pillories, and dunking stools were set up outside churches, village greens, and market places; gallows were erected at important crossroads or other conspicuous places where the largest number of people of an area could witness hideous lessons as they passed grotesquely dangling corpses left to rot.

Additional punishments included branding with a red-hot iron and amputation, both of which marked a criminal for what he was. Often the limb or member lost was appropriate to the crime. A thief lost his covetous eye or pilfering hand; a poacher lost the legs on which he made his stealthy rounds; a counterfeiter lost his right hand and his testicles; a scandalous woman lost her breasts. (Bibliog. 198)

tostao. See testoon.

tourn, sheriff's. See sheriff's tourn.

tournament, tourney, mock cavalry combat involving groups of warriors. In essence, this was the school of courage for a knight. In his training, a young noble left the control of women at age seven to serve as a valet or page; at fourteen he was created squire* and entered the service of some noble, usually not his father. He followed his master, sometimes as a pursuivant* to tournaments and combats, helping him arm and disarm, dressing his wounds, and serving on duty at the tree where his master's shield* was hung. At twenty-one he was knighted and donned a hauberk* for the first time (see knighthood). William Marshal,* for example, earned a good livelihood going from tournament to tournament; in less than one year, he and a fellow professional tourneyer reaped handsome profits by overcoming 103 knights in tourneys and from ransoming them, their equipment, and their horses* (see ransom), making no secret of their motive of maximum booty. Once William sat on an unhorsed opponent to keep him from escaping, and on another occasion after two captured horses were stolen from him, he pursued the thieves relentlessly until he recovered the beasts. When a large crowd was present, however, his actions changed. At Pleury near Epernay, he refused to take prisoners; and in grand public gestures at a tourney at Joigny in 1180, he granted a horse to a herald,* released prisoners on parole, and turned over most of his booty either to those he captured or to the cause of the crusades.* His act of granting booty to a prisoner over whom he had complete power and who was a source of profit was considered the epitome of magnaminity. His generosity at Joigny was prompted by the large number of women present in his stands.

Tournaments were exclusively the jealously guarded privilege of the aristocracy*; the rest of society could only approve or disapprove, admire or envy, but could not participate. The clergy were expressly forbidden by the church from taking part; the bourgeoisie were outsiders trying to buy access with their newly acquired wealth; the commoners were totally disbarred. Knights were not motivated by the lofty chivalric ideas of integrity, steadfastness, Christian love, and compassion to participate in tournaments, but rather by the more tangible aspects of honor*: valor, courtesy, and largesse.* (See chivalry.) These exercises had their practical side, too, because they trained knights for war.

Tournaments were a sport entailing physical endurance and calling for great personal courage, but one in which no animal should suffer death or pain, for even the accidental wounding of a horse caused a penalty to be imposed. It consisted of military exercises carried out in the spirit of comradeship, being a practice for war and a display of personal prowess. They were actual contests on horseback carried out within certain limitations by knights who had divided themselves into contending groups or parties to fight against each other like contending armies. The words "tourney" and "joust" often were confused for each other, but there was a marked difference. A tourney was a battle in miniature, an armed contest of courtesy on horseback, troop against troop using swords* as their main weapons. A joust, on the other hand, was a single combat between two mounted knights run in the lists* but not necessarily there, for they could be run in the street or a square of a town; they used lances* directed at the opponent's body only and were run in honor of ladies present to witness them. Tournaments trained knights for war; the games were meant to be the image of war just as war was the image of the games. They were the school of courage for a true knight. A young knight seeing his blood flow, feeling his teeth crack under the blows of his adversary, and being knocked to the ground from his horse countless times thus was better able to face real war with the hope of victory.

Its beginnings were impossible to trace. Mimic battles sometimes called the *ludus trojae* or the *conflictus gallicus** were held in ancient times and were reportedly continued by the Emperor Louis, Charlemagne's grandson, but the tourney rules were said to have been the creation of a French lord, Geoffroi de Preuilli* of Anjou, in the year 1066. However, Henry the Fowler, emperor* of Germany, 876–936, reputedly held a tournament at Magdeburg for which a list of twelve rules and ordinances was drawn up. This list merely set forth the qualifications of all those who were to be "fought and pursued" in the tourney: he who acted against his fealty*; he who has committed an act against the Holy Roman Empire* and his imperial majesty; he who had offended a woman or young girl by word or deed; he who had forged a seal or sworn a false oath, and so on.

These games were called *hastiludia** or spear-play, or *bohordicum* or behourd, an exercise with lance and shield. At first they were fought with blunted weapons, which the participants soon found insufficient in their search for a more stringent test of courage. Thus the tourney became a real imitation of war and wagers* of battle in which sharp swords and lances were used when the contests were said to be fought *à outrance*,* that is from French *outrer*, "to pierce your enemy with sword or lance." By the end of the 14th century these frequently were described as justs* or *pas d'armes*. Sometimes they even were called the *Pas de Saladin*, and represented the half-legendary exploits of King Richard I* (1189–1199) against the muslim leader, Saladin.* The just became the popular sport because in it, a single knight could demonstrate his individual skill and triumph before the ladies of the court who were the judges of the contests. By the 12th century these were characterized by all the romantic fire of knight errantry,* but frequently were rough and disorderly, degenerating into real battles in which participants were killed. At Neuss near Cologne in 1240, sixty combatants were killed. The rules and regulations imposed limitations on them to attempt control, but not until the reign of Edward I (1272–1307) was any regular system of control effective. Previous attempts to limit them had caused sovereigns to issue royal ordinances any infraction of which was punishable by forfeiture of horse and armor, imprisonment and other penalties, but these were loosely interpreted and largely ignored. King Stephen (1135–1154) was the first English king to agree to their being held, but his successor, Henry II (1154–1189) joined with the church to ban them. Yet, despite church opposition that resulted in a papal bull* in 1228 which decreed that any participant would be excommunicated and would be denied Christian burial if he were killed in one, Richard I allowed them to be held in England. He used that permission as a means to get money by licensing them and by imposing a fee on all who wished to participate: an earl* was charged twenty marks* of silver, a baron,* ten marks, a knight holding land, four marks, and a landless knight, two marks. King John (1199–1216) was opposed to them, so none were held during his reign, but under his son, Henry III (1216–1272), they became baronial affairs; and despite opposition by the king, who regarded them as veiled pretexts for conspiracy of war, about one hundred were held between 1216 and 1274. With the arrival on the throne of Edward I, tournaments became a social institution, officially recognized and formally attended by the court. One of the important regulations from Edward I's reign was a provision called the "Statute of Uncertain Date" (c. 1292) concerning the behavior of squires at tournaments. They were the subject of four of the twelve clauses of that statute:

(1) No earl, baron, or knight shall have more than three squires, (2) each of whom shall wear the device* (chapel des arms) of the lord whom he serves for the day; (3) no knight or squire is to carry a pointed sword or knife, stick or club, but only a broad sword for tourneying; (4) standard* bearers are to be armed with defensive armor* only: knee-cops, thigh pieces, and shoulder pieces of cane; (5) all are to obey the committee (named), and knights who do not are to lie in prison [see jail] at the will of the committee and lose their equipment; (6) squires who do not are to lose horse and arms and lie in jail for three years; (7) no one is to assist a fallen knight except his own squires under penalty of three years in jail; (8) a cadet is to be armed only with knee-cops and thigh pieces on pain of losing the horse he is riding for the day and three years in jail; (9) spectators are not to wear any kind of armor and to be penalized like squires; (10) no groom or footman is to carry a pointed sword, pointed knife, club, stick, or stone on pain of lying seven years in jail; (11) if any great lord holds a feast he is not to admit any squires except those who carve for their lord; (12) heralds and marshals* are to carry no concealed arms save their blunted swords, and the kings of heralds are to wear their mantles of arms and no more. (Bibliog. 88)

At first tourney fields were round within a palisade,* and then they grew oblong, ornamented with tapestry and heraldic devices, and became permanent sites enclosed by a ditch or a moat and had roofed-over wooden stands with sloping galleries for spectators placed at the sides of the list. Marshals of the lists, heralds, pursuivants-at-arms were stationed within the enclosure to note the actions of the fighters. The marshal had to enforce the rules of chivalry; valets helped squires look after their unhorsed masters. Trumpets announced the entrance of each competitor who was followed into the list by his squires. Each knight usually wore somewhere about his body—helmet,* lance, shield, sleeve— a token from his lady. The prize for the best knight was bestowed after his tournament with great pomp and circumstance, and the arms and armor of the vanquished fell to the victor as spoils unless ransomed.

Aside from the possible loss of horse and armor if one was vanquished, the tournament provided many other destructive aspects. In his eagerness to win at all costs, a knight often was driven to such unchivalrous conduct as grabbing an opponent around the waist to pull him from his horse. He would instruct his squires to pull down an adversary by sheer weight of numbers, to knock him from his horse with clubs, to carry a wooden cudgel with which to knock an opponent over the head, to set upon an opponent and force him and his horse into their own retreat or base from the main arena and thus capture him, or to surround their own lord and prevent any getting within attacking range. Such helpers were called kippers.* From such a *mêlée* men often emerged permanently disabled. William Longespee, son of the earl of Salisbury, natural son of King Henry II of England, received such injuries at a tourn in Blythe in 1256 that he never recovered. Count Robert of Clermont, youngest son of Louis IX and brother of King Philip* III, a handsome and generous youth of twenty-two years, was so severely beaten in his first tournament after being dubbed that he became an idiot. Others were killed: Geoffrey of Brittany, third son of Henry II, fell from his horse and was trampled to death in a tourney in 1186; Leopold VI of Austria fell under his horse as it fell in 1194 and died shortly thereafter. In 1216 Geoffrey de Mandeville died from a lance thrust. And Gilbert, earl of Pembroke, at Hertford was hit in his body so violently by the head of his galloping horse when it broke its reins that it knocked him from the saddle.* One foot, however, caught in a stirrup, and he was dragged such a great distance before the horse was brought under control that he died shortly thereafter.

A third aspect of the destructiveness lay in its conspicuous waste in the wholesale breaking of lances. Theoretically, the chief point of the tourney was to test the strength and skill of the contestants in horsemanship, in accuracy of aim, and in resistance to the shock of impact. Yet the splintering of as many lances as possible seemed to become the end in itself. These first lances were shafts of wood and gradually grew to become ornately painted and fitted with pennants of rich and embroidered material displaying armorial bearings (see charge) and other devices. Destruction of these ornate lances was deemed more honorable than that of the cheaper ones. For example, Moritz von Craün destroyed all 300 of his painted lances in a single day and still had time and energy to use some of his plain ones. Further, the tourney was destructive to shields, helmets, fabric of caparisons,* surcoats,* crests,* and the like, for exposing such costly articles to the hazards of combat was the essence of nobility,* which ignored the counsels of prudence and thrift and vainly wore expensive and irreplaceable items in the pursuit of honor and glory in the lists.

The words "*Laissez aller*" were uttered to start a particular tourney; "Hola" to stop it. "Largesse*" was the cry of the heralds for knights to seek rewards, and "*À logis, ployez les banniers*" to close the fête. However, sometimes ending the tourney proved to be more difficult than just the utterance of a few words. During the conflict, the kings of arms and the heralds had supreme authority, and they took steps to limit the number of blows struck with sword and mace,* but keeping order in such fractious times was never an easy matter, especially as blood was running hot in the veins of the participants. A number of means could be used to end the fighting. Sometimes an arrow* might be thrown into the lists by the lord in charge; sometimes the king of arms would throw his symbol of authority—a small white baton—at the contestants to force them apart; and sometimes direct external force was the only means possible. The final signal ending the affair was the blare of trumpets and the furling of banners.* (Bibliog. 72, 78, 88, 149)

tournois (Fr.), tournament.*

tournois, gros, coin of fine silver first struck by Louis IX (1250–1270) at the mint of the Abbey of St. Martin, and equal to four silver deniers (see denarius). Philip* II, his successor, struck the one-third gros* called the maille tierce. (Bibliog. 150)

Tournois du Roi René, 15th-century tourney book written and illustrated by King René d'Anjou himself. It detailed the rules, ceremonials, and courses of the great combat between the dukes* of Brittany and Bourbon. (Bibliog. 72)

tower, mural or flanking. See flanking tower; castle.

tower, heraldic charge* consisting of a single battlemented* tower, usually with a port at the base; it should not be confused with an heraldic castle.* (Bibliog. 43)

trace, footprint of a deer. See slot.

trailbaston, name given to certain 14th-century commissions, those of oyer and determiner, that dealt with hearing and determining the specific offenses involved in violence and breaches of the peace; it was first used in 1304–1305. The name originally referred to a powerful band of lawless men about 1300 who used bastons (clubs) to cudgel merchants. (Bibliog. 103, 163, 261)

train, live bird given to a hawk in a creance* to teach her to hunt their species as a particular quarry.* See hawking. (Bibliog. 26)

translation, moving and reburying a saint's body. See Holy Days.

traveler's gear. An English gentleman's* servant used a mnemonic verse every time he traveled with his master so that he would not forget any gear at an inn after an overnight stay:

> Purse, dagger, cloak, night-cap, kerchief, shoe-horn, budget and shoes.
> Spear,* male, hood, halter, saddle* cloth sposes [?], hat with your horse* comb.
> Bow,* arrow,* sword,* buckler, horn, leash, gloves, string, and your bracer.*
> Pen, paper, ink, parchment, reed wax, pumice, books to remember.
> Penknife, comb, thimble, needle, thread, pointer, lest your girth break.
> Bodkin, knife, lyngel [shoemaker's thread], give your horse food, see he be shod well.
> Make merry, sing as you can; take heed of your gear that you lose none.

(Bibliog. 76)

treasurer, servant in charge of the money* kept in a chest in the king's bedroom. (Bibliog. 262)

trebuchet, siege engine using a counterpoised arm constructed on the principle of the swing and the weighted lever, both for hurling and swinging a heavy stone against a rampart.* It also threw barrels* of "Greek fire."* (Bibliog. 71)

trefoil, three-leaved heraldic charge* resembling a clover leaf. (Bibliog. 116)

tremissis, triens, small Roman gold coin equal to one-third of a solidus (see sol) and widely copied throughout western Europe from the 6th to the 8th century, especially in Merovingian France, and circulating in England during the reign of Aethelbert, king* of Kent (c. 616). Its obverse contained a portrait and its reverse a cross.* (Bibliog. 150)

trial procedure. In Anglo-Saxon courts,* an accuser would swear that the defendant had done a certain deed. The defendant had to swear that he had not. In many cases, the defendant's oath was the definitive factor. He needed a certain number of oath-keepers or compurgators* to swear with him, the number varying according to the crime of which he stood accused. Should the accused be found in particularly damning circumstances, the burden of making the decisive oath fell upon the accuser, who then had to swear to the guilt of the accused. If he had sufficient compurgators, his side won. When a defendant could not raise sufficient oath, he could go to the "ordeal of red-hot iron"* or of cold or hot water (see "ordeal of") for the ordeal* was a direct appeal to the judgment of God, and according to Ethelred's law, the accuser could choose the ordeal which the accused would undergo. (Bibliog. 163)

trial by balance, species of ordeal* to test for witchcraft or sorcery in which the suspected sorcerer was weighed to ascertain his guilt, enabling him to escape except when the judges were so determined to obtain a conviction that they eluded the vigilance of the inspectors. A modification of this trial consisted of weighing the accused on one scale and the Great Bible on another. (Bibliog. 196)

trial by battle. See duel.

trial by combat. See duel.

trial by ordeal. See champion for ordeals.

triens. See tremissis.

trimoda necessitas, threefold necessity, the triple common burdens imposed in theory on all free Anglo-Saxon men but in practice on all in the land: fyrd* service (see also military duties), bridge building and repair, and work on burhs, or public defenses. (Bibliog. 47)

Triuwe, Treue (Ger. fidelity, loyalty), quality of loyalty highly praised in old German poetry, but not the ruthless, devastating force exemplified by Hagen in the *Nibelungenlied* when overpowering loyalty to his liege* lord or lady justified lying, treachery, and the assassination of Siegfried. Rather it had become tempered with gentler and more Christian virtues to become *diu maze.** See fealty. (Bibliog. 274)

tron weight. See weights and measures.

tronager, pesager, English customs official charged with weighing goods. (Bibliog. 163)

troops, raising. Troops could be raised in one of three ways: indenture,* commission of array,* and voluntary enlistment. (Bibliog. 222)

trou-de-loup (Fr. wolf traps), potholes dug in front of the Flemish lines of infantry at the battle of Courtrai* to break up the French cavalry charge. The French horses* inadvertently stepped into these holes and broke their legs and fell, rendering their riders highly vulnerable to the footsoldiers. (Bibliog. 241)

trouvères. See minstrels.

troy pound. See barleycorn.

truce, interlude in warfare. This was not an intermission as much as a suspension of war. No one was permitted to build new fortifications, repair old ones, or move troops within agreed-to distances of the border. Lands in which truces operated were considered strictly neutral ground; they were strictly *"hors de guerre"*—out of the war. This was similar to a safe-conduct,* but there were marked differences, the primary one being that whereas a safe-conduct secured a person against war, a truce placed an entire area, perhaps even an entire country, in security. Because of this wider scope, a truce needed a leader with authority over a wider area than just one small locale; it required a *chief de guerre*, a royal surety, someone with a rank equivalent to the king's* lieutenant.

As a truce was one of the conditions of war, its signs were of extreme importance. Because a truce suspended hostilities not necessarily everywhere, but for a local area or people, easily recognizable signs of the truce were essential. White* was its special color. Heralds* carried white batons as a sign of their personal immunity from war, and prisoners in some battles often carried a piece of white paper in their headcoverings. (Bibliog. 181)

Truce of God, *Truga Dei*, edict promulgated by the church in Normandy at the Synod of Caen (1042–1047) shortly after the accession of William* the Conqueror as duke* to quell a serious rebellion. This truce was to begin at sundown on Wednesday and end at sunrise on the following Monday. During that period, no assaults or wounds or killings were permissible, nor any attacks on castles* or houses. Violators were threatened with excommunication if they did not agree to do thirty years' penance in exile and make amends for what they had done against the peace. Anyone giving aid and comfort to a peacebreaker was to suffer the same punishment. This truce extended to land, beasts, and possessions in general, and anyone who stole something protected by this truce was to be excommunicated until he made amends first by returning the stolen property or its value and then by doing penance for seven years. Only the duke could make war. This truce was to extend from Advent until eight days after Epiphany, from the beginning of Lent until the octave* of Easter, and from the beginning of Rogation until eight days after Pentecost. (See Appendix A.) If anyone alleged that he had broken the peace unknowingly, he had to take an oath and then undergo the "ordeal of red-hot iron."* Additions were made to this document at the Council of Clermont in 1095. These included certain new periods for peace, continuous peace for all churches, sacred ground, monks, holy men, and clerical chattels, women, pilgrims, merchants and their servants, cattle and horses, and men at work. The plow was made sanctuary, for all men who fled to it were in peace, and every male over twelve had to swear to uphold the peace and to help any bishop or archdeacon in his attempts to preserve it. (Bibliog. 135)

truss, 1. hawk's clutching and holding the quarry* in her stoop* without letting it go; 2. measure of capacity for one-thirty-sixth load of hay, generally equal to fifty-six pounds. 3. to tuck in, said of eagle's* wings in heraldry. (Bibliog. 26, 116, 394)

trussel, measure of quantity for a number of skins or an amount of cloth that formed a convenient bundle. (Bibliog. 394)

tryst, place or stand where a hunter took his position to await the game he wished to shoot. The animal might be driven by him with hounds, or he might place himslf to shoot it as it went from its lair to its pasturing. These frequently were small enclosures with a roof to protect the hunter from the elements and to provide him with comfort while he awaited the game. (Bibliog. 96)

tun, measure of capacity for wine,* oil, honey, and other liquids generally containing 252 gallons* but occasionally 208, 240, and 250 gallon capacities were used. (Bibliog. 394)

tungerefan, Anglo-Saxon reeve* who managed the king's* private estate. (Bibliog. 132)

turnbedellus, court* official who gathered up all those who were involved in lawsuits at the hundred* and county* court to ensure their appearance. (Bibliog. 357)

turre del homenaje, great keep* or donjon,* the "tower of homage" of Spanish castles.* (Bibliog. 48)

turret, small tower built on corbels* often at the angles of large buildings to overhang the outer wall. (Bibliog. 100, 280)

Twici, Twety, William, grand huntsman* of Edward II, who composed one of the first French treatises on hunting.* (Bibliog. 334)

tyger, tiger, heraldic beast with a lion's* body, tufted hair, pointed ears, tusks, and a sort of beak at the end of its nose. (Bibliog. 43)

tzangara, name given by Princess Anna Comnena of Byzantium to crossbows* used as part of the armament of the crusaders on the first crusade.* (Bibliog. 71)

U

ulna, iron bar distributed to every county,* borough,* and city in England during Richard I's* reign as the official standard for a cloth yard* or an ell* against which all cloth measures were to be checked. (Bibliog. 213)

ulnage, aulnage, alnage, tax imposed in 13th-century England on all clothes produced for sale. (Bibliog. 163)

umbles. See numbles.

umbo, boss* or knob projecting from the center of a Saxon shield,* covering a hole in the wood into which the left hand was thrust as it grasped the handle that stretched across the shield. (Bibliog. 9)

undy, heraldic line of partition* resembling the waves of an ocean. (Bibliog. 43)

unharbor. See hunting.

unicorn, monoceros, one of the oldest and most popular of heraldic monsters.* It had a horse's body, a single twisted horn growing from its forehead, a lion's* tail, and the legs and cloven hooves of a stag. To capture such an animal, a hunter sent a young maiden into the forest* to sit with one breast uncovered. The unicorn would come to kiss it and would fall asleep with its head in the maiden's lap. Thus the hunter captured it easily. (Bibliog. 43, 258)

university discipline at Oxford. Every student lawfully convicted of breaking the peace was to be fined according to the quantity and quality of his offense in addition to other disciplinary penalties normally imposed for such infractions. Such fines,* in addition to satisfaction of the aggrieved party, ranged accordingly: for threats of personal assault, twelve pence (see penny); for bearing arms contrary to statutes, two shillings (see money); for drawing a weapon for violence or thrusting with a shoulder or striking with a fist, four shillings; for striking with a stone or staff, six shillings eightpence; for striking with a knife, dagger, baselard,* sword,* axe,* or any such weapon, ten shillings; for bearing a bow* and shooting it with intent to harm, twenty shillings; for assembling of armed or other persons, and conspiring and confederating against the execution of justice,* or inflicting bodily harm on any man, thirty shillings; for resisting the execution of justice or night-walking, forty shillings. (Bibliog. 263)

Upper Exchequer. See Exchequer.

usnea, sovereign remedy for many different ills, composed of moss from the skulls of criminals who had been hanged and exposed in chains. (Bibliog. 364)

utas, octave* of a Feast Day, the subsidiary observance a week later. (Bibliog. 246)

Utrum. See Assize Utrum.

V

vagiator, vadiator, servant who served writs and distrained goods and rents for the king.* See distraint. (Bibliog. 357)

Vaillantif, Veillantif, horse* Roland* won at age fifteen as part of booty (see spoils of war) fom Charlemagne's war in Italy described in the *chanson de geste,* Aspremont.* (Bibliog. 40)

vair, one of the two principal furs in heraldry,* the other being ermine.* Its design represented small animals' skins joined head to tail. (Bibliog. 116)

valletti, yeomen listed on the marshalsea* rolls as being squires* or knights of King Edward I or of the "king's household."* In other records, similar persons were called scutiferi* and sometimes armigers.* (Bibliog. 87)

value of money. See money.

vambraces, metal protection covering the arm from elbow to wrist. The earliest ones consisted of two gutter-shaped plates and a cuplike couter* strapped over the sleeve of the hauberk.* Each vambrace had two disc-shaped plates called besagews* secured by laces to the front of the shoulder and outside of the elbow respectively. By the end of the 14th century, the term rerebrace* had come to refer to shoulder protection and vambrace to refer to the rest of the arm defense including the couter. (Bibliog. 27)

vamplate, circular steel plate on a jousting (see joust) lance* to protect the hand. (Bibliog. 9)

Varangian Guard, hand-picked English and Scandinavian warriors recruited by the emperor* of Byzantium for service in his household guard (see household warriors). Harold Hardrata served with this group before becoming king* of Norway in 1047. (Bibliog. 49)

varvels, small rings of silver fastened to the end of the jesses* of a hawk, usually engraved with the owner's name. (Bibliog. 26)

vassal, vassalage, personal relationship between a lord and a servant. Originally the vassals of the 6th and 7th centuries were continuations of the German *gefolge* (see *gefolgschaft*) or *comitatus*,* bands of warriors loyal to their chief in return for his protection and generosity. Vassals were free men who became subjects of a warlord voluntarily because of their fighting ability in return for his protection and support. The word vassal came from the Celtic *gwas* meaning boy and meant basically a tough and rough fighter whose services were bought by an important man. These men lived in a stockade provided by the lord and were fed, clothed, and armed by him. As fighting methods changed over the centuries by the rise in military importance of the armed and mounted soldier,* the knight, lords found it necessary to invest a vassal with land of his own from which to derive the revenue needed to support him and his expensive equipment to array himself for battle. Thus he was changing from a thug of the early days to an important local lord with control over many manors.* Vassals by the 12th century began to seek out lords who could offer them land and to make the relationship inheritable for their descendants. In return for the land and fief,* the vassal owed the lord military service not to exceed forty days a year, money* payments called reliefs* on special occasions, and service and advice in the lord's court.* The protection which the lord extended to his weaker neighbors, his vassals, was called *mundium* or *mundeburdum*,* which became *mainbour** in French. (Bibliog. 28, 123)

vaunt chase. See parfitiers.

vavasour, lowest of vassals*; a vassal of vassals who was not himself the lord of any other warrior but exercised authority only over rustics and peasants (see villein). This term was common in Normandy, but in England it was used infrequently to refer to a freeman of little consequence. (Bibliog. 28)

Vegliantino, Orlando's famous horse.*

veltres, hound used for the chase* in hunting.* (Bibliog. 96)

venisection. See bloodletting.

ventail, ventaille, originally a flap which as part of the coif* could be drawn across the mouth and secured by a buckle or lace at the side of the head, but later the term referred to a part of a helmet* or heaume* which allowed in fresh air so the wearer could breathe. (Bibliog. 27)

verderer, special forest* official who was expected to be knowledgeable in the laws of the forest; he kept records of the "courts of attachment,"* checked on the activities of the foresters, and witnessed the execution of orders about forest management, such as which trees were to be felled for gifts or for sale. He was elected to this office in the county* court from the knightly or at least propertied landholders in the forest. (Bibliog. 163, 228)

verge, 1. area extending for twelve miles around the king's* court* regardless of where it might be, within which ("within the verge") the king's peace was enforced; it was so called from the staff or verge which the marshal* carried. 2. stick or wand which persons who were admitted to tenantcy held in their hands as they swore fealty*; such were called "tenants by the verge." (Bibliog. 171)

vert, 1. heraldic tincture (see colors) of green; 2. privilege of using wood in a forest.* Trespasses of vert were injuries to plant life and were heard in forest courts* which met approximately every six weeks. This court could fine* only up to fourpence (see penny); "courts of attachment"* handled more serious offenders, including all offenders of venison. (Bibliog. 163, 253)

vervelles, small staples fitting into openings in the helmet* through which a lace passed to fasten the camail* to it. (Bibliog. 9)

vespers, sixth "canonical hour"* said or celebrated toward evening, usually about 6 P.M.

via franca, also known as the *via Tolosana,* this was the route followed by pilgrims to shrines, especially the route through Saint Gilles, Montpellier, and Toulouse in southern France and past Roncevaux* in the Pyrenees to the shrine of St. James at Campostella (see Santiago de Compostella) in Spain. A popular detour on this route was a visit to the shrine of St. Guilhem-du-Desert at the monastery of Aniane near Gellone whose popularity came about through the *chansons de geste** dealing with the adventures against the Saracens of this saint when he was known as Count William of Toulouse, or Guillaume Court Nez, or Guillaume d'Orange. (Bibliog. 162)

vicomte. See viscount.

vielle, musical instrument played by a jongleur (see minstrel) to accompany the recitations of a *trouvère* or troubadour, or his own poetic creations; it was a stringed instrument sounded by turning a wheel inside it. (Bibliog. 166)

view of frankpledge. See frankpledge; tourn.

vif d'harnois, portion of a knight's body at the armpits which was unprotected by plate armor.* (Bibliog. 9)

vill, township; territorial unit or division consisting of a number of houses or buildings with their adjacent lands, more or less contiguous and having a common organization, and corresponding to the Anglo-Saxon tithing.* It was subordinate because it had no court* of its own, and its smallness made necessary only constables* for policing and reeves* for representing it in court. It was used as an administrative unit for fiscal, military, and judicial matters. It had to enforce the frankpledge,* raise the "hue and cry,"* arrest suspects, keep watches, and supervise the Assize of Arms.* In the 12th century, four lawful vill men had to present the cases of suspects before the justices and sheriffs*; in the 13th century, the reeve and four men were summoned to county court to meet eyre* justices and make presentments to them. (Bibliog. 28, 246)

villein, villani, peasant, native member of a village community, a rustic. Sometimes he performed duties as a servus, a serf,* but he was not a slave. His lord could do with him whatever he wished except kill or mutilate him. Normally, if the villein did what his lord demanded, his lord protected him. However, if he failed to perform his duties, he could be deprived of the lands he held in return for those duties. A villein was prohibited from grinding grain with a hand mill or baking bread* at his own home; instead he had to carry the grain, often a long way, to the lord's mill over abominable roads, to wait several days if the pool running the mill had gone dry, to accept poorly ground meal and burned or half-baked bread, and to endure the tricks and vexations of millers and bakers. Furthermore, he could not brew his own ale, sell his own beasts, give his daughter in marriage without the lord's permission "prayed and obtained." (See Marriage, lord's right to control.) He could not fish in the lord's river, hunt in the forests,* or prevent doves from attacking his crops. For his lord he had to do the field work of plowing, sowing, harvesting, harrowing, and so on. Once the land was plowed and sown, there were many chores still to be done. He had to cart dung from the stables and cowsheds and spread it on the lord's fields; to weed the fields; to tend the plants in the lord's garden; to cut, bind, and store hay in the lord's barn; to cut, glean, thresh, and winnow grain; to collect straw for roofing stacks; to scour ditches, trim hedges, mend fences, gather apples for cider, care for animals, and so on in an almost interminable list. He had to help repair the manor* house and its surrounding buildings by tearing down old walls, digging clay, bringing water to temper it, tearing off the old thatch, fetching and cutting stubble for new. He could not permit his daughter to marry without paying a fine* called merchet,* or permit his son to take holy orders, or sell his calf or horse.*

Sometimes he had to make payments in kind and in money.* Under different names and for various reasons he gave grain (corn*) to his lord: as gavelseed* in addition to money rent paid to the lord, as foddercorn* for feeding horses, as gathercorn* which a manorial servant collected from several homesteads for the lord's use, and as cornbole* which was the best sheaf at harvest time. Different from labor and rents were money payments to take the place of labor services: barlick-silver instead of barley, fish-silver instead of fish, malt-silver instead of malt; fold-silver as duty on sheep, scythe-penny as duty on scythe, bosing-silver as duty on every horse and cart*; pannage* for grazing swine in the woods; and ward-penny* as payment to substitute for the duty of keeping "watch and ward."* He paid a cornage tax according to the number of horns of cattle he had and hidage fee according to the size of his holding.

A person became a villein at birth. His father's status determined his status: the child of a villein father was a villein, of a free father and villein mother was free. If a free man married a villein, lived in a villein's tenement, and was bound there by villeinage tenure,* he lost all legal rights and became a villein. If a lord wished to free a villein, he could quit-claim the man from himself and his heirs, or he could sell him to another with the intent to free him. No villein, however, could buy his own freedom, because according to the law and custom of the realm, all his chattels belonged to the lord, and he could not use the lord's money to pay the lord for freedom. If a third party bought him with the intent to free him, he then remained free of the lord who sold him. If a freed villein appeared in court* to serve as a champion in a duel* of law, he could be lawfully excluded if his servile status was raised as an objection and proved, even if he had been knighted since achieving his freedom.

When a villein was freed, the act was performed solemnly and publicly, for it had to be made widely known that he was being released from bondage. Henry I proclaimed that such an act had to be done openly in the marketplace, church, or hundred* or county* court in the presence of witnesses, and the lord was to place in his hands the lance* or sword* or whatever were the arms of a freeman. Thus it paralleled the ceremony of knighthood* in which girding on the sword was an essential feature. (Bibliog. 24, 30, 103, 155, 172, 264)

villein sokemen, tenants on the estates of the "ancient demesne."* These men enjoyed many immunities denied to an ordinary villein.* They were relieved of the public burdens borne by regular tenants in villeinage; they could leave the tenement whenever they wished; and they were protected by special writs so that they could not be evicted or ejected nor have their services increased. (Bibliog. 264)

vintenaries, men in charge of twenty men on foot in the army of Edward III at Calais in 1347. These were equivalent to subalterns. (Bibliog. 104)

viper, snake which in its mating season attracted its female by songs which resembled a tune played on a flute. In mating, the male put his head down the throat of the female, who bit it off at the decisive moment; then the young killed their mother at their birth. (Bibliog. 258)

vireton, crossbow* bolt or quarrel* so named because its "feathering" of cuir-bouilli* caused it to rotate in flight along its longitudinal axis. (Bibliog. 9)

virgate, one-quarter of a hide*; the term came from the Latin word *virga* meaning a rod or rood. (Bibliog. 109)

viscount, vicomte, title given by William* I to the men he chose from among his comrades-in-arms to replace the English sheriffs.* Their duties in England were similar to those of the position of vicomte in Normandy. It retained this meaning until the word sheriff reasserted itself in the reign of Henry II (1154–1189). In time this rank became fourth in the peerage (see peer). The first English viscount was John, Lord Beaumont, when King Henry VI in 1440 gave him by "letters patent"* the title of Viscount Beaumont in England and France, hence the distinguished affix, "The Lord Viscount." (Bibliog. 246, 360)

visor, moveable plate with ventaille* and occularia* hung from the center or pivoted at the sides of a heaume.* (Bibliog. 9)

voie de fait. Se ransom.

voie de justice. See ransom.

voileurs. See falconry birds.

volant, blazon* term for a bird flying. (Bibliog. 116)

volante. See sharp-lance running.

vomeres igniti. See ordeal of red-hot iron.

vouge, voulge, French staff weapon from the 12th century onward similar to the English bill,* and from it the halbard* emerged. It had a broad axelike blade with a straight cutting edge and was pointed at the head. It was attached to the pole by means of two rings forged to the back of the blade so it pivoted around the staff always in the position to strike. Archers frequently carried one with a shorter staff as a secondary defense. (Bibliog. 9)

vow, sworn oath which knights often took to perform some sort of feat of arms in the lists* or some other emprise.* Often the knight wore the device* of a prisoner's chain as an outward and visible sign of a binding vow. The taking of a vow became a striking ritual of chivalrous society. For example, Sir John Webereton swore to guard the castle* of Lanark for a year as an undertaking sufficiently dangerous to be worthy of the woman he loved, and he died doing so. (Bibliog. 180)

Vow of the Heron, typical example of the chivalric vows.* This took place at the court of Edward III in 1337. Supposedly, it began the Hundred Years War. At that time, England and France were at peace. A French knight, Robert of Artois, had been exiled by the French King Philip* and swore vengeance. When his hawk brought down a heron one day, he saw a means to exact his revenge.

He took the heron to the palace, had it cooked still in its plumage, served at the king's hall* between two silver platters, and arranged for the meal to be accompanied by two fiddlers, a guitarist, and two ladies of noble blood. After the ladies had sung, Robert told the people in the hall that since the heron was the most cowardly of birds, the people of England should swear by it, and that it indeed was fitting to give this cowardly bird to Edward, the most cowardly of men, because he had allowed himself to be deprived of his inheritance in France. Furious, the English king vowed on the heron to renounce his allegiance to Philip and then carried the bird around to others there for their vows. The earl* of Salisbury, for example, asked his ladylove to put her finger over his right eye and swore never to open it until he had brought fire and destruction into France, and unless captured, he would aid Edward in fulfilling his vow. The lady took away her finger and the eye remained closed. (He had lost that eye in a battle in Scotland five years earlier!) The queen then vowed that the child she was carrying would not issue from her body until the king, whom she would accompany, undertook his vow. If the child tried to be born, she vowed to take a great steel knife and kill herself and the child as well. She kept her vow by going to Antwerp where her son, Lionel, was born before the king could keep his vow. (Bibliog. 379)

Vox in Excelso, papal bull* issued by Pope Clement V in 1311 which formally dissolved the order of the Templars* on suspicion of heresy; it ordered that all their property should go to the Hospitallers.* (Bibliog. 16, 317)

Voyde Place. See Siege Perilous.

vulned, heraldic description for wounded or disgorging blood, heraldically represented by a blotch of gules* from which drops of blood fell. (Bibliog. 43)

vuyders, pieces of mail* attached to a cloth garment at places where gussets* would occur to offer protection. (Bibliog. 9)

W

Wace, Anglo-Norman poet who completed his version of Geoffrey of Monmouth's *History of the Kings of Britain* in 1155; he introduced the "Round Table"* to the Arthurian story and the idea of Arthur's survival. (Bibliog. 200)

wad, pledges who were neighbors of people involved in a duel* who would become bail for their due appearance on the battle day. The word came from the Latin phrase *vadiare bellum* (to wage battle), hence the name wager of battle by which judicial duels were known to English law. (Bibliog. 229)

wager of battle, term by which judicial combat or the duel* of battle was known to English law. Introduced into England by William* I, this wager was used in the Court of Chivalry* in appeals (accusations) of felony* and in issues joined upon a "writ of right."* (Bibliog. 229)

wager of law, proceedings which consisted in a defendant's discharging himself from a claim of accusation by his own oath and supported at the same time by bringing into court eleven of his neighbors or compurgators* who swore that they believed his denial to be true. (Bibliog. 363)

wagging. See fumes.

wait on, for a hawk to fly in circles above the falconer* in expectation of the quarry* being sprung below. (Bibliog. 26)

waive, to deprive a woman of her lawful rights, to outlaw* her. Technically, women could not be outlawed because they had never had sworn to keep the law or peace as members of a tithing.* Thus when a woman was convicted of breaking the peace, she was waived. (Bibliog. 171)

wall-work, walkway along the top of a wall of a fortification. (Bibliog. 280)

Wallace, William, famous Scottish outlaw* (1270–1305) who led the Scots to a spectacular victory over the English at Stirling Bridge and who subsequently became legendary as the hero of a ten-year war against the English, rescuing his country three times from them. (Bibliog. 182)

Walter Tirel. See Tirel, Walter.

wambais, wambesium, wambs. See aketon.

wambeys. See gambeson.

wapentake, hundreds* in the Danelaw* area of England; the term came from the Old Norse word *vapnatak*, a meeting of armed warriors. (Bibliog. 163)

war, just. Any person of military status, a gentleman,* had the right to defy his enemies and levy wars against them given lawful cause. To be lawful and just, a war had to be just with regard to the persons waging it, that is, it had to be fought by laymen because clerics could not justly engage in warfare. It had to be just with regard to its object, that is, its aim was to redress some grievance or injury to persons, possessions, or rights. It had to be just with regard to its cause, that is, it had to be the only means possible to achieve its object. It had to be just in its intention and be waged by persons motivated by a genuine desire for justice* and not for greed or hate. And it had to be just by being waged on valid authority of a sovereign prince* or the church. John of Legnano divided just wars into four categories: Roman war waged against infidels on the authority of the church; war waged according to written law, that is, on the authority of a prince; war levied on the authority of a judge that guaranteed the justice of the objective to which the adversary refused to agree, such as a prisoner refusing to pay a lawful ransom* after he has been released on parole to raise the money; and necessary war waged in self-defense. Any war waged for a reason other than the authority of a prince was war in its original sense of "bellum hostile" in which the adversaries regarded themselves as lawful enemies. (Bibliog. 168, 181)

war scythe, single-edged staff weapon with a point which was slightly curved toward the cutting edge; similar to a gisarme.* (Bibliog. 7)

warantia, obligation of a person charged with a crime to produce guarantors who would assure his appearance at the trial and prove his innocence. Such guarantors generally included the accused's lord and members of his family when he was a member of the nobility* or the reeve* and a group of notable free men. A man without warantia could be declared an outlaw.* (Bibliog. 261)

warble, action of a hawk as she stretched both wings upward over her back until they nearly touched, and at the same time she spread her tail. (Bibliog. 26)

ward, inner court of a fortified place. See bailey. (Bibliog. 341)

ward-penny, payment to the king's* sheriff* in lieu of serving "watch and ward"* duty. Many places besides castles* demanded guard duty—town gates, bridges, roads, burghs*—and this payment was commutation of that duty for a money* payment. In 1124, for example, Henry I released the church of Ely from the forty-shilling (see money) payment he earlier had demanded as ward-penny from its land and men. Such an amount corresponded to the *servitium debitum* * of forty knights. (Bibliog. 159)

warden, official in charge of a particular forest* or group of forests. These men were executive officers of the crown to whom royal writs relating to forest business were addressed and who were attendants upon forest courts.* Sometimes called stewards,* bailiffs,* or chief foresters,* these men were to forests what sheriffs* were to shires.* (Bibliog. 156)

wardrobe, 1. location in early courts where the lords kept their precious objects of money, jewels, and clothing, which subsequently became a part of the treasury. In England it was controlled by the Exchequer* until during the minority of King Henry III (1216–1272) it became the king's private treasury whose revenues and expenditures were not controlled by the Exchequer or the baronage (see barony). 2. badger droppings. See fumes. (Bibliog. 96, 270)

wardship, "feudal obligation" which gave to the lord the right to the custody of an infant heir of a tenant by knight service (see knighthood), by military sergeanty, or by socage* and the right to the custody of the ward's property. Originally, it carried with it the right of the lord to dispose of the ward in marriage* and to retain the rents and profits of his land subject to the ward's right to suitable support. Guardianship by socage ended when the ward became fourteen years old but by sergeanty at twenty-one. As one of their articles of the eyre,* itinerant justices were given a list of the king's subjects about whom he wanted information. In 1194, for example, Richard I* wanted information about the wardships of boys which belonged to the king and about the marriages of girls and women belonging to him because he needed to know what price tag to place on widows and children in the marriage market and to determine if the estates in his custody under wardship were being properly and profitably managed. To set a proper price tag on the women, the king needed to know the age of the widow, the number of her children, and the value of her dowry. Young ladies gave their exact ages, but older widows were reluctant because a new husband couldn't enjoy their doweries for very long. Justices often hazarded guesses in round numbers of fifty, sixty, or even seventy and sometimes added "and a bit more."

About the condition of the estates under wardship, the justices found incredible neglect, mismanagement, and shameless profiteering by crown agents and the heirs suffering horribly. For example, in 1182, William de Vesci died and his manor* was placed in the hands of Adam Fitz Robert who mismanaged it so terribly that he was removed hastily. When Adam of Carlisle took over, he found twenty-eight oxen, one of which was dead; five draught horses, one dead; seven yearling pigs and eight smaller ones; 600 sheep of which 260 had been sold for ten pounds eleven shillings and eightpence, and of the remainder, 280 were dead and their fleeces sold for four pounds twelve shillings. Such abuses caused the barons to emphasize such feudal incidents as relief,* wardship, and marriage in the first few articles of the *Magna Carta Libertatum*.* (Bibliog. 261, 264)

warwolf, machine of the harrow family used as a second defense of a gate after the portcullis* had been forced. (Bibliog. 71)

Wash, the, indentation on the eastern coast of England fifteen miles* deep and fourteen miles across. Four rivers emptied into it. One, called the Wellstream in the time of King John, was four and one-half miles wide. At low tide, travellers could ride across it. On October 11, 1216, King John's baggage train tried to cross it, but a rapidly rising tide trapped both men and horses.* Administrative records, state documents, the royal wardrobe* and regalia,* the royal chapel and its relics,* and the king's treasure—dozens of gold and silver goblets, flagons, candelabra, the coronation* regalia, the regalia his grandmother (Mathilda, who was first married to Henry V, Holy Roman Emperor*) had worn as empress of Germany, the great crown and the sword* of Tristan—all were lost. Ironically, seven days later, King John was dead. (Bibliog. 262)

waste, if groves of trees were cut down to make assart* in such a way that one could see six trees felled in one spot, that was called waste—a place laid waste. (Bibliog. 261)

watch and ward, act of keeping guard by continuous and unbroken vigilance. Every man was to bear arms for home defense, so every man was expected to turn out on hearing the "hue and cry"* against some wrongdoer. Those who refused to pursue the hue and cry were subject to arrest by the sheriff.* According to an English royal writ of 1253, each township was to choose four or six men to follow the hue and cry hastily and swiftly, and if necessary armed with bows* and arrows* and other light arms provided them at the common cost of the township and maintained by the town for use by the watch and ward. Two of the most powerful men in the hundred* were to serve as overseers of the watch to ensure that no stranger stayed in the town except during the day, but left before nightfall; that no stranger abided for longer than two days except at harvest time, unless his host was willing to answer for him; and that if any merchant or stranger asked for safe-conduct* through the township, he must be conducted through it safely, for if he was robbed while there, his losses were to be repaid by the inhabitants of the township. Usually the watch was divided into inner and outer divisions. In London there was a marching watch which was separate from the body of ward watchmen, while in a small place like Sandwich, the sergeant* was ordered to summon fifteen men to stand watch and ward, stationing three groups of three at particular points and leading the remaining six around the town to question all people they met during the night. See keeping the peace. (Bibliog. 264)

water supply, essential but vulnerable commodity of a castle.* Sometimes it was available from streams, rivers, or lakes, but for a variety of reasons, most castles depended upon their own wells. Castles in southern Europe and Outremer* usually built huge cisterns to store water against the heat of summer and built aqueducts to replenish them. When wells failed, the castle was in trouble, especially during "siege warfare."* If besieging forces located and destroyed a castle's water supply, the castle's inhabitants frequently surrendered within only a few days. (Bibliog. 128)

week-work, one of the two main obligations of the peasants, that is, the villeins,* the other being boon-work.* Week-work was performed week by week during the year; boon-work was performed only as extra work. Normally the working year was divided into two parts: from Michaelmas (September 30) until the beginning of August, and from then until Michaelmas again. During this second period, on account of the grain harvest, more work was demanded of the villeins, so that during the greater part of his year, the peasant performed two to three days a week, but during harvest time, he worked three to five days with even some boon-work added. (Bibliog. 24)

weight of a bow, archery term referring to the power which a bow* required to draw it properly. (Bibliog. 100)

weights and measures. Rulers tried every means they could think of—proclamations, statutes, charters*—to secure uniformity in weights and measures. Even though judges in eyre* occasionally were asked to inspect weights, that job normally was performed by the coroner,* and presentments and fines* for unfair measures formed a regular part of the cases handled by "manor courts."* The weights and measures of the English standard for several hundred years after the Conquest were founded on a rude natural system: the weight of thirty-two grains* of average wheat taken from the middle of the ear. These thirty-two grains weighed twenty-two and a half troy grains, the legal weight of the penny,* and 240 such pence made the Saxon pound* of 5,400 grains and was the pound of account for money* and usually in weights.

Note that in the following list of English weights and measures, most terms can be found as separate entries, many with more elaborate definitions. The definitions given below those were those most commonly used in medieval England.

acre—amount of land one yoke of oxen could plow in one day

amber—four bushels

asine—measure without standard dimensions but equivalent to the load of one ass

barleycorn—3 medium-sized corns placed end to end equalled one inch

barrel—wet and dry measure of capacity varying between 32 and 42 gallons

besica—turf measure amounting to the amount of land one man could dig between May 1 and August 1

bind—10 sticks of eels

bovate—land plowed by 1 ox in a year; generally equivalent to 1/2 virgate* or to the eighth part of a carucate

bushel—4 pecks, 1/8 seam, 1/80 last

butt—same as pipe

cade—small barrel for fish holding 500 to 620 herring or 1,000 sprats

caritas—wine measure for monks, holding 3/4 to 2 gallons

carucate— see hide

chalder— coal measure equal to 1 ton

charge—see fother

choppin—1/2 Scots pint or 2 mutchkins

clove—1/2 stone

comble—measure heaped above the rim of any vessel of any capacity

coomb—grain measure equal to 4 bushels or 1/2 seam

costrel—indeterminate measure of capacity

crannock—grain measure varying from 7 to 14 bushels of oats; 4 to 8 of wheat

cubit—distance from elbow to tip of middle finger, equal to 6 palms

dicker—varying quantity of goods such as 10 animal hides, 10 pairs of gloves, 12 skins of leather

dozen—twelve of any commodity

ell—cloth measure generally of 45 inches but of varying lengths depending on locale

faggot—firewood measure 3 feet long and 24 inches in circumference; also weight for steel of 120 pounds

fardel—cloth capacity equal to a bale; also land measure of 1/4 virgate

farthingale—a land acre equal to 10 statute acres

fathom—length measure equal to 6 or 7 feet

ferling—land measure equal to 10 statute acres

fesse—hay unit varying between 7 and 56 pounds

firkin—capacity varying between 8 gallons of ale to 10-1/2 gallons of fish

fother—lead measure equal to 2,100 pounds

fotmal—lead weight equal to 1/30 of a fother

frail—capacity measure for small items ranging from 30 to 75 pounds

gallon—capacity equal to 4 quarts

garb—weight unit for 30 pieces of steel

grain—smallest unit of weight, equal to 2/875 avoirdupois ounce

hide—subdivision of feudal manor of varying sizes

hogshead—liquid capacity of varying number of gallons depending on item contained

hundred—measure of quantity but not necessarily 100 count

inch—length measure equal to a thumb's breadth

jar—capacity measure varying from 52 pounds of wheat to 100 of green ginger

kilderkin—capacity measure varying from 16 gallons of ale to 21 of fish

lagen—1 gallon

last—capacity measure greatly varying depending on item contained

league—measure of length varying from 1 1/2 to 3 miles

librate—area measure of land worth 1 pound per year

mease—herring measure varying from 520 to 630 pounds

met—capacity measure varying from 1/2 to 2 bushels

mile—land measure varying from 5,000 to 6,600 feet or 1,500 paces

mutchkin—capacity measure equal to 1/4 Scots pint

oenophorum—wine measure of 1 gallon

ounce—varying weight unit

oxgang—land measure equal to 1 bovate

pace—length measure equal to 2 steps or approximately 5 feet

pack—capacity measure varying from 10 pieces of cloth to 240 pounds of flax or wool

palm—unit of body measure equal to 1/3 span or about 3 inches

peck—1/4 bushel

pennyweight—weight of silver penny, 1/240 pound of tower silver

pensarius—see ponderator

perch—length measure generally varying from 9 to 16 1/2 feet but as many as 26 feet

piece—varying measure generally for cloth goods but for other goods as well

pint—capacity measure equal to 1/8 gallon

pipe—capacity measure varying from 84 gallons of salmon to 120 of cider to 126 for wine

poke—large bag or sack of varying size

pole—measure of varying lengths

pottle—two quarts of liquid

pound—varying measure of weight

quarter—measure equal to one seam

quartern—weight of 28 pounds of fruit

quintal—hundredweight of iron

quire—paper quantity equal to 1/20 ream of 480 to 500 sheets

rood—length measure equal to 1/8 mile

rundlet—wine measure equal to 18 or 18 1/2 gallons

sack—capacity measure varying between 3 1/2 bushels of apples to 364 pounds of wool

sarpler—wool measure equal to 2 sacks totalling 728 pounds

seam—measure of capacity and weight varying from 120 pounds of glass to 9 bushels of chopped bark

selion—land area betwen 2 furrows of open field

sester—capacity measure varying from 4 gallons of honey to 12 of ale and from 1 seam of grain to 4 of lime

sextary—6 gallons of wine

skep—capacity measure varying from 1 bushel to 2 seams

stang—land measure commonly equal to 1 acre of 3,240 square yards but sometimes smaller

stick—measure for 25 eels equal to 1/10 bind

stone—weight for dry products varying from 5 pounds for glass to 32 pounds for hemp

tey—measure for rope equal to 6 feet

thrave—measure for straw varying from 12 to 24 sheaves

timber—measure of quantity for 40 fur skins

toise—same as tey

truss—56 pounds of hay

trussel—quantity of skins or cloth to form a bundle

tun—liquid capacity for wine and oil varying from 208 to 252 gallons

wey—measure of capacity and weight varying from 40 bushels of barley to 180 pounds of cheese

yard—length measure of 36 inches for land and sometimes 37 inches for cloth

yoke—land measure in Kent equal to 4 virgates

(Bibliog. 289, 394)

werdekeit (Ger.), collective term for the virtues of the German chivalric/courtly warrior: honor,* loyalty, and courage. See chivalry. (Bibliog. 124)

wergild, wer, cash value set on a freeman's life in Germanic laws both in England and on the continent. As manslaughter and blood-feuds* were constant, attempts of wise men were imperfectly successful in keeping the peace and reconciling adversaries. In English the word was shortened to wer, and the amount of a man's wer often was a measure of the fine* to be paid for his offenses against public order. Recognizing the existence of both free and unfree people, Anglo-Saxon law codes by definition assumed that the unfree were under the protection of someone for whom they had value, so that if a slave were killed or injured, compensation was due to his owner. Many freemen similarly acknowledged lords who would expect compensation to be paid to themselves or their kinsmen if the freeman were killed; the only alternative was a feud in which he would be avenged by members of his family. Thus if a sum of money representing the value of the dead man could be paid to his family as wergild, a feud might be averted. This price determined a man's status in society. The value of his oath in legal proceedings depended upon his rank, and in 7th-century Kent, a noble could clear himself of an accusation by his unsupported oath while a ceorl,* an ordinary freeman, could do so only with three of his own class. In Aethelbert's reign (560–616) in Kent, the wergild of a ceorl was 100 shillings, while later in the century under King Ine's law (698–726) in Wessex, a ceorl had a wergild of 200 shillings, but a noble called a gesith had a wergild worth six times that amount. (Bibliog. 261, 305)

wet fire. See Greek fire.

wey, measure of capacity and a weight for dry products, but its size varied with the product: for barley, corn, and malt, it contained 40 bushels; for cheese, 180 pounds; and for grass, 60 bunches of uncertain weight. (Bibliog. 394)

whipping, material used to wrap the "nocking point"* of a bow.* (Bibliog. 100)

white, heraldic tincture (see colors) which was thought to be the noblest color after azure,* for it was nearer than any other to shining and luminous bodies. It was the color representing argent* or silver.* (Bibliog. 99)

white baton, sign of a truce.* See safe-conduct; signs of war.

White Ship disaster, maritime disaster in which William, the lord prince* of England and only legitimate son of King Henry I, drowned on November 25, 1120. This vessel was of the latest design in maritime transport, with the latest developments in shipbuilding, but when it left France for England, all its crew, marines, and passengers were drunk. In the excitement and haste to catch up with the rest of the main fleet which had sailed earlier, it struck a rock and sank with the loss of all aboard except for one survivor, a butcher from Rouen. Lost were two of the king's* twenty royal bastards, several earls* and barons,* and most of the "king's household"* who were returning to England after four years in Normandy. The loss of the heir to the throne placed a great deal of importance on the claim of William Clito, son of William II, for he was the surviving male of the line of William* the Conqueror, and this led ultimately to the anarchy in the dispute between Stephen of Blois and Henry's daughter, Matilda, over the throne when Henry I died in 1135. (Bibliog. 262)

wic reeve, Anglo-Saxon reeve* in charge of a royal vill,* the fortified place where the king* resided and held his court. He was a thane,* a landowner in his own right, and took precedence over all other reeves in the district; he became known as the king's reeve or the high reeve. (Bibliog. 132)

wildfire. See Greek fire.

William, names of two English kings*: William I, the Conqueror, called King of the Anglo-Normans, who ruled in Normandy from 1035 and England from 1066 until his death in 1087. He was a disagreeable man, masterful, stern, overbearing, and cruel, and he wanted his favorite son, William, to rule England. This favorite son ruled England as William II (Rufus) from 1087 until his death in 1100. Although brave, he was cynical, vain, capricious, ill-tempered, blasphemous, and irreverent, and morally was the worst English king. He was killed by an arrow* in his back shot by Walter Tirel,* one of his mercenaries.* (Bibliog. 262)

William Marshal. See Marshal, William.

windlass crossbow, *arbalète à cranquin.** See moulinet and pulleys crossbow.

windows, castle. Castle* windows were rarely glazed but instead were fitted with wooden shutters secured by iron bars. (Bibliog. 128)

Windsor Castle, royal English castle* occupied by royalty since the time of William* I. It has two baileys,* one on either side of the original motte*; its shell keep* called the Round Tower was built by Henry II and rebuilt by Edward III. Henry III built three huge drum towers. Edward III envisioned this structure to be Arthur's castle reincarnate, for it was here that he dreamed of recreating the Round Table,* and this castle was the spiritual home of his Order of the Garter.* (Bibliog. 45)

Windsor Herald, oldest English royal herald,* dating from 1338; his badge* was a sunburst ensigned* by the royal crown.* See heraldry.

wine, prize among all juices of trees and liquors, for when moderately drunk, wine most comforted the body, gladdened the heart, and healed wounds and evils. It strengthened all members of the body, giving to each might and strength. It allowed the soul to forget anguish of sorrow and woe; it sharpened the wit and let the mind understand quickly things that were difficult, hard and subtle. (Bibliog. 21)

witchcraft, punishment for. "Salic law"* merely imposed fines* for witchcraft even when the offender had eaten his victim bodily. Charlemagne allowed witchcraft suspects to be tortured* for confession, but not to the death, and after conviction they were imprisoned. The Ostrogoths punished such practices with death; the Visigoths by stripes delivered by severe blows with a lash or a rod, shaving the head, and exposure. Pope Gregory VII, the Great (1021–1085), directed slaves guilty of the offense should be punished with stripes and torments, but freemen were to be imprisoned and subjected to penance. The Anglo-Saxons at first banished witches who would not reform, then punished them with the penalty of death for disobedience. If a victim died, however, the offender was executed or delivered to the victim's kin to be punished at their pleasure. Scots condemned all to the stake who practiced witchcraft. By the 13th century, the "ordeal of cold water"* or "ordeal by hot or boiling water"* was still used as a special method of trying those unfortunates whose own folly or malice and fears of their neighbors pointed them out as witches or sorcerers. Even one hundred years after Pope Innocent III (1198–1216) put an end to the use of ordeals,* this still was used for witchcraft. Its continued use was probably due to the difficulty in proving guilt judicially and the handiness of the ordeal as a satisfactory solution to the doubts of timid judges. (Bibliog. 197)

wite, penal fine* payable to the king* or to some other public authority. See bot. (Bibliog. 261)

Witenagemot, national assembly before the Conquest when all the wise men of the land, the Witan, assembled to serve as the king's* counsellors. It consisted of five bishops, both archbishops of Canterbury and York, five abbots, and the earls.* Such a high position for churchmen was common to all of Europe at this time, partly because of the necessity to obtain advice from the only fully educated class of society—the clergy. (Bibliog. 267, 306)

"with banners displayed," mark of treason against one's king* when flown in his kingdom. Banners* flown gave the combatants clues as to the rules their enemies were to observe. Unfurling the oriflamme* at Crècy in 1346 told the English that the French would take no prisoners and would give no quarter. An Englishman, Henry Pomfret, in 1363 sued before the Parlement (see Parliament) of Paris his prisoner Jean de Melun for unpaid ransom.* Part of Melun's defense was that he had been taken at a time of truce* and therefore was not liable to ransom. Pomfret countered this by saying that Melun was riding under banners displayed, and thus was acting as though engaged in an open war; thus legally he could be taken and ransomed in accordance with the rules of public war. (Bibliog. 381)

wolf's head, have a, to be an outlaw,* an outcast from society, with a price or bounty upon one's head, just as a wolf had a price on its. (Bibliog. 182)

wood-penny, yearly prepayment required of a serf* before he could touch even a piece of dry wood. Cutting any wood meant a fine* at the "manor court,"* and the lord's officers were omnipresent looking for wood thieves because they recognized how essential wood was for the peasants (see villein). During the winter months, they carved spoons, platters, and bowls; they repaired the handles of tools such as scythes, rakes, hoes, and others; they shaped teeth for rakes and harrows, cut wooden shovels, fashioned ox-yokes, and so on; to say nothing of the need for fuel and material for cottage repairs. (Bibliog. 24)

woodward, officer appointed to safeguard the lord's woods and plantations or to become a forester* and watch over the lord's deer and his rights of chase.* As not all the woodland was owned by the king,* these owners could do with the land whatever they wished except interfere with the beasts of the forest.* They could not make essart,* purpesture,* or waste,* without the king's license. (Bibliog. 156)

woolfell. See maltote.

Worthies, Nine. See Nine Worthies.

wound treatment. Various medical authors wrote about treatment of wounds, but most showed remarkable consistency of directions. Bruno of Longoburgo in 1252 wrote in his *Chirurgia Magna* that wounds had to be examined more carefully in summer than in winter for putrefaction was greater in warm than in cold weather. He insisted on drainage, and for wounds in the extremities the limb always had to be placed to encourage drainage. If necessary, the wound was to be enlarged to secure it, even making a counteropening. To secure proper union of tissue, care had to be taken to bring the edges of the wound together accurately and not to allow hair or oil or dressing to come between them. In large wounds stitching was indispensable, preferably with silk or linen. In old wounds the edges should be cleansed, desiccated if required to refresh the edges. On the outer surface was to be laid lint steeped in wine,* for after washing, purifying, and drying the edges, wine evaporated; powder was too desiccating because it shut in decomposing matters. (Bibliog. 335, 364)

wreath, strands of material twisted and wreathed about the base of an heraldic crest* where it was fastened to the helmet.* (Bibliog. 43)

writ monstraverunt, right of the villeins* of the "ancient demesne"* not to have any increase in the services demanded of them by their lord. (Bibliog. 264)

writ of praecipe, new form of judicial writ created by King Henry II of England to replace the "writ of right"* which the litigant obtained from the Chancery* by paying a fee and which had been addressed to a local lord requesting him to take certain actions in matters connected with the possession and tenure* of land. Henry II's new writ was addressed to the sheriff* as a royal agent as opposed to the local lord, and it commanded him to take appropriate action in the matter specified and to return the writ to the court* of origin with a note of the action taken. (Bibliog. 132)

writ of right, document obtained from the Chancery* by a litigant on payment of a fee. This document was addressed to a local lord and requested him to take certain actions in matters connected with the possession and tenure of land. It was replaced by Henry II's ''writ of praecipe.''* (Bibliog. 132)

wyn ape. See ape wine.

wyvern, heraldic monster* resembling a dragon* but without hind quarters, its rear being like a serpent with a barbed tail. See cockatrice. (Bibliog. 116)

Y

yale, heraldic monster* with an antelope's body, lion's* tail, large tusks, and long curved horns which it could swivel at will. (Bibliog. 43, 116)

yard, measure of length of 36 inches* or 3 feet* for land, sometimes 37 inches for cloth, and generally was equal to 4/5 of an ell.* (Bibliog. 394)

years, dating of. Years were dated by the years a sovereign ruled, called "regnal years,"* but the date from which the regnal years were counted were not everywhere the same. The Franks began their year with the king's accession, but when Charlemagne became emperor* in A.D. 800, he dated from his coronation,* and this usually was followed by French kings.* In Germany the kings usually dated their years from their accession, but if they became emperor after their coronation as king, they might give both dates. In England, until the late 13th century, the year was reckoned from the king's coronation. With the death of Henry III (1272), however, because his son was absent on a crusade,* a change had to be developed, and so from that time on the king's years have been dated from accession and not coronation. Popes have always reckoned their years, pontifical years, not from their election but from their ordination or consecration. (Bibliog. 265)

yoke of land, measure of area in Kent generally equal to four virgates.* (Bibliog. 394)

youth, terms for. Two terms were used to describe well-born young men: *juvenis* (L., young) or *juventis* (L., youth). These were not synomous, but each had a specific meaning and indicated membership in a particular social group. It was used most often to assign warriors to clearly determined stages in their careers. A person as "young" clearly was no child, for he had passed through the educational process and exercises necessary to a military career (see knighthood). Other terms applied to the sons of nobility* who still were learning: *puer* (L. young man between twelve and eighteen years of age), *adulescentulus* (L. a very young boy), *adolencens emberbis* (L. beardless young man between fifteen and thirty) described boys who obviously were beyond childhood: they could be fifteen, seventeen, or nineteen but still had not completed their apprenticeships. A "youth" on the other hand already was an adult: he had been received into the company of warriors; he had taken up arms and had been dubbed; he was a knight. A knight could be called a youth until his marriage,* and often afterward. Knights who had not yet had children were called youths, while others who may actually have been younger but who had sired children were always called *vir* (L. man). Thus in the chivalric world, a warrior ceased to be called a youth when he had established himself and put down roots, became the head of a household, and founded a family. Youth, then, was between knighting and fatherhood. For example, William Marshal* left his father's house in 1155 at age twelve to be a *puer* with his uncle, William de Tancarville. In 1164 he took up the arms of knighthood; in 1166 and 1167 he took part in tournaments* and led a life filled with adventures and feats of valor. But he did not marry until 1189 when he was forty-five years of age; thus his youth lasted over twenty-five years.

This distinction was important, for one must consider what a youthful knight did. To him his youth was a time of turbulence, impatience, and instability. He already had been a child in a house of a mentor or tutor, and later on he was to marry and found his own house. In the interval he roamed abroad: wandering, searching constantly for adventure and prizes, conquering for reward and honor in war and in tournaments—in sum, living the kind of life characteristically descriptive of youth before marital responsibility anchored him to one place. (Bibliog. 94)

ypotryll, heraldic monster* with the head and tusks of a boar, the body of a camel* with two hairy humps, and the legs, hooves, and mane of an ox. (Bibliog. 43)

Z

zecchino, Italian gold coin of Venice where the first one was struck during the reign of Giovanni Dandolo (1280–1290). It derived its name from Zecca, the Venetian form of the name Guidecca where the mint lay. (Bibliog. 150)

Zifar, oldest surviving book in Castillian on chivalry.* Written about 1300, it contained an account of Arthur's fight with Cath Palug, the cat of Lausanne. (Bibliog. 200)

Appendices

Fixed Feast and Saint's Days Frequently Used to Date Documents

Feast and Saint's Days Listed Alphabetically

Adrian	9 January
Agatha	5 February
Agnes	21 January
Alban	22 June
Aldhelm	25 May
All Hallows	1 November
All Saints	1 November
All Souls	2 November
Alphege	19 April
Ambrose	4 April
Andrew	30 November
Anne	26 July
Annunciation	25 March
Audoneus	25 August
Ascension Day	39 days after Easter
Augustine (Canterbury)	26 May
Augustine (Hippo)	28 August
Barnabas	11 June
Bartholomew	24 August
Bede, Venerable	27 May
Benedict	21 March
(Translation)	11 July
Blasius	3 February
Boniface	5 June
Candlemas	2 February
Cathedri Peter	22 February
Catherine	25 November
Cecilia	22 November
Christmas	25 December
Christopher	25 July
Circumcision	1 January
Clement	23 November
Cornelius & Cyprian	14 September
Corpus Christi	Thursday after octave of Pentecost

Crispian	25 October
Cuthbert	20 March
(Translation)	4 September
Cyprian	26 September
David	1 March
Denis	9 October
Dunstan	19 May
Eadburga	15 June
Editha	16 September
Edmund (King of West Saxons)	20 November
Edmund (Archbishop of Canterbury)	16 November
Edward the Confessor	5 January
(Translation)	13 October
Edward (King of West Saxons)	18 March
(Translation)	20 June
Egidius	1 September
Enurchus	7 September
Epiphany	6 January
Ethelreda	17 October
Euphemia	16 September
Eustachius	2 November
Fabian & Sebastian	20 January
Faith	6 October
Felicitas	23 November
Franciscus	4 October
Geminianus (See Lucian)	
George	23 April
Giles	1 September
Gregory	12 March
Grimbold	8 July
Gule of August (See Peter ad Vincula)	
Guthlac	11 April
Hieronymus (See Jerome)	
Hilary	13 January
Holy Cross, Exaltation of	14 September
Holyrood Day	14 September
Innocents	28 December
James	25 July
Jerome (Hieronymus)	30 September
John the Baptist, Nativity	24 June
Beheading	29 August
John the Evangelist	27 December
Judoc	13 December
Lady Day (See Annunciation)	
Lambert	17 September
Lammas (See Peter ad Vincula)	
Laudus	21 September
Laurence	10 August

Leonard	6 November
Lucian & Geminianus	16 September
Lucian	8 January
Lucy	13 December
Luke	18 October
Margaret	20 July
Mark	25 April
Martin	11 November
(Translation)	4 July
Mary, Blessed Virgin	
Annunciation (Lady Day)	25 March
Assumption	15 August
Conception	8 December
Nativity	8 September
Purification	2 February
Visitation	2 July
Mary Magdalene	22 July
Mathias	24 February
Matthew	21 September
Maurice	22 September
Michael in Monta tumba	16 October
Michaelmas	29 September
Midsummer	24 June
Mildred	13 July
Name of Jesus	7 August
Nicholas	6 December
Nicomedes	1 June
Oswald	8 October
Patrick	17 March
Paul, Conversion	25 January
Commemoration	30 June
Perpetua	7 March
Peter (Peter and Paul)	29 June
(Cathedri Petri)	22 February
Peter ad Vincula (Lammas; Gule of August)	1 August
Petronilla, the Virgin	31 May
Philip & James	1 May
Prisca	18 January
Priscus	1 September
Remigius, Germanus, & Vedastus	10 October
Richard	3 April
Rogation	5th Sunday after Easter
Silvester	31 December
Simon and Jude	28 October
Stephen	26 December
Swithin	15 July

Thomas the Apostle	21 December
(Translation)	3 July
Thomas à Becket	29 December
(Translation)	7 July
Timotheus & Symphorianus	22 August
Transfiguration	6 August
Urban	25 May
Valentine	14 February
Vincent	22 January
Wilfred	12 October
Wulfstan	19 January
CHURCH DATES:	Septuagesima falls 9 weeks before Easter
	Sexagesima falls 8 weeks before Easter
	Quinquagesima falls 7 weeks before Easter
	Quadragesima falls 6 weeks before Easter
	Rogation falls on the 5th Sunday after Easter
	Whitsunday falls 7 weeks after Easter
	(See also ''Holy Days'' entry.)

Calendar of Fixed Feast and Saint's Days

January:	1	Circumcision
	5	Edward the Confessor
	6	Epiphany
	8	Lucian
	9	Adrian
	13	Hilary
	18	Prisca
	19	Wulfstan
	20	Fabian & Sebastian
	21	Agnes
	22	Vincent
	25	Paul, Conversion of
February:	2	Candlemas; Mary, Purification of
	3	Blasius
	5	Agatha
	14	Valentine
	22	Cathedri Peter
	24	Mathias
March:	1	David
	7	Perpetua
	12	Gregory
	17	Patrick
	18	Edward, King of West Saxons
	20	Cuthbert
	21	Benedict
	25	Annunciation

April:	3	Richard
	4	Ambrose
	11	Guthlac
	19	Alphege
	23	George
	25	Mark
May:	1	Philip and James
	19	Dunstan
	25	Aldhelm; Urban
	26	Augustine of Canterbury
	27	Bede, Venerable
	31	Petronilla, the Virgin
June:	1	Nicomedes
	5	Boniface
	11	Barnabas
	15	Eadburga
	20	Edward, King of West Saxons, Translation of
	22	Alban
	24	John the Baptist, Nativity of; Midsummer
	29	Peter (Peter and Paul)
	30	Paul, commemoration of
July:	2	Mary, Visitation
	3	Thomas the Apostle, Translation of
	4	Martin, Translation of
	7	Thomas à Becket, Translation of
	8	Grimbold
	11	Benedict, Translation of
	13	Mildred
	15	Swithin
	20	Margaret
	22	Mary Magdelene
	25	Christopher; James
	26	Anne
August:	1	Peter ad Vincula
	6	Transfiguration
	7	Name of Jesus
	10	Laurence
	15	Mary, Assumption of
	22	Timotheus & Symphorianus
	24	Bartholomew
	25	Audoneus
	28	Augustine of Hippo
	29	John the Baptist, Beheading of
September:	1	Egidius; Giles; Priscus
	4	Cuthbert, Translation of
	7	Enurchus
	8	Mary, Nativity of
	14	Holyrood Day; Cornelius & Cyprian; Holy Cross, Exaltation of

16	Editha; Euphemia; Lucian & Geminianus
17	Lambert
21	Laudus; Matthew
22	Maurice
26	Cyprian
29	Michaelmas
30	Jerome (Hienonymous)
October: 4	Franciscus
6	Faith
8	Oswald
9	Denis
10	Remigius, Germanus, & Vedastus
12	Wilfred
13	Edward the Confessor, Translation of
16	Michael in Monta tumba
17	Ethelreda
18	Luke
25	Crispian
28	Simon & Jude
November: 1	All Saints; All Hallows
2	All Souls; Eustachius
6	Leonard
11	Martin
16	Edmund, Archbishop
20	Edmund, King of West Saxons
22	Cecilia
23	Clement; Felicitas
25	Catherine
30	Andrew
December: 6	Nicholas
8	Mary, Conception of
13	Lucy; Judoc
21	Thomas, the Apostle
25	Christmas
26	Stephen
27	John the Evangelist
28	Innocents
29	Thomas à Becket
31	Silvester

Topical List of Entries

Animals and Other Creatures

adder, slaying
alphyn
amphisbene
ancipiter
apres
aptalon
argasill
asp
aspide
bagwyn
basilisk
bonacon
boreyne
Cabal
cacothephas
caladrius
calygreyhound
centaur
cetus
chough
cockatrice
corbie
cornu
cynophali
cynopodes
dragon
eagle
egrentyne
elephant
fourmi
goupil
griffin
herisson
hippogriff
hydra
hyena
leopard
lion
manticora
monster
mustelle
nebek
onager
opinicus
panther
phoenix
questing beast
regulus
salamander
satyr
satyral
scytale
serra
theow
tyger
unicorn
viper
wyvern
yale
ypotryll

Armor

aiguilette
ailette
aketon
alcato
arm and crown
armed all to rights

armed at all points
arming cap
arming doublet
arming nail
arming points
armor
armory
aubergel
avant-bras
avantail
backplate
baldric
baleyn
barbel
barbute
barded
barding
basinet
battle sark
bauderik
baviere
bei
besagews
bevor
brassarts
breastplate
brinied
button
byrnie
camail
cap-a-pie
caparisoned
casque
cervellière
chapelle-de-fer
chaplet
charnels
chausses
coif-de-mailles
colletin
contoise
coudieres
couters
crinet
crupper
cuir-bouilli
cuirass
cuirie

cuishes
cuissarts
cuisses
culiere
cyclas
demi-brassarts
demi-cuissarts
demi-greaves
demi-grevieres
demi-poulaines
demi-vambraces
epaulieres
estivals
flanchards
gadlings
gambeson
garde de bras
garde de cuisses
gauntlets
genouillieres
gisarme
glaive
gorged
gorget
Goswhit
grate
greave
grevieres
guige
gypciere
halbard
haqueton
harness
haubergeon
hauberk
hauberk of plates
heaume
helm
helm, frog-mouthed
helmet
hergeat
horn armor
horse armor
hosting harness
hour-glass gauntlet
hourt
jacque
jambarts

impost
keep
kitchen
latrine
loop hole
machicolation
merlon
meurtrières
motte
oriel
oylets
palisade
parados
parapet
perron
plinth
portcullis
postern
rampart
ring work
rubble
sally port
scarp
shell keep
stang
tasser
tower
turre del homenaje
turret
wall-work
ward
wardrobe
water supply
windows

Castles, Famous

Aggstein
Aix la Chapelle
Akershus
Albuquerque
Alcala de Guadaira
Alcazaba of Malaga
Alcazar of Segovia
Alençon
Alhambra
Alnwick
Arques-la-Bataille
Banos de la Encina

Beaufort
Beaumaris
Blachernes
Bodiam
Bolton
Bonaguil
Burghausen
Caen
Caerlaverock
Caerlon-on-Usk
Caernarvon
Caerphilly
Castle Sween
Château Gailiard
Châteaudun
Chepstow
Chillon
Chinon
Cobbie Row's
Cochem
Colchester
Conigsborough
Conway
Corfe
Fort St. Georges
Joyeuse Garde
Krak des Chevaliers
Windsor

Coinage

ambrosino
ange d'or
Anglo-Gallic money
aquilino
Arends groot
argento
aspro
augustale
ballard
barbuda
baseling
bemish
bezant
billon
blank
bolognino
botdragers
bourbonnais

taro
testoon
thrysma
tournois
tournois, gros
tremissis
ward-penny
zecchino

**Daily Life: Entertainment,
Life, and Death**

abbot
affer
agister
Albion
almerie
ambesas
ape wine
bard
basse-prime
bed
bedale
board lands
bragot
brasses, monumental
bread
Breton lai
breviary
bulbeggar
burial practices
buttery
candlesticks
canonical hours
capuchan
carpets
cart
cells
chansons de geste
chariot branlant
charnel house
Childermas
Christmas game
cloister
close
compline
conte
corn
Corpus Christi

coute
crepons
croft
curtilage
days of the week
demesne
dionysia
enfance
entertainment
feria
fesse
flail
forest
funerals
gab
gallery
geste
gestum
gite
gladius
gleeman
grail, graal
gregois
hall
harp
haute tierce
Hock Day
Holy Days
honour
hook or by crook
horologium
how to measure a sheaf
Hoxtide
huese
hypocras
jestours
lai
laisse
Lammas
Lamasse of Peter Apostle
langue de si
langue d'oc
langue d'oil
lauds
mabinogi
manor
manor court
Mappemonde de Pierre

mew
mews
musket
passage hawk
pitch
point, making her
put in
put out
quarry
rake away
reclaim
red hawk
ring
rufter hood
sails
seel
stoop
strike the hood
summed
swivel
tercel
train
truss
varvels
wait on
warble

Heraldry

abaised
abatements
accollé
achievement
Adam and Eve's arms
addorsed
affronty
allerion
allume
allusive arms
ambulant
amorette
annulet
apaume
arch
argent
argh
arm
armed
armigerous

arms
arms of assumption
arms of England
arms of France
arms of God
arms of office
aspect
aspersed
at gaze
at speed
attired
attributed arms
augmentation
aversant
azure
badge
bar
bar sinister
barrulet
barry
baton
battled
bearing
beasts, positions of
bend
bendlet
bendy
black
blazon
blazoning a shield
bordure
boss
bretessed
caboshed
cadency
cameleopard
canting arms
canton
castle
charge
chastons
chequy
chevron
chevronny
chief
cinquefoil
coat of arms
colors

nowed
octofoil
or
ordinaries
orle
ounce
pale
panache
Parliamentary Roll of Arms
partition, lines of
party
passant
pavon
pean
pile
plume
points of the shield
pomme
popinjay
potent
proper
purpure
quartering
queue
rampant
red
reremouse
roll of arms
Romanie
rose
roundel
sable
saltire
sanguine
sans
sejant
seme
shields of knighthood
sinister
soutiens
stains
statant
subordinary
supporters
swastika
tenne
thistle
tower

trefoil
undy
vair
vert
volant
vulned
white
wreath

Horses, Famous

Aarvak
Arion
Babieca
Baiart
Bayard
Blanchart
Bruiant
Bucephalus
Fadda
Ferrant
Ferrant d'Espagne
Grani
horses, famous
Pegasus
Sleipnir
Tencendur
Vegliantino

Hunting, Coursing, Archery

abai
abaite
acquiller
affeted
aland
alcube
allowance
ambler
anceps
argus
assise
athresten
beme
bemere
berner
billet
blench
boughs, breaking
broches

ruses
slot
soule
spayard
speytard
stables
staggart
stalling
staunch hound
stinking flight, beasts of
sued
suet
sweet flight, beasts of
talbot
tally ho
teaser
trace
tryst
veltres

Knighthood, Chivalry

accolade
Alcantara
armiger
attire
auxilium exercitus
aventiure
bachelor
banner
banneret knight
beau frère
bold
Book of the Order of Chivalry
bord fellow
brotherhood-in-arms
cadet
Chandos, Herald of
chevalchia
chevauchee
chivalry
Christian knighthood
cniht
colée
collar of SS
collar of Lancaster
collar of York
combat of chivalry
comitatus

commendation
constable's honor
constabularia
Court of Chivalry
degradation of a knight
démesuré
destrier
douzepeers
dreng
dub
dubbing ceremony
duel
emprise
erbarmde
ere
esquire
Exchequer
exchequer fashion
Feast of Swans
feoffment
feudal obligation
fief de haubert
fier
frouwendienst
fursten
gage
geldable
gentleman
German chivalry
great officers of state
grossmutigkeit
guidon
handbooks for knights
Histoire de Guillaume le Maréchal
hofisch
hoher muot
homage
honor, sense of
honorus
honours
Hospitallers
infant
intrinsic service
kiusche
knight bachelor
knight banneret
knight errant
knighthood

Knights of Calatrava
Knights of St. James
Knights of St. John of Jerusalem
Knights of St. Julian del Pereyo
Knights of the Round Table
knighthood
largesse
law of arms
leudes
liege
liege homage
Lull, Raimon
mannesmuot
manuum imixito
Maze, Diu
merker
mesure
miles
military duties
militia Christi
milk brother
milte
minnedienst
nail money
nithing
nobility
Olifant
Order of Santiago
Order of the Bath
Order of the Garter
Order of the Golden Fleece
Order of the Passion of Jesus Christ
Order of the Star
Order of the Sword
orders of chivalry and knighthood
ornest
preudhomme
pursuivant of arms
ritterschlag
scutage
Siege Perilous
squire
staete
Teutonic knights
thane, thegn
triuwe
vow

Vow of the Heron
werdikeit

Legal Terms

abece
abjuration of the realm
acoupen of
advowson
affeer
afon
age of majority
agistment
agueys
aids
aiel
alienated
allege
allegiance
allodium
aloue
alouten
amercement
ancient demesne
appeal
apposer
approver
arma patria
arms, come to
arrearage
arrent
assart
assize
Assize of Arms
Assize of Bread and Ale
Assize of Clarendon
Assize of Mort d'ancestor
Assize of Novel Disseisin
Assize of the Forest
Assize Utrum
assoin
attach
Attachment, Court of
attaint
attaint jury
aulnager
balk
barat
beadle-mead

bedemad
belligeration
bescia
blanching of farm rent
blood-feud
bodel silver
bonaghtie
bond
bondman
book-land
book-right
bord land
bordars
border
borgh
borough
borsilver
bos
bosing silver
bot
brenage
Britton
bull
Bulle d'Or
burdicia burg
burh
by-laws of a village
cagots
capias
capias utlagatum
capital
caruca
carucage
castellaria
Chancery
chancery fashion
charter
charter of liberties
charters of franchise
chases
chevage
chiminage
civilitermortuus
cocket
compurgation
compurgators
concord
consanguinity

Constitutions of Clarendon
conveyancing
copyhold
cornbole
cortes
county
court
court baron
court-leet
Court of Attachment
Court of Swanimote
cove et keye
craven
Criminous Clerks controversy
curia regis
customal
customary court
Danegeld
Danelaw
de gustu et fama
de malo lecti
deodand
Descriptio
Dialogus de Scaccario
disparage
distraint
distraint of knighthood
distringas
divorce
Domesday Book
dona
dooms
dower
douze
duchies
duel
English language
Englishry
escheat
escheator
essoin
exact
exactions
excommunication
execution
exigent
exoculation
eyre

usnea
wound treatment

Ordeals

ordeal
ordeal by bier right
ordeal by bread and cheese
ordeal by fire
ordeal by hot or boiling water
ordeal of cold water
ordeal of oaths on relics
ordeal of poison
ordeal of red-hot iron
ordeal of the cross
ordeal of the Eucharist
ordeal of the lot

People

Alberich
Alia-Aenor
Appolin
Assassins
Barbarossa
Blanche of Castile
Cahn
caliph
Dame Nicolla de la Haye
Dandolo, Enrico
Denis, St.
douzepeers
Eleanor of Aquitaine
Fabu
Ganelon
Geoffrey de Preuilli
Geoffroi de Villehardouin
Ghibelline
Gilbert of the Haye
Guelphs
Harold Godwineson
Henry II
Hospitallers
Isma'ilites
Kerbogha
Louis VII
Louis IX
Mahomet
Malet, William
Master James of St. George

Merlin
Neckham, Alexander
Nennius
Nine Worthies
Oliver
Paris, Mathew
Peasant's Revolt
Peggin, Elias
Pepin, the Short
Peter Bartholomew
Peter Igneus
Philip
Pinabel
Poor Knights of Christ
Prester John
Rannulf de Glanville
Raymond VI
Richard
Richard I
Richard, earl of Cornwall
Richard Fitz-Neale
Robert II, Curthose
Robin Hood
Roger Mortimer
Roger of Salisbury
Roland
Rotbart
Saladin
saracen
Stephen
Swein
Templars
Tervagant
Teutonic knights
Theoderic the Great
Tirel, Walter
Twici
Wace
Wallace, William
William
William Marshal

Places

Almayne
Amazonia
Antipodes
Cinque Ports
Dauphine

Glastonbury
Guienne
Guiennois
hotel de ville
hotel dieu
Île de France
Outremer
Oxydracca
Papal States
Roncevaux
St. Denis
Wash, the

Royalty

Ampulla or Golden Eagle
anointing
appanage
archduke
aristocracy
athel-man
atheling
baron
baroness
baronet
barony
cap of dignity
constable and marshal of England
coronation
coronation chair
Coronation Charter
coronation oath
coronet
count
countess
courtesy title
crown
dauphin
despotate
Dieudonné
dominus
duke
earl
earl marshal
emir
emperor
empire
German duchies
graf

House of Lords
king
kingmark
landgrave
law of descent
Liagh Fail
Lord Prince
Lords Appellant
marquess
noble
ordines
pater sancte
peer
planta genesta
Plantagenet
precedence
prince
Prince of Wales
ranking of nobles
regalia of England
rights of the King of France
royal houses of Europe
royal standard
royal touch
royal "we"
rumors
scepter
Scone, Stone of
tenants-in-chief
titles of dignity
viscount
White Ship disaster

Servants

achatour
ackermanni
agister
almoner
apothecary
argentarius
assessor
bailiff
barber-surgeons
beadle
bell man
biller
birle
bittar

blencher
boon-work
bouvier
boy
bulbegar
butler, king's
butlery
butsecarls
castellan
centenary
ceorl
chacechiens
chamberlain
chamberlains of the Exchequer
champion for ordeals
chancellor
chief butler
clerk of the market
congeners
conservator of the peace
constable
coroner
cottars
cursores
custos placitorum corone
custos rotulorum
dhimmis
Dienstmannen
ewerer
feodary
fewterer
forest dweller
forester
fusor
hayward
herald
house servants
housecarle
household knights
household warriors
justiciar
king of arms
king's champion
king's constable
king's household
king's knights and bannerets
kippers
marshal

messengers
messor
offices of state
ordainers
pauncenars
pittancer
ponderator
prevot
reeve
regardor
sacrabar
scutiferi
seneschal
serf
sergeant
sheriff
steward
treasurer
tronager
tungerefan
turnbedellus
vagiator
valletti
vassal
vavasour
verderer
villein
villein sokemen
vintenaries
warden
wic reeve
Windsor Herald
woodward

Swords, Famous

Balmung
Brownsteel
Caliburn
Caledfwlch
Corsheuse
Courtain
Curtana
Durendal
Epée aus Estranges Renges
Excaliber
Finamonde
Glorious
Gram

Halteclaire
Joyeuse
Sword of Tristan
Tizon

Tournaments

à logis, ployez les banniers
à mêlée
baston
baston course
behourd
bohort
bourdonasse
burdicia
clouage
conflictus gallicus
faites vos devoirs
foot tournament
free course
fussturnier
gestech
hastilude
Hohenzeuggestech
Hola
infamous
joust
jousts à outrance
jousts à plaisance
joutes plénières
just
laissez les aller
lists
mêlée
over the barrier
pas d'armes
pas de Saladin
passage of arms
passus
round tables
sharp-lance running
Statuum Armorum ad Tourniamentis
tilt
torneamentum
tournament
Tournois du Roi René

Warfare

à bonne usance
à butin

adalid
aesc-born
afornrider
ambulatory tower
antrustio
appatis
Aragonais
arbalastier
arciones
arcon
arms, bern of
arms, lede of
arms, mastery of
array
array, commission of
arrière-ban
arrière-garde
artillator
assail
assault
assay
astrolabe
attack first
avant-garde
bacele
balinger
bandcroll
banderole
bannerer
banners displayed
barge
barnacle
bataille
battle cry
Battle of Bouvines
Battle of Crécy
Battle of Courtrai
Battle of Falkirk
Battle of Hastings
Battle of Poitiers
Battle of the Standard
battle orders
battlefield actions and conditions
bausons
Beau Séant
bekin
belloculus
bern

bern-at-armes
bikeren
bitunen
bouget
braies
buccellarii
cingulum
commilitones
condotierri
conrois
constabularia
cottereaux
coule
coup de grâce
crakanel
crusades
crusading vows
cry of arms
dead angle
dromon
escalade
expeditio
falarica
favel
feudal army
feudal levy
fyrd
gonfanon
Henry I, laws of
here
heregild
herse
hobbies
hobelars
hoist
holmgang
hors de combat
immunity from war
law of King Richard about crusaders at sea
laws of William
letters of marque
lithsmen
lymphad
malvoisin
mantlet
mantlet wall
marche
master

mayhem
mercenaries
mesnie
mine gallery
Mont-joie
oriflamme of France
pel
pennon, guidon
pennoncelle
pommel
private wars
quintain
quota system
ransom
Reconquista
recreance
safe-conduct
"saint sepulchre"
servitium debitum
shield wall
shiltrons
Sicilian Vespers
siege warfare
signs of war
soldier
sovereign's role in battle
spoils of war
Stamford Bridge, battle of
standard
Strassbourg Oaths
striking point
tactics, battlefield
Tinchebrai
trimoda necessitas
troops, raising
trou-de-loup
truce
Truce of God
Varangian guard
with banners displayed

Weapons

adalid
Adventurous Shield
alborium
alkibrit
allonge
angon

mangon
marteau
martel-de-fer
maul
misericorde
morning star
moulinet and pulleys crossbow
mouse
partisan
pavise
pele
perriere
petraria
pick
pike
plançon-a-picot
plommee
poleaxe
pone
poniard
Pridwen
prodd
quarrel
quillons
ram
ranseur
Robinet
rondel dagger
saracen arrows
scimitar
scorpion
scramasax
scythe
seaxe
shaftment
sheath
sling
sow
sparth
spatha
spear
spontoon
springald
staff
staff sling
stele
sword
tang

targe, target
tenebra
terebra
testudo
therscol
throwing axe
tiller
Toledo test
tolleno
tortoise
trebuchet
tzangara
vireton
vouge
war scythe
warwolf
weight of a bow
whipping

Weights and Measures

acre
amber
arm long
arpentier
asine
avoirdupois
barleycorn
barrel
bilibre
bind
bitte
bovate
bushel
butt
cade
caritas
carucate
chalder
char
charge
choppin
clove
comble
coomb
costrel
crannock
cubit
cubit arm

Bibliography

1. Ackerman, Robert. "Knighting Ceremonies in Middle English Romances," *Speculum* XIX (1944), pp. 285–313.
2. Ackerman, Robert. *Index of the Arthurian Names in Middle English*, Palo Alto, CA: Stanford Publications in Language and Literature, X, 1952; repr. New York: AMS Press, 1967.
3. Aebischer, Paul. *Rolandiana et Oliveriana: Recueil d'études sur les chansons de geste*, Genève: Droz, 1967.
4. Akerman, John Y. "Furca and Fosssa: A Review of Certain Modes of Punishment in the Middle Ages," *Archeologia* XXXVIII (1860), pp. 54–65.
5. Allmand, Christopher T., ed. *War, Literature, and Politics in the Late Middle Ages*, Liverpool: Liverpool University, 1976.
6. *An Arabian-Syrian Gentleman and Warrior in the Period of the Crusades: Memoirs of Usamah Ibn-Munqidh*, tr. by Philip Hitti, New York, 1925.
7. Armitage, Ella. *Early Norman Castles of the British Isles*, London, 1912.
8. Armitage-Smith, Sir Sidney. *John of Gaunt*, London: Constable, 1904; repr. 1964.
9. Ashdown, Charles. *Armour and Weapons in the Middle Ages*, London, 1925; repr. West Orange, NJ: Albert Saifer, 1977.
10. Ashe, Geoffrey. *The Quest for Arthur's Britain*, St. Albans: Paladin, 1971.
11. Ashmole, Elias. *The Institution, Laws, and Ceremonies of the Most Noble Order of the Garter*, London, 1692; repr., Baltimore: Genealogical Publishing, 1971.
12. Atiya, Aziz. *Crusade, Commerce, and Culture*, Oxford University, 1962.
13. Ault, Warren. "Village By-Laws by Common Consent," *Speculum* XXIX (1954), pp. 378–394.
14. *The Babee's Book: Medieval Manners for the Young*, tr. by Edith Rickert, London, 1908; repr. New York: Cooper Square, 1976.
15. Baines, A. *Musical Instruments Through the Ages*, New York: Walker and Co., 1975.
16. Barber, Malcolm. *The Trial of the Templars*, Cambridge University, 1978.
17. Barber, Richard. *The Knight and Chivalry*, London: Longman, 1970.
18. Barber, Richard. *The Reign of Chivalry*, New York: St. Martin's, 1980.
19. Baring-Gould, Sabine. *Curious Myths of the Middle Ages*, London: Rivingtons, 1869; repr. New York: Gordon Press, 1977.
20. Barnie, J. *War in Medieval Society: Social Values and the Hundred Years War, 1337–1399*, Ithaca, NY: Cornell University, 1974.
21. Bartholomew Anglicus. *Medieval Lore*, ed. and tr. by Robert Steele, London, 1869; repr. New York: Cooper Square, 1966.

22. Bean, John M. W. *The Decline of English Feudalism: 1215–1540*, New York: Barnes and Noble, 1968.
23. Beeler, John. *Warfare in Feudal Europe: 730–1200*, Ithaca, NY: Cornell University, 1971.
24. Bennett, Henry S. *Life on the English Manor: 1150–1400*, Cambridge University, 1937, 1960.
25. Bisson, T. N. "Coinage and Royal Monetary Policy in Languedoc during the Reign of Saint Louis," *Speculum* XXXII (1957), pp. 443–469.
26. Blaine, Gilbert. *Falconry*, London, 1936.
27. Blair, Claude. *European Armor, c.1066–c.1700*, London: Batsford, 1971.
28. Bloch, Marc. *Feudal Society*, tr. by L. A. Manyon, London, 2nd ed., 1962; Chicago: University of Chicago, 1964.
29. Bloch, Marc. "The Problem of Gold in the Middle Ages," in *Land and Work in Medieval Europe*, ed. by Marc Bloch, London, 1938.
30. Boissonade, P. *Life and Work in Medieval Europe*, tr. by Eileen Power, New York: Harper & Row, 1964.
31. Bonet, Honoré. *The Tree of Battles*, tr. by G. M. Coopland, Liverpool, 1949.
32. Bordman, Gerald. *Motif Index of English Metrical Romances*, Helsinki: F. F. Communications, Vol. LXXIX, #190, 1963.
33. Borst, Arno. "Knighthood in the High Middle Ages: Ideal and Reality," in *Lordship and Community in the Middle Ages*, ed. by Frederic Cheyette, New York, 1968; repr. New York: Krieger, 1975, pp. 180–191.
34. Bossuat, Robert. *Manuel Bibliographique de la Littérature Française du Moyen Âge*, Melun, 1951.
35. ———. Supplement I (1949–1953), Paris: Librairie D'Argences, 1955.
36. ———. Supplement II (1954–1960), Paris: Librairie D'Argences, 1961.
37. Bostock, John. *Handbook of Old High German Literature*, Oxford University, 1955.
38. Boussard, Jacques. *The Civilization of Charlemagne*, New York: McGraw Hill, 1968.
39. Brault, Gerard. *Early Blazon: Heraldic Terminology in the 12th and 13th Centuries*, Oxford University, 1971.
40. Brault, Gerard. *The Song of Roland: An Analytical Edition*, University Park, PA: Pennsylvania State University, 1978, 2 vols.
41. *Breton Lays in Middle English*, Thomas Rumble, ed., Detroit: Wayne State University, 1965.
42. Briffault, Robert. *The Troubadours*, Bloomington, IN: Indiana State University, 1965.
43. Brook-Little, John P. *An Heraldic Alphabet*, New York: Arco, 1973.
44. Broughton, Bradford. *The Legends of Richard I, Coeur de Lion*, The Hague: Mouton, 1966.
45. Brown, R. Allen. *English Medieval Castles*, London: Batsford, 1976.
46. Brown, R. Allen. "The Norman Conquest and the Genesis of English Castles," *Chateau Gaillard: European Castle Studies* III, (Conference at Battle, Sussex, 19–24 September 1966), London, 1969, pp. 1–14.
47. Brown, R. Allen. *The Origins of English Feudalism*, London: Allen Unwin, 1973.
48. Brown, R. Allen. "Royal Castle Building in England, 1154–1216," *English Historical Review*, LXX, 1955.
49. Brown, R. Allen. *The Normans and the Norman Conquest*, London, 1969.

50. Bruce, J. D. *The Evolution of Arthurian Romance from the Beginning down to 1300*, Baltimore, 1923; repr. Magnolia, MA: Peter Smith, 1978.
51. *Bulletin Bibliographique de la Société Internationale Arthurienne*, Paris: Société Internationale Arthurienne, fascicles 21 through 34, 1969–1982.
52. *Bulletin Bibliographique de la Société Rencesvals*, Paris: A. G. Nizet, ed., fascicles 1 through 14, 1959-1981.
53. Bullough, D. A. "Games People Played: Drama and Ritual as Propaganda in Medieval Europe," *Transactions of the Royal Historical Society*, 5th Series, XXIV (1974), pp. 92–122.
54. Bumke, Joachim. *The Concept of Knighthood in the Middle Ages*, tr. W. T. H. Jackson, New York: AMS Press, 1972.
55. Burke, John. *Life in the Castle in Medieval England*, London and New York: British Heritage Press, 1978.
56. Burton, Sir Richard. *The Book of the Sword*, London, 1884.
57. Cabeen, D. C. *Critical Bibliography of French Literature, I: Medieval Period*, ed. U. T. Holmes, Syracuse, NY: Syracuse University, 1947.
58. Calin, William. *The Old French Epic of Revolt: Raoul de Cambrai, Renaud de Montauban, Gormond et Isembard*, Genéve: Droz, 1962.
59. Cam, Helen M. *The Hundred and the Hundred Rolls*, London, 1930; repr. New York: Burt Franklin, 1960.
60. *Cambridge History of English Literature*, I, ed. by A. W. Ward and A. R. Waller, Cambridge University, 1967.
61. *Cambridge Medieval History*, ed. by J. R. Tanner, C. W. Previte-Orton, and Z. N. Brooke, Cambridge University, repr. 1968:
    a. V. Contest of Empire and Papacy
    b. VI. Victory of the Papacy
    c. VII. Decline of Empire and Papacy.
62. Campbell, F. *The Celtic Dragon Myth*, Edinburgh: Blackwood, 1911.
63. Cannon, Henry L. "The Battle of Sandwich and Eustace the Monk," *English Historical Review*, XXVII (1912), pp. 649–670.
64. Caxton, William, ed. and tr. *The Book of the Ordre of Chyvalry*, Oxford: Early English Text Society, Original Series #168, 1926, repr. 1971.
65. *Chateau Gaillard: European Castle Studies*, Conference at Battle, Sussex, September 19–24, 1966.
66. Chauliac, Guy de. *Cyrurgie*, ed. by Margaret S. Ogden, London, Early English Text Society, Extra Series #265, 1963.
67. Chaytor, Henry. *The Troubadours*, Cambridge University, 1912.
68. Child, Clarence G. "The Natural History of Dragons," *University of Pennsylvania Bulletin*, XXI #18, Jan. 29, 1921, pp. 101–130.
69. Cipolla, Carlo. *Money, Prices, and Civilization in the Mediterranean World, Fifth to Seventeenth Centuries*, Princeton, NJ: Princeton University, 1965.
70. Cleator, P. E. *Castles and Kings: The Evaluation of Castles in England with Sketches of their Builders*, London, 1963.
71. Clephan, Robert C. *Defensive Armor and Weapons and Engines of War in Medieval Times*, London, 1900.
72. Clephan, Robert C. *The Tournament: Its Periods and Phases*, New York, 1919; repr. New York: Frederick Ungar, 1967.

73. Cline, R. "The Influences of Romances on the Tournaments of the Middle Ages," *Speculum* XX (1945), pp. 204–211.

74. Clouston, W. A. *Popular Tales and Fictions*, London, 1887; repr. Detroit: Gale, 1968.

75. Cockayne, George E. *The Complete Peerage*, rev. ed. London: St. Catherine Press, 1910–1940, 13 vols.

76. Coulton, George G. *Life in the Middle Ages*, Cambridge University, repr. 1967.

77. Coulton, George G. *Medieval Village, Manor, and Monastery*, New York: Harper & Row, repr. 1970.

78. Cripps-Day, F. H. *History of the Tournament in England and France*, London, 1918.

79. Crombie, A. C. *Medieval and Early Modern Science*, New York: Doubleday, 1959.

80. Crosby, Ruth. "Oral Delivery in the Middle Ages," *Speculum*, XI (1936), pp. 88–100.

81. Cutts, Edward L. *Scenes and Characters of the Middle Ages*, London, 1872; repr. Detroit: Gale, 1968.

82. Dahmus, Joseph. *History of Medieval Civilization*, New York: Odyssey, 1964.

83. Davies, William. *Life on a Medieval Barony*, New York: Harper & Row, 1923.

84. Davis, Henry W. C. *England Under the Normans and Angevins*, London, 13th ed. 1961.

85. Deaux, George. *The Black Death: 1347*, London, 1969.

86. Denholm-Young, N. "Feudal Society in the Thirteenth Century: the Knights," in N. Denholm-Young, *Collected Papers on Medieval Subjects*, Oxford University, 1946, pp. 56–67.

87. Denholm-Young N. *History and Heraldry, 1254–1310*, Oxford University, 1965.

88. ———. "The Tournament in the Thirteenth Century," *Studies in Medieval History presented to Sir Maurice Powicke*, ed. R. Hunt, R. Southern, and W. Pantin, Oxford University, 1948, pp. 240–268.

89. Diaz-Plaja, Guillermo. *A History of Spanish Literature*, tr. by H. Harter, New York: New York University, 1971.

90. *Dictionary of National Biography*, ed. by Sidney Lee, Oxford University, 1909.

91. Ditmas, Edith. "The Curtana or Sword of Mercy," *Journal of British Archeological Association*, Series 3, #29 (1966), pp. 122–133.

92. Dobson, R. B. and J. Taylor. *Rymes of Robyn Hood: An Introduction to the English Outlaw*, Pittsburgh: Pittsburgh University, 1976.

93. Du Bose, Hampden C. *The Dragon, Image and Demon*, London, 1886.

94. Duby, Georges. *The Chivalrous Society*, tr. Cynthia Postan, Berkeley, CA: University of California, 1977.

95. Dutton, Ralph. *The English Country House*, London: Batsford, 1962.

96. Edward, 2nd Duke of York. *The Master of Game*, London: Chatto and Windus, 1909.

97. Edwards, J. G. "Edward I's Castle-building in Wales," *Proceedings of the British Academy* XXXII (1946).

98. Elliott, T. J. *A Medieval Bestiary*, Boston, 1971.

99. Elvin, Charles N. *A Dictionary of Heraldry*, London, 1889, rev. by J. P. Brooke-Little, Baltimore: Genealogical Publishing, 1969.

100. *Encyclopedia Britannica*, 9th ed., London, 1875–1890.

101. *English and Scottish Popular Ballads*, ed. H. C. Sargent and G. L. Kittredge, Boston, 1932; repr. New York: Folklore Press, 1965.

102. *English Historical Documents, 1042–1189*, ed. by David C. Douglas and George Greenaway, Oxford University, 1953.

103. *English Historical Documents, 1189–1327*, ed. by Harry Rothwell, Oxford University, 1975.

104. *English Historical Documents, 1327–1485*, ed. by A. Reginald Myers, Oxford University, 1969.

105. Evans, Joan. *Life in Medieval France*, 3rd ed., London and New York: E. P. Dutton, 1969.

106. Ferrante, Joan and George Economou. *In Pursuit of Perfection: Courtly Love in Medieval Literature*, Port Washington, NY: Kennikat Press, 1975.

107. Ffoulkes, Charles. *Armour and Weapons*, Oxford University, 1909.

108. Ffoulkes, Charles. *Armourer and his Craft*, London: Methuen, 1912; repr. New York: Arno Press, 1967.

109. Finn, R. Weldon. *An Introduction to Domesday Book*, London and New York: Grossman, 1963.

110. *Five Middle English Narratives*, ed. by Robert Stevick, New York: Irvington, 1967.

111. Forde-Johnston, James. *Great Medieval Castles of Britain*, London: Bodley Head, 1979.

112. Foss, Michael. *Chivalry*, London and New York: McKay, 1975.

113. Foulet, Alfred. "Is Roland Guilty of *Demesure?*", *Romance Philology* X (1957), pp. 145–148.

114. Fourquin, Guy. *Lordship and Feudalism in the Middle Ages*, tr. by I. Sells and A. L. Sells, London and New York: Universe, 1976.

115. Fowler, Kenneth. *The Age of Plantagenet and Valois: The Struggle for Supremacy, 1328–1495*, London: Elek Books, 1967; Salem, NH: Merrimack Book Service, 1967.

116. Fox-Davies, Arthur. *Complete Guide to Heraldry*, London, 1909, rev. ed. by J. P. Brooke-Little, London, 1969. New York: Crown, 1978.

117. Frappier, Jean. *Chrétien de Troyes et le Mythe du Graal (Etude sur Perceval)*, Paris: Société d'Edition d'Enseignement Supérior, 1972.

118. Freeman, Gage, and Francis Salvin. *Falconry: Its Claims, History and Practice*, London, 1859; repr. Golden, CO: Falcon Head Press, 1972.

119. French, Walter H. and Charles B. Hale. *Middle English Metrical Romances*, New York, 1930; repr. New York: Russell and Russell, 1964.

120. Fry, Plantagenet. *British Medieval Castles*, Newton Abbot, England: David and Charles, 1964.

121. Galbraith, V. H. "The Death of a Champion (1269)," in *Studies in Medieval History presented to Frederick M. Powicke*, ed. by R. W. Hunt, Oxford University, 1948, pp. 283–295.

122. Galpin, F. W. *Old English Instruments of Music*, London, 1910; repr. St. Clair Shores, MI: Scholarly Press, 1976.

123. Ganshof, F. L. *Feudalism*, tr. by P. Grierson, London, 1952; repr. New York: Harper & Row, 1964.

124. Garland, Henry, and Mary. *Oxford Companion to German Literature*, Oxford University, 1976.

125. Gautier, Léon. *Chivalry*, tr. D. C. Dunning, New York, 1965.

126. Gautier, Léon. *Les Épopées Françaises*, Paris: Société Génerale de Librairie catholique, 4 vols., 1878–1882.
127. Génicot, Leonard. "The Nobility in Medieval Francia," *Lordship and Community in Medieval Europe*, ed. Frederic Cheyette, New York, 1968, repr. New York: Krieger, 1976, pp. 128–135.
128. Gies, Joseph and Frances. *Life in a Medieval Castle*, New York: Harper & Row, 1974.
129. Gies, Joseph and Frances. *Life in a Medieval City*, New York: Harper & Row, 1969.
130. Gilbey, Sir Walter. *The Great Horse, or the War-horse*, London, 1869.
131. Gist, Margaret. *Love and War in the Middle English Romances*, Philadelphia: University of Pennsylvania, 1947.
132. Gladwin, Irene. *The Sheriff: The Man and His Office*, London, 1974.
133. Glover, Richard. "English Warfare in 1066," *English Historical Review* LXVII (1952).
134. Godefrey, Frederic. *Dictionnaire de l'Ancienne Langue Française du IXe Siècle au XVe Siècle*, 10 vols., Paris, 1881–1902.
135. Goebel, Julius, Jr. *Felony and Misdemeanor*, Philadelphia: University of Pennsylvania, 1976.
136. Goitein, H. *Primitive Ordeal and Modern Law*, London: Unwin, 1923.
137. Goodrich, Norma. *The Ways of Love*, London, 1965.
138. Gould, Charles. *Mythical Monsters*, London: W. H. Allen, 1886; repr. Detroit: Singing Tree Press, 1969.
139. Grabois, Aryeh. *Encyclopedia of Medieval Civilization*, London: Octopus Books, 1980.
140. Grant, Edward. *Source Book in Medieval Science*, Cambridge, MA: Harvard University, 1974.
141. Graves, Edgar B. *Bibliography of English History to 1485*, Oxford University, 1975.
142. Grimm, Jacob. *Teutonic Mythology*, tr. by J. Stallybrass, 4th ed., New York, 1966; repr. Magnolia, MA: Peter Smith, 1977.
143. Hall, David. *Knights and Castles*, London: Edward Arnold, 1974.
144. Hall, Herbert. *Antiquities and Curiosities of the Exchequer*, London, 1898.
145. Hands, Rachael. "The Names of All Manner of Hawks and to Whom They Belong," *Notes and Queries* XVII (March 1971), pp. 85–88.
146. Hardy, R. *Longbow: A Social and Military History*, Cambridge University, 1976.
147. Harriss, G. L. "The Formation of Parliament," in *The English Parliament in the Middle Ages*, ed. by R. G. Davies and J. H. Denton, Manchester University, 1981.
148. Hartland, Edwin S. *The Legend of Perseus*, London, 1896; repr. New York: AMS Press, 1976.
149. Harvey, R. *Moriz von Craûn and the Chivalric World*, Oxford University, 1961.
150. Hazlitt, W. C. *The Coinage of the European Continent*, 2 vols. London, 1893–1897; repr. Chicago: Ares Press, 1975.
151. Henderson, Ernest, ed. *Select Historical Documents of the Middle Ages*, London, 1892; repr. New York: AMS Press, 1968.
152. Hibbard, Laura H. *Medieval Romance in England*, 2nd ed. New York: Burt Franklin, 1963.

153. Hill, Mary C. *The King's Messengers, 1199–1377*, London, 1961.
154. Hilton, R. H. *Bond Men Made Free*, New York: Viking, 1973.
155. Hilton, R. H. "Freedom and Villeinage in England," *Peasants, Knights, and Heretics*, ed. by R. H. Hilton, Cambridge University, 1976, pp. 174–191.
156. Holdsworth, Sir William. *A History of English Law*, 7th ed. (rev. by A. L. Goodhart and H. G. Hanbury), London, I, 1956.
157. Hollings, Marjorie. "The Survival of the Five-Hide Unit in the Western Midlands," *English Historical Review* LXIII (1948).
158. Hollister, C. Warren. *Anglo-Saxon Military Institutions*, Oxford University, 1962.
159. Hollister, C. Warren. *The Military Organization of Norman England*, Oxford University, 1965.
160. Hollyman, K. *La développement du vocabulaire féodal en France pendant la haute moyen âge*, Paris, 1957.
161. Holmes, U. T. *Daily Life in the Twelfth Century*, Madison, WI: University of Wisconsin, 1970.
162. Holmes, U. T. *History of Old French Literature*, New York: Crofts, 1936; repr. New York: Russell and Russell, 1962.
163. Holt, John C. *Magna Carta*, Cambridge University, 1965.
164. Holt, John C. *Robin Hood*, London: Thames and Hudson, 1982.
165. Holt, John C. "The Prehistory of Parliament," in *The English Parliament in the Middle Ages*, ed. by R. G. Davies and J. H. Denton, Manchester University, 1981.
166. Hoppin, Richard. *Medieval Music*, New York: Norton, 1978.
167. Houston, Mary C. *Medieval Costume in England and France, 13th, 14th, and 15th Centuries*, London, 1939; repr. New York: Barnes and Noble, 1965.
168. Howard, M. *War in European History*, Oxford University, 1976.
169. Huizinga, J. *The Waning of the Middle Ages*, New York: Doubleday, 1976.
170. Humble, Richard. *The Fall of Saxon England*, London: Arthur Barker, 1975.
171. Hunnisett, Roy F. *The Medieval Coroner*, Cambridge University, 1961.
172. Hyams, Paul R. *Kings, Lords, and Peasants in Medieval England: The Common Law of Villeinage in the Twelfth and Thirteenth Centuries*, Oxford University, 1980.
173. Ingersoll, Ernest. *Dragons and Dragon Lore*, New York, 1928; repr. Detroit: Singing Tree Press, 1968.
174. James, B. S. *Bernard of Clairvaux*, London, 1957; repr. New York: AMS Press, 1979.
175. Jewell, Helen M. *English Local Administration in the Middle Ages*, New York, 1972.
176. John, Eric. *Land Tenure in Early England*, Leicester, 1960.
177. Jones, William. *Credulities Past and Present*, London, 1880; repr. Detroit: Gale, 1968.
178. Jones, William. *Crowns and Coronations - A History of Regalia*, London, 1883; repr. Detroit: Gale, 1968.
179. Keen, Maurice. "Brotherhood in Arms," *History* 47 (1962), pp. 1–17.
180. Keen, Maurice. *Chivalry*, New Haven, CT: Yale University, 1984.
181. Keen, Maurice. *The Laws of War in the Middle Ages*, London, 1965.
182. Keen, Maurice. *The Outlaws of Medieval England*. London, 1961; repr. New York: Penguin, 1969.

183. Kimball, Elizabeth. *Sergeanty Tenure in Medieval England*, New Haven, CT: Yale University, 1936.

184. Kimble, George T. *Geography in the Middle Ages*, New York, 1938; repr. New York: Russell and Russell, 1968.

185. LaMonte, John L. *Feudal Monarchy in the Latin Kingdom of Jerusalem, 1100–1291*, Cambridge, MA, 1932; repr. New York: AMS Press, 1977.

186. LaMonte, John L. *World of the Middle Ages*, New York, 1949, repr. New York: Irvington, 1976.

187. Lane-Poole, Stanley. *Coins and Medals*, Chicago, 1968.

188. Langland, William. *Vision of William Concerning Piers Plowman*, ed. by W. W. Skeat, Oxford University, 1898.

189. Langlois, Charles V. *La Connaissance de la Nature et du Monde*, Paris, 1927. [Contains: Philippe de Thaon, *La Bestiaire*, pp. 1–43; *Les Merveilles de Prêtre Jean*, pp. 44–70; *La Mappemonde de Pierre*, pp. 122–134; *L'Image du monde*, pp. 135–197; Brunetto Latino, *Le Livre du Trésor*, pp. 335–390.]

190. Langlois, Charles V. *La Vie en France au Moyen Âge*, Paris, 1926. [Contains: *Galeron, L'Escoufle, Guillaume de Dole, Joufrois, Flamenca, Jehan et Blonde, La Chastellaine de Vergi, La Chatelain de Couci, Sone de Nansei*.]

191. Langlois, Ernest. *Table de Noms Propres de Tout Nature Compris dans les Chansons de Geste*, Paris: Librairie Émile Bouillon, 1904; repr. New York: Burt Franklin, 1971.

192. Lapsley, Gaillard. "Some Castle Officers in the Twelfth Century," *English Historical Review* XXXIII (1918), pp. 348–359.

193. Latino, Brunetto. *Le Livre du Trésor*, in Charles Langlois, *La Connaissance de la Nature et du Monde*, Paris, 1927, pp. 335–390.

194. Layamon. "Brut," *Arthurian Chronicles*, London: J. M. Dent, 1912; repr. New York: E. P. Dutton, 1962, pp. 115–264.

195. Lea, Henry C. *The Duel and the Oath*, Philadelphia: University of Pennsylvania, 1974.

196. Lea, Henry C. *The Ordeal*, Philadelphia: University of Pennsylvania, 1973.

197. Lea, Henry C. *Superstition and Force*, Philadelphia: University of Pennsylvania, 1895; repr. 1971.

198. Lea, Henry C. *Torture*, Philadelphia: University of Pennsylvania, 1973.

199. Lloyd, Alan. *King John*, Newton Abbot, England: David and Charles, 1973.

200. Loomis, Roger S. *Arthurian Literature in the Middle Ages*, Oxford University, 1959.

201. Loomis, Roger S. *Arthurian Tradition and Chrétien de Troyes*, New York: Columbia University, 1949.

202. Loomis, Roger S. "Chivalric and Dramatic Imitations of Arthurian Romance," in *Medieval Studies in Memory of A. Kingsley Porter*, ed. W. R. W. Koehler, Cambridge, MA: Arno, 1939, I, pp. 79–97.

203. Loomis, Roger S. "Edward I, Arthurian Enthusiast." *Speculum*XXVIII (1953), pp. 114–127.

204. Loomis, Roger S. "Morgain la Fée and the Celtic Goddess," *Speculum* XX (1945), pp. 183–203.

205. Lot, Ferdinand. *Étude sur le Lancelot en Prose*, Paris, 1918, repr. 1954.

206. Luchaire, Achille. *Social Life in France at the Time of Philip Augustus*, tr. E. B. Krehbiel, 2nd ed. New York: Harper & Row, 1967.

207. Lull, Ramon. *Book of the Ordre of Chyvalry*, tr. William Caxton, London: Early English Text Society, Original Series #168, repr. 1971.
208. Lyon, Bruce. *From Fief to Indenture*, New York, 1952; repr. New York: Octagon Books, 1971.
209. MacCulloch, J. A. *Celtic Mythology*, Boston, 1918; repr. New York: Cooper Square, 1976.
210. MacCulloch, J. A. *The Childhood of Fiction: A Study of Folktales and Primitive Thought*, London, 1905; repr. Detroit: Gale, 1976.
211. MacCulloch, J. A. *Eddic Mythology*, Boston, 1930; repr. New York: Cooper Square, 1976.
212. MacCulloch, J. A. *Medieval Faith and Fable*, Boston: Marshall Jones, 1932.
213. Maitland, F. W. *Domesday Book and Beyond*, Cambridge: Cambridge University, 1897; repr. London: Fontana Library, 1969.
214. Malory, Sir Thomas. *Le Morte D'Arthur*, ed. by E. Vinaver, Oxford University, repr. 1977.
215. Mannyng, Robert, of Brunne. *Handlyng Synne*. Oxford: Early English Text Society, Original Series #119 (1901), #123 (1903); repr. 1978.
216. Map, Walter. *De Nugis Curialium*, tr. by Frederick Tupper and M. B. Ogle, New York, 1924; repr. New York: AMS. Press.
217. "Mappemonde de Pierre." in C. V. Langlois, *La Connaissance De la Nature et du Monde*, Paris, 1927, pp. 122–134.
218. Mathew, G. "Ideals of Knighthood in Late Fourteenth-century England," *Studies in Medieval History presented to F. M. Powicke*, ed. by R. W. Hunt, Oxford University, 1948, pp. 354–362.
219. Mayhew, N. J. and D. R. Walker, "Crockards and Pollards," in *Edward's Monetary Affairs (1279–1344)*, British Archeological Report #36 (1977), pp. 125–146.
220. McCall, Andrew. *The Medieval Underground*, London: Hamish Hamilton, 1979.
221. McFarlane, K. B. *The Nobility of Later Medieval England*, Oxford University, 1973.
222. McKisack, May. *The Fourteenth Century*, Oxford University, 1959.
223. Mead, William E. *The English Medieval Feast*, New York: Gordon Press, 1967.
224. Meade, Marion. *Eleanor of Aquitaine*, New York: Hawthorne, 1977.
225. Meller, Walter. *Knight's Life in the Days of Chivalry*, New York: Greenberg, 1924.
226. *Middle English Dictionary*, ed. by Hans Kurath, Ann Arbor, MI: University of Michigan, 1954, et seq. fascicles A1 through N.
227. Mitchell, Sydney K. *Taxation in Medieval England*, New Haven, CT: Yale University, 1951; repr. Hamden, CT: Shoe String Press, 1971.
228. Morris, W. A. *The Medieval English Sheriff*, Manchester University, 1927.
229. Nielson, George. *Trial by Combat*, Glasgow: William Hodge and Company, 1890.
230. Neubecker, Ottfried. *Heraldry: Sources, Symbols, and Meaning*, New York: McGraw Hill, 1976.
231. Newton, Arthur P. *Travel and Travellers in the Middle Ages*, London: Kegan Paul, 1926; repr. New York: Arno, 1976.
232. *The Nibelungenlied*, tr. by A. T. Hatto, London: Penguin, 1965.
233. Nicholls, F. M. "On Feudal and Obligatory Knighthood," *Archeologia* XXXIX (1863), pp. 189–244.

234. Nitze, W A. "The Beste Glatissant in Arthurian Romance," *Zeitschrift für romanische Philologie* LVI (1953), pp. 409–418.
235. Norgate, Kate. *England under the Angevin Kings*, London: Macmillan, 1887; repr. New York: Burt Franklin, 1969.
236. Norgate, Kate. *Richard the Lion Heart*, New York: Macmillan, 1924; repr. New York: Russell and Russell, 1969.
237. North, J. J. *The Coinage of Edward I and Edward II*, London: Spink, 1968.
238. Nowell, Charles E. "The Historical Prester John," *Speculum*XXVIII (1953), pp. 435–445.
239. Oakshott, R. Ewart. *The Sword in the Age of Chivalry*, London, 1964.
240. Oman, Sir Charles. *The Coinage of England*, Oxford University, 1931.
241. Oman, Sir Charles. *A History of the Art of War in the Middle Ages*, Oxford University, 1924; repr. New York: Burt Franklin, 1959, 2 vols.
242. O'Neill, Bryan H. *Castles and Cannon*. Oxford University, 1960; repr. Westport, CT: Greenwood, 1975.
243. Oppenheimer, Sir Francis. *The Legend of the Sainte Ampoule*, London, 1953.
244. Orderic Vitalis. *The Ecclesiastical History*, ed. and tr. by Marjorie Chibnall, V, Oxford University, 1975.
245. *Oxford Companion to English Literature*, Oxford University, 1964.
246. *Oxford English Dictionary*, Oxford University, 1970.
247. Owings, Marvin. *The Arts in the Middle English Romances*. New York: Bookman Associates, 1952.
248. Painter, Sidney. *French Chivalry*, Baltimore: Johns Hopkins University, 1940; repr. Ithaca, NY: Cornell University, 1957.
249. Painter, Sidney. *William Marshall*, Baltimore: Johns Hopkins University, 1933, repr. 1967.
250. Painter, Sidney. *Studies in the History of the English Feudal Barony*, Baltimore: Johns Hopkins University, 1943; repr. New York: Octagon, 1969.
251. Pakula, Marvin. *Heraldry and Armor of the Middle Ages*, London, 1972.
252. Parker, F. H. M. "The Forest Laws and the Death of William Rufus," *English Historical Review* XXVII (1912), pp. 26–38.
253. Parker, James. *A Glossary of Terms used in Heraldry*, Devon, England, 1894; repr. Rutland, VT: C. E. Tuttle, 1970.
254. Parry, John J. "Geoffrey of Monmouth and the Paternity of Arthur," *Speculum* XIII (1938), pp. 271–277.
255. Paton, Lucy. *Studies in the Fairy Mythology of the Arthurian Tradition*, New York: Burt Franklin, 1970.
256. Percy, Bishop Thomas. *Reliques of Ancient English Poetry*, London, 1811; repr. New York: Dover, 1966.
257. Petit-Dutaillis, Charles. *The Feudal Monarchies in France and England from the Tenth to the Thirteenth Centuries*, tr. E. D. Hunt, New York: Harper & Row, 1964.
258. Philippe de Thaon. *La Bestiaire*, Charles Langlois, *La Connaissance de la Nature et du Monde*, Paris, 1927, pp. 1–43.
259. Pinches, J. H. and R. V. *The Royal Heraldry of England*, Rutland, VT: C. E. Tuttle, 1974.
260. Pirenne, Henri. *Medieval Cities*, Princeton, NJ: Princeton University, 1925.

261. Pollock, Edward, and F. W. Maitland. *History of English Law before the Time of Edward I*, 2nd ed., Cambridge University, 1968.

262. Poole, A. Lane. *From Domesday Book to Magna Carta, 1087–1216*, 2nd ed. Oxford University, 1955.

263. Poole, A. Lane. *Medieval England*, Oxford University, 1958.

264. Poole, A. Lane. *Obligations of Society in the XII and XIII Centuries*, Oxford University, 1946.

265. Poole, Reginald Lane. *Medieval Reckonings of Time*, London, 1918; repr. New York: Gordon Press, 1977.

266. Potter, Murray A. "The Horse as an Epic Character," *Four Essays*, Harvard Studies in Romance Languages, III (1917), pp. 109–139.

267. Powell, J. Enoch and Keith Wallis. *The House of Lords in the Middle Ages*, London, 1968.

268. Powell, James, ed. *Medieval Studies: An Introduction*, Syracuse, NY: Syracuse University, 1976.

269. Power, Eileen. *Medieval People*, New York: Barnes and Noble, 1963.

270. Powicke, F. *The Thirteenth Century*, 2nd ed. Oxford University, 1962.

271. Powicke, Michael R. "Distraint of Knighthood and Military Obligations under Henry III," *Speculum* XXV (1950), pp. 457–470.

272. Powicke, Michael R. *Military Obligations in Medieval England*, Oxford University, 1962.

273. Prawer, Joshua. *The World of the Crusaders*, New York: Octagon Books, 1972.

274. Prestage, Edgar. *Chivalry: A Series of Studies to Illustrate its Significance and Civilizing Influence*, London: Knopf, 1928; repr. New York: AMS Press, 1974.

275. Pullan, Brian. *Sources for the History of Medieval Europe*, Oxford University, 1971.

276. Puttock, Col. A. G. *A Dictionary of Heraldry and Related Subjects*, London: Genealogical Publishers, 1970.

277. Quaritch, Bernard. *A Catalogue of Medieval Literature, Especially of the Romances of Chivalry*, London: Bernard Quaritch, 1890.

278. Raimond of Agiles. "History of the Franks Who Captured Jerusalem," in *Source Book of Medieval History*, ed. by F. Ogg, New York, 1907; repr. New York: Cooper Square, 1972, pp. 201–202.

279. Reese, Gustave. *Music in the Middle Ages*, New York: Norton, 1940.

280. Renn, Derek F. *Norman Castles in Britain*, New York: Humanities Press, 1968.

281. Reuter, Timothy. *The Medieval Nobility*, Oxford University, 1978.

282. Richardson, H. G. "The Coronation in Medieval England," *Traditio*, 16 (1960), pp. 111–202.

283. Richardson, H. G. "The English Coronation Oath," *Speculum* XXIV (1949).

284. Richardson, H. G. and G. O. Sayles. *The Governance of Medieval England from the Conquest to the Magna Carta*, Edinburgh: Blackwood, 1963.

285. Rickard, Peter. *Britain in Medieval French Literature: 1100–1500*, Cambridge University, 1956.

286. Rieseman, E. *The Story of Medicine in the Middle Ages*, New York, 1935; Repr. Philadelphia: Porcupine Press, 1979.

287. Riley-Smith, Jonathan. *The Knights of St. John in Jerusalem and Cyprus c.1050–1310*, London, St. Martin, 1967.

288. Robertson, John G. *History of German Literature*, 6th ed. Edinburgh: Blackwood, 1970.

289. Rogers, J. E. T. *History of Agriculture and Prices*, I (1265–1400), II (1265–1400), Oxford University, 1866.

290. Ross, Susan. *The Castles of Scotland*, London: George Philip, 1973.

291. Round, J. H. "The Castles of the Conquest," *Archeologia*LVII (1902).

292. Round. J. H. *Feudal England*, London, 1964; repr. Westport, CT: Greenwood Press, 1979.

293. Round, J. H. "Tower and Castle," in J. H. Round, *Geoffrey de Mandeville*, London, 1892; repr. New York: Burt Franklin, 1972.

294. *Royalty, Peerage, and Aristocracy in the World*, 90, London and New York: International Publication Service, 1967.

295. Ruding, Rogers. *Annals of the Coinage of Great Britain*, London, 1840, 3 vols.

296. Rudorff, Raymond. *Knights in the Age of Chivalry*, New York: Viking, 1974.

297. Runciman, Steven. *History of the Crusades*, London: Penguin, 1978:
    a. I. *The First Crusade*
    b. II. *The Kingdom of Jerusalem*
    c. III. *The Kingdom of Acre*

298. Sabatier, Robert. *Histoire de la poésie française: La poésie du Moyen Âge*, Paris, 1975.

299. Saint Palaye, La Curne de. *Mémoires sur l'Ancienne Chevalerie*, tr. by Susannah Dobson, London, 1784.

300. Sanders, I. J. *Feudal Military Service in England*, Oxford University, 1956.

301. Sandquist, T. A. "The Holy Oil of St. Thomas of Canterbury," *Essays in Medieval History Presented to Bertie Wilkinson*, Toronto: Toronto University, 1969, pp. 330–344.

302. Sands, Donald B., ed. *Middle English Verse Romances*, New York: Holt Rinehart and Winston, 1966.

303. Saunders, John. *Cabinet Pictures of English Life*, London, 1845.

304. Savage, Hugh L. "Hunting in the Middle Ages," *Speculum* VII (1933), #1.

305. Sawyer, P. H. *From Roman Britain to Norman England*, London: St. Martin, 1978.

306. Sayles, George O. *Medieval Foundations of England*, Philadelphia: University of Pennsylvania, 1950.

307. Schmidt, A. V. C. and N. Jacobs, *Middle English Romances*,II, London, 1980.

308. Schramm, Percy E. *History of the Coronation*, London, 1937.

309. Schultz, James A. *The Shape of the Round Table: Structures of Middle High German Arthurian Romance*, Toronto: University of Toronto, 1983.

310. Setton, Kenneth, ed. *A History of the Crusades*, Madison, WI: University of Wisconsin, 1969–1975:
    a. I. *First Hundred Years*, ed. by M. W. Baldwin.
    b. II. *Later Crusades*, ed. by R. Wolff and H. Hazard.
    c. III. *Fourteenth and Fifteenth Centuries*, ed. by H. Hazard.

311. Severs, J. Burke. *Manual of the Writings in Middle English: 1050–1500*; fascicle 1--Romances, New Haven, CT: Connecticut Academy of Arts and Sciences, 1967.

312. Seward, Desmond. *The Hundred Years War: The English in France 1337–1453*, New York: Atheneum, 1978.

313. Shakespeare, William. *A Midsummer Night's Dream*, Variorum Edition, ed. by H. Howard Furness, Philadelphia, 1895.

314. Sharp, Harold S. *Footnotes to World History: A Bibliographic Source Book*, London and Metuchen, NJ: Scarecrow Press, 1979.

315. Shaw, William A. *The Knights of England from the Earliest Times*. London, 1906; repr. Baltimore: Genealogical Publishing, 1976.

316. Shepard, Odell. *Lore of the Unicorn*, London: Allen and Unwin; repr. New York: Harper & Row, 1979.

317. Simon, Edith. *The Piebald Standard: A Biography of the Knights Templar*, London, 1959; repr. New York: AMS Press, 1979.

318. Simpson, Jacqueline. *British Dragons*, London: Batsford, 1980.

319. *Sir Christopher Hatton's Book of Seals*, ed. by L. C. Lloyd and D. M. Stenton, Oxford University, 1950.

320. *Six Old English Chronicles*, ed. by J. A. Giles, London, 1885; repr. Philadelphia: R. West, 1977.

321. Skeel, Caroline, "Medieval Wills," *History* X (1926), pp. 300–310.

322. Smail, Raymond C. *Crusading Warfare, 1097–1193*, Cambridge University, 1956.

323. Spence, Lewis. *Dictionary of Medieval Romance and Romance Writers*, London, 1913; repr. New York: Humanities Press 1962.

324. Spufford, P. "Coinage and Currency," *Cambridge Economic History of Europe*, ed. by M. Postan, III, London, 1965, pp. 576–602.

325. Squibb, G. D. *The High Court of Chivalry*, Oxford University, 1959.

326. Stenton, Doris M. *English Justice between the Norman Conquest and the Great Charter: 1066–1215*, London, 1963; repr. Philadelphia: American Philosophical Society, 1964.

327. Stenton, Sir Frank. *Anglo-Saxon England*, 2nd ed. Oxford Unversity, 1947.

328. Stenton, Sir Frank. "The Changing Feudalism of the Middle Ages," *History* XIX (1935), pp. 289–301.

329. Stenton, Sir Frank. *The Development of the Castle in England and Wales*, Historical Association (England) Leaflet #22, 1910; rev. ed. 1933.

330. Stenton, Sir Frank. *The First Century of English Feudalism*, Oxford University, 1932.

331. Stone, George C. *Glossary of the Construction, Decoration, and Use of Arms and Armor*, New York, 1934; repr. New York: Jack Brussel, 1981.

332. Stothard, C. A. *The Monumental Effigies of Great Britain*, London, 1817.

333. Strayer, Joseph. "The Two Levels of Feudalism," in *Life and Thought in the Early Middle Ages*, ed. by Robert S. Hoyt, Minneapolis: University of Minnesota, 1967, pp. 51–65.

334. Strutt, Joseph. *The Sports and Pastimes of the People of England*, London, 1903; repr. Detroit: Gale, 1968.

335. Talbot, C. H. *Medicine in Medieval England*, New York: Elsevier, 1967.

336. Tappan, E. M. *In Feudal Times: Social Life of the Middle Ages*, London, 1939.

337. Tatlock, J. S. P. "The Dragons of Wessex and Wales," *Speculum* VIII (1933), pp. 223–235.

338. Tatlock, J. S. P. *The Legendary History of Britain*, Berkeley, CA: University of California, 1950; repr. 1974.

339. Tetlow, Edwin. *The Enigma of Hastings*, London: Peter Owen, 1974.

340. Thiebaux, Marcelle, "The Medieval Chase," *Speculum* XXXVII (1962), pp. 260–274.

341. Thompson, Alexander H. *Military Architecture in England during the Middle Ages*, Oxford University, 1912; repr. Totowa, NJ: Rowman and Littlefield, 1975.

342. Thompson, James W. *Economic and Social History of the Middle Ages (300–1300)*, New York,1928; repr. New York: Frederick Ungar, 1959.

343. Thompson, Stith. *Motif Index of Folk Literature*, Bloomington, IN: University of Indiana, 1955–1958, 6 vols.

344. Timbs, John and Alexander Gunn. *Abbeys, Castles, and Ancient Halls of England and Wales*, London, n.d.

345. Tout, T. F. "The Fair at Lincoln and the 'Histoire de Guillaume le Maréchal,' " *English Historical Review* XVIII (1903), pp. 240–265.

346. Tuchman, Barbara. *A Distant Mirror*, New York: Knopf, 1978.

347. Turner, T. Hudson. *Some Account of the Domestic Architecture in England from the Conquest to the End of the 13th Century*, Oxford University, 1851.

348. Twining, E. F. *A History of the Crown Jewels of Europe*, London, 1960.

349. Twining, E. F. *European Regalia*, London, 1967.

350. Vale, Malcolm. *War and Chivalry*, London: Duckworth, 1981.

351. Verbruggen, J. F. *The Art of Warfare in Western Europe during the Middle Ages*, tr. by S. Willard and S. C. M. Southern, Amsterdam: Elsevier, 1977.

352. Verney, Lady F. P. "Mythical and Medieval Swords," *The Contemporary Review* XXXVIII (July–December, 1880), pp. 595–613.

353. Vesey, Norman. *The Medieval Soldier*, London, 1971.

354. Vigneras, L. A. and Sidney Painter. "Monday as a 'Date for Tournaments,' " *Modern Language Notes* XLVIII (February, 1933), pp. 80–83.

355. Villehardouin and de Joinville. *Memories of the Crusades*,tr. by Sir Frank Marzials, New York: E. P. Dutton, 1958.

356. Vinaver, Eugene. "King Arthur's Sword or the Making of a Medieval Romance,"*Bulletin of the John Rylands Library* 40 (1958), pp. 513–526.

357. Vinogradoff, Paul. *Villainage in England*, Oxford University, 1892, repr. 1968.

358. Wace. "Le Roman de Brut," in *Arthurian Chronicles*, London: Everyman, 1928; repr. New York: E. P. Dutton, 1972, pp. 1–115.

359. Wagner, Sir Anthony, ed. *Aspilogia, Being Materials of Heraldry*:
    a. I. *Catalogue of English Medieval Rolls of Arms*, London, 1950.
    b. II. *Rolls of Arms of Henry III*, London, 1957.

360. Wagner, Anthony. *English Genealogy*, 2nd ed., Oxford University, 1972.

361. Wagner, Anthony. *Heralds and Heraldry in the Middle Ages*, 2nd ed., Oxford University, 1956.

362. Wagner, Edward. *Medieval Costume, Armour, and Weapons, 1350–1450*, tr. by Jean Layton, London, 1962.

363. Walsh, Clifford, ed. *Dictionary of English Law*, London, 1959.

364. Walsh, James J. *Medieval Medicine*, London, 1920; repr. New York: AMS Press, 1976.

365. *Walter of Henley's Husbandry, together with an Anonymous Husbandry, Seneschaunce, and Robert Grosseteste's Rules*, tr. by Elizabeth Lamond, London, 1890.

366. Ward, Henry L.D. *Catalog of the Romances in the Department of Manuscripts in the British Museum*, 3 vols., London, 1883–1910.

367. Ward, Philip. *Oxford Companion to Spanish Literature*, Oxford University, 1978.

368. Ware, R. Dean. "Medieval Chronology: Theory and Practice," in *Medieval Studies: An Introduction*, ed. by James Powell, Syracuse, NY: Syracuse University, 1976.

369. Way, A. "Illustrations of Medieval Manners: Chivalry and Costume," *Archeological Journal* V (1848).
370. Werner, Karl F. "Kingdom and Principality in Twelfth-century France," in *Medieval Nobility*, ed. by Timothy Reuter, Oxford University, 1978, pp. 243–290.
371. West, Francis. *The Justiciarship in England: 1066–1232*, Cambridge University, 1966.
372. West, G. D. *An Index of Proper Names in French Arthurian Prose Romances*, Toronto: Toronto University, 1978.
373. West, G. D. *An Index of Proper Names in French Arthurian Verse Romances, 1150–1300*, Toronto: Toronto University, 1969.
374. Weston, Jessie L. *The Legend of Perceval*, 2 vols., London, 1902.
375. Weston, Jessie L. *The Three Days Tournament*, repr. New York: AMS Press, 1965.
376. White, Beatrice. "Medieval Beasts," *English Historical Essays and Studies* XVIII (1965), pp. 34–44.
377. White, Lynn. *Medieval Technology and Social Change*, Oxford University, 1964.
378. White, T. H. *The Bestiary, a Book of Beasts*, New York: G. P. Putnam, 1954.
379. Whiting, B. J. "The Vow of the Heron," *Speculum* XX (1945), pp. 261–278.
380. Wildeblood, Joan. *The Polite World: A Guide to the Deportment of the English in Former Times*, London, 1973.
381. Wilkenson, Bertie. *The High Middle Ages in England, 1154–1377*, Cambridge University, 1978.
382. Wilkinson, Frederick, *The Castles of England*, London: George Philip, 1973.
383. Wimberly, Lowry. *Folklore in the English and Scottish Ballads*, repr. New York: Dover, 1965.
384. Wood, Charles T. *The Age of Chivalry: 1000–1450*, London: Wiedenfeld & Nicolson, 1970.
385. Wood, Margaret, *English Medieval Houses*, London and New York: Harper & Row, 1965.
386. Woodward, John and George Burnett. *Woodward's Treatise on Heraldry, British and Foreign*, London, 1892; repr. Rutland, VT: C. E. Tuttle, 1969.
387. Wright, John L. *Geographical Lore at the Time of the Crusades*, New York: American Geographical Society, 1925.
388. Wright, Thomas. *History of Domestic Manners and Sentiments in England During the Middle Ages*, London, 1862.
389. Wright, Thomas. *Political Songs of England from the Reign of John to that of Edward II*, Edinburgh, 1884; repr. New York: Johnson Reprints, 1977.
390. Yarwood, Doreen. *English Costume from the 2nd Century B.C. to 1967*, 3rd ed., Chester Springs, PA: Dufour, 1967.
391. York, Ernest C. "Legal Punishment in Malory's 'Le Morte d'Arthur,' " *English Language Notes* XI (1973), pp. 14–21.
392. Young, Sidney. *Annals of the Barber-Surgeons of London*, London, 1890; repr. New York: AMS, 1976.
393. Ziegler, Philip. *The Black Death*, New York: Harper & Row, 1971.
394. Zupko, Ronald E. *A Dictionary of English Weights and Measures from Anglo-Saxon Times to the 19th Century*, Madison, WI: University of Wisconsin, 1968.

Index

Numbers in **boldface** refer to illustrations.

corseque, 129
corsesca, 129
Corsheuse, 129
corsnaed, 350. *See also* ordeal by bread
    and cheese
cortes, 129
cost of armor, 253
cost of horses, 252
costrel, 129, 478
costume, herald's, 283
costume of pursuivant, 383
côte à plates. See hauberk, of plates
cottager, 69, 129
cottars, 129, 415
cotteraux, 130
couchant, 57, **58**, 130, 165
coudieres, 130
coule, glizade, 130
count, 44, 178, 345, 380, 451; of Anjou,
    220, 239; Charles II of Provence, and
    knighthood, 293; German, 221, 302; of
    Hainault, 206; of the marche, 324,
    401; of Provence, 129; of Rodez,
    Nimes, Narbonne, 393; territory of,
    361; of Toulouse, 129; of Toulouse,
    Raymond VI, 393
counte, 421
counter, 130
countercharged, 130
countermine, 83
counters, foreign coins as, 188
countess, 131; of Montfort as fighter,
    292; of Salisbury, 355–56
counties of England, 164
counting table, 188
county, 131, 421
county courts, 187
coup de grace, 131, 312
couped, ordinaries, 131
couple, 131
couriers, king's, 149
course, 131
courser, 131, 252
court, 131–32; appearance, sureties for,
    319; of Arms and Honors, 179; of at-
    tachment, records of, 466, 467; baron,
    132 (*see also* love-day; manor, court);
    of Chivalry, 132–34, 242; of Chivalry

and Edward III, 305; of Common
    Bench (*see curia regis*); of the Con-
    stable and Marshal, 242; of free ten-
    ants, 132; justices of, 277; of
    knighthood, 132; manor, 277; Military,
    132; official, 326; official to ensure ap-
    pearance in court, 461; right to hold,
    427; of Swanimote, 134
court-leet, 134
courtesy: knightly quality of, 290; lances
    of, 275; title, 134
coustel, coutelas, 135
coute, 135
couteau-de-breche, 135
coutel-axe, 148
couter, 398
cove et keye, 135
covert, 265
coward, 135, 344
cowardice, battlefield, 291
cowardly, 22
crakanel, 135
crannchur. *See* ordeal of the lot
crannock, 135, 478
crapaud, 208
craven, 135, 270, 313, 394
creance, 135, 458
Crecy, Battle of, 53, 357; and crossbow,
    137; and knightly conduct, 439
crenel, 135
crenellated, 135
crenellated parapet, 181
crenellation, 55, **93**, 150, 333, 417
crenelle, 135
crenels, 181, 333
crepons, 136
crescent, 79, **80**, 136, 269
crest, 28, 65, 104, 121, 136, 241, 340,
    484
cric, 21–22. *See also arbalète à cric*
crimes during war, 120
criminal clergymen, 120–21
Criminous Clerks controversy, 120–21,
    136
crinet, 47, 136
crisolite, 136
croat, 113
crockard, 136, 338

darnel, 343
dart, 43, 154
dart thrower, 96, 197
dating documents, 248
dating parliaments, 248
dating rents, 248
dauphin of France, 154–55; arms, 163; crown, 155
Dauphine, French territory, 154–55
David, King of Israel, 344
David, King of Scotland, 54
daybreak, 235
daylight, 380
days of week, 155
de dominio, 403
de excommunicato capiendo, writ of, 192
de excommunicato deliberando, writ of, 192
de gestu et fama, 155
de malo lecti, 155
dead angle, 92, 155
dead descendant, 305
death: concealed, 341; customs of, 245; duties on villeins, 339; of a knight (*see* knighthood); penalty, crimes calling for, 193; as punishment, 382; in tournaments, 456–57
death, horn call of, 262
decanummo, 346
deck feathers, 156
declare an outlaw, 381
decoration of shield, 242–43
decrescent, 156
deer: entrails, 346; footprint, 427, 458; of high grease, 226; killing, 263; lair, 309; red and fallow, 209; at rest, 385; resting place, 309; running, 268; scent, 214; slot, 251; started from lair, 334; stealing, 263; tricks to escape, 405
defeat in battle, effects of, 425
defeat in jousts, 275
defendant's proving innocence, 473
Degare, Sir, 168
degradation of a knight, 156–57, 292
Dei Gratia, 123, 157, 286
delf, 157
delivery of possession of fee, 202
dells, 206

demand to answer a charge, 194
demesne, 122, 157–58, 333, 339; French royal, administrator for, 380; lord's, 321; royal, 186
démesuré, 158, 401
demi-brassarts, 158
demi-cuissarts, 158
demi-grievieres, 158
demi-jambarts, 28, 158
demi-poulaines, 158
demi-vambrace, 158
denarius, 109, 158
denier, 111–13, 238, 309, 311, 336, 457; parisis, 113, 208; tournois, 113
denierat. *See* librate
denierat, 309
Denis, St., 408
deodand, 158–59
depositio, 247
descent, English law of, 305
Descriptio, 159, 164
desertion, 163
Despenser family, 156–57
despotate, 159
dessours, 274
destrier, 159, 252, 295; cost of, 163
destruction in tournaments, 457
device: heraldic, 159; of recognition, 241; for vow, 470; word, 182
Devil's whelp, 386
dexter: base, **242**; chief, **242**; forepaw raised, 365; in heraldry, 23, 268; side, **242**
dextrarius, 159
dhimmis, 159
diadem, 282
diadem, golden, 16
diadocos, 159–60
dialects: of northern France, 302; of northern Italy, 303; of Provence, 302
Dialogue of the Exchequer (1190), 160, 210
Dialogus de Scaccario, 160, 207
diapered, 160
dicker, 160
dienstmannen, 160–61, 451
dies amoris, 315
Dietrich von Bern, 448; sword of, 437

About the Author

BRADFORD B. BROUGHTON is Professor of Technical Communications at Clarkson University. His other books include *Legends of Richard I Coeur de Lion, Richard the Lion Hearted & Other English Metrical Romances*, and *Twenty-Seven to 1*.